Windows NT
Programming in Practice

From the Editors of
Windows Developer's Journal

R&D Books
Lawrence, KS 66046

R&D Books
an imprint of Miller Freeman, Inc.
1601 West 23rd Street, Suite 200
Lawrence, KS 66046
USA

Distributed in the U.S. and Canada by:
Publishers Group West
P.O. Box 8843
Emeryville, CA 94662
ISBN: 0-87930-472-3

 Miller Freeman
A United News & Media company

Table of Contents

Chapter 1

Writing Portable Windows Applications

David Van Camp

If you're a Windows programmer who's yet to start Windows NT development, chances are you've at least considered it. If so, the two questions you've most likely asked are: 1) How difficult is it to port to NT? and 2) What upfront development work can I do to simplify moving my current Windows 3.x apps to NT?

Obviously, the difficulty of porting any Windows application to NT depends on the program's features, not to mention the techniques used to develop it. Simple applications, such as Windows-supplied applets, are usually easy ports. (Microsoft claims File Manager was ported with the user interface running within a week.) With full-scale applications, however, the process is far more complicated and time consuming.

Why is Porting Difficult?

The 32-bit Windows API (Win32) supported by NT is similar to the 16-bit Windows 3.1 SDK (Win16), although there are subtle differences between the two platforms that can be overlooked. The greatest difficulty you'll likely encounter is when your application must be developed or maintained for both platforms simultaneously.

1

However, one way you can get a jump on potential porting problems when writing Win16 code is by following the guidelines summarized in Figure 1.1. For the most part, these guidelines are based on my experiences writing NT applications that require simultaneous single-source compatibility with Windows 3 (for instance, multiple tape backup systems).

Let's face it, hard-to-find portability problems cause the biggest headaches because it's impossible to fix a problem — no matter how simple — if you don't know where it is or what's causing it. Easy-to-find problems are less troublesome, even if a significant amount of work is required to correct them. Consequently, one of your basic tactics should be to make impossible-to-eliminate problems as easy as possible to find and fix (although you still want to try to remove as many problems as possible). One way to do this is mark that code with an NTPORT macro (Listing 1.1). In Listing 1.1(a), the NTPORT pragma macro shows a simple way of marking Win16 code you suspect may cause a problem when porting to NT. This macro should be defined in a header file, which is included with all your C files. As shown in Listing 1.1(b), you should put the macro close to the suspected problem and include a short description of it. Now the problem may be easily found when porting to NT either by searching your C files for NTPORT or by inspecting the compiler warning messages when compiling the code for NT.

Figure 1.1 Guidelines for writing portable Windows applications.

---

1. Eliminate all compiler and linker warnings.
2. Use the NTPORT macro to mark all potential portability problems.
3. Use WORD type data only when necessary; use INT or UINT otherwise.
4. Use SetClassLong or SetWindowLong to store widened types.
5. Never assign a handle or pointer to a short (16-bit) data type.
6. Use unique types for handles (HWND, HPEN, HBRUSH, and so on).
7. Avoid using obsolete API procedures whenever possible.
8. Portably declare all window and dialog procedures.
9. Use message crackers to process window messages.
10. Do not pack widened types into lParam words.
11. Do not use model-specific or segmented addressing.
12. Isolate operations that use globally shared memory.
13. Do not assume that filenames follow the DOS naming conventions.
14. Do not read or write system files.
15. Do not presume data elements are aligned on a specific byte.

Avoiding Portability Problems

Although tagging potential problems makes them easier to find, you can save more time by avoiding problems in the first place. With any multiplatform software project, many problems are prevented if you adhere to good structured programming techniques, avoid hard-coded values, and ensure that your code compiles without warnings or errors. Always compile your Windows code using the --W4 (warning level 4) and --DSTRICT command line options. When you use --W4, the compiler notifies you of any practice it considers suspect. The --DSTRICT option enables the strictest possible type checking and disallows many nonportable operations using incompatible data types.

Code that presumes a specific size of an int or a pointer isn't portable. The size of these data types depends on the platform or memory model used and differs across platforms. For Win32, all pointers and integers are widened to 32 bits and the near keyword is ignored. Further, Win32 uses 32-bit flat addressing, which means segmented addressing is obsolete. Never presume that allocated memory will be aligned on a 64Kb boundary, and avoid any operations that assume pointers are encoded as segment:offset. Do not compute offsets to arrays that combine a 16-bit computed offset to the high-order 16 bits of an address pointer, and never write code that assumes a pointer or integer will wrap around to 0 when adding 1 to 0xffff.

Many Win16 system resources have changed for NT. Do not directly read or write system files, including executables and resources, because the binary format of these files has changed. Also, the format of many system objects has changed, so you shouldn't access them directly. Never attempt to directly access a device port or any system code from an application; do so from a device driver. Always use the Windows API procedures to perform these types of operations and stay away from undocumented calls and data formats.

Listing 1.1 *Marking nonportable code with the* NTPORT *macro.*

(a)

```
#pragma NTPORT("warning, pointer stored in globally shared memory")
      gpszGlobalString = szLocalString;
```

(b)

```
#ifdef _WINNT_   /* if compiling for Windows NT, generate a compiler warning */
#define NTPORT(msg)  message(__FILE__ " NTPORT: " msg)
#else            /* we are compiling for Win16, so do nothing */
#define NTPORT(msg)
#endif
```

Changes to the Windows API

Under NT, many Windows API procedures have been widened to use 32-bit values. In most cases this means all pointers are 32 bits wide, and many WORD parameters have been changed to UINT. In general, it's a good idea to avoid using WORD data types except where they're required (for example, when a procedure parameter requires a pointer to a WORD). Graphics coordinates should be declared using UINT; INT should be used for general integers and array indexes. Widened types should never be assigned

---

Figure 1.2   Windows API procedures that have been eliminated.

(a) These procedures have been dropped from the 32-bit Windows API. No replacements are available. Consequently, code that calls these procedures will not be portable.
(b) These sound procedures have been dropped; use the multimedia sound support API instead.

(a)

AccessResource	AllocDSToCSAlias	AllocResource
AllocSelector	ChangeSelector	GetCodeHandle
GetCodeInfo	GetCurrentPDB	GetEnvironment
GetInstanceData	GetKBCodePage	GetTempDrive
GlobalDosAlloc	GlobalDosFree	GlobalPageLock
GlobalPageUnlock	LimitEMSPages	LocalNotify
SetEnvironment	SetResourceHandler	SwitchStackBack
SwitchStackTo	UngetCommChar	ValidateCodeSegment
ValidateFreeSpaces		

(b)

CloseSound	CountVoiceNotes	GetThresholdEvent
GetThresholdStatus	OpenSound	SetSoundNoise
SetVoiceAccent	SetVoiceEnvelope	SetVoiceNote
SetVoiceQueueSize	SetVoiceSound	SetVoiceThreshold
StartSound	StopSound	SyncAllVoices
WaitSoundState		

to a WORD, or any other 16-bit type, particularly pointers, ints, or any type of handle. And don't mix handle types — HANDLE, HWND, HINSTANCE, and HDC are separate and distinct types and not interchangeable.

A number of Win16 procedures have been replaced, modified, or eliminated altogether. For replaced functions, it's simple to find and modify the calls when porting to NT by using one of two techniques: either the functions are reimplemented by writing replacements that map the parameters and call the new API procedures, or the calls are changed to the Win32 replacement procedures. Win16 versions of those procedures are then created to map the parameters back to the original functions. Either way, it isn't much of a problem. For procedures that have undergone functional modification, however, the matter is often more serious. Finally, procedures that have been completely eliminated should be avoided (see Figure 1.2).

Of the API procedures that have been modified, the most important are the callbacks, particularly window and dialog procedures. Whenever you declare a pointer to a callback procedure, use the appropriate type, such as WNDPROC for window procedures, DLG-PROC for dialog procedures, HOOK-PROC for hook procedures, and so on. Do not use FARPROC or NEARPROC. Also, when declaring these procedures, use the proper function prototype. Always declare window and dialog procedures like this:

```
RESULT CALLBACK ProcName (HWND hwnd, UINT wMsg, WPARAM wParam, LPARAM lParam)
```

where, RESULT is LRESULT for window procedures or BOOL for dialog procedures. BOOL is widened to 32 bits for Win32, as are wMsg and wParam (both formally WORDs). See the Win16 or Win32 version of windows.h for a complete list of the callback types. Also note the use of CALLBACK instead of FAR PASCAL. This is a more portable modifier.

Modifications to Message Handling

The declaration prototype has changed for window procedures because the parameter packing for a number of messages has changed. For most messages, these changes were necessary because a widened value, usually a HWND, was originally packed into the upper or lower 16 bits of the LPARAM parameter. Because these values are widened, they have been typically moved to the WPARAM parameter, which is also widened. Additionally, other parameters were moved. Consequently, you can't write portable code that directly picks a value from the parameters of a modified message. Microsoft has provided a number of macros, collectively called "message crackers," that present different solutions for this.

One pair of message crackers, first introduced with the Windows 3.1 SDK, are called "handlers and forwarders." I recommend using these macros when writing new code to process window messages, because these macros not only solve the parameter packing changes introduced by Win32, but they also provide a highly structured method of message processing. These macros, defined in `windows.h`, allow an almost object-oriented approach to message handling that mimics the solution used by the Microsoft C++ Foundation Classes. Listing 1.2 shows an example of `WM_COMMAND` message processing for Win16. Listing 1.3 shows how this same code would be implemented using message handlers and forwarders. These macros use the following naming convention for message handlers:

```
HANDLE_message (hwnd, wParam, lParam, function_name);
```

In this convention, `message` is the window message ID and `function_name` is the name of your handler function. This macro unpacks the parameters in `lParam` and `wParam` and calls your handler function. Always declare the handler function using the example in the comment above the message-handler macro definition in `windows.h`. The naming convention for message forwarders is

```
FORWARD_message (paramlist, message_proc);
```

where `paramlist` is the list of parameters required for the particular message and `message_proc` is a message-passing procedure (`SendMessage`, `PostMessage`, `CallWindowProc`, and so on). This macro packs the parameters into `lParam` and `wParam` and calls the specified procedure. See the Microsoft Windows SDK documentation and `windows.h` for more information and a complete list of these macros.

Listing 1.2   WM_COMMAND message processing for Win16.

```
#include <windows.h>        /* normal include for all windows applications*/

/* The following window procedure declaration is NOT portable to WindowsNT! */

LONG FAR PASCAL MyWinProc (HWND hwnd, WORD wMsg, WORD wParam, WORD wParam)
{
    switch ( wMsg )
    {
        case WM_COMMAND:
        /* Nonportable reference to control ID in message params */
        switch ( wParam )
        {
        /* processing for WM_COMMAND based on control ID goes here...*/
        }
        case WM_SOMEMESSAGE:
        /* non-portable method to send WM_COMMAND message to parent */
        SendMessage ( GetParent (hwnd), WM_COMMAND, wMyID,
                    MAKELONG (hwnd, wNotifyCode) );
    }
}
```

The other pair of message crackers, simpler than handlers and forwarders, extract or pack the message parameters via a portable macro. Listing 1.4 shows how WM_COMMAND processing looks when extractors and packers are used. The general naming convention used for the extractors is

```
GET_message_item (wParam, lParam);
```

where message is the message ID and item is the particular data item you want to extract from the parameters. The return value type depends on the type of data extracted. The message packers follow the naming convention

```
GET_message_MPS (wParam, lParam, paramlist);
```

where paramlist is the list of parameters required for the particular message.

Listing 1.3   *WM_COMMAND processing using handlers and forwarders.*

```
#include <windows.h>      /* normal include for all windows applications */
#include <windowsx.h>     /* include macro definitions for Win16 or NT   */

/* Declare portable WM_COMMAND message handler function...  */

void MyWinProc_OnCommand (HWND hwnd, int id, HWND hwndCtl, UINT codeNotify)
{
    /* Portable reference to control ID in message params    */
    switch ( id )
    {
        /* processing for WM_COMMAND based on control ID goes here... */
    }
}

/* The following window procedure declaration IS portable to Windows NT! */

LRESULT CALLBACK MyWinProc (HWND hwnd, UINT wMsg, WPARAM wParam, LPARAM wParam)
{
    switch ( wMsg )
    {
        case WM_COMMAND:
        /* Portable WM_COMMAND processing using macro... */
        return HANDLE_WM_COMMAND (hwnd, wParam, lParam, MyWinProc_OnCommand );
        case WM_SOMEMESSAGE:
        /* portable method to send WM_COMMAND message to parent */
        FORWARD_WM_COMMAND ( GetParent (hwnd), wMyID, hwnd, wNotifyCode,
                             SendMessage);
    }
}
```

For Win32, Microsoft has only provided these macros for those messages whose parameter packing has changed. Microsoft didn't provide definitions of these macros for Win16, so I have (Listing 1.5). Because macros are only defined for changed messages, this code also serves as a quick reference to the changed messages. These macros are best suited for porting an existing code base to Windows NT, because less work is typically required to convert code using them than is needed for handlers and forwarders. Handlers and forwarders are better for new development because they can be used with all window messages and because of the highly structured solution they provide.

In Listing 1.5, the WM_CTLCOLOR message macros are an exception to the previously described naming convention. This Win16 message poses a problem because it contains two parameters widened to 32 bits and one 16-bit parameter. Consequently, there isn't enough room, so the message has to be split into a series of messages. When declaring your own messages, never pack more than two widened types, or one widened type and one 16-bit value, into message parameters.

Win32 dynamic data exchange (DDE) messages have undergone such significant changes that it's virtually impossible to write portable code that processes them. Consequently, always use the high-level DDEML procedures to perform DDE functions. Other aspects of message processing have changed as well. It isn't possible in Win32 to subclass a window belonging to another process. Also, global classes can only be registered in DLLs that are loaded during system initialization, never from an application. Avoid using these nonportable techniques whenever possible.

Listing 1.4   WM_COMMAND *processing using extractors and packers.*

```
#include <windows.h>     /* normal include for all windows applications  */
#include <windowsx.h>    /* include macro definitions for NT only        */
#include <move2nt.h>     /* include macro definitions for Win16          */

/* The following window procedure declaration IS portable to Windows NT!  */

LRESULT CALLBACK MyWinProc (HWND hwnd, UINT wMsg, WPARAM wParam, LPARAM wParam)
{
    switch ( wMsg )
    {
        case WM_COMMAND:
        /* Portable reference to control ID in message params     */
        switch ( GET_WM_COMMAND_ID (wParam, lParam) )
        {
        /* processing for WM_COMMAND based on control ID goes here */
        /* using GET_WM_COMMAND_xxx macros for portability...     */
        }
        case WM_SOMEMESSAGE:
        /*  Portable method to send WM_COMMAND message to parent */
            SendMessage ( GetParent (hwnd), WM_COMMAND,
                        GET_WM_COMMAND_MPS (wMyID,  hwnd, wNotifyCode));
    }
}
```

Win32 Features

Windows NT provides features not available under Win16, such as support for memory-mapped files, multiple users, advanced file systems, preemptive multitasking and multithreaded processes, C/2-level security, protected address spaces, and the Unicode character standard. Although you can't write truly portable code that uses these features, carefully crafted Win16 code simplifies the changes required to integrate these features when porting to NT. The most significant of these features are memory-mapped files. Globally shared memory, implemented in Win16 using GlobalAlloc with the GMEM_SHARE option or via named data segments, won't work for NT applications. Instead, your application needs to be modified to use memory-mapped files. For this reason, all code that uses shared memory should be isolated and marked with the NTPORT macro. Avoid storing addresses in shared memory, because this will often cause problems under NT. Additionally, due to preemptive multitasking, access to global memory must be carefully synchronized to ensure that different processes cannot attempt to modify and read information simultaneously.

You should never assume that file names follow standard DOS naming conventions. Both HPFS and NTFS, the advanced file systems supported by NT, allow long file names (up to 256 characters) and new characters (such as spaces and dots). C/2 security, a governmental classification, and protected address spaces ensure that certain "unsecured" operations fail under NT and should be avoided. These include shutting down the system, directly accessing devices or system memory, changing scheduling priorities, and modifying the system's CMOS or date and time. Also, if your application is expected to be used internationally, you should employ transparent character techniques so that you can properly utilize NT's Unicode support.

Listing 1.5   Win16 message extractor and packer macros.

```
/* File:    MOVE2NT.H - Message extractor and packer macros for Win16
 * Author:  David Van Camp, July 1993  */

#if !defined (MOVE2NT_INCL) && !defined (_WINNT_)
#define MOVE2NT_INCL

#define GET_EM_LINESCROLL_MPS(vert, horz)        (WPARAM)0, MAKELONG (vert, horz)
#define GET_EM_SETSEL_START(wp, lp)              (INT)HIWORD(lp)
#define GET_EM_SETSEL_END(wp, lp)                (INT)LOWORD(lp)

#define GET_EM_SETSEL_MPS(iStart, iEnd)          (WPARAM)0, MAKELONG(iStart, iEnd)
#define GET_WM_ACTIVATE_STATE(wp, lp)            (wp)
#define GET_WM_ACTIVATE_FMINIMIZED(wp, lp)       (BOOL)HIWORD(lp)
#define GET_WM_ACTIVATE_HWND(wp, lp)             (HWND)LOWORD(lp)
#define GET_WM_ACTIVATE_MPS(s, fmin, hwnd)       (WPARAM)(s), MAKELONG((hwnd), (fmin))
#define GET_WM_CHANGECBCHAIN_HWNDNEXT(wp, lp)    (HWND)LOWORD(lp)
```

Listing 1.5 (continued)

```
#define GET_WM_CHARTOITEM_CHAR(wp, lp)          (CHAR)(wp)
#define GET_WM_CHARTOITEM_POS(wp, lp)           HIWORD(lp)
#define GET_WM_CHARTOITEM_HWND(wp, lp)          (HWND)LOWORD(lp)
#define GET_WM_CHARTOITEM_MPS(ch, pos, hwnd)    (WPARAM)(ch), MAKELONG((hwnd), (pos))
#define GET_WM_COMMAND_ID(wp, lp)               (wp)
#define GET_WM_COMMAND_HWND(wp, lp)             (HWND)LOWORD(lp)
#define GET_WM_COMMAND_CMD(wp, lp)              HIWORD(lp)
#define GET_WM_COMMAND_MPS(id, hwnd, cmd)       (WPARAM)(id), MAKELONG(hwnd, cmd))

/* The WM_CTLCOLOR message was split in to multiple messages for NT, one
 * for each supported control type. For this reason, a extra macro is added,
 * GET_WM_CTLCOLOR_MSG which must be used to determine the message ID
 * to use for a particular type.  Use this macro in the following manner:
 *    SendMessage (hwnd, GET_WM_CTLCOLOR_MSG(type)
 *                     GET_WM_CTLCOLOR_MPS(hdc,hwnd,type));
 * where type is any of the types used in the Win16 WM_CTLCOLOR message.
 * Also notice that the extractor macros require the message ID in addition
 * to the two message parameters.  */
#define GET_WM_CTLCOLOR_HDC(wp, lp, msg)        (HDC)(wp)
#define GET_WM_CTLCOLOR_HWND(wp, lp, msg)
    (HWND)LOWORD(lp)#define GET_WM_CTLCOLOR_TYPE(wp, lp, msg)        HIWORD(lp)
#define GET_WM_CTLCOLOR_MSG(type)               (WORD)(WM_CTLCOLOR)
#define GET_WM_CTLCOLOR_MPS(hdc, hwnd, type)    (WPARAM)(hdc), MAKELONG(hwnd,type)
#define GET_WM_HSCROLL_CODE(wp, lp)             (wp)
#define GET_WM_HSCROLL_POS(wp, lp)              LOWORD(lp)
#define GET_WM_HSCROLL_HWND(wp, lp)             (HWND)HIWORD(lp)
#define GET_WM_HSCROLL_MPS(code, pos, hwnd)     (WPARAM)(code), MAKELONG(hwnd, pos)
#define GET_WM_MENUSELECT_CMD(wp, lp)           (wp)
#define GET_WM_MENUSELECT_FLAGS(wp, lp)         (UINT)LOWORD(lp)
#define GET_WM_MENUSELECT_HMENU(wp, lp)         (HMENU)HIWORD(lp)
#define GET_WM_MENUSELECT_MPS(cmd, f, hmenu)    (WPARAM)(wp), MAKELONG(f, hmenu)
/* These extractors are for MDIclient to MDI child messages only. */
#define GET_WM_MDIACTIVATE_FACTIVATE(hwnd, wp, lp)  (wp)
#define GET_WM_MDIACTIVATE_HWNDDEACT(wp, lp)        (HWND)HIWORD(lp)
#define GET_WM_MDIACTIVATE_HWNDACTIVATE(wp, lp)     (HWND)LOWORD(lp)
/* This packer is for sending to the MDI client window only. */
#define GET_WM_MDIACTIVATE_MPS(f, hwndD, hwndA)     (WPARAM)(hwndA), 0L

#define GET_WM_MDISETMENU_MPS(hmenuF, hmenuW)
    (WPARAM)!(hmenuF||hmenuW), MAKELONG(hmenuF, hmenuW)
#define GET_WM_MENUCHAR_CHAR(wp, lp)            (CHAR)(wp)
#define GET_WM_MENUCHAR_HMENU(wp, lp)           (HMENU)HIWORD(lp)
#define GET_WM_MENUCHAR_FMENU(wp, lp)           (BOOL)LOWORD(lp)
#define GET_WM_MENUCHAR_MPS(ch, hmenu, f)       (WPARAM)(ch), MAKELONG(f, hmenu)
#define GET_WM_PARENTNOTIFY_MSG(wp, lp)         (wp)
#define GET_WM_PARENTNOTIFY_ID(wp, lp)          HIWORD(lp)
#define GET_WM_PARENTNOTIFY_HWNDCHILD(wp, lp)   (HWND)LOWORD(lp)
#define GET_WM_PARENTNOTIFY_X(wp, lp)           (int)(short)LOWORD(lp)
#define GET_WM_PARENTNOTIFY_Y(wp, lp)           (int)(short)HIWORD(lp)
/* Use this packer for WM_CREATE or WM_DESTROY msg values only */
#define GET_WM_PARENTNOTIFY_MPS(msg, id, hwnd)  (WPARAM)(msg), MAKELONG(hwnd, id)
```

Addendum

Since I wrote this chapter back in 1993, a lot has changed in the world of Windows programming. However, the fundamental rule for writing single-source portable code between the newer 32-bit flavors of Windows and the older 16-bit version remains the same: program for the lowest common denominator. Any code that utilizes features or services not available on all platforms will not be single-source compatible and will require a potentially large effort to port.

Programming for the minimal set of compatible features, though, is seldom a reasonable solution. You will often find it difficult to limit yourself to only those features shared by all platforms. After all, why create an NT 4.0 application if it is only a Windows 3.1 application in disguise? Indeed, a key difference between today and 1993 is that most projects today are first designed for Win32 then ported to Win16 later, whereas in 1993 the opposite was the norm. This change in emphasis is important.

Users expect applications designed today for 32-bit Windows to act like 32-bit Windows applications: they must exhibit the newer user interface features and incorporate the more advanced system features. Take multithreading, for example. Multithreaded applications allow the user to perform operations while longer running tasks perform in the background. Design of such concurrent features is greatly simplified using threads, but threads are not available under Win16. Multithreaded services explicitly designed for Win32 applications are difficult to port to Win16. Two possible solutions are: 1) implement multithreaded services as nonportable tasks that must be re-implemented again later, or 2) break the multithreaded task into a series of short segments, which will be called by a loop in the multithreaded (Win32) version and triggered from a timer message in the Win16 version.

A more insidious problem is the shortening of address and integer sizes from 32 to 16 bits. Most code written originally for 16-bit applications will usually port easily to 32-bit applications, but the reverse is often not true. Code that may allocate blocks of memory greater than 64Kb or integers that presume a maximum memory larger than 32,767Kb will fail terribly when ported to 16-bit code. Consequently, programmers must try to consciously limit their usage of pointers and integers to the 16-bit realm when writing 32-bit code that will be ported to 16-bit code. However, as I suggested in 1993, the use of more specific data types and the incorporation of markers (such as the NTPORT macro) can aid significantly. The 32-bit programmer arguably has a harder job crafting portable code, but with care and diligence it can be done. Happy programming!

Listing 1.5 *(continued)*

```
/* Use this packer for all other msg values */
#define GET_WM_PARENTNOTIFY2_MPS(msg, x, y) (WPARAM)(msg), MAKELONG(x, y)

#define GET_WM_VKEYTOITEM_CODE(wp, lp)          (int)(wp)
#define GET_WM_VKEYTOITEM_ITEM(wp, lp)          HIWORD(lp)
#define GET_WM_VKEYTOITEM_HWND(wp, lp)          (HWND)LOWORD(lp)
#define GET_WM_VKEYTOITEM_MPS(code, item, hwnd)
    (WPARAM)(code), MAKELONG(item, hwnd)
#define GET_WM_VSCROLL_CODE(wp, lp)             (wp)
#define GET_WM_VSCROLL_POS(wp, lp)              LOWORD(lp)
#define GET_WM_VSCROLL_HWND(wp, lp)             (HWND)HIWORD(lp)
#define GET_WM_VSCROLL_MPS(code, pos, hwnd)     (WPARAM)(code), MAKELONG(hwnd, pos)
#endif /*MOVE2NT_INCL && _WINNT_*/
```

Chapter 2

Managing Memory in Win32 DLLs

Brian G. Myers

The rules for writing dynamic link libraries (DLLs) changed with 32-bit Windows. Although Microsoft went out of its way to preserve as much of the old Windows API as possible, some changes were inevitable. For example, DLLs must now cope with protected address spaces and multithreaded clients. The compile and link commands, the module definition file, the entry point procedure, and memory allocation techniques have all changed. The changes apply to Windows 95 as well as Windows NT. This chapter explains these changes, concentrating on the new ways to manage memory.

Under 16-bit versions of Windows, any variables a DLL declares are global to all callers, and extra precautions are necessary to prevent one caller from interfering with values set for another caller. Under 32-bit Windows, however, a DLL normally receives a new data segment for each new client. The fact that every process has a private address space prevents the different instances from conflicting with each other and eliminates the need to worry about multiple applications using the same data in your DLL.

Other modifications to the compiler, the linker, and the API collectively give you a complete set of tools for controlling the scope of any variable or allocated block. Each can be made visible to all the library's clients, to just one client, or even to just a single thread within a client.

Building a DLL for Windows NT and Windows 95

I'll begin with the new rules for building a DLL. A high percentage of the problems new Win32 developers experience with DLLs stems from difficulties with the build options and export mechanisms rather than from bugs in the actual code. Some of the advice in this section is compiler specific.

The New Entry Point Procedure

Under Win16, a DLL typically begins with a call to LibMain() and ends with a call to WEP(). In these two calls the library performs housekeeping chores as each new client summons or dismisses it. Win32 replaces LibMain() and WEP() with a single routine that responds whenever a thread or process uses or frees the library. The procedure is conventionally called DllMain() and must conform to the prototype shown in Listing 2.1. The first parameter is a handle to the DLL module. If other procedures in your library have any use for the handle, you should save it here in a static variable because calling GetModuleHandle() from a DLL returns the handle for the client program, not for the DLL. The next parameter, dwReason, signals the particular occasion for calling the entry point. It may be one of the four values you see in the switch statement. A DLL is not obligated to respond to all the possible values of dwReason. It can choose to handle some and ignore others. DllMain() returns a Boolean value, but the value matters only after DLL_PROCESS_ATTACH. If for any reason a DLL cannot complete necessary initialization tasks, it should return FALSE. The DLL_THREAD_ATTACH signal enables the entry point to initialize separately for individual threads. For example, in a program that creates a new thread to manage each new document window, a DLL might need to initialize a distinct data set for each thread.

Three warnings:

- A process' primary thread — the one that launches first — never generates a DLL_THREAD_ATTACH signal. In order to initialize for the primary thread, omit break from the DLL_PROCESS_ATTACH case and fall through to DLL_THREAD_ATTACH.

- Threads created before the DLL is loaded do not generate DLL_THREAD_ATTACH signals. This is only a problem in DLLs loaded dynamically using LoadLibrary() and GetProcAddress(). It means that a thread can call DLL routines that have not been initialized. You can work around the problem by making your DLL entry points check the ID of the calling thread and compare it to a list of initialized threads. [Use GetCurrentThreadId().]

- Don't assume every DETACH message will arrive. It is possible for threads to end without notifying DLLs. The TerminateProcess() and TerminateThread() commands both kill their targets immediately without notifying libraries. If a library's client is rudely terminated, any data the library holds for the client remains allocated until all the library's other clients also detach or terminate.

You do not have to provide a D11Main() at all. A DLL that performs no house-keeping — a resource DLL, for example — is not obliged to supply an entry point.

D11Main() *and the* **Runtime Library**

The C runtime library (RTL) has its own per-process and per-thread state variables. However, if your DLL uses the C runtime library, how does the RTL know when pro-cesses and threads attach and detach? The solution chosen by both Borland and Microsoft is to place the D11Main() procedure in the RTL and have the RTL call whatever entry point you provide. That way both you and the RTL receive all the noti-fications. For this to work, of course, the RTL has to know the name of the procedure you provide, meaning the name has to be hard coded into the RTL. Microsoft's RTL

Listing 2.1   Win32 DLL entry point skeleton.

```
BOOL WINAPI DllMain (
    HINSTANCE hinstDLL,           /* the DLL module */
    DWORD dwReason,               /* event code */
    LPVOID lpReserved)            /* not used */
{
    switch (dwReason)
    {
        case DLL_PROCESS_ATTACH:
            /* a process is loading the DLL */
            break;

        case DLL_THREAD_ATTACH:
            /* a process created a new thread */
            break;

        case DLL_THREAD_DETACH:
            /* a thread ended */
            break;

        case DLL_PROCESS_DETACH:
            /* a process is freeing the DLL */
            break;
    }
    return(TRUE);
}
```

assumes the name of your entry point is `DllMain()`. Borland accepts either `DllMain()` or `DllEntryPoint()`. The relevant excerpt from Microsoft's RTL appears in Listing 2.2 (with some parts omitted for clarity).

Microsoft's linker gets the name of the DLL entry point from the `-entry` switch. A DLL that uses the RTL should set the switch to `_DllMainCRTStartup@12`, the compiler's mangled name for the RTL startup routine. Microsoft DLLs that do not call C runtime routines can use any name at all for the optional entry procedure. Borland's linker always requires the name to be either `DllMain()` or `DllEntryPoint()`, so no `-entry` switch is needed.

Listing 2.2   Entry point for C/C++ runtime libraries.

```
/*
 * User routine DllMain is called on all notifications
 */

extern BOOL WINAPI DllMain(
        HANDLE  hDllHandle,
        DWORD   dwReason,
        LPVOID  lpreserved
        ) ;



/***
*BOOL WINAPI _DllMainCRTStartup(hDllHandle, dwReason, lpreserved) - C++ DLL
*       initialization.
*
*Purpose:
*       This is the entry point for DLL's linked with the C/C++ run-time libs.
*       This routine does the C runtime initialization for a DLL linked with
*       MSVCRT.LIB (whose C run-time code is thus in MSVCRT*.DLL.)
*       It will call the user notification routine DllMain on all 4 types of
*       DLL notifications.  The return code from this routine is the return
*       code from the user notification routine.
*
*       On DLL_PROCESS_ATTACH, the C++ constructors for the DLL will be called.
*
*       On DLL_PROCESS_DETACH, the C++ destructors and _onexit/atexit routines
*       will be called.
*
*Entry:
*
*Exit:
*
*******************************************************************************/
```

Exporting Procedures

In a flat, unsegmented address space, any function can call any other without worrying about near and far segments. The short assembly prolog formerly added to all callback and exported procedures no longer serves a purpose — another bump smoothed out by the flat memory model. Callback procedures do not need to be exported. Make-ProcInstance() now does nothing, and the __export keyword is obsolete in Win32. The functions in a DLL do still need to be exported, however, in order for the system to create header tables within the DLL image. There are two ways to export a function: the old way listed it in the .def file under EXPORTS; the new way preceded its declaration with the storage class specifier __declspec.

Listing 2.2 (continued)

```
BOOL WINAPI _DllMainCRTStartup(
        HANDLE  hDllHandle,
        DWORD   dwReason,
        LPVOID  lpreserved
        )
{
        BOOL retcode = TRUE;

        /*
         * If this is a process detach notification, check that there has
         * been a prior process attach notification.
         */
        if ( (dwReason == DLL_PROCESS_DETACH) && (__proc_attached == 0) )
            return FALSE;

        if ( dwReason == DLL_PROCESS_ATTACH || dwReason == DLL_THREAD_ATTACH )
        {
            // process attach notification
        }

        retcode = DllMain(hDllHandle, dwReason, lpreserved);


        if ( (dwReason == DLL_PROCESS_ATTACH) && !retcode )
            // Call a routine to clean up the RTL because the
            // user's DllMain routine returned failure.

        if ( (dwReason == DLL_PROCESS_DETACH) ||
             (dwReason == DLL_THREAD_DETACH) )
        {
            // process detach notification
        }

        return retcode ;
}
```

```
// as declared within the DLL
__declspec(dllexport) void MyExportedFunction();
// as declared within the code that calls the DLL
__declspec(dllimport) void MyExportedFunction();
```

In both Microsoft and Borland tools, the _declspec syntax replaces the old _export keyword. The examples in this chapter use _declspec for exporting.

The .def File

dllimport() and dllexport() make .def files nearly obsolete, but not quite. At times, you might still choose to have one; for example, to modify data segment memory characteristics, as demonstrated later. You still might choose to use a module definition file for exporting functions in order to call functions more efficiently by assigning ordinal numbers to them. A typical .def file might look like this:

```
LIBRARY MyLib BASE 0x400000000
EXPORTS
    AFunction        @1
    AnotherFunction  @2
```

Because it takes longer to look up string matches than numerical matches, you achieve a slight performance boost by using ordinal numbers.

The optional BASE keyword suggests a loading address for the DLL. You can suggest a base address by using a linker option instead of a .def file if you want. Either way, when a program invokes the DLL, the system tries to place the library at the suggested location in the caller's address space. If the location is already occupied, the system simply puts the library somewhere else. The only advantage of suggesting a base address is speed. Normally the linker cannot know in advance where in memory a DLL will reside, so at run time it must look up the current location of all the DLL procedures and copy the addresses into the client program's code. When you request a base address, the linker pencils in tentative addresses in advance. If the system manages to load the DLL at the requested location, then it can skip the lookup process and leave the tentative addresses intact. Some debuggers (such as TD32) will show you the address where the DLL was loaded.

The choice of a BASE address is arbitrary. The address must fall in the lower 2Gb of the address space. (For NT, the available range is more like 0x00010000–0x7FFEFFFF because of guard blocks at the top and bottom.) Within that range, very high and low addresses are likely to be occupied by the program itself or by the system DLLs. Use the middle of the range, and when a program calls several DLLs simultaneously, set the BASE addresses far enough apart that the file images don't overlap in memory.

Building with Microsoft Tools

Building a DLL requires three tools: the compiler, the linker, and the library manager. In Microsoft's SDK, these tools are Cl, Link, and Lib. Compiling a DLL is no different than compiling an executable file, but linking does require some new switches.

Run the library manager before the linker to create an export library. The linker learns about exported procedures from the export library, not from the .def file. In fact, Link never reads a .def file; only Lib does. A single run of Lib produces both an export library (.exp) and an import library (.lib). The export library is used only once, when the linker builds the DLL. Like .obj, .res, and .rbj files, the .exp file is an intermediate by-product, of no use after the DLL is finished. The import library, on the other hand, is used in building every program that calls the DLL. This command generates both libraries for MyDll:

```
lib -machine:i386 mydll.obj -def:mydll.def -out:mydll.lib
```

Linking a DLL requires a new command line switch, -DLL, telling the linker not to produce an executable file. In addition, the -entry switch must name the DLL's entry point procedure; the -out switch receives a name with the DLL extension instead of .exe; and the export library must appear with the object files.

```
link -incremental:no -nodefaultlib -DLL -entry:_DllMainCRTStartup@12 \
   -out:mydll.dll mydll.exp libcmt.lib kernel32.lib
```

The entry point name acquires three extra characters ("@12") because the linker needs to see the name in its decorated form. The _stdcall calling convention appends the number of bytes required for all the parameters to each procedure name. DllMain() takes a handle, a pointer, and a DWORD, so its parameters fill 12 bytes. A DLL may omit the -entry switch if it has no entry point of its own and does not call C runtime routines.

Building with Borland Tools

The Borland tools are Bcc32, Tlink32, and Implib. The Borland compiler requires a particular option for DLLs:

```
bcc32 -c -WD mydll.c
```

The -WD switch indicates that you want to build a DLL. Borland doesn't use .exp files for linking. Instead, run Implib after linking to create the import library. Here's a typical sequence:

```
tlink32 -Lc:\bc5\lib -Tpd c0d32 mydll, mydll.dll,, cw32mt import32, \
  mydll.def,
implib mydll.lib mydll.dll
```

-Tpd tells the linker to create a DLL instead of an .exe. cw32mt is the runtime library. Implib creates the import library to link with the DLL's clients.

The Three C Runtime Libraries

Borland C++ and Visual C++ both come with three different 32-bit versions of the C runtime library: static, static multithreading, and dynamic. Because the flat address space does away with 64Kb segments and the ds != ss problem, there are no special RTL versions for particular memory models or for dynamic link libraries. Executables and DLLs link to the same RTLs. The three 32-bit C libraries differ in their linking mechanism and their support for multithreading. Table 2.1 shows their names and contrasts their features.

Table 2.1 The three 32-bit C runtime libraries.		
	Features	*Compiler Options*
MS LIB		
LIBC	Standard	None
LIBCMT	Multithreading	-D_MT
MSVCRT	Multithreading	-D_MT
	Dynamic linking	-D_DLL
Borland LIB		
CW32	Standard	None
CW32MT	Multithreading	-D_MT
CW32MTI	Multithreading	-D_MT
	Dynamic linking	-D_RTLDLL

Listing 2.3   (a) Borland makefile for a multithreading DLL.

(a)

```
#
#  Builds the SECTIONS DLL and its TEST client
#  using Borland's MAKE and command line tools
#

!if !$d(BCROOT)
BCROOT = $(MAKEDIR)\..
!endif

CFLAGS = -c -D_MT
LFLAGS = -L$(BCROOT)\lib
LIBS   = cw32mt import32

!if $d(NODEBUG)
CFLAGS = $(CFLAGS) -O2
!else
CFLAGS = $(CFLAGS) -Od -v
LFLAGS = $(LFLAGS) -v
!endif

all: sections.dll test.exe

test.obj: test.c sections.h
  bcc32 $(CFLAGS) -W $*.c                    # Windows .EXE

global.obj: global.c sections.h
  bcc32 $(CFLAGS) -WD $*.c      # DLL, explicit functions exported

sections.obj: sections.c sections.h
  bcc32 $(CFLAGS) -WD $*.c      # DLL, explicit functions exported

sections.dll: global.obj sections.obj sections.def
  tlink32 $(LFLAGS) -Tpd c0d32 $* global, $*.dll,, $(LIBS), $*.def,
  implib $*.lib $<

test.exe: test.obj
  tlink32 $(LFLAGS) -Tpe c0x32 $*, $*.exe, , $(LIBS) sections,
```

The static library provides the traditional support familiar to C programmers. The linker copies code for C runtime routines from the library into the program's .exe file. The multithreading library also links statically, but all its routines are reentrant to support multithreading. Any DLL that might be called by a multithreading program should use the multithreading or DLL version of the RTL, not the static version. DLLs that support threaded clients should also add the -D_MT switch to the compiler command line. Some of the C header files alter their declarations for multithreading when _MT is defined.

Linking statically to a C library sometimes causes problems for DLLs. If a DLL and its client both call, for example, printf(), and both link statically to the RTL, then the printf() code is copied redundantly into both. Duplicated code is merely inefficient; a more serious problem is that the C routines in the client do not share internal data with C routines in the DLL. If, for example, something goes wrong in the DLL, the client cannot report the problem by calling perror() because it has a different copy of the errno variable. Similar problems arise if the client and the library try to share handles to buffered I/O streams, or if one allocates memory with malloc() and the other tries to free it.

Linking with the DLL version of the RTL solves both problems. Through it, a library and its callers may share a single instance of the internal runtime data. To use the RTL DLL, set two switches for the compiler — one to indicate multithreading support (-D_MT) and one to indicate use of the DLL RTL (-D_DLL for Microsoft, -D_RTLDLL for Borland). The _DLL or _RTLDLL symbol is required for any module — program or library — that links with the RTL DLL. The only catch in linking a DLL to the RTL DLL is that all its clients must also use the RTL DLL. Mismatched libraries cause unpredictable results. Do not choose to build your DLL with the RTL DLL unless you are sure all your library's clients use the RTL DLL too.

Listing 2.3(a) incorporates all the build rules into a sample Borland makefile for a multithreading DLL and a program to call the DLL. Listing 2.3(b) shows the Microsoft version. The sidebar "Win32 DLL Troubleshooting Tips" presents a checklist of troubleshooting tips for building DLLs.

Listing 2.3 (b) Microsoft makefile for a multithreading DLL.

(b)

```
#
#  Builds the SECTIONS DLL and its TEST client
#  using Microsoft's NMAKE and command line tools
#
all: test.exe sections.dll
test.exe: test.obj sections.lib
sections.lib: sections.obj sections.def sections.h
sections.dll: sections.obj sections.exp

# the environment variable CPU is not defined under WIN95
!ifndef CPU
CPU = i386
!endif

CFLAGS = -c -MD -W3 -DWIN32 -D_MT -D_DLL -D_X86_ -DWINVER=0x0400
LFLAGS = -incremental:no -pdb:none -nodefaultlib
SUBSYS = -subsystem:console,4
LIBS   = msvcrt.lib kernel32.lib oldnames.lib  # used in both targets
IMPLIB = sections.lib                          # used in building the EXE

!ifdef NODEBUG
CFLAGS = $(CFLAGS) -Ox
LFLAGS = $(LFLAGS) -release
!else
CFLAGS = $(CFLAGS) -Od -Z7
LFLAGS = $(LFLAGS) -debug:full -debugtype:cv
!endif

# to make header declare dllexport, define __DLL__
sections.obj: sections.c sections.h
   cl $(CFLAGS) -D__DLL__ $*.c

test.obj: test.c sections.h
   cl $(CFLAGS) $*.c

.obj.lib:
   lib -machine:$(CPU) $*.obj -out:$*.lib -def:$*.def

.obj.exe:
   link $(LFLAGS) $(SUBSYS) -out:$*.exe $*.obj \
   $(LIBS) $(IMPLIB)

.obj.dll:
   link $(LFLAGS) -DLL -entry:_DllMainCRTStartup@12 \
   -out:$*.dll $*.obj $*.exp $(LIBS)
```

Managing Memory

A Win32 programmer can decide whether each variable should be visible to all the library's clients, to just one client, or even to just a single thread within a client. At each level of visibility, memory objects can be static or dynamic. By a combination of .def file directives, compiler pragmas, variable storage classifiers, thread-local indexes, memory-mapped files, and conventional allocation functions, a DLL can arrange memory six different ways: statically or dynamically for one thread, for one process, or for all processes. Table 2.2 schematizes the possibilities.

Unfortunately, C and C++ have overloaded meanings for words like "static," and there are no universally agreed-upon terms for describing the visibility of variables in a shared library. This chapter applies the terms "public" and "private." For example, I will refer to global variables in Windows 3.x DLLs as "public" because Windows creates only a single instance of such variables (a single data segment), which is then shared among all the applications that call functions in that DLL. In this context, "public" and "private" do not refer to the scopes of variable names. For example, a Win32 DLL may have a public variable that is not exported and is therefore not directly visible to the DLL's client applications.

Win32 DLL Troubleshooting Tips

- Are the client and the library linked to the same version of the C runtime library?
- If the Microsoft library calls C runtime routines:

  Have you named the entry point DLLMain() and told the linker that _DllMainCRTStartup is the entry point?
  Have you added @12 to the entry point name on the linker command line?

- If the Borland library calls C runtime routines:

  Have you named the entry point DllMain() or DllEntryPoint()?

- If the library's clients are multithreading, have you linked to a multithreading version of the C runtime library (Table 2.1)? Have you defined _MT on the compiler command line?
- If the library links to the DLL version of the RTL, have you defined _DLL on the compiler command line?
- If you have named any data sections and are using Microsoft tools, have you assigned names of no more than eight characters, including the leading period?
- If you have named any data sections and are using Borland tools, do the #pragma option -z statements appear first (not counting comments) in the source file?

  If you have named any data sections and are using both tools and if you are using shared (public) data, are the public variables initialized?

Making Variables Public

By default, Win32 DLL variables are private because the operating system creates a fresh set of them for each new application that calls the DLL. With compiler pragmas, however, you can group variables into sections that you can designate either public or private. The following lines use Microsoft syntax to declare two variables, each in a different section:

```
#pragma dataseg( ".Global" )
UINT A_Public_Number = 0;
#pragma dataseg( ".Local" )
UINT A_Private_Number = 0;
#pragma dataseg( )
```

The first section is named .Global and the second .Local. In Win32 programming, data section names conventionally begin with a period in order to distinguish them easily from code sections, which begin with an underscore (.data vs. _code). However it is still true that variables in a public data section must be initialized explicitly. If the preceding lines of code failed to set A_Public_Number to zero, the variable would remain private even though the section is public.

The example lines only give names to data sections; they do not change the sections' memory attributes. That must happen in the .def file under the SECTIONS keyword (or on Microsoft's linker command line with the -section switch.)

```
LIBRARY MyDll
SECTIONS
     .Global     READ WRITE SHARED
     .Local      READ WRITE
```

Strictly speaking, the declaration for .Local is unnecessary because it merely reiterates the default attributes.

Table 2.2	Memory allocation methods for DLLs.		
	Public to All Processes	**Private to One Process**	**Private to One Thread**
Static	`#pragma data_seg()`	Variables	`_declspec(thread)`
	`#pragma option -zR/S/T`		
Dynamic	Memory-mapped file	`GlobalAlloc()`	`TlsAlloc()`
		`HeapAlloc()`	
		`VirtualAlloc()`	

Incidentally, the old SEGMENTS key word has no purpose in the unsegmented architecture of Windows NT. For compatibility, the build tools interpret SEGMENTS to mean SECTIONS. Also, the old DATA statement no longer has the power to change the default data attributes. This line has no effect:

```
DATA READ WRITE SHARED
```

You have to describe each shared section individually.

Public Variables with Borland Tools

Borland's method for naming data segments and assigning them memory characteristics is a bit more cumbersome. It's also a frequently asked question on the Borland forums. Each segment has a name, a class name, and a group name. You have to set all three using the compiler options -zR, -zS, and -zT:

```
#pragma option -zR.GLOBALDATA
#pragma option -zS.GLOBALGROUP
#pragma option -zT.GLOBALCLASS
UINT A_Public_Number = 0;
```

These options must always appear first in their source file — before any other code — and they always apply to the entire file. That means variables meant for different data segments must be declared in different files. In the Borland versions of my examples, you'll find an extra .C file containing just the public variable declarations.

Tlink32 recognizes this syntax in the .def file for making the Global segment public:

```
LIBRARY MyDll
SECTIONS
  .GLOBALDATA CLASS '.GLOBALCLASS' SHARED
```

Pros and Cons of Public Variables

Creating public data segments can ease the transition in porting a Win16 DLL to Win32. All the variables in a Win16 DLL are public by default. To maintain that status in Win32, move them all to a named data section and declare it public. The same strategy also helps when writing Win32s code that will also work under Windows NT and Windows 95, because variables in Win32s DLL are public, like Win16 variables. (For private variables in Win32s, use TlsAlloc(), discussed later.)

Even though the #pragma options make it easy to share variables through a DLL, it is not always profitable to do so. Many variables are useless when shared, particularly pointers and handles. For example, you can't declare a public lpGlobal variable and expect to share the buffer it names. The value placed in lpGlobal will be a virtual address from the process that was active when the DLL allocated the buffer. Other processes might be able to retrieve the pointer value stored in lpGlobal, but the allocated object doesn't exist in their address spaces, and for them, lpGlobal dangerously points to a random location. Win32 handles, too, are invalid except in the process where they originate.

An Example of Public and Private Data Sections

The program and .def file in Listing 2.4 demonstrates the DLL features I've explained so far, including the entry point procedure and public variables. The library merely counts the number of processes and threads that attach themselves to it. It creates both a public and a private section in order to keep a local total for individual callers and global totals for all callers. The exported GetNumClients() routine works as advertised only because the DLL declares its .Global data section to be SHARED. If data were private and each caller had its own copy of uNumClients, then GetNumClients() would always return 1. The complete code, available on the accompanying disk, includes a sample client that calls the DLL and prints the totals. With three instances of the client running, the output looks like this:

```
clients: 3
threads local: 1
threads global: 3
```

Listing 2.4 shows the Microsoft code; Borland equivalents are on the disk as well.

Listing 2.4 `sections.c` *counts the number of threads*
and processes that attach.

```
/*-------------------------------------------------
        SECTIONS.C

        A library that counts the number of threads
        and processes that attach themselves to it.
        The library's exported functions return the
        current tally values.

        written by Brian G. Myers
        --------------------------------------------------*/
#include <windows.h>
#include <stdio.h>
#include "sections.h"
```

Listing 2.4 (continued)

```
/*---------------------------------------------------
      GLOBAL VARIABLES

      uNumClients          total number of processes
      uNumThreadsGlobal    total number of threads
      uNumThreadsLocal     total threads from the
                              current process only
      --------------------------------------------------*/

#pragma data_seg( ".Global" )    /* SHARED section */
UINT uNumClients = 0;
UINT uNumThreadsGlobal = 0;

#pragma data_seg( ".Local" )     /* PRIVATE section */
UINT uNumThreadsLocal = 0;
#pragma data_seg( )              /* restore default */

/*---------------------------------------------------
      DLL MAIN
      Adjust totals as clients attach and
      detach themselves.
      --------------------------------------------------*/

BOOL WINAPI DllMain(HINSTANCE hinstDLL,
   DWORD dwReason, LPVOID lpReserved)
{
   switch (dwReason)
   {
      case DLL_PROCESS_ATTACH:
         uNumClients++;
         /* fall through for the primary thread */

      case DLL_THREAD_ATTACH:
         uNumThreadsLocal++;
         uNumThreadsGlobal++;
         break;

      case DLL_THREAD_DETACH:
         uNumThreadsLocal--;
         uNumThreadsGlobal--;
         break;

      case DLL_PROCESS_DETACH:
         uNumClients--;
         break;
   }
   return(TRUE);
}
```

Advanced Memory Management

The second DLL example (Listing 2.5) dynamically allocates a public buffer for all of its clients to share. Clients call a library routine to copy data into the buffer and another to display the contents of the buffer on the standard output device. As the library copies each new string to the buffer, it automatically prefixes a thread ID number to identify the source of the string. Allocating the buffer dynamically requires a

---

Listing 2.4 (continued)

```
/*-----------------------------------------------
      GET NUM CLIENTS
   --------------------------------------------*/

UINT GetNumClients(void)
{
   return(uNumClients);
}

/*-----------------------------------------------
      GET NUM THREADS LOCAL
   --------------------------------------------*/

UINT GetNumThreadsLocal(void)
{
   return(uNumThreadsLocal);
}

/*-----------------------------------------------
      GET NUM THREADS GLOBAL
   --------------------------------------------*/

UINT GetNumThreadsGlobal(void)
{
   return(uNumThreadsGlobal);
}


================================================

;  SECTIONS.DEF
;  module definition file for the Sections DLL

LIBRARY

SECTIONS
   .Global READ WRITE SHARED
   .Local  READ WRITE
```

Listing 2.5 `share.c` — *Allocating a shared global buffer.*

```c
/*----------------------------------------------------
      SHARE.C
      A library that dynamically allocates a single
      global buffer for all its clients to share.
      -------------------------------------------------*/

#include <windows.h>
#include <stdio.h>
#include "share.h"

#define BUFFER_SIZE         0x100000

PVOID SharedAlloc(DWORD dwBytes);
void SharedFree(PVOID pView);

#pragma data_seg(".Public")
DWORD dwOffset = 0;            /* position in buffer */
#pragma data_seg()

PSTR pBase;                    /* bottom of buffer */
HANDLE hFileMapping;           /* shared memory */
HANDLE hmxMappedFile;          /* protects buffer */

/* thread-local storage for client thread IDs */
_declspec(thread) DWORD dwThreadID;

/*----------------------------------------------------
      DLL MAIN
      -------------------------------------------------*/

BOOL WINAPI DllMain(HINSTANCE hinstDLL, DWORD dwReason, LPVOID lpReserved)
{
   switch (dwReason)   {
      case DLL_PROCESS_ATTACH:
         /* get a pointer to the shared buffer */
         pBase = (PSTR)SharedAlloc(BUFFER_SIZE);
         if (!pBase) {
            return(FALSE);
         }
         /* fall through for primary thread */

      case DLL_THREAD_ATTACH:
         dwThreadID = GetCurrentThreadId( );
         break;
```

memory-mapped file. Storing an ID for each thread requires thread-local storage (TLS). Before turning to the source code, I'll explain generally how these features are used in the context of a DLL.

Allocating Public Memory Dynamically

Like variables, dynamically allocated memory buffers are private by default under Windows NT. The values returned by functions such as VirtualAlloc(), GlobalAlloc(), and malloc() always refer to private objects. Even setting the GMEM_DDESHARE flag makes no difference; the memory is still private.

Listing 2.5 (continued)

```
        case DLL_PROCESS_DETACH:
            SharedFree(pBase);
            break;
    }
    return(TRUE);
}


/*-------------------------------------------------
    ADD STRING
    Determine the next empty byte in the buffer
    and copy a string there.
    ---------------------------------------------*/

BOOL AddString(PSTR pInput)
{
    PSTR pNext;        /* next empty space in buffer */
    char szDataString[256];    /* thread ID + input */
    UINT uLength;      /* byte count of szDataString */

    /* merge thread ID and data into one string */
    wsprintf(szDataString, "[0x%08lX] %s", dwThreadID, pInput);
    uLength = lstrlen(szDataString) + 1;

    /* Wait in line to use the buffer. */
    WaitForSingleObject(hmxMappedFile, INFINITE);

    /* If the buffer is too small, stop. */
    if ((dwOffset + uLength) > BUFFER_SIZE) {
        ReleaseMutex(hmxMappedFile);
        return(FALSE);
    }
```

Listing 2.5 (continued)

```c
      /* Copy the string into the buffer. */
      pNext = pBase + dwOffset;
      lstrcpy(pNext, szDataString);

      /* Make dwOffset point to the next empty space. */
      dwOffset += uLength;

      ReleaseMutex(hmxMappedFile);
      return( TRUE );
}

/*----------------------------------------------------
      SHOW ALL STRINGS
      Dump all the strings in the buffer to stdout.
      --------------------------------------------------*/

void ShowAllStrings(void)
{
   PSTR pCurrent = pBase;
   PSTR pEnd = pBase + dwOffset;

   while (pCurrent < pEnd) {
      puts(pCurrent);
      pCurrent += lstrlen(pCurrent) + 1;
   }
}

/*----------------------------------------------------
      SHARED ALLOCATE
      Allocate a block of memory to share among
      several processes.
      --------------------------------------------------*/

PVOID SharedAlloc(DWORD dwBytes)
{
   PVOID pView;

   /* Create the file mapping object.  If it already */
   /* exists, this still returns a handle to it. */
   hFileMapping =
         CreateFileMapping((HANDLE)0xFFFFFFFF,
         (LPSECURITY_ATTRIBUTES)NULL, PAGE_READWRITE,
         0, dwBytes, "shared_buffer");
```

In order to allocate a buffer of shared data at run time for several clients, a Win32 DLL must resort to the same means that other Win32 processes use: memory-mapped files. A thorough explanation of memory-mapped files is beyond the scope of this chapter, but briefly, memory mapping is a mechanism for making one block of physical memory visible in several address spaces. The block may appear at different addresses in different spaces, but its contents are the same for all processes. The `CreateFileMapping()` command establishes the block of physical memory, and `MapViewOfFile()` makes the block visible to one process. Processes share memory when several of them map views of the same block.

It may sound odd to use memory-mapped "files" to implement shared memory, but consider that Win32 is a virtual-memory operating system, in which almost any memory can be swapped out to disk. In fact, you could refer to the swap file as a memory-mapped file. Creating a memory-mapped file does not imply that Win32 has to access the file to access the memory. As with the rest of virtual memory, whether file I/O is actually required depends on the swapping algorithm and the amount of available physical memory.

The Share DLL creates one file-mapping object and maps it into the address space of each new client. This kind of "file mapping" actually has very little to do with files. In effect, the combination of `CreateFileMapping()` and `MapViewOfFile()` simply allocates a buffer that can become visible to other processes. The Share DLL packages the two calls in a single procedure named `SharedAlloc()`. When different processes call `SharedAlloc()`, they receive different pointers to the same block of memory. A corresponding `SharedFree()` routine releases the shared buffer. [The system doesn't actually destroy the mapped buffer until all the processes using it have called `SharedFree()`.]

Private Data for One Thread

Private variables in a DLL protect callers from interfering with each other. The actions of one client cannot interfere with values stored for another client. Multiple threads within a single client have the same destructive potential. The actions of one thread could interfere with values stored in the global variables it shares with other threads. One solution is thread-local storage (TLS), a way of making the system replicate a variable for each new thread.

Listing 2.5 (continued)

```
    /* Map the file object into the client's address */
    /* space and receive a pointer to the buffer. */
    pView = MapViewOfFile(hFileMapping,
        FILE_MAP_WRITE, 0, 0, dwBytes);

    /* Make a mutex to serialize buffer operations. */
    hmxMappedFile = CreateMutex(
        (LPSECURITY_ATTRIBUTES)NULL,
        FALSE, "buffer_mutex");

    return(pView);
}

/*----------------------------------------------------
    SHARED FREE
    Release a block of shared memory.
    --------------------------------------------------*/

void SharedFree(PVOID pView)
{
    UnmapViewOfFile(pView);
    CloseHandle(hFileMapping);
    CloseHandle(hmxMappedFile);
}


======================================================


;   SHARE.DEF
;   module definition file for the Share DLL

LIBRARY

SECTIONS
    .Public READ WRITE SHARED

EXPORTS
    AddString           @1
    ShowAllStrings      @2
```

You can make any static variable thread-local by declaring it with a storage class modifier:

```
__declspec(thread) UINT uMostRecentError;
```

This declaration causes the system to produce a new instance of the uMost-RecentError variable for every thread in the process. Each thread can see only the value it stores there; the values stored in the same variable by other threads are visible only to the other threads. The Win32 command GetLastError() presumably relies on a similar thread-local variable within the Win32 subsystem in order to remember the most recent error for each thread.

A little-known fact about thread-local storage may trip up DLL programmers: __declspec(thread) does not work with LoadLibrary(). A library that uses __declspec for TLS must load implicitly (meaning it must be linked directly to the client). To create thread-local storage in explicitly loaded DLLs, use the TLS functions: TlsAlloc(), TlsSetValue(), TlsGetValue(), and TlsFree(). They are more cumbersome than __declspec but also more flexible, easily managing dynamic allocations for individual threads. In cases where the thread-local data cannot be handled in a variable, use the TLS commands.

Sample: The Global Buffer Library

share.c (Listing 2.5) allocates a shared buffer to fill with strings that clients pass in. A public variable, dwOffset, maintains a high-water mark indicating the next available space in the buffer. Once the buffer is full, further attempts to add strings simply fail. The thread-local variable dwThreadID stores the system ID number for each new thread that attaches to the DLL. Every string in the buffer is stamped with the ID number of its thread. The AddString() procedure writes data to the buffer, and ShowAllStrings() displays the data in the buffer. In a program that created threads numbered 147 and 158, ShowAllStrings() would print data strings like these:

```
[147] entry #0
[147] entry #1
[158] entry #0
[147] entry #2
[158] entry #1
. . .
```

If several processes call AddString() concurrently, then ShowAllStrings() displays the combined input from all the clients.

The two procedures SharedAlloc() and SharedFree() are modeled on GlobalAlloc() and GlobalFree(). Unlike GlobalAlloc(), however, SharedAlloc() always returns a pointer to the same buffer. The first call creates the buffer, and subsequent calls from other processes map the buffer into new address spaces.

DllMain() calls SharedAlloc() to create a 1Mb memory-mapped file backed by the system's memory paging file. One great benefit of using memory-mapped files is that the system's virtual memory manager doesn't actually allocate much of the buffer until it's needed. If the buffer fills up to the 4Kb mark, for example, only 4Kb is taken from physical memory no matter how big the memory-mapped file is. That's why I didn't bother to write a SharedReAlloc() procedure to enlarge the buffer. It's easier and more efficient to give the object a large capacity from the start and let the virtual memory manager adjust the allocation size.

The Share DLL creates a mutex to prevent concurrent threads from corrupting the buffer contents and the dwOffset value. DLLs commonly need synchronization objects to protect variables. An animation library, for example, would use the caller's display DC frequently. If several threads drew simultaneously, the actions of one might interfere with the others. One thread might select a red brush, be interrupted by a thread that selects a blue brush, regain control, and draw a blue shape by accident. (A critical section object would solve the problem.) AddString() always waits for its mutex before consulting or modifying any global values. Waiting for the mutex ensures that all buffer modifications occur sequentially rather than simultaneously.

The Share library should check more often for errors; I've skimped for brevity.

Conclusion

The new features of Windows NT DLLs may at first slow you down as you adjust to the new system, but most of the changes confer clear benefits. The single entry point procedure is easier to manage than LibMain() and WEP(), and it's also more powerful because it responds to threads as well as processes. With linker switches and __declspec, you can avoid entirely the chore of listing exports in a .def file. The data_seg and option pragmas easily designate any variable public or private. And although you may have to cope with memory-mapped files and thread-local storage indexes, at least the system supports methods for both static and dynamic memory objects at all three levels of visibility — system, process, and thread.

## Chapter 3

Shared Memory and Message Queues

C++ Classes for OS/2, AIX, and Windows NT

Richard B. Lam

In the chapter, "Communication Classes for Cross-Platform Development" (*Dr. Dobb's Journal*, March 1995), I presented a method of separating a C++ class interface from the underlying implementation details when writing cross-platform classes for event and mutex semaphores. Although there are several ways to separate the interface and implementation, I'll continue with the same approach, applying it here to the cross-platform coding of named shared memory and message queues. In doing so, I'll support interprocess communication (IPC) mechanisms for OS/2, AIX, and Windows NT.

Shared Memory

Shared memory is a single address space allocated as a block of memory by some process (or thread). This process gives the memory to one or more additional processes, and all processes then use the memory as if it were part of their normal address space. To gain access to an existing shared-memory block, processes can either be given a pointer or handle to the block, or they can reference the block by a name agreed upon beforehand.

If the shared memory is unnamed, the memory pointer must be passed from the creating process to any other process that wants access to the shared memory. This can be done using other forms of IPC such as DDE, a message queue, or a pipe. In this chapter, I'll consider only named shared memory — a shared-memory block with a specific name that allows any process that knows the name of the block to gain access to the memory.

The interface to the generic shared-memory class is shown in Listings 3.1 and 3.2. There are two constructors for ipcSharedMemory. One is used by the process or thread that actually creates the memory block, and it takes the name of the block and the desired size of the block in bytes as input arguments. The second constructor is used by other processes or threads that need access to an existing block, and this constructor requires only the block name as a parameter.

Two member functions return the block name and a flag indicating whether the process or thread creates ("owns") or accesses the block. The Pointer() member function returns a void * pointer to the start of the memory block. The implementation of the member functions simply refers to the corresponding member functions in the implementation class osSharedMemory.

Listing 3.3 is the header file used to create the implementation code for shared memory on individual operating systems. The only difference in the constructor arguments to osSharedMemory is the additional pointer to the ipcSharedMemory interface class. This pointer is kept so that the myState variable in the interface class can be modified by the implementation-level member functions. Note that osSharedMemory is a friend of ipcSharedMemory so the myState variable can be set directly in case an initialization error occurs.

The implementation header file also defines a block ID required for the AIX and Windows NT implementations, along with CreateBlock(), OpenBlock(), and CloseBlock() methods, which call the corresponding operating-system-specific shared-memory API functions.

Listing 3.1   C++ class header file for `ipcSharedMemory`.

```
// ***********************************************************************
// Module:  ipcshmem.h  -- Author:  Dick Lam
// Purpose: C++ class header file for ipcSharedMemory
// Notes:  This is a base class. It is the interface class for creating and
//     accessing a memory block that is sharable between processes and threads.
// ***********************************************************************

#ifndef MODULE_ipcSharedMemoryh
#define MODULE_ipcSharedMemoryh

// forward declaration
class osSharedMemory;

// class declaration
class ipcSharedMemory {

friend class osSharedMemory;

public:

   // constructor and destructor
   ipcSharedMemory(const char *name,    // unique name for creating block
                long blocksize);        // requested size (in bytes)
   ipcSharedMemory(const char *name);   // name of block to open
   virtual ~ipcSharedMemory();
   // methods for getting memory block parameters [name, pointer to the block,
   // and whether this is the owner (creator) of the block]
   char *Name() const;
   void *Pointer() const;
   int Owner() const;

   // class version and object state data types
   enum version { MajorVersion = 1, MinorVersion = 0 };
   enum state { good = 0, bad = 1, badname = 2, notfound = 3 };

   // methods to get the object state
   inline int rdstate() const { return myState; }
   inline int operator!() const { return(myState != good); }
protected:
   osSharedMemory *myImpl; // implementation
   state myState;          // (object state (good, bad, etc.)
private:
   // private copy constructor and operator= (define these and make them
   // public to enable copy and assignment of the class)
   ipcSharedMemory(const ipcSharedMemory&);
   ipcSharedMemory& operator=(const ipcSharedMemory&);
};
#endif
```

Listing 3.2   C++ class source file for `ipcSharedMemory`.

```
// ***************************************************************************
// Module:  ipcshmem.C -- Author:  Dick Lam
// Purpose: C++ class source file for ipcSharedMemory
// Notes:  This is a base class.  It is the interface class for creating and
//   accessing a memory block that is sharable between processes and threads.
// ***************************************************************************

#include "ipcshmem.h"
#include "osshmem.h"

// ***************************************************************************
// ipcSharedMemory - constructor for creating

ipcSharedMemory::ipcSharedMemory(const char *name, long blocksize)
{
   // init instance variables
   myState = good;
   myImpl = new osSharedMemory(this, name, blocksize);
   if (!myImpl)
      myState = bad;
}
// --------------------------------------------------------------------------
// ipcSharedMemory - constructor for accessing
ipcSharedMemory::ipcSharedMemory(const char *name)
{
   // init instance variables
   myState = good;
   myImpl = new osSharedMemory(this, name);
   if (!myImpl)
      myState = bad;
}
// --------------------------------------------------------------------------
// ~ipcSharedMemory - destructor
ipcSharedMemory::~ipcSharedMemory()
{
   delete myImpl;
}
// --------------------------------------------------------------------------
// Name - returns the name of the memory block
char *ipcSharedMemory::Name() const
{
   if (!myImpl)
      return 0;
   return myImpl->Name();
}
```

The OS/2 implementation, os2shmem.C, is available on the companion code disk. The OS/2 API requires that all named shared-memory blocks have a name that starts with "\SHAREMEM\" (for example, \SHAREMEM\TEST, \SHAREMEM\MYBLOCK, and so on). Thus, memPath is defined at the top of the module as a constant string containing the name prefix, which is prepended to the block name passed to the constructors to form the complete shared-memory block name. The OS/2 API functions DosAlloc-SharedMem( ), DosGetNamedSharedMem( ), and DosFreeMem( ) are called to create, access, and close the memory block.

For AIX, the shared-memory API is handled similarly to the semaphore implementation — ftok( ) is called on a unique filename to get a key for use by the AIX IPC functions. In aixshmem.c (the AIX implementation is available on the companion code disk) the constructors prepend the string "/tmp/" to the input block name and then create a file with the full block name.

To create the block under AIX, the shmget( ) routine with an IPC_CREAT flag is used, and the memory is attached to the process with the function shmat( ). The block is accessed the same way, except that the creation flag is omitted in the call to shmget( ). The CloseBlock( ) member function calls shmdt( ) to detach the shared memory from the process, and calls shmctl( ) to remove the shared-memory ID from the system. The osSharedMemory destructor also deletes the temporary file created in the constructor if the shared-memory owner is destroyed. Windows NT implements shared memory via file mapping, which allows you to treat a file as a block of memory. The CreateBlock( ) member function in winshmem.c (available on the code disk) calls the NT function CreateFileMapping( ) with an input handle argument of

---

Listing 3.2 *(continued)*

```
// ------------------------------------------------------------------
// Pointer - returns a pointer to the start of the memory block
void *ipcSharedMemory::Pointer() const{
    if (!myImpl)
        return 0;
    return myImpl->Pointer();
}
// ------------------------------------------------------------------
// Owner - returns 1 if this is the owner (creator), and 0 otherwise
int ipcSharedMemory::Owner() const
{
    if (!myImpl)
        return 0;
    return myImpl->Owner();
}
```

Listing 3.3   C++ class header file for *osSharedMemory*.

```
// **************************************************************************
// Module:  osshmem.h  -- Author:  Dick Lam
// Purpose: C++ class header file for osSharedMemory
// Notes:  This is a base class.  It contains general implementation methods
//           for memory blocks shared between processes and threads.
// **************************************************************************

#ifndef MODULE_osSharedMemoryh
#define MODULE_osSharedMemoryh

#include "ipcshmem.h"

// class declaration
class osSharedMemory {

public:
   // constructor and destructor
   osSharedMemory(ipcSharedMemory *interface,const char *name,long blocksize);
   osSharedMemory(ipcSharedMemory *interface, const char *name);

   virtual ~osSharedMemory();

   // methods for getting memory block parameters [name, pointer to the block,
   // and whether this is the owner (creator) of the block]
   char *Name() const;
   void *Pointer() const;
   int Owner() const;
protected:
   ipcSharedMemory *myInterface;       // pointer to the interface instance
   unsigned long myID;                 // id of memory block
   char *myName;                       // shared memory block name
   int isOwner;                        // flag indicating owner

   void *myBlock;                      // pointer to the memory block

   // methods for handling the memory block
   void CreateBlock(long blocksize);
   void OpenBlock();
   void CloseBlock();
private:
   // private copy constructor and operator= (define these and make them
   // public to enable copy and assignment of the class)
   osSharedMemory(const osSharedMemory&);
   osSharedMemory& operator=(const osSharedMemory&);
};
#endif
```

OxFFFFFFFF. This tells the system to use the system swap file rather than an actual disk file to create a file-mapping object. The function returns a mapped file-object handle, which is passed to MapViewOfFile() to get a pointer to the block of shared memory. The OpenFileMapping() function is called to access an existing shared-memory block; the memory is freed by calling UnmapViewOfFile() and CloseHandle().

Message Queues

The message queues I deal with here are quite distinct but similar in function to the event queues used in Windows or OS/2. These event queues work only for windowed applications, whereas message queues are also valid in character-mode sessions. OS/2 and AIX provide direct API support for message queues on the same platform, but Windows NT provides an alternative mailslot API (also available on other platforms) that I'll use. Mailslots can be used for intersystem communications, but I will limit this ipcMessageQueue implementation to IPC.

There is a distinction for message queues between the owner or creator of the queue, which in general is the server process, and the clients that access the queue. Clients of the queue are allowed write-only access and queue owners read-only access. Member functions in the ipcMessageQueue interface class (Listings 3.4 and 3.5) are also provided for queue owners to peek at the number of messages currently waiting in the queue and to purge the queue of all messages.

Listing 3.4   C++ class header file for ipcMessageQueue.

```
// ***********************************************************************
// Module:  ipcqueue.h  -- Author:  Dick Lam
// Purpose: C++ class header file for ipcMessageQueue
// Notes:  This is a base class.  It is the interface class for creating and
//    accessing a message queue that handles messages between processes.
// ***********************************************************************

#ifndef MODULE_ipcMessageQueueh
#define MODULE_ipcMessageQueueh

// forward declaration
class osMessageQueue;
```

Listing 3.4 (continued)

```
// class declaration
class ipcMessageQueue {

friend class osMessageQueue;
public:
   // constructor and destructor
   ipcMessageQueue(const char *name);        // unique name to create queue
   ipcMessageQueue(const char *name,         // name of queue to open
                  unsigned long powner);     // process id of queue owner
   virtual ~ipcMessageQueue();

   // methods for accessing the queue and queue parameters [name, queue id,
   // queue owner process id, and whether this is the owner (creator)]
   char *Name() const;
   unsigned long ID() const;
   unsigned long Pid() const;
   int Owner() const;
   // read/write methods for the queue (only a queue owner may read from
   // the queue, and only queue clients may write to a queue)
   virtual int Read(void *data, long datasize, int wait = 0);
   virtual int Write(void *data, long datasize);

   // methods to examine and remove messages from the queue (owner only)
   virtual unsigned long Peek();
   virtual int Purge();

   // class version and object state data types
   enum version { MajorVersion = 1, MinorVersion = 0 };
   enum state { good = 0, bad = 1, badname = 2, notfound = 3, notowner = 4,
               notclient = 5, readerror = 6, writeerror = 7, badargument = 8 };
   // methods to get the object state
   inline int rdstate() const { return myState; }
   inline int operator!() const { return(myState != good); }
protected:
   osMessageQueue *myImpl; // implementation
   state myState;         // (object state (good, bad, etc.)
private:
   // private copy constructor and operator= (define these and make them
   // public to enable copy and assignment of the class)
   ipcMessageQueue(const ipcMessageQueue&);
   ipcMessageQueue& operator=(const ipcMessageQueue&);
};
#endif
```

In case direct access to the queue is required, the ID() member function returns the operating-system-specific queue handle. Also, there is a Pid() function that returns the process ID of the queue owner. This is provided because the OS/2 queue API functions require clients to know the queue owner's process ID in the call to Dos-OpenQueue(). Therefore, the ipcMessageQueue constructor for clients includes both the queue name and the process ID of the server, whereas the server constructor only needs the queue name.

Listing 3.5   C++ class source file for `ipcMessageQueue`.

```
// **************************************************************************
// Module:  ipcqueue.C  -- Author:  Dick Lam
// Purpose: C++ class source file for ipcMessageQueue
// Notes:  This is a base class.  It is the interface class for creating and
//    accessing a message queue that handles messages between processes.
// **************************************************************************

#include "ipcqueue.h"
#include "osqueue.h"

// **************************************************************************
// ipcMessageQueue - constructor for server
ipcMessageQueue::ipcMessageQueue(const char *name)
{
    // init instance variables
    myState = good;
    myImpl = new osMessageQueue(this, name);
    if (!myImpl)
        myState = bad;
}
// --------------------------------------------------------------------------
// ipcMessageQueue - constructor for clientsipcMessageQueue::ipcMessage-
Queue(const char *name, unsigned long powner)
{
    // init instance variables
    myState = good;
    myImpl = new osMessageQueue(this, name, powner);
    if (!myImpl)
        myState = bad;
}
// --------------------------------------------------------------------------
// ~ipcMessageQueue - destructor
ipcMessageQueue::~ipcMessageQueue()
{
    delete myImpl;
}
```

Listing 3.5 (continued)

```
// --------------------------------------------------------------------------
// Name - returns the name of the queue
char *ipcMessageQueue::Name() const
{
    if (!myImpl)
        return 0;
    return myImpl->Name();
}
// --------------------------------------------------------------------------
// ID - returns the queue id
unsigned long ipcMessageQueue::ID() const
{
    if (!myImpl)
        return 0L;
    return myImpl->ID();
}
// --------------------------------------------------------------------------
// Pid - returns the process id of the Queue owner
unsigned long ipcMessageQueue::Pid() const
{
    if (!myImpl)
        return 0L;
    return myImpl->Pid();
}
// --------------------------------------------------------------------------
// Owner - returns 1 if this is the owner (creator), and 0 otherwise
int ipcMessageQueue::Owner() const
{
    if (!myImpl)
        return 0;
    return myImpl->Owner();
}
// --------------------------------------------------------------------------
// Read - reads a message from the queue (queue owner only)
int ipcMessageQueue::Read(void *data, long datasize, int wait)
{
    if (!myImpl)
        return bad;
    return myImpl->Read(data, datasize, wait);
}
// --------------------------------------------------------------------------
// Write - writes a message to the queue (queue clients only)
int ipcMessageQueue::Write(void *data, long datasize)
{
    if (!myImpl)
        return bad;
    return myImpl->Write(data, datasize);
}
```

As before, the implementation details are delegated to an instance of `osMessage-Queue`, which calls the system-specific API functions.

In addition to requiring the server process ID, the OS/2 queue API uses an event semaphore that can inform the server that a client has posted data to the queue. Consequently, the implementation-class declaration in Listing 3.6 includes a pointer to an `ipcEventSemaphore`, which is created in the server constructor.

Listing 3.5 (continued)

```
// -------------------------------------------------------------------------
// Peek - returns the number of entries in the queue
unsigned long ipcMessageQueue::Peek()
{
   if (!myImpl)
      return 0L;
   return myImpl->Peek();
}
// -------------------------------------------------------------------------
// Purge - removes all entries from the queue
int ipcMessageQueue::Purge()
{
   if (!myImpl)
      return bad;
   return myImpl->Purge();
}
```

Listing 3.6   C++ class header file for `osMessageQueue`.

```
// ***************************************************************************
// Module:  osqueue.h  -- Author:  Dick Lam
// Purpose: C++ class header file for osMessageQueue
// Notes:   This is a base class.  It contains general implementation methods
//          for message queues for sending messages between processes.
// ***************************************************************************

#ifndef MODULE_osMessageQueueh
#define MODULE_osMessageQueueh

#include "ipcqueue.h"

// forward declaration
class ipcEventSemaphore;
```

Listing 3.6 (continued)

```
// class declaration
class osMessageQueue {

public:
   // constructors and destructor
   osMessageQueue(ipcMessageQueue *interface, const char *name);
   osMessageQueue(ipcMessageQueue *interface, const char *name,
                  unsigned long powner);
   virtual ~osMessageQueue();

   // methods for accessing the queue and queue parameters [name, queue id,
   // queue owner process id, and whether this is the owner (creator)]
   char *Name() const;
   unsigned long ID() const;
   unsigned long Pid() const;
   int Owner() const;

   // read/write methods for the queue (only a queue owner may read from
   // the queue, and only queue clients may write to a queue)
   virtual int Read(void *data, long datasize, int wait);
   virtual int Write(void *data, long datasize);

   // methods to examine and remove messages from the queue
   virtual unsigned long Peek();
   virtual int Purge();
protected:
   ipcMessageQueue *myInterface;    // pointer to the interface instance
   unsigned long myPid;             // process id of queue owner
   unsigned long myID;              // id of queue
   char *myName;                    // queue name
   int isOwner;                     // flag indicating owner

   ipcEventSemaphore *mySem;        // required for OS/2 only

   // methods for handling the message queue
   void CreateQueue();
   void OpenQueue();
   void CloseQueue();
private:
   // private copy constructor and operator= (define these and make them
   // public to enable copy and assignment of the class)
   osMessageQueue(const osMessageQueue&);
   osMessageQueue& operator=(const osMessageQueue&);

};
#endif
```

Three protected member functions also are declared in osMessageQueue for creating, opening, and closing a queue.

The OS/2 implementation (os2queue.c, available on the code disk) of message queues requires that all queue names begin with "\QUEUES\", so a constant string variable (queuePath) is defined at the top of the OS/2 module. A call to DosGetInfo-Blocks() in the server constructor is used to retrieve the server's process id, which is stored in the myPid variable. Finally, the event semaphore is created (using the same name as the queue input argument) and DosCreateQueue() is called. The client constructor simply forms the complete queue name and calls DosOpenQueue() to access the queue.

The osMessageQueue::Read() member function resets the event semaphore and then calls DosReadQueue() with either a DCWW_WAIT or DCWW_NOWAIT flag, depending on the value of the Read() function's wait input argument. The data is then copied to the input buffer, and the memory is freed. The Write() member function sets up an unnamed shared-memory block, gives the server process access to the block, and copies the data to be written into the block. The shared-memory block pointer, rather than a message-buffer structure, is then written directly to the queue. For each client write operation, the operating system automatically posts the event semaphore used in Dos-ReadQueue().

For AIX, the server process creates a file by prepending "/tmp/" to the input name and calling creat() — this name is used in the ftok() function call (see aixqueue.c, available on the code disk). The message queue is created or opened through a call to msgget() and closed with msgctl(). The read/write operations are handled by allocating a special msgbuf structure that is passed to msgsnd() for writing and msgrcv() for reading.

Windows NT message queues are implemented using the mailslot API. Mailslots must have a name that begins with "\\.\mailslot\" for use on the same machine, so this string is defined at the top of the NT implementation module (see winqueue.c, available on the code disk). The CreateQueue() member function calls the NT function CreateMailslot(), and the client constructor's OpenQueue() function call accesses the mailslot through a call to CreateFile().

Reading and writing to the mailslot is handled simply by calls to the NT functions ReadFile() and WriteFile(). The Peek() member function calls GetMailslotInfo() to return the number of waiting messages, and Purge() reads and discards each message until no further messages remain.

Test Programs

To test the shared-memory implementation, I've written a number of test programs (available on the code disk). The file mbtest.h defines a SharedVariables structure. The mbtest1.c program creates an ipcSharedMemory block, "myblock," large enough to hold the SharedVariables structure. The Pointer() function retrieves the pointer to the block of memory; the structure fields are initialized and their values are printed. The mbtest2.c program can then be started in a separate session to access the existing memory block, change the values of the structure fields, and print the results.

In practice, processes should synchronize their access to shared-memory blocks using a mutex semaphore. This controls access to the shared data to help provide data integrity and consistency.

The QMsg structure, defined in the file qtest.h, represents the contents of messages that will be written to the server process qtest1 in the file qtest1.c. The server test program creates a message queue named myque and starts the client program qtest2.c, passing the process id of the server as a command line argument to the client. The client then opens the queue and writes several messages to the server, which reads messages and purges the queue before ending.

Summary

Shared-memory blocks are perhaps the fastest IPC mechanism, especially for transferring large structures between processes. However, they require careful synchronization, or subtle bugs can occur in complex programs or systems. Message queues are quite useful for one-way communications between a server (say a display process) and a number of clients (data collection processes, for example). But the practical size of queue messages may be limited (particularly on AIX) to small chunks of information.

## Chapter 4

Memory-Mapped Files Made Easy

Mark R. Szamrej

Memory-mapped files are one of the most powerful and versatile features available in the Win32 API. Unfortunately most developers don't use memory-mapped files until they are faced with a situation that absolutely requires them. I will present a general C++ class that encapsulates the functionality and insulates the user from low-level details of memory-mapped files.

The class is compiler independent and so can be used with any Win32 compiler. All API function calls used by the class are available on all variants of Win32. It is capable of running unmodified on Win32, Windows 95, and Windows NT. A demo program, `poker.exe`, demonstrates memory-mapped files running on all Win32 platforms.

Quick Introduction

Memory mapping allows a disk file to be mapped into an address space. Once the memory has been mapped, the developer no longer has to `fseek()` around the file to access it. Mapping a file to memory returns a pointer as if the file were a contiguous block of memory. Any changes to this memory are reflected in the physical disk file as well.

There are several advantages to this approach. An example which immediately comes to mind is a data acquisition project I was involved in. The project had large data files with about 18 million data points per file. Storing this many data points with azimuth, elevation, range, and amplitude data resulted in file sizes approaching 80Mb each. These large files of raw data needed further processing. Quickly accessing multiple data points from several files was somewhat complicated. The files were too large to fit into memory and accessing the data from disk one value at a time was too slow to be useful. With memory-mapped files we were able to:

- create a "file mapping" for each file to process,
- map each file into memory and get a pointer to the data,
- use the pointer as if the entire file was really in memory, and
- process the large files using pointers.

This approach allows you to work as if all of the data could somehow fit into memory. You don't have to allocate and free memory or manipulate files. The data resides on disk but the operating system does all of the swapping, caching, and virtual memory management for you. This method worked well because data access was relatively sequential and the default caching scheme worked well. Depending on your needs, a custom caching method may perform better.

Maybe you want to convert all of the characters in a file from lower case to upper case? Simply map the file into memory and pass the pointer to strupr(). Want to find the occurrence of the string "Vampire" in a file? Map the file to memory and pass the pointer to strstr(). Comparing two text files? Map them both to memory and call strcmp(). One word of caution however; the C runtime routines assume that all pointers represent null-terminated strings, so be sure that a null is appended to the end of each file or use the general memcmp() routines.

Other Uses

Memory-mapped files have been documented as the only method in Win32 for sharing memory between applications. Memory-mapped files don't have to represent an actual disk file — they can represent regular memory as well (the memory is actually committed within the swapfile). Different applications can open the memory and share it. I don't agree that this is the only method for sharing data between applications. Clever developers could use LPC calls, global atoms tables, named pipes, and other methods. I do believe that using memory-mapped files is the easiest and most efficient method for sharing data.

Another good use for memory-mapped files is to monitor the status and performance of an application in real time while it is executing. To do this, simply fill a structure with the data that you want to monitor and map that structure into memory. Create a short monitoring application that uses memory-mapped files to read and display the contents of the structure. To minimize overhead, the application being monitored should pass a zero (0) as the parameter to CFileMap::Open(). This will prevent the application from waiting for the mapped memory to become available. If the mapped block of memory is not immediately available the call will return NULL rather than block on the function call.

I don't have quantitative numbers, but it is safe to assume that the performance of memory-mapped files is very good. Windows NT uses memory-mapped files internally for program execution and swapfile management. When Windows NT executes your application, it is actually mapping your .exe file into memory and beginning execution at the proper address. Once it's mapped, any required paging of your executable file will be automatic.

Limitations

There are certain limitations that you should be aware of when using memory-mapped files. One limitation is file size. Memory-mapped files allow up to 2^{64} (>18 billion Gb) to be mapped into memory. This isn't really a limitation for most users. The one limitation you will probably run into first is that large files can only be mapped into memory in 4.3Gb sections at a time. To create a file mapping, pass two 32-bit values for the file offset to use. My C++ class assumes that all files will be less than 4.3Gb and sets the high 32-bit value to zero.

Networked files can be mapped into memory, although it isn't necessarily a good idea to do so. File caching and other issues make it difficult for Windows to ensure that all users will have the same coherent view of a file. It is possible for another user to change a networked file without your system being aware of it.

Windows NT supports the concept of window stations and desktops. Each window station has its own desktop(s), clipboard, atom table, and namespace. This means that a memory-mapped file will not work when trying to share memory between processes that run in different window stations. A good example of this would be attempting to use memory-mapped files to communicate between an application and a service. Most services run under the system account, which resides in a different window station and desktop than the user's account.

The `CFileMap` Class

`filemap.h` (Listing 4.1) and `filemap.cpp` (Listing 4.2) show the interface and implementation for the CFileMap class. Of the six member functions in the class, you will likely use only three. The class should accomplish everything that users will want to do with memory-mapped files. All member functions are virtual and all internal structures are protected to make it easy to derive custom classes for specific needs. Although I use Visual C++ and the MFC library, I have kept the CFileMap class generic so it can be used with any compiler that supports Win32.

Listing 4.1   `filemap.h` — *Declaration of memory-mapped file class.*

```
/*========================================================
    CFileMap class header file.
    Written by: Mark Szamrej
    Date: November-1994
    Address: CompuServe 74261,1263

    Description: C++ class to facilitate the use of memory mapped
    files. Works with both disk files and shared memory. Class is
    safe in multithreaded and multitasking environments. Class
    cleanup will always be performed in the destructor.
    ======================================================*/

#ifndef __FILE_MAP_H__
#define __FILE_MAP_H__

class CFileMap
{
//----------------- Member Functions -----------------
public:
    CFileMap();                     // Standard constructor
    virtual    ~CFileMap();         // Destructor

    // ----- Map file to memory -----
    virtual BOOL    MapFile(const char*, DWORD dwAccess= READ | WRITE);

    // ----- Map shared memory -----
    virtual BOOL    MapMemory(const char*, DWORD dwBytes);
    // ----- Once mapped, use the following -----
    virtual LPVOID  Open(DWORD dwTimeOut= INFINITE);
    virtual BOOL    Close();
    virtual DWORD   GetLength(){return m_dwFileLen;}
    virtual void    UnMapFile();

protected:
    virtual BOOL    MapHandle(const char*, HANDLE);
```

Listing 4.1 (continued)

```
//----------------- Member Variables -----------------
public:
    enum{READ = 0x0001,         // READ access
         WRITE = 0x0002,        // WRITE access
        };

protected:
    DWORD   m_dwAccess;         // Access type (R/W)
    DWORD   m_dwFileLen;        // Length of mapped item

    LPVOID m_lpBaseAddress;     // Mapped file address
    HANDLE m_hMapping;          // File mapping handle
    HANDLE m_hFile;             // File handle
    HANDLE m_hMutex;            // File access mutex

    DWORD   m_dwOpen;           // Access count
};

#endif          // __FILE_MAP_H__
```

Listing 4.2 `filemap.cpp` — Implementation of memory-mapped file class.

```
/*=====================================================
    CFileMap class source file.
    Written by: Mark Szamrej
    Date: November-1994
    Address: CompuServe 74261,1263

    Description: See Filemap.h for more details.
=====================================================*/

#include "windows.h"
#include "filemap.h"

//=====================================================
// Standard constructor. Initialize all of
// the member variables to safe values.
//=====================================================
CFileMap::CFileMap()
{
m_hFile = INVALID_HANDLE_VALUE; // File handle
m_hMapping = NULL;              // File mapping handle
m_lpBaseAddress = NULL;         // Not mapped to a address
m_hMutex = NULL;                // No Mutex to sync withm_dwAccess =
0;              // No access rights
m_dwOpen = 0;                   // Lock count is zero
m_dwFileLen = 0;                // File length is zero
}
```

Listing 4.2 (continued)

```
//═══════════════════════════════════════
// The destructor simply calls UnMapFile()
// to remove any existing mapping.
//═══════════════════════════════════════
CFileMap::~CFileMap()
{
    CFileMap::UnMapFile();    // Remove any mapping before exit
}


//═══════════════════════════════════════
// Unmap any current file mapping we have.
// Note that this is done in the reverse
// order in which the view is mapped.
//═══════════════════════════════════════
void CFileMap::UnMapFile()
{
    while(Close());    // Remove all locks we have

    // Unmap any mapped views we have open
    if(m_lpBaseAddress != NULL)
    {
    FlushViewOfFile(m_lpBaseAddress, 0); // Flush to disk
    UnmapViewOfFile(m_lpBaseAddress);    // Unmap the view
    m_lpBaseAddress = NULL;              // Can't use this
    }

    // Close the file mapping object
    if(m_hMapping != NULL)
    {
        CloseHandle(m_hMapping);  // Close the mapping
        m_hMapping = NULL;        // Can't use this
    }

    // Close the file if open
    if(m_hFile != INVALID_HANDLE_VALUE)
    {
        CloseHandle(m_hFile);                // Close the file
        m_hFile = INVALID_HANDLE_VALUE; // Can't use this
    }

    if(m_hMutex != NULL)
    {
        CloseHandle(m_hMutex);    // Close the mutex
        m_hMutex = NULL;          // Can't use this
    }

    m_dwAccess = 0;              // No access
    m_dwFileLen = 0;             // No length
}
```

The class is completely self contained and performs any and all cleanup in its destructor. To use the class, simply create a `CFileMap` object, use it, and then throw it away when you are done. Before I get into the internals of the `CFileMap` class, I will take a closer look at how you might use this class.

Listing 4.2 (continued)

```
//================================================
// Maps memory for sharing. The name of the memory is 'pszName'
// and it has a length of dwBytes. Returns TRUE if successful.
//================================================
BOOL CFileMap::MapMemory(const char* pszName,DWORD dwBytes)
{
    UnMapFile();                     // Unmap current mapping

    m_dwFileLen = dwBytes;           // Set the file length
    m_dwAccess = READ | WRITE;       // Full R/W access

    if(! MapHandle(pszName, (HANDLE)0xFFFFFFFF))
    {
        UnMapFile();                 // Unmap if we failed
        return FALSE;                // Return failure
    }

return TRUE;                         // Return success
}


//================================================
// Maps a file into memory for access  or sharing. The file
// name is pszFileName and dwAccess indicates Read/Write
// access. Return is TRUE if function is successful.
// FALSE is returned if the file does not exist if the
// system is unable to map the file for any reason.
//================================================
BOOL CFileMap::MapFile(const char* pszFileName, DWORD dwAccess /* READ + WRITE */)
{
    UnMapFile();             // Remove any existing mapping
    m_dwAccess = dwAccess;   // Access type (Read/Write)

    // First set the flags for the function call
    DWORD dwFlags = 0;
    if(m_dwAccess & READ)
        dwFlags |= GENERIC_READ;
    if(m_dwAccess & WRITE)
        dwFlags |= GENERIC_WRITE;

    // Step #1 - Call CreateFile() to open the file
    m_hFile = CreateFile(pszFileName,
        dwFlags,                     // Access flags
        FILE_SHARE_READ | FILE_SHARE_WRITE,
        NULL,                        // Security attributes
        OPEN_EXISTING,               // Open existing file
        FILE_ATTRIBUTE_NORMAL,       // File Attributes
        NULL);                       // Template file to use
```

Listing 4.2 (continued)

```
    if(m_hFile == INVALID_HANDLE_VALUE)
    {
        UnMapFile();              // Unmap if we failed
        return FALSE;             // Return failure
    }

    // Get the size of the file that we have
    BY_HANDLE_FILE_INFORMATION bhInfo;
    if(GetFileInformationByHandle(m_hFile, &bhInfo))
        m_dwFileLen = bhInfo.nFileSizeLow;


    // File has been created!
    // Step #2 - Map the handle to memory
    if(! MapHandle(pszFileName, m_hFile))
    {
        UnMapFile();              // Unmap if we failed
        return FALSE;             // Return failure
    }
return TRUE;                       // Return success
}


//===============================================================
// Does the work to map a file handle (hFile) to memory.
// For real files (disk files) hFile is a file handle and
// for memory hFile is 0xFFFFFFFF. The code does the bulk
// of the work for the MapFile() and MapMemory() functions.
//===============================================================
BOOL CFileMap::MapHandle(const char* pszName, HANDLE hFile)
{
const int iLen = strlen(pszName);  // Get length of string

    // Create the mapping name.
    // The mapping name cannot contain any
    // '\' backslash charecters so we will
    // replace them with underscores ('_').
    char* pszMapName = new char[iLen+1];
    strcpy(pszMapName, pszName);    // Copy the base name
    strupr(pszMapName);             // Make it uppercase
    while(strchr(pszMapName, '\\'))// Replace '\' with '_'
        *(strchr(pszMapName, '\\')) = (char)'_';

    // Determine the flags to use for the function call
    DWORD dwFlags;
    if(m_dwAccess & WRITE)
        dwFlags = PAGE_READWRITE;
    else
        dwFlags = PAGE_READONLY;
```

Mapping a File to Memory

Before you can map a file to memory you must first create a `CFileMap` object. Once it is created, you can map a disk file with the `MapFile()` member function passing the filename and, optionally, the access rights as parameters. The access rights default to Read/Write if none were supplied. To create shared memory, call the `MapMemory()` member function, passing the name you want to give the memory along with the size of the memory block. This code snippet shows a typical example:

```
CFileMap map1;    // Create a CFileMap object

// Map a disk file to this object
BOOL bResult = map1.MapFile("c:\\Stuff\\somefile.bin");

// Map 1-Meg of memory named MyMemBlock
BOOL bResult = map1.MapMemory("MyMemBlock", 1024*1024);
```

Listing 4.2 (continued)

```
// Create a file mapping object
m_hMapping = CreateFileMapping(hFile,
              NULL,           // Security attributes
              dwFlags,        // Data protection
              0,              // High 32-bits of size
              m_dwFileLen,    // Low 32-bits of size
              pszMapName);    // Map name of object

if(m_hMapping == NULL)        // Create mapping failed
{
    delete[] pszMapName;      // Delete our buffer
    UnMapFile();              // Remove any mapping
    return FALSE;             // Return failure
}

// Determine the flags to use for the function call
if(m_dwAccess & WRITE)
    dwFlags = FILE_MAP_WRITE;
else
    dwFlags = FILE_MAP_READ;

// Have the file mapping!
// Map the file into an address space
m_lpBaseAddress = MapViewOfFile(m_hMapping,
        dwFlags,              // Read or write flags
        0, 0,                 // Offset (0=beginning)
        0);                   // Bytes to map (0=ALL)
```

Listing 4.2 (continued)

```
    if(m_lpBaseAddress == NULL)      // Unable to map a view
    {
    delete[] pszMapName;             // Delete our buffer
    UnMapFile();                     // Remove any mapping
    return NULL;                     // Return failure
    }

    //----------------------------------------------------
    // Create the mutex. We have to use a diffent name than
    // the file mapping object since they both share the
    // same global name space and the call will fail.
    //----------------------------------------------------
    const char* pSuffix = "Mutex"; // Suffix to use
    char* pszMutexName = new char[iLen+strlen(pSuffix)+1];
    strcpy(pszMutexName, pszMapName); // Copy existing name
    strcat(pszMutexName, pSuffix);   // Append the suffix
    strupr(pszMutexName);            // Make it uppercase

    m_hMutex = CreateMutex(NULL,     // Security attributes
            FALSE,                   // Don't want to own it
            pszMutexName);           // Name for our mutex

    delete[] pszMutexName;           // Delete the strings.
    delete[] pszMapName;             // We won't need them.

return TRUE;                         // Return success
}


//===============================================================
// Open - Does not actually do anything with the file
// mapping. It simply controls access to the data
// to prevent multiple threads from stomping over
// the data at the same time.
//===============================================================
LPVOID CFileMap::Open(DWORD dwTimeOut /* = INFINITE */)
{
    // If we are not mapped then our base address will
    // be NULL. Comply with the request and return NULL.
    if(m_lpBaseAddress == NULL)
        return NULL;

    // Wait for the mutex to be released or a timeout.
    DWORD dwResult=WaitForSingleObject(m_hMutex,dwTimeOut);

    if(dwResult == WAIT_OBJECT_0)
    {                                // We got the file
        m_dwOpen++;                  // Increment lock count
        return m_lpBaseAddress;      // Return memory pointer
    }

return NULL;                         // Couldn't get the file
}
```

Both functions return TRUE if the file was mapped and FALSE if the function failed. The first application to map memory will receive a zero-filled block of memory. Other tasks that use the same name will get the existing memory block. Calling MapFile() or MapMemory() will remove an existing file mapping. You can explicitly remove an existing file mapping by calling UnMapFile().

Accessing the Data

Once the mapping is complete, access the mapped data by using the pointer returned from the Open() member function. You can optionally tell Open() how many milliseconds to wait before timing out (this will happen if another thread has called Open() on the same object first). If not supplied, the time-out value defaults to INFINITE. You can also pass zero, in which case the function will return immediately. Open() returns a pointer to the object that has been mapped or NULL if the object isn't available.

When you are done with the data, call Close(). Close() takes no parameters and should be matched with every call to Open(). You should call Close() as soon as possible to avoid blocking other applications from accessing the data. Don't use the pointer previously returned from Open() after you have called Close(). When you are finished using the CFileMap object, simply let it go out of scope or delete it. The destructor will always perform the necessary internal cleanup.

Listing 4.2 (continued)

```
//=========================================
// Close - Does not actually do anything with the file
// mapping. Like Open(), it is used exclusively to
// control access to the data. Decrements the usage
// count and releases the mutex to waiting threads.
//=========================================
BOOL CFileMap::Close()
{
    if(m_dwOpen == 0)            // Return FALSE if file
        return FALSE;            // was not already open

    m_dwOpen--;                  // Decrement lock count
    ReleaseMutex(m_hMutex);      // Now release the mutex

return TRUE;                     // Return success
}
```

Safe in Any Task

Native Win32 memory-mapped files are not thread-safe in multitasking or multi-threaded environments. There is no built-in mechanism to protect several tasks or threads from reading or writing to the file simultaneously. My class takes this into consideration and protects itself by using an internal mutex (mutual exclusion semaphore). The Open() and Close() functions do not remove or modify any existing mapping. They exist for the sole purpose of managing access to the mapped item. The mutex guarantees that access to the memory-mapped file will be limited to one thread at a time.

A mutex is a system synchronization object that guarantees "MUTual EXclusion" to itself. The exclusion mechanism uses a thread as the unit of granularity. This means that only one thread at a time can own access to the mutex. The same thread can access the mutex several times, in which case the usage count of the mutex is incremented. When the usage count reaches zero, the next thread waiting for the mutex will receive ownership.

Other tasks or threads that try to access the mutex will be suspended until the mutex is released or until the time-out interval expires. The CFileMap object maintains its own internal usage count independent of the mutex. Internally, the class takes care of generating names for both the file mapping and the mutex system objects. Both of these names share the same system namespace so they must be unique and cannot contain any backslash characters. The class will generate proper names from the string passed to the MapFile() and MapMemory() functions.

An Example: poker.exe

I wanted to come up with a sample program that would show an interesting use for memory-mapped files. I wrote a short program poker.exe (Figure 4.1) which uses shared memory to play a game of poker between several instances of the same application. poker.exe was written using Visual C++ for NT and makes use of Microsoft's MFC library. The makefile for the poker application is targeted for the original version of MSVC++ for NT. To use the makefile with either VC++ 2.x or VC++ 4.x, simply open the .mak file and let Visual C++ convert the file to your current format. poker.exe and its source code are available on the companion code disk.

Each instance of the application creates a memory object named "PokerGame" which is then shared among all running instances. The mapped memory contains a POKER structure, which is described in the poker.h file. The various fields in this structure represent the number of players, the current state of the game, the amount of money in the jackpot, and all 52 playing cards in the deck. The playing cards and poker hands are handled by the CCard and CHand classes that are defined in the cards.cpp and cards.h files.

A very important field is the reference count field, which ensures that all players get access to the data. As the state of the game changes, this field is always set to the number of players in the game. As each player accesses the POKER structure, the player must decrement the reference count by one. The last player to access this structure will have decremented the count to zero. It is the last player's responsibility to update the state of the game and to reset the reference count back to the total number of players.

The game itself is a fairly routine game of seven card stud with common rules applied. One player cannot play against himself. The window title will display "Waiting for players" until a second player joins. A player cannot join in the middle of a hand. New players will display "Waiting to join..." until the start of the next hand. No more than six players are allowed, so any additional players will have to wait until someone leaves the game.

Figure 4.1   Poker program demonstrates shared memory.

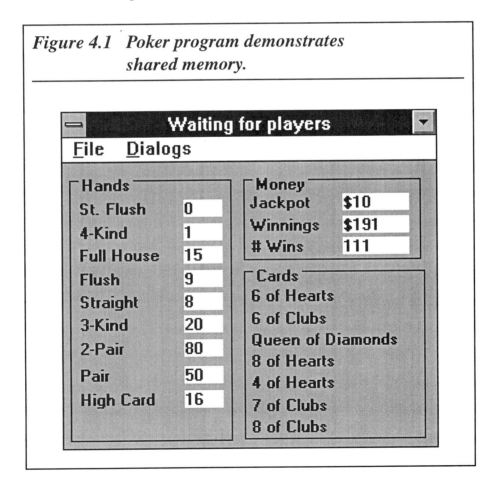

Players leave the game when they run out of money or when the application is closed. In the interest of maintaining order, players can leave only at the end of each hand. Closing the application will display "Leaving game..." which will change to "Out of the game" after the player has been officially removed.

Each player starts with $100 and the ante is $1. If nobody has the minimum pair required to open, another ante is placed into the jackpot and the cards are dealt again. Once a player can open, all bets are made and the hands are shown. The winner collects the jackpot and the next hand begins.

Summary

Memory-mapped files are ideal for manipulating disk files and for sharing data between applications. The class is easy to use and is useful for many Win32 programming tasks. The CFileMap class presented here will allow you to start using memory-mapped files in your Win32 applications today.

## Chapter 5

The Ultimate Windows Version Detector

Paula Tomlinson

In a perfect world, each successive version of the Windows API would be a superset of the previous version, with backwards compatibility fully intact. You could simply call the Windows API function GetVersion() to obtain the current Windows version number, which would be all you'd need to know about which operating system you were running under.

Of course, this has not been the case. For example, there are subtle differences between the 16-bit version of Windows and the Windows for Workgroups product — differences that are unrelated to Windows for Workgroups' built-in support for peer networking. The picture gets even more confused for Win32 applications. Win32 was first billed as a common API for applications running on Win32s, Windows NT, and Windows 95. In reality, each of these environments supports a different subset of the Win32 API. For example, although all three platforms support memory-mapped files, only Windows 95 and Windows NT support multithreaded applications. Win32s and Windows 95 use a 16-bit world coordinate system for graphics output whereas Windows NT uses a 32-bit system. Windows 95 supports the new plug-and-play messages, but Windows NT doesn't.

Another version-related problem is the way that backwards compatibility works under the Windows family of operating systems. Windows NT's WOW (Windows on Windows) module can load and execute a 16-bit .exe that was created for 16-bit Windows 3.1, but that .exe may encounter some subtle differences when running in the Windows NT environment. For example, your 16-bit .exe can directly access the I/O ports of custom hardware devices under 16-bit Windows 3.1, but when executed under Windows NT, the same action will cause your 16-bit .exe to terminate most ungracefully. Such an application could make a less unfavorable impression on users by detecting that it is being executed under Windows NT and either avoiding the illegal operation or simply informing the user that it cannot run under Windows NT.

The list goes on, but the end result is that programmers are typically left with the chore of trying to determine programmatically what platform their application is running on. Unfortunately, retrieving the Windows version and platform type isn't as

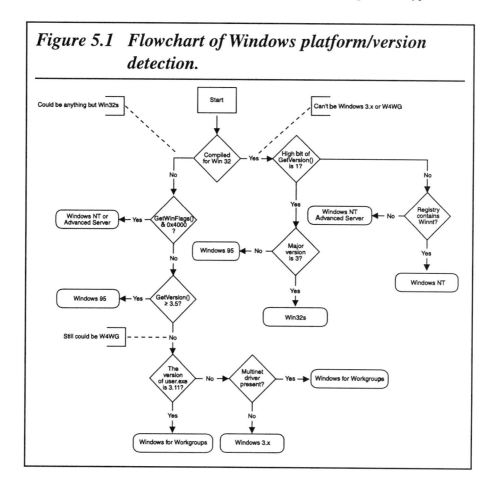

Figure 5.1   *Flowchart of Windows platform/version detection.*

easy as calling `GetVersion()` anymore. This chapter explains how to determine the platform you are running under, as well as which version of the operating system is in effect. I also supply a ready-to-use function that you can compile with any Windows program and call to identify the current Windows platform and version. Figure 5.1 contains a flowchart of the process; you may want to refer to it while reading the more detailed discussion below.

A Platform and Version Detector

Any decent version detection routine needs to retrieve the Windows version number in addition to distinguishing at least between Windows 3.x/Win32s, Windows 95, and Windows NT. It is also conceivable that applications might need to know if various networking services are available, so the "ultimate version detector" must also distinguish between Windows 3.x and Windows for Workgroups and between Windows NT and Windows NT Advanced Server. `wversion.h` (Listing 5.1) lists the constants I will use to refer to each of these platforms: `ENV_WIN3X`, `ENV_WFW`, `ENV_WIN32S`, `ENV_WIN32C`, `ENV_WINNT`, and `ENV_WINNTAS`.

Listing 5.1   `wversion.h`— *Version flags and defines.*

```
BOOL FAR PASCAL WVersion(LPDWORD, LPDWORD);

#define ENV_UNKNOWN       0x00000000
#define ENV_WIN3X         0x00000001
#define ENV_WFW           0x00000004
#define ENV_WIN32S        0x00000008
#define ENV_WIN32C        0x00000010
#define ENV_WINNT         0x00000020
#define ENV_WINNTAS       0x00000040

#define METHOD_MULTINET       0x01
#define METHOD_FILEVERSION    0x02

#define WNNC_NET_MULTINET          0x8000
#define WNNC_SUBNET_WINWORKGROUP   0x0004
#define WNNC_NET_TYPE              0x0002

typedef struct tagVS_VERSION
{
    WORD wTotLen;
    WORD wValLen;
    char szSig[16];
    VS_FIXEDFILEINFO vffInfo;
} VS_VERSION;
```

wversion.c (Listing 5.2) contains the source code for WVersion(), a platform and version number detection routine. WVersion() arguments consist of two pointers to DWORDs, where WVersion() will store the platform environment ID and the Windows version, respectively. You can compile WVersion() for either 16- or 32-bit Windows applications. As you will see, the version detection methods used are quite different for 16-bit and 32-bit Windows applications. I assume that either WIN32 or _WIN32 will be defined as a 32-bit Windows application is being compiled. If your compiler or its header files do not behave this way, you could always place an explicit

#define WIN32

in your source code (or set a corresponding command-line or IDE option) when building a 32-bit version of the code. I use these definitions to provide a completely different detection algorithm when WVersion() is compiled with a 16-bit compiler rather than a 32-bit compiler. This also lets me use Win32 routines for the 32-bit code path without generating unresolved externals in the 16-bit code path.

Listing 5.2 wversion.c *— Platform determination routines.*

```
#include "assert.h"
#include "windows.h"
#include "ver.h"
#include "wversion.h"

BOOL IsWindowsForWorkgroups(unsigned short);

/**-------------------------------------------------------**/
BOOL FAR PASCAL WVersion(LPDWORD lpdwEnviron,
    LPDWORD lpdwVersion)
{
    DWORD dwEnviron = ENV_UNKNOWN;
    DWORD dwVersion = GetVersion();

    //-------------------------------------------------
    // 32-bit code gets version info this way
    //-------------------------------------------------

    #if defined _WIN32 || defined WIN32
    {
        // if the highbit returned from GetVersion is 1, then
        // it's either Win32s or Win32c.

        if (dwVersion & 0x80000000)
        {           // check major version number to distinguish
            // Win32s from Win32c (in the LOBYTE of the LOWORD)
            if (LOBYTE(LOWORD(dwVersion)) == 3)
                dwEnviron = ENV_WIN32S;
            else dwEnviron = ENV_WIN32C;
        }
```

Listing 5.2 (continued)

```
        // if the highbit returned from GetVersion is 0, then
        // it's either Win NT or Win NT Advanced Server.

        else
        {
            // Check registry to distinguish NT from NTAS
            HKEY hKey;
            BYTE szValue[128];
            DWORD dwSize = 128;

            RegOpenKeyEx(HKEY_LOCAL_MACHINE,
                "SYSTEM\\CurrentControlSet\\Control",
                "\\ProductOptions", 0, KEY_READ, &hKey);
            RegQueryValueEx(hKey, "ProductType", 0, NULL,
                        szValue, &dwSize);
            RegCloseKey(hKey);

            if (stricmp(szValue, "Winnt") == 0)
                dwEnviron = ENV_WINNT;
            else
                dwEnviron = ENV_WINNTAS;
        }
    }

    // 16-bit code gets version info this way

#else
    {        // For 16-bit code, use GetWinFlags to tell if
        // running on the WOW layer of NT/NTAS

        if (GetWinFlags() & 0x4000)
            dwEnviron = ENV_WINNT;
        else
        {
            // check major version number to distinguish
            // Win 3.x from Win32c (in the LOBYTE of the LOWORD)
            if ((LOBYTE(LOWORD(dwVersion)) > 3) ||
                (HIBYTE(LOWORD(dwVersion)) > 50))
                dwEnviron = ENV_WIN32C;
            else
            {
                // finally, determine if Win 3.x or WFW
                if (IsWindowsForWorkgroups(METHOD_FILEVERSION))
                    dwEnviron = ENV_WFW;
                else if (IsWindowsForWorkgroups(METHOD_MULTINET))
                    dwEnviron = ENV_WFW;
                else dwEnviron = ENV_WIN3X;
            }
        }
    }
#endif
```

Consider the 32-bit code path first. If I compile WVersion() as part of a Win32 module, then I know it will only run on Win32s, Windows 95, Windows NT, or Windows NT Advanced Server; I can eliminate Windows and Windows for Workgroups as possible platforms. By definition, the high bit of the value that GetVersion() returns is 0 for Windows NT and 1 for Win32s or Windows 95. So, the first thing WVersion() does is check the value returned from GetVersion(). If the high bit is 1, then I know the code is running on either Win32s or Windows 95. At this point, a simple check of the major version number is sufficient to distinguish between Win32s and Windows 95; if the major version number is 3, I know it's Win32s; if the major version number is 4, I know it's Windows 95.

Listing 5.2 (continued)

```
*lpdwEnviron = dwEnviron;
*lpdwVersion = dwVersion;

    return TRUE;
} // WVersion

typedef WORD (WINAPI*NETCAPFUNC)(int);
/**----------------------------------------------------**/
BOOL IsWindowsForWorkgroups(unsigned short usMethod)
{
    HINSTANCE hLib = NULL;
    NETCAPFUNC lpWNetGetCaps = NULL;
    WORD wNetType;
    DWORD dwVerSize, dwVerHandle;
    HANDLE hMem;
    VS_VERSION FAR * lpVerInfo;
    BOOL bWfW = FALSE;  // assume failure

    // use the method that checks for a multinet driver
    if (usMethod == METHOD_MULTINET)
    {
        hLib = LoadLibrary((LPSTR)"user.exe");
        assert(hLib >= HINSTANCE_ERROR);
        lpWNetGetCaps = (NETCAPFUNC)GetProcAddress(hLib, (LPSTR)"WNetGetCaps");
        if (lpWNetGetCaps != NULL)
        {
            wNetType = (*lpWNetGetCaps)(WNNC_NET_TYPE);
            if (wNetType & WNNC_NET_MULTINET)
                if (LOBYTE(wNetType) & WNNC_SUBNET_WINWORKGROUP)
                    bWfW = TRUE;
        }
        if (hLib) FreeLibrary(hLib);
    }
```

On the other hand, if the high bit of the value returned from GetVersion() is 0, then the current platform must be either Windows NT or Windows NT Advanced Server. A simple yet reliable way for detecting Windows NT Advanced Server is querying the "ProductType" value of the

```
\HKEY_LOCAL_MACHINE\SYSTEM\CurrentControlSet\Control\ProductOptions
```

key in the registry. If the REG_SZ value stored there is Winnt then the workstation version of Windows NT is running. If the string is LANMANNT then Windows NT Advanced Server is running.

The second half of WVersion() performs platform and version number detection when compiled for a 16-bit Windows module. A 16-bit Windows application could be running on any of the platforms identified in wversion.h except for Win32s. Even if the Win32s components were installed and available on the currently running version of Windows 3.1, the 16-bit application is not taking advantage of them. So, in this case, I would classify the platform as ENV_WIN3X rather than ENV_WIN32S.

Listing 5.2 (continued)

```
    // use method that checks the file version of user.exe
    else
    {
        // allocate memory for the file info struct
        dwVerSize = GetFileVersionInfoSize((LPSTR)"user.exe",
            &dwVerHandle);
        hMem = GlobalAlloc(GMEM_MOVEABLE, dwVerSize);
        assert(hMem != NULL);
        lpVerInfo = (VS_VERSION FAR *)GlobalLock(hMem);

        // Get the file version
        // for Win32, the dwVerHandle is zero, ignored
        if (GetFileVersionInfo((LPSTR)"user.exe",
                        dwVerHandle, dwVerSize, lpVerInfo))
            if ((HIWORD(lpVerInfo->
                vffInfo.dwProductVersionMS) == 3) &&
                (LOWORD(lpVerInfo->
                vffInfo.dwProductVersionMS) == 11))
                bWfW = TRUE;
        GlobalUnlock(hMem);
        GlobalFree(hMem);
    }
    return bWfW;

} // IsWindowsForWorkgroups
```

For the 16-bit code path, the first thing I do is confirm or eliminate Windows NT as the current platform. Unfortunately, the 16-bit version of GetVersion() always returns version 3.1 from the Windows NT WOW layer, so it isn't particularly useful here. (See the sidebar "Windows NT and the 16-bit GetVersion() Routine.") However, I can AND the value returned from GetWinFlags() with 0x4000 to tell if Windows NT or Windows NT Advanced Server is running. Unfortunately, I don't know of any simple ways to distinguish between Windows NT and Windows NT Advanced Server from a 16-bit Windows application. Note that GetWinFlags() has been obsoleted from the Win32 API.

If the current platform is not Windows NT, then I check if the current platform is Windows 95. As with the 32-bit case, I can tell this by just checking the version number. There is a catch though — the 16-bit version of GetVersion() returns version 3.95 on Windows 95. Presumably this will be true in a later "service pack" release of Windows 95, but to be safe, I assume the platform is Windows 95 anytime the version number is greater than 3.50. If the current platform is not Windows NT or Windows 95, that just leaves Windows 3.x or Windows for Workgroups.

Windows NT and the 16-bit GetVersion() *Routine[1]*

The 16-bit version of GetVersion() returns 3.95 on Windows 95. However, on Windows NT, it returns 3.1 on all versions of Windows NT that have shipped to date (versions 3.1, 3.5, 3.51, and 4.0). Although the techniques described in this chapter enable 16-bit applications to determine if they're running on Windows NT, it doesn't help 16-bit applications know which version of Windows NT they're running on. This could be crucial information if, for example, an application needs to know whether some features of the new user interface and shell are available. Because the 32-bit version of GetVersion() returns the correct version number on Windows NT, perhaps the easiest solution to this problem is to have your 16-bit application thunk over to the 32-bit version of the GetVersion() routine.

Generic thunking support can be used by 16-bit applications to call 32-bit routines and is available on both the Windows 95 and Windows NT platforms. To use generic thunking to call the 32-bit version of GetVersion(), the 16-bit application would first call LoadLibraryEx32W() to load the DLL that contains the 32-bit GetVersion() routine (in this case, kernel32.dll) then call GetprocAddress32W() to retrieve the address of the 32-bit GetVersion() entry point. Finally, pass this address [no parameters are required in the GetVersion() routine] to CallProc32W(), which calls the 32-bit target routine (handling translations between 16 bits and 32 bits) and returns the value that the 32-bit version of GetVersion() returns.

1. This information is from an article by Gary S. Tresler that appeared in *Windows Developer's Journal.*

There are at least two documented methods for determining if Windows for Workgroups is running. One method involves checking the file version information for user.exe, and the other method involves checking for the presence of a multinet driver. I wrote a little routine called IsWindowsForWorkgroups() that takes a parameter to let it know which of these detection methods to use. (I will discuss this routine in more detail later.) The WVersion() routine calls IsWindowsForWorkgroups() first with the file version method (METHOD_FILEVERSION) and second with the multinet driver method (METHOD_MULTINET). If neither call to IsWindowsForWorkgroups() returns TRUE, then I can fairly safely assume that Windows 3.x is running. Finally, WVersion() returns the version number and the platform ID back to the caller.

IsWindowsForWorkgroups()

Apparently for backwards compatibility reasons, the original release of Windows for Workgroups returns version 3.1 for calls to GetVersion(), just like the ordinary version of Windows. This means you can't use GetVersion() to distinguish between Windows and Windows for Workgroups, so I needed a more creative approach. The Microsoft Knowledge Base lists at least two different methods for distinguishing between Windows 3.1 and Windows for Workgroups. IsWindowsForWorkgroups() demonstrates both of these methods.

If the usMethod type passed in to IsWindowsForWorkgroups() is METHOD_MULTINET, then I'll check for the presence of a multinet driver to indicate whether Windows for Workgroups is running. I first load user.exe and then attempt to get a procedure address for WNetGetCaps(). If WNetGetCaps() is present, then I call it with the WNNC_NET_TYPE parameter. If the value returned has the WNNC_NET_MULTINET and WNNC_SUBNET_WINWORKGROUP flags set, then a multinet driver is available and thus Windows for Workgroups is running. In this case, the routine returns TRUE, otherwise it returns FALSE. The WNNC flags are defined in wversion.h and the method is documented in the Microsoft Knowledge Base chapter Q114470.

An alternative method, documented in Knowledge Base chapters Q113998 and Q113892, involves retrieving the file version information for user.exe. IsWindowsForWorkgroups() uses this method if METHOD_FILEVERSION is passed as the usMethod parameter. The chapters are actually Visual Basic examples, but the concepts apply to C/C++ Windows applications as well. I use GetFileVersionInfoSize() and GetFileVersionInfo() routines (defined in ver.h, exported by ver.dll) to extract this file version. If Windows for Workgroups is installed, then the user.exe file will have a file version of 3.11; otherwise, Windows for Workgroups is not installed and so IsWindowsForWorkgroups() returns FALSE.

The WTest Sample Program

To demonstrate WVersion(), I wrote a simple Windows application, wtest.c (available on the code disk), which you can compile as a 16-bit or a 32-bit Windows application. The code has been compiled in the 16-bit environment with Borland, Microsoft, Symantec, and Watcom C++ compilers and in the 32-bit environment with Visual C++ v2.0. When compiling the 32-bit version, the compiler automatically used winver.h instead of ver.h (winver.h replaced ver.h for the Win32 development environments). Visual C++ 2.0 also ignores the STUB and EXETYPE settings in the module definition file.

Figure 5.2   Running the 16-bit wtest.exe **on Windows 95.**

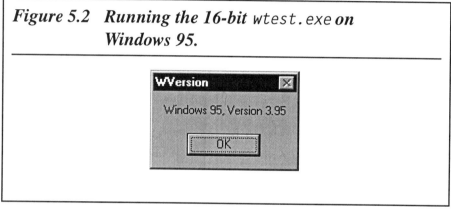

Figure 5.3   Running the 32-bit wtest.exe **on Windows NT.**

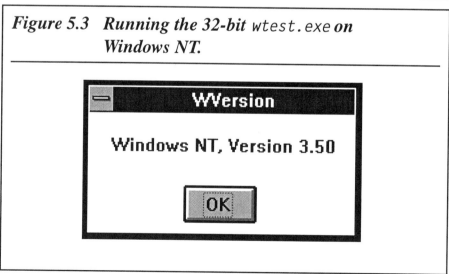

wtest.exe has a single menu item. When you select it, wtest.exe calls WVersion() and displays the result in a message box. Figure 5.2 shows the message box displayed when the 16-bit version of wtest.exe is run on Windows 95. Figure 5.3 shows the message box displayed when the 32-bit version of wtest.exe is run on Windows NT. Table 5.1 summarizes the information returned from GetVersion() for various operating systems.

What about DOS Applications?

A DOS application might also need to know whether it is running under a "pure" DOS environment or an emulated DOS environment, such as a DOS shell under Windows 3.1, Windows 95, or Windows NT. For example, if a DOS application needs to perform direct port I/O, it needs to know that this operation is allowed on Windows 3.x and Windows 95, but not allowed on Windows NT. Unfortunately, under DOS, I didn't come up with any simple methods for distinguishing between Windows NT and Windows NT Advanced Server (NTAS) or between Windows and Windows for Workgroups. It is, however, quite simple to distinguish between Windows 3.x, Windows 95, and the Windows NT family.

Table 5.1 GetVersion() *return codes.*		
	LOWORD returned from GetVersion()	*HIWORD returned from* GetVersion()
Win16 application on Windows 3.1	3.10	MS-DOS version
Win16 application on Windows for Workgroups	3.10	MS-DOS version
Win16 application on Windows 95	3.95*	MS-DOS version
Win16 application on Windows NT (WOW)	3.10	5.0 (MS-DOS version)
Win32 application on Win32s	3.10	High bit is 1
Win32 application on Windows 95	4.00	High bit is 1
Win32 application on Windows NT 3.5/NTAS	3.50	High bit is 0
*Beta 2 version of Windows 95		

dostest.c (Listing 5.3) is a simple DOS application I wrote to demonstrate the DOS-based platform detection techniques. INT 21h function 30h has been used since DOS 2.0 to retrieve the DOS version number. This version number might still be helpful to DOS applications, because it generally retrieves either the current DOS version or the version of DOS that is being emulated in a DOS shell of some kind. For completeness, dostest.exe displays the information returned from INT 21h function 30h.

Next, dostest.exe displays the version number retrieved by INT 21h function 3306h. Recall that INT 33h subfunctions 00h and 01h are used to get and set the

---

Listing 5.3 dostest.c — *A DOS-based platform detection program.*

```
#include "stdio.h"
#include "stdlib.h"
#include "string.h"

typedef unsigned char UCHAR;

#define LOBYTE(w) ((UCHAR)(w))
#define HIBYTE(w) ((UCHAR)(((unsigned int)(w)>>8)&0xFF))

void main(void)
{
    unsigned short usVersion=0, usWinVer=0;
    char *szEnvOS;

    // This method only returns emulated DOS version
    _asm  mov ah, 30h
    _asm  int 21h
    _asm  mov usVersion, ax
    printf("Real/Emulated DOS Version is %d.%d\n",
        LOBYTE(usVersion), HIBYTE(usVersion));

    // alternate DOS version, can be used to decide if its NT
    _asm  mov ax, 3306h
    _asm  int 21h
    _asm  mov usVersion, bx
    printf("Alternate DOS Version is %d.%d\n",
        LOBYTE(usVersion), HIBYTE(usVersion));

    // Is it Windows NT/NT Advanced Server?
    szEnvOS = getenv("OS");
    if (szEnvOS != NULL) {
        if (stricmp(szEnvOS, "Windows_NT") == 0) {
            printf("Running on a VDM under Windows NT/NTAS\n");
            return;
        }
    }
}
```

Ctrl-Break/Ctrl-C flag. Subfunction 06h is an alternative method for retrieving the DOS version number. In the case of Windows NT 3.5, the NT VDM (Virtual DOS Machine) reports a DOS version of 5.50. This can be used to determine if a DOS application is running under Windows NT (or NTAS). Note that INT 21h function 30h is affected by calls to SETVER, whereas INT 21h function 3306h is not.

An alternative method for determining whether a DOS application is running on the NT VDM (and the method I chose to use) is checking for the OS environment variable. I used the getenv() C runtime library routine to retrieve the value set, if any, for the OS environment variable. Both Windows NT and Windows NT Advanced Server set the OS environment variable to "Windows_NT".

If dostest.exe isn't running on NT, then I check whether it's running on either enhanced-mode Windows 3.x or Windows 95. Both platforms support the INT 2fh function 1600h method. As documented in the *Microsoft Windows Device Driver Adaptation Guide*, the value returned in AL will be either 00h or 80h if the application is not running on an enhanced-mode version of Windows. If the value in AL is something other than 00h or 80h, then I know it is either Windows 3.x or Windows 95. Further, the value in AX is the Windows version number (AL is the major Windows version number and AH is the minor Windows version number). I simply use this version number to distinguish between Windows 3.x and Windows 95.

Listing 5.3 (continued)

```
// Is a form of Enhanced mode Windows running?
_asm  mov ax, 1600h
_asm  int 2fh
_asm  mov usWinVer, ax
if ((LOBYTE(usWinVer)!=0) && (LOBYTE(usWinVer)!=0x80)) {
    // is it Windows 95?
    if (LOBYTE(usWinVer) >= 4)
        printf("Windows 95, version %d.%d\n",
            LOBYTE(usWinVer), HIBYTE(usWinVer));
    // must be Windows 3.x then
    else
        printf("enhanced-mode Windows version %d.%d\n",
            LOBYTE(usWinVer), HIBYTE(usWinVer));
    return;
}

// finally, by process of elimination,
// assume a pure DOS
printf("Running under a pure DOS environment\n");

} // main
```

Finally, by process of elimination, if it isn't Windows NT, Windows 95, or Windows 3.x, then I just assume that the application is running under a pure (nonemulated) version of DOS. Of course, this is not foolproof; the DOS application could be running under standard-mode Windows 3.x, for instance.

Table 5.2 summarizes the values returned from `INT 21h` function 30h, `INT 21h` function 3306h, the `OS` environment variable, and `INT 2fh` function 1600h.

Summary

As you can see, there really isn't a single right or wrong answer when it comes to programmatically determining what operating system you're running on. Some of these techniques I stumbled upon myself and many others I found through Knowledge Base chapters (see references) and CompuServe conversations. If you want to look at another sample detection routine, check out `winver.zip` (uploaded by John Howells) on the WINSHARE CompuServe forum in Library 5.4.

Also, if you're writing a Win32 module and you restrict your users to always running on the very latest operating system versions, then you might check out `GetVersionEx()`, a Win32 API function. `GetVersionEx()` fills in an `OSVERSIONINFO` structure with major and minor version information and a platform ID (either `VER_PLATFORM_WIN32s`,

Table 5.2	*Return values from various DOS version detection methods.*			
	DOS version from Int 21h, 30h	*DOS version from Int 21h, 3306h*	*OS environment variable*	*Windows version from Int 2fh, 1600h*
DOS 6.0	6.0	6.0	(None)	`AL = 00h`
DOS Shell on Windows 3.1	6.0	6.0	(None)	3.10
DOS Shell on Windows 95	7.0	7.0	(None)	4.0
DOS Shell on Windows NT 3.5	5.0	5.50	`Windows_NT`	`AL = 00h`

VER_PLATFORM_WIN32_WINDOWS, or VER_PLATFORM_WIN32_NT). I haven't used this routine much yet myself, but it reportedly is only supported on Windows NT v3.5 or later, Win32s v1.15 or later, and (presumably) Windows 95.

One more word of caution: the Knowledge Base chapter Q98723 describes a nasty bug in GetVersion() on Win32s. Apparently, an internal build number was inadvertently OR'd with the low word of the value returned from GetVersion() on Win32s v1.0. In this case, GetVersion() returns a value of 0x80000a3f (or 61.10).

References

Microsoft Knowledge Base Chapters: Q114470, Q113998, Q113892, Q92395, Q98723, Q96404.

Chapter 6

Unicode and Software Globalization

Software Design Guidelines for International Application Development

David Van Camp

Developers have traditionally produced software for the domestic U.S. market, then remarketed it overseas after a few simple modifications. This practice, however, is fast becoming unacceptable as more and more non-U.S. users expect software to "speak" to them in their native tongue and conventions. Furthermore, non-U.S. computer markets are growing rapidly, forcing software developers to begin thinking internationally. Currently, a variety of character standards and proprietary extensions are being used to address application internationalization. In many cases, however, the result is often inefficient code that's difficult to maintain, hard to port, and expensive to produce — all problems the Unicode standard addresses.

The Unicode Standard

Unicode is an international character code standard which replaces single-byte ASCII and ANSI, multibyte ANSI, and nearly every other character code standard currently defined. Unicode contains a one-to-one mapping of codes for ASCII and the ISO 8859/1 Latin character set used by Microsoft Windows, NextStep, and others. Additionally, Unicode contains a nearly complete superset of all fixed-size and multibyte standards currently in use and provides for symbol sets such as mathematical operators, technical symbols, geometric shapes, and dingbats. The initial release of Unicode, in fact, contained 26,000 characters. More importantly, when producing code, the Unicode character standard provides a global solution for application localization, which solves many of the problems associated with multibyte support. Specifically, it provides the ability to prepare your application code for supporting nearly all languages with little or no modification, at least in terms of data storage. (See the accompanying sidebar, "The Unicode Consortium.")

The good news is that it's relatively simple to modify most applications to transparently support multiple character standards. I now support Unicode whenever possible in my applications. The degree of difficulty for supporting Unicode depends on which and how many character standards were supported by the original code, what future requirements are expected, and how much support is provided by the underlying graphics engine and operating system.

Microsoft's NT operating system uses Unicode internally to represent all characters and strings. In addition to long filenames and extended attributes, NT supports Unicode characters in filenames. Consequently, it's possible for a single filename to contain a mix of characters from hundreds of modern languages and even a few archaic ones. Fortunately, Unicode prevents having to switch between character standards to process such filenames. This simplifies many string operations.

For example, in the common problem of splitting a filename off the end of a fully qualified path, you typically start at the rightmost character and traverse back to the first backslash, colon, or the beginning of the string (Figure 6.1).

Figure 6.1   Splitting off the filename from a path name.

```
for (pszTemp=szFName+strlen(szFName)-1;
     pszTemp>szFName && *pszTemp != '\\' &&  *pszTemp !=':';
     --szTemp);
```

The Unicode Consortium

The Unicode Consortium is responsible for defining and promoting the Unicode character standard. Consortium members include all the major international computer systems providers: Adobe, Apple, Borland, DEC, Go, Hewlett Packard, IBM, Lotus, Microsoft, Next, Novell, Sun, Symantec, Taligent, Unisys, WordPerfect, Xerox, and others.

Unicode derives its name from its three main characteristics: *universal* — it addresses the needs of world languages; *uniform* — it uses fixed-width codes for efficiency; and *unique* — duplication of character codes is minimized.

The Unicode Consortium was formally incorporated in 1991 as a joint effort between a number of the major computer software and hardware companies. However, the Unicode standard first began at Xerox in 1985 when Huan-mei Liao, Nelson Ng, Dave Opstad, and Lee Collins began working on a database to map the relationships between identical Japanese and Chinese characters. This lead to a technique called "Han Unification," which Unicode uses to minimize the codes it requires.

At the same time, discussions on the development of a universal character set got underway at Apple. In September of 1987, Joe Becker of the Xerox group and Mark Davis of Apple began discussions on multilingual issues with a new type of character encoding as a major topic. Later that year, Becker coined the term "Unicode."

The following year saw Collins working at Apple on Davis' new character-encoding proposals. By February Collins had incorporated the basic architecture for Unicode, and Becker presented it to a /usr/group international subcommittee meeting in Dallas. Apple decided to incorporate Unicode support into TrueType.

In February of 1989, bimonthly meetings to discuss Unicode began between these companies with Sun, Adobe, Claris, and the Pacific Rim Connections joining in. In addition, Glenn Wright of Sun began unicode@sun.com on the Internet for Unicode discussions. These discussions lead to the decision to incorporate all composite characters in existing ISO standards. In 1990 there was a flurry of activity, culminating in December when Becker presented Unicode at a UNIX International meeting. Cooperating with Apple on TrueType, Microsoft became interested in Unicode and assigned Asmus Freytag to attend meetings. By March all non-Han work had been completed, and work began on cross mappings and order. Meanwhile, Wright and Mike Kernaghan of Metaphor started the process of incorporating the Unicode Consortium, and the work continues today.

Much effort has been expended to meet the demands of each language represented by Unicode and each company and country involved in its development. International politics have often played a significant part in the definition of this standard. The result is a highly consistent and easily usable standard which will be around for a long time.

For more information, or to become a member of the Unicode Consortium, contact: The Unicode Consortium, P.O. Box 700519, San Jose, CA 95170-0519. (Phone: 408-777-5870, Fax: 408-777-5082, Internet: unicode-inc@unicode.org, WWW: http://www.stonehand.com/unicode/consortium/general.html)

For standards that use a variable number of bytes per character (such as Shift-JIS), it's impossible to cycle backwards through a string. You can't determine if any single byte is the first or second byte of a multibyte character, or if it's a single-byte character. Consequently, algorithms must be rewritten to start at the left and work toward the right. But with Unicode (or other fixed-size character code standards), you can traverse backwards, saving you from having to rewrite code for international support.

Implementing Unicode Support

A basic technique for implementing Unicode is transparent character support. This is a technique I used to develop multiple tape backup applications for NT. The goal of the project was to write and maintain a single, common set of source code such that Unicode would be supported if the underlying operating system provided sufficient support, and any other single-byte character set would be supported otherwise. This support had to be as portable and transparent as possible. Code that must specifically process strings of a known character standard, therefore, had to be isolated to a few specific files and code sections.

In order to achieve this goal, the following conditions had to be met:

- Transparent characters, macros, and functions had to be used.
- Operations that expect a specific byte size had to be avoided or encapsulated.

I've discovered a number of nonobvious stumbling blocks in implementing transparent character support, particularly when converting a non-Unicode application to either Unicode or transparent support. Also, you must consider how to program today for a non-Unicode environment, while preparing for an eventual migration to Unicode.

Multibyte character sets may be supported as well, but you must employ the same localization techniques you previously used. Those techniques need not be modified; just follow the simple rules outlined here. However, localization for multibyte character sets may reduce the efficiency of your code.

Code written following the guidelines in Figure 6.2 will transparently support Unicode, ASCII, or any other fixed-size character standard for all major languages and cultures, with only a minimal localization effort. The basic rule of transparent character support is that the size of a character code is determined at compile time. If a preprocessor macro named UNICODE is defined in your compiler's command line arguments and the platform supports Unicode, your application is compiled to support Unicode. Otherwise your application will support any 1-byte character set supported by the platform. You need only define another macro and modify your header files to support another 2- or 4-byte character standard if your platform provides sufficient support for that standard. If you do not compile for Unicode, the particular character standard supported is determined by the strings contained in your application's resources and the default code page selected by the user. This, of course, presumes that all strings that require language translation are placed in resource files. All modules should be compiled with Unicode explicitly enabled or disabled, and you should avoid mixing modules compiled for different character sizes whenever possible.

Programs written to support multiple-character standards transparently require a transparent character type. Many assumptions typically made about character variables are no longer valid. You must take care to ensure that code is truly transparent and, if multiplatform support is required, portable. The solution provided by transparent character support is based on never presuming the size of a character. Because a transparent character may be of any fixed size, a new type is used, TCHAR, which represents a character of unknown (but fixed) size. Other special types include:

- LPTSTR, a pointer to a null-terminated transparent character string.

- LPTCHAR, a pointer to a transparent character or array.

Figure 6.2 Guidelines for transparent character support.

1. Place all strings that require language translation in your application's resources.
2. Declare all text (not binary) data using TCHAR, LPTSTR, LPTCHAR.
3. Use transparent functions and macros for all TCHAR-type data.
4. Avoid using ASCII string functions that have no wide-character equivalent.
5. Check calls to strlen() and multiply by sizeof(TCHAR) if result is used as a byte size.
6. Ensure all memory allocations for strings are based on byte size, not character count.
7. Check all transparent character pointer arithmetic for validity; avoid using characters as indexes to 256-element arrays; remember that subtracting two character pointers yields a byte size, not a character count; always divide or multiply by sizeof(TCHAR) to convert between character counts and byte sizes.
8. Isolate operations on specific character code standards from transparent code.
9. Use wcstombs() and mbstowcs() to convert between Unicode and ASCII/ANSI-specific character codes.
10. Use the byte-order mark whenever processing text files and data streams.
11. Define UNICODE macro when compiling transparent modules for Unicode support.
12. Avoid mixing modules compiled to support different default character code standards.

Figure 6.3 provides definitions of these types for Unicode and ASCII/ANSI.

You can't use the standard C char type to store transparent characters, because char is the smallest atomic type, which is usually a byte. Neither can you use the ANSI wchar_t type, because it's a "wide" character type that will always be at least 2 bytes in size — too large for ASCII and other single-byte standards.

Consequently, the first steps performed when converting your code for transparent character support are:

1. Determine which data elements of type char, char *, or any other type derived from those are text (and not binary) data.

2. Change all of those to use TCHAR, LPTSTR, or LPTCHAR.

These steps can be trivialized if you adapt and rigidly enforce the following coding standard early on in your product's development style: define a type, such as BYTE, always use it to store binary data, and never store nontext data in a TCHAR. In the absence of such a standard, these steps can be tedious and time consuming.

Common Problems with Pointer Arithmetic

While most character pointer arithmetic is still valid, a number of widely accepted coding practices will no longer work when using transparent characters. These practices must be avoided or you may experience many wasted hours correcting them.

One of the most common invalid assumptions is that the length of a string plus one is equal to the number of bytes required to store it. This can be a particularly annoying and sometimes difficult problem to deal with when porting existing applications. You must learn to differentiate between string lengths and buffer sizes, or serious programming errors will result. These errors can be very difficult to resolve.

Figure 6.3   Type definitions for transparent characters.

```
#ifdef   UNICODE                  //  TCHAR's are Unicode
typedef   wchar_t     TCHAR;
typedef   wchar_t   * LPTSTR;
typedef   wchar_t   * LPTCHAR;
#else                             // TCHARS are ASCII/ANSI
typedef   char        TCHAR;
typedef   char      * LPTSTR;
typedef   char      * LPTCHAR;
#endif
```

The next steps are usually easy, but can be difficult if a string length is stored for later use or passed to other functions. The steps are:

1. Search for all calls to `strlen()`, and, if the return value is used to determine a byte size, multiply by `sizeof(TCHAR)`.

2. Search for all memory allocation calls (`malloc`, `GlobalAlloc`, and so on), and change those that allocate space for characters based on a character count to use a byte length.

Array indexing and general pointer arithmetic to determine an offset usually work fine, so changes are not normally required. In `*(achPtr+nIndex)=chSomeVal`, the contents of the `nIndex`th entry of the array `achPtr` would be assigned the correct value for any fixed-size character standard. As a general rule, whenever dealing with operations involving transparent characters and arrays, simply keep in mind that the size of each element may be larger than a byte.

Another common violation is using a character as an index into a 256-element array. Because a Unicode character is 2 bytes in length, you must either increase the size of the array to 65,536, or modify your algorithm. Also, remember that subtracting two pointers yields the number of bytes between those pointers, not the number of characters. Always multiply by `sizeof(TCHAR)` when calculating the byte size of a transparent character buffer. Likewise, always divide by `sizeof(TCHAR)` when calculating the number of transparent characters that can fit in a specified number of bytes.

Wide-Character Functions

Just as Unicode and transparent characters required new types, a set of new functions is needed to process them. It's critical that, for any function employed to process single-byte characters and strings, you have an equivalent wide-character function. Windows NT and the Microsoft C libraries provide a good starting set of routines. For the Microsoft C library, all wide-character string routines utilize one of two simple naming conventions to distinguish them from standard ASCII variants. In the first convention, as specified by the ANSI C standard, all ASCII string functions beginning with `str` have wide-character equivalents that begin with `wcs`. For example, the wide-character version of `strlen` is `wcslen`, which in both cases return the number of nonzero characters in a string.

The other naming identifies wide-character functions by either prefixing or embedding a "w" in the function name. For example, the wide version of `printf` is `wprintf`, whereas `vswprintf` is the wide version of `vsprintf`. The header files included with the Microsoft C compiler for NT provide a complete list of these functions. The Microsoft Win32 API uses a different naming convention to distinguish ASCII and wide-character variants of the API procedures. All ASCII/ANSI versions of the Win32 API end with the letter "A". Similarly, all Unicode (or wide) versions end with a "W". Therefore, CreateWindowA expects 1-byte characters, and CreateWindowW expects Unicode characters. This is an excellent naming convention in that it is easy both to remember the name of any character-specific routine and to identify all character-specific (that is, nontransparent) code at a glance.

Transparent Character Macros

What makes the Win32 naming convention particularly appealing is that, with only a few exceptions, whenever you use a Win32 API procedure without an A or a W suffix — that is, when you use the same name as the one used for Windows 3 applications — you support transparent characters by default. Consequently, code modifications to Windows API procedures usually aren't required to globalize an existing application. The exceptions are those Win32 API file procedures considered obsolete but provided for backwards compatibility to Windows 3: OpenFile and _lopen, for example. Consequently, you must use the Win32 CreateFile family of functions to support Unicode filenames. For C library functions, however, things aren't so easy. The Win32 naming convention replaces wcs with tcs and the prefixed or embedded w with t to create transparent equivalents. To convert your code for transparent character support, therefore, you must replace all calls to these string functions to use the transparent name instead. This usually entails a great deal of work.

There is an alternative method that requires less work for most existing applications. Instead of modifying the source code, create a header file that maps the standard string function names to the wide-character equivalents when compiling for Unicode (Figure 6.4). By doing this for each standard string function used in your code, you can often reduce the number of changes required. However, this technique effectively removes all of the standard character functions when you compile for Unicode. If you need to process ASCII data, you'll have to write your own ASCII-specific replacements. For each of these functions — including all those that use filenames, atoi(), and some others — you must implement the wide versions yourself, or avoid using them.

Figure 6.4 Part of the header file that maps the standard string function names to the wide-character equivalents.

```
#ifdef UNICODE
#define    strlen  wcslen
#define    sprintf swprintf
#endif
```

Mixing and Converting Character Standards

There are times when code must be written to support multiple character standards, either for backwards compatibility or for transferring data between platforms. Care must be taken when mixing transparent coding techniques with character-specific data types, or the resulting code will be very difficult to maintain.

Code that supports a specific character type is not transparent and should be isolated from transparent code, preferably by placing the code in a separate function. One method of handling this is to create two versions of your function — one that accepts Unicode strings and another for ASCII strings — along with a transparent mapping macro, as described earlier. An alternative method is to write a single function that takes and returns transparent characters. On entry to this function, the TCHAR parameters are converted to the required character standard and processed. Any resulting characters are then converted back to TCHAR, and the function returns (Listing 6.1).

Listing 6.1   Converting between transparent and ASCII characters.

```
VOID MyFunction ( LPTSTR pszXparent, int cchMaxBuf )
{
    char * pszMbyte;
    /* convert transparent parameter to ASCII if necessary */
#ifdef UNICODE
    /* allocate a buffer for the ASCII conversion of pszXparent */
    pszMbyte = malloc ( cchMaxBuf * sizeof (TCHAR) );
    _wcstombs (pszXparent, psAscii, cchMaxBuf * sizeof (TCHAR) );
#else
    /* string is already ASCII/ANSI so just use it directly */
    pszMbyte = pszXparent;
#endif
    /* perform ASCII-specific operations.... */
        . . .
    /* then convert the result back to a tranparent string... */
#ifdef UNICODE
    mbstowcs ( pszMbyte, pszXparent, cchMaxBuf );
    free ( pszMbyte );
#endif
    return;
}
```

Also, notice how the routines use the standard ANSI C functions wcstombs and mbstowcs, which convert single- or multibyte strings to wide-character strings and vice versa, using the current code page for the multibyte string. Keep in mind that a Unicode string converted using wcstombs may contain multibyte characters, which can complicate processing.

Reading and Writing Unicode Text Files

Unicode contains a special character code, called the "byte-order mark," which has a value of 0xfeff and is used to identify a text file or data stream as a collection of Unicode characters. It is important to use this mark whenever reading or writing text files. Additionally, this mark provides the information necessary to transfer data between Big- and Little-endian systems. Whenever a Unicode text file is created, or a stream of Unicode text is passed to another application or system, it is important to ensure that the first character written is the byte-order mark. Likewise, whenever you open a text file, or receive a stream of text, you should check for this mark. Then, you will need to convert the text as it is read to transparent characters before your application can use it. For this reason, you should encapsulate all file operations in a simple API.

The byte-order mark value was chosen because the possibility of 0xfeff occurring in the first 2 bytes of any non-Unicode text stream is highly unlikely. Also, its mirror image, 0xfffe, which is not a Unicode character, provides useful information for transferring data between Big- and Little-endian systems, because their byte orders are reversed. Therefore, if a text stream starts with 0xfffe, there is a good chance that it contains byte-swapped Unicode text, so you will need to reverse the byte order of each character as it is read.

The Future of Unicode

The Unicode standard is still new and not yet complete. The few issues that remain to be resolved will not significantly affect the development of transparent code. However, another character standard, which defines a superset of the Unicode standard, is under development — ISO 10646. Fortunately, applications developed to meet the guidelines presented in this chapter will require little or no modification to support the new standard as well. ISO 10646 comes in two flavors: 2-byte characters, which are essentially the same as Unicode, and 4-byte characters, which will eventually represent every character used in every known language. However, it's doubtful that ISO 10646 will ever become a common standard; it will likely be limited to special-purpose systems.

Unicode will probably become the predominant standard for all future systems. Unicode systems are currently under development by Microsoft, Apple, Novell, Next, Taligent, Metaphor, and others. By using transparent character support in your applications, you will be able to exploit the benefits of these systems as they become available and quickly enter new language markets with a minimum of effort, while maintaining compatibility with current systems and standards.

Chapter 7

A Windows NT C++ Class for Asynchronous I/O

Paula Tomlinson

Windows NT offers a preemptive multitasking environment based on a multithreaded application process model. Although Windows 95 also offers preemptive multitasking, this feature especially shines on Windows NT due to its support for systems with more than one processor. However, because multiprocessor systems are still expensive and fairly rare, your application will most likely execute on a single-processor machine. Simply dividing a program into multiple threads can result in multiple threads competing for the same processor with no increase in throughput. Given that, you might be wondering how your own program might benefit from a multithreaded operating system.

One place that a preemptive, multithreading operating system can produce measurable performance improvements (even on single-processor machines) for many programs is during device I/O. When a DOS program issues a file read or write request, everything pretty much grinds to a halt from the time the device begins processing the I/O until the I/O completes and control returns to the caller. On Windows NT, however, the operating system can continue to do useful work (such as executing other processes) while waiting for a device to complete an I/O request. If you restructure your program to use asynchronous I/O, your program can also perform other tasks while waiting for I/O to complete. Note that Windows 95 does not support asynchronous I/O with disk-based files.

Unlike some uses for multithreading, asynchronous I/O offers clear opportunities for making your program more efficient. Some devices, such as a CD-ROM, can take the biggest part of a second to complete an individual I/O request, enough time for your program to perform a large amount of processing. However, even the fastest hard-disk drive is still usually an order of magnitude slower than CPU speeds, making most file I/O potentially worth exploiting as an asynchronous activity. For example, if your Win32 program reads a file of records and processes them one at a time, it could overlap (asynchronous I/O is sometimes called overlapped I/O) the processing of one batch of records with an I/O request to read the next batch, potentially reducing the time required to process the file to roughly the time required to read the file.

Asynchronous I/O: Behind the Scenes

What's really happening behind the scenes when you start an asynchronous I/O operation on Windows NT? I will trace the progress of an asynchronous write request through the Windows NT operating system to a file on disk.

Suppose your application has already successfully opened a file for asynchronous I/O and has just called `WriteFile()`. `WriteFile()` calls into the Win32 environment subsystem (see Custer's *Inside Windows NT* for a description of environment subsystems), which then calls the `NtWriteFile` I/O manager service. The I/O manager creates an IRP (interrupt request packet) for the request and passes it to the appropriate device driver. For simplicity, I'll treat the device driver as a single component. In reality, the IRP would first be passed to the appropriate file system device driver for the partition that the file resides on. The file system device driver in turn passes the IRP on to the driver for the physical device. In the case of a SCSI hard disk, the device driver is further divided into class (applies to all devices of this type, such as a SCSI fixed disk), port (applies to all SCSI devices), and miniport (applies to the specific SCSI adapter controlling the SCSI device) driver components.

The device driver puts the IRP in its own queue and returns status back to the Win32 subsystem. `WriteFile()` returns back to the application [`GetLastError()` will report a status of `ERROR_IO_PENDING` at this point]. The application executes some code and then waits for the file handle, which it receives when the I/O operation is complete. When the device driver processes the request from its queue, it determines the physical location on the disk and transfers the data to that location. When the transfer is done, the driver interrupts the system, transferring control to the NT kernel. The kernel calls the ISR (interrupt service routine) registered for that driver/device. At this point, the driver is executing at a high IRQL (interrupt request level), so it does only what is absolutely necessary and schedules a DPC (deferred procedure call) to handle the work it needs to do to finish processing the interrupt. When the DPC eventually interrupts the system, the kernel again gains control, but this time it calls the driver's DPC routine. The DPC routine returns status information about the request that just completed back to the I/O manager. The I/O manager switches context to the calling application and copies the status information (and the data, in the case of a read operation) to the caller's address space. Finally, it signals the file handle, releasing the application's waiting thread.

Windows NT supports multiple installable file systems, and not all file systems support all Win32 features. For example, currently only NTFS supports file security. However, all three major file systems (FAT, HPFS, and NTFS) support asynchronous I/O. This chapter describes how asynchronous I/O works under Win32 and provides a C++ class (CFileIO) that implements asynchronous file I/O. The code disk contains a demonstration program that monitors a spool directory and asynchronously copies to the printer any files that appear in that directory. (See the sidebar "Asynchronous I/O: Behind the Scenes" for an overview of NT's processing of asynchronous I/O operations.)

Win32 File I/O Functions

Win32 provides a complete set of file and directory routines that are somewhat different than the analogous DOS routines. Table 7.1 shows the rough correspondences between the Win32 file and directory API and older DOS-style functions. Note that in the Win32 API, CreateFile() is used to open existing files, as well as to create and open new ones. You can use the Win32 file I/O routines to open and read a file normally (synchronously), just as you would use fopen() and fread() under DOS or Windows 3.1, but you can also use the Win32 API to accomplish asynchronous file operations.

Table 7.1 Win32 file and directory API comparison with DOS functions.

Win32	Action	DOS
File Input/Output Routines		
CloseHandle	Closes an open object handle	_close
CreateFile	Creates, opens, or truncates a file*	_creat, _open, _sopen
DeviceIoControl	Sends control directly to driver	(none)
DuplicateHandle	Duplicates an object handle	_dup
FileIOCompletionRoutine	Called when asynch I/O completes	(none)
FlushFileBuffers	Flushes buffered data to disk	_commit
LockFile, LockFileEx	Locks a byte range in an open file*	_locking
ReadFile, ReadFileEx	Reads from a file*	_read
SetEndOfFile	Sets end-of-file to current position	_chsize
SetFilePointer	Sets file pointer position	_lseek, _tell
WriteFile, WriteFileEx	Writes data to file*	_write
UnlockFile, UnlockFileEx	Unlocks a byte range in a file*	_locking

Table 7.1 (continued)

Win32	Action	DOS
File Management Routines		
CopyFile	Copies existing file to new file	(none)
DeleteFile	Deletes an existing file	remove, _unlink
MoveFile, MoveFileEx	Renames or copies a file	rename, (none)
Directory Routines		
CreateDirectory	Creates a new directory	_mkdir
GetCurrentDirectory	Gets current directory for process	_getcwd, _getdrive
RemoveDirectory	Removes an existing directory	_rmdir
SetCurrentDirectory	Changes the current directory	_chdir, _chdrive
File Search and Change Notification Routines		
FindClose	Closes a find file context	(none)
FindCloseChangeNotification	Stops change notification	(none)
FindFirstChangeNotification	Sets up change notification filter	(none)
FindFirstFile	Finds the first matching file	_dos_findfirst
FindNextChangeNotification	Asks for notification of next change	(none)
FindNextFile	Finds the next matching file	_dos_findnext
SearchPath	Searches for a file	_searchenv
File Information Routines		
GetDiskFreeSpace	Returns amount of free disk space	_dos_getdiskfree
GetDriveType	Returns type of specified drive	(none)
GetFile Attributes	Returns file attributes	_access
GetFileInformationByHandle	Retrieves file information	_stat, _fstat
GetFileSecutiry	Gets security of file object	_access
GetFileSize	Returns size of specified file	_filelength
GetFileType	Returns type of specified file	_isatty
GetFullPathName	Retrieves a full path and filename	_fullpath
GetLogicalDrives	Returns bitmask of valid drives	(none)
GetLogicalDriveStrings	Returns strings for valid drives	(none)
GetVolumeInformation	Returns file system information	(none)
SetFileAttributes	Sets file attributes	_chmod
SetFileSecurity	Sets security of file object	_chmod

The Win32 API provides three ways to perform asynchronous I/O. In all three cases, you have to pass the FILE_FLAG_OVERLAPPED flag to CreateFile() when you open the file. The other functions involved in these three methods are either Read-File() and WriteFile() or ReadFileEx() and WriteFileEx(). All four of these functions allow you to pass in a pointer to a structure of type OVERLAPPED, which is defined as shown in Figure 7.1.

All three methods have two components: how to start the asynchronous I/O and how to detect that it has completed. For example, suppose you want to process one record while reading the next one into a buffer. After the first record is in memory, you would start an asynchronous read to fetch the second record and then immediately start processing the first record. After you finish processing the first record, the read

Table 7.1 (continued)		
Win32	***Action***	***DOS***
File Information Routines — continued		
SetHandleCount	Sets number of available file handles	(none)
Set VolumeLabel	Sets a volume label	(none)
Temporary File Routines		
GetTempFileName	Creates a temporary filename	_mktemp
GetTempPath	Returns path for temporary files	(none)

Note: For compatibility, the following routines are still supported: _hread, _hwrite, _lclose, _lcreat, _lseek, _lopen, _lread, _lwrite, GetDriveType, GetSystemDirectory, GetTempFileName, GetWindowsDirectory, OpenFile, and SetHandleCount. The following routine has been obsoleted: GetTempDrive.

*In this case, a file could be a normal disk-based file, pipe, communications resource, disk device, or console.

Figure 7.1   Definition of OVERLAPPED *structure.*

```
typedef struct _OVERLAPPED {
    DWORD  Internal;      // reserved
    DWORD  InternalHigh;  // reserved
    DWORD  Offset;        // file offset (low bytes) to start transfer
    DWORD  OffsetHigh;    // file offset (high bytes) to start transfer
    HANDLE hEvent;        // event to signal when transfer is done
} OVERLAPPED;
```

request to fetch the second record may or may not have completed, so you need a way to say "now I want to wait until this I/O request is complete." Win32 offers a variety of methods for synchronizing; the sidebar "Win32 Synchronization Objects" provides an overview.

The first method for performing asynchronous I/O involves using `ReadFileEx()` and `WriteFileEx()`. In fact, you can only use these two routines asynchronously. In addition to a pointer to an `OVERLAPPED` structure, these routines take a pointer to a callback routine — the I/O completion routine. When the file operation finishes, Windows calls the completion routine. The completion routine will not be called in a preemptive fashion though; after the I/O completes, Windows waits until the calling thread is in an alertable state before calling your I/O completion routine. If you want

Win32 Synchronization Objects

When you take advantage of the power and flexibility of a fully preemptive, multithreaded operating system, one of the prices you pay is the complication of synchronization. Typical uses for synchronization include protecting shared data and serializing operations that depend on the completion of other operations. The Win32 API on Windows NT supports several dedicated synchronization objects (mutexes, semaphores, events, and critical sections), but other handles can also be used as synchronization objects (processes, threads, files, console, timers, and more). A synchronization object is always in one of two states: signaled or not signaled. In general, threads waiting on objects are released when the object is signaled and are blocked when the object is not signaled.

A mutex (from the phrase "mutual exclusion") is like a single-lane bridge that only one thread at a time can cross. If one thread successfully acquires ownership of a specific mutex, then no other threads can own it until the first thread releases it. Mutexes can be used to protect a global resource from being accessed by multiple threads at the same time. Note that a mutex (like a semaphore and an event) doesn't actually protect the resource directly; all threads wanting to access the resource just agree not to do so unless they have ownership of that particular mutex. Mutexes can be shared between processes.

Semaphores are like variable-lane bridges that allow a number of threads to cross at the same time. You specify how many threads can own the semaphore when you initialize it. Once the maximum number of threads have acquired ownership of a semaphore, other threads trying to own it are denied ownership until one of the owning threads releases it. Semaphores can be shared between processes.

Events are more like public broadcasts or triggers. Events are often used when one thread wants to let another thread know that a specific event occurred. There are two kinds of events — manual-reset (once they become set, they must be explicitly reset) and auto-reset (they are automatically reset after being set). You can have multiple threads waiting on an event. When a manual-reset event is signaled, all waiting threads are notified, but when an auto-reset event is signaled, only one thread at a time is notified. Events can be shared by processes.

Win32 Synchronization Objects — continued

Critical sections are similar to mutexes in that only one thread can own (enter) the critical section at a time. But critical sections can only be used to synchronize threads in one process. You can use several critical sections in a single process, but a thread will execute only if it is not in a critical section that has already been entered by another thread. Although critical sections are slightly more efficient (they have less overhead) than mutexes, they do not support timeouts for waiting.

On a trivial level, you can use Win32's InterlockedDecrement(), InterlockedIncrement(), and InterlockedExchange() to synchronize threads wanting to modify the same variable. In fact, if the variable is in shared memory, you can even use this method to synchronize between processes.

There are three methods for sharing a semaphore, mutex, or event between processes. First, the processes can agree on a unique name and then open the synchronization object by name. Second, you can use DuplicateHandle() to create a copy of the handle for another process to use. Finally, if you enabled inheritance for the object when it was created, child processes will inherit the object handle.

Synchronization is a foreign concept to those who have programmed only on nonpreemptive, nonreentrant DOS-based PCs. When writing Win32-based code, it is important to always assume the worst — that all threads are running at the same time (which theoretically could happen on a multiprocessor system) and that a thread can be preempted between any two machine instructions. The two most common pitfalls in using synchronization objects are deadlock conditions and race conditions. A deadlock condition occurs when threads end up waiting on each other indefinitely. If you avoid using infinite timeouts and always claim synchronization objects in the same order, you'll avoid many deadlock scenarios. A race condition occurs when you haven't synchronized events or threads properly. Then whether the program works or not comes down to the order in which the threads happen to execute.

You can synchronize program execution by passing a synchronization object handle to one of the Win32 wait routines. All the wait routines, with the exception of SleepEx(), accept as a parameter the object handle to be waited on. The object handle can be a handle of any synchronization object discussed above or any other waitable handle (which, as you'll see later, includes file handles). The wait routines differ based on how many conditions must be satisfied and whether a wait is alertable. The WaitForSingleObject() and WaitForSingleObjectEx() routines wait for only one object handle to be signaled, but you can pass an array of up to 64 object handles for the WaitForMultipleObjects() and WaitForMultipleObjectsEx() routines. In addition to waiting on object handles, the extended forms of the wait routines [WaitForSingleObjectEx() and WaitForMutlipleObjectsEx()] can also be triggered by queuing an I/O completion routine for that thread. And, finally, you can use GetOverlappedResult() to wait on a synchronization object or just to check whether the object is signaled or not. GetOverlappedResult() calls WaitForSingleObject() if the fWait flag is TRUE.

What about using a simple variable as a synchronization flag? This violates the rule of assuming that execution can be preempted between any two instructions. The thread could be preeempted after the flag is checked but just before it is set. The Windows NT scheduler treats operations to check and set Win32 synchronization objects as a single block of execution and will not preempt it in the middle. The Win32 synchronization objects are also much more efficient. Sitting in a loop waiting for a variable to change wastes precious clock cycles. When you use a wait function, the thread essentially goes to sleep (i.e., is not scheduled for execution) and does not consume CPU time.

the completion routine to be called once for each completed overlapped I/O operation, then you must call one of the alertable wait functions [WaitForSingleObjectEx(), WaitForMultipleObjectsEx(), or SleepEx()] from the thread that queued the overlapped I/O operation. The thread will sleep until an I/O operation completes and the completion routine is called. When there are no more queued operations, the wait function returns. You can name the completion routine anything you want, but it must have the following prototype:

```
VOID CompletionRoutine(DWORD fdwError, DWORD dwTransferred,
                       LPOVERLAPPED lpO);
```

The second method uses ReadFile() and WriteFile(). One of the fields in the OVERLAPPED structure (see Figure 7.1) whose address you pass to these functions is an event handle (field hEvent). You can call CreateEvent() to create a manual-reset event and then store its handle in the hEvent field of the OVERLAPPED structure. By passing a unique structure and event handle for each I/O operation, you can overlap multiple read or write requests and wait for one or more of them to complete by waiting on the corresponding manual-reset events. This method of overlapped I/O might be appropriate in a server process that uses a separate thread to handle each incoming client request.

The final method for asynchronous I/O has the most limitations, but is also the easiest to implement and requires the least program redesign to take advantage of. Once again, use ReadFile() and WriteFile() to perform I/O, but instead of creating separate events for each I/O, just set the hEvent field in the OVERLAPPED structure to NULL. This tells Win32 to signal the file handle when the I/O operation completes. (You can wait for a file handle to be signaled, just as you can wait for an event.) The limitation of this method (waiting on the file handle when you need to wait for the I/O to complete) is that you cannot start more than one overlapped I/O request; if you do, they will all signal the same file handle on completion and you will have no way to determine which I/O operation completed. However, for many programs, overlapping a single read or write request at a time is a natural model and an easy way to get the benefits of multithreading without much redesign work.

Creating the CFileIO *Class*

To demonstrate Win32's asynchronous file I/O capabilities, I wrote a very simple C++ class called CFileIO. The declaration is in asynch.h (Listing 7.1) and the implementation is in asynch.cpp (Listing 7.2). This code uses the simple method of waiting on a file handle to synchronize execution, which is appropriate for situations where you don't need more than one outstanding I/O request per file.

Listing 7.1   `asynch.h` — *Declaration of asynchronous I/O class.*

```c
/**-------------------------------------------------------------
** ASYNCH.H :     Simple Win32 File I/O Class Definition.
** Environment: Windows NT, MS Visual C/C++ (32-bit)
**-------------------------------------------------------------**/
#ifndef _ASYNCH_H_
#define _ASYNCH_H_
#include <stdio.h>

class CFileIO
{
    public:
        CFileIO(char *pFilename,
            DWORD dwAccess = GENERIC_READ | GENERIC_WRITE,
            DWORD dwCreate = OPEN_ALWAYS,
            DWORD dwAttribute = FILE_ATTRIBUTE_NORMAL,
            DWORD *dwStatus = NULL);
        virtual ~CFileIO();
        DWORD Read(BYTE *pBuffer, DWORD dwSize);
        DWORD Write(BYTE *pBuffer, DWORD dwSize);
        DWORD ReadWithAbandon(BYTE *pBuffer, DWORD dwSize);
        DWORD WriteWithAbandon(BYTE *pBuffer, DWORD dwSize);
        BOOL Close(void);
        BOOL Reopen(void);
        DWORD Seek(LONG lOffset, DWORD dwMethod = FILE_CURRENT);
        HANDLE GetHandle(void);
        BOOL IOComplete(BOOL bWait = FALSE, DWORD *dwBytes = NULL);

    private:
        // copying/assignment not supported, so declare but
        // do not define
        CFileIO(const CFileIO&);
        const CFileIO& operator=(const CFileIO&);

        HANDLE hFile;
        BOOL bAsynch;
        OVERLAPPED olFile;
        char reopenName[MAX_PATH * 2];
        DWORD reopenAccess, reopenCreate, reopenAttrib;
        DWORD dwPend;         // place holder
};
#endif
```

Listing 7.2 asynch.cpp — *Implementation of* CFileIO *class.*

```
/**-------------------------------------------------------
**   ASYNCH.CPP :  Simple Win32 File I/O Class methods.
**   Environment: Windows NT, MS Visual C/C++ (32-bit)
**-----------------------------------------------------**/
#include <windows.h>
#include "asynch.h"

/**-------------------------------------------------**/
CFileIO::CFileIO(char *pFilename, DWORD dwAccess, DWORD dwCreate,
    DWORD dwAttribute, DWORD *dwStatus)
{
    hFile = CreateFile(pFilename, dwAccess, 0, NULL,
        dwCreate, dwAttribute, NULL);
    if (hFile == INVALID_HANDLE_VALUE) *dwStatus = FALSE;
    else *dwStatus = TRUE;

    if (dwAttribute & FILE_FLAG_OVERLAPPED) bAsynch = TRUE;
    else bAsynch = FALSE;

    strcpy(reopenName, pFilename);
    reopenAccess = dwAccess;
    reopenCreate = dwCreate;
    reopenAttrib = dwAttribute;

    olFile.hEvent = NULL;
    olFile.Offset = olFile.OffsetHigh = 0;
} // CFileIO

/**------------------------------------------------**/
CFileIO::~CFileIO()
{
    if (hFile != NULL) {
        CloseHandle(hFile);
        hFile = NULL;
    }
} // CFileIO::~CFileIO

/**------------------------------------------------**/
DWORD CFileIO::Read(BYTE *pBuffer, DWORD dwSize)
{
    DWORD dwBytes;

    if (ReadFile(hFile, pBuffer, dwSize, &dwBytes, NULL))
        return dwBytes;
    else return (DWORD)0L;
} // CFileIO::Read
```

It's my personal programming style to stuff a lot of initialization work into the constructors of objects and thus avoid the requirement of an additional initialization or open method. If you prefer, this functionality could easily be pulled out and placed in an "Open" member function. The `CFileIO` constructor takes the name of the file to open, a creation flag, and an attribute flag [these are the same flags that `CreateFile()` accepts]. Because I can't return a status value from a constructor, I added a fifth parameter that I use to return status information back to the caller. Note that I also save the specified filename and attributes so that the file can be easily closed and reopened. This might be useful if, for instance, you need to occasionally close the file to let other processes or threads access it.

Listing 7.2 (continued)

```
/**------------------------------------------------------------**/
DWORD CFileIO::Write(BYTE *pBuffer, DWORD dwSize)
{
    DWORD dwBytes;

    if (WriteFile(hFile, pBuffer, dwSize, &dwBytes, NULL))
        return dwBytes;
    else return (DWORD)0L;
} // CFileIO::Write

/**------------------------------------------------------------**/
DWORD CFileIO::ReadWithAbandon(BYTE *pBuffer, DWORD dwSize)
{
    DWORD dwBytes;

    // Sorry, you didn't open it for asynchronous operation.
    if (!bAsynch) return Read(pBuffer, dwSize);

    IOComplete(TRUE, &dwBytes);
    olFile.Offset += dwBytes;
    return ReadFile(hFile, pBuffer, dwSize, &dwPend, &olFile);
} // CFileIO::ReadWithAbandon

/**------------------------------------------------------------**/
DWORD CFileIO::WriteWithAbandon(BYTE *pBuffer, DWORD dwSize)
{
    DWORD dwBytes;

    // Sorry, you didn't open it for asynchronous operation.
    if (!bAsynch) return Write(pBuffer, dwSize);

    IOComplete(TRUE, &dwBytes);
    olFile.Offset += dwBytes;
    return WriteFile(hFile, pBuffer, dwSize, &dwPend, &olFile);
} // CFileIO::WriteWithAbandon
```

Listing 7.2 (continued)

```
/**--------------------------------------------------------**/
BOOL CFileIO::Close(void)
{
    BOOL status = CloseHandle(hFile);
    hFile = NULL;
    return status;
} // CFileIO::Close

/**--------------------------------------------------------**/
BOOL CFileIO::Reopen(void)
{
    hFile = CreateFile(reopenName, reopenAccess, 0, NULL,
        reopenCreate, reopenAttrib, NULL);
    if (hFile == INVALID_HANDLE_VALUE) return FALSE;
    else return TRUE;
} // CFileIO::Reopen

/**--------------------------------------------------------**/
DWORD CFileIO::Seek(LONG lOffset, DWORD dwMethod)
{
    return SetFilePointer(hFile, lOffset, 0, dwMethod);
} // CFileIO::Seek

/**--------------------------------------------------------**/
HANDLE CFileIO::GetHandle(void)
{
    return hFile;
} // CFileIO::GetHandle

/**--------------------------------------------------------**/
BOOL CFileIO::IOComplete(BOOL bWait, DWORD *dwBytes)
{
    // Don't wait for completion, just return current status
    if (!bWait) {
        if (!GetOverlappedResult(hFile, &olFile, dwBytes, FALSE)
            && (GetLastError() == ERROR_IO_PENDING)) return FALSE;
        else return TRUE;
    }
    // Wait for the file I/O operation to complete
    else {
        if (GetOverlappedResult(hFile, &olFile, dwBytes, FALSE))
            GetOverlappedResult(hFile, &olFile, dwBytes, TRUE);
        return TRUE;
    }
} // CFileIO::IOComplete
```

The constructor initializes some fields in the OVERLAPPED olFile private data member. olFile must remain in scope while any overlapped I/O operations are in progress. To simplify the example, I always set the OffsetHigh field to zero. This limits the size of I/O operations to merely 32 bits or 4Gb — the NTFS file system uses 64-bit offsets allowing 17 million terabyte transactions! I set the hEvent field to NULL because I use the file handle itself to synchronize all operations. In the destructor for CFileIO, I simply close the file handle if it is currently open.

The CFileIO::Read() and CFileIO::Write() methods perform synchronous read and write operations by calling ReadFile() and WriteFile() routines with a NULL for the OVERLAPPED structure. With no valid OVERLAPPED structure, the operation is performed synchronously, even if the file was opened with the FILE_FLAG_-OVERLAPPED flag. But the opposite is not true — you must specify FILE_FLAG_-OVERLAPPED when a file is opened in order to perform asynchronous I/O operations on that file.

CFileIO::ReadWithAbandon() and CFileIO::WriteWithAbandon() routines perform asynchronous I/O operations. I first check whether the file was opened with the FILE_FLAG_OVERLAPPED flag. If it was not, I simply perform a synchronous rather than an asynchronous operation. If everything is in order to perform asynchronous operations, I check whether another operation is already pending. Remember that one of the limitations of using the file handle as a synchronization object is that you cannot have multiple I/O operations queued at the same time to the same file handle. To verify whether any I/O operations for this file are still in progress, I call CFileIO::IOComplete() (discussed later) with TRUE as the first parameter, indicating that I want to wait until any pending events complete. When CFileIO::IOComplete() returns, the dwBytes field contains the number of bytes transferred in the operation that just completed. This is crucial information, because ReadFile() and WriteFile() use the offset field of the OVERLAPPED structure as the current file position when operating asynchronously. So to keep the file pointer consistent, I increment the Offset field by the number of bytes in the last transaction.

I should point out that I've seen several documents, including Richter's *Advanced Windows NT*, state that the lpNumberOfBytesWritten and lpNumberOfBytesRead parameters of WriteFile() and ReadFile() routines can be NULL when performing asynchronous file I/O. This certainly should be the case because the value is meaningless; the operation has most likely not completed when WriteFile() or ReadFile() returns, so the system does not yet know how many bytes were actually transferred. However, specifying NULL as the fourth parameters of WriteFile() and ReadFile() (even when performing asynchronous I/O) causes an Access Violation Exception on earlier versions of the Windows NT operating system! This has been fixed in recent versions. (For example, on Windows NT 4.0 you may pass a NULL for this parameter.)

CFileIO::Close() and CFileIO::Reopen() provide a simple way to close and reopen the file without having to deallocate the object and reallocate it. In the case of CFileIO::Reopen(), no parameters are necessary because I automatically reopen the file with the parameters passed to the constructor.

CFileIO::Seek() calls the Win32 version of seek(), which is SetFilePointer(). Once again I have limited the CFileIO class to 32-bit transaction lengths by always passing zero as the third parameter of SetFilePointer(). The second parameter is the method type, which can be either FILE_BEGIN, FILE_CURRENT, or FILE_END depending on whether you want to seek from the beginning of the file, the current position in the file, or the end of the file.

I provided a GetHandle() member function that returns the open file handle. This may be useful if you need to call a Win32 file routine other than the ones I supply via CFileIO member functions.

CFileIO::IOComplete() lets you synchronize with the most recent asynchronous I/O request you made. If you pass FALSE to CFileIO::IOComplete(), it returns a TRUE or FALSE to indicate whether the pending operation has completed — without waiting for a completion if there are any pending transactions. If a transaction is currently in progress, then GetOverlappedResult() (passing the same file handle and overlapped structure that were used in the file I/O operation) will return FALSE and GetLastError() will return ERROR_IO_PENDING. If you pass TRUE to CFileIO::IOComplete(), it will not return until the pending transaction has completed.

To accomplish this, I first call GetOverlappedResult() with FALSE for the wait parameter, indicating I don't want to wait. This is important. If you call GetOver-lappedResult() with a value of TRUE for this parameter (indicating I want to wait) and there are no I/O operations in progress, then it will simply wait until another transaction starts and finishes. For this reason, I first check if a transaction is in progress and then call GetOverlappedResult() to wait for completion only if an event is in progress. If a transaction has finished, the third parameter of GetOver-lappedResult() returns the number of bytes actually transferred. I pass this on to the caller as the second parameter of the IOComplete method.

Using the CFileIO Class

I wanted to provide a simple yet useful program not only to demonstrate using the CFileIO class but also to show off a few more of the Win32 file API functions, so I wrote a console application that monitors a specified directory. When a file is copied to that directory, the console application uses the CFileIO class to asynchronously copy that file to the printer. Essentially, it operates like network utilities that print any files that happen to appear in a predefined spool directory.

The demonstration program is in `testmain.cpp` (Listing 7.3). In `main()`, I first query the user for the name of the spool file directory. If the directory does not already exist, I create it and select it as the current working directory for this process, using the Win32 functions `CreateDirectory()` and `SetCurrentDirectory()`. Then, just

---

Listing 7.3 `testmain.cpp` — *Asynchronous I/O*
demonstration program.

```
/**-------------------------------------------------------
** TESTMAIN.CPP : Demonstrates using CFileIO class.
** Environment: Windows NT, MS Visual C/C++ (32-bit)
**-------------------------------------------------------**/
#include <windows.h>
#include <string.h>
#include "asynch.h"

#define CHAR_FORMFEED     0x0c;     // formfeed character
#define BUF_SIZE          4096      // arbitrary buffer size

/**-------- private prototypes ----------------**/
BOOL FindNextSpoolFilename(char *);
BOOL SynchronousFileCopy(char *, char *);
BOOL AsynchronousFileCopy(char *, char *);

/**-------- global variables and defines -------**/
char spoolPath[MAX_PATH];
char rootName[MAX_PATH];
char fsName[MAX_PATH];
char fileName[MAX_PATH];
char findFile[MAX_PATH];

/**-------------------------------------------------------**/
VOID main(VOID)
{
    HANDLE hChange;
    DWORD dwWait, dwSPC, dwBPS, dwFC, dwTC;
    DWORDLONG DiskFree;

    // first prompt user for spool directory
    printf("Enter the print spool directory: \n");
    gets(spoolPath);
    if (!SetCurrentDirectory(spoolPath)) {
        CreateDirectory(spoolPath, NULL);
        SetCurrentDirectory(spoolPath);     }

    // show a little volume information
    strcpy(rootName, spoolPath);
    rootName[3] = '\0';                      // truncate to "x:\"
```

Listing 7.3 (continued)

```
        GetVolumeInformation(rootName, NULL, 0, NULL, NULL, NULL,
            fsName, MAX_PATH);
        printf("File system for volume %s is %s.\n", rootName, fsName);
        if (GetDiskFreeSpace(rootName, &dwSPC, &dwBPS, &dwFC, &dwTC)) {
            DiskFree = (DWORD)(((DWORDLONG)(dwFC * dwSPC * dwBPS))/1024);
            printf("Total free disk space: %d KB\n", DiskFree);
        }

        // form the search path, {spoolPath}\\*.*
        sprintf(findFile, "%s\\*.*", spoolPath);

        // monitor for create/deleted/renamed files in the spool dir
        if ((hChange = FindFirstChangeNotification(spoolPath, FALSE,
            FILE_NOTIFY_CHANGE_FILE_NAME)) == INVALID_HANDLE_VALUE)
                ExitProcess(GetLastError());

        // now wait (forever!) for notification of that event
        while (TRUE) {
            dwWait = WaitForSingleObject(hChange, INFINITE);
            if (dwWait != WAIT_OBJECT_0) ExitProcess(GetLastError());

            // find the filename
            if(FindNextSpoolFilename(fileName) {
                // copy the file asynchronously to the printer port
                AsynchronousFileCopy(fileName, "prn");

                // delete the file when done, triggers new search
                DeleteFile(fileName);
            }
            // now wait for the next event of this type
            if (FindNextChangeNotification(hChange) == FALSE)
                ExitProcess(GetLastError());
        } //while

    FindCloseChangeNotification(hChange);
} /* main */

/**---------------------------------------------------------------**/
BOOL FindNextSpoolFilename(char *fileName)
{
    WIN32_FIND_DATA lpFind;
    HANDLE hSearch;
    BOOL status = TRUE;

    if ((hSearch = FindFirstFile(findFile, &lpFind))
        == INVALID_HANDLE_VALUE) return FALSE;

    // if this is a hidden or system file, keep searching
    while (lpFind.dwFileAttributes != 32 && status)
        status = FindNextFile(hSearch, &lpFind);
    FindClose(hSearch);
```

for fun, I use GetVolumeInformation() and GetDiskFreeSpace() to display what kind of file system is present on the drive containing the spool directory and how much disk space is available. Figure 7.2 shows the output asynch.exe generated when executing on my own PC.

Listing 7.3 (continued)

```
    if (lpFind.dwFileAttributes == 32 && status) {
        sprintf(fileName, "%s\\%s", spoolPath, lpFind.cFileName);
        printf("Spooling file %s to the printer.\n", fileName);
        return TRUE;
    } //if
    return FALSE;
} /* FindNextSpoolFilename */

/**--------------------------------------------------------**/
BOOL SynchronousFileCopy(char *SourceName, char *DestName)
{
    unsigned long ulRead = 1, ulWritten = 1;
    BYTE formFeed = CHAR_FORMFEED;
    BYTE buffer[BUF_SIZE+1];
    DWORD dwStatus;

    CFileIO Source(SourceName, GENERIC_READ, OPEN_ALWAYS,
        FILE_ATTRIBUTE_NORMAL, &dwStatus);
    if (!dwStatus) return FALSE;

    CFileIO Dest(DestName, GENERIC_WRITE, OPEN_EXISTING,
        FILE_ATTRIBUTE_NORMAL, &dwStatus);
    if (!dwStatus) return FALSE;

    while (ulRead != 0)
    {
      ulRead = Source.Read(buffer, BUF_SIZE);
      ulWritten = Dest.Write(buffer, ulRead);
    }
    //send form feed to printer
    Dest.Write(&formFeed, sizeof(CHAR));
    return TRUE;
} // SynchronousFileCopy

/**--------------------------------------------------------**/
BOOL AsynchronousFileCopy(char *SourceName, char *DestName)
{
    DWORD dwStatus=TRUE, dwRead=0, dwWritten=0, dwPend=0;
    BOOL bMore = FALSE;
    BYTE formFeed = CHAR_FORMFEED;
    BYTE buf1[BUF_SIZE+1], buf2[BUF_SIZE+1], buf3[BUF_SIZE+1];
```

Listing 7.3 (continued)

```
CFileIO Source(SourceName,GENERIC_READ, OPEN_ALWAYS,
    FILE_FLAG_OVERLAPPED, &dwStatus);
if (!dwStatus) return FALSE;

CFileIO Dest(DestName, GENERIC_WRITE, OPEN_EXISTING,
    FILE_FLAG_OVERLAPPED, &dwStatus);
if (!dwStatus) return FALSE;

LPBYTE pRead = buf1;
LPBYTE pWrite = buf2;
LPBYTE pSwing = buf3;
LPBYTE pTemp = buf1;

// read the first buffer from the source file
Source.ReadWithAbandon(pRead, BUF_SIZE);

while (!bMore)
{
    // wait for pending read from source file
    while (!Source.IOComplete(TRUE, &dwRead));

    // swap buffer pointers
    pTemp = pRead; pRead = pSwing; pSwing = pTemp;

    // if more to read, start the next read from source file
    bMore = Source.ReadWithAbandon(pRead, BUF_SIZE);

    // wait for pending write to destination file
    while (!Dest.IOComplete(TRUE, &dwWritten));

    // swap buffer pointers
    pTemp = pWrite; pWrite = pSwing; pSwing = pTemp;

    // start the next write to parallel port
    Dest.WriteWithAbandon(pWrite, dwRead);
} //while

//send form feed to printer, wait until it's done
Dest.WriteWithAbandon(&formFeed, 1);
while (!Dest.IOComplete(TRUE, &dwWritten));
return TRUE;
} // AsynchronousFileCopy
```

Figure 7.2 Typical output from `asynch.exe`.

```
Enter the print spool directory:
c:\spool
File system for volume c:\ is FAT.
Total free bytes: 13361152
Spooling file c:\spool\AUTOEXEC.BAT to the printer.
Spooling file c:\spool\CONFIG.SYS to the printer.
```

Next, I use the Win32 file change notification routines to monitor activity in the specified spool directory. What I am really interested in is file creation events in that directory, but the finest granularity I can get with Win32's `FindFirstChangeNotification()` is notification of all file creations, deletions, and renames occurring in that directory (by specifying the `FILE_NOTIFY_CHANGE_FILE_NAME` flag). `FindFirstChangeNotification()` sets up the notification filter and returns a change notification handle that can be used in subsequent calls to `FindNextChangeNotification()` or any of the Win32 wait routines.

Once the notification filter is initialized I go into an infinite loop waiting for a change notification (don't panic; you can simply type Ctrl-C when the DOS shell that is running `asynch.exe` has the input focus or just close the DOS shell). The change notification handle is a waitable synchronization handle, so I can use `WaitForSingleObject()` to wait for any changes matching the filter I specified when calling `FindFirstChangeNotification()`. When such a change occurs, I call my private `FindNextSpoolFilename()` routine. Unfortunately, the notification routines do not return any specific information about the file that was created/deleted/renamed, so I used Win32's `FindFirstFile()` and `FindNextFile()` to search for any files in the spool directory.

Notice that if several files appear at once in the spool directory, `asynch.exe` will spool them to the printer in the order in which they were located by the find routines (generally in alphabetical order). If files appear in the spool directory while I am printing a previous file, then the next time I call `FindNextChangeNotification()` and `WaitForSingleObject()`, I will be signaled immediately. But if anything should go wrong with that notification mechanism, I also have a backup plan. Because I delete the file after I've finished printing, I will always get a second notification and thus another opportunity to search the spool directory for files that need printing. An example of how this check is crucial is when `asynch.exe` first loads. If files are already in the spool directory, it will catch those files the next time a new file is copied to the spool directory.

I can use either `SynchronousFileCopy()` or `AsynchronousFileCopy()` private routines to print the spooled file. Both routines use the `CFileIO` class. To make the test program more interesting, `testmain.cpp` always calls `AsynchronousFileCopy()`. `AsynchronousFileCopy()` is very general: you pass it two filenames and it copies the source file to the destination file. In this case the source file is the filename extracted from the spool directory and the destination file is the parallel printer port (`prn`).

To get the most efficiency from asynchronous file I/O while not allowing more than one I/O operation to be simultaneously queued to any file handle, I use an extra buffer as a sort of swing buffer. I start the first priming asynchronous read [`CFileIO::ReadWithAbandon()`] and immediately wait for it to complete. Once the read has completed I assign the `pSwing` pointer to that buffer and use the `pRead` buffer to start another asynchronous read operation. If the last asynchronous write operation [`CFileIO::WriteWithAbandon()`] has completed, I proceed to write the data pointed to by pSwing to the destination file, then I wait for the last read operation to complete. I repeat this sequence until I get to the end of the source file. This way I assure that the source file is never waiting on the destination file or vice versa. Of course you must be extremely careful to avoid accessing a buffer (or worse yet, deallocating it!) before pending I/O operations have completed. Also remember that you don't know how many bytes were actually transferred until the operation is completed.

All the sources file necessary to build the sample application can be found on the code disk.

Conclusion

Although this little utility is functional, there are several obvious enhancements I could make. For instance, I could design the program to use separate threads for the overlapped read and write operations -- on a multi-processor system, I could literally be writing one buffer while I'm reading the next buffer.

File locking is also a very powerful feature of the Win32 API. If there is a chance that another thread or process might need to access parts of the same file, I could open the file for sharing and then just protect the region I'm currently accessing by using Win32's LockFile() and UnlockFile().

And what about using the standard C runtime file routines? Although they are supported, the runtime routines are typically mapped directly to one of the new Win32 routines, so it's actually slightly faster to use the new routines. But more important, don't mix the Win32 file routines with the C runtime file routines. The file handles are not entirely interchangeable.

Asynchronous file I/O can significantly increase performance because your program no longer has to wait for a file transaction or the mechanical movements of the disk drive to finally complete. Asynchronous file I/O also increases overall system efficiency — when a thread really does need to wait for a file transaction to complete, it just goes to sleep without consuming any real CPU time. The technique contained in CFileIO provides an easy way to realize the benefits of multithreading for your application.

References

Custer, Helen. *Inside Windows NT.* Redmond, WA: Microsoft Press, 1993.

Microsoft Corp. Win32 Software Development Kit for Windows NT. Windows NT Device Driver Kit.

Myers, Brian, and Eric Hamer. *Mastering Windows NT Programming.* San Francisco, CA: Sybex, 1993.

Richter, Jeffrey. *Advanced Windows NT.* Redmond, WA: Microsoft Press, 1993.

Sheperd, George. "Getting in Synch with Windows NT." *NT Developer*, October 1993.

Chapter 8

Data Object List Dialog for Windows

Steve Welstead

If you have tried writing your own code for Windows dialog boxes, then chances are you have dealt with the issues of designing resources, identifying dialog controls with program variables, and writing callback procedures to define dialog box functionality. Even with today's "expert" and "wizard" application-building tools this process can be tedious. This chapter describes how to build a type of dialog, the data object list dialog, that can replace large complex input dialogs. This allows you to rapidly develop prototype Windows programs without getting bogged down in the details of dialog design.

The data object list dialog is based on a small C++ class library of dialogs that includes simple dialogs for commonly used data types as well as a list dialog class. The list dialog manages a list of data objects. Each data object knows how to update its own value through an appropriate input dialog. For example, string data objects call up a text input dialog, whereas objects representing RGB color values summon the standard Windows dialog for choosing colors. Once you have made the initial investment in designing this list dialog, you can provide your programs with a user input interface simply by inserting objects into the list. You don't need to design separate resources or callback procedures for each new application. The C++ class structure hides the issues of resources, control identifiers, and callback procedures. In the final section of this chapter, I will show how to implement the data object list dialog in a simple `WinMain()` application example.

The C++ code presented is compatible for compilation as both 16-bit and 32-bit Windows executables. You should be able to produce executables for Windows 3.1, Win32, Windows NT, and hopefully Windows 95. This code does not use any proprietary C++ Windows class libraries, such as Borland's OWL library or Microsoft's MFC library, although you can implement the concepts in those libraries. I have compiled and run this code using both Borland C++ v3.1 and v4.5, as well as Symantec's C++ v7.0 compiler.

The Object List

The object list is a simple C++ class that manages an array of pointers to objects. It is similar to a collection class in a container class library. This is the class I use to manage the items in the data object listbox. Listing 8.1 shows the header file cwobj.h, which defines this class. The code for the object list class is straightforward. Due to space limitations, it is not listed here, but is available on the code disk.

Listing 8.1 cwobj.h — *Header file for object list classes.*

```
#ifndef CWOBJ_H
#define CWOBJ_H

#define STRICT
#include <windows.h>

typedef void *p_void;

#define MAX_PATH 80
typedef char path_str[MAX_PATH + 1];

class object_list {
    public:
    p_void *the_list;
    int item_count;
    int max_count;
    object_list (int max_items);
    virtual int add_item (void *item_addr);
    virtual int insert_item (int index,void *item_addr);
    virtual void *at(int index);
    virtual int get_count ();
    virtual void delete_item (int index);
    virtual ~object_list (); };
```

Listing 8.1 (continued)

```
typedef struct {
   object_list *item_collection;
   int selected_item;
   } tlist_box_data;

#define MAX_DISPLAY_LEN 80

enum tdata_type {STR_DATA,PATH_DATA,COLOR_DATA};

class tdata_obj {
   public:
   void * value_addr;
   char * descr_addr;
   int item_no;
   tdata_obj (char * the_descr,void * value_ptr, int the_item_no)
     {descr_addr = the_descr;
     value_addr = value_ptr;
     item_no = the_item_no; } };

void build_display_str (tdata_type data_type,void
       *descr_addr,void *value_addr,int display_len,
       int maxlen,char *the_string);

class ttyped_data_obj: public tdata_obj {
   public:
   char display_str[MAX_DISPLAY_LEN + 1];
   tdata_type data_type;
   unsigned short display_len;
   char * wild_str;
   ttyped_data_obj (char * the_descr, void * value_ptr,
      tdata_type the_type, unsigned short the_len, char * the_wild_str,
      int the_item_no) : tdata_obj (the_descr, value_ptr,the_item_no) {
    data_type = the_type;
    display_len = the_len;
    if (display_len > MAX_DISPLAY_LEN)
        display_len = MAX_DISPLAY_LEN;
    wild_str = the_wild_str;
    build_display_str (the_type,the_descr, value_ptr,the_len,
     MAX_DISPLAY_LEN,display_str); }
   virtual char *get_display_str
    (int maxlen = MAX_DISPLAY_LEN);
   virtual void get_new_value (HWND parent,
      int max_display_len = MAX_DISPLAY_LEN); };
#endif
```

The array `the_list` stores the actual array of pointers. This array uses indexes one through `max_count` for its items rather than the usual C indexing starting with zero. The member function `insert_item` inserts a new object at the designated index using this convention, whereas the member function `at` returns the object at a given index value. It is important to note that the calling program supplies allocated objects for each item in `the_list`.

Because `object_list` does not allocate these objects, it does not destroy them either. (The calling program may, and probably will, want to use these objects after the `object_list` is destroyed.) Thus, `delete_item` does not actually delete the object at the given index, it only rearranges the list to skip over that item. Similarly, the destructor for `object_list` does not destroy items in the list, it only deletes the allocated array `the_list`.

Data Objects

File `cwobj.h` also defines the object types that the data object list dialog displays and manipulates. The class `tdata_obj` defines the basic data object type. Each data object contains a pointer to a value (`value_addr`), a description string (`descr_addr`), and an item number that indicates its position in an object list.

From `tdata_obj`, I derive the class `ttyped_data_obj`, which includes information about what type of data the object represents and how to update that data. Listing 8.2 shows the file `cwdatobj.cpp` with the code for this class.

Listing 8.2 `cwdatobj.cpp` — *Defines basic data objects.*

```
#include <stdio.h>
#include <string.h>

#include "cwobj.h"
#include "cwdialgs.h"

void value_str(tdata_type data_type, void *the_value_addr,int display_len,
    char *the_string) {
    switch (data_type) {
    case STR_DATA:
    case PATH_DATA:
      strncpy (the_string,(char *)the_value_addr, display_len);
      the_string[display_len-1] = '\0';
      break;
```

Listing 8.2 (continued)

```
   case COLOR_DATA:
     sprintf (the_string,"RGB(%hu,%hu,%hu)",
        GetRValue(*(DWORD *)the_value_addr),
        GetGValue(*(DWORD *)the_value_addr),
        GetBValue(*(DWORD *)the_value_addr));
     break;
   default:
     strcpy (the_string,"");  }  //End switch
     }  //End function

void build_display_str (tdata_type data_type,
     void *descr_addr,void *value_addr,
     int display_len,int maxlen, char *the_string) {
   char astring[256],the_value_str[MAX_DISPLAY_LEN];
   strcpy (astring,(char *)descr_addr);
   strcat (astring,": ");
   value_str (data_type,value_addr,display_len, the_value_str);
   strcat (astring,the_value_str);
   strncpy (the_string,astring,maxlen-2);
   the_string[maxlen-1] = '\0'; }

char *ttyped_data_obj::get_display_str (int maxlen){
     // Build display_str in case value has changed.
     build_display_str(data_type,descr_addr,value_addr,
        display_len,maxlen,display_str);
     return display_str; }

void ttyped_data_obj::get_new_value (HWND parent, int maxlen) {
     switch (data_type) {
     case STR_DATA:
       string_dialog (parent,descr_addr,descr_addr, display_len,value_addr);
       break;
     case PATH_DATA:
       get_file_name_dlg(parent,wild_str,
          descr_addr,(char *)value_addr,MAX_PATH);
       break;
     case COLOR_DATA:
       get_rgb_color (parent,(COLORREF *)value_addr);
       break;
       }  //end switch
     get_display_str(maxlen);  }
```

The job of a `ttyped_data_obj` object is to allow the user to update the value of the data that the object represents and to provide a string display of a description of this data and its current value. The function `value_str` formats the data value into a string, and the function `build_display_str` appends the value string to the description string for that item. The resulting string is what appears in the data object listbox. For example, suppose in a graphics program you had a `COLOR_DATA` item called "Line Color," and the current RGB values for this item were 255, 0, and 0 (pure red). The function `build_display_str` would produce the string

```
"Line Color: RGB(255,0,0)"
```

for this item, and this is what would appear in the listbox.

The typed data object obtains updates for its data value through the member function `get_new_value`, which presents to the user a dialog that is appropriate for that particular data type. The following sections discuss these dialogs in more detail.

Dialog Classes

At this point, I need to build some C++ classes that will define basic dialog behavior. If you are working with one of the Windows C++ libraries, such as Borland's OWL or Microsoft's MFC, you may want to substitute the basic dialog classes from one of those libraries. Listing 8.3 shows the header file `cwdlg.h` for these classes, and Listing 8.4 shows the file `cwdlg.cpp`, which contains the source code for the base class `tdialog` and the derived class `tinput_dialog`.

Listing 8.3 `cwdlg.h` — *Header file for* `tdialog` *classes.*

```
#ifndef CWDLG_H
#define CWDLG_H

#include "cwobj.h"

// Define this for Win32 and Windows NT:
// #define WIN_32
// Borland uses __FLAT__
// Symantec uses __NT__
#ifdef WIN_32
#define GET_WM_COMMAND_CMD(wp,lp)    HIWORD(wp)
#else   // 16 bit Windows
#define GET_WM_COMMAND_CMD(wp,lp)    HIWORD(lp)
#endif
```

Listing 8.3 (continued)

```
extern HINSTANCE gdlg_instance;
// Must be set to current instance before using any dialogs.

int check_gdlg_instance (void);

class tdialog {
    public:
    LPCSTR rc_title,caption_title;
    HWND hwndParent,hdialog;
    BOOL dlg_return_value;
    DLGPROC lpDialogProc;
    tdialog (HWND Parent,LPCSTR resource_name, LPCSTR caption_name);
    virtual void center_dialog (void);
    virtual BOOL respond_wm_initdialog (void);
    virtual BOOL respond_wm_command (WPARAM wParam, LPARAM lParam);
    virtual BOOL handle_message (HWND hwnd,UINT message,
        WPARAM wParam,LPARAM lParam);
    virtual BOOL exec_dialog (void);
    virtual ~tdialog (void); };

#define MAX_INPUT_LENGTH 80

class tinput_dialog: public tdialog {
    public:
    char input_text [MAX_INPUT_LENGTH + 1];
    LPCSTR input_caption;
    int input_id,input_caption_id;
    tinput_dialog (HWND Parent,LPCSTR caption_name,
        LPCSTR input_name,LPCSTR init_text);
    virtual BOOL respond_wm_initdialog(void);
    virtual BOOL respond_wm_command (WPARAM wParam, LPARAM lParam);
    virtual BOOL exec_dialog (void);
    virtual ~tinput_dialog (void); };

class tlist_dialog: public tdialog {
    public:
    int selected;
    tlist_box_data *list_box_data;
    LPCSTR list_box_descr;
    tlist_dialog (HWND Parent,LPCSTR caption_name,
        LPCSTR descr_name,tlist_box_data *the_data_rec,int init_selected);
    virtual void set_data (tlist_box_data *data_rec);
    virtual void get_data (tlist_box_data *data_rec);
    virtual BOOL respond_wm_initdialog(void);
    virtual BOOL respond_wm_command (WPARAM wParam, LPARAM lParam);
    virtual void set_selected (int sel);
    virtual LPSTR get_item_string (int item);
    virtual void clear_list_box (void);
    virtual BOOL exec_dialog (void);
    virtual ~tlist_dialog (void); };
```

C++ classes provide a convenient means for dealing with resource scripts and data-handling issues. The base class `tdialog` does not have a resource script associated with it because this dialog does not have any real functionality. However, it does provide a member variable, which descendant classes can use to store their resource identifiers.

Listing 8.3 (continued)

```
class tdata_list_dialog: public tlist_dialog {
   public:
   tdata_list_dialog (HWND Parent,LPCSTR caption_name,
      LPCSTR descr_name,tlist_box_data *the_data_rec, int init_selected):
   tlist_dialog (Parent,caption_name,descr_name, the_data_rec,
      init_selected) { } ;
   virtual BOOL respond_wm_command (WPARAM wParam, LPARAM lParam);
   virtual LPSTR get_item_string (int item);
   virtual BOOL exec_dialog (void);
   };
#endif
```

Listing 8.4   `cwdlg.cpp` — Dialog classes.

```
#include <stdio.h>
#include <string.h>

#include "cwdlg.h"
#include "dlgids.h"

HINSTANCE gdlg_instance = 0;
// This must be set to current instance before
// using any dialogs.

int check_gdlg_instance () {
    if (!gdlg_instance) {
       MessageBox (NULL,"gdlg_instance not set.",
       "UWDLG.CPP",MB_ICONEXCLAMATION | MB_OK);
       return 0; }
    return 1; }

tdialog *this_dialog = 0;

BOOL CALLBACK _export tdialog_proc(HWND hdlg,
    UINT message,WPARAM wParam, LPARAM lParam) {
    return this_dialog->handle_message(hdlg,message, wParam,lParam); }
```

Listing 8.4 (continued)

```
tdialog::tdialog (HWND Parent,LPCSTR resource_name, LPCSTR caption_name) {
    hwndParent = Parent;
    rc_title = resource_name;
    caption_title = caption_name; }

void tdialog::center_dialog () {
    RECT dlg_rect;
    int x_screen = GetSystemMetrics(SM_CXSCREEN),
        y_screen = GetSystemMetrics(SM_CYSCREEN);
    GetWindowRect (hdialog,&dlg_rect);
    int dlg_width = dlg_rect.right - dlg_rect.left,
        dlg_ht = dlg_rect.bottom - dlg_rect.top;
    int x_pos = (x_screen - dlg_width)/2,
        y_pos = (y_screen - dlg_ht)/2;
    SetWindowPos (hdialog,NULL,x_pos,y_pos,0,0, SWP_NOSIZE|SWP_NOZORDER);}

BOOL tdialog::respond_wm_initdialog () {
    center_dialog();
    return 1;}

BOOL tdialog::respond_wm_command (WPARAM wParam,LPARAM) {
    switch (LOWORD(wParam)) {
    case IDOK:
        dlg_return_value = 1;
        EndDialog(hdialog, TRUE);
        return 1;
    case IDCANCEL:
        dlg_return_value = 0;
        EndDialog(hdialog,FALSE);
        return 0;
    }  // end switch
    return 0; }

BOOL tdialog::handle_message (HWND hwnd,UINT message,
    WPARAM wParam,LPARAM lParam) {
    hdialog = hwnd; // hdialog must be set before any
        // handling any messages
    switch (message) {
    case WM_INITDIALOG:
        return respond_wm_initdialog ();
    case WM_COMMAND:
        return respond_wm_command (wParam,lParam);
    }  // end switch
    return FALSE; }
```

Member variables can also store the data that the dialog box obtains from the user. This allows you to associate the data with the dialog and avoid the use of global variables. You also avoid having to use that mysterious "extra" Windows parameter with its requirements for locking and unlocking local data. You can pass data to the dialog class through its constructor and obtain updated values from the class object after dialog execution.

Listing 8.4 (continued)

```
BOOL tdialog::exec_dialog () {
    if (!check_gdlg_instance()) return 0;
    tdialog *old_tdialog = this_dialog;
    this_dialog = this;
    lpDialogProc =
        (DLGPROC)MakeProcInstance((FARPROC)tdialog_proc, gdlg_instance);
        DialogBox(gdlg_instance,rc_title, hwndParent, lpDialogProc);
    FreeProcInstance((FARPROC)lpDialogProc);
    this_dialog = old_tdialog;
    return dlg_return_value; }

tdialog::~tdialog() { }

tinput_dialog *this_input_dialog = 0;

BOOL CALLBACK _export tinput_dialog_proc(HWND hdlg,
        UINT message,WPARAM wParam, LPARAM lParam) {
        return this_input_dialog->handle_message(hdlg,
            message,wParam,lParam); }

tinput_dialog::tinput_dialog (HWND Parent,
        LPCSTR caption_name,LPCSTR input_name,
        LPCSTR init_text):tdialog(Parent, "INPUT_DIALOG",caption_name){
    input_id = ID_DLG_INPUT;
    input_caption_id = ID_DLG_INPUT_CAPTION;
    input_caption = input_name;
    strncpy (input_text,init_text,MAX_INPUT_LENGTH);
input_text[MAX_INPUT_LENGTH] = '\0'; };

BOOL tinput_dialog::respond_wm_initdialog () {
    SetWindowText (hdialog,caption_title);
    SetWindowText (GetDlgItem(hdialog, input_caption_id),input_caption);
    SetWindowText(GetDlgItem(hdialog,input_id), input_text);
    SetFocus(GetDlgItem(hdialog,input_id));
    return tdialog::respond_wm_initdialog();}
```

It is somewhat more difficult to elegantly hide the issue of callback functions. The callback function defines the behavior of the dialog box; that is, how it responds to user input and system messages. Ideally, this function would be a member function of the dialog class. The problem is that when the dialog box is created, you must pass the address of the callback function to the Windows function `DialogBox`. C++ does not allow the address of a member function to be passed as a parameter, because this address is not known until a particular class object is instantiated at runtime. Even using the `this` pointer in front of a class member function to indicate a particular instantiation of the class is not sufficient for the C++ police. The callback function needs to be a stand-alone function whose definition is external to any C++ class.

To address this problem, I define a callback function for each dialog class that is external to that class. I also define a global pointer to that class that represents a particular object instance of that class. The callback function uses this global pointer to call a specific instance of a member function which defines the behavior of this dialog class. Listing 8.4 illustrates this approach in file `cwdlg.cpp`. The callback function for

Listing 8.4 (continued)

```
BOOL tinput_dialog::respond_wm_command (WPARAM wParam, LPARAM) {
    switch (LOWORD(wParam)) {
    case IDOK:
        GetDlgItemText(hdialog,input_id,input_text, MAX_INPUT_LENGTH);
        dlg_return_value = 1;
        EndDialog(hdialog, TRUE);
        return 1;
    case IDCANCEL:
        dlg_return_value = 0;
        EndDialog(hdialog,FALSE);
        return 0;
    } // end switch
    return 0; }

BOOL tinput_dialog::exec_dialog () {
    if (!check_gdlg_instance()) return 0;
    tinput_dialog *old_tinput_dialog = this_input_dialog;
    this_input_dialog = this;
    lpDialogProc = (DLGPROC)MakeProcInstance(
        (FARPROC)tinput_dialog_proc,gdlg_instance);
    DialogBox(gdlg_instance,rc_title, hwndParent, lpDialogProc);
    FreeProcInstance((FARPROC)lpDialogProc);
    this_input_dialog = old_tinput_dialog;
    return dlg_return_value; }

tinput_dialog::~tinput_dialog() { }
```

the base class `tdialog` is called `tdialog_proc`, and there is a global `tdialog` pointer called `this_dialog`. Member function `handle_message` determines the behavior of the dialog by defining how it responds to Windows messages. This is what should be the callback function. Thus, `tdialog_proc` calls a specific instantiation of `handle_message`, namely the one belonging to the global `tdialog` object that `this_tdialog` points to.

It is important to consider when to set the value of the global pointer used in the callback function. Member function `exec_dialog` makes the call to Windows that actually executes the dialog. It is here that the global pointer `this_tdialog` is set to the `this` pointer for the current instantiation of the dialog class object. Note that you don't want to set this pointer in the constructor for the class because any derived type will override the initial setting and reset the value to its own `this` value. This will cause problems if you have more than one dialog executing at one time. Also, `exec_dialog` saves the current value of the global pointer before resetting it and restores this value when it is done, in case two dialogs of the same class are executing at one time.

The first descendant class of `tdialog` is `tinput_dialog`, which takes text input from the user. Note that this dialog, as well as all other derived dialog classes, has its own global pointer (`this_input_dialog` in this case) and its own callback procedure (`tinput_dialog_proc`) defined external to the C++ class. The member function `exec_dialog` calls this procedure in the same way as was the case for the `tdialog` class.

Listing 8.5   `cwdialgs.h` — *Header for predefined dialog boxes.*

```
#ifndef CWDIALGS_H
#define CWDIALGS_H

#define STRICT
#include <windows.h>

extern HINSTANCE gdlg_instance;
// This must be set to current instance before using these dialogs.

int string_dialog (HWND Parent,LPCSTR dlg_title,
    LPCSTR descr,int maxlen,void *the_string);

int get_file_name_dlg (HWND hWnd,const char *pfilter,
    const char *ptitle_str, char *file_name, int max_len);

BOOL get_rgb_color (HWND hWnd,COLORREF *init_color);
#endif
```

The class `tinput_dialog` uses the resource script named `INPUT_DIALOG`, which defines a simple dialog box with a single edit control with the identifier `ID_DLG_INPUT`, a default "OK" button, and a "Cancel" button. Resource scripts are not listed here but are included with the code disk.

Dialogs

To use a C++ class, you need to create a particular instance of the class. For our dialog classes, this can be accomplished with a function that calls the class constructor for the particular dialog class then executes the dialog. This function also initializes the data presented to the user and brings input from the user back to the calling program. When the dialog terminates, this function obtains the data from the dialog class and then deletes the dialog class instance. The calling program never has to be aware of the existence of the C++ class.

Listing 8.5 shows the header file `cwdialgs.h` for the three dialog functions used in the example discussed here. These are the dialog functions that the `ttyped_data_obj` member function `get_new_value` calls when updating the object data values. The function `string_dialog` instantiates the `tinput_dialog` class and obtains string input from the user. Listing 8.6, file `cwinpdlg.cpp`, shows the code for this function. Recall that class `tinput_dialog` has the capability to override the dialog window caption and edit control caption. The function `string_dialog` supplies these captions, using string parameters `dlg_title` and `descr`.

Listing 8.6   `cwinpdlg.cpp` *— Input dialog box.*

```
#include <stdio.h>
#include <string.h>

#include "cwdlg.h"
#include "cwdialgs.h"

int string_dialog (HWND Parent,LPCSTR dlg_title,
     LPCSTR descr,int maxlen,void *the_string) {
    char buffer[80],buffer2[80];
    strncpy (buffer,(char *)the_string,maxlen);
    sprintf (buffer2,"Enter new %s:",descr);
    tinput_dialog *p= new tinput_dialog(Parent, dlg_title,buffer2, buffer);
    if (!(p->exec_dialog ())) {
        delete p;
        return 0; }
    strncpy ((char *)the_string,p->input_text,maxlen);
    ((char *)the_string)[maxlen-1] = '\0';
    delete p;
    return 1;
    } // end string_dialog
```

The two other dialog functions whose definitions appear in Listing 8.5, `get_file_name_dlg` and `get_rgb_color`, are actually not based on C++ classes. Rather, they call Windows common dialogs. The function `get_file_name_dlg` fills the Windows-defined structure `OPENFILENAME` and calls the Windows common dialog function `GetOpenFileName`. The function `get_rgb_color` fills the Windows structure `CHOOSECOLOR` and calls the Windows common dialog `ChooseColor`. The use of these structures and dialogs is fairly standard. You should be able to find examples of their use in the documentation for your Windows software development environment. For that reason, the code for these dialogs is not listed here but is included on the code disk in the file `cwcomdlg.cpp`.

List Dialog

The list dialog class `tlist_dialog` displays an object list by implementing a Windows listbox control in a dialog box. Listing 8.7, file `cwlstdlg.cpp`, shows the code for the class `tlist_dialog` and its descendant `tdata_list_dialog`. The items in the `object_list` may be strings, as in a standard Windows listbox, or they may be more complex structure or class types. The listbox displays string descriptions of these more general items. The `tlist_box_data` parameter sent to the `tlist_dialog` constructor contains the object list pointer `item_collection` as well as an integer indicating the currently selected item in the list. Note that this means that `tlist_dialog` does not instantiate, nor does it destroy, the object items in the list. This is because in many cases, such as the data object list dialog discussed below, you want the list items to have a life beyond that of the list dialog.

Listing 8.7 `cwlstdlg.cpp` *— List dialogs.*

```
#include "cwdlg.h"
#include "dlgids.h"

tlist_dialog *this_list_dialog = 0;

BOOL CALLBACK _export tlist_dialog_proc(HWND hdlg,
        UINT message,WPARAM wParam, LPARAM lParam) {
    return this_list_dialog->handle_message(hdlg, message,wParam,lParam); }

tlist_dialog::tlist_dialog (HWND Parent,
        LPCSTR caption_name,LPCSTR descr_name,
        tlist_box_data *the_data_rec,int init_selected):
        tdialog (Parent,"LIST_DIALOG",caption_name) {
    list_box_descr = descr_name;
    selected = init_selected;      list_box_data = the_data_rec; }
```

Listing 8.7 *(continued)*

```
BOOL tlist_dialog::respond_wm_initdialog () {
    SetWindowText (hdialog,caption_title);
    SetWindowText (GetDlgItem(hdialog,ID_LSTDIALG_DESCR), list_box_descr);
    set_data (list_box_data);
    SetFocus(GetDlgItem(hdialog,ID_LSTDIALG_LSTBOX));
    return tdialog::respond_wm_initdialog () ; }

BOOL tlist_dialog::respond_wm_command (WPARAM wParam, LPARAM lParam) {
    switch (LOWORD(wParam)) {
    case IDOK:
        selected = (int)SendDlgItemMessage(hdialog,
        ID_LSTDIALG_LSTBOX,LB_GETCURSEL,0,0L) + 1;
        dlg_return_value = 1;
        EndDialog(hdialog, TRUE);
        return 1;
    case IDCANCEL:
        dlg_return_value = 0;
        EndDialog(hdialog,FALSE);
    case ID_LSTDIALG_LSTBOX:
            switch (GET_WM_COMMAND_CMD(wParam,lParam)) {
            case LBN_DBLCLK:
            selected = (int)SendDlgItemMessage(hdialog,
            ID_LSTDIALG_LSTBOX,LB_GETCURSEL,0,0L) + 1;
            dlg_return_value = 1;
            EndDialog(hdialog, TRUE);
            return 1;
        }  // end switch
    }  // end switch
    return 0; }

void tlist_dialog::set_data (tlist_box_data *data_rec){
    int i;
    data_rec->selected_item = selected;
    clear_list_box();
    for (i=1;i<=(data_rec->item_collection)-> get_count();i++)
    SendDlgItemMessage(hdialog,ID_LSTDIALG_LSTBOX,
        LB_ADDSTRING,0,(LRESULT)get_item_string(i));
    set_selected(selected); }
void tlist_dialog::get_data (tlist_box_data *data_rec){
    // All we care about is getting the selected item
    // index. The object list updates itself.
    data_rec->selected_item = selected; }
```

The member functions of `tlist_dialog` implement listbox functionality by sending messages to Windows. Member function `set_data` fills the listbox with strings representing each item in the object list, using strings obtained from `get_item_string`. The key to modifying the basic behavior of `tlist_dialog` to handle objects more general than strings is to override `get_item_string`.

Listing 8.7 (continued)

```
LPSTR tlist_dialog::get_item_string (int item) {
    // Assumes item_collection in list_box_data is an
    // array of strings. Override this for list boxes
    // with more complex items.
    return (LPSTR)((list_box_data->
        item_collection)->at(item)); }

void tlist_dialog::set_selected (int sel) {
    SendDlgItemMessage(hdialog,ID_LSTDIALG_LSTBOX, LB_SETCURSEL,sel-1, 0); }

void tlist_dialog::clear_list_box () {
    SendDlgItemMessage(hdialog,ID_LSTDIALG_LSTBOX, LB_RESETCONTENT,0, 0); }

BOOL tlist_dialog::exec_dialog () {
    if (!check_gdlg_instance()) return 0;
    tlist_dialog *old_tlist_dialog = this_list_dialog;
    this_list_dialog = this;
    lpDialogProc = (DLGPROC)MakeProcInstance(
        (FARPROC)tlist_dialog_proc,gdlg_instance);
    DialogBox(gdlg_instance,rc_title, hwndParent, lpDialogProc);
    FreeProcInstance((FARPROC)lpDialogProc);
    this_list_dialog = old_tlist_dialog;
    return dlg_return_value; }

tlist_dialog::~tlist_dialog () {
    clear_list_box(); }

tdata_list_dialog *this_data_list_dialog = 0;

BOOL CALLBACK _export tdata_list_dialog_proc(HWND hdlg,
    UINT message,WPARAM wParam, LPARAM lParam){
    return this_data_list_dialog->handle_message(hdlg,
        message,wParam,lParam); }

LPSTR tdata_list_dialog::get_item_string (int item) {
    return (LPSTR)
        (((ttyped_data_obj *)((list_box_data-> item_collection)->at(item)))->
        get_display_str()); }
```

Data Object List Dialog

The descendant class tdata_list_dialog (cwlstdlg.cpp, Listing 8.7) manipulates a list of objects of type ttyped_data_obj (cwobj.h, Listing 8.1), rather than simple strings. In this case, the derived version of get_item_string() calls the ttyped_data_obj member function get_display_str to obtain the string that will appear in the listbox. Figure 8.1 shows a data object list dialog with some sample strings obtained from get_display_str(). The tlist_dialog member function, without any modification, takes care of inserting these strings in the listbox. This is a good example of how C++ classes can ease the job of Windows programming.

Listing 8.7 (continued)

```
BOOL tdata_list_dialog::respond_wm_command (WPARAM wParam,LPARAM lParam) {
    int list_selected;

    switch (LOWORD(wParam)) {
    case ID_LSTDIALG_LSTBOX:
        switch (GET_WM_COMMAND_CMD(wParam,lParam)) {
        case LBN_DBLCLK:
        list_selected = (int)SendDlgItemMessage(
            hdialog,ID_LSTDIALG_LSTBOX,LB_GETCURSEL,0,0L) + 1;
        ((ttyped_data_obj *)((list_box_data->
            item_collection)->at(list_selected)))->
            get_new_value(hdialog,MAX_DISPLAY_LEN);
        list_box_data->selected_item = list_selected;
        set_data (list_box_data);
        SetFocus(GetDlgItem(hdialog, ID_LSTDIALG_LSTBOX));
        return 1;
        }  // end switch
    }  /* end switch  */
    return tlist_dialog::respond_wm_command(wParam,lParam); }

BOOL tdata_list_dialog::exec_dialog () {
    if (!check_gdlg_instance()) return 0;
    tdata_list_dialog *old_data_list_dialog = this_data_list_dialog;
    this_data_list_dialog = this;
    lpDialogProc = (DLGPROC)MakeProcInstance(
        (FARPROC)tdata_list_dialog_proc,gdlg_instance);
    DialogBox(gdlg_instance,rc_title, hwndParent, lpDialogProc);
    FreeProcInstance((FARPROC)lpDialogProc);
    this_data_list_dialog = old_data_list_dialog;
    return dlg_return_value; }
```

The data object list dialog responds to a double-click on an item in the list by providing the user with an opportunity to update the value of that item. Objects of the class `ttyped_data_obj` know how to update their own values through the member function `get_new_value`. This function presents the user with a dialog box appropriate for updating the value of the data object. Thus, for example, items of type `STR_DATA` will call the dialog function `string_dialog` to obtain an updated text string from the user, whereas items of type `PATH_DATA` will summon the standard Windows file-opening dialog. After the user enters the new value, the listbox shows that new value in the display string for that item.

All of this is accomplished by having the listbox respond to a `LBN_DBLCLK` message in `respond_wm_command` with a call to the `ttyped_data_obj` member function `get_new_value`, and then calling its own member function `set_data`, which resets the listbox contents using the newly derived version of `get_item_string()`. Notice the use of a macro to handle the `LBN_DBLCLK` message. This is one of the messages that is handled differently in 16- and 32-bit Windows.

Figure 8.1   A sample data object list dialog.

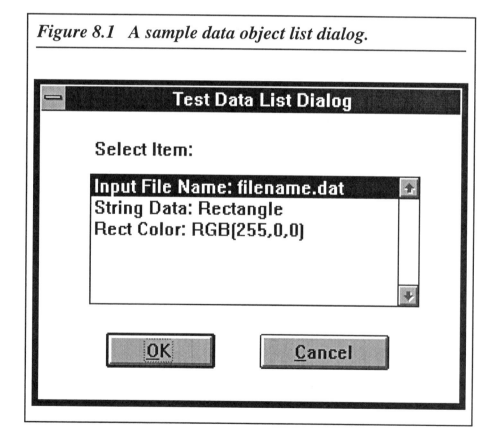

An Example

To implement a data object list dialog in a Windows application, you need to define the variables you want to obtain from the user and associate these variables with an object list. It is convenient, though not necessary, to collect these variables into a single structure. Listing 8.8 shows file tssetlst.h, which defines the structure setup_record containing three variables representing the different data types that the list dialog developed here can address. The function init_setup initializes this structure, and setup_to_collection inserts the structure variables into an object list. The code for these functions is contained in the file tssetlst.cpp, Listing 8.9. Note that setup_to_collection() instantiates a new ttyped_data_obj object for each variable in the setup_record structure then inserts these objects into the object list. This object list is the item_collection that is inserted in the list dialog. To use a data object list dialog in a different application, all you need to do is change the definitions of setup_record and setup_to_collection appropriately.

Listing 8.8 tssetlst.h *— Example of a typical function assigning setup structure fields to an* object_list.

```
#ifndef TSSETLST_H
#define TSSETLST_H

#include "cwobj.h"

#define MAX_ITEMS 10
#define STR_DATA_LEN 40

typedef struct {
      path_str input_file_name;
      char str_data [STR_DATA_LEN + 1];
      DWORD rect_color;
      } setup_record;

void init_setup (setup_record *the_setup);

void setup_to_collection (setup_record *the_setup,
   object_list *the_collection);

#endif
```

File `tstmain.cpp` (Listing 8.10) contains the `WinMain` function code for this example, which produces the application window shown in Figure 8.2. The menus are defined in the resource file `dlgtest.rc`, which also includes resource scripts for the dialogs. There are two menu choices: a "Dialog" submenu with a single option tied to the identifier `idm_dialog`, which summons the list dialog, and a "File" submenu whose single option "Exit" terminates the program.

Listing 8.9 `tssetlst.cpp` *— Example of a typical function assigning setup structure fields to an* `object_list`.

```
#include <string.h>
#include "tssetlst.h"

void init_setup (setup_record *the_setup) {
    strcpy (the_setup->input_file_name,"filename.dat");
    strcpy (the_setup->str_data,"Rectangle");
    the_setup->rect_color = RGB (255,0,0);  // Red
    return; }

void setup_to_collection (setup_record *the_setup,
        object_list *the_collection) {
    void *value_ptr = NULL;
    tdata_type the_type;
    unsigned short len;
    int item_no = 0;

    value_ptr = &the_setup->input_file_name;
    the_type = PATH_DATA;
    len = MAX_PATH;
    item_no++;
    the_collection->add_item (new ttyped_data_obj (
        "Input File Name",value_ptr,the_type,len, "*.DAT",item_no));
    value_ptr = &the_setup->str_data;
    the_type = STR_DATA;
    len = STR_DATA_LEN;
    item_no++;
    the_collection->add_item (new ttyped_data_obj (
        "String Data",value_ptr,the_type,len, "",item_no));
    value_ptr = &the_setup->rect_color;
    the_type = COLOR_DATA;
    len = 17;
    item_no++;
    the_collection->add_item (new ttyped_data_obj (
        "Rect Color",value_ptr,the_type,len, "",item_no));
    return; }
```

`WinMain()` takes care of registering and creating the main application window, as well as the message loop code that runs the program. In addition, this example contains function calls to initialize the listbox data, as well as code for deleting allocations associated with the listbox when the program terminates. You should be particularly careful about cleaning up your allocations in a Windows program; otherwise, they will live on beyond the end of your program.

The Window callback function `WndProc` creates and executes a data object list dialog in response to the menu command identified by `IDM_DIALOG`. When the dialog terminates, the latest information is displayed in the window, including a rectangle filled with the color designated by the latest value of `g_setup.rect_color`.

Table 8.1 lists the files needed to build the executable for this example. For 16-bit compilations, use the large memory model. For 32-bit executables, be sure to define the constant `WIN_32` at the top of file `cwdlg.h` (Listing 8.3).

Figure 8.2   A sample application window.

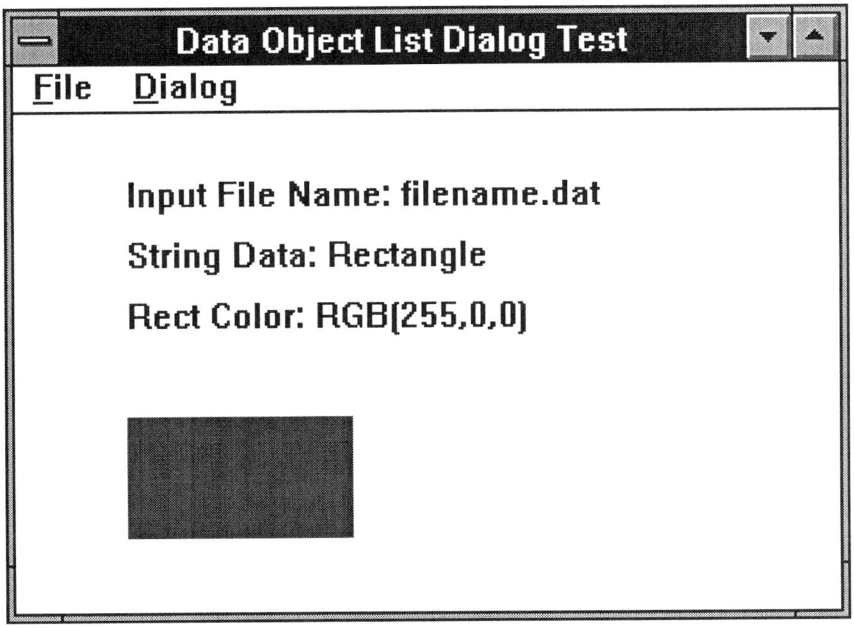

As you can see, the data object list dialog gives you a convenient way of getting information from the user into your Windows program with a minimum of development effort. This is handy for small programs you write for your own use and for prototype versions of larger programs. When you're ready to go to a full production version, you can replace the list dialog with a fancy dialog built with one of those "app wizard" resource workshops.

Table 8.1   Project files.

cwobjlst.cpp*
cwdatobj.cpp
cwdlg.cpp
cwinpdlg.cpp
cwinpdlg.cpp
cwcomdlg.cpp*
cwlstdlg.cpp
tssetlst.cpp
tstmain.cpp
dlgtest.rc*

*Not listed in chapter, but included with code disk.

Listing 8.10   `tstmain.cpp` — Test program for data object list dialog.

```
#include <stdio.h>
#include <string.h>

#include "cwdlg.h"
#include "cwdialgs.h"
#include "dlgids.h"
#include "tssetlst.h"

int init_item = 1;

setup_record g_setup;
tlist_box_data g_list_data;
```

Listing 8.10 (continued)

```
LRESULT CALLBACK _export WndProc(HWND hWnd,
    UINT message,WPARAM wParam, LPARAM lParam);

int WINAPI WinMain(HINSTANCE hInstance,
    HINSTANCE hPrevInstance, LPSTR,int nCmdShow){
        char AppName[]="DataListDlg";
        char MenuName[] = "DialogTestMenu";
        // Get full screen size dimensions:
        int i,xScreen = GetSystemMetrics(SM_CXSCREEN),
              yScreen = GetSystemMetrics(SM_CYSCREEN);

    HWND hWnd;
    MSG msg;
    gdlg_instance = hInstance; //used by uwdialgs.cpp
    WNDCLASS wndclass;

    if (!hPrevInstance) {
        wndclass.style          = CS_HREDRAW|CS_VREDRAW;
        wndclass.lpfnWndProc    = WndProc;
        wndclass.cbClsExtra     = 0;
        wndclass.cbWndExtra     = 0;
        wndclass.hInstance      = hInstance ;
        wndclass.hIcon          = LoadIcon (NULL,IDI_APPLICATION) ;
        wndclass.hCursor        = LoadCursor (NULL, IDC_ARROW) ;
        wndclass.hbrBackground = (HBRUSH)GetStockObject(WHITE_BRUSH);
        wndclass.lpszMenuName   = MenuName;
        wndclass.lpszClassName = AppName;
        if (!RegisterClass(&wndclass)) return FALSE;
        }
    hWnd = CreateWindow(AppName,
        "Data Object List Dialog Test",
        WS_OVERLAPPEDWINDOW,0,0,xScreen,yScreen, NULL,NULL,hInstance,NULL);
    if (!hWnd) return FALSE;

    init_setup (&g_setup);
    g_list_data.item_collection = new object_list(MAX_ITEMS);
    g_list_data.selected_item = 1;
    setup_to_collection (&g_setup, g_list_data.item_collection);

    ShowWindow(hWnd, nCmdShow);
    UpdateWindow(hWnd);

    while (GetMessage(&msg, NULL, 0, 0))
    {  TranslateMessage(&msg);
       DispatchMessage(&msg);
    }
```

Listing 8.10 (continued)

```
    // Clean up class allocations
    for (i=1;i<=g_list_data.item_collection-> get_count();i++)
    delete g_list_data.item_collection->at(i);
    delete g_list_data.item_collection;

    return msg.wParam;
}

LRESULT CALLBACK _export WndProc(HWND hWnd,
    UINT message,WPARAM wParam, LPARAM lParam){
    HDC hdc;
    PAINTSTRUCT ps;
    RECT rect;
    HBRUSH hbr;
    tdata_list_dialog *the_dialog;
    // used for device-independent line spacing:
    SIZE text_extent;
    int x_start,y_start,rect_y_start,line_spacing;
    int i;

    switch (message)
    {
    case WM_DESTROY:
        PostQuitMessage(0); break;
    case WM_COMMAND:
        switch (wParam) {
        case IDM_DIALOG:
            the_dialog = new tdata_list_dialog
                (hWnd,"Test Data List Dialog",
                "Select Item:",&g_list_data,init_item);
            the_dialog->exec_dialog ();
            delete the_dialog;
            InvalidateRect(hWnd,NULL,TRUE);
            UpdateWindow(hWnd);
            break;
        case IDM_EXIT:              // Exit the program
            SendMessage (hWnd, WM_CLOSE, 0, 0L) ;
            break ;
        } // end switch
        break;
```

Listing 8.10 (continued)

```
case WM_PAINT:
    hdc = BeginPaint(hWnd,&ps);
    GetTextExtentPoint (hdc,"X",strlen("X"), &text_extent);
    line_spacing = 1.5*text_extent.cy;
    y_start = line_spacing;
    rect_y_start = y_start;
    x_start = 5 * text_extent.cx;
    for (i=1;i<=g_list_data.item_collection-> get_count();i++) {
        TextOut(hdc,x_start,y_start + line_spacing*(i-1),
            ((ttyped_data_obj *) (g_list_data.item_collection->
            at(i))) ->get_display_str(), strlen ( ((ttyped_data_obj *)
            (g_list_data.item_collection->at(i))) ->get_display_str()));
    rect_y_start += line_spacing;
    }
    rect.left = x_start;
    rect.right = rect.left + 10*text_extent.cx;
    rect.top = rect_y_start + line_spacing;
    rect.bottom = rect.top + 2*line_spacing;
    hbr = CreateSolidBrush(g_setup.rect_color);
    FillRect (hdc,&rect,hbr);
    DeleteObject (hbr);
    EndPaint(hWnd,&ps);
    break;
default:
return DefWindowProc(hWnd,message,wParam,lParam);
}
return 0L;}
```

Chapter 9

Printing in Windows NT

Paula Tomlinson

Microsoft redesigned the printing subsystem for Windows NT with three primary goals in mind: decreased return-to-application time, improved WYSIWYG output, and enhanced remote printing support.

Return-to-application time refers to the amount of time the application is tied up with the job of printing, as opposed to how much time the printing actually takes. The assumption is that users care more about getting back to work in their applications than about the overall print time. To accommodate this, the print subsystem itself has been redesigned to perform high-level spooling, or journaling, of device calls. Journaling automatically gives Win32 applications a much faster return-to-application time, because the printer driver now does its rendering in the background during unspooling.

WYSIWYG, or what-you-see-is-what-you-get, for Windows 3.1 has generally represented the desire to match printed output as closely as possible to the screen output. Win32 on Windows NT takes this a step further: the goal is not just WYSIWYG between a specific application's output on a given screen and a given printer, but consistency across applications and across output devices and even across networks.

Windows NT supports true remote printing. You can use the Print Manager to browse through remote printers and install and configure printer drivers remotely. In fact, if you are printing to a remote printer, you needn't even install the printer driver (or any associated soft fonts) locally. Windows NT also supports print pooling, which allows you to set up one logical (named) printer that offloads print jobs to a pool of printers. This remote printing architecture increases network printing performance and enhances WYSIWYG output across the network.

Inside the Windows NT Print Subsystem

I'll begin by describing the components of the Windows NT print subsystem (see Figure 9.1 and the sidebar "Printing on Windows NT v4.0"). You may notice a subtle change in terminology with respect to GDI (graphics device interface). GDI is usually referred to as a component of the Windows operating environment. In the context of the print subsystem, this component is referred to as the graphics engine and GDI represents the interface between the application and the graphics engine.

When a Win32 application calls `CreateDC()` to create a printer device context (DC), the request is routed to the print spooler. The spooler is a Win32 executable module. It is loaded when Windows NT starts up and continues to run until Windows NT is shutdown. The Print Manager provides the user interface for accessing the spooler, but the spooler will still continue to run if the Print Manager is closed. In a network, a spooler runs on each client/workstation. The spooler loads the printer driver specified in the `CreateDC()` call, and then determines from the driver which data type to use for saving print jobs targeted for that printer. The supported data types are Journal (default) and Raw. These data types will be discussed in more detail later.

DDI (device driver interface) is the interface that the graphics engine uses to communicate with printer drivers. If the printer driver is located on a remote machine (the print server), then the printer driver will be copied from the server and loaded into the client's memory. If an application calls query functions such as `GetDeviceCaps()` or `GetTextExtent()` to the printer DC, the graphics engine converts these calls into DDI calls to the printer driver. The printer driver returns the corresponding information to the graphics engine, which in turn passes the information back to the calling

---

Printing on Windows NT v4.0

From the original version of Windows NT (3.1) through version 3.51, the graphics (GDI) and user interface (USER) subsystems were implemented in user mode. Starting with version 4.0, much of the graphics and user-interface subsystems were moved to kernel mode for performance reasons. Although this change has little or no effect on applications that display or print graphics, it has had an impact on the internal printing architecture. The print spooler is still a user-mode process and print processors and monitors are still 32-bit user-mode DLLs. Printer drivers, on the other hand, are now kernel-mode modules. Because printer drivers are now capable of causing a "blue screen" on Windows NT, it is more important than ever for developers to build robust printer drivers and for printing applications to ensure they are communicating correctly with the print subsystem.

Figure 9.1   Diagram of printer architecture.

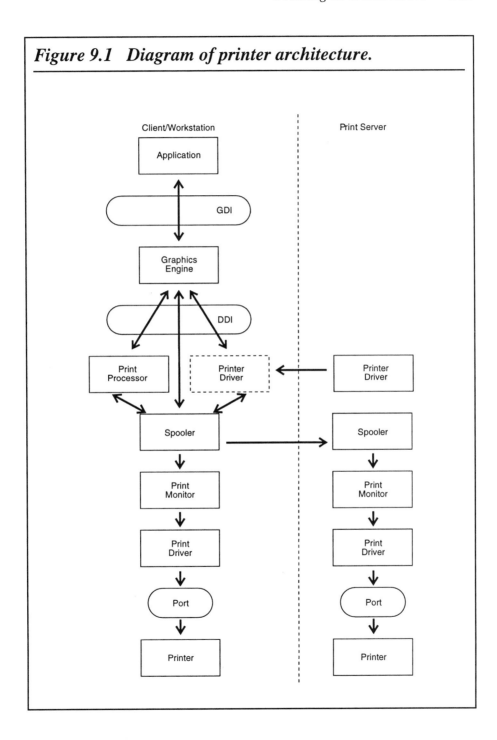

application. When an application performs graphics output such as TextOut() or BitBlt() to the printer DC, the graphics engine again translates those calls into DDI calls using information (such as resolution and supported fonts) from the printer driver. But instead of being rendered by the printer driver now, the DDI calls are saved in the data type specified by the spooler. For the Journal data type, the graphics engine passes the DDI calls to the spooler, which records them in a Journal file. For the Raw data type, the graphics engine calls the printer driver to render the DDI calls into device-specific, low-level commands and passes the Raw data to the spooler.

It's the spooler's job to create and maintain a list of print jobs for each printer and to schedule those jobs for printing. Once the spooler determines that a job is ready to be printed, it passes the spooled document to the print processor. The default print processor for Windows NT interprets both Journal and Raw data types, but custom print processors that support additional data types or perform additional processing of the Raw or Journal spool files can be added to the print subsystem. If the data type is Raw, it is already in a format the printer can accept, so the print processor simply returns the document to the spooler. If the data type is Journal, the print processor passes the journal file to the graphics engine, which passes it on to the printer driver for rendering into device-specific data. The printer driver converts the journal file into raw device data and passes it back to the spooler.

At this point the spooler has raw device data that is ready to be printed. If the target printer is a remote printer on the print server, the client spooler passes the file, via a router and print provider, to the server's spooler. The router and print provider isolate any network-specific protocols and transport layers from the other components in the print subsystem. The spooler then passes the file to the appropriate print monitor for the target port. The print monitor provides a common interface to the spooler, hiding the specifics of the port I/O and the NT I/O subsystem. The print monitor generally handles any device-specific software protocols, whereas a kernel-mode port driver handles the port-specific hardware protocol. When the printer has finished printing the document, the print monitor displays a message in the Print Manager indicating the print job is complete.

Even jobs printed from DOS applications or Windows 3.x applications get redirected to the spooler in Windows NT.

New Win32 Print Routines

How does the redesigned Windows NT print architecture affect Win32 applications? First, if you aren't already using the common print dialogs, now is the time to make the switch. The common print dialogs are by far the easiest way to acquire a handle to a printer device context. The Foundation Classes also provide a CPrintDialog and CPrintInfo class for this purpose. Except for a few very minor user interface changes and a few additional options, the Win32 common print dialogs, contained in comdlg32.dll, are identical to those in Windows 3.x. If you don't want to use the common dialogs, you should at the very least replace any code that parses the win.ini file for printer information with calls to the new Win32 routines, such as EnumPrinters() and OpenPrinter(). You should also replace code that still uses LoadLibrary() and GetProcAddress() to call the printer driver's ExtDeviceMode() routine directly with calls to DocumentProperties(). In fact, don't even assume that the printer driver is located locally on your machine. If you need to access it directly for any reason, use GetPrinterDirectory(). The Win32 API provides a whole new set of routines for enumeration, information retrieval, installation, and configuration of the components of the NT print subsystem (Table 9.1). You can also view printer property information in the Registry key HKEY_LOCAL_MACHINE\SYSTEM\Current-ControlSet\Control\Print.

Table 9.1   List of Win32 print routines.

Document Print Control Functions

AbortDoc	Terminate a print job, replaces ABORTDOC escape
AbortProc	Application-defined callback, process canceled print job
AdvancedDocumentProperties	Configure printer advanced settings
DeviceCapabilities	Return device driver capabilities
DeviceCapabilitiesEx	Not implemented; use DeviceCapabilities
DocumentProperties	Configure printer settings
Escape	Allow access to a device capability
EndDoc	End a print job, replaces ENDDOC escape
EndPage	Mark end of page, replaces NEWFRAME escape
ExtEscape	Allow access to private device capability
SetAbortProc	Set the abort function for a print job, replaces SETABORTPROC escape
StartDoc	Start a print job, replaces STARTDOC escape
StartPage	Mark start of page, replaces NEW-FRAME/STARTDOC escapes

Table 9.1 (continued)

Spooler and Print Job Functions

AddJob	Start a print job
AbortPrinter	Delete printer spool file
EndDocPrinter	End a print job
EndPagePrinter	End a printer page
EnumJobs	Get print job information
GetJob	Get print job information
PrinterMessageBox	Display printing job error message
ScheduleJob	Schedule an added job for printing
SetJob	Set print job information
StartDocPrinter	Start print job
StartPagePrinter	Start a printer page

Printer Form Functions

AddForm	Add a printer form
DeleteForm	Remove printer form
EnumForms	Enumerate supported printer forms
GetForm	Get printer form information
SetForm	Set printer form information

Monitor and Port Functions

AddMonitor	Add a printer monitor
AddPort	Add a printer port
ConfigurePort	Configure printer port
DeleteMonitor	Remove a printer monitor
DeletePort	Delete a printer port
EnumMonitors	Enumerate available monitors
EnumPorts	Enumerate available printer ports

You should also consider replacing any remaining calls to Escape() with the corresponding print job control routines (see Table 9.1). In Windows 3.0, applications controlled the flow of print jobs by using Escape() with a whole host of escape codes (64 to be exact!). Windows 3.1 introduced a new set of routines to serve as an alternative to these job control escape codes. In particular, the introduction of specific routines for StartPage() and EndPage() eliminated the ambiguity between page breaks that resulted from using the NEWFRAME escape sequence (NEWFRAME ended the current page and started the next). In Windows 3.1 it is still necessary to use several of the escape codes (to acquire information about the printer and physical page and to perform banding by the application), but in Windows NT there is little need for them. Of the 64 escape codes, only two are truly supported in Windows NT (QUERYESCSUPPORT and PASSTHROUGH); nine others are supported for compatibility with Windows 3.x (ABORTDOC, ENDDOC, GETPHYSPAGESIZE, GETPRINTINGOFFSET, GETSCALINGFACTOR, NEWFRAME, NEXTBAND, SETABORTPROC, and STARTDOC).

Table 9.1 (continued)	
Print Processor Functions	
AddPrintProcessor	Copy a print processor to a server
DeletePrintProcessor	Remove printer processor
EnumPrintProcessors	Enumerate installed print processors
GetPrintProcessorDirectory	Get path for print processor
Print Provider Functions	
AddPrintProvidor	Add a printer provider
DeletePrintProvidor	Remove printer provider
Printer Driver Functions	
AddPrinterDriver	Copy a printer driver to a print server
DeletePrinterDriver	Remove printer driver
EnumPrinterDrivers	Enumerate installed printer drivers
GetPrinterDriver	Get printer driver information
GetPrinterDriverDirectory	Get path for printer driver

Background Banding

Printers that cannot image a full page of output all at once use a technique called banding. In Windows 3.x, the graphics engine supported banding transparently by saving output commands to a metafile. It then played the metafile back once for each band, clipping the output to just the current band. Replaying the entire metafile multiple times was so painfully slow that Windows 3.x applications often performed banding themselves by calling `Escape()` with the `BANDINFO` and `NEXTBAND` escape codes.

Table 9.1 (continued)

Printer Functions

`AddPrinter`	Create a printer on a printer server
`AddPrinterConnection`	Add connection to printer for current user
`ClosePrinter`	Close an open printer
`ConnectToPrinterDlg`	Display dialog for browsing and connecting to network printers
`DeletePrinter`	Delete a printer on a printer server
`DeletePrinterConnection`	Delete a connection to a printer
`EnumPrinters`	Enumerate available printers
`GetPrinter`	Get printer information
`GetPrinterData`	Get printer configuration information
`OpenPrinter`	Get handle for specified printer
`PrinterProperties`	Modify printer properties
`ReadPrinter`	Read printer data
`ResetPrinter`	Set printer data type and device mode values
`SetPrinter`	Set printer information
`SetPrinterData`	Set printer configuration information
`WaitForPrinterChange`	Wait for change(s) on a printer or print server
`WritePrinter`	Write data to printer

Print Messages

`WM_SPOOLERSTATUS`	Send whenever a print job is added or removed

With the information returned, applications could limit output to only one band at a time. To find out whether a printer is a banding printer, applications can call GetDe-viceCaps() with the RASTERCAPS index and check the return value for the RC_BANDING bit.

In a journaling print system, if banding support is required, the graphics engine takes care of it when the journal file is unspooled, and thus is completely out of the hands of the application. Consequently, even though Windows NT supports the NEXT-BAND and BANDINFO escapes for compatibility, removing application-level banding code will minimize return-to-application time. You can further optimize performance by using fewer, more complex primitives (for example, Bezier curves instead of line segments), because it takes less time to record the smaller set of DDI calls to the journal file. If the printer driver or printer cannot accept the more complex primitives, the graphics engine will break them down (in the background during unspooling) into simpler primitives.

No More Brute Functions

The general principles for WYSIWYG display that govern Windows 3.x applications (such as creating screen fonts to match the printers' fonts) still apply for Win32 applications. However, the new graphics engine plays a much bigger role in supporting cross-application and cross-device output consistency and so overcomes some of the problems inherent with Windows 3.x. For instance, in Windows 3.x there was a gray area between where the graphics engine left off and where the display and printer drivers began (you might have noticed in Windows 3.x that changing display drivers often caused printed output to look different).

The brute functions are the culprit in this perplexing dependency of printer drivers on video display drivers. The brute functions consist of a series of helper routines provided by the Windows 3.x graphics engine to assist printer drivers with many operations involving memory bitmaps. Banding printer drivers in particular use the brute routines, because they typically image their output to a memory bitmap before dumping that bitmap to the printer. Unfortunately, the brute functions operate by calling corresponding routines in the display driver, and there is no guarantee that all display drivers will implement those functions in exactly the same way. Windows NT solves this problem by providing services for display drivers and printer drivers within the graphics engine itself. Locating these services in the graphics engine makes them truly common services and thus helps to ensure more consistent output across devices.

Graphics-Engine-Supported Halftoning

Another feature of the new graphics engine is sophisticated internal support for halftoning. The fact that different applications halftone grayscale and color images differently has been a significant problem in Windows 3.x. Worse yet, applications and printer drivers often fight over who should perform the halftoning. If the application halftones the image before printing and the image somehow gets scaled in the printing process, the printed image displays ugly interference patterns.

Disk space issues aside, you should consider using grayscale and color images within your Win32 applications and letting the graphics engine (with the help of the printer driver) take care of halftoning to a particular device. Users can adjust some of the properties of halftoning from the Print Manager; an application can do so by using CreateHalftonePalette(), SelectPalette(), RealizePalette(), and SetColorAdjustment().

Listing 9.1   cprint.h — Creating the CPrint class.

```
// CPRINT.H     Windows NT, MS Visual C/C++ (32-bit) 1.1
#include <windows.h>
#define IDC_DOCTITLE     9000

class CPrint {
public:
   CPrint(HWND hWindow, LPTSTR lpDocName = "(Untitled)");
   virtual ~CPrint();
   HDC PrintDialog(void);
   DWORD PrinterSetupDialog(void);
   DWORD DocumentStart(HINSTANCE hInst);
   DWORD PageStart(void);
   DWORD PageEnd(void);
   DWORD DocumentAbort(void);
   DWORD DocumentEnd(void);
   char szDriver[32], szDevice[32], szOutput[32];
   DWORD lastError;

private:
     // prevent copy by declaring without defining
   CPrint(const CPrint&);   const CPrint& operator=(const CPrint&);
   HDC hdcPr;
   HWND hWnd;
   DOCINFO docInfo;
   PRINTDLG printDlg;
};  // CPrint
```

Listing 9.2 `cprint.cpp` — *Using the common print dialogs and print job control functions.*

```
//  CPRINT.CPP    Windows NT, MS Visual C/C++ (32-bit) 1.1
#include <windows.h>
#include "cprint.h"

LRESULT CALLBACK AbortDlg(HWND, UINT, WPARAM, LPARAM);
BOOL CALLBACK AbortProc(HDC, int);
char lpDocTitle[128];
BOOL bAbort = FALSE;
HWND hDlgAbort = 0;


/**-------------------------------------------------------**/
CPrint::CPrint(HWND hWindow, LPTSTR lpDocName) {
    hdcPr = NULL;
    lastError = NULL;
    szDriver[0] = szDevice[0] = szOutput[0] = '\0';
    lstrcpy(lpDocTitle, lpDocName);
    docInfo.cbSize = sizeof(DOCINFO);
    docInfo.lpszDocName = lpDocTitle;
    docInfo.lpszOutput = 0;
    memset((void *)&printDlg, 0, sizeof(PRINTDLG));
    printDlg.lStructSize = sizeof(PRINTDLG);
    printDlg.hwndOwner = hWnd = hWindow;
} // CPrint

/**-------------------------------------------------------**/
CPrint::~CPrint() { if (hdcPr) DeleteDC(hdcPr); } // ~CPrint

/**-------------------------------------------------------**/
HDC CPrint::PrintDialog(void) {
    LPDEVNAMES pNames;
    printDlg.Flags = PD_RETURNDC;
    if (PrintDlg(&printDlg)) {        hdcPr = printDlg.hDC;
        pNames = (LPDEVNAMES)GlobalLock(printDlg.hDevNames);
        lstrcpy(szDriver, (LPSTR)pNames + pNames->wDriverOffset);
        lstrcpy(szDevice, (LPSTR)pNames + pNames->wDeviceOffset);
        lstrcpy(szOutput, (LPSTR)pNames + pNames->wOutputOffset);
        GlobalUnlock(printDlg.hDevNames);
    } else hdcPr = FALSE;
    lastError = CommDlgExtendedError();
    if (printDlg.hDevMode != NULL) GlobalFree(printDlg.hDevMode);
    if (printDlg.hDevNames != NULL) GlobalFree(printDlg.hDevNames);
    return hdcPr;
} // CPrint::PrintDialog
```

Listing 9.2 (continued)

```
/**--------------------------------------------------------**/
DWORD CPrint::PrinterSetupDialog(void) {
    DWORD dwStatus = TRUE;
    printDlg.Flags = PD_PRINTSETUP;
    if (PrintDlg(&printDlg)) dwStatus = TRUE;
    else dwStatus = FALSE;
    lastError = CommDlgExtendedError();
    if (printDlg.hDevMode) GlobalFree(printDlg.hDevMode);
    if (printDlg.hDevNames) GlobalFree(printDlg.hDevNames);
    return dwStatus;
} // CPrint::PrinterSetupDialog


/**--------------------------------------------------------**/
DWORD CPrint::DocumentStart(HINSTANCE hInst) {
    if (hdcPr == NULL) hdcPr = PrintDialog();
    bAbort = FALSE;
    hDlgAbort = CreateDialog(hInst, (LPSTR)"DlgAbort", hWnd,
        (DLGPROC)AbortDlg);
    SetAbortProc(hdcPr, (ABORTPROC)AbortProc);
    return StartDoc(hdcPr, &docInfo);
} // CPrint::DocumentStart


/**--------------------------------------------------------**/
DWORD CPrint::PageStart(void) { return StartPage(hdcPr); }

/**--------------------------------------------------------**/
DWORD CPrint::PageEnd(void) { return EndPage(hdcPr); }

/**--------------------------------------------------------**/
DWORD CPrint::DocumentAbort(void) { return AbortDoc(hdcPr); }

/**--------------------------------------------------------**/
DWORD CPrint::DocumentEnd(void) {
    if (!bAbort) DestroyWindow(hDlgAbort);
    return EndDoc(hdcPr);
} // CPrint::DocumentEnd


/**--------------------------------------------------------**/
LRESULT CALLBACK AbortDlg(HWND hDlg, UINT msg, WPARAM wParam,
        LPARAM lParam) {
    switch(msg) {
        case WM_INITDIALOG:
            SetDlgItemText(hDlg, IDC_DOCTITLE, lpDocTitle);
            return TRUE;
        case WM_COMMAND:
            bAbort = TRUE;
            DestroyWindow(hDlg);
            hDlgAbort = 0;
            return TRUE;
    } return 0;
} // AbortDlg
```

Creating the `CPrint` *Class*

To demonstrate the use of the common print dialogs and the print job control functions, I wrote a simple C++ class called `CPrint`. The declaration and methods for this class are in `cprint.h` (Listing 9.1) and `cprint.cpp` (Listing 9.2).

The constructor for `CPrint` takes as parameters a window handle and the name of the document to print (this name shows up in the Print Manager while the job is pending). The constructor initializes some variables, including some members of the `PRINTDLG` and `DOCINFO` data structures (see Figure 9.2). The `PRINTDLG` data structure is passed to `PrintDlg()` to control display of the common print dialogs. Although the common print dialogs can be heavily customized, for simplicity I used default settings. The `DOCINFO` structure is used later in a call to `StartDoc()`. The destructor, `~CPrint()`, closes the printer DC if it is currently open.

`PrintDialog()` sets the `Flags` field of the `PRINTDLG` structure to `PD_RETURNDC` and calls `PrintDlg()` to display the Print common dialog. If the user chooses OK in the Print dialog, a printer DC is created for the default printer and returned from `PrintDlg()`. `PrintDialog()` saves the DC in a member variable and returns it to the caller. `PrintDialog()` also saves the driver name, the device name, and the port name in member string variables that can be accessed by the caller at a later time.

`PrinterSetupDialog()` similarly sets the `Flags` field of the `PRINTDLG` structure to `PD_PRINTSETUP` and calls `PrintDlg()`. This displays the Printer Setup common dialog, which allows the user to select and configure printers.

Both `PrintDialog()` and `PrinterSetupDialog()` set the member variable `lastError` to the value returned by `CommDlgExtendedError()`. `CommDlgExtendedError()` returns the most recent error to have occurred during execution of any of the common dialogs. The common print dialogs use the error range of `0x1000` to `0x1fff` (PDERR_*).

Listing 9.2 (continued)

```
/**-----------------------------------------------------**/
BOOL CALLBACK AbortProc(HDC hDC, int iCode) {
   MSG msg;
   while (!bAbort && PeekMessage(&msg,NULL,0,0,PM_REMOVE)) {
      if (!hDlgAbort || !IsDialogMessage(hDlgAbort, &msg)) {
         TranslateMessage(&msg);
         DispatchMessage(&msg);
      }
   } return !bAbort;
} // AbortProc
```

DocumentStart() first calls PrintDialog() to return a printer DC if there is no valid printer DC open. DocumentStart() also hides most of the work involved in setting up an Abort dialog box and an abort procedure for the print job. For simplicity, I assume that a dialog box template named "DlgAbort" exists and that I can access it using the instance handle passed to DocumentStart(). The dialog box template has only two restrictions: it can have only one control (a Cancel button), and it must have a static text field with the identifier ID_DOCTITLE (which I defined to be 9000). DocumentStart() creates a modeless dialog box using AbortDlg() as the dialog box procedure. Implementing callback functions as member functions is rather complicated,

---

Figure 9.2   *PRINTDLG and DOCINFO data structures.*

PRINTDLG Data Structure

```
// Contains information the operating system uses to
// initialize the system-defined Print dialog boxes.
typedef struct tagPD {
    DWORD            lStructSize;
    HWND             hwndOwner;
    HANDLE           hDevMode;
    HANDLE           hDevNames;
    HDC              hDC;
    DWORD            Flags;
    WORD             nFromPage;
    WORD             nToPage;
    WORD             nMinPage;
    WORD             nMaxPage;
    WORD             nCopies;
    HINSTANCE        hInstance;
    DWORD            lCustData;
    LPPRINTHOOKPROC  lpfnPrintHook;
    LPSETUPHOOKPROC  lpfnSetupHook;
    LPCSTR           lpPrintTemplateName;
    LPCSTR           lpSetupTemplateName;
    HANDLE           hPrintTemplate;
    HANDLE           hSetupTemplate;
} PRINTDLG;
```

DOCINFO Data Structure

```
// Contains the input and output filenames used by the
// StartDoc function.
typedef struct {
    int    cbSize;        // size in bytes of struct
    LPTSTR lpszDocName;   // name of document
    LPTSTR lpszOutput;    // name of output file
} DOCINFO;
```

so, again, for simplicity, I made both the dialog box procedure [AbortDlg()] and the abort procedure [AbortProc()] standard functions in the cprint.cpp file. Finally, DocumentStart() calls StartDoc().

The PageStart(), PageEnd(), and DocumentAbort() methods simply call the corresponding Win32 routines: StartPage(), EndPage(), and AbortDoc(). The caller is not required to pass in the handle to the printer DC because the CPrint object already has access to the printer DC through a member variable. The DocumentEnd() method destroys the Abort dialog box (if it hasn't already been canceled) and calls EndDoc().

The Abort dialog box procedure, AbortDlg(), initializes a static text control to the name of the document that was passed to the constructor. If the Cancel button is pressed, AbortDlg() sets bAbort flag to TRUE and destroys the dialog box. The abort procedure [AbortProc()] contains a fairly standard PeekMessage() loop to allow other applications to process their messages. When an abort procedure is registered using SetAbortProc(), the system guarantees that the abort procedure will be called periodically, usually every couple of seconds. If the abort procedure returns a nonzero value, the system responds by aborting the current print job. AbortProc() returns the negated value of the bAbort flag, so that the print job will be aborted whenever the bAbort flag is set to TRUE.

Listing 9.3   ntprint.cpp — *Demonstrates the CPrint class.*

```
// NTPRINT.CPP    Windows NT, MS Visual C/C++ (32-bit) 1.1
#include <windows.h>
#include "ntprint.h"
#include "cprint.h"
#include "cform.h"

HINSTANCE hInst;                          // app instance
char szAppName[] = "NTPrintSample";       // app name
char lpName[] = "Index Card";             // new form name
char lpString[128], lpStr1[128];          // temp strings
CPrinterForm form;                        // form object


/**------------------------------------------------------------**/
int APIENTRY WinMain(HINSTANCE hInstance, HINSTANCE
     hPrevInstance, LPSTR lpCmdLine, int nCmdShow) {
   MSG msg;
   lpCmdLine;  // just to avoid an unused formal parameter
   if (!InitApplication(hInstance, nCmdShow)) return FALSE;
   while (GetMessage(&msg, NULL, 0, 0)) {
      TranslateMessage(&msg);
      DispatchMessage(&msg);
   } return msg.wParam;
} // WinMain
```

Listing 9.3 (continued)

```
/**-----------------------------------------------------**/
BOOL InitApplication(HINSTANCE hInstance, int nCmdShow) {
   HWND hWnd;
   WNDCLASS  wc;
   wc.style = CS_HREDRAW | CS_VREDRAW;
   wc.lpfnWndProc = (WNDPROC)WndProc;
   wc.cbClsExtra = wc.cbWndExtra = 0;
   wc.hInstance = hInstance;
   wc.hIcon = LoadIcon(NULL, IDI_APPLICATION);
   wc.hCursor = LoadCursor(NULL, IDC_ARROW);
   wc.hbrBackground = (HBRUSH)(COLOR_WINDOW+1);
   wc.lpszMenuName = wc.lpszClassName = szAppName;
   if (!RegisterClass(&wc)) return FALSE;
   hInst = hInstance;
   if (!(hWnd = CreateWindow(szAppName,
       "Sample NT Printing Application", WS_OVERLAPPEDWINDOW,
       CW_USEDEFAULT, 0, CW_USEDEFAULT, 0, NULL, NULL,
       hInstance, NULL))) return FALSE;
   ShowWindow(hWnd, nCmdShow);
   UpdateWindow(hWnd);
   return TRUE;
} // InitApplication


/**-----------------------------------------------------**/
LRESULT CALLBACK WndProc(HWND hWnd, UINT msg, WPARAM uParam,
      LPARAM lParam) {
   switch (msg) {
      case WM_COMMAND:
         switch (LOWORD(uParam)) {
            case IDM_PRINT:
               DWORD dwThreadID;
               CloseHandle(CreateThread(NULL, 0,
                  (LPTHREAD_START_ROUTINE)PrintingThread,
                  (LPVOID)hWnd, 0, &dwThreadID));
               break;
            case IDM_PRINTSETUP: {
               CPrint print(hWnd, "Document.plt");
               print.PrinterSetupDialog();
               } break;
            case IDM_ENUMFORMS:
               DialogBox(hInst, "DlgForms", hWnd,
                  (DLGPROC)EnumDlgProc);
               break;
            case IDM_ADDFORM:
               form.Add(lpName,76200,127000,0,0,76200,127000);
               break;
```

Using the `CPrint` Class

To demonstrate using the `CPrint` class, I wrote a very simple Win32 application (ntprint.exe). Source for the application is in Listings 9.3, 9.4, and 9.5 (`ntprint.cpp`, `ntprint.h`, `ntprint.rc`). In `WinMain()`, you'll notice that I don't pay any attention at all to the `hPrevInstance` parameter. In Windows NT, the instance handle is actually the base address of the executable after it's mapped into its private address space. Because different instances of an executable will load at the same base address, but in different address spaces, all instances of an executable will have the same instance handle. But because window classes aren't shared in Windows NT, each instance needs to register its own window classes. The system always passes `NULL` for the value of `hPrevInstance`, so you can safely eliminate the check or leave it in for backwards compatibility.

The main window procedure, `WndProc()`, in response to a `WM_PAINT` message, passes a handle to a display device context to `DrawOnSurface()`. `DrawOnSurface()` also takes as parameters a window handle and `x` and `y` scaling factors (in this case,

---

Listing 9.3 (continued)

```
            case IDM_CHANGEFORM:
                form.Set(lpName,127000,177800,0,0,127000,177800);
                break;
            case IDM_DELETEFORM:
                form.Delete(lpName);
                break;
            case IDM_EXIT:
                DestroyWindow (hWnd);
                break;
            default:
                return DefWindowProc(hWnd, msg, uParam, lParam);
        } break;
        case WM_PAINT: {
            PAINTSTRUCT ps;
            HDC hDC = BeginPaint(hWnd, &ps);
            DrawOnSurface(hDC, hWnd, (float)1, (float)1);
            EndPaint(hWnd, &ps);
        } break;
        case WM_DESTROY:
            PostQuitMessage(0);
            break;
        default:
            return DefWindowProc(hWnd, msg, uParam, lParam);
    } return 0;
} // WndProc
```

Listing 9.3 (continued)

```
/**------------------------------------------------------**/
void DrawOnSurface(HDC hDC, HWND hWnd, float sx, float sy) {
   BITMAP bm;
   COLORADJUSTMENT ca;
   HDC hdc = GetDC(hWnd);
   HANDLE hMemDC = CreateCompatibleDC(hdc);
   ReleaseDC(hWnd, hdc);
   HANDLE hBmp = LoadBitmap(hInst, MAKEINTRESOURCE(IDB_WINLOGO));
   SelectObject(hMemDC, hBmp);
   GetObject(hBmp, sizeof(BITMAP), (LPSTR)&bm);
   HPALETTE hPal = CreateHalftonePalette(hDC);
   SelectPalette(hDC, hPal, TRUE);
   RealizePalette(hDC);
   GetColorAdjustment(hDC, (LPCOLORADJUSTMENT)&ca);
   ca.caBrightness = 50;
   SetColorAdjustment(hDC, (LPCOLORADJUSTMENT)&ca);
   StretchBlt(hDC, 0, 0, (int)((float)bm.bmWidth * sx),
      (int)((float)bm.bmHeight * sy), hMemDC, 0,0, bm.bmWidth,
      bm.bmHeight, SRCCOPY);
   DeleteDC(hMemDC);
   DeleteObject(hBmp);
} // DrawOnSurface


/**------------------------------------------------------**/
void PrintingThread(LPVOID hWnd) {
   CPrint print(hWnd, "Document.plt");
   HDC hPDC, hDC;
   float fx1, fx2, fy1, fy2, fsx, fsy;
   if (!(hPDC = print.PrintDialog())) return;
   if (!(GetDeviceCaps(hPDC, RASTERCAPS) & RC_BITBLT)) return;
   hDC = GetDC(hWnd);
   fx1 = (float)GetDeviceCaps(hDC, LOGPIXELSX);
   fy1 = (float)GetDeviceCaps(hDC, LOGPIXELSY);
   fx2 = (float)GetDeviceCaps(hPDC, LOGPIXELSX);
   fy2 = (float)GetDeviceCaps(hPDC, LOGPIXELSX);
   if (fx1 > fx2) fsx = (fx1/fx2);
   else fsx = (fx2/fx1);
   if (fy1 > fy2) fsy = (fy1/fy2);
   else fsy = (fy2/fy1);
   ReleaseDC(hWnd, hDC);
   print.DocumentStart(hInst);
   print.PageStart();
   DrawOnSurface(hPDC, hWnd, fsx, fsy);
   print.PageEnd();
   print.DocumentEnd();
} // PrintingThread
```

both scaling factors are 1). DrawOnSurface() loads a bitmap from the application's resources (I just used the winlogo.bmp bitmap file). It next asks the graphics engine to create a halftone palette for this device context and then selects and realizes the logical halftone palette into the device context. The code also demonstrates the use of the new Win32 GetColorAdjustment() and SetColorAdjustment() routines. The values specified in the COLORADJUSTMENT data structure (see Figure 9.3) are used by subsequent calls to StretchBlt() and StretchDIBits() if the StetchBltMode is HALFTONE (the default for Win32). You can set StretchBltMode by calling Set-StretchBltMode(). Although the HALFTONE mode is typically a little slower than other StretchBltModes, it usually yields higher image quality. For demonstration purposes, I increased the brightness before drawing the bitmap to the device context.

Listing 9.3 (continued)

```
/**------------------------------------------------------**/
LRESULT CALLBACK EnumDlgProc(HWND hDlg, UINT msg,
    WPARAM wParam, LPARAM lParam) {
  long i, dx, dy, lf, tp, rt, bt;
  switch (msg) {
    case WM_INITDIALOG:
      for (i = 0; (DWORD)i < form.dwForms; i++) {
        form.Enumerate((DWORD)i, lpString);
        SendDlgItemMessage(hDlg, IDC_FORMS, LB_ADDSTRING,
          0, (int)(LPSTR)lpString);
      } return TRUE;
    case WM_COMMAND:
      switch (LOWORD(wParam)) {
        case IDC_FORMS:
          if (HIWORD(wParam) == LBN_DBLCLK) {
            i = SendDlgItemMessage(hDlg, IDC_FORMS,
              LB_GETCURSEL, 0, 0);
            SendDlgItemMessage(hDlg, IDC_FORMS,
              LB_GETTEXT, i, (int)(LPSTR)lpString);
            form.Get(lpString, &dx, &dy, &lf, &tp, &rt, &bt);
            wsprintf(lpStr1, "Form: %s\nWd: %ld\nHt: %ld",
              lpString, dx, dy);
            MessageBox(hDlg, lpStr1, "Get Form Info", MB_OK);
          } return TRUE;
        case IDOK:
          EndDialog (hDlg, TRUE);
          return TRUE;
      } break;
  } return FALSE;
}  // EnumDlgProc
```

In response to a user selecting the "Print..." menu item, WndProc() creates a thread that executes the PrintingThread() routine. Printing is commonly implemented as a separate thread, because it allows the user to continue working in the application while the thread prints in the background. A word of caution: GDI objects aren't shareable among threads. I have not prevented a user from starting a new print job before the current print job is completed, so there could be multiple Printing-Thread() threads running in addition to the main thread. None of these threads can share GDI objects (such as a global handle to a font). However, each thread does get its own stack, so as I've implemented them, the threads create any GDI objects they need as local variables on their stacks.

By closing the thread handle immediately after the thread is created, I let the system know that the main application thread won't be referencing the thread directly. This allows the system to free up any memory associated with the thread once the thread terminates. If the handle to the thread is extant, the system cannot free the memory until the process terminates.

PrintingThread() allocates a CPrint object and calls PrintDialog() to display the common print dialog and return a handle to the printer device context. Printing-Thread() also checks whether the printer is capable of transferring bitmaps by using the RASTERCAPS index and comparing the return value with the RC_BITBLT flag. To preserve the aspect ratio and size of the image when printed, I calculate an x and y scaling factor using the logical resolution of the printer device context and the display device context. Finally, to print the image, I call DocumentStart() and PageStart()

Listing 9.4   nprint.h

```
/*  NTPRINT.H    Windows NT, MS Visual C/C++ (32-bit) 1.1 */
#define IDM_EXIT          3000
#define IDM_PRINT         3001
#define IDM_PRINTSETUP    3002
#define IDM_ENUMFORMS     3003
#define IDM_ADDFORM       3004
#define IDM_CHANGEFORM    3005
#define IDM_DELETEFORM    3006
#define IDNULL            -1
#define IDC_FORMS         4000
#define IDB_WINLOGO       5000

BOOL InitApplication(HANDLE, int);
LRESULT CALLBACK WndProc(HWND, UINT, WPARAM, LPARAM);
void DrawOnSurface(HDC, HWND hWnd, float, float);
void PrintingThread(LPVOID);
LRESULT CALLBACK EnumDlgProc(HWND, UINT, WPARAM, LPARAM);
```

Listing 9.5 ntprint.rc

```
/* NTPRINT.RC   Windows NT, MS Visual C/C++ (32-bit) 1.1 */
#include "windows.h"
#include "ntprint.h"
#include "cprint.h"


IDB_WINLOGO  BITMAP  winlogo.bmp

NTPrintSample MENU
BEGIN
    POPUP "&File" {
        MENUITEM "&Print...",            IDM_PRINT
        MENUITEM "P&rint Setup...",      IDM_PRINTSETUP
        MENUITEM SEPARATOR
        MENUITEM "&Enumerate Forms...",  IDM_ENUMFORMS
        MENUITEM "&Add Form",            IDM_ADDFORM
        MENUITEM "&Change Form",         IDM_CHANGEFORM
        MENUITEM "&Delete Form",         IDM_DELETEFORM
        MENUITEM SEPARATOR
        MENUITEM "E&xit",                IDM_EXIT
    }
END

DlgForms DIALOG 16, 16, 118, 94
LANGUAGE LANG_ENGLISH, SUBLANG_ENGLISH_US
STYLE DS_MODALFRAME|WS_POPUP|WS_VISIBLE|WS_CAPTION|WS_SYSMENU
CAPTION "Forms (default printer)"
FONT 8, "MS Sans Serif"
BEGIN
  LISTBOX    IDC_FORMS, 10, 10, 98, 60, WS_VSCROLL|WS_TABSTOP
  PUSHBUTTON "OK", IDOK, 68, 70, 40, 14
END

DlgAbort DIALOG 16, 16, 156, 72
LANGUAGE LANG_ENGLISH, SUBLANG_ENGLISH_US
STYLE DS_MODALFRAME | WS_POPUP | WS_VISIBLE | WS_CAPTION
CAPTION "Sample Application"
FONT 8, "MS Sans Serif"
BEGIN
  CTEXT      "Printing", IDNULL, 10, 10, 135, 8
  CTEXT      "(Untitled)", IDC_DOCTITLE, 10, 20, 135, 8
  PUSHBUTTON "Cancel", IDCANCEL, 53, 48, 49, 14
END
```

Figure 9.3 *COLORADJUSTMENT data structure (Win32).*

```
// defines color adjustment values used by StretchBlt and
// StretchDIBits when StretchBltMode is HALTONE
typedef struct  tagCOLORADJUSTMENT {
  WORD   caSize;              // size of structure in bytes
  WORD   caFlags;             // specifies how image is prepared
  WORD   caIlluminantIndex;   // luminance of light source
  WORD   caRedGamma;          // 2500-65000, 10000=no correction
  WORD   caGreenGamma;        // 2500-65000, 10000=no correction
  WORD   caBlueGamma;         // 2500-65000, 10000=no correction
  WORD   caReferenceBlack;    // 0-4000, darker colors are black
  WORD   caReferenceWhite;    // 6000-10000, lighter colors are white
  SHORT  caContrast;          // -100 to 100, 0 = no adjustment
  SHORT  caBrightness;        // -100 to 100, 0 = no adjustment
  SHORT  caColorfulness;      // -100 to 100, 0 = no adjustment
  SHORT  caRedGreenTint;      // -100 to 100, 0 = no adjustment,
                              // positive adjusts more towards red,
                              // negative adjusts more towards green

} COLORADJUSTMENT;
```

Listing 9.6 *cform.h — The CPrinterForm class.*

```
//   CFORM.H      Windows NT, MS Visual C/C++ (32-bit) 1.1
#include <windows.h>
#define BUF_SIZE 10240

class CPrinterForm {
public:
   CPrinterForm(void);
   CPrinterForm(LPSTR lpName);
   virtual ~CPrinterForm(void);
   BOOL Enumerate(DWORD iIndex, LPSTR lpName);
   BOOL Add(LPSTR, long, long, long, long, long, long);
   BOOL Delete(LPSTR);
   BOOL Get(LPSTR, long*, long*, long*, long*, long*, long*);
   BOOL Set(LPSTR, long, long, long, long, long, long);
   DWORD dwForms;
private:
      // prevent copy by declaring without defining
   CPrinterForm(const CPrinterForm&);
   const CPrinterForm& operator=(const CPrinterForm&);
   void CPrinterForm::FillForm(FORM_INFO_1 *, LPSTR, long,
      long, long, long, long, long);
   HANDLE hPrinter;
   BYTE lpData[BUF_SIZE];
   FORM_INFO_1 *pFI;
   DWORD dwSize;
};  // CPrinterForm
```

to signal the beginning of a print job. To draw the bitmap to the printer, I pass a printer DC to DrawOnSurface( ), the same routine I use to draw the bitmap to the display surface. Then I end the print job by calling PageEnd( ) and DocumentEnd( ).

Creating the *CPrinterForm* Class

Windows NT uses the term "form" to refer to a physical surface characterized by a descriptive name, a physical size, and an imageable (or printable, in this case) area that excludes any physical margins. The Registry contains a database of all forms available on all installed printers (on a per-server basis). When you add a new form using the Win32 form routines, you are adding to the list of forms a user can choose from in the Print Manager. A given form will be displayed as an option for a particular printer only if it doesn't exceed the physical limitations of the current printer. You can also use the Print Manager to add new forms and specify which type of form is in each tray.

Listing 9.7   *cform.cpp* — *Demonstrates its Win32 forms routines.*

```
//  CFORM.CPP     Windows NT, MS Visual C/C++ (32-bit) 1.1
#include <windows.h>
#include "cform.h"

/**------------------------------------------------------**/
CPrinterForm::CPrinterForm(void) {
    dwForms = 0;
    dwSize = BUF_SIZE;
    HKEY hKey;
    RegOpenKeyEx(HKEY_CURRENT_USER, "Printers", 0,
        KEY_QUERY_VALUE, &hKey);
    RegQueryValueEx(hKey, "Default", 0, NULL, lpData, &dwSize);
    RegCloseKey(hKey);
    if (OpenPrinter((LPTSTR)lpData, &hPrinter, NULL))
        EnumForms(hPrinter, 1, (LPBYTE)lpData, BUF_SIZE,
            &dwSize, &dwForms);
} // CPrinterForm(void)


/**------------------------------------------------------**/
CPrinterForm::CPrinterForm(LPSTR pName) {
    dwForms = 0;
    if (OpenPrinter(pName, &hPrinter, NULL))
        EnumForms(hPrinter, 1, (LPBYTE)lpData, BUF_SIZE,
            &dwSize, &dwForms);
} // CPrinterForm(LPSTR)
```

Listing 9.7 (continued)

```
/**----------------------------------------------------**/
CPrinterForm::~CPrinterForm(void) {
    if (hPrinter != NULL) ClosePrinter(hPrinter);
} // ~CPrinterForm

/**----------------------------------------------------**/
BOOL CPrinterForm::Enumerate(DWORD iIndex, LPSTR lpName) {
    if (iIndex == 0 || dwForms == 0) {
        EnumForms(hPrinter, 1, (LPBYTE)lpData, BUF_SIZE,
            &dwSize, &dwForms);
    }
    if (iIndex >= dwForms) return FALSE;
    pFI = (FORM_INFO_1 *)lpData;
    lstrcpy(lpName, pFI[iIndex].pName);
    return TRUE;
} // CPrinterForm::Enumerate

/**----------------------------------------------------**/
BOOL CPrinterForm::Add(LPSTR lpName, long width, long height,
        long left, long top, long right, long bottom) {
    FORM_INFO_1 fi;
    FillForm(&fi, lpName, width,height,left,top,right,bottom);
    return AddForm(hPrinter, 1, (LPBYTE)&fi);
} // CPrinterForm::Add

/**----------------------------------------------------**/
BOOL CPrinterForm::Delete(LPSTR lpName) {
    return DeleteForm(hPrinter, lpName);
} // CPrinterForm::Delete

/**----------------------------------------------------**/
BOOL CPrinterForm::Get(LPSTR lpName, long *width, long *height,
        long *left, long *top, long *right, long *bottom) {
    BYTE lpBuff[BUF_SIZE];
    FORM_INFO_1 *p;
    GetForm(hPrinter,lpName,1,(LPBYTE)lpBuff,BUF_SIZE,&dwSize);
    p = (FORM_INFO_1 *)lpBuff;
    *width  = p[0].Size.cx;
    *height = p[0].Size.cy;
    *left   = p[0].ImageableArea.left;
    *top    = p[0].ImageableArea.top;
    *right  = p[0].ImageableArea.right;
    *bottom = p[0].ImageableArea.bottom;
    return TRUE;
} // CPrinterForm::Get
```

To demonstrate the Win32 forms routines, I wrote a simple class (CPrinterForm) to enumerate, add, delete, get, and set printer forms. The declaration and methods for this class are in cform.h (Listing 9.6) and cform.cpp (Listing 9.7). The CPrinterForm class has two overloaded constructors. If a CPrinterForm object is allocated without any parameters being passed to the constructor, then I assume the caller is asking for forms available on the default printer. Alternatively, a caller can pass a string containing the name of a printer. The prescribed way of determining the name of the default printer is to call EnumPrinters() with the PRINTER_ENUM_DEFAULT type. Unfortunately, using the PRINTER_ENUM_DEFAULT type with EnumPrinters() returns a success code but returns zero for the number of PRINT_INFO_1 structures returned. As a workaround for this unexpected behavior, I just resorted to reading the name of the default printer from the Registry under the HKEY_CURRENT_USER\Printers\Default key. Both constructors open the printer and save a handle to the printer in a member variable. Then the constructors enumerate the forms for that printer so that the dwForms member variable can be initialized to the number of forms currently available. The destructor closes the handle to the printer.

I wrote the Enumerate() method so that it would be easy to call in a loop of code. The caller passes an index and a pointer to a string to Enumerate(), which returns the corresponding form name. I didn't want to re-enumerate the forms each time Enumerate() is called in a loop, so I only call EnumForms() if the index is zero or if there are currently no forms enumerated at all (if dwForms is zero).

Listing 9.7 (continued)

```
/**------------------------------------------------------------**/
BOOL CPrinterForm::Set(LPSTR lpName, long width, long height,
      long left, long top, long right, long bottom) {
   FORM_INFO_1 fi;
   FillForm(&fi, lpName, width,height,left,top,right,bottom);
   return SetForm(hPrinter, lpName, 1, (LPBYTE)&fi);
} // CPrinterForm::Set

/**------------------------------------------------------------**/
void CPrinterForm::FillForm(FORM_INFO_1 *p, LPSTR pName,
      long dy, long dx, long x1, long y1, long x2, long y2) {
   p->pName = pName;
   p->Size.cx = dx;
   p->Size.cy = dy;
   p->ImageableArea.left = x1;
   p->ImageableArea.top = y1;
   p->ImageableArea.right = x2;
   p->ImageableArea.bottom = y2;
} // CPrinterForm::FillForm
```

The Add() method creates a new form based on the name and size information passed to it. It accomplishes this by filling in a FORM_INFO_1 structure (Figure 9.4) and calling AddForm(). Delete() deletes a form matching the name passed to it (you can't delete a form that is enumerated by a printer). Get() takes the name of a form and returns the size and imageable area of that form. Set() takes the name of a form and changes its size and imageable area to the values passed to it.

Figure 9.4 FORM_INFO_1 *data structure (Win32).*

```
// Identifies a printer form
typedef struct _FORM_INFO_1 {
    LPTSTR pName;              // name of form
    SIZEL  Size;              // width/height of form (.001 mm)
    RECTL  ImageableArea;     // printable area (.001 mm)
} FORM_INFO_1;
```

Figure 9.5 Screen capture from ntprint.exe.

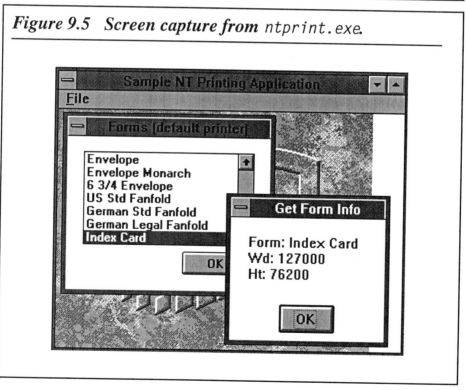

Using the `CPrinterForm` Class

The sample `ntprint.exe` program also demonstrates using the `CPrinterForm` class. When the "Enumerate Forms..." menu item is selected, `WndProc()` creates a dialog box using `EnumDlgProc()` as the dialog box procedure. `EnumDlgProc()` uses the `dwForms` field of the globally allocated `CPrinterForm` and the `Enumerate()` method to enumerate all of the forms available on the default printer. If a user double-clicks on an item in the listbox, I call `Get()` to retrieve information about the selected form (Figure 9.5). Notice that Win32 uses the high word of `wParam` for listbox notification codes, rather than the high word of `lParam` (as was the case for Win16).

When the "Add Form" menu item is selected, I call `Add()` to add a sample form called "Index Card" to the forms database. The units of size are given as thousands of millimeters, so I multiplied the dimensions in inches (3" x 5") by a factor of 25,400. You can view the new form by selecting the "Enumerate Forms..." menu item again or by selecting the Print Manager "Forms..." menu item under the "Printer" menu. The "Delete Form" menu item deletes the newly created Index Card form by calling `Delete()`. The "Change Form" menu item changes the size of the Index Card form to 5" x 7" by calling `Set()`.

The Source Code

All the source code described in this chapter, as well as a makefile are included on the code disk.

References

Custer, Helen. *Inside Windows NT*. Redmond, WA: Microsoft Press, 1993.

Microsoft Corp. Win32 Software Development Kit for Windows NT. Windows NT Device Driver Kit.

Microsoft Corp. *Windows NT Resource Kit*, Volume 1 of 3. Redmond, WA: Microsoft Press, 1993.

Richter, Jeffrey. *Advanced Windows NT*. Redmond, WA: Microsoft Press, 1994.

Chapter 10

Enumerating Processes in Windows NT

Brian G. Myers

The Win32 API can enumerate windows, child windows, window properties, dependent services, clipboard formats, metafile records, fonts and font families, pens and brushes, printers, printer drivers, print jobs, ports, resource languages, and resource types, but no API routine exists for enumerating the currently running processes. The means to correct the omission lurk deep in the system Registry.

A list of ID numbers for running processes might be useful, for example, when a debugger seeks a process to debug. But you can do much more by first passing a process ID to `OpenProcess()` and getting a handle in return. Assuming your user access token permits such actions, a handle lets you change a process' priority, read from and write to its address space, determine how long it's been running and how much processor time it uses, wait for it to end, and retrieve its closing error code. You can even create new threads within the other process. [Curious or devious readers may wish to know that the functions needed for all those actions are `DebugActiveProcess()`, `SetPriorityClass()`, `ReadProcessMemory()`, `WriteProcessMemory()`, `GetProcessTimes()`, `WaitForSingleObject()`, `GetExitCodeProcess()`, and `CreateRemoteThread()`.] Although I won't have room here to enumerate threads as well as processes, my code could easily be extended to create an `EnumThreads()` procedure as well, permitting a similar range of actions on foreign threads.

I've implemented a process enumeration function that sifts through performance data from the system Registry to pass back the name and ID of each running process. To use the library, compile the code and call the exported `EnumProcesses()` function from within your own program. You'll need to provide a callback function just as you would for any other enumeration function. Besides introducing the complex structure of performance data in the system Registry, `enumproc.c` also shows how to implement enumeration procedures generally.

The techniques described here apply only to Windows NT. Currently there is no portable way to enumerate processes under both Windows NT and Windows 95. For information about enumerating processes under Windows 95, search the Win32 SDK for Microsoft's PVIEW95 example and read Matt Pietrek's article "An Exclusive Tour of the New TOOLHELP32 Functions in Windows 95."

Understanding System Registry Performance Data

Conceptually, the system registry is nothing more than a big bin where any application may store any information it likes. The system uses the Registry to remember hardware and software configurations, File Manager associations, OLE servers, the identities of different users on a single machine, and many other things as well. All the data is organized into keys, where each key represents a node on a hierarchical tree. Unlike most registry data, NT's performance data does not reside permanently in the Registry. Instead, a request to read from the performance data nodes causes NT to gather the data on the fly and hand it over in a single large block. To get performance data, you read from subkeys of the root called `HKEY_PERFORMANCE_DATA`. The subkeys hold data (or cause data to be gathered) about the CPU, the paging file, the disk, system memory, threads, processes, network drivers, and other objects.

The performance data block must cope with information retrieved from a variety of systems, some of them remote, some of them perhaps not even running Windows NT. The set of objects and the types of values gathered could vary. The number and size of the structures in the data block is not considered constant, so the data needs to describe itself. Each structure in the block contains offsets for navigating to subsequent structures. You move a pointer from structure to structure by adding offsets to it.

Figure 10.1 diagrams the performance structures. Understanding the block of data requires a little terminology. An "object" is something whose performance you might want to watch. Disk drives, processes, and CPUs are types of objects. One type may have several instances. There are always many process objects, for example, but only one system object. For each object, the performance monitor tracks a set of values called "counters." To monitor processes, for example, you might want to know when the process started, what its ID number is, what percentage of processor time it has consumed, and how many file operations it has performed. For the system object, you might want to know the number of thread context switches occurring per second or the processor queue length. Each object has different counters, and each instance of an object has its own set of values for those counters. If ten processes are running, then you'll retrieve ten sets of counter values.

Figure 10.1   The structure of performance data in the system Registry.

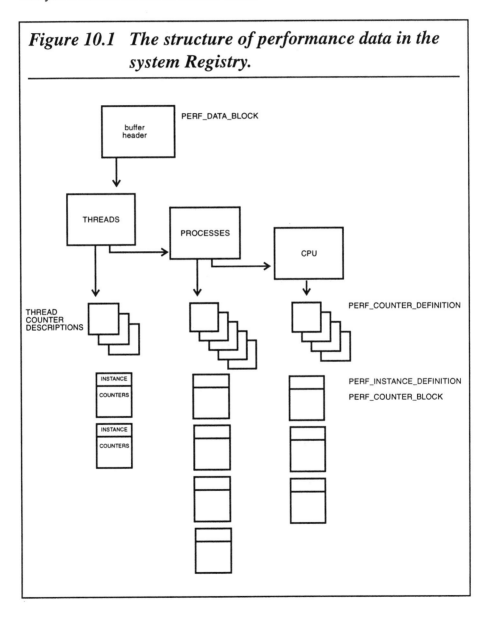

The initial PERF_DATA_BLOCK structure tells how many kinds of objects are represented in the current sample. It also tells its own size, as do most of the structures, to help you find the PERF_OBJECT_TYPE structures that follow, one for each object type. If the object name is "Process," then it probably has 23 counters and many instances. Each PERF_OBJECT_TYPE is followed by a string of PERF_COUNTER_DEFINITION structures, one for each of the object's counters. The definition structures do not contain values; they tell how to interpret the values once you find them. They tell whether a counter is a 32- or 64-bit value, a timer, a percentage, or an average; what calculations to perform before presenting the value; and whether the value should be displayed with a particular suffix such as "/sec" or "%". After the object types and their counter definitions come instance definitions — if there are instances — and counter blocks. Instance definitions tell the name of the instance, if it has one. Counter blocks (at last!) contain all the actual counter values for one particular object instance. You can't interpret the counter block without referring back to the counter definitions. All these structures are defined in winperf.h, which a program must include in order to read the data.

Retrieving Object and Counter Names

Because the kinds of performance data retrieved may vary on other systems, it is not safe to assume that a given object will always present the same counters in the same order. The PERF_COUNTER_DEFINITION structures give enough information to evaluate and display each counter value, but not enough to know exactly what the value represents. That information comes from a block of label strings stored separately in the Registry. The counter definition structures contain index values that identify strings in the name block. To use the performance data you usually have to read in both blocks: the data itself and the associated names. Table 10.1 shows the structure of the name block. A double null marks the end of the list. The quotation marks shown in the table are, of course, not stored in the name block: they indicate that the

Table 10.1   The structure of the name block.

Index String	*Separator*	*Name String*	*Separator*
"2"	NULL	"System"	NULL
"4"	NULL	"Memory"	NULL
"6"	NULL	"% Processor Time"	NULL
[...]			
"822"	NULL	"Pages Input/sec"	NULL NULL

entries are strings. The name strings help to make the performance data self-describing. If a PERF_OBJECT_TYPE contains the value 4 in its ObjectNameTitleIndex field, then you can look in the name block to discover that the object type is "Memory". To perform the lookup you must convert the DWORD value 4 to the string "4", scan through the name block for the matching string, then return the string that follows "4".

If you find this proliferation of data blocks and structures confusing, you might not want to know that the Registry also contains a parallel block of explanatory strings to supplement the name strings. In the name block, "4" precedes "Memory", and in the help block it precedes a long string of several sentences explaining what "Memory" is. Patient readers can find all the labels and help strings for themselves by running the Performance Monitor application that comes with Windows NT. Pull down the Edit menu, choose Add To Chart, and click on the Explain button. Figure 10.2 shows the resulting dialog box. When you choose an object, such as Thread, a listbox displays all the counter names. Selecting a counter brings up the help text in the Counter Definition box. You don't have to worry about the help strings now, though, because EnumProc doesn't use them.

Figure 10.2 NT Performance Monitor Add to Chart dialog box.

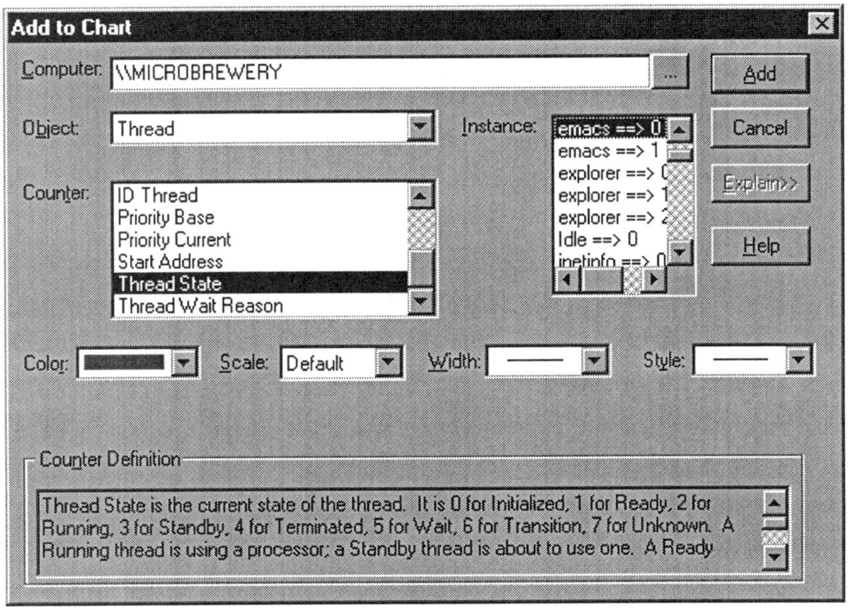

The `LoadNameStrings()` procedure in Listing 10.1 reads the name block into memory. The names reside under HKEY_LOCAL_MACHINE under a subkey with the cumbersome name

```
SOFTWARE\\Microsoft\\Windows NT\\CurrentVersion\\Perflib\\009
```

Listing 10.1   Read the name block into memory.

```
/*------------------------------------------------
  LOAD NAME STRINGS
  Read in the block of object name strings.
  Return a valid pointer to the block of
  MULTI_SZ strings or NULL if an error occurs.
  ----------------------------------------------*/
PTSTR LoadNameStrings ( PTSTR szComputerName )
{
  HKEY hNamesKey;
  LONG lResult;
  DWORD dwDataType;
  DWORD dwDataSize;
  PTSTR pstrNameBlock; /* points to block of name strings */
  HKEY hMachineKey = HKEY_LOCAL_MACHINE;

  /* attempt a remote connection if caller requests it */
  if (szComputerName)
  {
    lResult = RegConnectRegistry( szComputerName,
                          HKEY_LOCAL_MACHINE, &hMachineKey );
    if (lResult != ERROR_SUCCESS)
      return( NULL );
  }

  /* open the key where the block of names is kept */
  lResult = RegOpenKeyEx( hMachineKey, NAME_BLOCK_SUBKEY,
                     RESERVED, KEY_QUERY_VALUE, &hNamesKey );
  if (lResult != ERROR_SUCCESS)
    return( NULL );

  /* find out how big the data block is */
  lResult = RegQueryValueEx( hNamesKey, TEXT("Counters"), RESERVED,
                        &dwDataType, NULL, &dwDataSize );
  if (lResult != ERROR_SUCCESS)
    return( NULL );

  /* allocate room for all the names */
  pstrNameBlock = (PTSTR) GlobalAlloc( GMEM_ZEROINIT, dwDataSize );
  if (!pstrNameBlock)
    return( NULL );
```

Listing 10.1 (continued)

```
  /* load all the names into the buffer */
  lResult = RegQueryValueEx( hNamesKey, TEXT("Counters"), RESERVED,
                           &dwDataType, (PBYTE)pstrNameBlock, &dwDataSize );
  if (lResult != ERROR_SUCCESS)
    return( NULL );

  /* close the key that holds the names */
  RegCloseKey( hNamesKey );
  RegCloseKey( hMachineKey );
  return( pstrNameBlock );
}


/*--------------------------------------------------
  GET TITLE INDEX VALUE
  Search through the name block for the given string
  pTitle. If convert the corresponding index string
  (e.g. "230") to an unsigned integer. Return the
  integer, or if not found, return GET_INDEX_FAILURE.
  --------------------------------------------------*/

UINT GetTitleIndexValue ( PTSTR pstrNameBlock, PTSTR pTitle )
{
  PTSTR pIndexString;
  UINT uValue = GET_INDEX_FAILURE;

  if ((!pstrNameBlock) || (!pTitle))
    return( GET_INDEX_FAILURE );

  pIndexString = GetTitleIndexString( pstrNameBlock, pTitle );

  if (pIndexString) {
    uValue = tstr_to_uint( pIndexString );
    LocalFree( pIndexString );
  }

  return( uValue );
}


/*--------------------------------------------------
  GET TITLE INDEX STRING
  Search through the name block for the given string
  pTitle. If found, copy and return the corresponding
  index string (e.g. "230"). Caller must free the
  string.  NULL return for errors.
  --------------------------------------------------*/
PTSTR GetTitleIndexString ( PTSTR pstrNameBlock, PTSTR pTitle )
{ BOOL bEndOfData = FALSE;
  PTSTR pThisIndex, pThisTitle;
  PTSTR pReturn = NULL;
```

The final three digits of the string indicate a language. "009" stands for the default language, U.S. English. Under this node, ask for the subkey "Counters" to get the name strings or "Help" to get the explanatory strings.

Listing 10.1 (continued)

```
    if ((!pstrNameBlock) || (!pTitle))
      return( NULL );

    /* point to first two strings in the name block */
    pThisIndex = pstrNameBlock;
    pThisTitle = NextString( pstrNameBlock );

    /* search through the name block for a match */
    while (!bEndOfData &&
           (lstrcmp(pTitle, pThisTitle) != 0)) {

      pThisIndex = NextString( pThisTitle );
      if (*pThisIndex != NULL_CHAR)
        pThisTitle = NextString( pThisIndex );
      if (*pThisTitle == NULL_CHAR)
        bEndOfData = TRUE;
    }

    /* if a match was found, copy and return the string *//* */
    if (!bEndOfData) {
      pReturn = LocalAlloc( LPTR, lstrlen(pThisIndex)+1 );
      if (pReturn)
        lstrcpy( pReturn, pThisIndex );
    }
    return( pReturn );
}


/*-------------------------------------------------
  NEXT STRING
  Return a pointer to the subsequent string in
  a data block of MULTI_SZ strings.
  -------------------------------------------------*/
PTSTR NextString ( PTSTR pstr )
{
  if (pstr == NULL)
    return( NULL );

  while (*pstr != NULL_CHAR)
    pstr++;

  return( ++pstr );
}
```

Loading the Data Block

The other function that queries the registry is LoadCounterData() (Listing 10.2), which returns a pointer to the block that holds all the performance structures and counter values. If the caller passes in the name of a remote computer, then Load-CounterData() begins by calling RegConnectRegistry() to open the HKEY_PERFORMANCE_DATA key on the remote machine. Next comes a loop that allocates a data buffer and then repeatedly enlarges it until the call to RegQueryValueEx() succeeds. According to the Win32 documentation for RegQueryValueEx(), such a loop should not be necessary. If the buffer is too small, then the required size is returned through the function's last parameter, here called dwDataSize. That's how LoadNameStrings() determines the proper size for its buffer. Performance data, however, is an exception. The quantity of performance data varies from moment to moment. As the set of running processes grows or shrinks, so does the quantity of related performance data. Between the time RegQueryValueEx() fails once and the time you call it again, the system might start more processes. Therefore, when dwDataSize requests a buffer of a certain size for performance data, the value is unreliable.

The data buffers required for processes are not huge. The performance data on my home machine fits easily into the library's initial 30Kb buffer, but the data for my work machine, which is attached to a network and returns network data along with the process data, expands the buffer to about 63Kb. Here's the central command that actually loads the data block:

Listing 10.1 (continued)

```
/*-------------------------------------------------
   TSTR TO UINT
   Convert the given string (e.g. "230") from
   a TCHAR string to an unsigned integer.
   -------------------------------------------------*/
UINT tstr_to_uint ( PTSTR pNumString )
{
  UINT uValue = 0;

  while (isdigit( *pNumString )) {
    uValue *= 10;
    uValue += (BYTE)*pNumString - TEXT('0');
    pNumString++;
  }

  return( uValue );
}
```

Listing 10.2   Read counter values from the Performance Monitor.

```
/*-------------------------------------------------
   LOAD COUNTER DATA
   Read from the performance monitor a block of data holding
   counter values for the given object. Return a pointer to the
   data block, which the caller must free, or NULL on errors.
   -------------------------------------------------*/
PPERF_DATA_BLOCK LoadCounterData ( PTSTR szComputerName,
                                   PTSTR pObjectTitleIndex )
{
  PPERF_DATA_BLOCK pCounters;
  DWORD dwDataSize = 30*BUFFER_INCREMENT;      /* 30k */
  LONG lResult;
  DWORD Type;
  HKEY hPerfKey = HKEY_PERFORMANCE_DATA;

  /* attempt a remote connection if caller requests it */
  if (szComputerName)
  {
    lResult = RegConnectRegistry( szComputerName,
                          HKEY_PERFORMANCE_DATA, &hPerfKey );
    if (lResult != ERROR_SUCCESS)
      return( NULL );
  }

  /* allocate buffer for data (guessing its size) */
  pCounters = (PPERF_DATA_BLOCK)
    LocalAlloc(   LMEM_FIXED, (UINT)dwDataSize );
  do {
    /* try to load the data */
    lResult = RegQueryValueEx (hPerfKey, pObjectTitleIndex, NULL,
                      &Type, (PBYTE)pCounters, &dwDataSize );

    /* if there wasn't room, expand the buffer */
    if (lResult == ERROR_MORE_DATA) {
      LocalFree( pCounters );
      dwDataSize += BUFFER_INCREMENT;
      pCounters = (PPERF_DATA_BLOCK)
        LocalAlloc( LMEM_FIXED, (UINT)dwDataSize );
    }
    /* if some other error occurred, quit */
    else if (!pCounters)
      return( NULL );

  } while (lResult == ERROR_MORE_DATA);

  /* close key so system won't lock monitored objects */
  RegCloseKey( hPerfKey );
  return( pCounters );
}
```

```
dwResult = RegQueryValueEx (
     HKEY_PERFORMANCE_DATA,    /* key where data resides */
     TEXT("230"),              /* process name title index */
     NULL,                     /* reserved */
     &Type,                    /* data type returned here */
     (PBYTE)pDataBlock,        /* buffer pointer */
        &dwDataSize );         /* size of data copied to buffer */
```

HKEY_PERFORMANCE_DATA is a predefined key. The second parameter names a sub-key. The subkeys under HKEY_PERFORMANCE_DATA take their names from the title index values in the name block (Table 10.1). "230" is usually the index for the string "Process". Change the subkey to gather information about different objects. "002", for example, retrieves data for the system object. "700" gets data for the paging file. You can combine several numbers in one string. "234 236" gets data for both physical and logical disk objects. To monitor all objects at once, use the subkeys "Global" and "Costly". "Global" retrieves all the data that can be collected quickly. "Costly" retrieves the remaining counters but is likely to be slow.

LoadCounterData() ends by closing HKEY_PERFORMANCE_DATA. Opening the key was unnecessary because it is always open, but closing it is necessary because the system cannot install or remove components while they are being monitored. Network drivers, for example, are locked in place while being monitored until the performance data key is closed.

Finding Specific Counters

In that breezy explanation, I've ignored the difficulty of figuring out which index value belongs to which counter. The index numbers are not guaranteed to be constant across systems. "Process" may not always be at index "230". What is constant are the English object names such as "Process". So in order to retrieve thread data, for example, you have to:

- Load the name block.
- Search the block for the string "Thread".
- Back up and find the string that precedes "Thread" (usually "232").
- Pass the string as a subkey name to RegQueryValue() or RegQueryValueEx().

GetTitleIndices() (Listing 10.3) looks up the index values for some of the strings that pertain to processes and stores them in the global variable Index. The function's purpose is to avoid hard coding the index values. The task of searching for a string and returning its index is performed by GetTitleIndexString() and GetTitleIndexValue(). Which you call depends on whether you want the index as a string or a number. One field of Index holds the string (usually "230") for reading the process object subkey from the performance Registry. The other Index fields store numbers for use in identifying process counters. You'll see how that works soon.

The performance Registry collects much more information about processes than I make use of here. I'm assuming that the point of enumerating processes is to get the name and ID number. If you need other relatively esoteric information, such as the maximum amount of virtual address space the process has used at any one time or the rate of bytes transferred per second in the process' file I/O operations, then you probably want to work directly with the performance Registry yourself. To find out more

---

Listing 10.3   Avoid hard coding index values.

```
/*-------------------------------------------------
  GET PROCESS COUNTER TITLE INDICES
  Loads block of strings from performance
  monitor and searches for string index
  values for process-related counters.
  Stores the values in the global Index
  structure.  Returns FALSE for errors.
  -----------------------------------------------*/
BOOL GetTitleIndices ( PTSTR szComputerName )
{
  PTSTR pstrNameBlock;

  pstrNameBlock = LoadNameStrings( szComputerName );
  if (!pstrNameBlock)
    return( FALSE );

  /* search data block for index numbers to  */
  /* process counters  */
  Index.ThreadCount  = (UINT)GetTitleIndexValue( pstrNameBlock,
                                      TEXT("Thread Count") );
  Index.PriorityBase = (UINT)GetTitleIndexValue( pstrNameBlock,
                                      TEXT("Priority Base") );
  Index.IDProcess    = (UINT)GetTitleIndexValue( pstrNameBlock,
                                      TEXT("ID Process") );
  /* get string and value of index to object name  */
  Index.ProcessIndexString = GetTitleIndexString( pstrNameBlock,
                                      TEXT("Process") );
  Index.ProcessIndexValue = tstr_to_uint( Index.ProcessIndexString );

  GlobalFree( pstrNameBlock );

  /* return TRUE if all indices were found */
  return( (Index.ThreadCount != GET_INDEX_FAILURE)
          && (Index.PriorityBase != GET_INDEX_FAILURE)
          && (Index.IDProcess != GET_INDEX_FAILURE)
          && (Index.ProcessIndexString != NULL) );
}
```

about what information the Registry holds and how to process more complicated counter values, you might begin with the comments in `winperf.h`, but you'll want to end with Russ Blake's "Optimizing Windows NT", which is devoted entirely to performance-monitoring issues.

Parsing the Data Block

Parsing the data block requires many statements like this one, which advances a pointer from one `PERF_OBJECT_TYPE` structure to the next.

```
pProcessObjectType =
(PPERF_OBJECT_TYPE)((PBYTE)pProcessObjectType + pProcessObjectType->HeaderLength);
```

Most of the structures have a `HeaderLength` or `ByteLength` field containing the offset in bytes to the next structure. For pointer arithmetic, you must cast the pointer to type `PBYTE` before adding the offset, then cast the result back to a structure pointer. Using `sizeof()` to calculate the offset doesn't always work because sometimes other data intervenes between two structures. Each `PERF_INSTANCE_DEFINITION` structure is followed immediately by a variable-length string containing the instance name. In this case, the offset from one instance definition to the next is the sum of the `Byte-Length` and `NameLength` fields.

All the strings stored in the Registry as part of the data block or the name block are stored as Unicode strings. For the most part, `enumproc.c` doesn't care about the width of the characters because it uses generic character types such as `TCHAR` and `PTSTR` along with the `TEXT` macro and so works equally well with either width. When the `UNICODE` constant is not defined, `RegQueryValueEx()` becomes the narrow-character function `RegQueryValueExA()` and silently converts all the strings in the name block to narrow characters. But the instance name, embedded in a complex structure containing many data types, cannot be converted automatically. As you see in Listing 10.4, I've added an `#ifdef` to force the conversion if `UNICODE` is not defined. [`WideCharToMultiByte()` does not necessarily produce multibyte characters; it produces normal 1-byte characters unless the original string contains foreign characters that require multibyte representations.] My code assumes that the library and its client program are compiled with the same `UNICODE` setting. With `UNICODE` defined, enumproc.c passes process names to the client as Unicode strings. Without the `UNICODE` constant, it passes narrow-character strings.

Listing 10.4   Lists all processes currently running.

```
/*-----------------------------------------------
   ENUM PROC LIBRARY
   Library clients call EnumProcesses to list
   all the processes currently running.
   -----------------------------------------------*/

/* library must match caller's UNICODE setting */
#define UNICODE             /* for windows headers */
#define STRICT

#include <windows.h>
#include <winperf.h>        /* performance structures */
#include <limits.h>         /* UINT_MAX */
#include "enumproc.h"


/*-----------------------------------------------
   MANIFEST CONSTANTS
   -----------------------------------------------*/

#ifdef UNICODE
#define NULL_CHAR UNICODE_NULL
#else
#define NULL_CHAR '\0'
#endif

#define GET_INDEX_FAILURE   UINT_MAX
#define RESERVED            0
#define BUFFER_INCREMENT    1024
#define NAME_BLOCK_SUBKEY \
    TEXT("SOFTWARE\\Microsoft\\Windows NT\\CurrentVersion\\Perflib\\009")


/*-----------------------------------------------
   PROTOTYPES
   -----------------------------------------------*/

PWSTR GetInstanceName( PPERF_INSTANCE_DEFINITION pInstance );
BOOL CollectCounterValues( PPERF_OBJECT_TYPE pProcessObjectType,
    PPERF_INSTANCE_DEFINITION pProcess, PPROCESSENUMDATA pProcessEnumData );
BOOL StoreProcessCounterValue( PPERF_COUNTER_DEFINITION pPerfCounterDef,
    PBYTE pCounter, PPROCESSENUMDATA pProcessEnumData );
PPERF_INSTANCE_DEFINITION NextInstance( PPERF_INSTANCE_DEFINITION pInstanceDef );
PPERF_DATA_BLOCK LoadCounterData( PTSTR szComputerName,
    PTSTR pObjectIndexString );
BOOL GetTitleIndices( PTSTR szComputerName );
PTSTR LoadNameStrings( PTSTR szComputerName );
UINT GetTitleIndexValue( PTSTR pNameBlock, PTSTR pTitle );
PTSTR GetTitleIndexString( PTSTR pNameBlock, PTSTR pTitle );
PTSTR NextString( PTSTR pstr );
UINT tstr_to_uint( PTSTR pNumString );
```

The *EnumProcesses* **Procedure**

Listing 10.4 begins with EnumProcesses(), the library's primary function. EnumProcesses() executes these steps:

1. Loads the name block and gets title index values for counter names.
2. Loads the data block.
3. Finds the PERF_OBJECT_TYPE structure for processes.
4. Finds the first PERF_INSTANCE_DEFINITION structure.
5. For each instance it copies the process name and counter values into a structure, and passes the structure back to the caller.

Most of the variables in the program are dynamic rather than static, so issues of multithreading do not arise. Each thread pushes its own values onto its own stack. However, the program's one static variable, Index, must be thread-local. If EnumProcesses() always queried only the local machine, then all inquiries would use the

---

Listing 10.4 (continued)

```
/*------------------------------------------------------
   GLOBAL VARIABLE
   The Index structure holds title string index values
   for all the counters the library passes to its caller.
   It must be thread-local in case concurrent threads
   retrieve performance data from different machines.
   ------------------------------------------------------*/
typedef struct {
  UINT IDProcess;
  UINT ThreadCount;
  UINT PriorityBase;
  UINT ProcessIndexValue;
  PTSTR ProcessIndexString;
} TITLE_INDEX_STRUCT;

/* Older Borland compilers used __thread instead of    */
/* Microsoft's declspec.  More recent Borland compilers */
/* support both.  The THREADLOCAL macro provides a      */
/* portable syntax.                                     */

#ifdef __BORLANDC__
#define THREADLOCAL( type, name ) type __thread name
#else  // using Microsoft tools
#define THREADLOCAL( type, name ) __declspec( thread ) type name
#endif

THREADLOCAL( TITLE_INDEX_STRUCT, Index );
```

Listing 10.4 (continued)

```
/*-------------------------------------------------
   ENUMERATE PROCESSES (exported function)
   Call up the performance monitor data for
   process objects and pass some information
   about each existing process to the caller.
   Return TRUE if enumeration succeeds and
   FALSE if an error interrupts enumeration.
   -----------------------------------------*/
BOOL WINAPI EnumProcesses ( PTSTR szComputerName, UINT uProcessID,
                            PROCESSENUMPROC ProcessEnumProc, LPARAM lParam )
{
   PPERF_DATA_BLOCK pDataBlock;
   PPERF_OBJECT_TYPE pObjectType;
   unsigned long lNumProcesses;
   PPERF_INSTANCE_DEFINITION pThisProcess;
   unsigned i;
   PROCESSENUMDATA ProcessEnumData;
   BOOL bFound = FALSE;
   BOOL bSuccess = TRUE;

   /* get name string index values for process counters */
   if (!GetTitleIndices( szComputerName ))
     return( FALSE );

   /* query performance monitor for process data */
   ZeroMemory( &ProcessEnumData, sizeof(ProcessEnumData) );
   pDataBlock = LoadCounterData( szComputerName, Index.ProcessIndexString );
   if (!pDataBlock)
     return( FALSE );   /* unable to load data */

   /* set a pointer to start of data for first object */
   pObjectType = (PPERF_OBJECT_TYPE)
     ((PBYTE)pDataBlock + pDataBlock->HeaderLength);

   /* loop through objects to find Process object */
   for (i=0; i<pDataBlock->NumObjectTypes; i++)
   {
     if (pObjectType->ObjectNameTitleIndex
         == Index.ProcessIndexValue) {
       bFound = TRUE;
       break;
     } else {                   /* next object */
       pObjectType = (PPERF_OBJECT_TYPE)
         ((PBYTE)pObjectType + pObjectType->HeaderLength);
     }

   }
   if (!bFound)            /* no processes found! */
     return( FALSE );   /* (this shouldn't happen) */
```

same name block and there would be no need for thread-local instances of Index. But because remote inquiries could conceivably produce various name blocks, each thread must be allowed to keep its own version of the index values.

For the third step, I've written a loop that walks through all the PERF_OBJECT_TYPE structures to find the one for process objects. Normally the loop is not necessary because asking for process data yields only one object type ("Process"). Sometimes, however, asking for one object yields information about several. The system can't monitor threads, for example, without monitoring processes as well, and it returns the information for both. Similarly, asking for logical disk data pulls up physical disk data, too. The loop allows for the possibility that some other system might return multiple objects even for a process query, and it makes the code more easily adapted to inquiries about objects other than processes.

EnumProcesses() calls CollectCounterValues() to pick out the performance values for one process. CollectCounterValues() loops through all the counters to read them. For each iteration it sets one pointer to a counter definition and another to

---

Listing 10.4 (continued)

```
/* how many processes were found? */
lNumProcesses = pObjectType->NumInstances;

/* point to first process instance definition */
pThisProcess = (PPERF_INSTANCE_DEFINITION)
  ((PBYTE)pObjectType + pObjectType->DefinitionLength);

/* Loop through all instances.  Send info about */
/* each process object back to the client program */
/* through its callback function, ProcessEnumProc. */

for (i = 0; i < lNumProcesses; i++)  {

   /* Copy instance name to ProcessEnumData. */
   /* If UNICODE is not defined, convert to */
   /* a narrow-character string. */

#ifdef UNICODE
   lstrcpy( ProcessEnumData.InstanceName, GetInstanceName(pThisProcess) );
#else
   WideCharToMultiByte( CP_ACP, 0, GetInstanceName(pThisProcess), -1,
                        ProcessEnumData.InstanceName,
                        sizeof(ProcessEnumData.InstanceName), NULL, NULL );
#endif
```

the corresponding counter value. It passes both pointers to `StoreProcessCounter-Value()`, which uses the counter definition to identify and interpret the data in the counter. When it finds the process ID, priority, or thread count, it copies the value into the structure that is later passed to the client.

Listing 10.4 (continued)

```
    /* copy counter values to ProcessEnumData */
    if (!CollectCounterValues( pObjectType, pThisProcess, &ProcessEnumData )) {
      bSuccess = FALSE;    /* no values found (this */
      break;               /* (shouldn't happen) */
    }

    /* if caller wants info for this process, send it */
    if ((uProcessID == ENUM_PROCESSES_ALL)
        || (uProcessID == ProcessEnumData.IDProcess)) {

      if (!ProcessEnumProc( &ProcessEnumData, lParam ))
        break; /* caller wants no more data */
    }

    /* point to the subsequent process */
    pThisProcess = NextInstance( pThisProcess );
  }

  LocalFree( Index.ProcessIndexString );
  LocalFree( pDataBlock );
  return( bSuccess );
}

/*-------------------------------------------------
  GET INSTANCE NAME
  Given a pointer to an instance definition
  structure, return a pointer to the name of that
  instance.  Return a pointer to Unicode name
  string, if successful, or UNICODE_NULL if for
  any reason the name cannot be found.
  -------------------------------------------------*/
PWSTR GetInstanceName ( PPERF_INSTANCE_DEFINITION pInstance )
{
  PWSTR pNameString;

  if (!pInstance)
    pNameString = UNICODE_NULL;
  else if ((pInstance->NameLength != 0) && (pInstance->NameOffset != 0))
    pNameString = (PWSTR)((PBYTE)pInstance + pInstance->NameOffset);

  return( pNameString );
}
```

Listing 10.4 *(continued)*

```
/*-----------------------------------------------
   COLLECT COUNTER VALUES
   Run through all the counters associated with
   one process. Interpret counter values and copy
   them into fields of a PROCESSENUMDATA structure.
   Return TRUE if any values are copied into
   pEnumData.
   -----------------------------------------------*/
BOOL CollectCounterValues ( PPERF_OBJECT_TYPE pObjectType,
                            PPERF_INSTANCE_DEFINITION pProcess,
                            PPROCESSENUMDATA pEnumData )
{
  UINT i;
  UINT uNumCounters;
  PPERF_COUNTER_BLOCK pCounterBlock;
  PPERF_COUNTER_DEFINITION pThisCounterDef;
  PBYTE pThisCounter;
  BOOL bSuccess = FALSE;

  uNumCounters = (UINT)pObjectType->NumCounters;

  /* point to the first counter definition */
  pThisCounterDef = (PPERF_COUNTER_DEFINITION)
    ((PBYTE)pObjectType + pObjectType->HeaderLength);

  /* point to the first counter block */
  pCounterBlock = (PPERF_COUNTER_BLOCK)
    ((PBYTE)pProcess + pProcess->ByteLength);

  for (i = 0; i < uNumCounters; i++) {

    /* point to the counter data that */
    /* corresponds to the counter definition */
    pThisCounter = (PBYTE)pCounterBlock + pThisCounterDef->CounterOffset;

    /* copy a counter value into pEnumData */
    if (StoreProcessCounterValue( pThisCounterDef, pThisCounter, pEnumData ))
      bSuccess = TRUE;

    /* point to the next counter definition */
    pThisCounterDef = (PPERF_COUNTER_DEFINITION)
      ((PBYTE)pThisCounterDef + pThisCounterDef->ByteLength);
  }

  return( bSuccess );
}
```

Calling the Library

The library's exported procedure, EnumProcesses(), mimics the prototypes of other enumeration procedures in Windows.

```
BOOL WINAPI EnumProcesses( PTSTR szComputerName,
        UINT uProcessID, PROCESSENUMPROC ProcessEnumProc, LPARAM lParam );
```

Listing 10.4 (continued)

```
/*-------------------------------------------------
    STORE PROCESS COUNTER VALUE
    Interpret the value in pCounter and store it in
    the appropriate field of pEnumData. To interpret
    the value, the procedure needs to see the related
    counter definition structure. Returns TRUE if
    pCounter is identified and stored.
    ---------------------------------------------*/
BOOL StoreProcessCounterValue ( PPERF_COUNTER_DEFINITION pPerfCounterDef,
                                PBYTE pCounter, PPROCESSENUMDATA pEnumData )
{
    DWORD dwCounterIndex = pPerfCounterDef->CounterNameTitleIndex;

    if (dwCounterIndex == Index.ThreadCount) {
      pEnumData->ThreadCount = *(PDWORD)pCounter;
    } else if (dwCounterIndex == Index.PriorityBase) {
      pEnumData->PriorityBase = *(PDWORD)pCounter;
    } else if (dwCounterIndex == Index.IDProcess) {
      pEnumData->IDProcess = *(PDWORD)pCounter;
    } else
      return (FALSE);         /* no value was stored */

    return( TRUE );      /* a value was stored */
}


/*-------------------------------------------------
    NEXT INSTANCE
    Given a pointer to an instance definition
    structure, return a pointer to the next
    instance definition structure that follows.
    ---------------------------------------------*/
PPERF_INSTANCE_DEFINITION NextInstance ( PPERF_INSTANCE_DEFINITION pInstanceDef )
{
    PPERF_COUNTER_BLOCK pCounterBlock;

    pCounterBlock = (PPERF_COUNTER_BLOCK)
      ((PBYTE)pInstanceDef + pInstanceDef->ByteLength);

    return( (PPERF_INSTANCE_DEFINITION)
          ((PBYTE)pCounterBlock + pCounterBlock->ByteLength) );
}
```

   The first parameter names the machine whose processes you want to enumerate. Machine names begin with two backslashes: \\MachineName. (Remember though, that as a C literal string, it would be written "\\\\MachineName".) If the name pointer is NULL, EnumProcesses() defaults to the local machine. The second parameter, if used, limits the enumeration to a single process ID in order to retrieve the data for one known process without the overhead of many callbacks from the DLL. ProcessEnum-Proc, the third parameter, is a callback procedure with the following prototype:

```
BOOL CALLBACK ProcessEnumProc( PPROCESSENUMDATA pProcessData, LPARAM lParam )
```

Listing 10.4 (continued)

```
/*-------------------------------------------------
  GET PROCESS COUNTER TITLE INDICES
  Loads block of strings from performance monitor
  and searches for string index values for process-
  related counters. Stores the values in the global
  Index structure. Returns FALSE for errors.
  -------------------------------------------------*/
BOOL GetTitleIndices ( PTSTR szComputerName )
{
  PTSTR pstrNameBlock;

  pstrNameBlock = LoadNameStrings( szComputerName );
  if (!pstrNameBlock)
    return( FALSE );

  /* search data block for index numbers to  */
  /* process counters  */
  Index.ThreadCount  = (UINT)GetTitleIndexValue( pstrNameBlock,
                                      TEXT("Thread Count") );
  Index.PriorityBase = (UINT)GetTitleIndexValue( pstrNameBlock,
                                      TEXT("Priority Base") );
  Index.IDProcess    = (UINT)GetTitleIndexValue( pstrNameBlock,
                                      TEXT("ID Process") );

  /* get string and value of index to object name  */
  Index.ProcessIndexString = GetTitleIndexString( pstrNameBlock,
                                      TEXT("Process") );
  Index.ProcessIndexValue = tstr_to_uint( Index.ProcessIndexString );

  GlobalFree( pstrNameBlock );

  /* return TRUE if all indices were found */
  return( (Index.ThreadCount != GET_INDEX_FAILURE)
        && (Index.PriorityBase != GET_INDEX_FAILURE)
        && (Index.IDProcess != GET_INDEX_FAILURE)
        && (Index.ProcessIndexString != NULL) );
}
```

pProcessData points to a structure defined in enumproc.h whose fields hold the name, ID, base priority, and thread count for one process. lParam contains whatever value was passed as lParam to EnumProcesses(). Using this parameter, a program can pass signals to its own callback procedure.

Here's how a sample client, ShowProc(), calls the library:

```
#define ENUM_PROCESSES_ALL     0

/* print column titles */
printf( "%5s%9s%8s %s\n", "PID", "Threads", "PriBase", "Name" );
if (!EnumProcesses( NULL, ENUM_PROCESSES_ALL, ProcessEnumProc, 0L ))
      printf( "Enumeration failed.\n" );
```

And here is how the callback function handles the data received for each process:

```
BOOL CALLBACK ProcessEnumProc ( PPROCESSENUMDATA pProcessData,
                                LPARAM lParam )
{
   TCHAR szOutputLine[FILENAME_MAX * 2];
   HANDLE hStdOut;

   hStdOut = GetStdHandle( STD_OUTPUT_HANDLE );
   if (!hStdOut)
        return( FALSE );

   wsprintf( szOutputLine, TEXT("%5lu%9lu%8lu %s\n"),
           pProcessData->IDProcess,
           pProcessData->ThreadCount,
           pProcessData->PriorityBase,
           pProcessData->InstanceName    );

   WriteConsole( hStdOut, szOutputLine, lstrlen(szProcessData),
                NULL, NULL );
   return( TRUE );
}
```

WriteConsole() works better than printf() here because, depending on the UNICODE setting, pProcessData->InstanceName may point to a Unicode string. The printf() in Microsoft's C runtime library handles wide-character strings, but not everyone's libraries do, so WriteConsole() is more portable.

ShowProc() produces a list like this:

```
PID  Threads PriBase Name
  0        1       0 Idle
  2       23       8 System
 18        6      11 smss
 22        8      13 csrss
 32        2      13 winlogon
 38       18       9 services
 41       12       9 lsass
 63        7       8 spoolss
 75        7       8 rpcss
 64       11       8 tapisrv
135        1       8 nddeagnt
143        3       8 explorer
157        2       8 systray
150        4       8 ntvdm
163        2       8 SHOWPROC
```

The fact that process names appear in different cases is insignificant; the case depends merely on how the process name was first typed. The processes with cryptic names belong to the system. Here are a few you might see:

```
smss  = Session Manager Subsystem
csrss = Client Server Runtime Subsystem (Win32 SubSystem)
lsass = Local Security Authority Subsystem
rpcss = Remote Procedure Call Subsystem
```

The code listings here have shown all the procedures that compose the Enum-Proc() DLL. For the complete code listing, with header, .def, and makefiles for both Borland and Microsoft compilers, see the disk that accompanies this book.

Conclusion

EnumThreads() would follow almost exactly the same steps as EnumProcesses() and call many of the same subroutines. Threads have different counters such as "ID Thread", "ID Process", "Thread State", and "Current Priority". GetTitleIndices() would have to find and remember the index values for thread titles instead of process titles. StoreThreadCounterValue() would replace StoreProcessCounterValue(), and of course the header file would define a data structure to hold thread counter values and a callback function to receive the structure.

With the information `EnumProcesses()` returns, you can discover and manipulate other processes. Or you can use the library code to find your way into the performance data for any object the system monitors, enabling you to make better programming decisions based on how your code affects the paging file, disk operations, CPU, physical memory, and other system resources.

Chapter 11

Windows NT Console Programming

Tom Haapanen

With Microsoft Windows' emphasis on the graphical user interface, it has generally been difficult to port (or create) character-based applications for Windows. Windows NT, however, addresses this problem by providing a Console API for creating text-based applications.

The Console API, a part of the Win32 API, was introduced in the original Windows NT 3.1 and has continued essentially unchanged through versions 3.5, 3.51, and 4.0 (Table 11.1). It was also included in the Win32 implementation on Windows 95 but, unfortunately, is not included in the Win32s API subset.

The choice between a traditional Windows application and a console application is often easy. If you are porting a text-based package from the MS-DOS or UNIX platform, you can use the Console API to produce a rapid port to Windows NT. However, if you need a more complex interaction with the user — especially if you are writing an application from scratch — it may well be best to write a graphical user interface for the application. Many UNIX-based tools, however, do not readily move to a graphical environment with a message loop, dialogs, and scalable proportional fonts.

Table 11.1   Windows NT Console API functions.

Stream Input

ReadFile*	Read characters only from the event queue
getchar*	Read a character only from the event queue (other C library standard input functions may also be used)

Stream Output

WriteFile*	Write text to console buffer at current cursor location
printf*	Write formatted text to console buffer at current cursor location (other C library standard output functions may also be used)
SetConsoleTextAttribute	Set the current text attribute (color) for stream output

Structured Input

ReadConsoleInput	Read an event from the input queue
PeekConsoleInput	Examine an event in the input queue without removing it
WriteConsoleInput	Append an event to the end of the input queue
GetNumberOfConsoleInputEvents	Return the number of pending input events
FlushConsoleInputBuffer	Clear the queue of pending input events

Structured Output

WriteConsoleOutput	Write a block of text and attributes to console at specified cursor location
WriteConsoleOutputCharacter	Write a buffer of text to console at specified cursor location
WriteConsoleOutputAttribute	Write a buffer of attributes to console at specified cursor location

At its most basic, Windows NT's Console API includes the standard C library's `stdio` functions: you can use `printf()`, `getch()`, `puts()`, and other standard routines simply by including `stdio.h`, with no need for further changes — the traditional K&R "Hello, world!" (from *The C Programming Language*) shown in Listing 11.1 compiles and runs just fine on Windows NT. You could also use ANSI control codes for full-screen control with standard I/O, but there is a better solution: the Win32 Console API. It provides for full-screen control, colors, two input modes, mouse support, attribute management, and more — all the building blocks you need to create advanced text-mode applications.

Table 11.1 (continued)	
Structured Output — continued	
ReadConsoleOutput	Read a block of text and attributes from console at specified cursor location
ReadConsoleOutputCharacter	Read a buffer of text from console at specified cursor location
ReadConsoleOutputAttribute	Read a buffer of attributes from console at specified cursor location
Structured Output Fill	
FillConsoleOutputCharacter	Write a single character repeatedly to console at specified cursor location
FillConsoleOutputAttribute	Write a single attribute repeatedly to console at specified cursor location
Cursor Control	
GetConsoleCursorInfo	Get the size and visibility of the cursor
SetConsoleCursorInfo	Set the size and visibility of the cursor
SetConsoleCursorPosition	Set the position of the cursor
Input/Output Modes	
GetConsoleMode	Get a set of bit flags indicating current console modes
SetConsoleMode	Set current console modes using a set of bit flags

Listing 11.1   K&R "Hello, world!"

```
#include <stdio.h>

main()
{
    printf("Hello, world!\n");
}
```

Table 11.1 (continued)

Console Management

AllocConsole	Create a console if one does not exist
FreeConsole	Destroy the console
GetConsoleTitle	Get the title on the console title bar
SetConsoleTitle	Set the title on the console title bar

Console Window Management

GetLargestConsoleWindowSize	Return the size of the largest console window that will fit on the physical display
SetConsoleWindowInfo	Set the size of the console window and its origin in the screen buffer

Console Buffer Management

CreateConsoleScreenBuffer	Create a new screen buffer
SetConsoleActiveScreenBuffer	Activates an existing screen buffer
SetConsoleScreenBufferSize	Sets the size of the screen buffer
GetConsoleScreenBufferInfo	Return screen buffer size, console window origin, cursor position, and current output attribute

Miscellaneous

ScrollConsoleScreenBuffer	Scroll, move and/or copy characters in screen buffer
GetNumberOfConsoleMouseButtons	Return the number of mouse buttons
SetConsoleCtrlHandler	Installs or deinstalls a console break handler

Getting Started with Console I/O

If your application is invoked from the Windows NT command line (SCP, or Single Command Prompt), it will inherit the console window of the standard command line. All the subprocesses will share a single window (as opposed to OS/2, which creates a new window for a DOS process started from the OS/2 command line), reducing flickering and allowing the user to continue to see the information already in the console window.

If your application is invoked by a nonconsole application, such as File Manager, though, there is no console to be inherited; thus, your application will not have a valid console handle. To ensure that your application has a console window available, call AllocConsole() in your initialization. This call will fail if a console already exists. To start with a separate window from the SCP, precede AllocConsole() with a call to FreeConsole() to release the existing console (if one exists).

Once you have a console handle, basic console output is exceedingly simple. You can use either WriteConsoleOutput() to write a block (string) of characters to the standard output or WriteFile() to do the same using the standard Windows functions. Alternatively, you can continue to use the C library's standard I/O functions.

Unless you use the file-oriented ReadFile(), console input is somewhat more complex. The basic function ReadConsoleInput() will read mouse events as well as key presses. Although you could just ignore the mouse clicks, this could be considered impolite behavior for a Windows NT application, even if it is a console application. Using just the basics for now, though, we can easily implement a Windows NT version of the traditional K&R "Hello, world!" application.

By default, the Windows NT console API processes input line-by-line. To process keystroke-by-keystroke using the file I/O functions, you need to set the console input mode to "raw", which requires clearing the flags for line-mode input, input edit key processing, character echo, output control character processing, and end-of-line wrap. Although in most applications it makes sense to use either none ("raw" mode) or all ("cooked" mode) of these, you can also set each one individually — for example, to temporarily enable single-character input.

The ReadFile() and WriteFile() functions work well, but they are needlessly complex for console I/O. Furthermore, to read just a single keystroke, you need to get the console mode, reset the input bits to raw, read the keystroke, and then restore the original console mode. Listing 11.2 includes this capability and introduces a whole new level of complexity. However, by writing simple Console API equivalents for the getch() and putstr() functions, StdioGetch() and StdioPutStr(), we can clean up and simplify this new and improved "Hello, world!" to the level of the typical ANSI C version (Listing 11.3).

A basic set of Console API equivalents for the standard C library I/O calls is shown in Listing 11.4; you can use these directly or #define the standard calls to refer to the Stdio*() versions for ease of porting. You might want to complete the set of functions if you plan to use them in your own application.

Full-Screen Addressing

Although doing standard stream I/O seems pretty straightforward, at least once you have worked your way past the imposing argument lists to ReadFile() and Write-File(), you have really only just begun. More complex applications require you to reposition the cursor and display colors other than just black-on-white. For such purposes, you will find the more advanced console API functions preferable to struggling with ANSI escape codes.

Listing 11.2   Console API "Hello, world!"

```
#include <windows.h>

main()
{
    int n;

    AllocConsole();

    WriteFile(GetStdHandle(STD_OUTPUT_HANDLE), "Hello, world!\n",
            strlen("Hello, world!\n"), &n, NULL);
}
```

Listing 11.3   "Hello, world!" using the StdioNT library.

```
#include <StdioNT.h>

main()
{
    StdioInit();
    StdioPutStr("Hello, world!\n");
    StdioGetch();
}
```

Listing 11.4 `StdioNT.c`

```c
#include <windows.h>

HANDLE StdIn, StdOut, StdErr;

void StdioInit()
{
   AllocConsole();

   StdIn = GetStdHandle(STD_INPUT_HANDLE);
   StdOut = GetStdHandle(STD_OUTPUT_HANDLE);
   StdErr = GetStdHandle(STD_ERROR_HANDLE);

   SetConsoleMode(StdIn, ENABLE_LINE_INPUT | ENABLE_ECHO_INPUT |
                  ENABLE_PROCESSED_INPUT );
   SetConsoleMode(StdOut, ENABLE_PROCESSED_OUTPUT | ENABLE_WRAP_AT_EOL_OUTPUT );
   SetConsoleMode(StdErr, ENABLE_PROCESSED_OUTPUT | ENABLE_WRAP_AT_EOL_OUTPUT );
}

void StdioPuts(char *s)
{
   int n;

   // Write the string to StdOut
   WriteFile(StdOut, s, strlen(s), &n, NULL);
}

int StdioGetch()
{
   DWORD dwFlags;
   int n;
   char c;

   // Reset the console into single-character no-echo input
   GetConsoleMode(StdIn, &dwFlags);
   SetConsoleMode(StdIn, dwFlags & ~(ENABLE_LINE_INPUT | ENABLE_ECHO_INPUT));

   // Read in a single character, no echo
   ReadFile(StdIn, &c, 1, &n, NULL);

   // Reset the console mode
   SetConsoleMode(StdIn, dwFlags);
   return(c);
}
```

If you have used DOS interrupt calls and a variety of the C screen management libraries, you might expect to see calls such as SetCursorPosition() and SetCurrentColor() for the Console API. Microsoft, however, decided on a different approach and incorporated cursor positioning into the WriteConsoleOutputCharacter() call, which makes it necessary to change colors for each output string using the WriteConsoleOutputAttribute() function.

Incorporating cursor positioning into the screen output function may clean up some code. For example, you often see code such as:

```
SetCursor(y++, x);
DisplayString("Menu choice 1");
SetCursor(y++, x);
DisplayString("Menu choice 2");
. . .
```

The integrated cursor movement simplifies this to something similar to:

```
DisplayStringAt(y++, x, "Menu choice 1");
DisplayStringAt(y++, x, "Menu choice 2");
. . .
```

With the Console API, an implementation of the latter method would consist of a sequence of calls to WriteConsoleOutputAttribute(). Unfortunately, the window coordinates are passed as a COORD structure, which would require you to fill in the values on the fly. Thus, you may either increment separately before each call:

Listing 11.4 (continued)

```
int StdioGetchE()
{
    char c;

    // Get a character, echo it back
    c = StdioGetch();

    WriteFile(StdOut, &c, 1, &n, NULL);

    return(c);
}

int StdioPrintf(format, ...)
{
    char szBuff[256];

    vsprintf(szBuff, format, va_arg);
    StdioPuts(szBuff);
}
```

```
WriteConsoleOutputText(StdOut, coords, ... );
++coords.Y;
WriteConsoleOutputText(StdOut, coords, ... );
++coords.Y;
...
```

or write a function to define coordinates on the fly (a macro does not appear possible for this problem):

```
COORD
MakeCoord(int y, int x)
{
   COORD coord;
   coord.X = x;
   coord.Y = y;
   return(coord);
}
...
WriteConsoleOutputText(StdOut, MakeCoord(y++, x, ... );
WriteConsoleOutputText(StdOut, MakeCoord(y++, x, ... );
...
```

It would be nice to have a choice of these two methods, because frequently you may need only to reposition the cursor once then make a series of output calls. This approach is still possible, however, by using both the WriteFile(), which writes its output starting at the current cursor location, and WriteConsoleOutput() functions. However, the process is not obvious because an explicit SetCursorPosition() call is lacking.

Controlling Color Attributes

Color handling is more unconventional. The only way to control color is to explicitly change a string's attributes after it has been output to the screen. After calling SetConsoleOutputCharacter(), either call WriteConsoleOutputAttribute() with a buffer the size of the output string containing the correct attributes, or call FillConsoleOutputAttribute() to set the entire output string to a single attribute value. Neither method is optimal for unstructured output in which you may need to output a string in a specific color at a previously unknown location. Color attributes are probably best hidden behind an abstraction layer to keep the interface presented to your application clean.

Note, however, that the screen text and screen attributes are completely independent of each other. You can set screen attributes without affecting text, and display text does not change screen attributes. With a structured screen display, you can use this behavior to your advantage. If, for example, a data entry screen has color-coded fields, you can set the display attributes to the correct values for the fields, background, and message areas, then just update the text within as the user enters data.

Reading Character Input

As mentioned earlier, the Console API provides two basic input modes, raw and cooked. Line-oriented input (e.g., for a UNIX-like tool using stream I/O, such as a command shell, a stream editor, or an expression evaluator) is best handled in the cooked mode, in which the Console API manages backspaces, breaks, and editing keys automatically. You receive the input only after the user presses the Return key.

In raw mode, which is suitable for use with a full-screen editor, a spreadsheet, or a word processor, your application is expected to handle all the editing keys. In exchange, though, it will receive all keystrokes immediately. For Ctrl-C processing, you should probably install a break handler using the `SetConsoleCtrlHandler()` function.

Using `ReadFile()`, both modes work as a traditional character-oriented C program does: simply wait for input characters at the appropriate location(s) in the application, with no message loop, accelerator table, dialog key checking, or other GUI complexities to worry about.

Mouse Support

The Console API interface, unlike the traditional MS-DOS text screen, allows you to handle mouse movement and clicks and operate in different sizes of console windows easily. Adding mouse support to a character-mode DOS application is a difficult task. Apart from the work of communicating with the mouse driver, integrating mouse events into the input can be confusing.

To take advantage of the mouse support, use `ReadConsoleInput()` instead of `ReadFile()`. The latter only processes keystrokes, whereas the former can recognize GUI input on the console window and pass it along to the Console API application. `ReadConsoleInput()` returns the event(s) to your application in an `INPUT_RECORD` structure that contains either a keyboard event, a mouse event, or a window resize event. You can use the event flags to determine the type of event, the mouse position, the mouse buttons pressed, and so on.

To receive mouse input, enable the `ENABLE_MOUSE_INPUT` mode for the console (this is the default). Note that using `ReadConsoleInput()` effectively sets the console input into raw mode, disabling echo and returning keystrokes immediately. The `SetConsoleMode()` raw and cooked settings are ignored.

Suppose, for example, that you are in the main keyboard processing loop for the vi editor, which uses the h, j, k, and l keys for cursor movement. You want to add the capability to move the cursor to wherever you double-click in the window. The code fragment to handle this might look something like that in Listing 11.5. If you are porting an existing application and want to hide the mouse functionality from it, you should call ReadConsoleInput() at the lowest level and translate mouse actions into their keyboard equivalents within that module. In the vi example, you might place the event-reading routine in the getch() module and include code like that shown in Listing 11.6 for a mouse double-click cursor movement.

Listing 11.5   Processing mouse input.

```
while (1) {
    ReadConsoleInput(StdIn, &Input, sizeof(Input), &n);
    if (Input.EventType == KEY_EVENT) {
        if (!Input.Event.KeyEvent.bKeyDown)
            continue;
        switch (Input.Event.KeyEvent.uChar) {
            case 'h':
                SetCursor(row, --col);
                break;
            case 'j':
                SetCursor(--row, col);
                break;
            }...
    } else if (Input.EventType == MOUSE_EVENT) {
        if (~Input.Event.MouseEvent.dwEventFlags & DOUBLE_CLICK)
            continue;
        row = Input.Event.MouseEvent.dwMousePosition.Y;
        col = Input.Event.MouseEvent.dwMousePosition.X;
        SetCursor(row, col);
    }
}
```

Listing 11.6   Handling mouse double-clicks.

```
x = Input.Event.MouseEvent.dwMousePosition.X;
y = Input.Event.MouseEvent.dwMousePosition.Y;
for ( ; y < row; y++ )
    PushKeyOnStack(CURSOR_UP);
for ( ; y > row; y-- )
    PushKeyOnStack(CURSOR_DOWN);
for ( ; X < col; y++ )
    PushKeyOnStack(CURSOR_RIGHT);
for ( ; x > col; y-- )
    PushKeyOnStack(CURSOR_LEFT);
```

This rather simplistic approach requires the implementation of a keyboard stack in your getch() module. Although it might seem that two rapid double-clicks (the second before the first cursor movement has been completed) could throw your cursor positioning completely off, it is actually not a problem as long as you empty the keyboard stack before making new calls to ReadConsoleInput().

Note that ReadConsoleInput() can read multiple events per call, even though the sample in Listing 11.5 needs only a single event at a time. The model of reading a single event at a time often fits in better with the typical single-character input used in text-type applications. In neither case, though, does calling ReadConsoleInput() impose any load on the system, because the Console API will idle until it receives an input event from the user.

Scrolling and Window Resizing

If the Console application is window aware (the default), Windows NT allows the user to resize the window. You can disable window awareness, and thus resizing, by calling SetConsoleMode() with the ENABLE_MOUSE_INPUT flag cleared.

If the Input.EventType flag is set to WINDOW_BUFFER_SIZE_EVENT, the new size of the window is contained in the Input.Event.WindowBufferSizeEvent.dwSize fields (X for width and Y for height). Upon receiving this event, adjust your screen-handling parameters and redraw your application's screen within the new boundaries of the console window.

An Intermediate API Layer

Although the Console API is quite powerful in its own right, especially in allowing some GUI-type input into a character-based console application, it was clearly not designed to port existing character-based applications to Windows NT easily. Many of the paradigms are different, the function parameter lists are unfamiliar, and cursor positioning and color control only provide one model of functionality.

The StdioNT call set shown in Listing 11.4 is useful for writing and porting basic character-based utilities, which do not require full-screen control, mouse input, or window resizing. For more complex applications, however, this call set is clearly insufficient. One possible solution is to use the Windows NT port of the UNIX curses full-screen library, available in the WIN32SDK forum on CompuServe. Unfortunately, curses is often cursed by novice programmers, and it is probably not the best choice for a new application.

Chapter 12

Cross-Platform Communication Classes

C++ semaphore classes for OS/2, AIX, and Windows NT

Richard B. Lam

Numerous C++ libraries are available that ease the burden of programming graphical user interfaces (GUIs) in a cross-platform environment. However, few libraries address the interprocess communications (IPC) facilities built into today's sophisticated PC and workstation operating systems. Interprocess communication is a vital part of client/server computing, and processes and threads running on the same system can communicate in many ways other than the familiar clipboard, DDE, and OLE standards.

In this chapter, I'll summarize the common techniques for IPC and present one way to build cross-platform C++ libraries. In doing so, I'll write an example library that implements semaphores in a platform-independent manner to allow signaling or controlling of shared resources between processes and threads. Implementations are presented for OS/2, AIX, and Windows NT.

Communication Mechanisms

Clipboard, DDE, and OLE facilities are familiar to many programmers because they are supported by Windows 3.x. However, Windows does not support the IPC capabilities built into 32-bit operating systems such as AIX, OS/2, and Windows NT. These powerful APIs enable sophisticated access to and sharing of information between processes and threads running in the same environment. The most common of these communication mechanisms are semaphores, shared memory, queues, and named pipes.

A semaphore is really just a flag indicating that an event has occurred or that data is locked and should not be changed by another process. While you can certainly define your own flag as a global variable in a DLL that other processes can use for signaling or resource locking, problems can arise. For instance, in a preemptive-multitasking environment, a task may be preempted at any time, even while trying to access or change a flag. This can cause synchronization problems unless the flag is controlled at the kernel level of the operating system in cooperation with the task scheduler. Thus, operating systems provide a semaphore API for creating and controlling semaphores.

There are two basic types of semaphores: mutex (mutual exclusion) and event. Mutex semaphores are used primarily to control access to some kind of shared resource: shared memory, database records, files, and the like. Event semaphores signal that an event has occurred, allowing other processes waiting on that event to continue. This facilitates synchronizing tasks that need to cooperate or allowing a process to wait until some kind of required initialization is complete.

Shared-memory address space is a block of memory created by one process or thread and made available to other running processes. Any process or thread that has access to the memory can use it just as if the memory were a part of the application's own address space. Memory is usually accessed through a unique name known to all processes needing to use it. Obviously, if two or more processes are writing to the shared-memory space simultaneously, the resulting data could be garbled, so a mutex semaphore is typically used to ensure that access is sequential.

Figure 12.1 schematically shows how two processes share the same address space. Shared memory typically offers the best performance in sharing data among applications, but other techniques may be more appropriate for client/server programming.

Message queues are familiar to GUI programmers who use event-driven message loops to dispatch messages to window procedures. Windowing systems typically provide functions for posting messages to windows in the same or other applications, but these functions do not work for character-mode programs. However, a message queue communication mechanism exists that is valid for both character-mode and window-mode applications: A queue may be created by a server application, which then reads messages from the queue and processes them one at a time. Multiple client applications can then access the queue and write messages to the server, and the operating system synchronizes the queue so that messages originating from different sources will not intermingle (Figure 12.2).

The server can examine the queue to see if any messages are waiting and can optionally purge all messages from the queue. Because this queue API is separate from the underlying window system API, both window–message loops and queue–message loops may be running in the same application, possibly in different threads.

Pipes are buffer areas that allow processes to communicate with each other as if they were reading and writing files. Pipes can be either named or unnamed. Some operating systems (such as OS/2 and NT) allow named-pipe communications not only between applications on the same system, but also between applications running on

Figure 12.1   Shared memory between two processes
(P1 and P2).

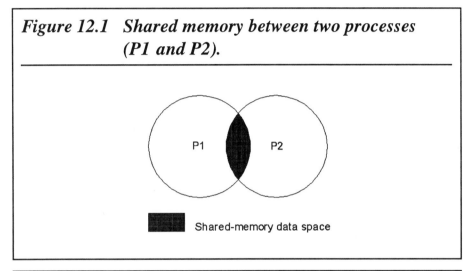

Figure 12.2   A message queue with a server and two
client processes.

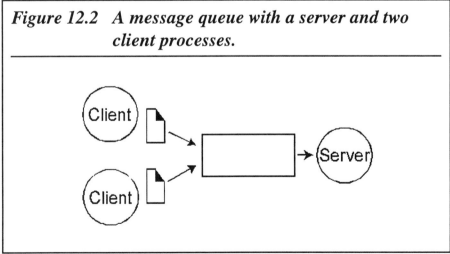

different systems connected via a network. A server process creates a named pipe, and one or more client processes open it and establish connections (Figure 12.3). Once the connection is established, the pipe is treated as a regular file handle, and the standard file I/O methods are used to transfer data across the pipe.

Writing Cross-Platform Classes

OS/2, AIX, and Windows NT implement the IPC features described up to this point. Unfortunately, there is no standard for these features' functional interface, so each vendor provides a custom API. What programmers need is an API that is consistent across all platforms to minimize the operating-system-dependent part of their code.

The preprocessor definitions, macros, and data types for each operating system are all different. To avoid having users of your communication library deal with this at the API level, you can separate the library class APIs from the implementation of the classes, which must necessarily be different on each platform. While there are many ways of doing this in C++, I'll undertake the separation for this library by defining a single interface class (InterfaceClass) that contains an instance of the operating-system-specific implementation class (ImplementationClass).

InterfaceClass is packaged as a class declaration (in ifclass.h) as in Figure 12.4(a). The file ifclass.C contains method invocations which call the corresponding method in the ImplementationClass instance [Figure 12.4(b)]. Now the implementation class header (defined in imclass.h) can still be operating system independent (or #ifdefs can be included to encapsulate the dependent parts) [Figure 12.4(c)]. Furthermore, as Figure 12.4(d) shows, you can define three separate implementations of the constructor and destructor ImplementationClass to handle the individual operating systems (os2impl.C, aiximpl.C, and winimpl.C).

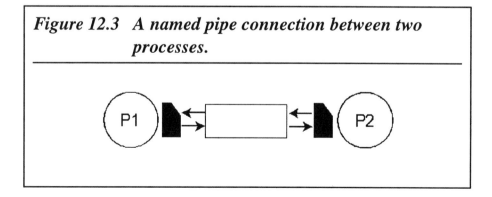

Figure 12.3   A named pipe connection between two processes.

To package the class library for distribution, compile the `ifclass.C` module and the appropriate implementation module for the current operating system (for OS/2, compile `os2impl.C`). You then either link the modules as a DLL or make a static library. The distribution files are simply the `ifclass.h` file and the library module for each operating system. Each platform uses the same header file containing the class declaration, so platform-independent applications can be written using `InterfaceClass`.

Figure 12.4 Defining a single interface class.

(a) `InterfaceClass` packaged as a class declaration;
(b) method invocations which call the corresponding method in `ImplementationClass`;
(c) implementation of class header can still be independent of the operating system;
(d) defining three separate implementations of the constructor and destructor `ImplementationClass`.

(a) `ifclass.h`
```
// forward declaration
class ImplementationClass;

// interface class declaration
class InterfaceClass {
friend class ImplementationClass;
public:
   // constructor and destructor
   InterfaceClass();
   virtual ~InterfaceClass();
   void SomeMethod();            // invoked by class user
protected:
   ImplementationClass *myImpl; // pointer to implementation
};
```

(b) `ifclass.C`
```
void InterfaceClass::SomeMethod()
{
  myImpl->SomeMethod();
}
```

Semaphores

To illustrate, I'll implement named semaphores, because AIX requires a name for the ftok() function I'll use later. Also, you may need to query for the name and type of semaphore and perhaps access the semaphore ID created by the underlying operating system. You can implement all of these generic methods in an abstract base class, and derive specialty classes for the mutex and event semaphores from the base class.

Figure 12.4 (continued)

(c) `imclass.h`

```
class ImplementationClass {
public:
    // constructor and destructor
    ImplementationClass();
    virtual ~ImplementationClass();
    void SomeMethod();   // invoked by InterfaceClass
};
```

(d)

```
// os2impl.C
#define INCL_DOS
#include <os2.h>
void ImplementationClass::SomeMethod()
{
    // call OS/2 specific functions
}
// aiximpl.C
#include <sys/ipc.h>
void ImplementationClass::SomeMethod()
{
    // call AIX specific functions
}
// winimpl.C
#include <windows.h>
void ImplementationClass::SomeMethod()
{
    // call Windows NT specific functions
}
```

The Abstract Base Class

Listing 12.1 shows the class declaration for the abstract base class ipcSemaphore. All of the interface classes and data types are given an ipc prefix to avoid possible namespace collisions when linking with other libraries. Two enumerated types are defined in this file: ipcSemaphoreType holds the type of semaphore (mutex or event), and ipcSemaphoreOp defines whether the semaphore is being created by the owner of the semaphore (semcreate) or already exists and is being accessed (semaccess).

Listing 12.1   Declaration for ipcSemaphore *class.*

```
// ************************************************************************
// Module:  ipcsem.h   --  Author:  Dick Lam
// Purpose: C++ class header file for ipcSemaphore
// Notes:   This is an abstract base class.  It is the interface class for
//          semaphores used in signalling between processes and threads.
// ************************************************************************

#ifndef MODULE_ipcSemaphoreh
#define MODULE_ipcSemaphoreh

// semaphore type designation and operation type
enum ipcSemaphoreType { unknown = 0, mutex = 1, event = 2 };
enum ipcSemaphoreOp { semcreate = 0, semaccess = 1 };

// forward declaration
class osSemaphore;

// class declaration
class ipcSemaphore {

friend class osSemaphore;

public:
    // constructor and destructor
    ipcSemaphore(const char *name,         // unique name for semaphore
                 ipcSemaphoreType type,     // mutex or event
                 ipcSemaphoreOp operation);// create or access the semaphore
    virtual ~ipcSemaphore();

    // methods for getting semaphore parameters [name, semaphore id, type of
    // semaphore (mutex or event) and whether this is the owner (creator)
    // of the semaphore]   char *Name() const;   unsigned long ID() const;
    ipcSemaphoreType Type() const;
    int Owner() const;

    // pure virtual query method for number of requests made for the semaphore
    // (must be redefined in derived classes)
    virtual unsigned long Query() = 0;
```

Listing 12.1 (continued)

```
// class version and object state data types
enum version { MajorVersion = 1, MinorVersion = 0 };
enum state { good = 0, bad = 1, badname = 2, notfound = 3 };

// methods to get the object state
inline int rdstate() const { return myState; }
inline int operator!() const { return(myState != good); }
protected:
  osSemaphore *myImpl;     // implementation
  state myState;           // (object state (good, bad, etc.)
private:
  // private copy constructor and operator= (define these and make them
  // public to enable copy and assignment of the class)
  ipcSemaphore(const ipcSemaphore&);
  ipcSemaphore& operator=(const ipcSemaphore&);
};
#endif
```

Listing 12.2   `ossem.h` — Declaration for `osSemaphore` class.

```
// ************************************************************************
// Module:  ossem.h  --  Author:  Dick Lam
// Purpose: C++ class header file for osSemaphore
// Notes:   This is a base class.  It contains general implementation methods
//          for semaphores used in signalling between processes and threads.
// ************************************************************************

#ifndef MODULE_osSemaphoreh
#define MODULE_osSemaphoreh
#include "ipcsem.h"
// class declaration
class osSemaphore {

public:
  // constructor and destructor
  osSemaphore(ipcSemaphore *interface, const char *name,
              ipcSemaphoreType type, ipcSemaphoreOp operation);
  virtual ~osSemaphore();
  // methods for getting semaphore parameters [name, semaphore id, type of
  // semaphore (mutex or event) and whether this is the owner (creator)
  // of the semaphore]
  char *Name() const;
  unsigned long ID() const;
  ipcSemaphoreType Type() const;
  int Owner() const;
```

The base class constructor takes arguments corresponding to a unique name for the semaphore, type, and operation. Processes or threads that access the semaphore only need to know the name and type of the semaphore to use it.

Methods are also defined for returning the semaphore name, underlying operating system semaphore ID (as an unsigned long), semaphore type, and whether the current process or thread is the owner (creator) of the semaphore. The last method, Query(), is a pure virtual method that queries the semaphore and returns the number of requests pending on it.

The last member is a pointer to the osSemaphore class. This friend class has its declaration in ossem.h (Listing 12.2). osSemaphore is the operating-system-independent implementation class corresponding to the imclass.h mentioned earlier.

Listing 12.2 *(continued)*

```
   // mutex semaphore methods
   void CreateMutex();
   void OpenMutex();
   void RequestMutex();
   void ReleaseMutex();
   unsigned long QueryMutex();
   void CloseMutex();

   // event semaphore methods
   void CreateEvent();
   void OpenEvent();
   void PostEvent();
   void ResetEvent();
   void WaitEvent();
   unsigned long QueryEvent();
   void CloseEvent();
protected:
   ipcSemaphore *myInterface;    // pointer to the interface instance
   char *myName;                 // semaphore name, id and type
   unsigned long myID;
   ipcSemaphoreType myType;
   int isOwner;                  // flag indicating whether this is owner
private:
   // private copy constructor and operator= (define these and make them
   // public to enable copy and assignment of the class)
   osSemaphore(const osSemaphore&);
   osSemaphore& operator=(const osSemaphore&);
};
#endif
```

Listing 12.3 `ipcsem.C`— *Implementation of* `ipcSemaphore` *class.*

```
// **************************************************************************
// Module: ipcsem.C   -- Author: Dick Lam
// Purpose: C++ class source file for ipcSemaphore
// Notes:   This is an abstract base class.  It is the interface class for
//          semaphores used in signalling between processes and threads.
// **************************************************************************
#include "ipcsem.h"
#include "ossem.h"
// **************************************************************************
// ipcSemaphore - constructor
ipcSemaphore::ipcSemaphore(const char *name, ipcSemaphoreType type,
                           ipcSemaphoreOp operation)
{
   // init instance variables
   myState = good;
   myImpl = new osSemaphore(this, name, type, operation);
   if (!myImpl)
      myState = bad;
}
// --------------------------------------------------------------------------
// ~ipcSemaphore - destructor
ipcSemaphore::~ipcSemaphore()
{
   delete myImpl;
}
// --------------------------------------------------------------------------
// Name - returns the name of the semaphore
char *ipcSemaphore::Name() const
{
   if (!myImpl)
     return 0;
   return myImpl->Name();
}
// --------------------------------------------------------------------------
// ID - returns the semaphore id
unsigned long ipcSemaphore::ID() const{
   if (!myImpl)
      return 0L;
   return myImpl->ID();
}
// --------------------------------------------------------------------------
// Type - returns the type of semaphore
ipcSemaphoreType ipcSemaphore::Type() const
{
   if (!myImpl)
    return unknown;
   return myImpl->Type();
}
```

Listing 12.3 is the interface class. The `ipcSemaphore` constructor simply creates an instance of `osSemaphore` that is deleted by the destructor. The other member functions use this instance of the implementation class to call the corresponding function in that class. For example, the `ipcSemaphore::Name()` method calls `myImpl->Name()`.

Mutex Semaphores

Mutex semaphores control access to some resource. They have two basic functions which our class must implement — request and release. When a process (or thread) requests a mutex semaphore, the process either obtains "ownership" of the semaphore immediately or is blocked until another process releases the semaphore.

Listing 12.3 (continued)

```
// -----------------------------------------------------------------------
// Owner - returns 1 if this is the owner (creator), and 0 otherwise
int ipcSemaphore::Owner() const
{
    if (!myImpl)
      return 0;
    return myImpl->Owner();
}
```

Listing 12.4   *ipcmutex.h — Declaration for ipcMutexSemaphore class.*

```
// ***********************************************************************
// Module:  ipcmutex.h  -- Author:  Dick Lam
// Purpose: C++ class header file for ipcMutexSemaphore
// Notes:   This class is derived from ipcSemaphore.  It is an interface class
//          for mutex semaphores that can be used to control access to a shared
//          resource across processes or threads.
// ***********************************************************************

#ifndef MODULE_ipcMutexSemaphoreh
#define MODULE_ipcMutexSemaphoreh
#include "ipcsem.h"
// class declaration
class ipcMutexSemaphore : public ipcSemaphore {

public:
    // constructor and destructor
    ipcMutexSemaphore(const char *name, ipcSemaphoreOp operation = semcreate);
    virtual ~ipcMutexSemaphore();
```

The semaphore is then "owned" by the requesting process, and requests for the semaphore by other processes are blocked until the "owner" releases the semaphore.

Listing 12.4 shows the class declaration for ipcMutexSemaphore, which is derived from our abstract base class. The Query() method provides an implementation for the pure virtual method in the base class and Request() and Release() methods for the allowed operations on mutex semaphores.

The implementation of this class is given in ipcmutex.C (Listing 12.5). In the constructor, the ipcSemaphoreOp operation is checked and used to call either CreateMutex() or OpenMutex() in the osSemaphore class instance myImpl (defined as "protected" in the base class). The destructor calls the myImpl->CloseMutex() method, and the other three methods call their corresponding methods in myImpl. Listing 12.2 shows prototypes for these five member functions included in the public section of osSemaphore.

Listing 12.4 (continued)

```
    // query method for number of requests made
    virtual unsigned long Query();

    // request and release methods (to lock and unlock resources)
    virtual void Request();
    virtual void Release();
private:
    // private copy constructor and operator= (define these and make them
    // public to enable copy and assignment of the class)
    ipcMutexSemaphore(const ipcMutexSemaphore&);
    ipcMutexSemaphore& operator=(const ipcMutexSemaphore&);
};
#endif
```

Listing 12.5 ipcmutex.C — Implementation of ipcMutexSemaphore class.

```
// ************************************************************************
// Module:  ipcmutex.C  -- Author:  Dick Lam
// Purpose: C++ class source file for ipcMutexSemaphore
// Notes:   This class is derived from ipcSemaphore.  It is an interface class
//          for mutex semaphores that can be used to control access to a shared
//          resource across processes or threads.
// ************************************************************************
#include "ipcmutex.h"
#include "ossem.h"
```

Listing 12.5 (continued)

```
// ************************************************************************
// ipcMutexSemaphore - constructor
ipcMutexSemaphore::ipcMutexSemaphore(const char *name,ipcSemaphoreOp operation)
   : ipcSemaphore(name, mutex, operation)
{
   // check the state of the object
   if (myState != good)
       return;
   // create or open the semaphore
   if (operation == semcreate)
     myImpl->CreateMutex();
   else if (operation == semaccess)
     myImpl->OpenMutex();
}
// ------------------------------------------------------------------------
// ~ipcMutexSemaphore - destructor
ipcMutexSemaphore::~ipcMutexSemaphore()
{
   // close the semaphore
   if (myState == good)
       myImpl->CloseMutex();
}
// ------------------------------------------------------------------------
// Query - returns the number of requests made of the semaphore
unsigned long ipcMutexSemaphore::Query()
{
   if (myState == good)
      return myImpl->QueryMutex();
   return 0L;
}
// ------------------------------------------------------------------------
// Request - requests the semaphore
void ipcMutexSemaphore::Request()
{
   if (myState == good)
     myImpl->RequestMutex();
}
// ------------------------------------------------------------------------
// Release - releases the semaphore
void ipcMutexSemaphore::Release()
{
   if (myState == good)
       myImpl->ReleaseMutex();
}
```

Event Semaphores

Event semaphores synchronize operations between processes or threads. The terminology is different from mutex semaphores, and there are three basic operations instead of two. For example, if application A wants to start application B and wait for AppB to perform some operation before continuing, AppA first creates and resets an event semaphore. AppB is then started, and AppA does a wait on the event semaphore. When AppB is done with its operation, it accesses the event semaphore and posts it, causing AppA to unblock and continue execution.

Listing 12.6 `ipcevent.h` *— Declaration of* `ipcEventSemaphore` *class.*

```
// ***********************************************************************
// Module:  ipcevent.h -- Author:  Dick Lam
// Purpose: C++ class header file for ipcEventSemaphore
// Notes:   This class is derived from ipcSemaphore.  It is an interface class
//          for event semaphores that can be used to signal events across
//          processes or threads.
// ***********************************************************************

#ifndef MODULE_ipcEventSemaphoreh
#define MODULE_ipcEventSemaphoreh

#include "ipcsem.h"

// class declaration
class ipcEventSemaphore : public ipcSemaphore {

public:
   // constructor and destructor
   ipcEventSemaphore(const char *name, ipcSemaphoreOp operation = semcreate);
   virtual ~ipcEventSemaphore();
   // query method for number of requests made
   virtual unsigned long Query();
   // post, reset and wait methods
   virtual void Post();
   virtual void Reset();
   virtual void Wait();
private:
   // private copy constructor and operator= (define these and make them
   // public to enable copy and assignment of the class)
   ipcEventSemaphore(const ipcEventSemaphore&);
   ipcEventSemaphore& operator=(const ipcEventSemaphore&);
};
#endif
```

Listings 12.6 and 12.7 show the declaration and implementation for ipcEvent-Semaphore. This closely parallels the structure of ipcMutexSemaphore, except that the Request() and Release() methods are replaced by Reset(), Wait(), and Post(). The constructor also tests the operation flag argument and calls either CreateEvent() or OpenEvent(); the destructor calls CloseEvent(). Note that all of these functions are also included in the public section of the declaration for osSemaphore. Now that the interface to the two semaphore types has been defined, we are ready to look at the actual implementations on each operating system.

Listing 12.7 ipceven.C — *Implementation of* ipcEventSemaphore *class.*

```
// ************************************************************************
// Module:  ipcevent.C  -- Author:  Dick Lam
// Purpose: C++ class source file for ipcEventSemaphore
// Notes:   This class is derived from ipcSemaphore.  It is an interface class
//          for event semaphores that can be used to signal events across
//          processes or threads.
// ************************************************************************
#include "ipcevent.h"
#include "ossem.h"
// ************************************************************************
// ipcEventSemaphore - constructor
ipcEventSemaphore::ipcEventSemaphore(const char *name,ipcSemaphoreOp operation)
   : ipcSemaphore(name, event, operation)
{
   // check the state of the object
   if (myState != good)
      return;
   // create or open the semaphore
   if (operation == semcreate)
     myImpl->CreateEvent();
   else if (operation == semaccess)
     myImpl->OpenEvent();
}
// ----------------------------------------------------------------------
// ~ipcEventSemaphore - destructor
ipcEventSemaphore::~ipcEventSemaphore()
{
   // close the semaphore
   if (myState == good)
     myImpl->CloseEvent();
}
```

The *os Semaphore* Implementations

The modules that implement the os Semaphore class for OS/2 (os2sem.C), AIX (aixsem.C), and Windows NT (winsem.C) are available on the code disk. Each module includes the header files specific to that operating system plus ossem.h, the class declaration for os Semaphore. Because the operating system dependencies are buried here, users of these classes need not compile with complicated preprocessor definitions and Include files that specify the target operating environment.

The constructors for all three implementations are almost identical. OS/2 requires system semaphores to have a path name such as \SEM32\name, and AIX requires a name for the ftok() function, which returns a key required to obtain UNIX interprocess communication identifiers. Therefore, both os2sem.C and aixsem.C define a

---

Listing 12.7 (continued)

```
// -----------------------------------------------------------------
// Query - returns the number of requests made of the semaphore
unsigned long ipcEventSemaphore::Query()
{
    if (myState == good)
     return myImpl->QueryEvent();
    return 0L;
}
// -----------------------------------------------------------------
// Post - posts the semaphore
void ipcEventSemaphore::Post()
{
    if (myState == good)
        myImpl->PostEvent();
}
// -----------------------------------------------------------------
// Reset - resets the semaphore
void ipcEventSemaphore::Reset()
{
    if (myState == good)
        myImpl->ResetEvent();
}
// -----------------------------------------------------------------
// Wait - waits for a semaphore event to be posted
void ipcEventSemaphore::Wait()
{
    if (myState == good)
        myImpl->WaitEvent();
}
```

semPath string constant at the top of the module, and semPath and the name argument are used to form the full semaphore name stored in the myName instance variable. Also, a file with the name of the semaphore must exist on AIX, and it is created in aixsem.C if the ipcSemaphoreOp type is semcreate.

Note that the constructor takes a pointer to the ipcSemaphore interface instance that creates the osSemaphore. Because osSemaphore is also declared as a friend of ipcSemaphore, the osSemaphore methods can change the myState variable (declared in ipcsem.h). The user can then call rdstate() (or use the ! operator) to get information on the state of the semaphore.

The destructors delete the memory allocated in the constructors for the full semaphore path name, and the AIX destructor also deletes the file and removes the semaphore using a call to semctl(). The other methods for returning the name, ID, type, and owner are all the same in each file and could arguably be put in the interface base class implementation. However, this would require exposing the protected variables representing these values to the user of the semaphore classes. You also could have placed the common code in an abstract implementation base class and derived specific implementation classes from it, but the current structure is adequate for our needs.

CreateMutex(), OpenMutex(), and the like are the remaining methods, and they simply call the API functions appropriate for each operating system. For example, DosCreateMutexSem() is the OS/2 function that creates a mutex semaphore, whereas the ftok() and semget() functions are required under AIX. For Windows NT, macros are defined in winbase.h that must be undefined to avoid conflicts with the CreateMutex(), OpenMutex(), CreateEvent(), and OpenEvent() methods. Then the Win32 functions ::CreateMutexA(), ::OpenMutexA(), and the like are called directly.

Conclusion

I have defined a cross-platform implementation of mutex and event semaphores with an interface class that has no operating system dependencies. You only need to compile the modules on the appropriate system and distribute the object module or DLL and the three header files ipcsem.h, ipcmutex.h, and ipcevent.h.

The test programs semtest1.C and semtest2.C (available on the code disk) can be compiled on all three systems using the code presented in this chapter. These programs illustrate how the mutex and event semaphores can synchronize two processes.

## Chapter 13

How to Write an NT Service

Paula Tomlinson

Windows 95 and Windows NT share a common API for the most part, but some important features are only available under NT. One such feature, NT services, not only offers the NT equivalent of UNIX "daemons," but also makes it possible to create programs that can perform privileged operations on behalf of less privileged users. Services are a logical choice for the server side of client/server NT software. This chapter explains what NT services are and provides a template program that you can easily alter to get your own NT service up and running.

What Is a Service?

The term "service" in Windows NT is used to denote both a special kind of Win32 process and Windows NT kernel-mode device drivers. In fact, a component of the operating system known as the "service controller" (or "service control manager," or SCM) is used to load and control both types of services. For the rest of this chapter, when I use the term "service," I will be referring to the special Win32 processes (not device drivers). In that context, a service is more or less a program that gets executed by NT (as opposed to getting directly executed by a user) and that responds to special requests to start, pause, or stop execution.

Services have some special capabilities beyond those of the typical Win32 process. For one thing, you can tell NT to start your service when the system loads, before any users have logged on. That makes services a good choice for software that needs to start automatically and run constantly in the background, whenever the system is up. For example, if you want to write a program that continually monitors changes to files in a particular directory [using the `FindFirstChangeNotification()` function], you might want to implement that program as a service so that users cannot make unobserved changes to the file before your monitor program starts running.

Another important feature of services has to do with NT security. When you log onto NT, your account gives you certain privileges. Every program you execute has only those privileges, no more. Under UNIX, it's possible to create a privileged program that unprivileged users can execute, but you can't do that under NT (there's no "setuid bit" in NT).

Services, however, are executed by NT (not directly by you) and are associated at installation time with a particular account. In effect, a service logs on as a separate user, so although your account may not have the privileges needed to access some special file, you can ask NT to start up a service that does have the necessary privileges to do so (assuming a privileged user created such a service and gave you permission to use it). When you want to allow users to perform some privileged operation or access some special file in very restricted circumstances, consider writing a service.

Figure 13.1   The Services control panel applet.

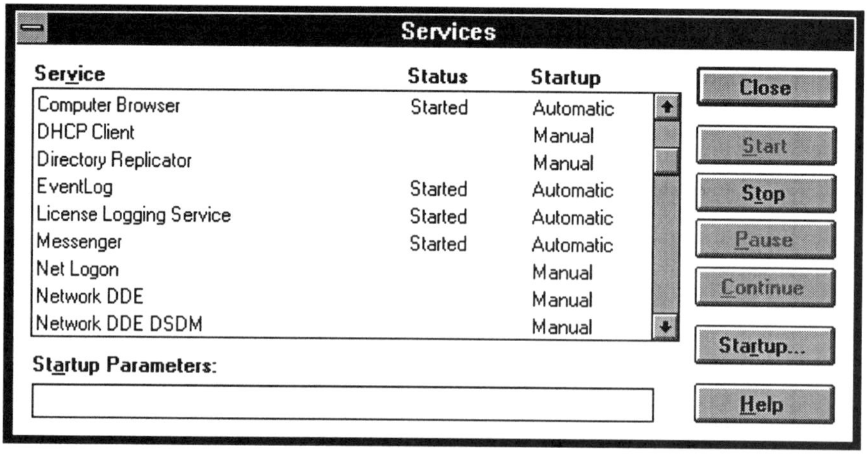

That way, the user gets to perform the privileged operation — but only via your program. [The new NT function LogonUser() offers an alternative, but less secure, method of writing programs that acquire the privileges of some other account.]

Another handy feature of services is that they obey a common API for starting, pausing, stopping, etc. Once you write your service, any user can use the standard "Services" control panel applet (Figure 13.1) to control it (assuming you have the necessary privileges). For instance, the user can pause a service and then continue it later. The configuration information (such as when and how a service starts) can be viewed and modified via the service controller. Services can even establish elaborate dependency lists on other services and control their load order among other services. What's even nicer is that much of the capability of the service controller is made available to applications in the form of a service controller API. These routines are implemented as an RPC server and are thus extensible to other machines (i.e., you can control services on other machines if you have sufficient privilege). The "Services" control panel applet uses these routines to allow users to view and configure all the services currently installed on a system. That's one reason why services are an attractive choice for the server side of client/server software; if you implement your server program as a service, all the work of letting client-side users administer your program (start it up, check if it's running, and so on) is already done for you.

Services have many uses. Background processes that used to be implemented as DOS TSRs or perhaps UNIX daemons are good candidates for Windows NT services. Other examples of processes that are well suited as services include RPC servers, communications programs, utility programs such as virus scanners, and backup programs. The Windows NT operating system itself uses services extensively. The Event-Log service is a classic example of a Win32 service. It is implemented as a service within the services.exe process (which contains several other services) and uses RPC, so that the event log routines it exports are available to remote machines. Of course, the EventLog service must be available before logon so that it can receive events that occur while the system is booting. The network subsystem also makes extensive use of services to manage network communication.

Installing a Service

It might seem a bit odd to discuss how something is installed before you've even written it, but demonstrating how services are installed highlights some of the major design decisions and characteristics of a service. (Also see the sidebar "Design Decisions for Services.") The service controller manages services by maintaining a database of information in the Registry. Each service has a subkey under HKEY_LOCAL_MACHINE\System\CurrentControlSet\Services. Each service entry contains standard information that tells the service controller how to manage the service. Although some developers install their services by writing information directly to the Registry, I strongly discourage this practice. The location and format of the service database is internal to the Windows NT operating system and thus could change in future versions. A much safer practice is to use the service controller routines.

In `instsrv.c` (Listing 13.1) I wrote a very simple console application to demonstrate installing a service programmatically. You must call `OpenSCManager()` first to establish a connection with the service controller. When I call `CreateService()`, the service controller adds the information I've specified about this new service to its service database. In addition to the handle to the service controller, `CreateService()`

Design Decisions for Services

When you create a service that is not a device driver, you have to make a few decisions before calling `CreateService()` to install your service in the service controller database:

- *What name will you use for your service?* The convention is to use the name of the module containing your service (e.g., `mysrvice.exe` uses a service name of `mysrvice`).

- *What display name will you use for your service?* This is just a text string that the "Services" applet will display to users.

- *Where will you store your service?* By convention, most services reside in the `windows\system32` directory.

- *What access will you grant to your service?* The easiest (but least secure) choice is `SERVICE_ALL_ACCESS`, which allows all the possible operations on your service.

- *Are you creating a single executable that exports more than one service?* If so, use a service type of `SERVICE_WIN32_SHARE_PROCESS` rather than `SERVICE_WIN32_OWN_PROCESS`.

- *Does your service need to start automatically when the system starts?* If so, you will pass `SERVICE_AUTO_START` instead of `SERVICE_DEMAND_START`.

- *Does your service start automatically at boot time?* If so, you need to decide how important a failure is. `SERVICE_IGNORE_ERROR` is the parameter to use for demand load services or if you want to log an error, but not display a message to the user.

- *Does your service depend on any other service?* If your service starts automatically at boot time, you can control the load order.

- *Does your service share a `.exe` with other services?* If not, you can specify what account the service will run under. Otherwise, if you selected `SERVICE_WIN32_SHARE_PROCESS` for the service type, the service will run under the default account: "LocalSystem." If the account has a password, you will also have to pass that to `CreateService()`. Make sure the account has the privileges and access that your service needs to execute (e.g., ODBC access).

Listing 13.1 `instsrv.c`— *Program to install a service.*

```c
#include <windows.h>
#include <stdio.h>
#include <tchar.h>
#include "srvctmpl.h"

// Borland C++ v4.52 does not support VC-specific
// Unicode functions _tprintf, etc.
#ifdef __BORLANDC__
// therefore, don't compile this with Unicode enabled!
#    define _tprintf    printf
#    define _stprintf   sprintf
#endif

VOID main(VOID)
{
    SC_HANDLE   hSCManager = NULL, hService = NULL;
    TCHAR       szWinDir[MAX_PATH], szImagePath[MAX_PATH];

    if((hSCManager = OpenSCManager(NULL, NULL,
        SC_MANAGER_CREATE_SERVICE)) == NULL) {
            _tprintf(TEXT("OpenSCManager Failed\n"));
            return;
    }

    GetWindowsDirectory(szWinDir, MAX_PATH);
    _stprintf(szImagePath, TEXT("%s\\system32\\%s.exe"),
        szWinDir, GENSRV_ServiceName);

    if ((hService = CreateService(hSCManager,
        GENSRV_ServiceName,
        GENSRV_DisplayName, SERVICE_ALL_ACCESS,
        SERVICE_WIN32_OWN_PROCESS, SERVICE_DEMAND_START,
        SERVICE_ERROR_IGNORE, szImagePath, NULL, NULL,
        NULL, NULL, NULL)) == NULL) {
            _tprintf(TEXT("CreateService Failed, %d\n"),
                GetLastError());
                return;
    }

    CloseServiceHandle(hService);
    CloseServiceHandle(hSCManager);
    _tprintf(TEXT("%s installed successfully\n"),
        szImagePath);
}
```

requires a long list of other parameters, including several forms of the service name. The second parameter is the name that the service controller uses internally and by convention is usually the file name of the service without the .exe extension. The third parameter is the name you want to be displayed in the services applet for users to see. The eighth parameter is the fully qualified path of the service file (by convention, services are placed in the windows\system32 directory). In srvctmpl.h (Listing 13.2), I added definitions for both the internal service name (WDJSrvc) and the display name (WDJ Sample Service) of my sample service so that I can refer to these names in several files.

The fourth parameter to CreateService() specifies what kind of access to your service you're granting to other processes. When a process attempts to query or control this service, the service control manager will check the access token of the calling process against the access you specified when you created the service. For my sample service, I chose to grant broad access by specifying SERVICE_ALL_ACCESS.

Because this is a Win32 service (as opposed to a kernel-mode device driver), the only two choices for service type are SERVICE_WIN32_OWN_PROCESS and SERVICE_WIN32_SHARE_PROCESS. Because my sample executable image will only contain a single service, I specified SERVICE_WIN32_OWN_PROCESS.

The dwStartType parameter controls how the service will be started. The options available to Win32 services are SERVICE_AUTO_START (the service will be started when the system starts), SERVICE_DEMAND_START (the service will be started if another process starts it), and SERVICE_DISABLED (the service is installed but can't be started). I chose SERVICE_DEMAND_START for the sample service because it's not required to be running before logon. The dwErrorControl parameter is not really relevant for services that are demand started, because this parameter controls how the system will respond if the service fails to start during boot. Just to be safe, I specified

---

Listing 13.2 srvctmpl.h *— Definitions for generic service.**

```
#define GENSRV_ServiceName        TEXT("WDJSrvc")
#define GENSRV_DisplayName        TEXT("WDJ Sample Service")

// prototypes
BOOL ServiceInitialization(DWORD, LPTSTR *);
VOID ServiceTermination(VOID);
DWORD MainServiceThread(LPDWORD);
```

SERVICE_ERROR_IGNORE so that any problems my service might encounter while starting will not affect the rest of the operating system.

Although my simple service is a stand-alone, you can also specify dependencies and load order in the call to CreateService(). Dependencies can refer to specific services or groups of services, so in addition to specifying services that your service is dependent on, you can also specify that your service is part of a group of services which another service can claim a dependency on. Further, you can specify a tag value that indicates what order your service is loaded in among its group.

Finally, you can specify what account the service will run under when it's started. Remember that your service may start before a user even logs on, so services get to make selections about their own logon account. When the service process is started, the service controller logs onto the account specified and attaches the resulting access token to the newly started service. The default account, "LocalSystem," is the only option available to services of type SERVICE_WIN32_SHARE_PROCESS. Single-service processes can specify an account in either the local (built-in), primary, or trusted domains. If the account has a password, then you'll be required to provide that in the lpPassword parameter. One disadvantage of specifying a particular logon account is that you would need to reinstall [or reconfigure using ChangeServiceConfig()] your service if the account name or password changed. Remember that your service will have only the privileges of that account. So, for example, if you install a database library that your service uses, make sure the service's account has the permissions needed to access the library. Also remember that your service may run before any user has logged on, which means that the registry key HKEY_LOCAL_USER may not be set to what you expect. Ideally, your service will only depend on machine-specific Registry information, not user-specific Registry information.

If CreateService() returns successfully, the service is installed. A demand start service can then be immediately controlled by calling the service controller routines or using the "Services" control panel applet (or the console "net" command). CreateService() will fail if the service is already installed. Services can only be demand started by calling the StartService() service controller routine, not by starting them from the command line.

The Service Interface

A service may start running before any users are logged on, so services generally don't have an extensive user interface and are often written as console programs, rather than windowed programs. Apart from that, the main thing that distinguishes a service from an ordinary NT program is that a service cooperates with the service control manager. Figure 13.2 shows a rough overview.

The situation is made slightly complicated by the fact that you are allowed to create a single .exe that contains more than one logical service. To accomplish this, your .exe has to pass the service controller the address(es) of the function(s) that do the work of the service(s). The service controller then uses each of these functions to create a thread that does the actual work of the service.

Figure 13.2   Overview of how a service works.

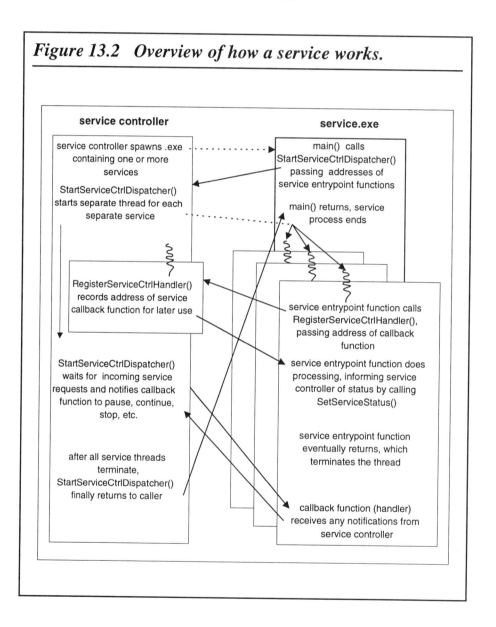

Here is a more detailed description of the process: immediately after a service starts up, it calls StartServiceCtrlDispatcher() to notify the service controller that it is executing and to provide the addresses of the service functions. It sounds a little confusing, but StartServiceCtrlDispatcher() does not return until much later. That's because it starts a thread for each of your services and then waits for them to terminate. In fact, StartServiceCtrlDispatcher() does not just wait for the threads to terminate, it also waits for any incoming commands aimed at your service (e.g., pause, continue, stop) and notifies the appropriate thread of such events. To make things simpler, I'll assume in the rest of this discussion that your .exe is only providing one service.

So, while your main() is still waiting for StartServiceCtrlDispatcher() to return, a separate thread starts up and calls the function whose address you passed to StartServiceCtrlDispatcher(). This function is expected to do the main work of your service, but first it has to establish a protocol for communicating with the service controller. It does this by passing the address of a callback function to RegisterServiceCtrlHandler(), which returns a handle. As your service thread is executing, the service controller may have to call the callback function to notify your service that it should pause, stop, continue, etc. Your service thread will have to pass to SetServiceStatus() the handle that RegisterServiceCtrlHandler() returned, in order to inform the service controller that it has responded to the notification correctly.

It seems odd that you have to explicitly call SetServiceStatus() to respond to a notification from the service controller, rather than just returning some value from the callback function. The idea is that your service may need a bit of time to respond to an individual request. Thus, for example, when you receive a notification to pause your service, you are expected to respond immediately with a code that means "the pause is pending." Then, when you finally achieve the paused state, you are supposed to call SetServiceStatus() again with a code that means "I'm paused now." In fact, you can even use SetServiceStatus() to tell the service controller how long you think it will take to respond to a given request; if it takes longer than that, the service controller can then assume something went wrong in your service.

The Service Template

I've created a sample service that you can revise to create your own service. To make it easier to reuse this code, I've structured the service in two files. The first file, srvctmpl.c (Listing 13.3), contains the standard header part of a service and can be used directly with little modification for most basic service applications. The second file, wdjsrvc.c (Listing 13.4), is a trivial example of the service-specific code you would provide to fill out the rest of the service.

Listing 13.3 *srvctmpl.c — Stub functions for generic service.*

```c
#include <windows.h>
#include <stdio.h>
#include "srvctmpl.h"

// private prototypes
BOOL NotifySCM(DWORD, DWORD, DWORD);
VOID ServiceMain(DWORD, LPTSTR *);
VOID ServiceHandler(DWORD);

HANDLE   hDoneEvent = NULL, hThread = NULL;
DWORD    dwCurrentState;
SERVICE_STATUS_HANDLE  hService;

//------------------------------------------------------------
void main(void)
{
    SERVICE_TABLE_ENTRY ServiceTable[] = {
        {GENSRV_ServiceName, (LPSERVICE_MAIN_FUNCTION)ServiceMain},
        {NULL, NULL}
    };

    // connect to  the service control manager
    StartServiceCtrlDispatcher(ServiceTable);
}

//------------------------------------------------------------
VOID ServiceMain(DWORD dwArgc, LPTSTR *lpszArgv)
{
    DWORD    ThreadId;

    if (!(hService = RegisterServiceCtrlHandler(
          GENSRV_ServiceName,
          (LPHANDLER_FUNCTION)ServiceHandler)))
        return;

    NotifySCM(SERVICE_START_PENDING, 0, 1);

    if (!ServiceInitialization(dwArgc, lpszArgv))
        return;

    NotifySCM(SERVICE_START_PENDING, 0, 2);
```

By definition, a service is supposed to call StartServiceCtrlDispatcher() from its main() routine. It has only 30 seconds in which to do so, or else the service controller will assume the process died and terminate it. For this reason you should put off as much initialization work as possible until later. A common guideline is to only perform initialization tasks that are common to all services supplied by this process (which is none for my sample process because it contains only one service) before calling StartServiceCtrlDispatcher(). If you really must do lengthy initialization tasks, you may need to create a separate thread to do so.

Listing 13.3 (continued)

```
    if ((hDoneEvent=CreateEvent(NULL,FALSE,FALSE,NULL)) == 0)
        return;

    NotifySCM(SERVICE_START_PENDING, 0, 3);

    if ((hThread = CreateThread(0, 0,
            (LPTHREAD_START_ROUTINE)MainServiceThread, 0, 0,
            &ThreadId)) == 0) {
        CloseHandle(hDoneEvent);
        return;
    }

    NotifySCM(SERVICE_RUNNING, 0, 0);

    WaitForSingleObject(hDoneEvent, INFINITE);

    CloseHandle(hThread);
    ExitThread(ThreadId);
    CloseHandle(hDoneEvent);
    return;
}

//-------------------------------------------------------------
VOID ServiceHandler(DWORD fdwControl)
{
    switch(fdwControl) {
        case SERVICE_CONTROL_STOP:
            OutputDebugString("Stop\n");
            NotifySCM(SERVICE_STOP_PENDING, 0, 1);
            SetEvent(hDoneEvent);
            NotifySCM(SERVICE_STOPPED, 0, 0);
            break;
```

Listing 13.3 (continued)

```
            case SERVICE_CONTROL_PAUSE:
                OutputDebugString("Pause\n");
                NotifySCM(SERVICE_PAUSE_PENDING, 0, 1);
                SuspendThread(hThread);
                NotifySCM(SERVICE_PAUSED, 0, 0);
                break;

            case SERVICE_CONTROL_CONTINUE:
                OutputDebugString("Continue\n");
                NotifySCM(SERVICE_CONTINUE_PENDING, 0, 1);
                ResumeThread(hThread);
                NotifySCM(SERVICE_RUNNING, 0, 0);
                break;

            case SERVICE_CONTROL_INTERROGATE:
                OutputDebugString("Interrogate\n");
                NotifySCM(dwCurrentState, 0, 0);
                break;

            case SERVICE_CONTROL_SHUTDOWN:
                OutputDebugString("Shutdown\n");
                ServiceTermination();
                break;
    }
}


//-------------------------------------------------------------
BOOL NotifySCM(DWORD dwState, DWORD dwWin32ExitCode,
        DWORD dwProgress)
{
    SERVICE_STATUS ServiceStatus;

    // fill in the SERVICE_STATUS structure
    ServiceStatus.dwServiceType = SERVICE_WIN32_OWN_PROCESS;
    ServiceStatus.dwCurrentState = dwCurrentState = dwState;
    ServiceStatus.dwControlsAccepted = SERVICE_ACCEPT_STOP |
        SERVICE_ACCEPT_PAUSE_CONTINUE | SERVICE_ACCEPT_SHUTDOWN;
    ServiceStatus.dwWin32ExitCode = dwWin32ExitCode;
    ServiceStatus.dwServiceSpecificExitCode = 0;
    ServiceStatus.dwCheckPoint = dwProgress;
    ServiceStatus.dwWaitHint = 3000;

    // send status to SCM
    return SetServiceStatus(hService, &ServiceStatus);
}
```

StartServiceCtrlDispatcher() takes only one parameter, which is an array of at least two SERVICE_TABLE_ENTRY structures. Each SERVICE_TABLE_ENTRY structure describes a service that is provided by the calling process, and the last one in the array is a sentinel (all values NULL). For simplicity, in srvctmpl.c, I've assumed the process provides only one service. If your application calls for multiple independently managed services, it's better to provide all services in a single process rather than in

---

Listing 13.4 wdjsrvc.c— *Framework code for generic service.*

```c
#include <windows.h>
#include <stdio.h>
#include "srvctmpl.h"

TCHAR szSomeThreadInfo[] = TEXT("SomeThreadInfo");


//------------------------------------------------------------
#ifdef __BORLANDC__
#    pragma argsused
#endif
BOOL ServiceInitialization(DWORD dwArgc, LPTSTR *lpszArgv)
{
   OutputDebugString(TEXT("ServerInitialization\n"));
   return TRUE;
}


//------------------------------------------------------------
VOID ServiceTermination(VOID)
{
   OutputDebugString(TEXT("ServiceTermination\n"));
}


//------------------------------------------------------------
DWORD MainServiceThread(LPDWORD ThreadParam)
{
   OutputDebugString((LPTSTR)ThreadParam);

   while (TRUE) {
     Sleep(5000);
     OutputDebugString(TEXT(".\n"));
   }
}
```

multiple processes, because threads are less expensive to create and manage than processes are. The `lpServiceName` field specifies the internal name of the service [supplied in the call to `CreateService()`] and the `lpServiceProc` field specifies the service's main entry point. To indicate that there are no more services, you should provide one additional `SERVICE_TABLE_ENTRY` that contains `NULL` for both fields. For processes that provide a single service, the `lpServiceName` parameter is supposed to be ignored, but I've experienced problems with this in the past so I always specify the service name explicitly.

Once `StartServiceCtrlDispatcher()` is called, it manages the service via the service's main entry point and its handler routine and only returns if the service fails to start or when the service is stopped. If the process supports multiple services, `StartServiceCtrlDispatcher()` won't return until all services have stopped. The thread that `StartServiceCtrlDispatcher()` is called from is also significant. This is the thread that subsequent control requests will be sent to, so the service's handler routine will be in the same thread that made the call to `StartServiceCtrlDispatcher()`. In other words, when your callback function gets notified of a service control request, it is executing in the context of the thread that originally called `StartServiceCtrlDispatcher()` (usually the main thread of your process), not the separate thread that was started for your service.

The service controller then creates a new thread in which to execute the service's main entry point routine. Because you specify the service's entry point routine in the call to `StartServiceCtrlDispatcher()`, you can give it any name you want, but it must have the following prototype:

```
VOID ServiceMain(DWORD dwArgc, LPTSTR *lpszArgv)
```

The very first thing `ServiceMain()` should do is call `RegisterServiceCtrlHandler()`. This routine takes as parameters the service name and the name of the service handler routine. It returns a handle to the service, which is used in subsequent calls to `SetServiceStatus()`. `SetServiceStatus()` is called to let the service controller know the current state of the service. These are the states that a service can be in at any given time:

```
SERVICE_STOPPED
SERVICE_START_PENDING
SERVICE_RUNNING
SERVICE_PAUSED_PENDING
SERVICE_PAUSED
SERVICE_CONTINUE_PENDING
SERVICE_STOP_PENDING
```

The pending states are used to indicate that the service is in transition between two states. In these cases, you should make frequent calls to SetServiceStatus(), incrementing the dwCheckPoint field each time. This lets the service controller know that the service is still making progress toward the transition to the next state. The dwWaitHint field lets the service controller know how long to wait before expecting another SetServiceStatus() call. To simplify this repeated calling of SetService-Status(), I wrote a wrapper function called NotifySCM(), which also saves the current status in a global parameter for use later.

In ServiceMain(), SERVICE_START_PENDING will be in transition to the SERVICE_RUNNING state. After calling RegisterServiceCtrlHandler() to register ServiceHandler() as my service's handler routine, I call a predefined ServiceIni-tialization() routine. The prototype is defined in srvctmpl.h (Listing 13.2). I intend for this routine to be provided by the service-specific part of the code, which will then be linked to the template header part of the code to produce the complete service. ServiceInitialization() is where you would put service-specific code to perform initialization tasks. I pass along any command line parameters that were passed in to ServiceMain().

If the service-specific initialization succeeds, I create an event that I will use later to signal when the service has terminated. Then I create a separate thread that will perform the real work of the service. Again, this thread routine will be provided by the service-specific part of the code. In my simple custom service example, MainSer-viceThread() simply wakes up every five seconds and outputs a "." to any running debugger. You would put your own code inside MainServiceThread() to do whatever it is your service is supposed to do at run time. All this time, ServiceMain() has been calling NotifySCM() [which calls SetServiceStatus()] frequently to let the service controller know the service is still in the process of starting. Once the main service thread is successfully created, I can let the service controller know my service is officially running.

Creating a separate thread (in addition to the thread created to run the service) to do the main work of the service is not required, but it can be convenient. For one thing, I can't return from ServiceMain() until my service has been stopped, so I want to be able to have the thread that is running ServiceMain() go into a wait loop until my termination event is signaled. (I'll discuss this more later.) As I'll describe later, having a separate thread perform the main work of the service is very convenient for pausing and continuing the service.

The last routine that the service needs to provide is the callback function, or handler. Because service handlers often perform the same basic tasks, I've included the handler as part of the service template code. If your service has more complex needs, the handler in srvctmpl.c can be extended accordingly. A service can receive control requests from the service controller itself or from applications that call the service controller API routines. The most common example of this is the control panel "Services" applet (the "Devices" applet performs a similar task for kernel-mode drivers), which uses the service controller routines to allow users to view and control any services currently installed on the system. Because I specified SERVICE_ALL_ACCESS when I created this service, I've stated that my service can respond to all the standard control requests. All services must respond at least to the SERVICE_CONTROL_INTERROGATE control request.

If my service receives a control request to pause, I simply suspend the main thread by calling SuspendThread(). As always, I need to inform the service controller of my change in state. Likewise, when the service is continued from a paused state, I simply resume the thread by calling ResumeThread().

The SERVICE_CONTROL_INTERROGATE control simply represents the service controller's prerogative to call a service at any time and request its current status. For this reason, whenever my service changes state, I update the global dwCurrentState value and return this information during SERVICE_CONTROL_INTERROGATE requests.

The SERVICE_CONTROL_SHUTDOWN event is sent when the operating system itself is in the process of shutting down. According to SDK information, your service has about 20 seconds to complete cleanup. If you don't finish in that time, shutdown will proceed anyway. Because the shutdown event is so time critical, only critical cleanup activities should be performed (flushing files, etc.).

The SERVICE_CONTROL_STOP request is sent when the service itself is explicitly stopped. At this point, I call the service-specific ServiceTermination() routine to perform any routine cleanup tasks and then signal the termination event so that the WaitForSingleObject() in ServiceMain() can be released.

Services can also respond to user-defined control codes in the range of 128–255.

To get started writing your own service, follow these steps to modify the code supplied with this chapter:

1. In srvctmpl.h, change the text for GENSRV_ServiceName to the name of your service and the text for GENSRV_DisplayName to the display name of your service.

2. In wdjsrvc.c, insert any initialization code you need to perform in the function ServiceInitialization().

3. In wdjsrvc.c, insert the code that does the main work of your service into MainServiceThread().

4. In wdjsrvc.c, insert any termination code you need into ServiceTermination().

The code disk includes build.bat, a batch file that builds the code for either Visual C++ v2.2 or Borland C++ v4.52.

Debugging a Service

Once a service is running, most debuggers provide a mechanism for attaching to the running process. At that point you can set breakpoints and debug the service in a normal fashion. The tricky part is debugging a service during startup. Even if your service is an autostart service, during the debugging phase it is much simpler to install it as a demand start service, until you're sure the service initialization is working properly.

Although it's possible for services to communicate directly with the user, most services will communicate important status and error information via the event logging routines (refer to the References section for information on the event logging routines).

If you can't seem to get any service at all to start, make sure the account you are logged onto has the "log on a service" privilege. To check this, select User Rights from the Policies menu, then select Show Advanced User Rights, and add that right if necessary.

If you have the Microsoft Developer's Network CD-ROM, check out `sc.exe`, a utility that lets you interactively make calls to the service controller functions. For example, you can type:

```
sc qc MyService
```

to dump information about a service called "MyService," to see if it was installed correctly. `sc.exe` provides more control and more detailed information than the "Services" control panel applet.

Managing Services from an Application

In some cases, a service and a companion application that manages the service can be a powerful combination. To communicate with an installed service, the application calls `OpenService()`, specifying the internal service name. The returned handle can be used in calls to the other service controller routines. You might also decide to have the application and the service communicate via shared memory or other mechanisms.

In addition to starting, stopping, pausing, and resuming a service, you can also query or modify its configuration. You can query the list of running services or a list of services that are dependent upon a given service. See the SDK documentation for a list of the available service controller API routines.

Summary

That Win32 services can be specified to start when the system starts is, alone, a very useful feature. That services have a uniform interface that can be managed and controlled via a standard set of Win32 routines and that services can define complex sets of dependencies and load ordering make them a very powerful tool. The biggest potential drawback of services is that they aren't supported in Windows 95. On the other hand, because services are often used in distributed application and server environments, they are particularly well-suited to Windows NT.

References

Brain, Marshall. *Win32 System Services, the Heart of Windows NT.* Englewood Cliffs, NJ: Prentice Hall, 1994.

Microsoft Corp. Win32 SDK Reference.

Tomlinson, Paula. "Using Windows NT Event Logging". *Windows/DOS Developer's Journal*, July 1994 (Vol. 5, No. 7), pp. 19–32.

## Chapter 14

Using Windows NT Event Logging

Paula Tomlinson

After you build and ship your Windows application, inevitably, customers report problems. And no matter how hard you worked to phrase those abort messages in plain English, you will get reports like, "Um, it said it couldn't get a file or something." Wouldn't it be nice if there was a tool you could use to see what those error messages really said, and in what order they appeared? There is such a tool for Windows NT, the Event Viewer, and this chapter will show you how to use it.

The Windows NT event-logging mechanism is a useful tool that has, unfortunately, been something of a well-kept secret due to poor and incomplete documentation. The event log can not only help you monitor program execution during development, but also furnish crucial information to users of your Win32 applications in the field. The event log provides a mechanism whereby applications, device drivers, and the operating system can log useful information to a common location that administrators can access. The Event Viewer (eventvwr.exe) in the Program Manager's Administrative Tools group offers a standard means of viewing software and hardware event notifications, and the Win32 event log routines provide a standard interface for logging and reading events programmatically.

The Windows NT event-logging API is quite complicated. Fortunately, though, the normal application or device driver need not understand or make use of every possible feature of NT event logging. Typically, you have to perform only three basic tasks:

- Use a tool called the message compiler to create a resource that describes each event your application might generate.

- At install time, add information about your application (mainly, the path of the DLL that contains your message resource) to a particular location in the Registry.

- At run time, use the Windows NT API functions `RegisterEventSource()`, `ReportEvent()`, and `DeregisterEventSource()` to log events.

The Windows API provides a full set of functions for reading and operating on the event logs that are generated by your application, but these are mostly unnecessary, because NT's Event Viewer gives you the ability to view and clear event logs interactively. This chapter presents a reusable C++ class that handles most of the details of event logging for you.

What Is the Message Compiler?

The Windows NT documentation contains scattered references to a "message compiler," to "message tables," and to "message files" but never actually documents what any of these things are. For example, under the topic "Resources," the SDK documentation contains a table that lists the various types of predefined Windows resources and the chapters that describe them. However, it contains an entry for a resource called "message-table entry" and only tells you to refer to "your message-compiler documentation." What is "your message compiler," and where is its documentation? It turns out that the message compiler is one of those Microsoft products that fell through the cracks and did not get properly documented. You can find some information in code samples that come with the Windows NT SDK (refer to the following example on the Win32 SDK, `\samples\win32\winnt\msgtable`), and you can find some information in a help file called `mc.hlp` (located in the `bin` directory in the Win32 SDK installation directory or the Visual C++ installation directory).

A message table is a new predefined Windows resource (resource type 11) that contains "messages," which are the text descriptions for events that an application wants to log. Each message consists of an integer ID, a severity (used by the Event Viewer for filtering), a symbolic name, a language, and the text that describes that event. The message compiler defines its own unique syntax (described later) for constructing these messages. The message compiler produces a binary resource file that you can then compile into a `.res` file by using a resource compiler statement of the form:

```
TableID MESSAGETABLE filename.bin
```

The message compiler actually generates a `.rc` file that contains the correct statement to include the binary file that it generates. A message file is typically just a DLL that happens to contain a MESSAGETABLE resource.

I see no reason why Microsoft could not have just used the resource compiler and a new resource type to accomplish the same task as the message compiler. This would have been a simpler design and would have helped publicize the existence of the event logging capabilities. But the message compiler is what we've got, so it's what we'll use.

What Constitutes an Event?

Obviously, if every application and operating system component logged every insignificant aspect of its execution as an event, not only would there be a drain on precious disk space (this is Windows NT after all!), but the overhead would reduce overall system performance. Although there is nothing to prevent an application from abusing the event log in just such a way, there are some general guidelines for logging events.

There are three basic types of events: information, warnings, and errors. The security service uses the additional event types of Success Audit and Failure Audit, but normal applications can ignore these two. An information event is typically used to indicate the occurrence of an important activity, such as a service starting or a DDE client connecting to a DDE server. A warning event is used to indicate some kind of recoverable anomaly, such as low disk space or failure to load an optional module. An error event is used to report a nonrecoverable problem, such as failure to locate an important data file. Standard information is associated with each type of event, but you can also add event-specific information. Events can be further subdivided into categories. You can use the Event Viewer to filter by event type and event category, as well as event source (a name describing the module that logged the event).

When deciding what events to log, realize that these events may pile up in the log file without anyone looking at them, unless something goes wrong with your application. That means you probably do not want to include a lot of informational trace information in a production version of your software. However, if your code contains assertion checking or abort messages, those would be good candidates for logging as events: you could then have the end user use the Event Viewer to give you an exact history of what went wrong.

Modifying the Registry

Figure 14.1 shows the modifications your application should make to the Registry at install time. Event log management information is maintained in the `HKEY_LOCAL_MACHINE\SYSTEM\CurrentControlSet\Services\EventLog` key of the Registry. This key contains three default subkeys: "Application", "Security", and "System". Each subkey represents a separate log file; if you look in `\windows\system32\config`, you should see files named `secevent.evt`, `sysevent.evt`, and `appevent.evt`, where the physical event log data is stored. Each log file subkey can contain unique source subkeys for each process or service that is submitting events to the event log. An application that wants to log events would first create a unique source subkey (typically based on the name of the application or a component of the application, such as DrWatson) under the "Application" log file subkey.

The application then adds two subkeys to its source subkey. The "EventMessageFile" (type `REG_EXPAND_SZ`) value specifies the complete path and filename of the associated message file (usually in the form of a resource-only DLL that contains event message information). The "TypesSupported" (type `REG_DWORD`) value is a bitmask specifying which event types this source supports (typically `EVENTLOG_ERROR_TYPE | EVENTLOG_WARNING_TYPE | EVENTLOG_INFORMATIONAL_TYPE)`.

Figure 14.1   Registry modifications required for logging events.

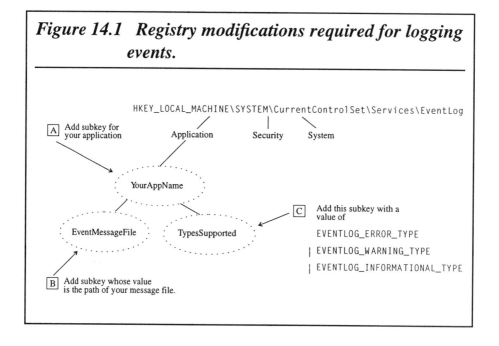

If your application supports event categories, then you can also add the "CategoryMessageFile" (type REG_EXPAND_SZ) and "CategoryCount" (type REG_DWORD) subkeys to specify the category message file and the total number of categories supported. In theory, supporting categories might be a good strategy for applications or services that provide a lot of complex event information. In practice, however, I've yet to find an application or service that supports categories.

Creating a Message File

What the NT SDK documentation calls a "message file" is just a DLL that happens to contain a MESSAGETABLE resource. You may find it convenient to use a resource-only DLL for this purpose, in which case, you will follow these steps to create your message file:

- Create a .mc file that contains the script for the message compiler (syntax described later).
- Compile the .mc file with the message compiler to produce one or more .bin files containing compiled messages, a .rc file containing MESSAGETABLE statements and references to the .bin files, and an Include file containing message definitions.
- Compile the .rc file with the resource compiler to obtain a .res file.
- Compile a stub DLL entry point function (see eventmsg.c in Listing 14.1) and link it with the .res file.

Listing 14.1 eventmsg.c — Entry code for resource-only DLL.

```
// eventmsg.c
#include <windows.h>

BOOL APIENTRY DllMain(HANDLE hInst, DWORD dwReason, LPVOID lpResrv)
{
  return TRUE;
}
```

The message file for the sample program I've included on the code disk is in eventmsg.mc (Listing 14.2). The message file should include a list of all messages that the source application may need to log. (As I'll show later in the WriteCustom() method of the EventLog class, the application can also generate messages on the fly and log them as events.) A message file has two sections, a header section and a message section. The header section defines values that are used in the message section.

The header section contains the following keywords and values:

```
MessageIdTypedef=[type]
SeverityNames=(name=number[:name])
FacilityNames=(name=number[:name])
LanguageNames=(name=number:filename)
```

Listing 14.2   *eventmsg.mc* — *Example message table script.*

```
MessageIdTypedef=DWORD
SeverityNames=(Success=0x0:SEVERITY_SUCCESS
            Informational=0x1:SEVERITY_INFORMATIONAL
            Warning=0x2:SEVERITY_WARNING
            Error=0x3:SEVERITY_ERROR)

MessageId=0x1
Severity=Informational
Facility=Application
SymbolicName=MSG_LOADSUCCESS
Language=English
The %1 module was loaded successfully.
.


MessageId=0x2
Severity=Warning
Facility=Application
SymbolicName=MSG_LOWDISKSPACE
Language=English
Disk space on drive %1 is getting low.
.


MessageId=0x3
Severity=Error
Facility=Application
SymbolicName=MSG_CANTFINDFILE
Language=English
Could not locate file %1.
.
```

The `MessageIdTypedef` value specifies the type casting that will be applied to message codes listed in the automatically created Include file. Because the message code is a 32-bit value, I specified `DWORD` for this value. If the `MessageIdTypedef` keyword is omitted, the default behavior is for no type casting to be applied to message codes.

The `SeverityNames` keyword allows you to list up to four severity codes (delimited by open and closed parentheses) that can be used in the message section. The severity code includes a name, a 2-bit numeric value, and an optional symbolic name. The severity code is stored in the high 2 bits of the automatically generated message code. If the `SeverityNames` keyword is omitted, the following default values are used: Success (0x0), Informational (0x1), Warning (0x2), and Error (0x3). I used the standard default values but added symbolic names for use in the message file; symbolic names are easier to remember and make the message file more readable.

The `FacilityNames` keyword defines a list of valid facility names (delimited by open and closed parentheses) that can be used in the message section. The list includes facility names, codes, and optional symbolic names. The facility code is stored in the low 12 bits of the high word (bits 16–27) in the automatically generated (32-bit) message code. If the `FacilityNames` keyword is omitted, the default values are System (0x0ff) and Application (0xfff). You can assign your own private facility codes, but the first 256 codes are reserved for use by the Windows NT system. Because I only use the predefined Application facility in the sample `eventmsg.mc` (Listing 14.2) message file, I omitted the `FacilityNames` keyword all together.

The `LanguageNames` keyword defines a list of valid language names (delimited by open and closed parentheses) that can be specified in the message section. You specify the symbolic name for the language, the language ID (listed in `winnt.h`), and an arbitrary but unique filename for the automatically generated binary message file. English is predefined and English messages are by default stored in a binary message file called `msg00001.bin`. Because I only support English in this simple example, I omitted the `LanguageNames` keyword. To specify additional languages, use the `LANG_` values listed in `winnt.h` for the language ID and specify unique binary message files (such as `msg00002`).

The message section consists of a set of message definitions of the following form:

```
MessageID=[number|+number]
Severity=serverity_name
Facility=facility_name
SymbolicName=name
Language=language_name
textual message
.
```

The MessageID keyword marks the beginning of a new message, so it is a required keyword. However, the MessageID value is optional. If no value is given, the previously used message value plus one will be assigned. Alternatively, you can specify a "+n" format, which causes the message compiler to assign a value of n plus the previous message value. The MessageID value cannot occupy more than 16 bits. In eventmsg.mc, I simply assigned sequential numbers, starting with 0x1, to each of my messages.

The Severity and Facility keywords are optional. If they are omitted, they default to the last values specified. If no values had been specified previously, they default to "Severity=Success" and "Facility=Application." The only valid names for these keywords are the names listed in the SeverityNames and FacilityNames keywords in the header section. In eventmsg.mc (Listing 14.2), I specified "Application" for the facility in all cases. I added three messages to eventmsg.mc, one for each severity type.

The SymbolicName keyword allows you to assign a convenient symbolic name for the message code. The symbolic name is defined in the automatically generated Include file and thus can be used by any source file that incorporates that Include file. My sample messages have the following symbolic names: MSG_LOADSUCCESS, MSG_LOWDISKSPACE, and MSG_CANTFINDFILE.

The next components of the message section are the Language statement and the body of the textual message itself. Messages are terminated by a line containing only a period and carriage return. To support more than one language, list a language and message pair for each language supported. The message text itself can contain white space and blank lines in addition to the special format escape codes listed in

Table 14.1 Message text format escape codes.

%0	Terminates the message text line without adding a trailing newline.
%%	Generates a single percent sign in the formatted message text.
%\	If occuring at the end of a line, generates a hard line break.
%r	Generates a hard carriage return without adding a trailing newline.
%b	Generates a space character in the formatted message text.
%.	Generates a single period character (as opposed to terminating the message).
%!	Generates a single exclamation point (as opposed to the string insert symbol).
%n	Specifies a string insertion. n can range from 1 to 99. This escape code can also be used to specify printf style format specifiers (refer to mc.hlp).

Table 14.1. I embedded a single insertion string escape code (indicated by "%1") in each of the sample messages in eventmsg.mc. Remember that the language-specific version of the message is not chosen until the event is viewed or read. This is because the current language is specific to the particular user logged on to the machine and thus can change. To allow for this, use only insertion strings for data fields, such as filenames and numeric values, rather than phrases.

The message compiler automatically generates an Include file and a resource file with the same prefix as the message file. Because my message file is named event-msg.mc, the message compiler generated eventmsg.h (Listing 14.3) and eventmsg.rc

---

Listing 14.3 *eventmsg.h — Header generated by message compiler.*

```
//
//  Values are 32 bit values layed out as follows:
//
//   3 3 2 2 2 2 2 2 2 2 2 2 1 1 1 1 1 1 1 1 1 1
//   1 0 9 8 7 6 5 4 3 2 1 0 9 8 7 6 5 4 3 2 1 0 9 8 7 6 5 4 3 2 1 0
//  +---+-+-+------------------------+-------------------------------+
//  |Sev|C|R|     Facility           |               Code            |
//  +---+-+-+------------------------+-------------------------------+
//
//  where
//
//      Sev - is the severity code
//
//          00 - Success
//          01 - Informational
//          10 - Warning
//          11 - Error
//
//      C - is the Customer code flag
//
//      R - is a reserved bit
//
//      Facility - is the facility code
//
//      Code - is the facility's status code
//
//
// Define the facility codes
//
```

(Listing 14.4). eventmsg.h contains a fair number of inline comments, as well as a #define for each value I listed in the header section and a #define for each message listed in the message file. The message definition also contains some helpful inline comments, including the text of the message (for the first language listed). eventmsg.rc (Listing 14.4) contains only a reference to the automatically generated binary file for each language. Because I only specified English, eventmsg.rc contains a

---

Listing 14.3 (continued)

```
//
// Define the severity codes
//
#define SEVERITY_WARNING                    0x2
#define SEVERITY_SUCCESS                    0x0
#define SEVERITY_INFORMATIONAL              0x1
#define SEVERITY_ERROR                      0x3


//
// MessageId: MSG_LOADSUCCESS//
// MessageText:
//
//   The %1 module was loaded successfully.
//
#define MSG_LOADSUCCESS              ((DWORD)0x40000001L)

//
// MessageId: MSG_LOWDISKSPACE
//
// MessageText:
//
//   Disk space on drive %1 is getting low.
//
#define MSG_LOWDISKSPACE            ((DWORD)0x80000002L)

//
// MessageId: MSG_CANTFINDFILE
//
// MessageText:
//
//   Could not locate file %1.
//
#define MSG_CANTFINDFILE            ((DWORD)0xC0000003L)
```

LANGUAGE resource statement listing the language ID (LANG_ENGLISH is defined as 0x9) and sublanguage ID (SUBLANG_ENGLISH_US is defined as 0x1) and a reference to the generated binary message file (msg00001.bin).

Be careful when adding comments to the message file. The message compiler tries to carry these comments over to the generated Include file and sometimes does not succeed in substituting the "//" comment specifier correctly. If you add inline comments to your message file, check the generated Include file to ensure that the comments were transferred correctly.

eventmsg.mak is included with the source distribution (see the code disk). It contains the basic information necessary for building a simple DLL plus a section for the message compiler. The only command line argument required by the message compiler is the message filename: mc eventmsg.mc

The *EventLog* Class

I created a simple C++ class that encapsulates the event-logging routines. The Event-Log class is defined in eventlog.h (Listing 14.5) and the methods are implemented in eventlog.cpp (Listing 14.6). Five basic operations can be performed on the event log, and each is represented by a method in the EventLog class: Backup(), Clear(), Query(), Read(), and Write().

The EventLog constructor accepts several parameters. The first parameter is a string specifying the name of the event-logging source. The source name is generally the name of the application (or module) that is logging events. This is merely a convention; you can specify any unique string as the source name. The second parameter is a string specifying the name of the message DLL. This DLL contains binary message information in its resources. The third parameter is a flag indicating whether the entries added to the Registry should be deleted when the EventLog destructor is called. For testing purposes, you might want to pass a value of TRUE for this parameter, to avoid cluttering the Registry with old source information. You can also, of course, delete old information in the Registry by using regedt32.exe. If you specify

---

Listing 14.4 *eventmsg.rc — Resource compiler instructions generated by message compiles.*

```
LANGUAGE 0x9,0x1
1 11 MSG00001.bin
```

Listing 14.5 `eventlog.h`— *Interface for* `EventLog` *class.*

```
// EVENTLOG.H - Include file for EVENTLOG.CPP
#ifndef _EVENTLOG_H_
#define _EVENTLOG_H_

class EventLog
{
    public:
        EventLog(char *szSourceName, char *szMessageDLL,
            BOOL bClearOnExit = FALSE, DWORD *dwStatus = NULL);
        virtual ~EventLog();
        DWORD Backup(LPTSTR szBackup);
        DWORD Clear(LPTSTR szBackup);
        DWORD Query(DWORD *dwNumRecords, DWORD *dwOldestRecord);
        DWORD Read(DWORD dwRec, EVENTLOGRECORD *pData, DWORD dwSize);
        DWORD Write(DWORD dwEventID, WORD wEventType, WORD wStrings,
            LPCTSTR *pszStrings, DWORD dwData, LPBYTE lpData);
        DWORD WriteCustom(LPTSTR szString, WORD wEventType);

    private:
        char szSource[MAX_PATH];
        char szRegKey[MAX_PATH];
        BOOL bClearReg;
        // prevent copy by declaring without defining
        EventLog(const EventLog&);
        const EventLog& operator=(const EventLog&);
};
#endif
```

Listing 14.6 `eventlog.cpp`— *Source code for* `EventLog` *class.*

```
// EVENTLOG.CPP - Methods for EventLog class
#include <windows.h>
#include "eventlog.h"

#define EVENT_APP  "SYSTEM\\CurrentControlSet\\Services\
\\EventLog\\Application\\"
```

TRUE for this flag, be aware that you will be able to view detailed event information only while the EventLog object is still allocated — once the object is destroyed and the Registry entries are deleted, the Event Viewer can no longer find the associated message DLL for any events that source had logged previously. The final parameter is a status value the constructor returns to indicate whether or not the tasks performed in the constructor succeeded.

Listing 14.6 (continued)

```
/**------------------------------------------------------------**/
EventLog::EventLog(char *szSourceName, char *szMessageDLL,
    BOOL bClearOnExit, DWORD *dwStatus)
{
    HKEY hKey;
    DWORD dwData;

    bClearReg = bClearOnExit;
    strcpy(szSource, szSourceName);

    // just try creating it, if it exists, it will be opened
    strcpy(szRegKey, EVENT_APP);
    strcat(szRegKey, szSource);
    if (RegCreateKeyEx(HKEY_LOCAL_MACHINE, szRegKey, 0, "\0",
        REG_OPTION_NON_VOLATILE, KEY_ALL_ACCESS | KEY_WRITE,
        NULL, &hKey, &dwData) == ERROR_SUCCESS) {

        // add the message file value
        strcpy(szRegKey, "%SystemRoot%\\System32\\");
        strcat(szRegKey, szMessageDLL);
        RegSetValueEx(hKey, "EventMessageFile", 0, REG_EXPAND_SZ,
            (LPBYTE)szRegKey, strlen(szRegKey)+1);

        // add the supported types value
        dwData = EVENTLOG_ERROR_TYPE | EVENTLOG_WARNING_TYPE |
            EVENTLOG_INFORMATION_TYPE;
        RegSetValueEx(hKey, "TypesSupported", 0, REG_DWORD,
            (LPBYTE)&dwData, sizeof(DWORD));
        RegCloseKey(hKey);
        *dwStatus = TRUE;
    }
    else *dwStatus = FALSE;
} // EventLog::EventLog
```

Listing 14.6 (continued)

```
/**----------------------------------------------------------**/
EventLog::~EventLog()
{
   HKEY hKey;

   if (bClearReg) {
      // caller specified for registry entry to be removed
      if (RegOpenKeyEx(HKEY_LOCAL_MACHINE, EVENT_APP, 0,
         KEY_WRITE, &hKey) == ERROR_SUCCESS) {
            RegDeleteKey(hKey, szSource);
            RegCloseKey(hKey);
      }
   }} // EventLog::~EventLog

/**----------------------------------------------------------**/
DWORD EventLog::Backup(LPTSTR szBackup)
{
   HANDLE hSource;

   if ((hSource = OpenEventLog(NULL, szSource)) != NULL) {
      BackupEventLog(hSource, (LPCTSTR)szBackup);
      CloseEventLog(hSource);
      return TRUE;
   } else return FALSE;
} // EventLog::Backup

/**----------------------------------------------------------**/
DWORD EventLog::Clear(LPTSTR szBackup)
{
   HANDLE hSource;

   if ((hSource = OpenEventLog(NULL, szSource)) != NULL) {
      ClearEventLog(hSource, (LPCTSTR)szBackup);
      CloseEventLog(hSource);
      return TRUE;
   } else return FALSE;
} // EventLog::Clear
```

The `EventLog` constructor creates a new subkey, using the name passed as the `szSourceName` parameter, in the Registry under the `HKEY_LOCAL_MACHINE\SYS-TEM\CurrentControlSet\Services\EventLog\Application` key. It then adds the `EventMessageFile` subkey with a value equal to the message DLL path. Note that I'm assuming the message file will be located in the `%SystemRoot%\System32` directory. The constructor also adds a value for `TypesSupported`, specifying all three basic event types as supported by this source. The `EventLog` destructor deletes the source key added by the constructor if the `bClearOnExit` flag is `TRUE`. When a key is deleted from the Registry, all subkeys and values underneath it are deleted as well. Note that whenever you specify a string length in a registry function, you must include the null terminator.

Listing 14.6 *(continued)*

```
/**----------------------------------------------------------**/
DWORD EventLog::Query(DWORD *dwNumRecords, DWORD *dwOldestRecord)
{
    HANDLE hSource;

    if ((hSource = OpenEventLog(NULL, szSource)) != NULL) {
        GetNumberOfEventLogRecords(hSource, dwNumRecords);
        GetOldestEventLogRecord(hSource, dwOldestRecord);
        CloseEventLog(hSource);
        return TRUE;
    } else return FALSE;
} // EventLog::Query

/**----------------------------------------------------------**/
DWORD EventLog::Read(DWORD dwRec, EVENTLOGRECORD *pData,
    DWORD dwSize)
{
    HANDLE hSource;
    DWORD dwRead, dwRequired, dwStatus = TRUE;

    if ((hSource = OpenEventLog(NULL, szSource)) != NULL)
        return FALSE;
    if (!ReadEventLog(hSource, EVENTLOG_FORWARDS_READ |
        EVENTLOG_SEEK_READ, dwRec, pData, dwSize, &dwRead,
        &dwRequired)) dwStatus = dwRequired;
    CloseEventLog(hSource);
    return dwStatus;
} // EventLog::Read
```

EventLog::Backup() uses BackupEventLog() to save the current contents of the Application log file to the filename passed in as a parameter. If the filename already exists, BackupEventLog() will not overwrite it. EventLog::Clear() deletes the current Application log file. If you pass in a valid, unique filename to Clear(), the Application log file will be saved to that filename before it is cleared. By convention, saved log files have a .evt extension. Although I didn't provide a method, saved log files can be opened by calling OpenBackupEventLog(). Log files can also be restored by selecting "Open..." from the Log menu in the Event Viewer.

Listing 14.6 (continued)

```
/**--------------------------------------------------------------**/
DWORD EventLog::Write(DWORD dwEventID, WORD wEventType,
    WORD wStrings, LPCTSTR *pszStrings, DWORD dwData, LPBYTE lpData)
{
    HANDLE hSource;

    if ((hSource = RegisterEventSource(NULL, szSource)) != NULL) {
        ReportEvent(hSource, wEventType, 0, dwEventID, NULL,
            wStrings, dwData, pszStrings, lpData);
        DeregisterEventSource(hSource);
        return TRUE;
    } else return FALSE;
} // EventLog::Write


/**--------------------------------------------------------------**/
DWORD EventLog::WriteCustom(LPTSTR pString, WORD wEventType)
{
    HANDLE hSource;

    if ((hSource = RegisterEventSource(NULL, szSource)) != NULL) {
        ReportEvent(hSource, wEventType, 0, 0, NULL, 1, 0,
            (LPCTSTR *)&pString, NULL);
        DeregisterEventSource(hSource);
        return TRUE;
    } else return FALSE;
} // EventLog::WriteCustom
```

`EventLog::Query()` returns the total number of events currently in the Application log file and the record number of the oldest event in the Application log file. `EventLog::Read()` returns the requested event record in an EVENTLOGRECORD structure (see Figure 14.2). Notice that the EVENTLOGRECORD is followed immediately by several variable-length fields. These variable-length fields may contain padding at the end to ensure that subsequent fields are DWORD aligned. If the size of the buffer passed to `EventLog::Read()` is not large enough to hold the entire record, then Event-Log::Read() returns the required buffer size back to the caller. You should call `EventLog::Query()` before calling `EventLog::Read()`, so that you'll know how many event records are available to read in the Application log file.

I provided both `EventLog::Write()` and `EventLog::WriteCustom()` methods so that callers can easily log events based on message IDs or on message strings created on the fly, using `ReportEvent()`. To log an event that is listed in the message DLL,

---

Figure 14.2 EVENTLOGRECORD structure.

```
typedef struct _EVENTLOGRECORD {
    DWORD   Length;                      //length of event record (bytes)
    DWORD   Reserved;                    //reserved
    DWORD   RecordNumber;                //use with ReadEventLog
    DWORD   TimeGenerated;               //time event submitted
    DWORD   TimeWritten;                 //time event written to logfile
    DWORD   EventID;                     //source-specific event ID
    WORD    EventType;                   //error,warning,info (audit)
    WORD    NumStrings;                  //number of strings in message
    WORD    EventCategory;               //source-specific subcategory
    WORD    ReservedFlags;               //reserved
    DWORD   ClosingRecordNumber;         //reserved
    DWORD   StringOffset;                //offset of Strings
    DWORD   UserSidLength;               //length of UserSid member
    DWORD   UserSidOffset;               //offset of UserSid
    DWORD   DataLength;                  //length of event-specific
Data
    DWORD   DataOffset;                  //offset of event-specific
Data
    // Then follow:
    // WCHAR SourceName[]                //variable-length source name
    // WCHAR Computername[]              //variable-length computer name
    // SID   UserSid                     //security ID of active user
    // WCHAR Strings[]                   //message replacement strings
    // BYTE  Data[]                      //data accompanying event
    // CHAR  Pad[]                       //pad for DWORD alignment
    // DWORD Length;                     //length of event record (bytes)
} EVENTLOGRECORD;
```

just pass the message ID and the event type ID to `EventLog::Write()`. You can also pass an array of insertion strings and an arbitrary, event-specific buffer of data. If you want to log an event that is not listed in the message DLL, use `EventLog::WriteCustom()`. `EventLog::WriteCustom()` passes 0 for the message ID, indicating that the message is being passed in and is not contained in the message DLL. Although you can pass insertion strings and event-specific data even when not using a message from the message DLL, for simplicity I limited `EventLog::WriteCustom()` to a single, preformatted string and did not allow inclusion of event-specific data. Notice that instead of opening and closing the event log [using `OpenEventLog()` and `CloseEventLog()`], as I did when reading, writing to the event log requires that I sandwich calls to `ReportEvent()` between calls to `RegisterEventSource()` and `DeregisterEventSource()`.

Using the `EventLog` Class

To demonstrate the `EventLog` class, I wrote a simple Win32 program. The source files are `eventapp.cpp`, `eventapp.h`, and `eventapp.rc`, and are all included on the code disk, along with the makefile and executable.

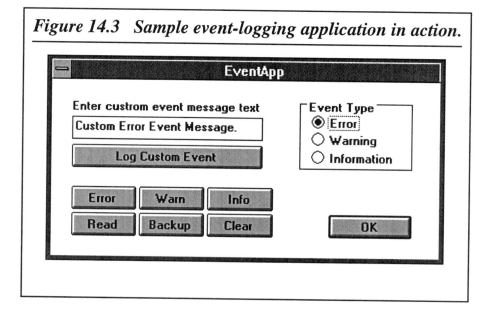

Figure 14.3 Sample event-logging application in action.

The sample program displays the dialog box shown in Figure 14.3. The dialog procedure also creates a static local `EventLog` object, specifying `EventApp` as the source name and `eventmsg.dll` as the message file. The top half of the dialog box is related to custom (on-the-fly) event messages. To log a custom event, type a message in the edit box, select the appropriate event type radio button, and press the Log Custom Event button. The dialog procedure calls `EventLog::WriteCustom()` to log a custom event based on the information you specified. To view the event you've just logged, bring up the Event Viewer in the Administrative Tools group of the Program Manager. If the Event Viewer was already running, you may have to select Refresh from the View menu to see the newly logged event. Also, to make sure you are viewing the Application log file, select Application under the Log menu.

The Error, Information, and Warning buttons in the dialog box call `EventLog::Write()` to log an event based on a message ID in the message DLL. The sample message DLL I wrote (`eventmsg.dll`) contains an information message, a warning message, and an error message. Each message contains a placeholder for one insertion string. I hard coded some insertion strings to pass to `EventLog::Write()` in response to any of these three buttons being pushed. The sample warning message describes a low-disk message, so for demonstration purposes, I also pass a buffer of disk space information as event-specific data. This allows a user to view the event log at a later time and determine how much disk space was free when the warning event was logged. Figure 14.4 shows the Event Viewer after three custom events and the three predefined events have been logged. Figure 14.5 shows the Event Viewer Details dialog box, with information for the predefined warning message.

Figure 14.4   Event Viewer after logging some events.

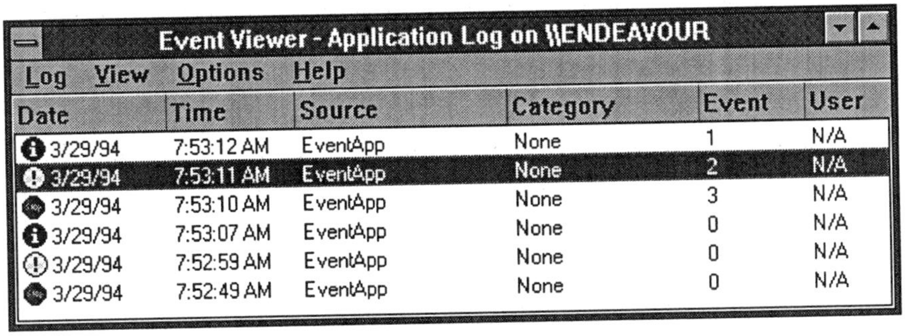

In response to the Read button being pushed, the sample application first calls `EventLog::Query()` to determine how many records are currently stored in the Application log file. The code then reads the records one at a time, using `Event-Log::Read()`, and displays some of the information from the `EVENTLOGRECORD` structure in a message box.

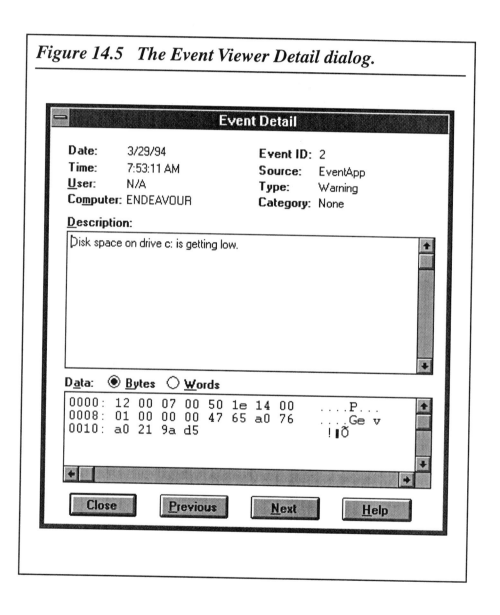

Figure 14.5   The Event Viewer Detail dialog.

The Backup and Clear buttons call the corresponding methods in `EventLog`. For simplicity, I've hard coded the log file names passed to `EventLog::Backup()`. This isn't generally a good idea, because existing log files won't be overwritten by subsequent calls to backup the log file. I pass a `NULL` as the filename for `EventLog::Clear()`, indicating that I don't want the Application log file to be saved before clearing.

Conclusion

It's unfortunate that the event-logging facility and the message file format are not better documented. But if you can wade through the sparse documentation that does exist and use this code as an example, I think you'll find the benefit of a consistent, uniform place for applications and services to log information well worth the extra work. The event log is not only useful during the development cycle but also extremely helpful in tracking down problems real customers may encounter in the field.

References

Microsoft Corp. *Win32 Programmer's Reference*, Volume II. Software Development Kit for Windows NT.

## Chapter 15

Windows NT Remote Procedure Calls

Guy Eddon

Windows NT was designed to support distributed computing; that is, the ability to distribute a single logical computing task across multiple physical computers connected to a network. One example of distributed computing in the PC market is a database server, such as that of Oracle. You can dedicate a machine on your network to running the database server; it "listens" for requests (such as an SQL query) from client applications connected to the network. To access the database server, you link your client application with a library supplied by the database server vendor. When your client application calls a library function (to retrieve a row from a table, for example), it appears to work just like a function call to any library. In reality, though, the library function is just a "stub" that packages up its parameters in some proprietary format, sends them across the network to the database server (which does all the hard work), and waits for a reply packet, which it then uses to return a status or any other information required by that particular function.

No matter what the application, the mechanics of making calls to remote applications look like local function calls will be similar. Function parameters must be placed into packets that can be sent across a network and delivered to the correct remote functions, then return values must make the return trip to the calling application. If the server does not respond in a reasonable amount of time, the client must treat this as an error or find another server on the network to satisfy the request. Because this aspect of distributed computing is the same for any distributed application, wouldn't it be nice if the operating system provided a standard interface for this work? That is just one of the problems that the Windows NT Remote Procedure Call (RPC) mechanism solves. This chapter describes NT's RPC facilities and provides an example of distributed computing, in the form of a distributed application that uses multiple computers to compute prime numbers faster than a single CPU can.

RPC: The Foundation of Distributed Computing

Applications that use remote procedure calls are inherently distributed. Such applications are usually divided into two parts: a client and a server. The client always makes requests of the server, whose only purpose is to provide the client with whatever information it requests. You can classify such servers by the type of resource they offer. For instance, vendors already offer file servers, print servers, and communication servers. Windows NT makes it possible for a server to share not only its peripherals, such as hard disk space, printers, and modems, but also its computational horsepower, via compute servers.

If you were to measure the percentage of resources used on most networks over a period of a month, you would probably determine that the network was busy about 10 to 15 percent of the time. The number of wasted CPU cycles is enormous. Using RPC, you can take advantage of this wasted processing power by distributing work across the network to all available compute servers. Compute servers do not necessarily have to be locked in a room with the file server; any computer on the network running Windows NT can be considered a compute server. If it is not currently working at full capacity, then work can be sent to it from another computer that is overloaded.

Distributed systems offer many advantages over more conventional centralized systems. In a centralized system, upgrading the main computer is difficult at best. Sometimes the entire computer must be replaced with a more powerful one. This requires that the current system be brought down and replaced before the new one can be used. During that period all the users who depend on those systems are out of luck.

In a distributed system, upgrading often consists of merely adding another computer to the network. For most users, the only noticeable effect is that their work gets processed faster. In addition, distributed systems are more fault tolerant than centralized ones. In a centralized system, if the main computer goes down, the users go down. A failure in a properly constructed distributed system causes at most a few resources and some computing power to be temporarily unavailable. A successful distributed system results in an exponential increase in available computational power.

Although client/server architecture offers many benefits, it also extracts a price in complexity. Systems built using this paradigm are usually much more complex, and often require longer to develop. They are also more apt to have reliability problems than their centralized counterparts. RPC was designed to directly address these issues.

Microsoft RPC is compatible with the Open Software Foundation (OSF) Distributed Computing Environment (DCE). This allows it to interoperate with DCE servers and any other RPC tool compatible with the OSF DCE standards. The low-level network communication done to facilitate the remote procedure call mechanism is implemented in a hardware-independent manner. The RPC runtime module can communicate in many standard network protocols. Microsoft RPC even deals with the different "endian" schemes found on some computers. Even IBM has announced an OSF-DCE-compatible environment for OS/2 v2.0, meaning that Windows NT applications may soon be able to call remote procedures running under OS/2. All things considered, RPC is a very powerful tool for communication and distribution.

The Design and Purpose of RPC

Remote procedure calls are designed to alleviate the difficulties commonly associated with building distributed applications. These difficulties consist of all the possible errors that can occur in applications that communicate over a network. When an application sends a message to another application, such as a DDE message, that application can be reasonably sure that the other application will receive it. However, even with DDE, a lot of programming effort is focused on error handling. What if the application engaged in the conversation does not follow the DDE protocol properly? What if it crashes? What if it sends garbage? These types of problems increase exponentially when communicating over a network. As anyone who has ever done low-level network programming knows, the number of errors that can occur is mind boggling. Someone can trip over the network cable, the server can crash, an application can fail to acknowledge a message. When working with network communication, the following rule of thumb applies: if it can go wrong, it will.

RPC addresses these problems by providing a procedural interface to the network. Without such an interface, distributed computing is centered on the problem of I/O. Centralized systems, however, were not built on I/O, but rather on a procedural foundation. RPC solves this by providing a facility to build distributed systems based on the procedural model of its centralized ancestors. Figure 15.1 shows an overview of the RPC mechanism.

The goal of RPC in action is to be as transparent and unobtrusive as possible. The remote procedure call model attempts to adhere closely to the normal local procedure call model. It accomplishes this so well, in fact, that even a programmer need not know if a function will execute remotely or locally. This is made possible by a special RPC language called the Interface Definition Language.

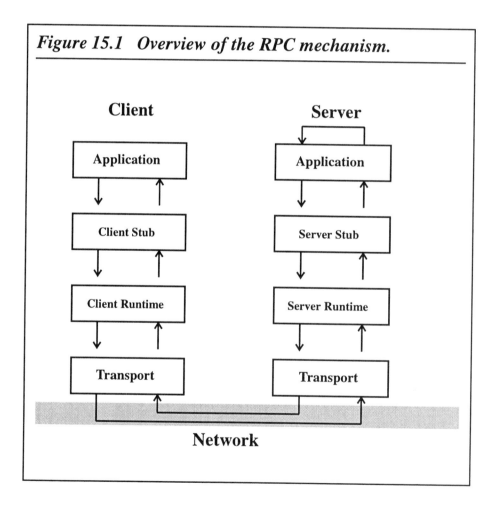

Figure 15.1 Overview of the RPC mechanism.

Interface Definition Language

The Interface Definition Language (IDL) lets you define the interface between a client and a server. Once the interface is defined, all the communication between the client and the server passes through it. In projects involving communications between applications written by different teams, the problem is to define a common interface to which both sides will adhere. With IDL, this process is automated. Once the interface has been defined with IDL, both sides must adhere to it, or they will not be able to compile their programs.

In an IDL definition file you specify the name, version, and UUID of the interface. The UUID, or Universally Unique IDentifier, is a special number that the RPC runtime code uses to ensure it sends remote procedure calls to the correct server (the UUID of the server must match that of the client). Besides identification information, you also place in the IDL definition file a prototype for each function that the server exports.

You compile an IDL file with a special compiler, the Microsoft Interface Definition Language (MIDL) compiler, which translates the IDL description into C. The C code generated by MIDL forms the remote procedure stubs in both the client and the server. Thus, the master IDL file produces code that is compiled and linked by both sides of the distributed application. If one side does not follow the specified interface, the compilation or link will fail.

Binding

Binding is the mechanism by which the client connects to the server at run time. Because the server resides on a separate machine, the client application has no way to know at compile time the address of the remote procedure it wants to call. The binding is the means by which the client has the server call the correct remote procedure on its behalf. Two types of binding are available to RPC applications: manual and automatic. Manual binding is the typical choice, although it requires more programming effort. When using automatic binding, the MIDL compiler generates all the code necessary to create and maintain the binding. This makes the programmer's job much easier at the cost of less control. Automatic binding is usually restricted to very general applications that do not care which server they bind to. For example, an application that wants to get the time from a remote server is a good candidate for automatic binding.

You can view binding to a remote server as a process similar to opening a file. When you open a file, you do so symbolically with a filename — your program is insulated from having to know precisely where and on what disk the file resides. If the file exists and the open succeeds, you get a file handle that you have to pass to the file I/O functions. The file handle lets the file I/O package maintain information about the state of the file, so that your program is insulated from its physical details. Likewise, when you bind to a remote server, you don't have to specify details such as network addresses. If the desired server exists and the binding succeeds, you get a handle that you will use to perform remote procedure calls to that server.

Binding Handles

An RPC application has to deal with two types of handles: binding handles and context handles. Binding handles contain information about the binding between the client and the server, and context handles maintain state information.

A client initiates the binding process by calling several RPC runtime functions. If everything goes smoothly (a valid server is found), then the client receives a binding handle. A binding handle is an opaque data structure that the client must use when making remote procedure calls to that server. The binding handle is always the first parameter passed to a remote procedure. There are two methods of passing binding handles in an RPC application: implicit and explicit.

Implicit handles are easier to use than explicit handles, because the code to pass the handle is generated by the MIDL compiler. When using implicit handles, the binding handle is declared as a global variable so that the C code generated by the MIDL compiler can package it for transmission to the remote procedure's stub. All binding handles are eventually converted to explicit handles. The only difference is whether you write the code to pass the explicit handle or whether you let the MIDL compiler generate the code to pass it. If you use explicit handles, you have to pass the handle to each RPC call yourself, but you can manage simultaneous connections to multiple servers. The RPC application presented in this chapter uses explicit handles.

RPC versus Normal Calls

A remote procedure call looks like a normal procedure call to the client, but you should be aware of some differences. Because the client and the server are two different executable programs, you cannot use global variables to communicate. Another difference is in the performance of pointer parameters. With a simple function call, passing a pointer (to a string, for example) can be much more efficient than passing the entire string itself. With a remote procedure call, however, the MIDL compiler has to generate code to copy the entire string anyway; just passing a pointer would be of no use to a server that resides on a separate machine. The IDL gives you some options in dealing with pointer parameters. You can group the pointers transmitted to remote procedures into three basic categories: reference pointers, unique pointers, and full pointers.

Reference pointers are the most efficient of all, but allow you less power in manipulating the pointer. A reference pointer points to valid data, and does not change its value. It is basically like a constant pointer to a specific address in memory. In addition, a reference is not allowed to cause aliasing. This means that a reference pointer is the only way to access the block of memory it is pointing to. Using a reference pointer, you allow the compiler to significantly optimize the mechanism of data transfer and pointer emulation.

Unique pointers are less efficient than reference pointers but allow you more flexibility. A unique pointer can be NULL and can change the memory address it is pointing to on the fly. A unique pointer cannot be aliased.

A full pointer is the least efficient of the three pointer types, but it allows the most flexibility with what your pointer can do. A full pointer can be NULL and change the memory address it is pointing to. Also, a full pointer can be aliased. Using this method does not allow the compiler to make any assumptions about the pointer or about memory referenced by this pointer. The memory can be accessed at any time and by any pointer. Full pointers are most useful for distributing existing code with RPC. This way, you can get your application up and running in the shortest time possible and then later go back and improve it. Unfortunately, full pointers are not supported by Microsoft RPC v1.0.

Complex structures pose more problems. Consider what happens if you attempt to pass a pointer to a doubly-linked list as a parameter to a remote procedure. In such cases the code generated by the MIDL compiler is insufficient because it cannot know the exact structure of your linked list. Microsoft RPC provides the solution to this problem in the form of user-defined marshalling (packetizing) and unmarshalling routines. In these cases, you have to supply special callback functions, executed by the client and server stubs, that transfer all or part of the special memory structure into a standard array that MIDL can transmit to the server. On the server, the unmarshalling routine is called to convert the array back into the structure expected by the remote procedure.

An RPC Example

The RPC application provided in this chapter computes prime numbers using most of the RPC features I've described. Prime numbers provide a simple example of a computationally intensive task that can benefit from distributed computing. To keep the code brief, this example uses the Win32 console functions to create a text-mode Windows NT application. The console functions in this example are handled by two source files, directio.c (Listing 15.1) and directio.h (Listing 15.2).

I designed the client side of the prime number application so that it can operate whether or not the server side is available. When executed, it creates a thread for each server. Each thread then attempts to bind to its designated server, then the client sends work to all servers with which it bound successfully. Each thread that was unable to bind to a server waits a predetermined period of time before trying to rebind. In addition, the client creates one local thread that computes prime numbers on the client's computer. The source code for the prime number client is in client.c (Listing 15.3).

Listing 15.1 directio.c — Bit text mode routines.

```
#include "directio.h"

HANDLE hStdOut;
CONSOLE_SCREEN_BUFFER_INFO csbi;

void set_vid_mem(void) {
    hStdOut = GetStdHandle(STD_OUTPUT_HANDLE);
    GetConsoleScreenBufferInfo(hStdOut, &csbi);
    }

DWORD dummy;
void mxyputs(UCHAR x, UCHAR y, char *str, unsigned  attr) {
    COORD Coord = { x , y };
    WORD Color[MAX_STR];
    unsigned count;
    WriteConsoleOutputCharacter(hStdOut, str, strlen(str), Coord, &dummy);
    for(count = 0; count < strlen(str); count++)
        Color[count] = attr;
    WriteConsoleOutputAttribute(hStdOut, Color, strlen(str), Coord, &dummy);
    }

void mxyputc(UCHAR x, UCHAR y, char ch, UCHAR num, UCHAR attr) {
    COORD Coord = { x, y };
    ConsOutChar(ch, num, attr);
    }
```

The client searches for prime numbers using a divide and conquer algorithm. Each thread takes a number and tests it to see if it is prime. To ensure that work is not replicated between the threads, the client keeps one global variable, NextNumber, that contains the value of the next number to be tested. Each thread increments this number

---

Listing 15.1 *(continued)*

```
void box(UCHAR x1, UCHAR y1, UCHAR x2, UCHAR y2, char S_D) {
    COORD Coord;
    UCHAR count;
    for(count = y1 + 1; count < y2; count++) {
        PutStruct(x1, count, (char)(S_D ? 186 : 179), 1, WHITE_ON_CYAN);
        PutStruct(x2, count, (char)(S_D ? 186 : 179), 1, WHITE_ON_CYAN);
        }
    count = x2 - x1 - 1;
    PutStruct(x1+1 ,y1, (char)(S_D ? 205 : 196), count, WHITE_ON_CYAN);
    PutStruct(x1+1 ,y2, (char)(S_D ? 205 : 196), count, WHITE_ON_CYAN);
    PutStruct(x1, y1, (char)(S_D ? 201 : 218), 1, WHITE_ON_CYAN);
    PutStruct(x1, y2, (char)(S_D ? 200 : 192), 1, WHITE_ON_CYAN);
    PutStruct(x2, y1, (char)(S_D ? 187 : 191), 1, WHITE_ON_CYAN);
    PutStruct(x2, y2, (char)(S_D ? 188 : 217), 1, WHITE_ON_CYAN);
    }

void clearscreen(WORD attr) {
    COORD Coord = { 0, 0 };
    ConsOutChar((char)32, 2000, attr);
    }

char get_character(int wait) {
    HANDLE hStdIn;
    DWORD dwInputMode, dwRead;
    INPUT_RECORD aInputBuffer;
    char chBuf;
    hStdIn = GetStdHandle(STD_INPUT_HANDLE);
    GetConsoleMode(hStdIn, &dwInputMode);
    SetConsoleMode(hStdIn, dwInputMode&~ENABLE_LINE_INPUT&~ENABLE_ECHO_INPUT);
    if(wait) {
        ReadFile(hStdIn, &chBuf, sizeof(chBuf), &dwRead, NULL);
        SetConsoleMode(hStdIn, dwInputMode);
        return chBuf;
        }
    else {
        PeekConsoleInput(hStdIn, &aInputBuffer, 1, &dummy);
        SetConsoleMode(hStdIn, dwInputMode);
        FlushConsoleInputBuffer(hStdIn);
        if(aInputBuffer.EventType == KEY_EVENT)
            return (char)(aInputBuffer.Event.KeyEvent.wVirtualKeyCode);
        }
    }
```

Listing 15.2   `directio.h` — *Header file for* `directio.c.`

```
#include <stdio.h>
#include <string.h>
#include <stdlib.h>
#include <stdarg.h>
#include <limits.h>
#include <ctype.h>
#include <windows.h>
#include <rpc.h>
#include "prime.h"

#define BACKGROUND_CYAN (WORD)0x0030
#define WHITE_ON_BLUE    (WORD)0x0007|(WORD)0x0008|(WORD)0x0010
#define WHITE_ON_CYAN    (WORD)0x0007|(WORD)0x0008|(WORD)0x0030
#define RED_ON_BLUE      (WORD)0x0004|(WORD)0x0008|(WORD)0x0010
#define RED_ON_CYAN      (WORD)0x0004|(WORD)0x0008|(WORD)0x0030
#define CYAN_ON_CYAN     (WORD)0x0003|(WORD)0x0030
#define SINGLE           0
#define DOUBLE           1
#define MAX_STR          100
#define PRIME            1
#define NOT_PRIME        0
#define MAX_CALLS        10
#define ERROR_EXIT       2
#define SUCCESS_EXIT     0
#define STRING_LENGTH    256
#define WAIT             350
#define WAIT_DISPLAY     2000
#define C_N_LENGTH       7
#define NO_WAIT          0
#define TEST_X1          3
#define TEST_Y1          3
#define TEST_X2          23
#define TEST_Y2          18
#define PRIME_X1         30
#define PRIME_Y1         3
#define PRIME_X2         50
#define PRIME_Y2         18


#define ConsOutChar(1, c, z) FillConsoleOutputCharacter(hStdOut, 1, c,\
        Coord, &dummy); FillConsoleOutputAttribute(hStdOut, z, c, Coord,\
        &dummy)
#define CoordStruct(x, y) Coord.X = x, Coord.Y = y
#define PutString(x, y, clr, frmt, var1, var2) { sprintf(Buffer, frmt, var1,\
        var2); mxyputs((UCHAR)(x), (UCHAR)(y), Buffer, clr); }
#define PutStruct(x, y, 1, c, z) CoordStruct(x, y); ConsOutChar(1, c, z);
#define CheckStatus(comment) if(status) { printf("comment %d\n");\
        exit(status); }
```

within a critical section to ensure that no other thread is accessing it simultaneously. Once the increment is complete, the thread copies it to a local variable, `temp`, and exits the critical section. `temp` can then be used safely because it is local to the thread and no other thread can modify it. Another thread can then access the already incremented

Listing 15.2 (continued)

```
extern HANDLE hStdOut;
extern CONSOLE_SCREEN_BUFFER_INFO csbi;
extern void clearscreen(WORD), box(UCHAR, UCHAR, UCHAR, UCHAR, char);
extern void mxyputs(UCHAR, UCHAR, char *, unsigned);
extern void mxyputc(UCHAR, UCHAR, char, UCHAR, UCHAR), set_vid_mem(void);
extern char get_character(int);
```

Listing 15.3 `client.c` *— Client side of prime number application.*

```
#include "directio.h"

#define MAX_THREADS     9
#define REMOTE_TRY   100000

extern void thread_local(void), thread_remote(int), thread_client(void);
extern void Usage(void);
extern char ServerStatus(char);

PCONTEXT_HANDLE_TYPE phContext[MAX_THREADS];
HANDLE hthread_client, hthread_remote[MAX_THREADS];
CRITICAL_SECTION GlobalCriticalSection;
UCHAR  pszRName[MAX_THREADS][STRING_LENGTH], IsPrime(ULONG TestNumber);
ULONG IDThrdClient, StartNumber = 1, Notry[MAX_THREADS];
ULONG PrimeSHandle[MAX_THREADS], NoPrimeRemote[MAX_THREADS];
ULONG NextNumber = 1, StartTime, CurrTime, NoPrimeLocal, NoPrimeRemoteT;
WORD Color[TEST_X2-TEST_X1-3], Normal[TEST_X2-TEST_X1-3];
SMALL_RECT pRectTest = { TEST_X1+1, TEST_Y1+2, TEST_X2-1, TEST_Y2-1 };
SMALL_RECT pRectPrime = { PRIME_X1+1, PRIME_Y1+2, PRIME_X2-1, PRIME_Y2-1 };
COORD coordTest = { TEST_X1+1, TEST_Y1+1 };
COORD coordPrime = { PRIME_X1+1, PRIME_Y1+1 };
CHAR_INFO pchiFill = { (char)32, WHITE_ON_BLUE };
COORD ComputTestCoord = { TEST_X2-7, TEST_Y2-1 };
COORD ComputPrimeCoord = { PRIME_X2-7, PRIME_Y2-1 };
DWORD dummy;
int ipszNetAdd = 0, NumThreads, count, i;
char IsActiveServer[MAX_THREADS], comp_name[STRING_LENGTH];
handle_t BindHandle[MAX_THREADS];
```

Listing 15.3 (continued)

```c
void _CRTAPI1 main(int argc, char **argv) {
    RPC_STATUS status;
    UCHAR *pUuid = NULL, *pProtocolS = "ncacn_np";
    UCHAR *pOpts = NULL, *pSBind[MAX_THREADS] = { NULL };
    UCHAR *pNetworkA[MAX_THREADS] = { NULL };
    UCHAR pEndp[MAX_THREADS][STRING_LENGTH];
    DWORD Max_CompName_Length = STRING_LENGTH, IDThrd[MAX_THREADS];
    char tokensep[] = " \t,;", *token;
    int loop;
    for(loop = 0; loop < TEST_X2-TEST_X1-3; loop++) {
        Color[loop]  = RED_ON_BLUE;
        Normal[loop] = WHITE_ON_BLUE;
        }
    for(count = 0; count < MAX_THREADS; count++)
        strcpy(pEndp[count], "\\pipe\\prime");
    for(count = 1; count < argc; count++) {
        if((*argv[count] == '-') || (*argv[count] == '/')) {
            switch(tolower(*(argv[count]+1))) {
                case 'p': /* protocol sequence */
                    pProtocolS = argv[++count];
                    break;
                case 'n': /* network address */
                    token = strtok(argv[++count], tokensep);
                    while(token != NULL) {
                        pNetworkA[ipszNetAdd] = token;
                        token = strtok(NULL, tokensep);
                        strcpy(pszRName[ipszNetAdd],
                            strupr(&pNetworkA[ipszNetAdd][2]));
                        pszRName[ipszNetAdd][C_N_LENGTH] = 0;
                        printf("   (%d) -  %s\n", ipszNetAdd + 1,
                            pNetworkA[ipszNetAdd]);
                        ipszNetAdd++;
                        }
                    printf("\n   Please wait.\n");
                    break;
                case 'e': /* endpoint */
                    token = strtok(argv[++count], tokensep);
                    while(token != NULL) {
                        strcpy(pEndp[ipszNetAdd], token);
                        token = strtok(NULL, tokensep);
                        printf("%d %s\n", ipszNetAdd, pEndp[ipszNetAdd]);
                        ipszNetAdd++;
                        }
                    break;
                case 'f': /* first number */
                    NextNumber = StartNumber = atol(argv[++count]);
                    break;
```

value of NextNumber. This ensures that no two threads will compute the same number. The client has several runtime options. Type "client /?" for a list of these features. You can execute the client by typing:

```
CLIENT -N \\FIRST_SERVER_NAME;\\SECOND_SERVER_NAME;...
```

Client Initialization

After parsing the command line arguments, the client uses the RpcStringBindingCompose() function to create a string binding for each server it intends to bind with:

```
status = RpcStringBindingCompose(
  pszUuid, pszProtocolSequence,
  pszNetworkAddress[i], pszEndpoint[i],
  pszOptions, &pszStringBinding[i]);
```

Listing 15.3 (continued)

```
            default:
                Usage();
            }
        }
    else
        Usage();
    }
if(pNetworkA[0]) {
    for(i = 0; i < ipszNetAdd; i++) {
        status = RpcStringBindingCompose(pUuid, pProtocolS, pNetworkA[i],
            pEndp[i], pOpts, &pSBind[i]);
        CheckStatus(RpcStringBindingCompose);
        }
    /* Set the binding handle that will be used to bind to the server */
    for(i = 0; i < ipszNetAdd; i++) {
        status = RpcBindingFromStringBinding(pSBind[i], &BindHandle[i]);
        CheckStatus(RpcBindingFromStringBinding);
        }
    }
else {
    printf("\n\n\tCOMPUTING LOCALLY ONLY!\n\n\tFor Server Specify:\n");
    printf("\t -n network_address (client -n \\\\server1;\\\\server2;..)\n");
    get_character(WAIT);
    }
```

RpcStringBindingCompose() is a convenience function that combines all the pieces of a string binding together and returns the combined string in a character array allocated by the function. This memory is later freed by calling RpcStringFree().

A string binding is a string of characters that defines all the attributes for the binding between the client and the server. A string binding consists of the UUID, protocol sequence, network address, end point, and options. All the parameters used to create the string binding can be modified by the user through the use of command line arguments.

The UUID specifies an optional number used for identification purposes. This UUID allows clients and servers to distinguish different objects from one another. In this example the field is set to NULL by default.

Listing 15.3 (continued)

```
GetComputerName(comp_name, &Max_CompName_Length);
InitializeCriticalSection(&GlobalCriticalSection);
    for(i = 0; i < ipszNetAdd; i++)
        ServerStatus((char)i);
for(count = 1; count <= ipszNetAdd ; count++)
    hthread_remote[count-1] = CreateThread(NULL, 0,
        (LPTHREAD_START_ROUTINE)thread_remote, count, 0, &IDThrd[count-1]);
set_vid_mem();
clearscreen(BACKGROUND_CYAN);
StartTime = GetTickCount();
box(0, 0, 79, 24, DOUBLE);
mxyputs(37, 0, " CLIENT ", WHITE_ON_CYAN);
mxyputs(TEST_X1, 2, "Testing...", WHITE_ON_CYAN);
box(TEST_X1, TEST_Y1, TEST_X2, TEST_Y2, SINGLE);
mxyputs(PRIME_X1, 2, "Prime!", WHITE_ON_CYAN);
box(PRIME_X1, PRIME_Y1, PRIME_X2, PRIME_Y2, SINGLE);
mxyputs(32, 23, "Press Esc to exit", WHITE_ON_CYAN);
hthread_client = CreateThread(NULL, 0,
    (LPTHREAD_START_ROUTINE)thread_client, NULL,CREATE_SUSPENDED,
    &IDThrdClient);
SetThreadPriority(hthread_client, THREAD_PRIORITY_NORMAL);
ResumeThread(hthread_client);
thread_local();
DeleteCriticalSection(&GlobalCriticalSection);
if(pNetworkA[0])
    for(count = 0; count < ipszNetAdd; count++)
        if(RpcStringFree(&pSBind[count]))
            exit(ERROR_EXIT);
exit(SUCCESS_EXIT);
}
```

Listing 15.3 (continued)

```
void thread_local(void) {
   ULONG temp;
   char Buffer[STRING_LENGTH];
   while(1) {
      EnterCriticalSection(&GlobalCriticalSection);
      if((temp = ++NextNumber) >= ULONG_MAX)
         break;
      ScrollConsoleScreenBuffer(hStdOut, &pRectTest, NULL, coordTest,
         &pchiFill);
      PutString(TEST_X1+2, TEST_Y2-1, WHITE_ON_BLUE, "%d", temp-1, "");
      WriteConsoleOutputAttribute(hStdOut, Normal, 7, ComputTestCoord,
         &dummy);
      mxyputs((UCHAR)(TEST_X2-7), (UCHAR)TEST_Y2-1, "LOCAL ", WHITE_ON_BLUE);
      LeaveCriticalSection(&GlobalCriticalSection);
      if(IsPrime(temp - 1) != 0) {
         EnterCriticalSection(&GlobalCriticalSection);
         ScrollConsoleScreenBuffer(hStdOut, &pRectPrime, NULL, coordPrime,
            &pchiFill);
         PutString(PRIME_X1+2, PRIME_Y2-1, WHITE_ON_BLUE, "%-17d", temp-1, "");
         WriteConsoleOutputAttribute(hStdOut, Normal, 7, ComputPrimeCoord,
            &dummy);
         mxyputs((UCHAR)(PRIME_X2-7), (UCHAR)PRIME_Y2-1, "LOCAL ",
            WHITE_ON_BLUE);
         LeaveCriticalSection(&GlobalCriticalSection);
         NoPrimeLocal++;
         }
      }
   }

void thread_remote(int count) {
   ULONG temp;
   char Buffer[STRING_LENGTH];
   while(1) {
      if(!IsActiveServer[count-1]) {
         if(Notry[count-1]++ > REMOTE_TRY) {
            mxyputs((UCHAR)10, (UCHAR)21,
               "Attempting to connect to Prime Server:", WHITE_ON_CYAN);
            mxyputs((UCHAR)49, (UCHAR)21,pszRName[count-1], WHITE_ON_CYAN);
            Notry[count - 1] = 0;
            EnterCriticalSection(&GlobalCriticalSection);
            ServerStatus((char)(count - 1));
            LeaveCriticalSection(&GlobalCriticalSection);
            mxyputc(10, (UCHAR)(21), (char)32, 48, CYAN_ON_CYAN);
            }
         else
            continue;
         }
```

Listing 15.3 (continued)

```
            if(!IsActiveServer[count-1])
               continue;
            EnterCriticalSection(&GlobalCriticalSection);
            if((temp = ++NextNumber) >= ULONG_MAX)
               break;
            ScrollConsoleScreenBuffer(hStdOut, &pRectTest, NULL, coordTest,
               &pchiFill);
            PutString(TEST_X1+1, TEST_Y2-1, RED_ON_BLUE," %-17d", temp-1, "");
            WriteConsoleOutputAttribute(hStdOut, Color, 7, ComputTestCoord,
               &dummy);
            mxyputs((UCHAR)(TEST_X2-7), (UCHAR)TEST_Y2-1, pszRName[count-1],
               RED_ON_BLUE);
            LeaveCriticalSection(&GlobalCriticalSection);
            RpcTryExcept {
               if(RemoteIsPrime(BindHandle[count-1], PrimeSHandle[count-1],
                     temp - 1) != 0) {
                  EnterCriticalSection(&GlobalCriticalSection);
                  ScrollConsoleScreenBuffer(hStdOut, &pRectPrime, NULL,
                     coordPrime, &pchiFill);
                  PutString(PRIME_X1+1, PRIME_Y2-1, RED_ON_BLUE, " %-17d", temp-1, "");
                  WriteConsoleOutputAttribute(hStdOut, Color, 7, ComputPrimeCoord,
                     &dummy);
                  mxyputs((UCHAR)(PRIME_X2-7), (UCHAR)PRIME_Y2-1,
                     pszRName[count-1], RED_ON_BLUE);
                  LeaveCriticalSection(&GlobalCriticalSection);
                  NoPrimeRemote[count-1]++;
                  NoPrimeRemoteT++;
                  }
               }
         RpcExcept(1) {
            EnterCriticalSection(&GlobalCriticalSection);
            ServerStatus((char)(count - 1));
            LeaveCriticalSection(&GlobalCriticalSection);
            }
         RpcEndExcept
         }
      }

UCHAR IsPrime(ULONG TestNumber) {
   ULONG count, HalfNumber = TestNumber / 2 + 1;
   for(count = 2; count < HalfNumber; count++)
      if(TestNumber % count == 0)
         return NOT_PRIME;
   return PRIME;
   }
```

The protocol sequence specifies the low-level network protocol to be used for the network communication. Several network protocols are currently supported. This example uses the named pipes ("ncacn_np") protocol native to Windows NT.

The network address is the address of the server with which the client wants to bind. When using the named pipes protocol sequence, the network address is described in the following form: "\\servername", where "servername" is the name of the server computer. The type of valid network address depends on the protocol sequence used. Different protocol sequences have very different methods of defining network addresses.

The endpoint used to create the binding specifies the network endpoint at which the server application is listening. The endpoint is like a street address to a particular server application, and the network address is like the city where your server lives. As is the case with the network address, the type of endpoint reflects the protocol sequence being used. When using the named pipes protocol sequence, the valid endpoint specifies the pipe that the server is listening to. A valid endpoint for the named pipes protocol sequence is as follows: "\pipe\pipename", where "pipename" is an application-defined name for the pipe used for the low-level network communication between the client and the server.

Listing 15.3 (continued)

```
void Usage(void) {
    printf("Usage: CLIENT\n");
    printf(" -p protocol_sequence\n");
    printf(" -n network_address (\\\\server1;\\\\server2;...\n");
    printf(" -e endpoint\n");
    printf(" -f first number\n");
    exit(1);
    }

char ServerStatus(char iserver) {
    char value = FALSE;
    RpcTryExcept {
        PrimeSHandle[iserver] = InitPServer(BindHandle[iserver],
            &phContext[iserver], comp_name);
        IsActiveServer[iserver] = TRUE;
        }
    RpcExcept(1) {
        value = TRUE;
        IsActiveServer[iserver] = FALSE;
        }
    RpcEndExcept
    return value;
    }
```

Listing 15.3 (continued)

```
void thread_client(void) {
    UCHAR no_active = 0;
    while(1) {
        char Buffer[STRING_LENGTH];
        int i;
        if(VK_ESCAPE == get_character(NO_WAIT)) {
            EnterCriticalSection(&GlobalCriticalSection);
            Sleep(WAIT);
            for(i = 0; i < ipszNetAdd; i++) {
                RpcTryExcept {
                    TerminatePServer(BindHandle[i], PrimeSHandle[i]);
                }
                RpcExcept(1) {
                    clearscreen(0);
                    exit(0);
                }
                RpcEndExcept
            }
            clearscreen(0);
            exit(0);
            LeaveCriticalSection(&GlobalCriticalSection);
        }
        mxyputs(58, 2, "Number of Primes", WHITE_ON_CYAN);
        PutString(60, 4, WHITE_ON_CYAN, "%s:%5d", "LOCAL    ", NoPrimeLocal);
        EnterCriticalSection(&GlobalCriticalSection);
        for(no_active = i = 0; i < ipszNetAdd; i++)
            if(IsActiveServer[i])
                PutString(59, 5+no_active++, RED_ON_CYAN, " %7s:%5d ",
                        pszRName[i], NoPrimeRemote[i]);
        box(58, 3, 74, (UCHAR)(5+no_active), SINGLE);
        mxyputc(58, (UCHAR)(6+no_active), (char)32, 17, CYAN_ON_CYAN);
        for(no_active = i = 0; i < ipszNetAdd; i++)
            if(!IsActiveServer[i])
                PutString(59, 19+no_active++, RED_ON_CYAN," %7s:%5d ",
                        pszRName[i], NoPrimeRemote[i]);
        if(no_active) {
            mxyputs(58, (UCHAR)(17), "Inactive Servers", WHITE_ON_CYAN);
            box(58, (UCHAR)(18), 74, (UCHAR)(19+no_active), SINGLE);
            mxyputc(58, (UCHAR)(20 + no_active), (char)32, 17, CYAN_ON_CYAN);
        }
        else
            for(i = 0; i < 5; i++)
                mxyputc(58, (UCHAR)(17+no_active+i), (char)32, 17, CYAN_ON_CYAN);
        LeaveCriticalSection(&GlobalCriticalSection);
        CurrTime = (GetTickCount() - StartTime) / 1000;
        PutString(58, 7+ipszNetAdd, WHITE_ON_CYAN, "Primes =  %d",
            NoPrimeLocal+NoPrimeRemoteT, "");
        PutString(58, 8+ipszNetAdd, WHITE_ON_CYAN, "Time = %d.%02d min.",
            CurrTime/60, CurrTime%60);
        PutString(58, 9+ipszNetAdd, WHITE_ON_CYAN, "First = %d", StartNumber, "");
    }
}
```

The options parameter is a miscellaneous string to be used for whatever special settings are appropriate for a particular protocol sequence. For the named pipes protocol sequence, the only currently available option is "security=true". This turns on security mechanisms for the remote procedure call.

RpcStringBindingCompose() combines the parts of a string binding together. The purpose of a string binding is to specify all the parameters for the protocol sequence (network protocol) used. The client then transforms each string binding into the actual binary binding with RpcBindingFromStringBinding().

```
status = RpcBindingFromStringBinding( pszStringBinding[i], &BindingHandle[i]);
```

The binding can then be thought of as a magic cookie or handle with which you can make remote procedure calls.

The client calls CreateThread() to create a thread to manage each server. Each thread is passed a number designating a server it is responsible for. In addition, the client initializes a critical section object for use later, when accessing global variables from the threads. Finally, the client calls GetComputerName() so that it can pass the returned string to the server. The server displays this string so that the user can see which client is making remote procedure calls.

Once the client has obtained a valid binding to each server, it attempts to initialize these servers on a logical level. To do so, it calls a special remote procedure available on each prime number server: InitPServer(). This function is designed to notify the server that a client is planning to make requests. InitPServer() accepts a binding handle, context handle, and the name of the computer retrieved by GetComputer-Name().

Client Computation

After the client initialization is completed, prime number computation begins. thread_local() computes prime numbers locally on the client computer via IsPrime(). thread_remote() makes a remote procedure call to determine if a number is prime via RemoteIsPrime(). In this case, because RemoteIsPrime() is a remote procedure call, it is embedded in an exception handler.

If an exception occurs, the client attempts to recognize the error and provide an error message on the console display. If the exception that occurred indicates that the server is off-line, the client thread waits a specified period of time before attempting to rebind to that server.

When the client terminates normally, via the Escape key, a special remote procedure call, TerminatePServer(), is made to notify the server of the client's plans to exit. The server can then take action to free memory and update its display to reflect the new status.

The Server

The prime number server has an important, if unrewarding, job. It must register its interface and begin to listen for client requests. The source code for the prime number server resides in `server.c` (Listing 15.4) and `remote.c` (Listing 15.5).

Listing 15.4   *server.c— Server side of primer number application.*

```
#include "directio.h"

extern char IsPrime(ULONG TestNumber), GCompName[MAX_CALLS][STRING_LENGTH];
extern void Usage(void), thread_server(void);
extern ULONG NoPrimes[MAX_CALLS], handles;

DWORD  IDThrd;
HANDLE hthread_server;
CRITICAL_SECTION GlobalCriticalSection;

void _CRTAPI1 main(int argc, char *argv[]) {
   RPC_STATUS status;
   UCHAR *pProtocolS = "ncacn_np", *pSecurity = NULL,
      *pEndp = "\\pipe\\prime";
   unsigned cMinCalls = 1, cMaxCalls = MAX_CALLS, i;
   for(i = 1; (int)i < argc; i++) {
      if((*argv[i] == '-') || (*argv[i] == '/')) {
         switch(tolower(*(argv[i]+1))) {
            case 'p':
               pProtocolS = argv[++i];
               break;
            case 'e':
               pEndp = argv[++i];
               break;
            default:
               Usage();
         }
      }
      else
         Usage();
   }
   status = RpcServerUseProtseqEp(pProtocolS, cMaxCalls, pEndp, pSecurity);
   CheckStatus(RpcServerUseProtseqEp);
   status = RpcServerRegisterIf(prime_ServerIfHandle, NULL, NULL);
```

RpcServerUseProtseqEp() notifies the RPC runtime module to register a protocol sequence, endpoint, and security attribute on which to accept remote procedure calls. This is the station the server listens to, to hear the client's cries for help. RpcServerRegisterIf() registers the server's interface. It accepts the handle to the interface being registered and two optional management parameters not used in this example. This interface is defined in the IDL file.

Listing 15.4 (continued)

```
   CheckStatus(RpcServerRegisterIf);
   InitializeCriticalSection(&GlobalCriticalSection);
   set_vid_mem();
   clearscreen(BACKGROUND_CYAN);
   box(0, 0, 79, 24, DOUBLE);
   mxyputs(37, 0, " PRIMES ", WHITE_ON_CYAN);
   mxyputs(TEST_X1, 2, "Testing...", WHITE_ON_CYAN);
   box(TEST_X1, TEST_Y1, TEST_X2, TEST_Y2, SINGLE);
   mxyputs(PRIME_X1, 2, "Prime!", WHITE_ON_CYAN);
   box(PRIME_X1, PRIME_Y1, PRIME_X2, PRIME_Y2, SINGLE);
   mxyputs(32, 23, "Press Esc to exit", WHITE_ON_CYAN);
   hthread_server = CreateThread(NULL, 0,
       (LPTHREAD_START_ROUTINE)thread_server, NULL, CREATE_SUSPENDED,
       &IDThrd);
   SetThreadPriority(hthread_server, THREAD_PRIORITY_LOWEST);
   ResumeThread(hthread_server);
   mxyputs(23, 21, "Listening for prime number requests.", RED_ON_CYAN);
   status = RpcServerListen(cMinCalls, cMaxCalls, FALSE);
   CheckStatus(RpcServerListen);
   }

void Usage(void) {
   printf("Usage: SERVER\n");
   printf(" -p protocol_sequence\n");
   printf(" -e endpoint\n");

   exit(EXIT_SUCCESS);
   }

void __RPC_FAR *__RPC_API midl_user_allocate(size_t len) {
   return(malloc(len));
   }

void __RPC_API midl_user_free(void __RPC_FAR *ptr) {
   free(ptr);
   }
```

The last RPC runtime function the prime number server calls begins listening for client requests. In this example, RpcServerListen() never returns. Until a client makes a remote procedure call, the server cannot do anything. To avoid this problem, I create a special thread for the server to perform maintenance tasks even when not in use. This thread is created with the CREATE_SUSPENDED attribute so that it can be subsequently modified with the THREAD_PRIORITY_LOWEST attribute. This ensures that the maintenance thread consumes the least amount of CPU cycles possible when it is restarted with ResumeThread(). In this example the maintenance thread provides some prime number statistics and checks to see if the Escape key was pressed.

Listing 15.4 (continued)

```
void thread_server(void) {
   while(1) {
      char Buffer[STRING_LENGTH], Buffert[STRING_LENGTH];
      UCHAR i;
      if(VK_ESCAPE == get_character(NO_WAIT)) {
         EnterCriticalSection(&GlobalCriticalSection);
         Sleep(WAIT);
         clearscreen(0);
         exit(EXIT_SUCCESS);
         LeaveCriticalSection(&GlobalCriticalSection);
         DeleteCriticalSection(&GlobalCriticalSection);
         }
      if(handles) {
         mxyputs(58, 2, "Number of Primes", WHITE_ON_CYAN);
         EnterCriticalSection(&GlobalCriticalSection);
         for(i = 0; i < handles; i++) {
            strncpy(Buffert, strupr(GCompName[i]), C_N_LENGTH);
            Buffert[C_N_LENGTH] = 0;
            PutString(59, 4+i, WHITE_ON_BLUE, " %7s:%5d ", Buffert,
               NoPrimes[i]);
            }
         box(58, 3, 74, (UCHAR)(4 + handles), SINGLE);
         mxyputc(58, (UCHAR)(5+i), (char)32, 17, CYAN_ON_CYAN);
         LeaveCriticalSection(&GlobalCriticalSection);
         }
      else
         for(i = 0; i < 13; i++)
            mxyputc(58, (UCHAR)(2+i), (char)32, 17, CYAN_ON_CYAN);
      if(!handles) {
         mxyputs(23, 21, "Listening for prime number requests.",
            RED_ON_CYAN);
         Sleep(WAIT_DISPLAY);
         }
      mxyputc(23, 21, (char)32, 36, CYAN_ON_CYAN);
      }
   }
```

Listing 15.5 `remote.c` — *Server support routines.*

```c
#include "directio.h"

extern CRITICAL_SECTION GlobalCriticalSection;

ULONG handles = 0, handlesp = 0, handle_mod = 1, NoPrimes[MAX_CALLS];
ULONG GlobalComputerHandleBuffer[MAX_CALLS];
char GCompName[MAX_CALLS][STRING_LENGTH];

ULONG InitPServer(handle_t h1, PPCONTEXT_HANDLE_TYPE pphContext,
        UCHAR *CompName) {
    ULONG unique_handle;
    char Buffer[STRING_LENGTH];
    EnterCriticalSection(&GlobalCriticalSection);
    unique_handle = handles + 10 * handle_mod++;
    strcpy(GCompName[handles], CompName);
    mxyputc(2, 21, (char)32, 75, CYAN_ON_CYAN);
    PutString(27, 21, RED_ON_CYAN, "Computer %s", CompName, "");
    PutString(54, 21, RED_ON_CYAN, "(%ld)", unique_handle, "");
    Sleep(2 * WAIT_DISPLAY);
    mxyputc(2, 21, (char)32, 75, CYAN_ON_CYAN);
    GlobalComputerHandleBuffer[handles] = unique_handle;
    *pphContext = (PCONTEXT_HANDLE_TYPE)unique_handle;
    NoPrimes[handles] = 0;
    handlesp = ++handles;
    LeaveCriticalSection(&GlobalCriticalSection);
    return unique_handle;
    }

UCHAR RemoteIsPrime(handle_t h1, ULONG PrimeSHandle, ULONG TestNumber)
    {
    ULONG count, HalfNumber = TestNumber / 2 + 1;
    SMALL_RECT pRectTest = { TEST_X1+1, TEST_Y1+2, TEST_X2-1, TEST_Y2-1 };
    SMALL_RECT pRectPrime = { PRIME_X1+1, PRIME_Y1+2,PRIME_X2-1, PRIME_Y2-1 };
    COORD coordTest = { TEST_X1+1, TEST_Y1+1 };
    COORD coordPrime = { PRIME_X1+1, PRIME_Y1+1 };
    CHAR_INFO pchiFill = { (char)32, WHITE_ON_BLUE };
    COORD ComputTestCoord = { TEST_X2-7, TEST_Y2-1 };
    COORD ComputPrimeCoord = { PRIME_X2-7, PRIME_Y2-1 };
    DWORD dummy;
    WORD Local[C_N_LENGTH];
    char Buffer[STRING_LENGTH], LocalCompName[STRING_LENGTH];
    unsigned loop;
    EnterCriticalSection(&GlobalCriticalSection);
    for(loop = 0; loop < handles; loop++)
        if(GlobalComputerHandleBuffer[loop] == PrimeSHandle) {
            strcpy(LocalCompName, GCompName[loop]);
            PrimeSHandle = loop;
            break;
            }
```

Listing 15.5 *(continued)*

```
    LeaveCriticalSection(&GlobalCriticalSection);
    for(loop = 0; loop < C_N_LENGTH; loop++)
        Local[loop] = WHITE_ON_BLUE;
    if(VK_ESCAPE == get_character(NO_WAIT)) {
        EnterCriticalSection(&GlobalCriticalSection);
        Sleep(WAIT);
        clearscreen(0);
        exit(SUCCESS_EXIT);
        LeaveCriticalSection(&GlobalCriticalSection);
        DeleteCriticalSection(&GlobalCriticalSection);
        }

    EnterCriticalSection(&GlobalCriticalSection);
    ScrollConsoleScreenBuffer(hStdOut, &pRectTest, NULL, coordTest,
        &pchiFill);
    PutString(TEST_X1+2, TEST_Y2-1, WHITE_ON_BLUE, "%d", TestNumber, "");
    WriteConsoleOutputAttribute(hStdOut, Local, C_N_LENGTH,
        ComputTestCoord, &dummy);
    LocalCompName[C_N_LENGTH] = 0;
    mxyputs((UCHAR)(TEST_X2-7), (UCHAR)TEST_Y2-1, LocalCompName,
        WHITE_ON_BLUE);
    LeaveCriticalSection(&GlobalCriticalSection);
    for(count = 2; count < HalfNumber; count++)
        if(TestNumber % count == 0)
            return NOT_PRIME;
    EnterCriticalSection(&GlobalCriticalSection);
    ScrollConsoleScreenBuffer(hStdOut, &pRectPrime, NULL, coordPrime,
        &pchiFill);
    PutString(PRIME_X1+2, PRIME_Y2-1, WHITE_ON_BLUE, "%d", TestNumber, "");
    WriteConsoleOutputAttribute(hStdOut, Local, C_N_LENGTH,
        ComputPrimeCoord, &dummy);
    mxyputs((UCHAR)(PRIME_X2-7), (UCHAR)PRIME_Y2-1, LocalCompName,
        WHITE_ON_BLUE);
    NoPrimes[PrimeSHandle]++;
    LeaveCriticalSection(&GlobalCriticalSection);
    return PRIME;
    }

void TerminatePServer(handle_t h1, ULONG PrimeSHandle) {
    UCHAR loop, loopshift;
    char Buffer[256+STRING_LENGTH];
    EnterCriticalSection(&GlobalCriticalSection);
    for(loop = 0; loop < (UCHAR)handles; loop++) {
        if(GlobalComputerHandleBuffer[loop] == PrimeSHandle) {
            mxyputc(2, 21, (char)32, 75, CYAN_ON_CYAN);
            PutString(27, 21, RED_ON_CYAN, "Computer %s Exited!",
                GCompName[loop], "");
            mxyputc(59, (UCHAR)(4+loop), (char)32, 15, CYAN_ON_CYAN);
            Sleep(WAIT_DISPLAY);
            mxyputc(2, 21, (char)32, 75, CYAN_ON_CYAN);
            break;
            }
        }
```

The server also has a special context rundown routine that can be seen in remote.c (Listing 15.5). As you may recall, the client calls TerminatePServer() when the user presses the Escape key. What happens if the client terminates abnormally? Perhaps the client crashed, the power went out, or the computer failed. In any case, the server must be fault tolerant and not allow such a possibility to impair its performance for other clients that may still be on-line. Whatever TerminatePServer() would have done, the server needs to do. The designers of RPC took this situation into account and came up with a special facility known as a rundown. This rundown is a user-defined function called automatically by the RPC runtime whenever the client terminates. If the client terminates normally by calling TerminatePServer(), the rundown routine is skipped. However, if the client terminates abnormally, the rundown routine is called to perform the necessary clean-up.

The prime number interface definition file specifies the RPC interface between the client and server. The prime interface is defined in prime.idl (Listing 15.6). The UUID, version number, and pointer type used are defined here for the interface header. Following that is the actual interface definition, consisting of the function prototypes with special IDL flags.

Listing 15.5 (continued)

```
    if(loop < handles-1) {
       loopshift = loop;
       for(loop = loopshift; loop < (UCHAR)(handles-1); loop++) {
          strcpy(GCompName[loop], GCompName[loop+1]);
          GlobalComputerHandleBuffer[loop] =
             GlobalComputerHandleBuffer[loop+1];
          NoPrimes[loop] = NoPrimes[loop+1];
          }
       }
    handles--;
    LeaveCriticalSection(&GlobalCriticalSection);
    }

void PCONTEXT_HANDLE_TYPE_rundown(PCONTEXT_HANDLE_TYPE phContext)
    {
    handle_t dummmy;
    if(handlesp == handles) {
       mxyputs(27, 2, "Rundown Executed", RED_ON_CYAN);
       TerminatePServer(dummmy, (ULONG)phContext);
       Sleep(WAIT_DISPLAY);
       mxyputs(27, 2, "                ", CYAN_ON_CYAN);
       }
    handlesp = handles;
    }
```

Building the Example

The makefile used to build the prime number application is available in `prime.mak` (Listing 15.7). This file handles the building of the entire example, including execution of the MIDL compiler, C compiler, and linker. Figure 15.2 shows the overall build process.

To build and run this example you need to have at least one computer capable of running Windows NT. This is possible because both the client and the server can be run on one computer. If you want to test this application across a network, you will need at least two computers running Windows NT, both with supported network cards. You must also have Windows NT and the Microsoft Win32 Preliminary SDK for Windows NT.

Microsoft RPC v1.0 provides support for MS-DOS and Windows for Workgroups. Applications on both of these platforms can make remote procedure calls to servers running Windows NT. MS-DOS and Windows applications cannot, however, become RPC servers as these platforms lack the multithreading capability required.

Debugging distributed RPC applications is slightly different from debugging conventional applications because of the added factor of the network. For this reason it is best to separate the server initialization code from the remote procedures themselves. This is done in the Prime RPC application with `server.c` and `remote.c`. Both files are linked together to produce the server, but during the debugging stage this separation can be invaluable. By dividing the server into two parts, you permit yourself the

---

Listing 15.6 `prime.idl` — Interface definition language file for distributed application.

```
[ uuid (62387AFE-C34B-1ABE-B235-98765233AFEA),
  version(1.0),
  pointer_default(unique)]
interface prime
   {
   typedef [context_handle] void *PCONTEXT_HANDLE_TYPE;
   typedef [ref] PCONTEXT_HANDLE_TYPE *PPCONTEXT_HANDLE_TYPE;
   char RemoteIsPrime([in] handle_t h1, [in] unsigned long PrimeSHandle,
      [in] unsigned long TestNumber);
   unsigned long InitPServer([in] handle_t h1,
      [out] PPCONTEXT_HANDLE_TYPE pphContext,
      [in, string] unsigned char *CompName);
   void TerminatePServer([in] handle_t h1, [in] unsigned long PrimeSHandle);
   }
```

option of linking the remote procedures directly with the client to produce one standard application. In this manner you can test the application as a whole without worrying about the network. Once your program works properly, you can divide it into a client and server to test it in a distributed environment.

Listing 15.7   `prime.mak` — *Makefile for prime number application.*

```
!include <NTWIN32.MAK>
cflags = $(cflags:G3=Gz)

.c.obj:
   $(cc) $(cflags) $(cvarsmt) $<

all : client server

client : client.exe
client.exe : client.obj prime_c.obj directio.obj
    $(link) $(conflags) -out:client.exe \
       client.obj prime_c.obj directio.obj \
       rpcrt4.lib rpcndr.lib rpcns4.lib $(conlibsmt)

client.obj : client.c prime.h

directio.obj : directio.c directio.h
   $(cc) $(cflags) $(cvarsmt) directio.c

prime_c.obj : prime_c.c prime.h
   $(cc) $(cflags) $(cvarsmt) prime_c.c

server : server.exe
server.exe : server.obj remote.obj prime_s.obj directio.obj
    $(link) $(conflags) -out:server.exe \
       server.obj prime_s.obj remote.obj directio.obj \
       rpcrt4.lib rpcndr.lib rpcns4.lib $(conlibsmt)

server.obj : server.c prime.h

remote.obj : remote.c prime.h

prime_s.obj : prime_s.c prime.h
   $(cc) $(cflags) $(cvarsmt) prime_s.c
prime.h prime_c.c prime_s.c : prime.idl
   midl -cpp_cmd $(cc) -cpp_opt "-E"  prime.idl
```

What advantage is there to computing prime numbers in a distributed manner across a network, compared to the conventional way on one computer? The prime example presented in this chapter provides some simple timer routines to let you know how long the computations are taking. Figure 15.3 shows that when computations are relatively small (1–1,000), distributing an application can actually cause the performance to worsen. This is because the overhead of RPC is significant compared to the work done by the server. In addition, these times were clocked with the March

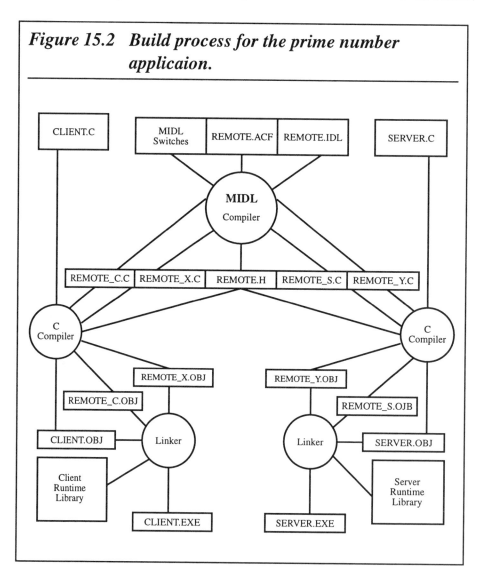

Figure 15.2   Build process for the prime number applicaion.

1993 beta version of Windows NT. Perhaps the release version will have better performance. In any case, you can still observe that under some circumstances, much better performance can be achieved with RPC. Once the calculations required become very large (10,000,000 and up), the overhead of RPC becomes insignificant. When I clocked these times, the improvement with the distributed prime computations approached an order of 3.5 times faster with four computers than with only one. [Editors' note: While all the examples given here are dated, the ratios of the computations remain the same. If the times were clocked today, all samples would be proportionally faster.] A smart application might make remote procedure calls only when the possible gain outweighed the overhead. As networks and operating systems that support distributed computing become more and more common, RPC more likely will play a part in your next application.

Figure 15.3 Performance of prime number application in conventional and distributed environments.

Range	1 computer (sec.)	4 computers (sec.)	Ratio
1-1,000	35	40	0.88
100,000-101,000	40	42	0.95
1,000,000-1,001,000	100	61	1.64
10,000,000-10,001,000	581	170	3.42

Chapter 16

Inside Windows NT Security

Rob Reichel

One of the design goals for Microsoft's Windows NT operating system is that it meet the requirements for government C/2 security certification. C/2-level security requires the operating system to supply "discretionary access control" (DAC) mechanisms that allow it to protect objects (such as files) from unauthorized use.

Discretionary access control means that the creator of an object has the ability to permit anyone to access the object in any way. You can contrast this with such stronger forms of security as "mandatory access control," which enforces access rules that even the creator of an object may not override (for example, preventing you from copying a file marked "Top Secret" to a directory owned by someone with only "Secret" clearance).

Even if you are not planning to write a security-intensive application (such as a database server or a file manager), understanding Windows NT security makes the behavior and proper administration of the system easier to understand, which in turn leads to making systems more secure. Anyone administering a system or writing applications for a system containing sensitive information must have an in-depth understanding of how the various pieces fit together; otherwise, they will eventually make mistakes that compromise their data.

Think of it this way: the person trying to break into your system will have read every line of documentation and will have figured out all of the holes that you might have left open. The best defense against such an attack is to understand the system thoroughly enough to ensure that there are no holes to exploit.

First, I will describe Windows NT security and the discretionary access control mechanisms it provides. Finally, I will illustrate some of these concepts with a small program that allows an administrator to override the normal security on a file.

What Is Security?

The goal of a security system such as that in Windows NT is to ensure that the wrong people don't do the wrong things on the computer or on the network, either unintentionally or maliciously. When a user attempts to access a file, for example, the system must evaluate two pieces of information to determine if that user may access that file: who the user is, and who is allowed to access the file.

Although this may seem obvious, the mechanisms that Windows NT uses to represent who you are and who may access that file are very flexible and complex. This flexibility allows organizations to tailor their use of the security system very closely to their needs, but it puts an extra burden of understanding on application developers who plan to take advantage of it.

Although the details of Windows NT security are complex, the big picture is fairly simple. The main items of interest are users and objects. A user is a person or process that logs onto the system and an object is something that a user can access (for example, a file). Whenever a user wants to access an object, Windows NT security comes into play. As Figure 16.1 shows, Windows NT maintains security information for both users and objects. The answer to whether or not the security system will grant a user access to an object depends on the detailed security information associated with both the user and the object. Most of the remainder of this chapter explores the details of user information and object information and the algorithms by which Windows NT security uses this information to decide whether or not to grant a particular access request.

User Information Overview

In order to understand who you are when you are logged onto the system, Windows NT maintains a database (called the Security Account Manager, or SAM) of all the users who have accounts in each network domain. When you log onto a Windows NT system (either directly or via the network), the logon process validates your logon name and password, and if they are correct, retrieves everything that it knows about you from the database. At this point, you are what is known as a subject.

A subject may be either sitting at the keyboard or accessing the machine over the network. The ability to allow multiple subjects to access a machine simultaneously is the basis of Windows NT's claim to be a multi-user operating system. Despite the fact that only one user may have a Windows desktop at a time, any number of users may connect to the machine and be represented as themselves in order to access objects in the system.

Each Windows NT process is associated with a subject. Windows NT itself is a special subject that is always present. This allows the parts of the operating system that run in user (or nonsupervisor) mode to have a context to use when accessing objects, which means that Windows NT is subject to restrictions from its own security system.

When a subject (you, for example) logs on, the first thing the system retrieves from the database is your security identifier, or SID. The SID is the Windows NT equivalent of your name and provides just about as much information about you (that is, not much). The purpose of the SID is to identify you uniquely across all of the machines on your network in a format that is easy for the operating system to manipulate.

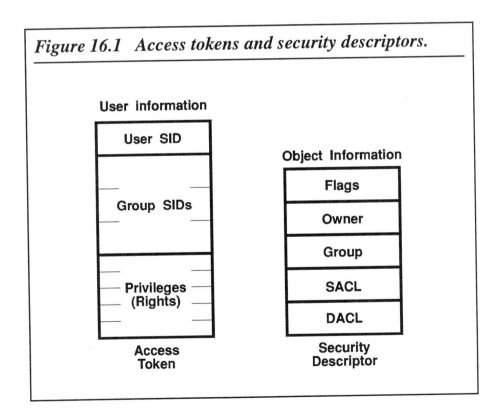

Figure 16.1 Access tokens and security descriptors.

But there is more to who you are on the computer than your SID, just as there is more to who you are in real life than your name. Windows NT supports combining users into groups, which also have names (like "Administrators" or "Power Users") and SIDs. Groups allow a single group SID to represent an arbitrarily large number of group members, and thus are very useful. For example, if I specify that all members of the group "My Friends" can read a certain file, then I can simply maintain the membership of that group to grant access to the file. Every Windows NT user is in one or more groups, and the security system retrieves these group memberships when you log on.

Finally, in addition to your SID and your groups, the logon process retrieves your privileges. Privileges are difficult to understand without knowledge of the details of the security system, because they permit extensions and allow special overrides to the normal security mechanisms. Privileges may be granted either to an individual or to a group, and every user gets the sum total of his or her individual privileges, plus those granted to all of his or her groups.

Windows NT gathers all of this information (SID, groups, and privileges) together into a structure called an access token. This structure is not directly addressable by applications, but you can manipulate it in certain ways through system calls (for example, you can enable and disable privileges). It is this access token that truly represents "who you are" to the operating system.

Every Windows NT process has an associated access token. If the user has logged on interactively (by sitting down at the keyboard and typing Ctrl-Alt-Del), then this access token is attached to the Program Manager when it is created. Any process created by the Program Manager will inherit a copy of the access token attached to the Program Manager, and any child process of those processes will inherit a copy, and so forth. So even though many access tokens in the system represent the user, most of the time they will be identical. This allows you to ignore the details and speak of "the user's token" as if there were only one in the system.

The purpose of the access token is twofold: first, to keep all the necessary security information about the user together to speed access validation; and second, to allow each process to modify its security information in limited ways without affecting other processes running on behalf of the user. An example of how a process may modify information in its access token would be to enable a privilege before performing a privileged operation. It would obviously be bad if all of the security information for the user were kept in one system-wide place, such that enabling a privilege for one process enabled it for all of them.

Object Information Overview

Knowing who you are is only half of the information the system needs so that it knows what you can do. The other half is attached to each system object that you might want to access and is contained in a structure called a security descriptor. The security descriptor contains data structures that describe very precisely who (by SID) can do what to the object. By examining the security descriptor and comparing what is in it to what is in your access token, the system can decide whether or not you are allowed to access the object in the way you want.

As Figure 16.1 shows, the security descriptor is a collection of security information about an object, just as the access token is a collection of security information about a user. I discuss these fields in more detail later, but here is brief overview of the key fields:

- *Owner* — the security ID (SID) of the owner of the object. The owner of an object can perform almost any action on that object.
- *Group* — a field that exists mainly to support Windows NT's POSIX subsystem; as a Win32 programmer, you can always ignore it.
- *SACL* — the System Access Control List. This specifies what kinds of operations on the object should generate audit messages.
- *DACL* — the Discretionary Access Control List. This is the main field you will be concerned with, because it grants and denies access to individual users and groups.

What Are NT Objects?

Most PC programmers only run into security in the context of files on a network. Under Windows NT, security is not a special concept just for files. Instead, Windows NT security applies uniformly to several different operating system resources, each of which Windows NT treats internally as an object. To understand the security system, then, you need to understand how Windows NT uses objects.

Every entity that Windows NT creates is an object. Files are objects, as are threads, semaphores, timers, windows, and so on. Windows NT creates all of its objects in a uniform way through a body of code in the kernel called the object manager. The object manager is responsible for creating, opening, and destroying objects on behalf of applications.

You can divide Windows NT objects into two groups: named and unnamed. When you create an unnamed object, you get a handle to that object, and the handle is the only way to refer to it. Named objects, on the other hand, are useful because they have a name that other processes can use to obtain a handle to the object. For example, if Process A is to synchronize itself with Process B, it might create a named event object and pass the name of the event to Process B. Process B would then open and use that event object. However, if Process A is simply to use the event to synchronize two threads within itself, it would probably choose to create an unnamed event object, because no other process need be able to use that particular event.

Any type of object other than a file may be either named or unnamed. It is up to the application to decide what best meets its needs. However, there is one important difference between named and unnamed objects in NT: all named objects always have security information associated with them. The security information may not restrict access to the object, but the system will always maintain internal data structures describing the security attributes of the object.

The reason named objects have security information is for the same reason that names make them useful: they may be accessed by any process by name. If Process A creates an unnamed semaphore, Process B has no way to ask for access to that particular semaphore. Thus, there is no need to protect it. However, Process A may create a named semaphore with the intent that only processes it knows about should be able to open and use that semaphore. To guarantee that the semaphore is not improperly used by an unauthorized process, Process A must place security information on the semaphore when creating it.

Windows NT uses objects internally, but the interface that you use (the Win32 API) is a procedural one — you always manipulate Windows NT objects indirectly, by passing their handles to Win32 API functions. When your application attempts to open an object, it must pass in a bit mask describing the desired access (such as "read" or "write") to the object. If all of the desired accesses to the object are granted, the Win32 function returns a handle to the object. The desired access mask you pass when opening the object is retained by the system and stored internally with the handle in the process's handle table. A handle may only be used in ways permitted by its desired access mask. Attempting to use the handle for any other purpose will result in an "Access Denied" error code.

Planning an Access Request

That all handles are not created equal (because they may have different access masks) is a source of confusion to many programmers who have never written applications for a secure system before. It means that your application has to know in advance exactly what it intends to do with a particular object handle and make sure it gets the access it needs up front. It also means that even though the user may have some access to the underlying object, if that access is not reflected in the corresponding object handle, the attempt to use that access will fail.

For example, suppose user "BartS" wants to access a word processing file that he has read and write access to. His word processor has the option to open the file for read access, write access, or both (it is an error to attempt to open an object for no access). If the word processor opens the file for read access only and then attempts to use that handle for writing the file, the write operation will fail even though "BartS" has write permission to the file. The word processor must know when it opens the file that it may have to read and write the file and must request both accesses.

Suppose your application does not know all of the operations that it is going to be asked to perform on an object. You have three choices of what to do in that case.

First, you could attempt to open the object for all possible accesses. This is generally a bad thing to do, because each access requested is another access that may be denied (remember that all of the accesses in the desired access mask must be granted to receive a handle to the object). This can result in unfortunate situations where the application will not let a user operate on an object in any way, even though the user has all of the access rights needed for the task at hand. Another disadvantage of asking for more access than necessary is that it prevents the system from helping you debug your application. Having a handle that may only be used in limited ways is a great debugging aid, because the system will detect errant uses of the handle. It is like extending virtual memory protection to files and other objects and can be very useful.

Second, your application could open a new handle to the object each time it attempts to perform a different kind of operation on the object. This is the preferred method, because it will not deny or allow more access than necessary. However, it has the overhead of opening and closing several handles.

Finally, you could attempt to open the object for as much access as the system will permit. I describe the best way to do this later in this chapter, via the MAXIMUM_ALLOWED access type. The advantage of this method is that the user will not be artificially denied access to the object, but the disadvantage is the same as mentioned above: the handle may have more access than it needs, which may help mask bugs.

It is rare for an application not to be able to determine reasonably well what access it is going to need to an object, so you should not find yourself having to evaluate the pros and cons of the above strategies very often.

SIDs in Detail

As I mentioned earlier, the first piece of security information the system retrieves about you when you log on is your security identifier (SID). Each user and group in Windows NT is assigned an SID that the system uses to differentiate one user from another, much as the IRS uses Social Security and taxpayer ID numbers to differentiate taxpaying entities. This gives Windows NT a uniform way to manipulate security information for individual users and groups.

An SID consists of a series of integers representing an "authenticating authority" (typically, "Windows NT"), a subauthority (representing the network domain that will be the user's primary domain), and a "relative ID," representing a particular group or user in that domain. For example, a typical SID might look like:

S-1-5-462442-37204

where "S-1-5" means that the SID was created by a Windows NT system, "462442" represents a network domain in the organization, and "37204" is the unique ID of an individual employee whose account is in that domain.

A unique SID is created for each user when that user's account is created in a network domain. One important thing to note is that because each user's primary domain is coded into his or her SID, switching domains forces the creation of a new SID to represent the user, which in turn causes that user to lose access to much of the information he or she had previously been able to get to.

To understand why this is desirable behavior, take the example of a user "Megan," who works in the payroll department and has access to company payroll records. For one reason or another, Megan is transferred to some other part of the company, a part that does not normally have access to payroll records (such as the advertising department). Megan no longer needs, and in fact should not have, access to the company payroll records, yet if she kept her old SID, it might be very difficult to make sure that she can no longer access the files she used to work with. The easiest way to ensure this is to "re-create" Megan's account from scratch and add the ability to access what she needs for her new job.

This example illustrates that SIDs may be thought of as representing a specific job within the company rather than a specific individual. When an individual changes assignments, the security information associated with the old position should not move with the user to the new job.

Privileges

As Figure 16.1 shows, the main piece of user information you have to understand besides SIDs is privileges, which permit extensions and allow special overrides to normal security. Privileges have two states: enabled and disabled. This allows a user to have a privilege and not necessarily be able to use it. Because privileges function as security overrides, the enable/disable capability is a safety feature to prevent their accidental use, like a lock on a pistol trigger. In my experience using Windows NT and privileges, I have found that unintentional uses of privileges tend to result in damage at best, disaster at worst, and are thus to be used with care.

Administrators grant privileges via the Windows NT User Manager. For example, an administrator may choose to create a group called "Backup Operators" and assign to that group SeBackupPrivilege. Users who have SeBackupPrivilege are allowed to use a backup tool and back up files that they normally would not be able to read. Every member of "Backup Operators" would have this privilege while logged on. If there was no need for an entire group of backup operators, the administrator could just choose one or two people and grant them SeBackupPrivilege individually. It is up to the administrator to decide which is the best method.

Security Descriptors

Looking again at Figure 16.1, I have described some of the structure and purpose of the user information that the security system maintains. I now turn to the details of the object security information, which is contained in the security descriptor structure. The security descriptor contains control flags and pointers to an owner SID, a group SID, a system access control list (SACL), and a discretionary access control list (DACL).

Security descriptors come in two formats: absolute and self relative. Absolute format means that the pointers to the owner SID, group SID, DACL, and SACL fields are genuine pointers into memory. Self-relative format means that, instead of pointers, these fields contain offsets to the actual data, which has been appended to the end of the structure.

The reason for the self-relative format is that security descriptors must be stored on disk and transmitted over network connections, and a structure containing pointers is not suitable in either of these cases. If you are familiar with Remote Procedure Call (RPC) conventions, you will recognize the self-relative format as simply a marshalled version of the absolute format descriptor.

When applications create security descriptors, they create them in absolute format. The Win32 API provides a number of functions to help you construct security descriptors, and all of them construct absolute format descriptors. When Windows NT receives an absolute format security descriptor, it converts it to self-relative format before storing it. When the application queries the security descriptor of an object, it will always get it in self-relative format.

Figure 16.2 shows a security descriptor structure. The meanings of the fields follow.

Revision — The Revision field allows Microsoft to revise the security descriptor structure sometime in the future without breaking existing software.

Sbz1 — The abbreviation "Sbz" stands for "should be zero." This means that Windows NT does not currently force these fields to be zero, but may at any future time require that they be so. This allows the Windows NT designers to start to use these fields at some time in the future without having to worry about breaking correctly written applications. An application that uses these fields for its own purposes is almost guaranteed not to work on some future release of Windows NT.

Control — The flags in a security descriptor indicate what is in it. This field contains flags describing whether or not the SACL and DACL are present, whether or not they were placed on the object by a defaulting mechanism, and whether the security descriptor is in self-relative or absolute format.

Owner — Every security descriptor contains an owner security ID (SID). If you don't specify an owner when you create the object, Windows NT will examine your token and usually assign your user SID as the owner. Anyone may change the owner of an object to any SID that is in the current token. For example, if Joe is a member of groups "Power Users" and "Managers," any process he runs may only change the owner of an object to either his SID or one of the SIDs representing "Power Users" or "Managers." If the owner SID is set to either of the groups, then all of the members of the owning group are owners of the object.

Figure 16.2   A security description structure.

```
typedef struct _SECURITY_DESCRIPTOR {
    UCHAR Revision;
    UCHAR Sbz1;
    SECURITY_DESCRIPTOR_CONTROL Control;
    PSID Owner;
    PSID Group;
    PACL Sacl;
    PACL Dacl;
} SECURITY_DESCRIPTOR, *PISECURITY_DESCRIPTOR;
```

Why can't Joe make anyone he wants the owner of the object? Because then he would be able to cover his tracks if he has accessed the file illegitimately. Users may only take ownership of objects, they may never give ownership of an object to other users.

The owner can always perform one very important operation on the object: change its DACL, which grants and denies accesses to the object. In essence, given this control, the owner of an object cannot be prevented from performing almost any action on the object.

Group — As I mentioned earlier, the group field is for POSIX compatibility — you can ignore it.

Sacl — The SACL field contains a pointer to the system access control list, which contains auditing and alarm information. This list contains access control entries (which I discuss in detail later), which describe what operations should generate audit messages in the audit log. Applications must have a privilege (SeSecurityPrivilege) in order to read or write the SACL on any object. This is to prevent unauthorized applications from reading SACLs (and thereby knowing what not to do in order to avoid generating audits) or setting them (to generate lots of spurious audits in order to cause an illicit operation to go unnoticed).

Dacl — This field (often pronounced "dackle"), is a list that grants or denies specific accesses to specific users or groups of users. The DACL contains the bulk of the object security information, and it can be one of the most confusing parts of Windows NT security to understand. Much of the rest of this chapter is devoted to explaining DACLs.

DACLs

Given a Windows NT object, you can grant or deny specific kinds of access to that object for specific users by adding entries to the object's Discretionary Access Control List (DACL). An object may get its DACL from an explicit assignment or a defaulting mechanism.

An explicit DACL is assigned when a user process constructs a DACL and passes it to the system with instructions to apply it to a particular object. However, most DACLs in a running system will be assigned to their objects by default. The most common defaulting mechanism is where protection on a file is inherited from that file's directory.

The other defaulting mechanism is rarely employed but occasionally useful. One of the user-modifiable fields in the access token is the default DACL. This default DACL will be applied to every object created by the process that owns the token. This mechanism is useful if a large number of objects must be created with identical DACLs, but in practice it often has unintended side effects.

DACL Structure

Conceptually, the DACL is just a list of entries, each of which grants or denies a set of accesses to a user or group of users. However, if you are going to write code that deals with security, it will be helpful to look at the structure of a DACL in detail.

As shown in Figure 16.3, a DACL consists of header information followed by a variable number of structures called access control entries (or ACEs). An ACEs consists of header information, a set of access bits (in the form of an access mask), and an SID that may represent either a user or a group of users.

Part of what makes NT security confusing is that its mechanisms are very flexible and easy to extend. Access control entries do not have to look like the ones described here. However, the Windows NT kernel will only recognize and interpret ACE that it understands. The definitions of the data structures I am going to describe may look unnecessarily complex, but they are defined so that they may be used in many ways.

Figure 16.3 Access control list layout.

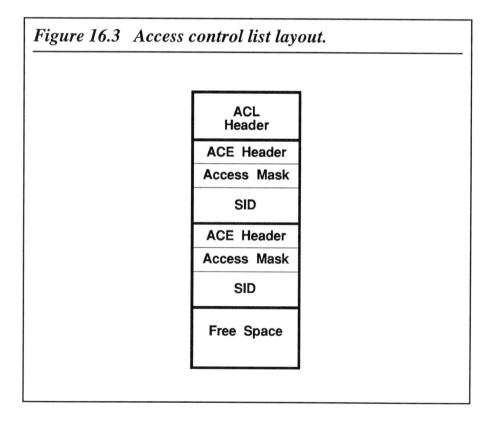

Header Information

A DACL is a structure of type `ACL`, defined as follows:

```
typedef struct _ACL {
  UCHAR AclRevision;
  UCHAR Sbz1;
  USHORT AclSize;
  USHORT AceCount;
  USHORT Sbz2;
} ACL, *PACL;
```

There isn't much information here. As with the security descriptor structure, the `Acl-Revision` field and `Sbz1` and `Sbz2` fields exist to allow for future changes in the data structure. The `AclSize` field contains the total size of the structure, which may be larger than the sum total of the ACEs in the list to allow for future growth. The `Ace-Count` field indicates the number of ACEs in the ACL.

Although it is entirely permissible for you to fill in the fields of an ACL or ACE structure "by hand," it isn't necessary. The Win32 API provides `InitializeAcl()`, which takes a buffer and initializes the various parts to look like a valid, empty ACL. (I will demonstrate this later in the chapter.)

Access Control Entry Structure

As Figure 16.3 shows, the DACL header is immediately followed by some number (which may be zero) of ACEs. Like the DACL itself, each ACE starts with a header:

```
typedef struct _ACE_HEADER {
  UCHAR AceType;
  UCHAR AceFlags;
  USHORT AceSize;
} ACE_HEADER, *PACE_HEADER;
```

The `AceType` field may be one of two values: `ACCESS_ALLOWED_ACE_TYPE` and `ACCESS_DENIED_ACE_TYPE`. As might be obvious from the names, these indicate whether or not the access control entry is meant to grant or deny accesses.

The `AceFlags` field holds flags describing if and how the ACE is to be inherited. As described earlier, ACEs may be marked so that if they appear on a directory and a file is created in that directory, the ACEs will be passed to that file. ACE inheritance is complex and beyond the scope of this chapter, but suffice it to say that it is a very powerful means of setting up a secure system in that it ensures that newly created files will be protected, even if the user creating them does not know the principles of Windows NT security.

Figure 16.4 shows the structures that describe the "known ACEs," which define the structure that Windows NT expects to find for the ACCESS_ALLOWED and ACCESS_DENIED ACE types. Because the Win32 API provides AddAccessAl-lowedAce() and AddAccessDeniedAce(), few applications will have to make direct use of the ACE structure. However, understanding what's going on under the covers helps in understanding how the ACEs are interpreted.

The Access Mask

The mask field in the ACE is the same as the desired access mask that you pass to the Win32 API when you create or open an object. Figure 16.5 shows the structure of an access mask. Bits 16 through 25 of this mask contain standard access types that are common to all objects, and are used as follows:

- WRITE_DAC access allows the application to modify the protection on the object. This means the application can obtain the object's DACL, edit it in any way it pleases, and replace the old DACL with the new one. With this access, an application could even remove all protection from the object.

- WRITE_OWNER access allows a program to modify the owner of the object. This is useful because the owner of an object can always change the protection on the object (or, more formally, the owner of an object may not be denied WRITE_DAC access to the object). Remember that the SID of the owner of an object resides in a field of the object's security descriptor.

Figure 16.4   Access control entry sructure.

```
typedef struct _ACCESS_ALLOWED_ACE {
    ACE_HEADER Header;
    ACCESS_MASK Mask;
    ULONG SidStart;
} ACCESS_ALLOWED_ACE;

typedef ACCESS_ALLOWED_ACE *PACCESS_ALLOWED_ACE;

typedef struct _ACCESS_DENIED_ACE {
    ACE_HEADER Header;
    ACCESS_MASK Mask;
    ULONG SidStart;
} ACCESS_DENIED_ACE;

typedef ACCESS_DENIED_ACE *PACCESS_DENIED_ACE;
```

- READ_CONTROL access allows the application to query the owner, DACL, and certain control information from the object's security descriptor.

- DELETE access allows the application to delete the object. Note that even though an object may be deleted and no longer usable, the memory associated with the object will not be freed until all handles to the object are closed.

- SYNCHRONIZE access allows the handle to be passed into WaitForSingleObject() and related calls. In other words, this access gives you permission to synchronize execution with some event associated with the given object.

- ACCESS_SYSTEM_SECURITY access allows modifying audit and alarm control for the object. This access may not be granted via an object's DACL, but in fact requires that the caller have a particular privilege.

- MAXIMUM_ALLOWED is not really an access bit that you can grant or deny in an ACE. This is a bit that you can set in a desired access mask that modifies Windows NT's algorithm for scanning the DACL.

Object-Specific vs. Generic Access Types

In the diagram of the access mask shown in Figure 16.5, the lower 16 bits of the access mask are labeled "Specific Rights". "Specific" means that the meaning of these bits is different for each type of object. For example, requesting bit 0 for a file object means that you're asking for FILE_READ_DATA, whereas bit 0 for an event object is EVENT_QUERY_STATE. There is no pattern to how these bits are used; you must know what access you need to accomplish what you want to do.

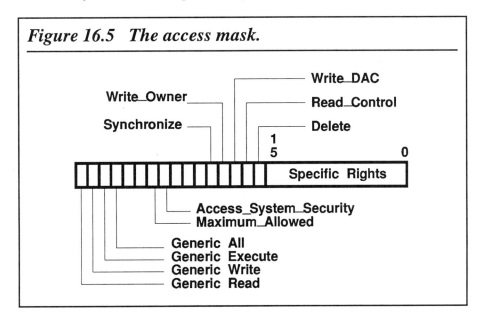

Figure 16.5   The access mask.

The fact that object-specific access bits are different for each type of object often makes them difficult to use. For example, suppose an application wants to create several types of objects and ensure that users have "read" access to the objects, even though "read" may mean slightly different things for each object. In order to protect each object of each type, the application would have to construct a different DACL for each type of object and be careful to pass the correct DACL in when creating each object. It would be much more convenient to be able to create a single DACL that expresses the concept "allow read." Simply apply this DACL to each object that is created, and have the right thing happen. Generic access types allow precisely this kind of shortcut.

Each object type (file, event, process, etc.) has something called a generic mapping. A generic mapping is a description of all of the accesses that correspond to the concepts of "read," "write," "execute," and "all" access for that object. When Windows NT receives a request to place a DACL on an object, it first looks up the generic mapping for objects of that type. It then examines all of the ACCESS_ALLOWED and ACCESS_DENIED access control entries in the DACL, examining the generic access bits in each entry's access mask. For each generic access bit it finds set, it sets the specific bits corresponding to that generic bit in the access mask and clears the generic bit.

For example, for a file object, the bit GENERIC_READ maps to the standard bits READ_CONTROL and SYNCHRONIZE and to the object-specific bits FILE_READ_DATA, FILE_READ_ATTRIBUTES, and FILE_READ_EA. Placing a DACL on a file that grants someone GENERIC_READ will grant those five accesses as if they had been specified individually in the access mask.

The DACL Evaluation Algorithm

Having described the DACL structure in detail, I can now give a formal description of how Windows NT evaluates the DACL to decide whether or not to grant a particular access request. Figure 16.6 shows the pseudocode for the algorithm.

If a program requests access to an object that has a DACL, the operating system will walk the access control entries in the DACL in order, from first to last. For each ACCESS_ALLOWED ACE it finds, it will see if the SID in that entry is in the current token (meaning, is it the SID of the user or one the user's groups?). If it is present, the operating system clears the bits found in common between that ACE's access mask and the desired access mask. For each ACCESS_DENIED entry, the operating system will again make sure the SID is in the current token, and if so, it will see if any of the bits in the ACE's access mask remain in the desired access mask. This continues until there are no more ACEs (in which case the operating system denies access), any of the desired bits are denied (which will also deny access), or all of the desired access bits are granted.

This implies two rules to keep in mind. First, all accesses are denied unless explicitly granted. If anything is left in the desired access mask after the DACL is evaluated, the request will be denied. Second, the order of ACEs is extremely important. Once an access is granted by an ACE, it may not be denied by a subsequent ACE. Likewise, once an access is denied, the presence of an ACE that grants the access further down the list is not going to change that denial. In order to guarantee that an ACCESS_DENIED ACE will have the desired effect, you have to place that entry near the front of the list.

The Windows NT File Manager's ACL editor supports this convention. It builds DACLs such that all ACCESS_DENIED ACEs are at the head of the DACL, followed by all the ACCESS_ALLOWED ACEs. A DACL in this form is referred to as being in "canonical form."

Missing DACLs vs. Empty DACLs

There is a subtlety to the DACL algorithm. Windows NT makes the distinction between an object having no DACL and having an empty DACL. An empty DACL is one that is structurally complete but has no ACEs in it. If an object has no DACL, the object is said to have "no security," and all accesses to the object are granted (except for those requiring a privilege). If a DACL is present but empty, the "all accesses are denied unless explicitly granted" rule kicks in, and all accesses are denied — a completely opposite result for what would appear to be a similar situation.

Figure 16.6   Pseudocode for the DACL evaluation algorithm.

```
while (more ACEs and DesiredAccess != 0)
    if ACE.AceType == ACCESS_ALLOWED_ACE_TYPE
        if ACE.Sid is in token
            DesiredAccess &= ~ACE.Mask
            continue
    if ACE.AceType == ACCESS_DENIED_ACE_TYPE
        if ACE.Sid is in token
            if (DesiredAccess & ACE.Mask) != 0
                return(ACCESS_DENIED)

if DesiredAccess == 0
    return(ACCESS_ALLOWED)
else
    return(ACCESS_DENIED)
```

Whether a DACL is present is determined by the DACL_PRESENT bit in the header of the security descriptor and the DACL pointer field. The chart in Figure 16.7 shows all the possible combinations. The "evaluate DACL" field may be expanded further into the cases of whether ACEs are present (in which case they are evaluated) or absent (in which case the request is denied).

Privileges and DACL Evaluation

As I mentioned earlier, privileges are basically overrides of the normal security mechanisms. They exist because there are times when the DACL security on objects should not be enforced for one reason or another. For example, many companies have their MIS department perform backup and restore operations on machines in their organization. Without a backup privilege that allows overriding the DACLs on files, it would be necessary for every file in the organization to grant explicit access to some account in the MIS department. In a large organization the chances of this sort of setup working smoothly are vanishingly small and irritating regardless. So, Windows NT provides a backup privilege that allows its holder to read (but not write) any file on the disk.

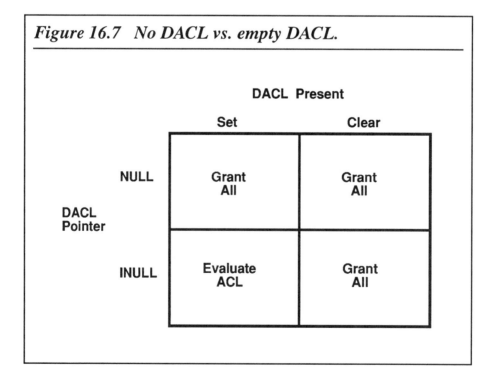

Figure 16.7   No DACL vs. empty DACL.

Privileges are very powerful in Windows NT, because there is no mechanism to override their effects. If user Joe is in a group that normally has access to a file, it is still possible to deny Joe access to that file with another ACE. Privileges cannot be restricted, so they must be given out sparingly and only when a need is clear and definite.

MAXIMUM_ALLOWED Access

One final access type is different from all of the others: MAXIMUM_ALLOWED access. MAXIMUM_ALLOWED may only be requested in a desired access mask: it cannot be granted or denied in an ACE.

When Windows NT sees a request for MAXIMUM_ALLOWED access to an object, it walks down the DACL of the object and computes the maximal access that the caller has to the object. The algorithm it uses is as follows:

```
Denied=0;
Granted=0;
for each ACE
  if ACE.Type== \
  ACCESS_ALLOWED_ACE_TYPE
    Granted |= \
    (ACE.Mask & ~Denied);
  else Denied |=
  (ACE.Mask & ~Granted);
if Granted==0 return ACCESS_DENIED
```

Keep two special cases in mind when using MAXIMUM_ALLOWED. First, if any bit in the desired access mask is set in addition to MAXIMUM_ALLOWED, the system interprets it to mean that bit is required, meaning that the access request will fail if that bit does not end up being granted by the MAXIMUM_ALLOWED algorithm. Second, for an object with no DACL, which may be opened for any access, Windows NT returns the GENERIC_ALL bits in the handle and returns success.

MAXIMUM_ALLOWED is a cheap and easy way to deal with the situation where you don't know what access you're going to need to an object. The downside is that you don't know what accesses were granted to the object, so you have to be prepared for operations on the returned handle to fail with ACCESS_DENIED.

A Security Example

I will describe how to write a small program (take.exe) that lets an administrator override the normal security on a file. I say "an administrator" because the Administrator account has special privileges (or "rights") not normally found in regular user accounts. These privileges allow the administrator to perform security-related actions that no other user of the machine should be allowed to do. The source to take.exe is in Listing 16.1 (newtest.c), and you may want to refer to it as you read the description that follows.

Listing 16.1 *newtest.c — Source code for* take.exe *lets administrator override file security.*

```
#include <windows.h>
#include <malloc.h>
#include <stdio.h>
#include <process.h>

BOOL EnableTakeOwnershipPrivilege(
    HANDLE TokenHandle,
    PTOKEN_PRIVILEGES OldPrivileges
    );

BOOL OpenToken(
    PHANDLE TokenHandle
    );

VOID _CRTAPI1 main  (int argc, char *argv[])
{
    int i;
    PACL Dacl;
    LPSTR FileName;
    TOKEN_PRIVILEGES OldPrivileges;
    SID_IDENTIFIER_AUTHORITY NtAuthority = SECURITY_NT_AUTHORITY;
    PSID AdminAliasSid;
    BOOL Result;
    ULONG DaclSize;
    HANDLE TokenHandle;
    SECURITY_DESCRIPTOR SecurityDescriptor;

    if ( argc <= 1 ) {
        printf("No file specified\n");
        exit(-1);
    }
```

Listing 16.1 (continued)

```
Result = AllocateAndInitializeSid(
            &NtAuthority,    2,
            SECURITY_BUILTIN_DOMAIN_RID,
            DOMAIN_ALIAS_RID_ADMINS,
            0, 0, 0, 0, 0, 0,
            &AdminAliasSid
            );

if ( !Result ) {
    printf("Unable to allocate memory for SIDs\n");
    exit(-1);
}

Result = OpenToken( &TokenHandle );

if ( !Result ) {
    printf("Unable to open token\n");
    exit(-1);
}

// Build the new Security Descriptor to put on
// the file.
// This will only fail if the revision is wrong, but
// it's good to be prepared for anything.

Result = InitializeSecurityDescriptor( &SecurityDescriptor,
                    SECURITY_DESCRIPTOR_REVISION );


if ( !Result ) {
    printf("Unable to initialize Security Descriptor\n");
    exit(-1);
}

// Compute the size of the buffer needed for the
// DACL.

DaclSize = sizeof( ACL )                +
            sizeof( ACCESS_ALLOWED_ACE ) -
            sizeof( ULONG )              +
            GetLengthSid( AdminAliasSid );

Dacl = malloc( DaclSize );

if ( Dacl == NULL ) {
    printf("Out of memory\n");
    exit(-1);
}
```

Even though this program duplicates features found in the File Manager, under-standing it and the problem it solves is important to understanding the basics of NT security. Anyone who wants to write applications that manipulate the security attributes of files or other objects in NT should be comfortable with the concepts I dis-cuss here.

An important note: NT currently supports three file systems — FAT, HPFS, and NTFS. Of the three, only NTFS allows placing security information on files. Although take.exe will appear to work on FAT and HPFS, it quietly does nothing. It is much more interesting to run it on NTFS, where you can readily observe its actions.

Listing 16.1 (continued)

```
Result = InitializeAcl ( Dacl, DaclSize, ACL_REVISION2 );

if ( !Result ) {
    printf("Unable to initialize ACL, error = %d\n",GetLastError());
    exit(-1);
}

Result = AddAccessAllowedAce (
            Dacl,
            ACL_REVISION2,
            GENERIC_ALL,
            AdminAliasSid
            );

if ( !Result ) {
    printf("Unable to add ACE, error = %d\n",GetLastError());
    exit(-1);
}

Result = SetSecurityDescriptorDacl (
            &SecurityDescriptor,
            TRUE,
            Dacl,
            FALSE
            );

if ( !Result ) {
    printf("Unable to add ACL to security descriptor,
        error = %d\n",GetLastError());
    exit(-1);
}
```

The Problem

In order to make this an interesting exercise, log onto Windows NT as a normal user (not an administrator). Create a dummy file on an NTFS partition and select it in the File Manager. From the File Manager's Security menu, select Permissions. Remove any permissions and add an entry giving "Everyone" "No Access." This tells the File Manager to put an empty DACL on the file. Because you are the creator of the file, your SID is now the owner of the file.

Because you are the owner of the file, you could start File Manager again and put another DACL on the file that does whatever you'd like. But suppose you are the system administrator, you discover this file, and its owner is no longer available. You can't just change its DACL, because its current DACL denies everyone (including an administrator) access. You would have to run a program that does something similar to what take.exe does.

Listing 16.1 (continued)

```
Result = SetSecurityDescriptorOwner(
            &SecurityDescriptor,
            AdminAliasSid, FALSE
            );

if ( !Result ) {
    printf("Unable to set owner, error = %d\n",GetLastError());
    exit(-1);

}

for (i=1; i<argc; i++) {
    FileName = argv[i];
    printf("\nFile: %s\n",FileName);
    Result = SetFileSecurity(
                FileName,
                DACL_SECURITY_INFORMATION,
                &SecurityDescriptor
                );
    if ( Result ) {
        printf("%s: Dacl replaced\n",FileName);
        continue;
    }
```

Listing 16.1 (continued)

```
        // If the attempt to change the DACL didn't work,
        // we have to make Admin the owner.  Just try it
        // first, and then try it with a privilege.

        Result = SetFileSecurity(
                    FileName,
                    OWNER_SECURITY_INFORMATION,
                    &SecurityDescriptor
                    );
        if ( !Result ) {
            // The attempt to make Admin the owner of
            // the file failed.  Use SeTakeOwnership
            // privilege.
            Result = EnableTakeOwnershipPrivilege(
                        TokenHandle,
                        &OldPrivileges
                        );
            if ( !Result ) {
                // This account doesn't have SeTakeOwnership
                // privilege.  Tell them to try running it again
                // from an account that does.

                printf("Unable to enable SeTakeOwnership privilege\n");
                printf("Try running take again from the Administrator
                        account\n");
                printf("%s: skipped\n",FileName);
                continue;
            }
            Result = SetFileSecurity(
                        FileName,
                        OWNER_SECURITY_INFORMATION,
                        &SecurityDescriptor
                        );
            if ( !Result ) {
                // This shouldn't fail, but it can.
                printf("Unable to set file owner with privilege\n");
                printf("Terminating\n");
                exit(-1);
            }

            // Turn off SeTakeOwnership privilege.
            (VOID) AdjustTokenPrivileges ( TokenHandle, FALSE, &OldPrivileges,
                        sizeof( TOKEN_PRIVILEGES ), NULL, NULL );
            if ( GetLastError() != NO_ERROR ) {
                // This is unlikely to happen,
                printf("AdjustTokenPrivileges failed turning off SeTakeOwnership
                        privilege\n");
            }
```

To demonstrate the problem you're up against, log onto the Administrator account and try to do something to the file. Try anything. Try to delete the file or even just type it out. You'll be told "Access Denied." There's no way for you to get rid of the file (and reformatting the disk is cheating!). take.exe tackles the problem by taking steps to:

- initialize data structures,
- attempt to replace the DACL on the file by the most straightforward approach,
- enable SeTakeOwnership privilege, if necessary, and replace the owner on the file, and
- once again attempt to replace the DACL on the file.

Figure 16.8 provides a schematic of roughly what happens up to the first attempt to set the file security.

Listing 16.1 (continued)

```
                Result = SetFileSecurity(
                        FileName,
                        DACL_SECURITY_INFORMATION,
                        &SecurityDescriptor
                        );
                if ( Result ) {
                    printf("%s: Dacl replaced\n",FileName);
                    continue;

                } else {
                    // This shouldn't fail, but it can.
                    printf("Unable to set DACL of file owned by Admin\n");
                    printf("Terminating\n");
                    exit(-1);
                }
            }
        }
    }
}

BOOL EnableTakeOwnershipPrivilege( HANDLE TokenHandle,
    PTOKEN_PRIVILEGES OldPrivileges )
{
    TOKEN_PRIVILEGES NewPrivileges;
    BOOL Result;
    LUID TakeOwnershipValue;
    ULONG ReturnLength;

    Result = LookupPrivilegeValue(
                NULL, "SeTakeOwnershipPrivilege",
                &TakeOwnershipValue
                );
```

Listing 16.1 *(continued)*

```
      if ( !Result ) {
          printf("Unable to obtain value of TakeOwnership privilege\n");
          return FALSE;
      }

      // Set up the privilege set we will need
      NewPrivileges.PrivilegeCount = 1;
      NewPrivileges.Privileges[0].Luid = TakeOwnershipValue;
      NewPrivileges.Privileges[0].Attributes = SE_PRIVILEGE_ENABLED;

      (VOID) AdjustTokenPrivileges (
                  TokenHandle, FALSE,
                  &NewPrivileges,
                  sizeof( TOKEN_PRIVILEGES ),
                  OldPrivileges, &ReturnLength
                  );
      if ( GetLastError() != NO_ERROR )
          return( FALSE );
      else
          return( TRUE );
  }

BOOL OpenToken( PHANDLE TokenHandle )
{
      HANDLE Process;
      BOOL Result;

      Process = OpenProcess(
                  PROCESS_QUERY_INFORMATION,
                  FALSE, GetCurrentProcessId()
                  );
      if ( Process == NULL ) {
          // This can happen, but is unlikely.
          return( FALSE );
      }

      Result = OpenProcessToken (
                  Process,
                  TOKEN_ADJUST_PRIVILEGES | TOKEN_QUERY,
                  TokenHandle
                  );
      CloseHandle( Process );
      if ( !Result ) {
          // This can happen, but is unlikely.
          return( FALSE );
      }
      return( TRUE );
  }
```

Constructing the Data Structures

The first thing `take.exe` has to do is initialize its data structures. Because `take.exe` is going to loop through all the files specified on its command line to perform its initialization upfront, it will have ready all the data it needs to interact with the Win32 security functions.

Building the SID

`take.exe` will attempt to create a DACL that allows administrators full access to the file and then will place that DACL on the file. It may first have to make "Administrators" the owner of the file. It can use the same SID both for the new owner and in the new DACL, so it builds the SID once here with a call to `AllocateAndInitialize-Sid()`. This routine figures out how much memory will be required by the SID, allocates the memory, and fills in the passed values. The call in `take.exe` is:

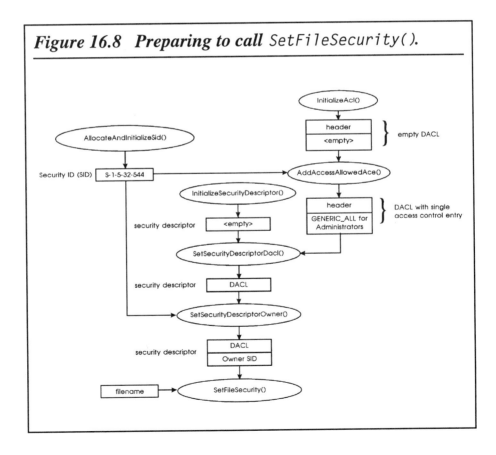

Figure 16.8 Preparing to call `SetFileSecurity()`.

```
Result = AllocateAndInitializeSid( &NtAuthority, 2,
        SECURITY_BUILTIN_DOMAIN_RID, DOMAIN_ALIAS_RID_ADMINS,
        0, 0, 0, 0, 0, 0, &AdminAliasSid);
```

which results in the following SID:

```
S-1-5-32-544
```

Building the DACL

Once the SID has been assembled, the new DACL for the file can be constructed. take.exe calculates exactly how much space will be required by the new DACL and allocates just that much. Calculating how much space is needed requires knowing what the various data structures that are going to go into the DACL look like. Unfortunately, DACLs are so arbitrarily complex that it isn't possible to have an Allocate-AndInitializeACL() routine, although such a thing would be quite helpful. This calculation requires the size of the SID in order to know how much space to allocate for the DACL, which is why I constructed the SID first.

The buffer allocated for the DACL must be initialized with a call to Initial-izeAcl(). This builds the header information at the beginning of the buffer and generally prepares the way for placing ACEs into the DACL.

I will put one ACE into the ACL, which will grant GENERIC_ALL access to anyone who is in the Administrators group. Because assembling the pieces of an ACE and getting it right is tedious and prone to error, Windows NT provides an easy-to-use Win32 function that takes all the necessary information and correctly puts it into the DACL. In take.exe this call is:

```
Result = AddAccessAllowedAce( Dacl, ACL_REVISION2,GENERIC_ALL,AdminAliasSid);
```

The corresponding call to put an ACCESS_DENIED ACE into the ACL would be AddAccessDeniedAce().

Building the Security Descriptor

Once I've finished building the DACL, I can put it into the security descriptor. I do this with a call to SetSecurityDescriptorDacl(). I also indicate that the DaclPresent flag should be set in the security descriptor, and that the DACL was not derived from a defaulting mechanism. In addition to setting the DACL in the security descriptor, I also put the AliasAdminSid into the owner field.

The reason for doing it this way is that I can load up a security descriptor with all four possible pieces of information (the owner, group, DACL, and SACL) but tell the system to only pay attention to certain pieces at a time. At one point in the program I want to set the DACL on the file, and at another point I'm going to want to set the owner, so I might as well load up both pieces now and just use what I need when I need it. This will become clearer when I get to the `SetFileSecurity()` calls.

Applying the Security Descriptor to a File

Because all I really want to do is change the DACL on the file, that is what I'll try first. If it doesn't work, I'll take stronger measures that I know will work.

Why not start with the stronger measures? First, the program makes a better learning tool by illustrating how to use increasingly sophisticated measures to achieve a goal. But more important, it's bad design methodology to employ security overrides you don't really need. Frequently, it isn't the right thing to do at all. For example, suppose you want to write a program like the File Manager that allows users to copy and delete files. To immediately employ every possible security override in order to accomplish a file copy or delete operation would be a bad design decision, because the user may have made a mistake in requesting that operation.

Security-aware programs like the File Manager should make the user issue a specific order before attempting to override the normal security on a file. Such programs may then turn around and use every trick in the book to accomplish the operation, but not before.

`take.exe` calls `SetFileSecurity()` to change the DACL on the file. `SetFileSecurity()` performs several operations on behalf of the user. First, it examines which part of the file's security descriptor is being changed and attempts to open up the file for the access required to make the change. If that succeeds, it replaces the specified piece of the security descriptor, closes the handle it got during the open call, and returns. Because the security of files receives more attention than the security of most other objects, Microsoft provided `SetFileSecurity()` to make common operations easier for applications to perform.

In fact, `SetFileSecurity()` may sometimes be the only way to change the security on a file. Alternatively, you could call `CreateFile()` for the access needed to change the security descriptor, followed by `SetKernelObjectSecurity()` to perform the changes. There is one subtle problem with this approach, however: `CreateFile()` will always attempt to open the file for `SYNCHRONIZE` access in addition to whatever other access you pass in. This can interfere with attempts to change the security descriptor of the file. `SetFileSecurity()` always tries to open the file for the least amount of access needed to change the security descriptor.

The second parameter to SetFileSecurity() tells the system which part of the passed security descriptor to pay attention to. Even though an owner is set in the passed security descriptor, passing DACL_SECURITY_INFORMATION causes it to be ignored.

Using Privileges to Override the DACL

If SetFileSecurity() does the job, take.exe will move on to the next file specified. If you set up the file to allow no access, as I suggested earlier, then this call to SetFileSecurity() won't be able to do anything. The next step is to try to change the owner on the file, which, like the attempt to change the DACL, may or may not fail.

I set the owner field of the security descriptor earlier on, so I can use this same security descriptor to try to change the owner by specifying OWNER_SECURITY_INFORMATION in the call to SetFileSecurity(). If this attempt to change the owner fails, a privilege will be necessary to get the job done. The subroutine EnableTakeOwnershipPrivilege() sets things up so that this is possible.

The first thing EnableTakeOwnershipPrivilege() must do is look up the value of the privilege (it is a good idea not to hard-code privilege values into applications, but rather to query their values at startup or when needed). Once the value of the privilege is known, I put it into a TOKEN_PRIVILEGES structure and pass it into the system. This is a variable-length structure composed of a header and any number of privilege values. If you need to adjust more than one privilege, you will have to compute the size of the structure with a calculation similar to the one I used to compute the required size of the ACL.

The call to AdjustTokenPrivileges() is the heart of the subroutine. Notice one important thing about the call to AdjustTokenPrivileges() — you don't need to examine its return value because, unlike most other API calls, AdjustTokenPrivileges() has three possible results: complete failure, complete success, and somewhere in between. The "somewhere in between" case occurs when you pass in multiple privileges, and some are found in the token and some are not. In this case, those that are found are enabled and the rest are ignored, but the API function will set LastError to tell you what happened. So the rule of thumb is, always call GetLastError() for the true story of what happened during a call to AdjustTokenPrivileges(). [AdjustTokenGroups() has similar semantics.]

Windows NT places privileges in an access token when the token is created, based on the groups and rights assigned to the subject. Not all tokens will contain all privileges, and in fact, most tokens will contain very few of the available privileges. There is no way to change the privileges in an existing token. Rather, the system administrator would have to modify the account information for the user and specify that the desired privileges be placed in the user's token the next time the user logs in.

Changing the Owner

Now that `SeTakeOwnership` privilege has been enabled, I can be sure that I'll be able to change the owner of the file, and once that is done, I will be able to modify the DACL of the file. Note that immediately after setting the owner of the file, I turn off `SeTakeOwnership` privilege in my token. In general, it is good practice to have privileges enabled only for the duration of the time you know that you're going to need them. Otherwise, they may have unintended and undesirable side effects (such as deleting at some later point a file that should not be deleted).

Rather than simply turning off the privilege, I call `AdjustTokenPrivileges()` again with the previous state of the privilege I changed. This allows me to restore the privilege to the state it was in before I started modifying it, rather than to just turn it off and potentially cause problems to the calling code (assuming this is taking place in the framework of a larger application).

Summary

Windows NT security is designed to meet the government C/2 security standards for discretionary access control. The operating system maintains security information both for users and for the objects they want to access, such as files, events, processes, and so on. Windows NT also supports privileges, which provide a way to override the normal security mechanisms to handle special problems, such as allowing someone to back up all files. The operating system uses a flexible scheme (the DACL) to specify the security on each object, providing a uniform interface to security features for a variety of different operating system resources.

The sample program is not meant to be as efficient as possible, but to illustrate design principles for security-aware applications. Were this to be a true "quick and dirty" tool, it would enable the privilege once up-front, blast the owner and DACL information onto each file, and be done with it. However, in complex applications that are not as straightforward as this one, it pays to wield the power of the security system carefully and only when necessary. In fact, most applications will never need to manipulate security information at all; those that do must be very careful not to cause dangerous side effects that could destroy large amounts of information.

Understanding how this program works also helps you to understand why it is bad practice to use accounts with lots of privileges except when really necessary. take.exe can only use SeTakeOwnership privilege in an account that has that privilege, which is normally only an Administrator account. Although it may be tempting for a system administrator to set up all of the users of the system as administrators or near administrators, such users are open to attacks by "Trojan Horse" programs that use the same techniques as take.exe to either steal or destroy data. It is for this reason that privileges should be granted sparingly, or not at all, and those who have privileges should be very careful only to run software that they trust absolutely.

References

Custer, Helen. *Inside Windows NT.* Redmond, WA: Microsoft Press, 1993. ISBN 1-55615-481-X.

Gasser, Morrie. *Building a Secure Computer System*, 1st ed. New York: Van Nostrand Reinhold, 1988. ISBN 0-442-23022-2.

## Chapter 17

Setting Breakpoints in a Windows NT Debugger

Brian G. Myers

One problem encountered when writing a debugger for 16-bit Windows is that it needs to modify code to insert breakpoints, but because Windows assumes read-only code pages, it may discard a code page and then swap it back by reading it directly from the executable file, wiping out any breakpoints that were set. A more complex problem arises because the Windows message system is synchronous, which makes it difficult to avoid situations in which the debugger's user interface cannot receive user input because the debuggee has not finished processing one or more messages.

Windows NT's Win32 API solves some of these problems. Preemptive multitasking and localized input queues prevent a debugging session from interfering with other tasks in the system, so there is no need for synchronous and asynchronous debugging modes. NT provides copy-on-write protection for code pages, so that as soon as the debugger attempts to modify a code page, NT makes a separate copy of the page for that instance of the application — the debugger's modifications will not be wiped out by swapping. New debugging API routines tell the debugger about events in the process it is debugging. And a multithreaded debugger can dedicate a thread to waiting for event notifications without having to merge the polling mechanism into its user interface code.

In the interest of portability, however, Win32 does not directly support single-step, breakpoint, or watchpoint capabilities in the host CPU. To use these features, the debugger must manipulate directly the hardware context of individual threads. UNIX, OS/2, and Windows 3.1 (the latter through undocumented means) give the debugger more direct support for the hardware's debugging features. A hardware-independent debugger for Win32 must use different low-level code depending on which hardware platform it is executing. Win32 also does not support the TOOLHELP API, which provides 16-bit Windows with many useful debugging functions, such as notifications of debugging events. You may have to construct your own equivalents from more primitive functions in the Win32 debugging API.

As an introduction to the process of writing a Windows API, this chapter explains the Win32 debugging API and shows how to set breakpoints on an Intel CPU. My first sample program watches for its child to call `OutputDebugString()` and displays the messages as they come. My second sample loads a short program and lets the user set breakpoints on source code lines. It shows how to structure an interactive debugger, how to set and remove breakpoints, and how to manage both hard and soft breakpoints.

Attaching the Debuggee Process

The Windows NT system recognizes and supports the special relationship that arises between two processes when one is debugging the other. The debugger acquires special privileges for intruding on its "child." (For convenience, I will call the program being debugged the child, although it need not be a child process launched by the debugger.) In order to acquire special debugging privileges, the debugger attaches itself to the child. There are two ways of attaching to a process. The easy way is to create the process yourself and set a debugging flag.

```
STARTUPINFO sui;
PROCESS_INFORMATION pi;
/* fill in the process's startup information */
ZeroMemory(&sui, sizeof(STARTUPINFO));
sui.cb = sizeof(STARTUPINFO);
sui.wShowWindow = SW_SHOWDEFAULT;
/* create the debuggee process */
CreateProcess(NULL, lpszFilePath,
        NULL, NULL, TRUE,    DEBUG_PROCESS,
        NULL, NULL, &sui, &pi);
```

The DEBUG_PROCESS flag in the last command has two effects. First, it requests extra access privileges such as PROCESS_VM_READ and PROCESS_VM_WRITE. A debugger needs these privileges in order to read and write data from the child's protected address space. The handle that CreateProcess() returns in pi.hProcess will have the extra debugging privileges. Second, the DEBUG_PROCESS flag also tells the system that the parent process wants to know when the child does anything important, such as load DLLs, create threads, cause exceptions, or terminate. In a minute I'll explain what else the debugger must do to receive debugging notifications, but they won't arrive at all unless the debugger uses the DEBUG_PROCESS flag.

A debugger may also attach itself to a process that already exists, but that is more difficult, because the debugger must know the process ID number first. To attach to a running process, use this function:

```
BOOL DebugActiveProcess(DWORD dwProcessId)
```

DebugActiveProcess() lets the debugger adopt a child it did not create. It's easy to adopt children you wrote because you can make them pass their own IDs to the debugger, perhaps in a message or through a pipe. The only way to determine the ID of an unknown process, however, is to enumerate the IDs of all the active processes from the system Registry. (See Chapter 10, "Enumerating Processes in Windows NT".)

Receiving Event Notifications

At the core of any debugger written for Windows NT, you'll use some version of this loop.

```
DEBUG_EVENT DebugEvent;
BOOL bDebugging = TRUE;
while (bDebugging) {

    /* block until a debugging event occurs */
    WaitForDebugEvent(&DebugEvent, INFINITE);

    switch (DebugEvent.dwDebugEventCode) {
        /* recognize and handle debugging events */
    }

    /* allow child to resume execution */
    ContinueDebugEvent(DebugEvent.dwProcessId,
        DebugEvent.dwThreadId, DBG_CONTINUE);
}
```

WaitForDebugEvent() makes the debugging thread block until the child process does something noteworthy. When an event occurs and WaitForDebugEvent() returns, the system automatically freezes all the child's threads. The child remains frozen until the debugger calls ContinueDebugEvent(). A debugger must call both WaitForDebugEvent() and ContinueDebugEvent() in order to receive event notifications from the child. Furthermore, the thread that calls the commands must be the same thread that created or adopted the child. If a different thread calls WaitForDebugEvent(), the function always returns FALSE.

The requirements of the debugging loop influence the structure of a debugger. Most debuggers spin off a new thread when the user chooses a process to debug. The new thread handles debugging events, and the original thread handles the debugger's user interface. The debugging thread attaches to a child, enters an event loop, and ends when the child ends.

Listing 17.1   Launch child and wait for events.

```
/*---------------------------------------------------
    DO LAUNCH
---------------------------------------------------*/
void DoLaunch( HWND hWnd )
{
  TCHAR szName[_MAX_FNAME*sizeof(TCHAR)] = TEXT("");
  TCHAR szPath[_MAX_PATH*sizeof(TCHAR)] = TEXT("");
  BOOL bSuccess;
  HANDLE hThread;               /* debugging thread */
  DWORD dwThreadID;

  /* ask user for name of file to open */
  bSuccess = GetFileName(hWnd, szPath, szName);
  if (!bSuccess)
    return;

  /* create a thread to wait for debugging events */
  gbContinueDebug = TRUE;
  hThread = CreateThread(NULL, 0, (LPTHREAD_START_ROUTINE)DebuggingThread,
    (LPTSTR)szPath, 0, &dwThreadID);
  if (!hThread) {
    ShowErrorMsg(__LINE__);
    gbContinueDebug = FALSE;
    return;
  }
  CloseHandle(hThread);
}
```

A Simple Debugging Monitor

That's enough background to build a simple debugging monitor that logs messages from the child process to its window. One of the events a debugger hears about is called OUTPUT_DEBUG_STRING_EVENT, and it occurs whenever the child calls Output-DebugString(). Under 16-bit Windows, OutputDebugString() results in an event notification that you can receive through the ToolHelp function NotifyRegister-Callback() [which is how Microsoft's DBWIN utility displays the output from Out-putDebugString()]. Under Windows NT, OutputDebugString() sends information only to a debugger. Without a debugger, you cannot see the trace messages. My DBTrace utility waits for these messages and displays them. DBTrace fills its client area with an edit control and prints the messages there. It begins by asking the user to choose an .exe file, which it then launches. Listing 17.1 shows the parts of DBTrace that launch the child and wait for events. (The complete code is on the disk that accompanies this book.) Figure 17.1 shows a typical DBTrace session in progress.

Listing 17.1 (continued)

```
/*-------------------------------------------------------
      DEBUGGING THREAD
   ----------------------------------------------------*/
LRESULT DebuggingThread( LPCTSTR lpszFilePath )
{
   STARTUPINFO sui;
   PROCESS_INFORMATION pi;
   BOOL bSuccess;
   DEBUG_EVENT DebugEvent;

   /* fill in the process's startup information */
   ZeroMemory( &sui, sizeof(STARTUPINFO) );
   sui.cb = sizeof(STARTUPINFO);
   sui.wShowWindow = SW_SHOWDEFAULT;

   pi.hProcess = NULL;

   /* create the debuggee process */
   bSuccess = CreateProcess(NULL, lpszFilePath, NULL, NULL, TRUE,
     DEBUG_PROCESS | DEBUG_ONLY_THIS_PROCESS, NULL, NULL, &sui, &pi);
   if (!bSuccess) {
     ShowErrorMsg(__LINE__);
     gbContinueDebug = FALSE;
     ExitThread( 1 );
   }
   CloseHandle( pi.hProcess );
   CloseHandle( pi.hThread );
```

The challenge in handling OUTPUT_DEBUG_STRING_EVENT notifications is extracting the message text. OutputDebugString() does not send anything from the child to the debugger; it merely transfers control to the debugger. The structures that come with the notification tell the debugger where the child's execution broke off. The debugger must use that information to peek into the child's address space, find the message text, and copy the message into its own space as follows.

```
length = DebugEvent.u.DebugString.nDebugStringLength;
bSuccess = ReadProcessMemory(pi.hProcess,
  DebugEvent.u.DebugString.lpDebugStringData,
  szDebugString, length, &dwBytesRead);
szDebugString[length] = '\0';
Edit_Append(ghEditBox, szDebugString);
```

Listing 17.1 (continued)

```
  while (gbContinueDebug) {
    DWORD dwBytesRead;
    TCHAR szDebugString[256];

    /* block until a debugging event occurs */
    WaitForDebugEvent(&DebugEvent, INFINITE);

    switch (DebugEvent.dwDebugEventCode) {

      case OUTPUT_DEBUG_STRING_EVENT:
        bSuccess = ReadProcessMemory(pi.hProcess,
          DebugEvent.u.DebugString.lpDebugStringData, szDebugString,
          DebugEvent.u.DebugString.nDebugStringLength, &dwBytesRead);
        if (!bSuccess)
          ShowErrorMsg(__LINE__);
        Edit_Append(ghEditBox, szDebugString);
        break;

      case EXIT_PROCESS_DEBUG_EVENT:
        Edit_Append(ghEditBox, "DETACHING" );
        gbContinueDebug = FALSE;
        break;
    }
    /* allow debuggee to resume execution */
    ContinueDebugEvent(DebugEvent.dwProcessId,
      DebugEvent.dwThreadId, DBG_CONTINUE);
  }
  return(0L);
}
```

ReadProcessMemory() copies information from the address space of one process into the address space of another. The handle passed in the first parameter must permit PROCESS_VM_READ access. The DebugEvent structure, filled in by WaitForDebug-Event(), contains information relevant to the most recent event. The DebugEvent.u field of the structure is a union. What you look for in the union field depends on the event that just occurred. After an OUTPUT_DEBUG_STRING_EVENT, the union contains an OUTPUT_DEBUG_STRING_INFO structure in a field called DebugString. This structure gives the length and location of the message string in the child process. ReadPro-cessMemory() copies the string into the debugger's own buffer, szDebugString. Edit_Append() adds the string to the end of the edit control buffer where DBTrace displays messages.

Figure 17.1 DBTrace session in progress.

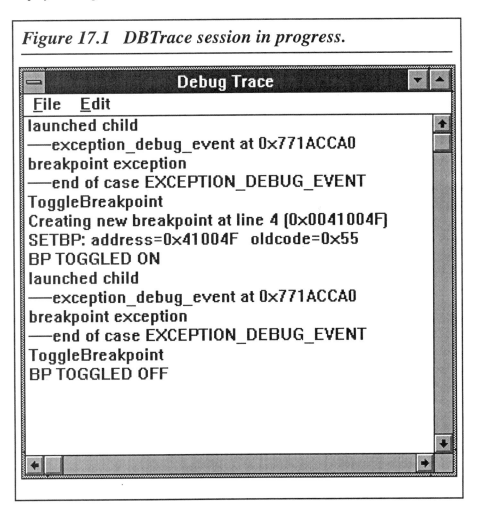

As an enhancement to DBTrace, it would be easy to expand the `switch` statement in the event loop and log other events as well.

```
switch (DebugEvent.dwDebugEventCode) {
    case CREATE_PROCESS_DEBUG_EVENT:
        Edit_Append(ghEditBox, "created process");
        break;

    case CREATE_THREAD_DEBUG_EVENT:
        Edit_Append(ghEditBox, "created thread");
        break;

    case LOAD_DLL_DEBUG_EVENT:
        Edit_Append(ghEditbox, "loaded DLL");
        break;

    case EXIT_PROCESS_DEBUG_EVENT:
        Edit_Append(ghEditBox, "process ended" );
        bContinueDebug = FALSE;
        break;
}
```

From the `DebugEvent` structure, each case could gather information about the event and print more specific messages. Table 17.1 lists all the possible events a debugger might receive.

Common Debugging Tasks

Debuggers do more than log events. Once you have gained a debugger's access privileges, you might undertake a variety of useful tasks.

Map the child's address space. For this, you need the `VirtualQueryEx()` function to retrieve information about blocks of memory in another process. By starting with an address of 0 and working your way up to the top of the child's address space, you can map every block of memory and show whether it is free, reserved, or committed and how it is protected.

Freeze and thaw the child's threads. From the `CREATE_THREAD` events, you can build a list of all the child's threads. `SuspendThread()` and `ResumeThread()` can make individual threads stop and start at will. This may be useful to help solve thread synchronization problems.

Change execution priority. To fine-tune the child's performance, modify the process's base priority [SetPriorityClass()] or the dynamic priority of individual threads [SetThreadPriority()].

Execute in single-stepping mode. Using GetThreadContext() and SetThread-Context(), you can toggle the CPU's single-step register bit. (Not all CPUs support this, but Intel does.) In single-step mode, the processor stops after executing each machine instruction. This is good for stepping through disassembled code, but has other uses too, as you'll see in my Stepper program below.

Retrieve symbolic information. A symbolic debugger is one that understands the symbols, such as variable and function names, used in the source code. If you set the compiler to leave symbol information in the .exe file, then the debugger can read the

Table 17.1   Win32 debugging events.

CREATE_THREAD_DEBUG_EVENT	The child created a new thread. Creation of the primary thread does not generate a CREATE_THREAD event.
CREATE_PROCESS_DEBUG_EVENT	The child has been created. Its DLLs have not yet been loaded.
EXIT_THREAD_DEBUG_EVENT	One of the child's threads ended. When the last thread ends you get only an EXIT_PROCESS event.
EXIT_PROCESS_DEBUG_EVENT	The child has ended or been terminated.
LOAD_DLL_DEBUG_EVENT	The child has loaded a DLL, either at load time or at run time.
UNLOAD_DLL_DEBUG_EVENT	The child has unloaded a DLL. When the process exits, no unload events are generated for libraries loaded statically at load time.
EXCEPTION_DEBUG_EVENT	The child produced a system exception. the DEBUG_EVENT structure to determine the exception was, for example, a breakpoint or an access violation.
OUTPUT_DEBUG_STRING_EVENT	The child called OutputDebugString. Examine the DEBUG_EVENT structure to find the message and copy it from the child's address space.
RIP_EVENT	A system debugging error occurred.

.exe file to interpret your symbols. A symbolic debugger needs the information in order to step through source code lines, inspect variables by name, or show what procedures have been called by reading the stack.

Set breakpoints. Most of the rest of this chapter concentrates on breakpoints.

Breakpoints: The Stepper Program

Microsoft's examples for the Win32 debugging API don't go much beyond the kind of passive monitoring that DBTrace performs. As you might expect, unanticipated complications arise in any nontrivial example. Interpreting symbol information could be the subject of a book in itself, so I've settled more modestly on breakpoints for my example. A debugger inserts breakpoints into the program's code in order to interrupt execution at strategic moments. All Intel processors in the 80x86 family support interrupting the sequential execution of machine code with the INT instruction. Normally this is a 2-byte instruction, because the first byte is an opcode (0xcd) and the second byte specifies one of 256 possible interrupt numbers. However, Intel also created a special 1-byte form of this opcode (0xcc) for INT 03h specifically to support software debuggers. The general idea is that the debugger installs its own INT 03h handler and then sets breakpoints by altering the first byte of the instruction where it wants to break, replacing it with 0xcc. When execution reaches that point, the inserted opcode generates an INT 03h and the debugger's registered handler gets control, performs any required task, then restores the original instruction byte and resumes execution of the debuggee.

The reason it is crucial to have a 1-byte form of the INT instruction is that some 80x86 instructions are only 1 byte long. If the debugger tried to write a 2-byte INT over a 1-byte instruction, it would be modifying both the instruction where it wants to break and the first byte of the next instruction as well. There is no way of ensuring that the child does not contain a jump directly to that second instruction, and if it did, the CPU would execute the last half of the interrupt instruction as though it were the first byte of a regular instruction, and disaster would ensue.

My Stepper program launches a single-threaded child program called foo.exe. Stepper displays the source code from foo.c, as shown in Figure 17.2. The minus signs ("-") indicate lines where a breakpoint can legally occur. It doesn't make sense to break, for example, on the line

```
#include <windows.h>
```

because the line generates no machine instructions. Also, if the programmer happens to split the code for a single function call over several lines, only one line supports a breakpoint. Stepper marks the legal break lines with a minus sign in the left margin.

A plus sign in the left margin marks a line where the user has set a breakpoint (using commands from the Run menu.) The F9 key runs foo.exe but execution halts at any breakpoint. A ">>" character marks the line where the program halted. You can also put the cursor on a line and press F4 to make the program run up to the cursor line. As you'll see, the run-to-line feature adds considerable complexity to the debugger code.

A Shortcut to Symbol Information

I'm going to describe the interesting parts of Stepper from the top down, but one bottom-level detail requires attention first: the problem of matching source code lines with machine code. To set breakpoints in source code, a debugger needs to know at what address the instructions corresponding to each line begin. The linker's debugging switches make it copy line information (and much else besides) into the .exe file. Both Borland and Microsoft have published the format of their symbolic debugging information. Microsoft's specification is on the Microsoft Developer's Network CD-ROM and Borland's is in the Borland Open Architecture Handbook, available for

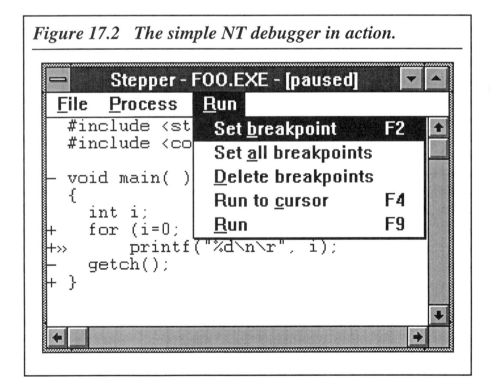

Figure 17.2   The simple NT debugger in action.

download from CompuServe in the BCPPWIN forum. Under Windows NT a debugger has easy access to the symbol information because when a CREATE_PROCESS_-DEBUG_EVENT occurs, the system passes the debugger a pointer to the beginning of the child's executable image and an offset from there to the beginning of the child's symbolic debugging information.

You can see the information for yourself by running one of the many utilities that dump information from an .exe file. All Stepper needs is line number information. In order to dump line number information from an .exe file, you must build the program with debug switches. For Borland, this means using the -v switch and calling TDUMP.exe.

```
TLINK32 -Tpe -ap -v -Lc:\bc4\lib c0x32 foo, foo,, cw32 import32,,
TDUMP foo.exe
```

For Microsoft, it means telling LINK32 to use COFF debug information only and then calling LINK32 a second time to dump the information.

```
LINK32 -debug:full -debugtype:COFF \
  -subsystem:console -out:foo.exe foo.obj libc.lib kernel32.lib
LINK32 -dump -linenumbers foo.exe
```

Both TDUMP and LINK32 -dump parse the .exe file and translate the debugging information into a more readable format. The dump listings match line numbers to code offsets. I have hard coded foo.exe line breaks into Stepper. Table 17.2 shows partial dumps from both the Microsoft and Borland utilities, along with the arrays that Stepper declares to hold the necessary information. A real debugger would gather the information for itself from foo.exe.

Both dump utilities match line numbers to offsets, but they measure the offsets from different origins. Microsoft gives offsets from the base of the loaded executable file image. Borland gives offsets from the first instruction in the program [main() or WinMain()]. The system supports both models. When the linker loads an executable image into memory, the first byte of the image is not the first byte of code. The image begins with a header describing the sections that follow. Where the actual code begins varies. When the debugger launches a program to debug, Windows NT tells the debugger both addresses, the image base, and the starting address. To determine the address where a specific source line begins, add its offset to one of those origins. The functions in Stepper that work with line addresses calculate offsets the Borland way, starting from the first instruction. To modify the code for Microsoft tools, look for the lines that refer to the value stored in Debuggee.pStartAddress and change them to use Debuggee.pImageBase instead. To determine at runtime which kind of offset the program uses, you would have to parse the .exe file and find its debug directory table.

Command Events and Debugging Events

When Stepper begins executing, it creates a second thread to perform the debugging. The second thread launches foo.exe and enters a debugging loop. Meanwhile the first thread continues to process window messages and manage the user interface. The code for the user interface thread resides in a file called stepper.c, whereas most of the debugging thread's code resides in debug.c. A third file, bpnode.c, contains functions for managing a linked list of breakpoints. All the code listed in this chapter comes from debug.c. The other two modules are available on the code disk for this book.

The need for interaction between the user interface thread and debugger thread poses a problem that did not arise in DBTrace, where the user interface thread has its message loop and the debugging thread has its event loop. Until the program ends, neither loop cares what the other is doing. In Stepper, on the other hand, the debugging thread must also respond to commands received through the user interface. The

---

Table 17.2   Symbolic line information dumped from
. *exe*.

***Output from Microsoft's* LINK32 -dump**

```
COFF LINENUMBERS #1
1000    5    1009    7    1022    8
1038    9    103D    A
```

***Output from Borland's* TDUMP.exe**

```
Source files:
    File: foo.c [002]  Offset: 082BA
    Range: 0001:0007C-0009A
      Line numbers:
      0004:0007C    0007:0007D    0008:0007F    0009:00093
      0010:00098    0000:0009A
```

How Stepper records Borland's line number data

```
    int LineAddress[] = {0x7C, 0x7D, 0x7F, 0x93, 0x98, 0x9A};
    UINT BreakLines[] = {4, 7, 8, 9, 10, 0};
    int iBreakLineCount = 6;
```

user signals where to set breakpoints, when to resume execution, and when to terminate the child. But if the debugging thread spends most of its time blocking in Wait-ForDebugEvent( ), how can the user interface thread interrupt to signal a menu command event?

The answer is a larger loop that calls WaitForMultipleObjects( ) on each iteration to wait for one of three event synchronization objects that Stepper creates during initialization. Two of them represent user interface commands: EVENT_RESUME and EVENT_KILL. If the user interface thread sets either of these event objects, the debugging thread notices and responds. Most of the time, however, both are off and the third object, EVENT_RUNNING, remains on. Because one event is usually on, the WaitForMultipleObjects( ) command usually returns at once. Then each iteration of the large loop checks briefly for a debugging event, responds if necessary, and returns back to the larger command loop. Here, in code stripped of unessential details, is an outline of the main DebuggingThread( ) procedure.

```
LaunchDebuggee();
gbAttached = TRUE;
SetEvent(ghCommandEvent[EVENT_RUNNING]);
__try {
    __try {
        while (gbAttached) {
            /* wait for event signals */
            iCmdEvent = WaitForMultipleObjects(&ghCommandEvent);

            switch (iCmdEvent) {
                case EVENT_RUNNING:
                    CheckForDebugEvent();
                    break;
                case EVENT_RESUME:
                    SetEvent(ghCommandEvent[EVENT_RUNNING]);
                    ContinueDebugEvent(Debuggee.dwProcessId,
                        Debuggee.dwThreadId, DBG_CONTINUE);
                    break;
                case EVENT_KILL:
                    TerminateProcess();
                    gbAttached = FALSE;
                    break;
            }
        }
    } __finally {
        ResetEvent(ghCommandEvent[EVENT_RUNNING]);
        gbAttached = FALSE;
    }
}__except (EXCEPTION_EXECUTE_HANDLER) {
    MessageBox();
}
```

Within this command loop, the task of receiving debug notifications falls to CheckForDebugEvent(), shown in Listing 17.2. When it calls WaitForDebug-Event(), this function sets a maximum blocking time of 100 milliseconds. If the time limit passes uneventfully, execution returns to the main command loop. If the RUNNING_EVENT signal is still on, the program comes back for another 100-millisecond wait.

Listing 17.2 Excerpts from stepper.h and DEBUG.C.

```
/*----------------------------------------------------
        STEPPER.H (excerpts)
   ----------------------------------------------*/

typedef struct bpnode{
  UINT uLine;          /* source line of bp */
  PBYTE pAddress;      /* code address of bp */
  BYTE Opcode;         /* displaced instruction */
  BOOL bOnceOnly;      /* TRUE for soft break */
  struct bpnode *pNext; /* next node in list */
} BPNODE;
typedef BPNODE *PBPNODE;

enum EVENTS {
  EVENT_RUNNING, EVENT_RESUME, EVENT_KILL
};
#define NUM_COMMAND_EVENTS  3

/* flags for SetLinePrefix() */
enum PREFIX_MARK {
  PREFIX_BREAK_LINE, PREFIX_BREAKPOINT, PREFIX_CURRENT_LINE
};

#define ERROR_MSG(h) ShowErrorMsg((h), __FILE__, __LINE__)


^^^^^^^^^^^^^^^^^^^^^^^^^^^^^^^^^^^^^^^^^^^^^^^^^^^^^


/*----------------------------------------------------
    DEBUG.C
    Routines for the debugging thread of the
    STEPPER program.
   ----------------------------------------------*/
#define STRICT
#include <windows.h>
#include <windowsx.h>
#include <stdlib.h>      /* _MAX_PATH */
#include "stepper.h"
```

Listing 17.2 (continued)

```
/*----------------------------------------------------
     TYPES AND DEFINITIONS
     -------------------------------------------------*/
#define BP_OPCODE 0xCC   /* INT 3 instruction */
#define TF_BIT 0x100     /* single-step register bit */

typedef struct tagDEBUGGEE {
  PBYTE pStartAddress;   /* address of main() */
  HANDLE hProcess;       /* process under scrutiny */
  HANDLE hThread;        /* primary thread */
  DWORD dwProcessId;
  DWORD dwThreadId;
  BOOL bBreakSeen;  /* FALSE until first bp occurs */
} DEBUGGEE;
typedef DEBUGGEE *PDEBUGGEE;

/*----------------------------------------------------
     GLOBAL VARIABLES (all modules)
     -------------------------------------------------*/
extern HWND ghMainWnd;
extern TCHAR gszAppTitle[];
extern BOOL gbAttached;
extern BOOL gbPaused;
extern HANDLE ghCommandEvent[NUM_COMMAND_EVENTS];

/*----------------------------------------------------
     STATIC VARIABLES (this module only)
     -------------------------------------------------*/
DEBUGGEE Debuggee;
PBPNODE pbpPending = NULL;

/* FOO.EXE line information (assumes */
/* Foo was compiled with Borland tools) */

int LineAddress[] = {0x4F, 0x53, 0x57, 0x66, 0x6C, 0x71, 0x73};
int BreakLines[] = {4, 7, 8, 7, 9, 10, 0};
int iBreakLineCount = 7;

/*----------------------------------------------------
     DEBUGGING THREAD
     -------------------------------------------------*/
LRESULT DebuggingThread( LPCTSTR pszFilePath )
{
  PROCESS_INFORMATION pi;
  TCHAR szMsg[_MAX_PATH + 25];
  int iCmdEvent;
```

The addition of an exception and a termination handler make the debugger much more robust. When a debugger picks at the innards of its child many things can go wrong. The exception handler ensures that even if an unexpected error causes the debugging thread to end, the debugger itself continues to run. The termination handler ensures that the gbAttached variable always accurately reflects the program's state even after an unexpected error. (The primary thread reads gbAttached when deciding what menu commands to enable or disable.)

Listing 17.2 (continued)

```
/* create the debuggee process */
if (!LaunchDebuggee(pszFilePath, &pi)) {
  wsprintf( szMsg, TEXT("Cannot launch %s"),
    (PSTR)pszFilePath);
  MessageBox( ghMainWnd, szMsg, gszAppTitle,
    MB_OK | MB_ICONEXCLAMATION );
  gbAttached = FALSE;
} else {
  gbAttached = TRUE;   /* creation succeeded */
  SetEvent(ghCommandEvent[EVENT_RUNNING]);
}
SetWindowTitle();

__try {
  __try {
    while (gbAttached) {
      /* proceed only when a command event permits it */
      iCmdEvent = WaitForMultipleObjects(
        NUM_COMMAND_EVENTS,  (PHANDLE)&ghCommandEvent,
        FALSE, INFINITE);

      switch (iCmdEvent) {

        case EVENT_RUNNING:
          CheckForDebugEvent(pi.hProcess);
          break;

        case EVENT_RESUME:
          SetEvent(ghCommandEvent[EVENT_RUNNING]);
          gbPaused = FALSE;
          SetWindowTitle();
          ContinueDebugEvent(Debuggee.dwProcessId,
            Debuggee.dwThreadId, DBG_CONTINUE);
          break;
```

Listing 17.2 (continued)

```
                case EVENT_KILL:
                  /* the termination handler cleans up */
                  TerminateProcess(pi.hProcess, 0);
                  gbAttached = FALSE;
                  break;

            } /* end switch (iCmdEvent) */

          } /* end while (bAttached) */

      } __finally {
        /* clean up */
        ResetEvent(ghCommandEvent[EVENT_RUNNING]);
        gbAttached = FALSE;
        SetWindowTitle();
        DestroyList();
        CloseHandle(pi.hProcess);
        CloseHandle(pi.hThread);
      }

    }__except (EXCEPTION_EXECUTE_HANDLER) {
      MessageBox(ghMainWnd, "An unexpected error occurred.",
        gszAppTitle, MB_OK | MB_ICONSTOP);
    }
    return(0L);
}

/*----------------------------------------------------
    LAUNCH DEBUGGEE
  ------------------------------------------------*/
BOOL LaunchDebuggee( LPCTSTR pszFilePath, PPROCESS_INFORMATION ppi )
{
  STARTUPINFO sui;
  BOOL bSuccess;

  /* fill in the process's startup information */
  ZeroMemory(&sui, sizeof(STARTUPINFO));
  sui.cb = sizeof(STARTUPINFO);
  sui.wShowWindow = SW_SHOWDEFAULT;
  sui.dwFlags = STARTF_USESHOWWINDOW;
  ppi->hProcess = NULL;

  /* create the debuggee process */
  bSuccess = CreateProcess(NULL, pszFilePath,
    NULL, NULL, FALSE, DEBUG_PROCESS |
    DEBUG_ONLY_THIS_PROCESS, NULL, NULL, &sui, ppi);
  if (!bSuccess) ERROR_MSG(ghMainWnd);

  return(bSuccess);
}
```

When the debugger discovers that the child has encountered a breakpoint, Check-ForDebugEvent() skips its usual call to ContinueDebugEvent(). Skipping the call leaves the child completely frozen so the user can examine the state of the program at leisure. When the user issues a command such as Run, the user interface thread sets the Resume event. When the debugger finds that event set, it finally makes the deferred call to ContinueDebugEvent(), allowing the child to resume execution.

Listing 17.2 (continued)

```
/*-------------------------------------------------
    CHECK FOR DEBUG EVENT
---------------------------------------------------*/
void CheckForDebugEvent(HANDLE hDebuggee)
{
  DEBUG_EVENT DebugEvent;
  BOOL bContinue = TRUE;

  /* wait up to 100 ms for a debug event to occur */
  if (WaitForDebugEvent(&DebugEvent, 100)) {

    /* determine what event occurred */
    switch (DebugEvent.dwDebugEventCode) {

      case EXCEPTION_DEBUG_EVENT:
        bContinue = DoExceptionEvent(&DebugEvent, hDebuggee);
        break;

      case CREATE_PROCESS_DEBUG_EVENT:
        gbAttached = TRUE;
        Debuggee.pStartAddress =
          (PBYTE)DebugEvent.u.CreateProcessInfo.lpStartAddress;
        Debuggee.hProcess = hDebuggee;
        Debuggee.dwProcessId = DebugEvent.dwProcessId;
        Debuggee.hThread = DebugEvent.u.CreateProcessInfo.hThread;
        Debuggee.dwThreadId = DebugEvent.dwThreadId;
        Debuggee.bBreakSeen = FALSE;
        break;

      case EXIT_PROCESS_DEBUG_EVENT:
        gbAttached = FALSE;
        SetWindowTitle();
        MessageBox(ghMainWnd, "The program ended.",
          gszAppTitle, MB_OK | MB_ICONINFORMATION);
        break;

    } /* end switch (EventCode) */
```

Only three debugging events interest Stepper: process creation, process termination, and exceptions. When the child is created, Stepper stores some thread and process ID values in a static structure for future reference. Stepper also sets the bBreakSeen field of this structure to FALSE. The first break signal a debugger receives is not a true breakpoint. After the system creates a child process and loads its DLLs, it needs to tell the debugger the child is about to begin execution. To do this it simulates a breakpoint at the place where the system code is about to jump into main() or Win-Main(). From the debugger's point of view this first breakpoint differs from all others because no actual 0xcc instruction was inserted in the child's code to produce it. The bBreakSeen flag helps Stepper avoid tidying up a mess that isn't there.

Breakpoint Exceptions

Process creation and termination events, however, interest Stepper much less than exceptions because breakpoint instructions surface in the debugger as exceptions. The two routines that handle exceptions, DoExceptionEvent() and OnBreakpointException(), appear in Listing 17.3. DoExceptionEvent() recognizes breakpoint exceptions and single-step exceptions. (I'll return to single-stepping in a few paragraphs.) On encountering a breakpoint, DoExceptionEvent() calls OnBreakpointException() to ask three questions about the breakpoint that just occurred.

- Is this the very first breakpoint?
- Is this a known breakpoint that Stepper set?
- Is this breakpoint permanent or temporary?

Listing 17.2 (continued)

```
    /* Unless the debuggee is paused at a */
    /* breakpoint, resume execution of debuggee */
    if (bContinue)
      ContinueDebugEvent(DebugEvent.dwProcessId,
        DebugEvent.dwThreadId, DBG_CONTINUE);
    else {
      gbPaused = TRUE;
      SetWindowTitle();
      ResetEvent(ghCommandEvent[EVENT_RUNNING]);
    }
  }
}
```

The very first breakpoint is the one the system sets, so `OnBreakpointException()` simply resets the `bBreakSeen` flag and returns. On subsequent breakpoint exceptions, the program compares the address where the exception occurred to the addresses of all the breakpoints in its linked list. It is entirely possible for a breakpoint to occur without the debugger setting it. The child may cause breakpoints to occur if it calls the `DebugBreak()` Win32 function. For breakpoints it doesn't recognize, Stepper

Listing 17.3   Exception handling code for a simple debugger.

```
/*-----------------------------------------------------
    DO EXCEPTION EVENT
    Respond to EXCEPTION_DEBUG_EVENTS, particularly
    breakpoints.  Return TRUE if the debug loop
    may continue immediately to the next event, FALSE
    if it should wait for the user to resume.
    ------------------------------------------------*/
BOOL DoExceptionEvent(
  LPDEBUG_EVENT pde, HANDLE hDebuggee )
{
  BOOL bContinue;
  UINT uXCode =
    pde->u.Exception.ExceptionRecord.ExceptionCode;
  PBYTE pXAddress =
    pde->u.Exception.ExceptionRecord.ExceptionAddress;

  switch (uXCode) {

    case EXCEPTION_BREAKPOINT:
      pbpPending = OnBreakpointException(pXAddress);
      bContinue = FALSE;
      break;

    case EXCEPTION_SINGLE_STEP:
      /* end single-step mode */
      SetStepFlag(Debuggee.hThread, FALSE);
      /* restore the breakpoint we just stepped over */
      if (pbpPending)
        SetBreakpoint(hDebuggee, pbpPending);
      pbpPending = NULL;
      bContinue = TRUE;
      break;
  }
  return(bContinue);
}
```

Listing 17.3 (continued)

```
/*-------------------------------------------------
    ON BREAKPOINT EXCEPTION
-----------------------------------------------------*/
PBPNODE OnBreakpointException( PBYTE pXAddress )
{
  PBPNODE pBP;
  PBPNODE pbpPassed = NULL;

  /* The first breakpoint is supplied by */
  /* NT when the program loads */
  if (!Debuggee.bBreakSeen) {
    Debuggee.bBreakSeen = TRUE;
    return(NULL);
  }

  /* is this a known breakpoint? */
  pBP = FindBPbyAddress(pXAddress);

  /* has the debuggee stopped on a known breakpoint? */
  if (pBP) {
    SetLinePrefix(pBP->uLine, PREFIX_CURRENT_LINE);

    /* get the INT3 opcode out of there */
    RemoveBreakpoint(Debuggee.hProcess, pBP);

    if (!pBP->bOnceOnly) {        /* For a hard break, turn on single-step-
ping */
      /* to restore the INT 3 opcode later */
      SetStepFlag(Debuggee.hThread, TRUE);
      pbpPassed = pBP;
    } else
      /* for a soft break, remove all traces */
      DeleteNode(pBP);

      /* Reset the IP to execute the instruction */
      /* displaced by the INT 3 opcode */
      DecrementIP(Debuggee.hThread);

  } else { /* unknown breakpoint */
    SetLinePrefix(0, PREFIX_CURRENT_LINE);
  }

  /* Return pointer to the breakpoint if it must */
  /* be restored after the next single-step exception */
  return(pbpPassed);
}
```

takes no special action, but known breakpoints do require action. The debugger must remove the 0xcc opcode and restore the original instruction in order for the program to continue its normal execution.

Removing the breakpoint is easy but may not be exactly what the user wants. If you remove the breakpoint code and resume execution, the breakpoint disappears entirely. If the program later happens to reiterate the same instruction, it won't stop the second time. On the other hand, if the user has said "run to the cursor and stop," then the debugger *should* remove the breakpoint entirely. Breakpoints that disappear after the first encounter are called soft or once-only breakpoints. Breakpoints that persist are called hard or sticky, and they take more work.

Listing 17.3 (continued)

```
/*****************************************************
      THE FOLLOWING ROUTINES ASSUME AN INTEL CPU
 *****************************************************/

/*---------------------------------------------------
    SET STEP FLAG
    Turn the TF (trap flag) off or on to enable or
    disable single-stepping mode.
 ---------------------------------------------------*/
BOOL SetStepFlag( HANDLE hThread, BOOL bOn )
{
  CONTEXT Context;
  BOOL bSuccess;

  Context.ContextFlags = CONTEXT_CONTROL;

  __try {
    bSuccess = GetThreadContext(hThread, &Context);
    if (bSuccess) {
      if (bOn)
        Context.EFlags |= TF_BIT;
      else
        Context.EFlags &= ~TF_BIT;
        bSuccess = SetThreadContext(hThread, &Context);
    }
  } __except (EXCEPTION_EXECUTE_HANDLER) {
    bSuccess = FALSE;
  }
  return(bSuccess);
}
```

Before showing how to handle a sticky breakpoint, I'll explain what OnBreak-pointException() is doing with the EIP register. A breakpoint exception occurs when the instruction pointer in the EIP register advances to an address that contains the instruction 0xcc. Executing that instruction causes the breakpoint exception. By the time the debugger learns of the exception, the EIP pointer has already advanced 1 byte past the place where the breakpoint was inserted. (Not all CPUs handle breakpoints the same way; I'm describing an Intel processor.) In order to execute the original instruction that the breakpoint replaced, the debugger must restore the displaced byte *and* set the EIP register back. DecrementIP() performs this machine-specific task.

Listing 17.3 (continued)

```
/*---------------------------------------------------
    GET IP ADDRESS
    Return the current value of the instruction
    pointer from the context of a given thread.
--------------------------------------------------*/
PBYTE GetIPAddress( HANDLE hThread )
{
  CONTEXT Context;

  __try {
    Context.ContextFlags = CONTEXT_CONTROL;
    GetThreadContext(hThread, &Context);

  } __except (EXCEPTION_EXECUTE_HANDLER) {
    Context.Eip = 0L;
  }
  return((PBYTE)Context.Eip);
}


/*---------------------------------------------------
    DECREMENT IP
    Set the instruction pointer back one byte.
--------------------------------------------------*/
BOOL DecrementIP( HANDLE hThread )
{
  CONTEXT Context;
  BOOL bSuccess;

  Context.ContextFlags = CONTEXT_CONTROL;
  bSuccess = GetThreadContext(hThread, &Context);
  if (bSuccess) {
    Context.Eip--;
    bSuccess = SetThreadContext(hThread, &Context);
  }
  return(bSuccess);
}
```

Single-Stepping Over a Sticky Breakpoint

To make a persistent breakpoint, the debugger must manage to execute the original instruction and then reinsert the breakpoint opcode before the program moves on. The following sequence of events must occur when the debugger receives an exception event for a sticky breakpoint:

• Restore the original instruction.
• Call `ContinueDebugEvent()` and let the child execute past the original instruction.
• Pause the child program.
• Reinsert the breakpoint instruction.
• Continue execution.

The third step, pausing the child, is the hard one. `SuspendThread()` is not precise enough. Between the time the child resumes and the time the debugger calls `SuspendThread()`, the child may already have iterated several more times past the instruction where the breakpoint is supposed to be. Fortunately, Intel CPUs support a single-stepping mode that automatically generates a trap after executing each machine instruction.

Here is the revised sequence for reinserting a sticky breakpoint:

• Restore the original instruction.
• Set single-stepping mode.
• Call `ContinueDebugEvent()` and let the child resume execution.
• Wait for the subsequent single-step exception to pause the child.
• Reinsert the breakpoint instruction.
• Turn off single-stepping mode.
• Continue normal execution.

Be reassured that single-step mode affects only one thread at a time. A bit flag in the CPU turns it on and off. Because Windows NT saves and restores the CPU registers each time it switches from one thread to another, other threads remain unaffected.

Also in Listing 17.3 is `SetStepFlag()`, which turns the single-stepping flag on and off. The single-stepping flag is the trap fault bit (`TF_BIT`) of the `EFlags` register. `GetThreadContext()` retrieves the CPU register values for a single thread. Stepper tweaks the `TF_BIT` and then calls `SetThreadContext()` to push the new setting back into the thread state. Next time the system switches to the thread, it begins by loading the thread's context and so sets `TF_BIT`.

```
#define TF_BIT 0x100
CONTEXT Context;
Context.ContextFlags = CONTEXT_CONTROL;

GetThreadContext(hThread, &Context);
if (bSetFlag)
    Context.EFlags |= TF_BIT;           /* set bit to 1 */
else
    Context.EFlags &= ~TF_BIT;          /* set bit to 0 */
```

The Context structure contains all the register information and must be defined differently for different CPUs. Its fields are documented only in winnt.h.

OnBreakpointException() distinguishes between hard and soft breakpoints by examining a Boolean field in the breakpoint list node structure. When Stepper inserts a soft breakpoint that should disappear as soon as the program reaches a certain line, it makes the bOnceOnly field TRUE. When the user sets a sticky breakpoint, Stepper makes the field FALSE. When Stepper receives an exception from a hard breakpoint, it turns the single-step mode on and saves a pointer to the relevant breakpoint node in the static pbpPending variable. The next debugging event to occur (assuming the child is single-threaded) will be a single-step exception. That's the other signal that DoExceptionEvent() recognizes. It turns off single-stepping, restores the 0xcc breakpoint instruction, and continues.

```
case EXCEPTION_SINGLE_STEP:
    /* end single-step mode */
    SetStepFlag(Debuggee.hThread, FALSE);

    /* restore the breakpoint we just stepped over */
    if (pbpPending)
        SetBreakpoint(hDebuggee, pbpPending);
    pbpPending = NULL;
    bContinue = TRUE;
    break;
```

Before restoring the breakpoint instruction, the program confirms that the pbp-Pending variable still points to a BPNODE structure. That's in case the user deleted the breakpoint while the program was suspended. The bContinue flag is passed back to the main debugging event routine where it tells the program not to suspend execution for this exception. The program keeps running without the user realizing a second exception occurred.

The processor's single-step mode comes in very handy for restoring persistent breakpoints. Its usefulness might suggest an easier way for Stepper to make the program stop on source code lines. Stepper could keep the child running permanently in single-step mode, watch the instruction pointer, and pause whenever it reaches an address that corresponds to a source code line. That way Stepper would never have to insert and remove breakpoint instructions.

This works but is unacceptably slow. The number of machine instructions corresponding to a single source code line may be quite high. The instructions may step into system code. In practice, debuggers never use this logical algorithm for stepping through source code. Even the brute force method of silently setting invisible breakpoints on all the program's lines and running from one to the next is usually faster. (Stepper lets you do that, by the way. One of the menu commands sets all the possible breakpoints.)

Some of the processors that run Windows NT lack single-step support. RISC chips in particular avoid single-stepping because it slows all instructions. To restore a sticky breakpoint on these machines, most debuggers disassemble the instruction where the breakpoint occurred in order to discover which instruction will execute next. The debugger then sets a soft break at the next instruction, runs to the soft break, puts the sticky breakpoint back behind, removes the soft break, and continues.

Setting and Removing Breakpoint Instructions

Now I can show the code that sets and removes breakpoints. The breakpoint routines also initialize new breakpoint nodes for the linked list. Here's the structure that defines each breakpoint node:

```
typedef struct bpnode{
    UINT uLine;             /* source line of bp */
    PBYTE pAddress;         /* code address of bp */
    BYTE Opcode;            /* displaced instruction */
    BOOL bOnceOnly;         /* TRUE for soft break */
    struct bpnode *pNext;   /* next node in list */
} BPNODE;
typedef BPNODE *PBPNODE;
```

Setting a breakpoint means modifying the code of another program, and the protected address space that NT provides every process is designed to prevent such modification. Besides isolating programs from each other, the system protects the pages of physical memory where a program's executable image resides and any attempt to write there produces an access violation. To set a breakpoint you must change the page protection at the given address, save the original instruction, write a breakpoint opcode, and restore the protection.

Listing 17.4   Code for setting and removing breakpoints.

```
/*---------------------------------------------------
    SET BREAKPOINT
    Write a breakpoint instruction into the debuggee's
    code.  Save the original instruction first.
    --------------------------------------------------*/
BOOL SetBreakpoint( HANDLE hProcess, PBPNODE pBP )
{
  BOOL bSuccess;
  BYTE byOpcode = BP_OPCODE;
  char szMsg[256];

  __try {
    bSuccess = ReadOpcode(hProcess, pBP->pAddress,
      &pBP->Opcode);
    if (bSuccess)
      bSuccess = WriteOpcode(hProcess, pBP->pAddress,
        &byOpcode);

  } __except (EXCEPTION_EXECUTE_HANDLER) {
    bSuccess = FALSE;
  }

  return(bSuccess);
}


/*---------------------------------------------------
    REMOVE BREAKPOINT
    Remove a breakpoint instruction from the
    debuggee code.  (Does not remove the BPNODE
    structure from the list of breakpoints.)
    --------------------------------------------------*/
BOOL RemoveBreakpoint( HANDLE hProcess, PBPNODE pBP )
{
  BOOL bSuccess;
  __try {
   bSuccess = WriteOpcode(hProcess, pBP->pAddress,
       &pBP->Opcode);

  } __except (EXCEPTION_EXECUTE_HANDLER) {
    bSuccess = FALSE;
  }
  return(bSuccess);
}
```

Listing 17.4 shows the four procedures I use to set and remove breakpoints: WriteOpcode(), ReadOpcode(), and SetBreakpoint(), and RemoveBreakpoint(). WriteOpcode() overwrites a single byte at any address in the child's address space. It calls VirtualProtectEx() to change the page protection and WriteProcess-Memory() to put a new byte there. A termination handler ensures that the protection is

Listing 17.4 (continued)

```
/*----------------------------------------------------
    WRITE OPCODE
    Write a byte into the address space of the given
    process.  (Call this to insert breakpoints.)
-------------------------------------------------*/
BOOL WriteOpcode(
  HANDLE hProcess, PBYTE pAddress, PBYTE pOpcode )
{
  BOOL bSuccess;
  DWORD dwBytes;
  DWORD dwNewFlags, dwOldFlags;

  /* change mem protection in debuggee for writing */
  bSuccess = VirtualProtectEx(hProcess, pAddress,
    1L, PAGE_READWRITE, &dwOldFlags);
  if (!bSuccess) {
    ERROR_MSG(ghMainWnd);
    return(FALSE);
  }

  __try {
    __try {
      /* write new byte to memory */
      bSuccess = WriteProcessMemory(hProcess,
        pAddress, pOpcode, 1L, &dwBytes);

    } __except (EXCEPTION_EXECUTE_HANDLER) {
      bSuccess = FALSE;
    }

  } __finally {
    /* restore original protection */
    dwNewFlags = dwOldFlags;
    VirtualProtectEx(hProcess, pAddress, 1L,
      dwNewFlags, &dwOldFlags);
  }

  if (!bSuccess || (dwBytes != 1))
    ERROR_MSG(ghMainWnd);
  return(bSuccess);
}
```

restored to its previous state even if an exception occurs. ReadOpcode() is simpler because the normal protection state of code pages allows read access, so a single call to ReadProcessMemory() accomplishes the task. SetBreakPoint() calls both of the other routines. First, ReadOpcode() returns the child's original instruction, which must be saved, and then WriteOpcode() inserts the 0xcc byte that causes an INT 03h exception.

Other Breakpoint Functions

Once you have the low-level routines for setting breakpoints, the linked list for maintaining a list of breakpoints, and the basic program structure that lets the debugging thread respond to commands from the user, Stepper's other breakpoint functions fall into place. SetAllBreakpoints() reads the hard-coded arrays of line number information and creates breakpoint list nodes for each address stored there. ClearAll-Breakpoints() walks the linked list of breakpoints and restores all the original

---

Listing 17.4 (continued)

```
/*---------------------------------------------------
     READ OPCODE
     Read one byte from the address space of the given
     process.  (Call this to save an instruction
     before over-writing it.)
     ---------------------------------------------------*/
BOOL ReadOpcode(
   HANDLE hProcess, PBYTE pAddress, PBYTE pOpCode )
{
   BOOL bSuccess = FALSE;
   DWORD dwBytes;

   __try {
     bSuccess = ReadProcessMemory(hProcess,
        pAddress, pOpCode, 1L, &dwBytes);
   } __except (EXCEPTION_EXECUTE_HANDLER) {
     bSuccess = FALSE;
   }

   if (!bSuccess || (dwBytes != 1))
     ERROR_MSG(ghMainWnd);
   return(bSuccess);
}
```

instructions, deleting each list node it passes. ToggleBreakpoint() searches the existing list to determine if any breakpoint exists for the current line. If so, it removes the breakpoint. If not, it creates one. These routines appear in Listing 17.5.

Stepper greatly simplifies its task by assuming that the child process never creates extra threads. A full-featured Win32 debugger would need to let the user set breakpoints that interrupt only a single thread. It would monitor CREATE_THREAD_DEBUG_EVENT signals and maintain a list of all the current threads. Each thread might have its own linked list of breakpoints, or each breakpoint node might have a field to store a thread ID. To accommodate conditional breakpoints that occur only when some condition is true, the BPNODE structure would also need to record the condition associated with a breakpoint.

Listing 17.5 Code to manage breakpoints.

```
/*-------------------------------------------------------
    TOGGLE BREAKPOINT
--------------------------------------------------------*/
BOOL ToggleBreakpoint( UINT uLine )
{
  PBPNODE pBP = NULL;
  BOOL bFound = FALSE;

  if (!CanBreakOnLine(uLine))
    return(FALSE);

  /* search to end of list for */
  /* hard breaks on uLine */

  pBP = FindNextBPbyLine(NULL, uLine);
  while (pBP != NULL) {
    if (!pBP->bOnceOnly) {
      bFound = TRUE;
      RemoveBreakpoint(Debuggee.hProcess, pBP);
      DeleteNode(pBP);
      if (pBP == pbpPending)
        pbpPending = NULL;
      SetLinePrefix(pBP->uLine, PREFIX_BREAK_LINE);
    }
    /* any more breakpoints on this line? */
    pBP = FindNextBPbyLine(NULL, uLine);
  }
```

One complication that Stepper does partially accommodate is the possibility of several breakpoints existing on a single line of source code. Consider how Borland's compiler encodes the for loop in foo.exe:

```
#foo#7:  for (i=0; i<3; i++)
:00410053 31FF              xor    edi,edi
:00410055 EB10              jmp    F00.00410067 (00410067)
#foo#8:  printf("%d\n\r", i);
:00410057 B86C004300        mov    eax,0043006C
:0041005C 57                push   edi
:0041005D 50                push   eax
:0041005E E8450C0000        call   printf
:00410063 83C408            add    esp,00000008
#foo#7:  for (i=0; i<3; i++)
:00410066 47                inc    edi
:00410067 83FF03            cmp    edi,00000003
:0041006A 7CEB              jl     #foo#8 (00410057)
```

Listing 17.5 (continued)

```
/* if no breakpoints were found, create one */
if (!bFound) {
  int iIndex = 0;
  PBYTE pAddress;

  pAddress = GetNextAddressForLine(&iIndex, uLine);
  while (pAddress) {
    pBP = NewNode();
    if (!pBP) return(FALSE);
    pBP->uLine = uLine;
    pBP->pAddress = pAddress;
    pBP->bOnceOnly = FALSE;
    if (!SetBreakpoint(Debuggee.hProcess, pBP)) {
      DeleteNode(pBP);
      return(FALSE);
    }
    pAddress = GetNextAddressForLine(&iIndex, uLine);
  }
  SetLinePrefix(pBP->uLine, PREFIX_BREAKPOINT);
}
return(TRUE);
}
```

Addresses 0x00410053 and 0x00410066 both contain instructions that correspond to a line 7 of the source code, with the code for line 8 falling in the middle. (Microsoft codes the for loop differently, as you can tell from the data in Table 17.2, where only one address falls on line 7.) In the first draft of Stepper, if I asked to set a breakpoint on line 7, the debugger found the first address for line 7 and stopped, setting a breakpoint there only. I expected the program to stop every time it returned to the top of the for loop, but in fact it stopped only the first time through the loop. That's why ToggleBreakpoint() now searches for all the addresses that correspond to a single line when setting or removing any breakpoint.

Listing 17.5 (continued)

```
/*------------------------------------------------
    RUN TO LINE
------------------------------------------------*/
BOOL RunToLine( UINT uLine )
{
  int iIndex = 0;
  PBYTE pAddress;
  PBPNODE pBP = NULL;

  if (!CanBreakOnLine(uLine))
    return(FALSE);

  pAddress = GetNextAddressForLine(&iIndex, uLine);
  if (pAddress == GetIPAddress(Debuggee.hThread))
    return(TRUE);

  pBP = NewNode();
  if (!pBP) return(FALSE);
  pBP->uLine = uLine;
  pBP->pAddress = pAddress;
  pBP->bOnceOnly = TRUE;
  if (!SetBreakpoint(Debuggee.hProcess, pBP)) {
    DeleteNode(pBP);
    return(FALSE);
  }
  /* do not show breakpoint glyph on screen */

  /* initiate the Run command */
  FORWARD_WM_COMMAND(ghMainWnd, CMD_RUN, NULL,
    0, SendMessage);
  return(TRUE);
}
```

Listing 17.5 (continued)

```
/*----------------------------------------------------
     SET ALL BREAKPOINTS
  ----------------------------------------------------*/
BOOL SetAllBreakpoints( void )
{
  PBPNODE pBP;
  int i;

  for (i=0; i<iBreakLineCount; i++) {
    pBP = NewNode();
    if (!pBP) return(FALSE);
    pBP->uLine = BreakLines[i];
    pBP->pAddress = Debuggee.pStartAddress + LineAddress[i];
    pBP->bOnceOnly = FALSE;
    if (!SetBreakpoint(Debuggee.hProcess, pBP)) {
      DeleteNode(pBP);
      return(FALSE);
    }
    SetLinePrefix(pBP->uLine, PREFIX_BREAKPOINT);
  }
  return(TRUE);
}


/*----------------------------------------------------
     CLEAR ALL BREAKPOINTS
  ----------------------------------------------------*/
BOOL ClearAllBreakpoints( void )
{
  PBPNODE pTemp, pBP;
  BOOL bSuccess = TRUE;

  pBP = FirstNode();
  while (pBP && bSuccess) {
    bSuccess = RemoveBreakpoint(Debuggee.hProcess, pBP);
    if (bSuccess) {
      /* remove the breakpoint glyph */
      if (pBP->uLine != 0)
        SetLinePrefix(pBP->uLine, PREFIX_BREAK_LINE);

      /* remember not to restore bp after */
      /* next single-step */
      if (pBP == pbpPending)
        pbpPending = NULL;

      pTemp = NextNode(pBP);
      DeleteNode(pBP);
      pBP = pTemp;
    }
  }
  return(bSuccess);
}
```

A single line may also have to bear several breakpoints if the user asks for them. Even in Stepper the user might toggle all the breakpoints on, put the cursor on the first breakpoint, and choose "Run to cursor" from the Run menu. The Run-to-cursor command inserts a soft breakpoint where there is already a hard one. Stepper solves this problem by making NewNode( ) always insert new nodes at the beginning of the list so that FindBPbyAddress( ) always finds the most recent breakpoint first. That way the debugger never accidentally removes a hard breakpoint by mistake. In a full-featured debugger the situation becomes more complicated if the user, for example, sets a thread-specific hard break on one line, a conditional break for any thread, and then single-steps through the code. At each stop the debugger must find and evaluate all the relevant breakpoints.

Listing 17.5 (continued)

```
/*-----------------------------------------------------
    CAN BREAK ON LINE
    Return TRUE if it is possible to set a breakpoint
    on the given line of source code.
    -------------------------------------------------*/
BOOL CanBreakOnLine( UINT uLine )
{
  int i = 0;
  BOOL bFound = FALSE;

  while ((i<iBreakLineCount) && !bFound)
    bFound = (uLine == BreakLines[i++]);

  return(bFound);
}


/*-----------------------------------------------------
    GET NEXT ADDRESS FOR LINE
    Starting from the given array index, search for
    the next machine code address associated with
    a given line number.  Use this function to find
    all the stoppable instructions that fall on a
    particular source code line.
    -------------------------------------------------*/
PBYTE GetNextAddressForLine( PINT pIndex, int iLine )
{
  PBYTE pAddress = NULL;
  BOOL bFound = FALSE;
  int iIndex = *pIndex;

  iIndex = max(iIndex, 0);        /* assert *pIndex >= 0 */
```

Conclusion

The Win32 debugging API imposes a basic program structure on any 32-bit Windows debugger. A `WaitForDebugEvent()` loop must poll for debugging events, and an interactive debugger needs synchronization objects to coordinate command events from the user interface with debugging events from the system. The Win32 API gives a debugger much of the control it needs over any process it launches, but it lacks the commands for machine-specific features such as breakpoints and single-step mode. A debugger aimed at all the possible NT platforms must still provide a toolbox of machine-specific routines such as Stepper's `SetStepFlag()`, `GetIPAddress()`, and `DecrementIP()`.

Listing 17.5 (continued)

```
  while (!bFound && (iIndex < iBreakLineCount))
    bFound = (BreakLines[iIndex++] == iLine);

  if (bFound) {
    *pIndex = iIndex--;
    pAddress = LineAddress[iIndex] + Debuggee.pStartAddress;
  }
  return(pAddress);
}


/*----------------------------------------------------
   MARK ALL BREAK LINES
   Place a PREFIX_BREAK_LINE character in front of
   each source line where a breakpoint may be set.
   --------------------------------------------------*/
void MarkAllBreakLines( void )
{
  int i;
  for (i=0; i<iBreakLineCount; i++)
    SetLinePrefix(BreakLines[i], PREFIX_BREAK_LINE);
}
```

References

Crawford, John H., and Patrick P. Gelsinger. *Programming the 80386*. Sybex, 1987. Written by engineers on the CPU design team, this book tells much about the 80386 processor.

Hansen, Marion, and Nick Strueklen. "Investigating the Debugging Registers of the Intel 386 Microprocessor", *Microsoft System Journal*, May 1989. A detailed explanation of the CPU's support for debugging.

Hummel, Robert L. *PC Magazine Programmer's Technical Reference: The Processor and Coprocessor*. Ziff-Davis Press, 1992. Contains an excellent discussion of the 80x86's support for debugging.

Pietrek, Matt. "Writing a Windows Debugger," *Windows/DOS Developer's Journal*. June 1992. Discusses the technical problems involved in writing a debugger for 16-bit Windows.

Rosenberg, Jonathan B. *How Debuggers Work: Algorithms, Data Structures, and Architecture*. John Wiley & Sons, 1996. Surveys available methods for all the tasks debuggers commonly perform. Takes platform differences into account.

## Chapter 18

Symmetric Multiprocessing for PCs

Tips, Tricks, and Tools for Fortran NT Applications

John Norwood and Shankar Vaidyanathan

The traditional definition of supercomputing is generally restricted to Fortran and mainframe computers. But with the advent of the 80486, Pentium, MIPS, and DEC Alpha processors and 32-bit operating systems, such as Windows NT, PC computational power has come to rival that of heavy-metal systems. This chapter, describes techniques that provide this computational power, focusing on multithreaded application development for single-processor and symmetric-multiprocessor machines. It covers DLLs, shared common blocks, multiprocess/multithreaded programming, and the Win32 API. It also provides Fortran interface statements for the Win32 console API and a black-box solution for calling 32-bit DLLs from 16-bit applications (such as Visual Basic) under NT.

To illustrate, a simple matrix-multiplication algorithm is implemented (Listing 18.1), then functionality is added gradually.

Matrix multiplication is an easy algorithm to multithread because you do not have to handle memory contention when writing to the final output matrix. The driver module (Listing 18.2) is a minimal program that calls the computation routine and provides the matrices to be multiplied, their dimensions (assuming conformation), and the number of threads to perform the task. In the compute module (compute.for), a common block stores matrices A, B, and C and keeps track of the number of spawned threads through MaxThreadCount. The subroutine Initiate() initializes the common-block variables from the parameters provided by the driver module — an inefficient but simple approach. The subroutine Compute() then spawns the specified number of threads. Each thread has as one of its parameters a number corresponding to the iteration that spawned it.

Listing 18.1   A simple matrix-multiplication algorithm.

```
C The triple DO loop that performs matrix multiplication
      Do i = 1, A_ROWS
        Do j = 1, B_COLUMNS
          Do k = 1, A_COLUMNS
            C(i, j)  =  C(i, j) + A(i, k) * B(k, j)
          End Do
        End Do      End Do
```

Listing 18.2   The driver module.

```
      include 'mt.fi'
      include 'flib.fi'

*** Driver program to do the Matrix Multiplication. Input matrices are ***
*** initialized to random values here. Maximum number of threads to be ***
*** spawned is also identified here. ***
      Program Driver
      include 'flib.fd'
      real*4 ranval
      integer*4 i, j, k, inThreadCount
      integer*4 A_Rows, A_Columns, B_Columns
      real*4 A[Allocatable](:,:), B[Allocatable](:,:), C[Allocatable](:,:)

      A_Rows = 50          ! size of A array
      A_Columns = 100      ! size of B array
      B_Columns = 100      ! size of C array
      inThreadCount = 8    ! number of threads to be spawned
```

Listing 18.2 (continued)

```fortran
      Allocate (A(A_Rows, A_Columns), B(A_Columns, B_Columns),
     +   C(A_Rows, B_Columns) )
      Do  i = 1, A_Columns
          Do j = 1, A_Rows
              Call Random (ranval)
              A (j, i) = ranval
          End Do
          Do k = 1, B_Columns
              Call Random (ranval)
              B(i, k) = ranval
          End Do
      End Do
      Call Compute (A, B, C, A_Rows, A_Columns, B_Columns, inThreadCount)
      End
*** Initiate transfers data from the arguments into the common block. ***
      Subroutine Initiate(In_A, In_B, In_A_Rows, In_A_Columns,
     +                    In_B_Columns, In_Thread_count)
      real*4 In_A(In_A_Rows, In_A_Columns)
      real*4 In_B(In_A_Columns, In_B_Columns)
      integer*4 In_A_Rows, In_A_Columns, In_B_Columns
      integer*4 In_Thread_count, i, j, k
      include 'common.inc'
      MaxThreadCount = In_Thread_count
      A_Rows = In_A_Rows
      A_Columns = In_A_Columns
      B_Columns = In_B_Columns
      Do  i = 1, A_Columns
          Do j = 1, A_Rows
            A (j, i) = In_A(j, i)
          End Do
          Do k = 1, B_Columns
            B(i, k) = In_B(i, k)
          End Do
      End Do
      End ! Initiate
*** MatMult is where the actual calculation of a row times a column is ***
*** performed. This is the thread procedure. ***
      Subroutine MatMult (CurrentThread)
      include 'common.inc'
      integer*4 CurrentThread
      automatic
      integer*4 i, j, k
```

Listing 18.2 (continued)

```
C The loop variable i ranges from the current thread number to the
C maximum number of rows in A in steps of the maximum number of threads
      Do i = CurrentThread, A_Rows,  MaxThreadCount
         Do j = 1, B_Columns
            Do k = 1, A_Columns
               C(i, j)  =  C(i, j) + A(i, k) * B(k, j)
            End Do
         End Do
      End Do
      End ! MatMult
*** Compute does the actual computation by spawning threads. ***
      Subroutine Compute
     +                    (In_A, In_B, In_C, In_A_Rows, In_A_Columns,
     +                    In_B_Columns, In_Thread_count)
      real In_A(In_A_Rows, In_A_Columns)
      real In_B(In_A_Columns, In_B_Columns)
      real In_C(In_A_Rows, In_B_Columns)
      integer In_A_Rows, In_A_Columns, In_B_Columns
      integer In_Thread_count
      include 'common.inc'
      external MatMult
      integer*4 ThreadHandle [Allocatable](:), threadId
      integer*4 CurrentThread[Allocatable](:), count
      integer*4 waitResult
      integer*4 i, j
      Call Initiate (In_A, In_B, In_A_Rows, In_A_Columns,
     +      In_B_Columns, In_Thread_count)
      Allocate (ThreadHandle(MaxThreadCount),
     +      CurrentThread(MaxThreadCount) )
      Do count = 1, MaxThreadCount
        CurrentThread(count) = count
        ThreadHandle(count) = CreateThread( 0, 0, MatMult,
     +           CurrentThread(count), 0, threadId)
      End Do
C Can't wait on more than 64 threads
      waitResult = WaitForMultipleObjects(MaxThreadCount,
     +      ThreadHandle, .TRUE.,  WAIT_INFINITE)
C Transfer result from common back into return argument.
      Do i = 1, A_Rows
         Do j = 1, B_Columns
            In_C(i,j) = C(i,j)
            C(i, j) = 0.0
         End Do
      End Do
      Deallocate ( ThreadHandle, CurrentThread )
      End ! Compute
```

The essence of the implementation is the thread function MatMult( ), in which each thread begins on the row corresponding to its thread number. When the thread is finished multiplying that row by all columns of the second matrix, it jumps by the total number of threads to a new row. Thus, the threads "leapfrog" to the end of the matrix. This implementation can, at the end, leave a few final threads operating, but it's simple to implement and avoids memory contention issues when writing to the final matrix.

SMP Issues and Results

Still, the approach just described doesn't avoid memory contentions on read access to the input arrays. This isn't a problem on single-processor machines because only one thread is accessing memory at any given instant. On symmetric multiprocessor (SMP) machines, however, it becomes a potentially serious issue. SMP machines are coarse-grained, parallel machines that excel in performing separate, discrete tasks, but don't have fine-grained memory arbitration and messaging facilities like those in vector or other super-scalar implementations. This can result in processors "stalling" on simultaneous access to a memory location that another processor is using. Listing 18.3 is a simple first pass at minimizing this problem by staggering the rows and columns each thread accesses. Each thread not only leapfrogs on the rows of the first matrix, but also "chases" the subsequent threads on the columns of the second matrix, thus minimizing the chances of simultaneous memory access in the columns.

Listing 18.2 (continued)

```
!###################################################################
C File Name: common.inc
        include 'mt.fd'      ! Data declarations for Multithreading API
        include 'flib.fd'    ! Data declarations for runtime library
        real*4 A, B, C    ! Input Matrices A & B and Output Matrix C
        integer*4 A_Rows, A_Columns, B_Columns  ! Matrix Dimensions
        integer*4 MaxThreadCount  ! Maximum numner of Threads
        common  MaxThreadCount,      ! common block
     +          A_Rows,              ! Rows in A = Rows in C
     +          A_Columns,           ! Columns in A  = Rows in B
     +          B_Columns,           ! Columns in B = Columns in C
     +          A(1000, 1000),
     +          B(1000, 1000),
     +          C(1000, 1000)        ! Maximum Array size is 1000 X 1000
```

Changing the process and thread priorities achieved little measurable benefit. Pushing all threads and processes to the maximum available priority may steal a few more time slices from other user-level threads, but the NT kernel still maintains its core activities. The net result is that the machine becomes totally unresponsive to user input, while net performance hardly changes. An additional side effect of real-time priority is that on a four-processor machine, using more than four threads is inefficient — the first four threads totally lock out any subsequent threads until they terminate. Thus, the best mix of performance and utility is achieved by eliminating all unnecessary applications and services and allowing the sophisticated NT thread and processor scheduler to deliver its designed functionality.

The example ran under default priority with a flexible number of threads and the external interferences minimized by stopping all the extraneous applications and services possible. However, without claim to any particular rigor in the results, they simply illustrate the benefits of using SMP machines with minimal code redesign.

Listing 18.2 ran with the Listing 18.3 modifications on an NCR 3400 machine with four processors and 64Mb of physical RAM. The results of various numbers of threads on a 300 x 300 matrix for A, B, and C and averaged over 100 runs are shown in Table 18.1. The compiler options used were /0x and /0b2.

On a four-processor machine, a simple task such as matrix multiplication with four threads was about 3.8 times faster than a task with a single thread and 3.7 times faster than a nonthreaded task. As more and more threads are generated, thread overhead and context switching take their toll.

Listing 18.3 Minimize memory contention on an SMP machine.

```
C This is variation in the MatMult subroutine Do loops. Loop variable i ranges
C from current thread number to maximum number of rows in A in steps of
C maximum number of threads. Loop variable j ranges across all columns of B,
C but is staggered according to current thread number to minimize memory
C contention on an SMP machine. Loop variable jj translates (maps) value of j
C to fall within permissible range of B, that is from 1 to B_Columns

      Do i = CurrentThread, A_Rows,  MaxThreadCount
        Do j = (CurrentThread-1)*MaxThreadCount,
     +          B_Columns + (CurrentThread-1)*MaxThreadCount - 1
          jj =  1 + mod(j, B_Columns)
          Do k = 1, A_Columns
            C(i, jj)  =  C(i, jj) + A(i, k) * B(k, jj)
          End Do
        End Do
      End Do
```

Build Option Considerations

To convert this computational module into a DLL that can be called from different applications (and dynamically loaded), simply add the `dllexport` attribute to the `Compute()` subroutine and use the `/LD` compiler option. This automatically creates an import library for linking calling applications. Although there are a number of options for linking NT Fortran executables, `/LD` is the only supported option for linking DLLs. `/LD` causes the DLL to be linked with a runtime import library. The actual runtime code resides in `MSFRT10.DLL`, which must be in the path. This has the following implications for applications that intend to call the DLL: If the calling executable is a console application, you should compile it with the `/MD` option. The executable can then be linked to the runtime import library, and both the application and the DLL will share the same instance of the runtime from the runtime DLL. Unit numbers opened in the executable will be accessible in the DLL and vice versa, and screen I/O using `WRITE` or `PRINT` statements will coordinate correctly.

If the calling application is compiled and linked using the `/ML` (single-threaded static runtime) or `/MT` (multithreaded static runtime) options, the executable and DLL will use separate instances of the runtime code. Then unit numbers will be local and separate for the executable, and the DLL and screen I/O from the executable might not appear as expected if the DLL also does screen I/O.

Table 18.1 Matrix multiplication results on an SMP.

Threads	*Time (sec)*
None	21.77
1	22.21
2	11.33
3	7.62
4	5.91
5	5.82
6	5.89
7	5.82
8	5.82
30	5.94
60	6.02

A Win32 application can be either a console subsystem executable or a Windows subsystem application. Console applications are always in text mode and can't attain higher resolution screen output, but screen output is rapid. Windows applications have full access to the user interface functionality provided by the Win32 API. If a Microsoft Fortran application is compiled and linked to be a console application, the user interface consists of character-mode input and output in a console window using READ, WRITE, or PRINT statements. There's no default for text positioning or mouse input. Microsoft Fortran allows you to generate Windows subsystem applications using the QuickWin implementation and /MW compiler option. Because QuickWin has its own API — similar to that for graphics output under DOS and 16-bit Windows in earlier versions of the compiler — it's very easy to generate a Windows subsystem application.

QuickWin applications must be statically linked (implied by /MW). Furthermore, Windows subsystem applications don't have console windows available by default. Thus, screen I/O from a Fortran DLL (which is, by definition, console I/O) won't be visible.

Common Blocks Across Processes

All threads of a given process share the same address space and can access the process' global variables; this can vastly simplify communication between threads. However, suppose we want to accomplish the same task of matrix multiplication by spawning processes instead of threads, which is a possible scenario on an SMP. We need to allow the same common block to be accessed across all the processes. Spawned processes inherit handles to files, console buffers, named pipes, serial-communication devices, and mailslots, but they don't inherit global variables.

Listing 18.4, a modified version of Listing 18.3, spawns processes instead of threads. The common block is named bridge with the attribute dllexport and is contained in the source file bridge.for along with a DATA statement. Because this module contains only data, the linker can be used with the /EDIT option to rename the .data section and set the new section attributes as read, write, and shared. The common block for the shared data must have at least one data item initialized in a DATA statement or it will not be stored in a section that can be modified. If there's any run-time functionality in this file, renaming the .data section will cause the code to fail. The parent process could wait for all the child processes to signal events, but for simplicity, here the parent process sleeps for 10 seconds before it prints out the results. The initialization and driver routines remain the same, and the child process (process.for) identifies its number from the command line argument passed to it by its parent (compute.for).

Listing 18.4   Spawns processes instead of threads.

```fortran
C File Name: Driver.for
C Include contents of Program Driver from Listing 18.2 here
C Then modify all occurrences of InThreadCount to InProcCount


C###############################################################################
C File Name: Compute.for
      include 'mt.fi'
      include 'flib.fi'

C Include contents of Subroutine Initiate from Listing 18.2 here
C Then modify all occurrences of InThreadCount to InProcCount


C Compute does the actual computation by spawning processes

      Subroutine Compute(In_A, In_B, In_C, In_A_Rows, In_A_Columns,
     +     In_B_Columns, In_Proc_Count)
      real*4 In_A(In_A_Rows, In_A_Columns)
      real*4 In_B(In_A_Columns, In_B_Columns)
      real*4 In_C(In_A_Rows, In_B_Columns)
      integer*4 In_A_Rows, In_A_Columns, In_B_Columns
      integer*4 In_Proc_Count
      include 'mt.fd'
      include 'flib.fd'
      include 'common.inc'
      logical*4 ProcHandle                   ! Process Handle
      integer*4 x, y, count
      character*32 inbuffer [Allocatable] (:)
      record /PROCESS_INFORMATION/ pi        ! Process Information
      record /STARTUPINFO/ si                ! Startup Information

      si.cb = 68                             ! Size of Startup Info
      si.lpReserved = 0
      si.lpDeskTop = 0
      si.lpTitle = 0
      si.dwFlags = 0
      si.cbReserved2 = 0
      si.lpReserved2 = 0
      si.hStdInput = 0
      si.hStdOutput = 0
      si.hStdError = 0

      Call Initiate (In_A, In_B, In_A_Rows, In_A_Columns, In_B_Columns,
     +     In_Proc_Count)

      Allocate (inbuffer(MaxProcCount) )

      Do count = 1, MaxProcCount
         write(inbuffer(count),"(A7, 1X, I4)") 'process', count
         ProcHandle = CreateProcess( 0, loc(inbuffer(count)),
     +               0, 0, .TRUE. , 0, 0, 0, loc(si), loc(pi))
         print"('+',a,i5)", "Generating Process # " , count
      End Do
```

Listing 18.4 (continued)

```
      write(*,*)
      write(*,*)

      Call sleepqq(10000)    ! Sleep for 10000 milliseconds

      Do x = 1, A_Rows
        Do y = 1, B_Columns
            In_C(x,y) = C(x,y)
            C(x,y) = 0.0
        End Do
      End Do

      End   ! Compute

C##################################################################
C File Name: Process.for
C MatMult is the Process that  multiplies the
C appropriate Row of A with the appropriate column of B

      Program MatMult
      include 'common.inc'
      automatic
      integer*4 CurrentProc, i, j, k, jj
      character*32 buffer
      integer*2 status

C Obtaining the command line arguments

      Call GetArg (1, buffer, status)
      read (buffer(1:status), '(i4)') CurrentProc

      Do i = CurrentProc, A_Rows,  MaxProcCount
        Do j = (CurrentProc-1)*MaxProcCount,
     +          B_Columns + (CurrentProc-1)*MaxProcCount - 1
          jj =  1 + mod(j, B_Columns)
          Do k = 1, A_Columns
             C(i, jj)  =  C(i, jj) + A(i, k) * B(k, jj)
          End Do
        End Do
      End Do
      End
```

Console Input and Output

Many Fortran applications rely on character-mode input and output for speed and simplicity. Although the default functionality of READ and WRITE statements is largely sufficient, sometimes more control is required (for text positioning and trapping mouse input, for example). Windows NT provides these text-mode services via the console API. The Win32 API documentation gives detailed descriptions of these functions and an overview of the console API. Complete interface files that can be included in Fortran console applications and DLLs for increased text-mode services are included on the code disk.

Interfacing console output from Windows subsystem applications is largely unexplored territory. For example, if a Windows application calls a DLL that does console output, that output is normally just sent to the bit bucket. If the DLL calls AllocConsole() to create a console window, the output can be displayed.

Listing 18.4 (continued)

```
C#############################################################################
C File Name: Bridge.for
C
C The common block for shared data must have one data item initialized
C in a DATA statement or it will not be stored in a section that can be
C modified. The LINK /EDIT command is used to rename the .data section
C and set the new sections attributes as read, write, shared. The source
C file should contain only the common declaration and the DATA
C statement.  If there are any runtime statements then renaming the
C .data section will cause the code to fail.

      Subroutine dllsub[dllexport]
      real*4 A, B, C
      integer*4 A_Rows, A_Columns, B_Columns
      integer*4 MaxProcCount     ! Maximum number of processes
      common /bridge[dllexport]/ MaxProcCount,
     +                           A_Rows,
     +                           A_Columns,
     +                           B_Columns
     +                           A(100, 100),
     +                           B(100, 100),
     +                           C(100, 100)
      data MaxProcCount /0/
      End
```

But there's another level of complexity in this situation. By default in console applications, runtime screen I/O functions like READ, PRINT, and WRITE are associated with the handles stdin and stdout. These handles are, in turn, associated with the console input screen buffer and the output screen buffer. A Windows subsystem application calling AllocConsole() creates a console window, but it won't automatically

---

Listing 18.4 *(continued)*

```
C##########################################################################
C File Name: Common.inc
C Common Block contents
      real*4 A, B, C
      integer*4 A_ROWS, A_COLUMNS, B_COLUMNS
      integer*4 MaxProcCount
      common /bridge[dllimport]/ MaxProcCount,
     +                           A_ROWS,
     +                           A_COLUMNS,
     +                           B_COLUMNS,
     +                           A(1000, 1000),
     +                           B(1000, 1000),
     +                           C(1000, 1000)
###########################################################################
# File Name: Makefile

all: bridge.dll process.exe driver.exe

bridge.dll: bridge.obj
   link /edit bridge.obj /section:.data=.bridge,srw
   fl32 /LD bridge.obj

bridge.obj: bridge.for
   fl32 /LD /c bridge.for

process.exe: process.obj bridge.lib
   fl32 /MD process.obj bridge.lib

process.obj: process.for common.inc
   fl32 /MD /c process.for

driver.exe: driver.obj compute.obj bridge.lib
   fl32 /MD driver.obj compute.obj bridge.lib

driver.obj: driver.for common.inc
   fl32 /MD /c driver.for

compute.obj: compute.for common.inc
   fl32 /MD /c compute.for
```

associate the runtime screen I/O file handles with that console window. This isn't a concern when using the console APIs, because they directly use the console input and output handles; however, READ or WRITE statements to the screen will fail. The solution is to force an association between the runtime standard handles and the console standard handles. This is illustrated in the InitConsole() routine (available on the companion code disk). The logical sequence is as follows. First, the console input and output handles are obtained by calling CreateFile() with the special filenames of CONIN$ and CONOUT$. These console file handles are converted to C runtime file handles using the _open_osfhandle() routine. The _dup2() C runtime function then forces stdin, stdout, and stderr to be identical to the C file handles pointing to the console. The C routines are always available to the Fortran code in this chapter, because the interface statements are included in the console.fi and console.fd files (available on the companion code disk).

InitConsole() allows a self-contained DLL capable of doing console I/O using both the console API and runtime screen I/O. The DLL needs to know the type of application (console, Windows subsystem, or other) calling it, so it can adjust its functionality accordingly. This information is provided in the final parameter from the calling application. The code displays the progress of the matrix multiplication using different colors for different threads. This requires the use of a global critical section to synchronize access to the console output buffer. Console output is limited in resolution, but it is very rapid and easy to implement.

Mixed-Language Considerations

Microsoft Fortran PowerStation 32 for Windows NT is capable of mixing with Microsoft Visual C/C++ for Windows NT. Although this process is easier than with prior versions, certain tricks make the process even easier. For example, the default naming and passing convention for a Fortran subroutine is a modified version of stdcall that has the following effect on routine names: They are prepended with an underscore, appear in all capital letters, and are appended with "@", followed by the number of bytes passed on the stack for the argument list. The passing convention is that arguments are pushed on the stack from right to left. Unlike the cdecl convention, however, the callee, not the caller, cleans up the stack. By default, Fortran passes all arguments by reference, but this can be overridden using the value attribute. Passing by reference means that every argument will usually require 4 bytes of stack space for its address. The only exception is character variables, which require 8 bytes: four for the address, followed by four for an integer passed by value that contains the string length. The hidden string length parameter is required by the character*(*) indeterminate size type allowed in Fortran. The hidden string parameter following character variables can be suppressed using the stdcall or C attribute on the name of the subroutine or in an interface statement to the Fortran subroutine. The amount of stack space for an argument passed by value is always rounded up to the next multiple of 4 bytes that can contain the data item.

The default structure packing for both Microsoft C/C++ and Fortran is 8-byte packing. The only allowed metacommands or compiler options for Fortran are for 1-, 2-, and 4-byte packing, so 8-byte packing is only possible as the default. Common blocks are accessible from C as global static structures owned by Fortran. The dllexport attribute allows common blocks to be exported from DLLs, as demonstrated in the previous example illustrating shared memory in a common block.

Microsoft C/C++ and Fortran development environments let you manage projects in their respective languages. The Fortran Visual WorkBench allows debugging of mixed-language applications because it has access to both C and Fortran expression evaluators. It is often convenient to use the Fortran Visual WorkBench debugger from the C/C++ Visual WorkBench. Using the Tools menu makes this easy. In the C/C++ Visual WorkBench, go to the Options menu and select Tools. Click the Add button and browse for the Fortran f32vwb.exe file. Enter $(TARGET) in the Arguments text field. When you select the Fortran Visual WorkBench under the Tools menu, it will automatically start debugging the application you're working on in the C/C++ Visual WorkBench.

Linking mixed-language C/C++ applications with Fortran object modules requires that the Fortran library LIBF.LIB (static single thread), LIBFMT.LIB (static multi-thread), or MSFRT.LIB (DLL runtime import library) precede the equivalent LIBC.LIB, LIBCMT.LIB, or MSVCRT.LIB. The versions of both libraries should come from the Fortran LIB directory. Because the order is important, the libraries should be added from the Options Projects Linker Input text field. You should not add them via the Additional Libraries text field or by including them in a project. To link a C/C++ Win32 Windows application that includes Fortran object files, use all the libraries normally used by C/C++ and add LIBF.LIB and CONSOLE.LIB. The latter is necessary to provide routines for file I/O.

32-bit DLLs and 16-bit Applications

At times it is desirable to call a 32-bit DLL from a 16-bit application. In such cases, the 16-bit application could run either under 16-bit Windows 3.x or under the WOW layer on Windows NT. In the first case, you'd use Win32s and Universal thunk facilities. In the second, you'd turn to Generic thunk functionality. This chapter is mainly about running on NT and threading, so only the second case will be examined.

Peter Golde of Microsoft has graciously shared a 16-bit C DLL that can be used in conjunction with Visual Basic to access 32-bit DLLs under NT. The scope of this chapter doesn't permit a discussion of the implementation details of this solution, but the DLL is provided with a VB example in Listing 18.5, which calls our multi-threaded matrix-multiplication DLL. Peter's solution is elegant because it can be used to call any 32-bit DLL under NT without creating a new 16-bit DLL each time. DLLs called from 16-bit applications can't do console I/O [AllocConsole() fails], thus requiring the "other" (WIN16$) case in the final parameter that is passed in to the DLL from the driver module. This will suppress all console I/O from the example code.

Conclusion

The advent of SMP machines at affordable prices promises to bring to the desktop more computational horsepower then ever before. The granularity of the parallelism they offer needs to be considered, but even simple modifications to conventional algorithms combined with multithreading can result in a tremendous boost beyond single-processor expectations.

Listing 18.5   A 16-bit C DLL used with Virtual Basic.

```
VERSION 2.00
Begin Form Form1
    Caption         =   "Form1"
    ClientHeight    =   6045
    ClientLeft      =   1095
    ClientTop       =   1485
    ClientWidth     =   9180
    Height          =   6450
    Left            =   1035
    LinkTopic       =   "Form1"
    ScaleHeight     =   6045
    ScaleWidth      =   9180
    Top             =   1140
    Width           =   9300
    Begin CommandButton Compute
        Caption     =   "Compute"
        Height      =   375
        Left        =   1200
        TabIndex    =   1
        Top         =   5040
        Width       =   1575
    End
    Begin Grid grdC
        Height      =   4335
        Left        =   1200
        TabIndex    =   0
        Top         =   480
        Width       =   6495
    End
End
```

Listing 18.5 *(continued)*

```
' These declarations set up the two core functions to access the CALL32 DLL:
' Declare32 and CALL32. These are the only two functions you need to use to
' get access to any 32-bit DLL. The Option Base is used to start arrays at
' index 1 just as in Fortran
Option Base 1
Declare Function Declare32 Lib "call32.dll" (ByVal Func As String, ByVal
Library As String, ByVal Args As String) As Long
Declare Sub Compute Lib "call32.dll" Alias "Call32" (A As Single, B As
Single, C As Single, A_ROWS As Long, A_COLUMNS As Long, B_COLUMNS As
Long, MaxThreadCount As Long, DO_CONSOLE As Long, ByVal id As Long)
Const A_ROWS% = 30
Const A_COLUMNS% = 200
Const B_COLUMNS% = 30
Const DO_CONSOLE% = 3
Dim A(A_ROWS, A_COLUMNS) As Single
Dim B(A_COLUMNS, B_COLUMNS) As Single
Dim C(A_ROWS, B_COLUMNS) As Single
Dim MaxThreadCount As Long
Dim idCompute As LongDim i As Long
Dim j As Long
Sub Compute_Click ()
' This code simply initializes the two input arrays and then calls the
' 32-bit DLL to multiply them.  It then puts the result in the grid.
  MaxThreadCount = 8
  Randomize
  For i = 1 To A_COLUMNS
    For j = 1 To A_ROWS
        A(j, i) = Rnd
    Next j
    For k = 1 To B_COLUMNS
        B(i, k) = Rnd
    Next k
  Next i
  Call Compute(A(1, 1), B(1, 1), C(1, 1), A_ROWS, A_COLUMNS, B_COLUMNS,
                                MaxThreadCount, DO_CONSOLE,
idCompute)
  For i = 1 To A_ROWS
    grdC.Row = i
    For j = 1 To B_COLUMNS
      grdC.Col = j
      grdC.Text = Str$(C(i, j))
    Next j
  Next i
End Sub
```

References

Norwood, John. "Mixed Language Windows Programming". *Dr. Dobb's Journal,* October 1991.

Vaidyanathan, Shankar. "Multitasking Fortran and Windows NT". *Dr. Dobb's Sourcebook of Windows Programming,* Fall 1993.

Vaidyanathan, Shankar. "Building Windows NT Applications using Fortran". *Proceedings of the Tech*Ed Conference,* FR-301, Volume 2, March 1993.

Listing 18.5 (continued)

```
Sub Form_Load ()
' This code sets up the call to the CALL32 DLL by first using the Declare32
' function to get an id number. At this point CALL32 creates a function
' pointer to that 32-bit DLL subroutine and all access to the routine will be
' through that function pointer. The code also initializes the row and column
' number and sets the size of the grid fields.
  idCompute = Declare32("COMPUTE", "compute", "pppppppp")
  grdC.Rows = A_ROWS + 1
  grdC.Cols = B_COLUMNS + 1
  grdC.Row = 0
  For i = 1 To B_COLUMNS
    grdC.Col = i
    grdC.Text = Str$(i)
    grdC.ColWidth(i) = TextWidth("123.1234567")
  Next i
  grdC.Col = 0
  For i = 1 To A_ROWS
    grdC.Row = i
    grdC.Text = Str$(i)
    grdC.RowHeight(i) = TextHeight("1") + 10
  Next i
End Sub
```

Chapter 19

Multiprecision Integer Arithmetic Using C++

John K. Gotwals

In the last few years a need has developed for programming packages that can carry out integer arithmetic involving hundreds or thousands of digits. The advent of the RSA public key cryptosystem has contributed to this need by creating interest in factorization and testing for primality. Multiprecision arithmetic also allows researchers to observe patterns that appear in calculations, formulate conjectures about the patterns, and perhaps find counterexamples to others' erroneous conjectures.

This chapter describes the implementation and usage of a multiprecision integer arithmetic package on a 32-bit computer running Windows NT. I've written the high-level portions of the package in C++; I've found a clear and compelling reason for using C++ when operator overloading leads to a simplified programming interface. The system can perform arithmetic with integers of any reasonable length. For reasons to be discussed shortly, I've written the low-level routines in assembly language, but the interfaces to these routines are fully documented in the complete package. I've built and tested this package with Microsoft's 32-bit Visual C++ v1.0, and the full version, including assembly language source, is available on the code disk. I've also included a program (Listing 19.1) to demonstrate the capabilities of this package.

Design Issues and Implementation Choices

This design uses the signed-magnitude representation for numbers, in which negative and positive numbers of the same magnitude receive identical representation except in their signs. The implementation represents negative, zero, and positive numbers by sign values of -1, 0, and +1 respectively. Furthermore, the implementation assumes that at the end of every arithmetic operation, the result will be normalized. With the exception of zero, a normalized number does not have any leading zero digits. Zero is a special case and consists of one digit which contains zero.

The design process always involves tradeoffs between such things as performance, portability, size, ease of implementation, and ease of use. In any extended-precision

---

Listing 19.1 Program to demonstrate `LargeInt` class.

```
/* fact1.cpp
   demo factorial program
   -------------------- */
#include <stdio.h>
#include <string.h>
#include "largeint.h"
#include "misc.h"

int main() {
   const int bufSize = 50000; // max decimal digits
   char buf[bufSize];
   int choice;
   LargeInt result = 1;

   printf("Calculate factorial of: ");
   scanf("%d", &choice);
   for (int i = 2; i <= choice; i++)
      result *= i;
   if (result.binToDec(buf, bufSize) != NULL) {
      printf("\n%d! = \n%s\n", choice, buf);
      printf("\nwhich has %d digits\n", strlen(buf));
   }
   else
      printf("Output string buffer too small\n");

   return 0;
}
```

system, it is necessary to detect overflow or underflow before applying a carry or borrow to the next most significant digit. Because C doesn't provide a standard and efficient way to detect overflow in computations involving unsigned operands, I decided to implement the low-level arithmetic routines in assembly language. (I also used assembly language for performance reasons.)

The use of assembly language threatens to make a good portion of the system nonportable and to throw me into the nefarious intricacies of extended-precision arithmetic at the CPU register level. To avoid this scenario in my particular implementation, I "wrap" a multiple-precision integer as an object of the LargeInt class. As shown in Listing 19.2, just below the access specifier private:, each object of this class contains a pointer (adr) to the most significant digit of a radix-2^{32} multi-precision integer, a count (len) of the number of radix-2^{32} digits, and the sign (sign) of the LargeInt object.

Listing 19.2   `largeint.h`— *Definition of the* `LargeInt` *class.*

```
/* largeint.h : interface of the LargeInt class
   multiple precision integer arithmetic
   -------------------------------------------- */
class LargeInt {
friend LargeInt divRem(const LargeInt& u,
   const LargeInt& v, LargeInt* r);
friend char* evalFrac(const LargeInt& u,
   const LargeInt& v, int precision,
   char* dest, int lim);

public:
   LargeInt();
   LargeInt(int num);
   LargeInt(unsigned num);
   LargeInt(const char* str);
   LargeInt(const LargeInt& lint);
   ~LargeInt() {delete [] adr;}
   int lintLen() {return len;}
   int operator==(const LargeInt& lint) const;
   int operator==(int num) const;
   int operator<(const LargeInt& lint) const;
   int operator<(int num) const;
   const LargeInt& operator=(const LargeInt& lint);
```

My implementation allocates memory for multiprecision integers from the heap. Because the arithmetic and assignment operations will always result in the creation and deletion of LargeInt objects, a large amount of heap activity occurs during program execution. I made no attempt to provide for a custom memory manager, because preliminary measurements made while running under Windows NT indicated a performance hit of only about 10% from the system memory manager.

Listing 19.2 (continued)

```
    const LargeInt& operator=(int num);
    const LargeInt& operator=(unsigned num);
    const LargeInt& operator=(const char* str);
    LargeInt operator+(const LargeInt& lint) const;
    LargeInt operator-(const LargeInt& lint) const;
    LargeInt operator*(const LargeInt& lint) const;
    LargeInt operator/(const LargeInt& lint) const;
    LargeInt operator%(const LargeInt& lint) const;
    LargeInt operator-() const; // unary minus
    void operator*=(int num);
    void powerTwo(int power);
    char* binToDec(char* dest, int lim) const;
    void decToBin(const char* str);
    void lintDump() const;

private:
    int* adr;  // address of most significant digit
    int len;   // number of radix-2^32 digits
    int sign;  // 1 ==> +; 0 ==> zero; -1 ==> -
    LargeInt(int digits, int fill);
    void normalize();
};

/* manifest constants and other misc items
------------------------------------- */
const LargeInt tenTo9   = 1000000000u;
const int intTenTo9     = 1000000000u;
    // change both to 10^18 for 64-bit machine
const LargeInt zero     = 0;
const LargeInt one      = 1;
const LargeInt two      = 2;
const int numBitsStar3 = sizeof(int) * 8 * 3;
const int PackFactor    = numBitsStar3 / 10;
    // log of 2 to base 10 is approx. 3/10
```

Constructing a Multiprecision Integer

Listing 19.2 shows the header file for the `LargeInt` class and lists the five `LargeInt` constructors available for creation of multiprecision integers. The following example invokes all five constructors to create and initialize n1 through n5. In this code fragment, the default constructor initializes n1 to zero and the copy constructor is used to initialize n5 with the value contained in n4:

```
LargeInt n1, n2 = -123, n3 = 1234u;
LargeInt n4 = "12345678901234567890";
LargeInt n5 = n4;
```

Note that although n4 has been initialized with a string constant, it could have been initialized from a file input buffer. The only upper limit on the string initializer's length (assuming adequate virtual memory) is the maximum length that can be returned by `strlen()`. The string initializer is converted from decimal to radix-2^{32} binary via the C function `strtoul()`, which converts blocks of nine decimal digits (starting at the left of the string) at a time to binary. The constructor adds each converted block to the radix-2^{32} multiple-precision integer, and multiplies the resultant integer by 10^9. The `LargeInt` member function `decToBin()` carries out the conversion. A portion of this code is presented in Listing 19.3.

Listing 19.2 (continued)

```
/* int version of memcmp()
   ----------------------- */
inline int memcmpInt(const int* u, const int* v,int n) {
    while (n--) {
        if (*u != *v)
            return ((unsigned)*u < (unsigned)*v)? -1 : 1;
        u++;
        v++;
    }
    return 0;
}

/* LargeInt function prototypes
   ---------------------------- */
LargeInt sqrt(const LargeInt& lint);
```

decToBin() uses Horner's method to evaluate a polynomial whose coefficients are formed from blocks of nine decimal digits each. (Note that the listing does not include the code that picks off the optional sign from the front of the string, gets rid of any leading zeros, and tests for the special case of zero.) str is the address of the string to be converted, PackFactor is a constant with a value of 9 for a 32-bit system, and the implicit this pointer points to the LargeInt object, which contains the result of the conversion.

Listing 19.3   Definition of member functions decToBin() **and** get9().

```
void LargeInt::decToBin(const char* str) {
//
// code to determine value of strSign belongs here
//
    sign = 1; // sign adjusted below
    // find out how many blocks will be transferred
    numblocks = numchars = strlen(str);
    if (numblocks % PackFactor != 0)
        numblocks = numblocks / PackFactor + 1;
    else
        numblocks /= PackFactor;
    // carry out the intial coversion
    last = get9(buf, str, 1 + (numchars-1)%PackFactor);
    *this = (unsigned)strtoul(buf, 0, 10);
    // carry out the rest of the conversion
    while (--numblocks > 0) {
        last++;
        last = get9(buf, last, PackFactor);
        *this = (*this) * tenTo9;
        *this = (*this) + (unsigned)strtoul(buf, 0, 10);
    }
    sign = strSign;
}


/* Copy qty characters and store as string
   Return adr of last source character transferred
   ---------------------------------------------- */
const char* get9(char*dest, const char*src, int qty) {
    assert (*src != '\0');
    for (int i = 0; i < qty  && (dest[i]=src[i]); i++)
        { };
    dest[i] = '\0';
    return src + i - 1;
}
```

Comparing Multiprecision Integers

Almost any calculation creates a need to perform arithmetic comparisons. Because C++ has provisions for overloading operators, a multiprecision comparison of lint1 with lint2 can be as simple as writing the code

```
if (lint1 < lint2)
// do this
else
// do this
```

As currently written, the LargeInt package overloads only the == and < operators, but additional comparison operators could be added easily. In this implementation, the left operand must be a LargeInt object, but the right operand can be either another LargeInt object or the built-in int type. Listing 19.4 contains the code for overloading the operator<.

Listing 19.4   Overloading of operator<.

```
/* signed comparison : lint1 < lint2
   (assumes normalized operands)
   -------------------------------- */
int LargeInt::operator<(const LargeInt& lint) const {
    if (sign < lint.sign)
        return 1;
    if (sign > lint.sign)
        return 0;
// at this point, the signs are the same
    if (sign == 0)
        return 0;
    if ((sign == -1  &&  len > lint.len)  ||
        (sign ==  1  &&  len < lint.len))
        return 1;
    if ((sign == -1  &&  len < lint.len)  ||
        (sign ==  1  &&  len > lint.len))
        return 0;
// here the signs and the lengths are both the same
    int compare = memcmpInt(adr, lint.adr, len);
    if ((sign ==  1  &&  compare < 0)  ||
        (sign == -1  &&  compare > 0))
        return 1;
    return 0;
}
```

The routine begins by checking the signs and number of radix-2^{32} digits of each operand. Only if the signs and lengths are the same is it necessary to perform a digit-by-digit compare. Although the code is fairly simple, I endured a fair amount of mental anguish while testing, until I realized that I could not use the system memcmp() to compare digits, because it compares bytes instead of 32-bit words. See the bottom of Listing 19.2 for the definition of the memcmpInt function.

Multiprecision Arithmetic

As shown in Listing 19.2, LargeInt objects can participate in the standard signed arithmetic operations of addition, subtraction, multiplication, and division by using the overloaded operators +, -, *, and /. In addition, I've also overloaded the modulus, multiply assignment, and unary minus operators %, *=, and -, although the *= operator requires the right operand to be of type int. The code for overloading the * operator is given in Listing 19.5.

The multiplication routine performs three steps:

1. Check whether either operand is zero (in which case, the routine is essentially finished).

2. Create a LargeInt result with sufficient space to hold the product.

3. Determine the sign of the result, and call the low-level multiply().

The multiply() prototype at the top of Listing 19.5, takes five parameters. Pointers u and v point to the multipliers, w points to their product, and n and m are the number of radix-2^{32} digits for u and v respectively. (The low-level multiply routine is shown in Listing 19.9. The full assembly language source for all routines is provided on the code disk.)

Listing 19.4 (continued)

```
/* signed comparison : lint < 123
   ------------------------------- */
int LargeInt::operator<(int num) const {
    LargeInt test;
    test = num;
    return *this < test;
}
```

The `LargeInt` package includes several additional useful functions such as `powerTwo()`, `sqrt()`, `divRem()`, and `evalFrac()`. The prototypes of these functions are given in Listing 19.2. The friend function `divRem()` performs division between `LargeInt` variables, but unlike the division operator, `divRem()` generates both the quotient and the remainder. The friend function `evalFrac()` evaluates the fraction u/v, where u and v are both multiprecision integers, to any desired precision. This function is useful when you want to approximate some quantity with the rational number u/v.

Binary to Decimal Conversion

In the factorial calculation program shown in Listing 19.1, `LargeInt` variable `result` contains the factorial of a number that was entered by the user. To convert this result to a decimal number, the statement

```
result.binToDec(buf, bufSize)
```

Listing 19.5 Overloading of operator*.

```
void multiply(const int *u, const int *v, int *w,
     int n, int m); // multiply prototype

/* multiplication : lint3 = lint1 * lint2;
---------------------------------------- */
LargeInt LargeInt::operator*(const LargeInt& lint) const {
    if (sign == 0 || lint.sign == 0)
        return zero;
    LargeInt result(len + lint.len, 0);
    if (sign == lint.sign)      result.sign = 1;
    else
        result.sign = -1;
    multiply(adr, lint.adr, result.adr, len, lint.len);
    if (*result.adr == 0)
        result.normalize();
    return result;
}
```

calls `binToDec()` with parameter `buf` pointing to an output string buffer and `bufSize` equal to the size of the string buffer. `binToDec()` converts the radix-2^{32} integer into a decimal integer string and stores the string in the buffer. The function returns `buf` if the conversion is successful, but if there is insufficient string buffer space, the conversion process is halted and `binToDec()` returns `NULL`.

A description of the binary to decimal conversion procedure is as follows: The routine creates blocks of nine decimal integers at a time by dividing `result` repeatedly by 10^9 and stopping when the final quotient is zero. After each division the routine calls `sprintf()` to convert the remainder from the division to a string of nine decimal digits. Each string of nine digits is stored at successive positions in the string buffer, and the quotient from the division becomes the dividend for the next division. Because this conversion procedure generates the least significant block of digits first and the most significant block last, the output string must be reversed, in blocks of nine.

Listing 19.6 contains the code for the binary to decimal conversion. (Code to remove leading zeros from the result string and possibly insert a minus sign has been omitted from this listing.) `PackFactor` is a constant with a value of 9 for a 32-bit system. Because the `LargeInt` object to be converted may not be changed, the routine must create a copy (stored in variable `copy` in the listing). The low-level division routine `divrem()` carries out the real work of the conversion process. The prototype of `divrem()` is shown at the top of Listing 19.6.

Listing 19.6   Definition of `divrem()`.

```
int divrem(int *u, int v, int m); // divrem prototype

char* LargeInt::binToDec(char* dest, int lim) const {
    LargeInt copy = *this;   // convert this copy
    int* copyAdr = copy.adr; // this will be changed
    int copyLen  = copy.len; // this will be changed
    int binDec; // holds one 10^PackFactor binary digit
    char* initDest = dest;
    int blkCnt, i, j;

    // special case of 0
    if (sign == 0) {
        strcpy(dest, "0");
        return initDest;
    }
```

This routine divides the m-place integer pointed at by u by the single-precision integer v. When the function has finished the division, the dividend has been replaced by the quotient and the remainder is returned on the stack.

Listing 19.6 (continued)

```
// convert to string in blocks of PackFactor
blkCnt = 0;
while (*copyAdr != 0  ||  copyLen > 1) {
    binDec = divrem(copyAdr, intTenTo9, copyLen);
    if (copyLen > 1  &&  *copyAdr == 0) {
        copyAdr++;
        copyLen--;
    }
    if (lim - (PackFactor + 1) > 0) { // 1 for '\0'
        sprintf(dest, "%09u", binDec);
        lim  -= PackFactor;
        dest += PackFactor;
    }
    else
        return 0; // short of room for output string
    blkCnt++;
} // on exit, dest points at null byte
lim--; // account for the null byte

// swap output in blkCnt groups of size PackFactor
i = 0; // subscript of beginning of 1st block
j = (blkCnt - 1) * PackFactor; // last block
blkCnt &= -2; // only need an even number of swaps
while (blkCnt > 1) {
    swap9(initDest + i, initDest + j);
    blkCnt -= 2;
    i += PackFactor;
    j -= PackFactor;
}
```

Testing

Testing a package of this type is difficult. As an example, the low-level divide function is quite complex and consists of over 200 lines of assembly language code with a fair number of conditional branches. The code is a derivative of a program by Knuth which was written for his fictional MIX computer. Knuth has written that "some portions of that program would probably never get tested even if a million random test cases were tried." Because I developed this package for "recreational computing," my main method of testing was to run some programs that have known results.

For very basic debugging and testing, `lintDump()` displays the sign and hex contents of each radix-2^{32} digit. The following code fragment provides an example; the output can be checked by using a scientific calculator.

```
LargeInt n1 = "-12345678901234567890";
printf("n1: ");
n1.lintDump();
// n1: sign = -1  AB54A98C EB1F0AD2
```

Listing 19.6 (continued)

```
//
// Code to remove leading zeros and possibly insert
// minus sign belongs here
//
    return initDest;
}

inline void swap9(char* s1, char* s2) {
    char hold;

    for (int i = 0; i < PackFactor; i++) {
        hold  = s1[i];
        s1[i] = s2[i];
        s2[i] = hold;
    }
}
```

At a more advanced level of testing, a test program can use sqrt() to take the square root of a large integer, square the result, and compare it with the original. Listing 19.7 shows a surprisingly simple function from this package which uses Newton's method to compute the square root of an integer. Using this function will exercise the add, multiply, and divide operations.

The Lucas–Lehmer algorithm tests the primality of a Mersenne number. Mersenne numbers are those of the form $2^p - 1$. The Lucas–Lehmer test determines if, for a particular prime number p, the corresponding Mersenne number is also prime. Listing 19.8 shows a program that asks the user to enter a prime number and then determines if $2^p - 1$ is prime. This program calls the timer function to measure execution time, and the if statement inside the for loop displays information about the progress of the calculation.

Performance

A program that can calculate and display the factorial of any reasonably sized number is given in Listing 19.1. (The bufSize constant will have to be adjusted if the result contains 50,000 or more digits.)

Listing 19.7 Computing the square root within Newton's method.

```
/* Compute the greatest integer less than or equal
    to the square root of lint.  From "Factorization
    and Primality Testing", Bressoud
    --------------------------------------------- */
LargeInt sqrt(const LargeInt& lint) {
    LargeInt a = lint;
    LargeInt b = (lint + one) / two;

    while (b < a) {
        a = b;
        b = (a * a + lint) / (two * a);
    }
    return a;
}
```

Listing 19.8   The Lucas–Lehmer test.

```
/* test3.cpp
   Lucas-Lehmer test for primality of 2^p - 1
   If p > 2 is a prime, then 2^p - 1 is prime if
   and only if L[p-2] = 0, where the sequence L[i]
   is defined as follows: L[0] = 4,
   L[i+1] = (L[i]^2 - 2) modulo (2^p - 1)
   -------------------------------------------- */
#include <stdio.h>
#include "largeint.h"

void pause();
void timer(int f);

int main() {
   int p, i;
   LargeInt L, mod;

   printf("Enter a prime number: ");
   scanf("%d", &p);
   timer(0); // start timer
   mod.powerTwo(p);
   mod = mod - 1; // mod = 2^p - 1
   L = 4;
   for (i = 2; i <= p - 1; i++) {
      if (i % 100 == 0)
         printf("%4d\r", i);
      L = (L * L - 2) % mod;
   }
   printf("\n2^%d - 1 is ", p);
   if (L == zero)
      printf("prime\n");
   else
      printf("not prime\n");
   printf("and the calculation took "), timer(1);

   return 0;
}
```

Although this package performs signed arithmetic on integers of almost any length, as the precision increases the processing time increases, and probably in a nonlinear fashion. This time increase is illustrated by the program in Listing 19.1. Table 19.1 summarizes the data obtained from several different runs on a 33MHz 486DX computer under Windows NT. Note the significant amount of time needed to perform the binary to decimal conversions.

The Lucas–Lehmer primality test is another CPU-intensive process. Although the algorithm is simple, the program processes large numbers. Table 19.2 shows some representative times.

Conclusion

Using C++ to overload the arithmetic operators and to create a LargeInt class of extended precision integer objects provides an easy-to-use package for multiprecision integer arithmetic. A package of this type allows the user to carry out calculations that are simply not feasible with most standard languages.

Be forewarned that your calculation results may sometimes be challenged. After calculating and printing all 1,512,852 digits of 300,000 factorial, I proudly showed the results to my neighbor. After looking at several pages of the output, he stopped on

Table 19.1   Results of calculating factorials of a number.

Number	*Run Time (sec)*	*Conversion Time (sec)*	*Output Digits*
3,000	3	1	9,131
10,000	41	12	35,660
30,000	431	131	121,288
300,000	59,114	21,250	1,512,852

Table 19.2   Results of Lucas–Lehmer test.

p	*Run Time (sec)*	*Digits for 2p – 1*
1279	9	386
2203	49	664
11213	5749	3376

page 367 and circled one of the numbers with his pen. He then informed me that my output was wrong, because the digit he circled should be a "4" and not a "3," as was represented by my calculations. We had quite a heated exchange of words, and he told me that I could only make him change his mind by redoing the calculations by hand!

References

Bressoud, D. *Factorization and Primality Testing*, Springer-Verlag, 1989.

Knight, D. "An Ada Package for Multi-Precision Integer Arithmetic," *SIGSMALL/PC Notes*. ACM Press, November 1993.

Knuth, D. *The Art of Computer Programming*, Volume 2. Addison-Wesley, 1981.

Nievergelt, J., J. Farrar, and E. Reingold. *Computer Approaches to Mathematical Problems*. Prentice-Hall, 1974.

Listing 19.9 Assembly language multiply() *routine for an 80x86.*

```
/* multiply.cpp  Multiplication of nonnegative
   integers forms the radix-2^32 product of arrays
   u[n] and v[m]. Returns the result in array
   w[n + m]. After Knuth, volume 2, section 4.3.1
   Copyright (C) 1994 John K. Gotwals
   --------------------------------------------- */
void multiply(const int *u, const int *v, int *w,
              int n, int m) {
    int edisav, esisav;
    int carry;

__asm {
    mov edisav,edi      ; edi and esi must be preserved
    mov esisav,esi

    ; set w[m] to w[m+n-1] to zero inclusive
    mov eax,0
    mov ecx,n           ; ecx = n
    mov esi,w           ; esi -> w[0]
    mov edx,m           ; edx = m
    init:
        mov [esi+edx*4],eax
        inc edx
    loop init
```

Listing 19.9 (continued)

```
  ; rI1 = ecx = i
  ; rI2 = esi = j
  ; rI3 = edi = i + j
  ; edx = k = carry
  ; rIn are the index registers of Knuth's MIX

  mov esi,m
  dec esi                    ; j = m - 1
  h1:                        ; M2. zero multiplier?
    mov ebx,v                ; ebx -> v[0]
    mov edx,[ebx+esi*4]
    cmp edx,0 ;if v[j] = 0, goto h8 and set w[j] = 0
    je h8
    mov ecx,n                ; M3. initialize i = n;
    lea edi,[ecx+esi]        ; (i+j) = (n+j)
    dec ecx                  ; i = n - 1
    mov edx,0                ; k = 0
    h2:                      ; M4. multiply and add
      mov carry,edx
      mov ebx,u
      mov eax,[ebx+ecx*4]    ; eax = u[i]
      mov ebx,v
      mul DWORD PTR[ebx+esi*4] ; edx:eax=u[i]*v[j]
      mov ebx,w
      add eax,[ebx+edi*4] ; add w[i+j] to lower half
      adc edx,0       ; add carry bit into upper half
      add eax,carry   ; add k to lower half
      adc edx,0       ; add carry bit into upper half
      mov [ebx+edi*4],eax ; w[i+j] = t mod 2^32
                      ; where t = u[i]*v[j]+w[i+j]+k
      dec edi              ; decrease i and (i+j) by 1
      dec ecx              ; M5. loop on i
    jge h2                 ; note: edx = t/b
    h8:
    mov ebx,w
    mov [ebx+esi*4],edx  ; w[j] = k
    dec esi              ; M6. loop on j
  jge h1

  mov edi, edisav          ; restore edi and esi
  mov esi, esisav
  }
}
```

Chapter 20

Multitasking Fortran and Windows NT

Calling the Win32 API directly from Fortran

Shankar Vaidyanathan

A Windows NT application can consist of more than one process, and a process can consist of more than one thread. The Win32 API supports multitasking, which allows the simultaneous execution of multiple threads and processes. In a single-processor system, multitasking is achieved by dividing the CPU time among all threads competing for it. With systems having multiple processors and symmetric multiprocessing, more than one thread or process can be executed simultaneously, resulting in a dramatic improvement in application performance.

However, NT applications that jive well in such environments usually are written in C and C++ because the Win32 APIs involve C type character strings, null pointers, pointers to valid data types, structures, arrays of structures, cyclic/recursive structures, pointers to structures, and dynamic allocation of memory. Trying to develop Fortran applications to make use of these APIs can be a challenging and arduous task.

Numerically intensive Fortran applications, both existing and new, are suited to Windows NT because they naturally yield to subdivision of computational tasks.

Matrix computations, solutions of linear algebraic equations, partial differential equations, interpolations and extrapolations, integration and evaluation of functions, Eigen systems, Fourier and fast Fourier transformations, and statistical simulation and modeling are typical of this divide-and-conquer paradigm. Some of these functions are inherently parallelizable and traditionally run on mainframes and supercomputers. With a 32-bit, flat-memory-model operating system like Windows NT, however, all these applications can run on a PC. With the guidelines and interface statement file provided in this chapter, you can write Fortran applications that call the Win32 API directly, gaining all the benefits of its multitasking and multiprocessing abilities.

Processes and Threads

A process can be considered as a program loaded into memory and prepared for execution. Each process has a private virtual address space and consists of code, data, and other system resources. Threads, on the other hand, are the basic entity to which the operating system allocates CPU time. Each process is started with a single thread, but additional, independently executing threads can be created. Each thread maintains a set of structures for saving its context while waiting to be scheduled for processing time. The context includes the thread's set of machine registers, the kernel stack, a thread environment block, and a user stack in the address space of the thread's process. The most important feature of threads is that all threads of a process share the same virtual address space, and can access global variables (like the Fortran common block) and system resources of the process. This makes communication between threads easy and cheap. Furthermore, the system can create and execute threads more quickly than it creates processes. The code for threads has already been mapped into the address space of the process, whereas the code for the new process must be loaded during run time. In addition, all threads of a process can use open handles to resources such as files and pipes. Hence, it's usually more efficient for an application to implement multitasking by distributing tasks among the threads of one process rather than by creating multiple processes.

Time Slicing

The Win32 API in Windows NT is designed for preemptive multitasking. Under preemptive multitasking, the system allocates small slices of CPU time among the competing threads. The currently executing thread is suspended when its time slice elapses, allowing another thread to run. When the system switches from one thread to another, it saves the context of the suspended thread and restores the saved context of the next thread in queue. To the application developer, the advantage of multitasking is the ability to create applications that use more than one process and to create processes that use more than one thread of execution.

If, for example, you make a simple Fortran application, like matrix multiplication, multithreaded, you can create separate threads for multiplying every row with a particular column. Because each time slice is small, it may appear that multiple threads are multiplying the subcomponents of the matrix simultaneously. This is true on multiprocessor systems, where the executable threads are distributed among the available processors.

Figure 20.1   *(a) Prototype of* `CreateThread( )`,
                  (b) structure for security attributes,
                  (c) implementing the security attributes
                  structure using `STRUCTURE/ END STRUCTURE`.

(a)

```
HANDLE WINAPI CreateThread (
    LP_SECURITY_ATTRIBUTES lpThreadAttributes,    DWORD  dwStack-
Size,
    LPTHREAD_START_ROUTINE  lpStartAddress,
    LPVOID  lpParameter,
    DWORD  dwCreationFlags,
    LPDWORD  lpThreadId
    );
```

(b)

```
typedef struct _SECURITY_ATTRIBUTES {
    DWORD nLength;
    LPVOID lpSecurityDescriptor;
    BOOL bInheritHandle;
} SECURITY_ATTRIBUTES, *LPSECURITY_ATTRIBUTES;
```

(c)

```
STRUCTURE /SECURITY_ATTRIBUTES/
    integer*4 length
    integer*4 lpSecurityDescriptor
    logical*4 bInheritHandle
END STRUCTURE
```

Thread Creation

The Win32 API CreateThread() creates a new thread for a process. Figure 20.1(a) shows how this API function is prototyped in winbase.h (shipped with the NT SDK). Looking at the listing of kernel32.lib, you'll notice that this function is listed as _CreateThread@24. This Win32 API is invoked with the __stdcall convention, which means that all the function arguments are pushed on the stack, and the stack is cleaned up by the callee. The __stdcall function names are prefixed by an underscore and suffixed with @<number> when decorated. The number is the number of bytes in decimal used by the widened arguments pushed on the stack.

CreateThread() returns a HANDLE which is an integer*4 (double word) entity in Fortran. The creating thread must specify the starting address of the code that the new thread is to execute — loc() in Microsoft Fortran can provide the address of variables as well as functions. By default, all parameters are passed by value in C and by reference in Fortran. Because all functions are external by specification in Fortran, declaring the function in Figure 20.1(a) as external isn't necessary.

A process can have multiple threads simultaneously executing the same function. The arguments specifying the stack size of the new thread and the creation flags are double words in C, and they are once again integer*4 data types in Fortran. In the function prototype in Figure 20.1(a), the argument to the thread function is passed through a long pointer. On the Fortran side, this object can be passed by reference; this will pass a long pointer (integer*4) to that object. CreateThread() returns the identifier of the thread through a long pointer to a double word, and, on the Fortran side, that parameter can be specified as integer*4 with the reference attribute.

The first argument to CreateThread() is a structure prototyped in winbase.h, as in Figure 20.1(b). This structure can be implemented using STRUCTURE/END STRUC-TURE statements in Fortran, as in Figure 20.1(c). Note that BOOL in C is a logical*4 in Fortran capable of taking either a .TRUE or .FALSE value. Because the parameter in the C function prototype is a long pointer to the structure, the structure itself can be

---

Figure 20.2 Interface statement for CreateThread().

```
interface to integer*4 function CreateThread [stdcall, alias:
                                        '_CreateThread@24']
+    (security, stack, thread_func, arguments, flags, thread_id)
    integer*4  security, stack     [value]
    integer*4  thread_func [value] ! loc(thread_func) is passed by value
    integer*4  arguments   [reference]
    integer*4  flags       [value]
    integer*4  thread_id   [reference]
   end
```

passed by reference, or the loc() of the structure can be passed by value in Fortran. The same is true for character strings. Passing the loc() of the structure or character string has a distinct advantage because if I want to pass a C null pointer, I can simply pass a 0 in Fortran.

With all the arguments of CreateThread() squared away, the interface statement can be specified as in Figure 20.2.

Synchronization

In a multitasking environment, it's sometimes necessary to coordinate the execution of multiple processes or multiple threads within a process. Win32 provides a set of synchronization objects for this. A synchronization object is essentially a data structure whose current state is signaled or not-signaled. A thread can interact with any of these objects either by modifying its state or by waiting for it to be in a signaled state. When a thread waits for an object, the execution of the thread is blocked as long as the state of the object is not-signaled. Typically, a thread will wait for a synchronization object before performing an operation that must coordinate with other threads; it will also wait when using a shared resource such as file, shared memory, or a peripheral device.

There are four types of synchronization objects: critical section, mutual exclusion (mutex), semaphores, and events. Two generic functions, WaitForSingleObject() and WaitForMultipleObjects(), are used by threads to wait for the state of a waitable object to be signaled. In addition to event, mutex, and semaphore objects, these functions may be used to wait for process and thread objects. The prototypes for WaitForSingleObject() and WaitForMultipleObjects() are provided in winbase.h in the NT SDK; the interface statements for them are provided in mt.fi (Listing 20.1).

Listing 20.1   mt.fi —Interface statements for thread, process, and synchronization Win32 APIs.

```
     interface to logical*4 function CloseHandle
+     [stdcall, alias: '_CloseHandle@4'] (handle)
+     (security, owner, string)
     integer*4 handle [value]
     end
```

Listing 20.1 (continued)

```
      interface to integer*4 function CreateEvent
  +     [stdcall, alias: '_CreateEventA@16']
  +     (security, reset, init_state, string)
      integer*4 security [value]
      Logical*4 reset [value]
      Logical*4 init_state [value]
      integer*4 string [value]
    end

    interface to integer*4 function CreateMutex
  +     [stdcall, alias: '_CreateMutexA@12']
  +     (security, owner, string)
      integer*4 security [value]
      Logical*4 owner [value]
      integer*4 string [value]
    end

    interface to logical*4 function CreateProcess
  +     [stdcall, alias: '_CreateProcessA@40']
  +     (lpApplicationName, lpCommandLine, lpProcessAttributes,
  +      lpThreadAttributes, bInheritHandles, dwCreationFlags,
  +      lpEnvironment, lpCurrentDirectory, lpStartupInfo,
  +      lpProcessInformation)
      integer*4 lpApplicationName [value]
      integer*4 lpCommandLine [value]
      integer*4 lpProcessAttributes [value]
      integer*4 lpThreadAttributes [value]
      logical*4 bInheritHandles [value]
      integer*4 dwCreationFlags [value]
      integer*4 lpEnvironment [value]
      integer*4 lpCurrentDirectory [value]
      integer*4 lpStartupInfo [value]
      integer*4 lpProcessInformation [value]
    end

    interface to integer*4 function CreateSemaphore
  +     [stdcall, alias: '_CreateSemaphoreA@16']
  +     (security, InitialCount, MaxCount, string)
      integer*4 security [value]
      integer*4 InitialCount [value]
      integer*4 MaxCount [value]
      integer*4 string [value]
    end
```

Critical Section

A critical section is a synchronization object that can be owned by only one thread at a time, enabling threads to coordinate mutually exclusive access to a shared resource. The restriction on this object is that it can only be used by threads of a single process. The critical-section object is a cyclic data structure, which makes its representation interesting and challenging in Fortran; winnt.h (in the NT SDK) declares the structure, as in Figure 20.3(a). Figure 20.3(b) is the Fortran implementation of the cyclic

---

Listing 20.1 (continued)

```
      interface to integer*4 function CreateThread
   +    [stdcall, alias: '_CreateThread@24']
   +    (security, stack, thread_func,
   +    argument, flags, thread_id)
      integer*4 security [value]
      integer*4 stack [value]
      external thread_func
      integer*4 argument [reference]
      integer*4 flags [value]
      integer*4 thread_id [reference]
    end

      interface to subroutine DeleteCriticalSection
   +    [stdcall, alias: '_DeleteCriticalSection@4'] (object)
      integer*4 object [value]
    end

      interface to logical*4 function DuplicateHandle
   +    [stdcall, alias: '_DuplicateHandle@28']
   +    (hSourceProcessHandle, hSourceHandle,
   +     hTargetProcessHandle, lpTargetHandle,
   +     dwDesiredAccess, bInheritHandle, dwOptions)
      integer*4 hSourceProcessHandle [value]
      integer*4 hSourceHandle [value]
      integer*4 hTargetProcessHandle [value]
      integer*4 lpTargetHandle [reference]
      integer*4 dwDesiredAccess [value]
      logical*4 bInheritHandle [value]
      integer*4 dwOptions [value]
    end
```

Listing 20.1 (continued)

```
      interface to subroutine EnterCriticalSection
 +    [stdcall, alias: '_EnterCriticalSection@4'] (object)
      integer*4 object [value]
      end

      interface to subroutine ExitProcess
 +    [stdcall, alias: '_ExitProcess@4'] (ExitCode)
      integer*4 ExitCode [value]
      end

      interface to subroutine ExitThread
 +    [stdcall, alias: '_ExitThread@4'] (ExitCode)
      integer*4 ExitCode [value]
      end

      interface to integer*4 function GetCurrentProcess
 +    [stdcall, alias: '_GetCurrentProcess@0'] ()
      end

      interface to integer*4 function GetCurrentProcessId
 +    [stdcall, alias: '_GetCurrentProcessId@0'] ()
      end

      interface to integer*4 function GetCurrentThread
 +    [stdcall, alias: '_GetCurrentThread@0'] ()
      end

      interface to integer*4 function GetCurrentThreadId
 +    [stdcall, alias: '_GetCurrentThreadId@0'] ()
      end

      interface to logical*4 function GetExitCodeProcess
 +    [stdcall, alias: '_GetExitCodeProcess@8']
 +    (hProcess, lpExitCode)
      integer*4 hProcess [value]
      integer*4 lpExitCode [reference]
      end

      interface to logical*4 function GetExitCodeThread
 +    [stdcall, alias: '_GetExitCodeThread@8']
 +    (hThread, lpExitCode)
      integer*4 hThread [value]
      integer*4 lpExitCode [reference]
      end
```

structure in Figure 20.3(a). loc( ) points the first structure to the second, and the second structure back to the first. Although the LIST_ENTRY item in the C typedef statement could be complex, I don't need to go into the implementation details in Fortran, because all that's required is a 4-byte space for the address of that data structure.

Listing 20.1 (continued)

```
   interface to integer*4 function GetLastError
+    [stdcall, alias: '_GetLastError@0'] ()
 end

   interface to integer*4 function GetPriorityClass
+    [stdcall, alias: '_ GetPriorityClass@4'] (hProcess)
     integer*4 hProcess [value]
 end

   interface to integer*4 function GetThreadPriority
+    [stdcall, alias: '_GetThreadPriority@4'] (hThread)
     integer*4 hThread [value]
 end

   interface to logical*4 function GetThreadSelectorEntry
+    [stdcall, alias: '_GetThreadSelectorEntry@12']
+    (hThread, dwSelector, lpSelectorEntry)
     integer*4 hThread [value]
     integer*4 dwSelector [value]
     integer*4 lpSelectorEntry [value]    ! Pass loc of the struct
 end

   interface to subroutine InitializeCriticalSection
+    [stdcall, alias: '_InitializeCriticalSection@4'] (object)
     integer*4 object [value]
 end

   interface to subroutine LeaveCriticalSection
+    [stdcall, alias: '_LeaveCriticalSection@4'] (object)
     integer*4 object [value]
 end

   interface to integer*4 function OpenEvent
+    [stdcall, alias: '_OpenEventA@12']
+    (dwDesiredAccess, bInheritHandle, lpName)
     integer*4 dwDesiredAccess [value]
     logical*4 bInheritHandle [value]
     integer*4 lpName [value]
   end
```

Listing 20.1 (continued)

```
      interface to integer*4 function OpenMutex
   +     [stdcall, alias: '_OpenMutexA@12']
   +     (dwDesiredAccess, bInheritHandle, lpName)
      integer*4 dwDesiredAccess [value]
      logical*4 bInheritHandle [value]
      integer*4 lpName [value]
   end

      interface to integer*4 function OpenProcess
   +     [stdcall, alias: '_OpenProcess@12']
   +     (dwDesiredAccess, bInheritHandle, lpName)
      integer*4 dwDesiredAccess [value]
      logical*4 bInheritHandle [value]
      integer*4 IdProcess [value]
   end

      interface to integer*4 function OpenSemaphore
   +     [stdcall, alias: '_OpenSemaphoreA@12']
   +     (dwDesiredAccess, bInheritHandle, lpName)
      integer*4 dwDesiredAccess [value]
      logical*4 bInheritHandle [value]
      integer*4 lpName [value]
   end

      interface to integer*4 function PulseEvent
   +     [stdcall, alias: '_PulseEvent@4'] (hEvent)
      integer*4 hEvent [value]        end

      interface to Logical*4 function ReleaseMutex
   +     [stdcall, alias: '_ReleaseMutex@4'] (handle)
      integer*4 handle [value]
   end

      interface to Logical*4 function ReleaseSemaphore
   +     [stdcall, alias: '_ReleaseSemaphore@12']
   +     (handle, ReleaseCount, LpPreviousCount)
      integer*4 handle [value]
      integer*4 ReleaseCount [value]
      integer*4 LpPreviousCount [reference]
   end

      interface to integer*4 function ResumeThread
   +     [stdcall, alias: '_ResumeThread@4'] (hThread)
      integer*4 hThread [value]
   end
```

To illustrate, I'll develop code for finding the sum of the first 50 whole numbers and apply various facets of multitasking to it. I'll start by generating 50 threads, each passing a particular value to ThreadFunc(). Each of the threads adds its value to a global variable result, which is inside a common block. Because you shouldn't allow simultaneous access to the global variable by all the threads, I protect this resource inside a critical section. This calls for an initialization of the critical-section object [done by InitializeCriticalSection()], and the modification of the global variable result is enclosed within EnterCriticalSection() and LeaveCriticalSection().

Listing 20.1 (continued)

```
    interface to integer*4 function SetEvent
+    [stdcall, alias: '_SetEvent@4'] (handle)
    integer*4 handle [value]
    end

    interface to subroutine SetLastError
+    [stdcall, alias: '_SetLastError@4'] (dwErrorCode)
    integer*4 dwErrorCode [value]
    end

    interface to logical*4 function SetPriorityClass
+    [stdcall, alias: '_SetPriorityClass@8'](hProcess, nPriority)
    integer*4 hProcess [value]
    integer*4 nPriority [value]
    end

    interface to logical*4 function SetThreadPriority
+    [stdcall, alias: '_SetThreadPriority@8'](hThread, nPriority)
    integer*4 hThread [value]
    integer*4 nPriority [value
    end

    interface to integer*4 function SuspendThread
+    [stdcall, alias: '_SuspendThread@4'] (hThread)
    integer*4 hThread [value]
    end

    interface to logical*4 function TerminateProcess
+    [stdcall, alias: '_TerminateProcess@8']
+    (hProcess, uExitCode)
    integer*4 hProcess [value]
    integer*4 uExitCode [value]
    end
```

Listing 20.1 (continued)

```
   interface to logical*4 function TerminateThread
+    [stdcall, alias: '_TerminateThread@8']
+    (hThread, dwExitCode)
     integer*4 hThread [value]
     integer*4 dwExitCode [value]
   end

   interface to integer*4 function TlsAlloc
+    [stdcall, alias: '_TlsAlloc@0'] ()
   end

   interface to logical*4 function TlsFree
+    [stdcall, alias: '_TlsFree@4'] (dwTlsIndex)
     integer*4 dwTlsIndex [value]
   end

   interface to integer*4 function TlsGetValue
+    [stdcall, alias: '_TlsGetValue@4'] (dwTlsIndex)
     integer*4 dwTlsIndex [value]
   end

   interface to logical*4 function TlsSetValue
+    [stdcall, alias: '_TlsSetValue@8'] (dwTlsIndex, lpTlsVal)
     integer*4 dwTlsIndex [value]
     integer*4 lpTlsVal [value]
   end

   interface to integer*4 function WaitForMultipleObjects
+    [stdcall, alias: '_WaitForMultipleObjects@16']
+    (Count, LpHandles, WaitAll, Mseconds)
     integer*4 Count [value]
     integer*4 LpHandles [reference]
     logical*4 WaitAll [value]
     integer*4 Mseconds [value]
   end

   interface to integer*4 function WaitForSingleObject
+    [stdcall, alias: '_WaitForSingleObject@8']
+    (handle, Mseconds)
     integer*4 handle [value]
     integer*4 Mseconds [value]
   end
```

However, if the primary thread exits before the completion of all the other threads, the child threads are "orphaned," and hence we wait for all the threads to complete through WaitForMultipleObjects(). I've made the function wait on the handle to all the threads indefinitely until all the threads complete their execution. The critical section object, GlobalCriticalSection, is also inside the common block so that it need not be passed as a parameter to ThreadFunc(). The code is given in Listing 20.3. Also refer to the Include file mt.fd (Listing 20.2) for data type declarations.

Figure 20.3 *(a) Declaration of the cyclic data structure in* winnt.h *(in the NT SDK).*
(b) Fortran implementation of the cyclic structure.

(a)
```
typedef struct _RTL_CRITICAL_SECTION_DEBUG {
        WORD    Type;
        WORD    CreatorBackTraceIndex;
        struct _RTL_CRITICAL_SECTION *CriticalSection;
        LIST_ENTRY ProcessLocksList;
        DWORD EntryCount;
        DWORD ContentionCount;
        DWORD Depth;
        PVOID OwnerBackTrace[ 5 ];
} RTL_CRITICAL_SECTION_DEBUG, *PRTL_CRITICAL_SECTION_DEBUG;

typedef struct _RTL_CRITICAL_SECTION {
        PRTL_CRITICAL_SECTION_DEBUG DebugInfo;
        LONG LockCount;
        LONG RecursionCount;
        HANDLE OwningThread    // from the thread's ClientId->UniqueTh-
read        HANDLE LockSemaphore;
        DWORD Reserved;
} RTL_CRITICAL_SECTION, *PRTL_CRITICAL_SECTION;
```

(b)
```
STRUCTURE /RTL_CRITICAL_SECTION_DEBUG/
    integer*4 Type
    integer*4 CreatorBackTraceIndex
    integer*4 Address
    integer*4 ProcessLocksList
    integer*4 EntryCount
    integer*4 ContentionCount
    integer*4 Depth
    integer*4 OwnerBackTrace(5)
END STRUCTURE
```

Figure 20.3 (continued)

```
STRUCTURE /RTL_CRITICAL_SECTION/
    integer*4 Address
    integer*4 LockCount
    integer*4 RecursionCount
    integer*4 OwningThread
    integer*4 LockSemaphore
    integer*4 Reserved
END STRUCTURE

record /RTL_CRITICAL_SECTION/ GlobalCriticalSection
record /RTL_CRITICAL_SECTION_DEBUG/ AuxCriticalSection

GlobalCriticalSection.Address = loc(AuxCriticalSection)
AuxCriticalSection.Address = loc(GlobalCriticalSection)
```

Listing 20.2   `mt.fd`— *Interface file for the data structures.*

```
PARAMETER (MAX_THREADS = 50)
PARAMETER (WAIT_INFINITE = -1)
PARAMETER (STANDARD_RIGHTS_REQUIRED = #F0000)
PARAMETER (SYNCHRONIZE = #100000)

STRUCTURE /PROCESS_INFORMATION/
integer*4 hProcess
integer*4 hThread
integer*4 dwProcessId
integer*4 dwThreadId
END STRUCTURE

STRUCTURE /RTL_CRITICAL_SECTION_DEBUG/
integer*4 Type
integer*4 CreatorBackTraceIndex
integer*4 Address
integer*4 ProcessLocksList
integer*4 EntryCount
integer*4 ContentionCount
integer*4 Depth
integer*4 OwnerBackTrace(5)
END STRUCTURE
```

Mutexes, Semaphores, and Events

A mutex (mutual exclusion) is similar to a critical-section object except that it can be used by the threads belonging to more than one process. A semaphore object is used as a resource gate and maintains a count between zero and some maximum value, thus limiting the use of a resource by counting threads as they pass in and out of the gate.

Listing 20.2 (continued)

```
      STRUCTURE /RTL_CRITICAL_SECTION/
      integer*4 Address
      integer*4 LockCount
      integer*4 RecursionCount
      integer*4 OwningThread
      integer*4 LockSemaphore
      integer*4 Reserved
      END STRUCTURE

      STRUCTURE /SECURITY_ATTRIBUTES/
      integer*4 nLength
      integer*4 lpSecurityDescriptor
      logical*4 bInheritHandle
      END STRUCTURE

      STRUCTURE /STARTUPINFO/
      integer*4 cb
      integer*4 lpReserved
      integer*4 lpDesktop
      integer*4 lpTitle
      integer*4 dwX
      integer*4 dwY
      integer*4 dwXSize
      integer*4 dwYSize
      integer*4 dwXCountChars
      integer*4 dwYCountChars
      integer*4 dwFillAttribute
      integer*4 dwFlags
      integer*2 wShowWindow
      integer*2 cbReserved2
      integer*4 lpReserved2
      integer*4 hStdInput
      integer*4 hStdOutput
      integer*4 hStdError
      END STRUCTURE
```

Listing 20.3   Program to demonstrate thread creation and
critical section object.

```
        include 'mt.fi'

Thread Function as a subroutine

        subroutine ThreadFunc (param)
        include 'mt.fd'
        integer*4 param, result
        record /RTL_CRITICAL_SECTION/ GlobalCriticalSection
        record /RTL_CRITICAL_SECTION_DEBUG/ AuxCriticalSection
        common result, GlobalCriticalSection

Critical Section region begins...

        Call EnterCriticalSection ( loc(GlobalCriticalSection))
            result = param + result

Critical Section region ends...

        Call LeaveCriticalSection ( loc(GlobalCriticalSection))
        Call ExitThread(0)
        return
        end

Main program begins here
        program test
        include 'mt.fd'
        external ThreadFunc
        integer*4 ThreadHandle(MAX_THREADS), inarray(MAX_THREADS)
        integer*4 CreateThread, threadId
        integer*4 waitResult, WaitForMultipleObjects
        integer*4 loop, result
        record /RTL_CRITICAL_SECTION/ GlobalCriticalSection
        record /RTL_CRITICAL_SECTION_DEBUG/ AuxCriticalSection
        common result, GlobalCriticalSection

Creating the cyclic structure for the critical section object

        GlobalCriticalSection.Address = loc(AuxCriticalSection)
        AuxCriticalSection.Address = loc(GlobalCriticalSection)

        result = 0
```

The Win32 API calls associated with mutex are `CreateMutex( )`, `OpenMutex( )`, and `ReleaseMutex( )`; there's a similar set for semaphores. The semaphore functions typically take an additional set of parameters that manipulate the semaphore count. Semaphores are quite powerful, because they are mutexes with the additional ability to control the number of threads. The Fortran prototypes for these APIs are provided as interface statements in `mt.fi` (Listing 20.1).

As another example, I'll modify the previous example to incorporate semaphores and mutex objects. I'll also try to save space by not requiring that you save the handles of all the threads waiting on them. Here, I generate 50 threads as before and enclose the global common-variable result within the mutex region. Instead of waiting on all the threads to complete, however, I wait for the last thread to complete; this is an indication of all the threads having completed. To this end, a semaphore object is created with an initial count of 0. Because this is a not-signaled state of the semaphore, the call to `WaitForSingleObject( )` blocks the main thread until the last spawned thread releases the semaphore by incrementing the semaphore count by 1. The handles to the mutex and semaphore objects are `hMutex` and `hSemaphore`, respectively, and they're inside the common block so that they need not be passed as parameters. `ThreadCounter` is an additional parameter in the common block to keep track of the number of threads that have modified the global result variable (Listing 20.4).

Listing 20.3 (continued)

```
Initializing Critical Section ...

    Call InitializeCriticalSection(loc(GlobalCriticalSection))

    do loop = 1, MAX_THREADS
       inarray(loop)= loop
       write(*, '(1x, A, I3)') 'Creating Thread # ', loop
       ThreadHandle(loop) = CreateThread( 0, 0, ThreadFunc,
                                          inarray(loop), 0, threadId)
    end do

    write(*,*) 'Waiting for all the threads to complete ...'
    waitResult = WaitForMultipleObjects
   +   (MAX_THREADS, ThreadHandle, .TRUE. , WAIT_INFINITE)
       write(*, '(1x, A, I6, A, I10)' )
   +   'The sum of the first ', MAX_THREADS,' #s is ', result
    end
```

Listing 20.4   Program to demostrate the semaphore and mutual exclusion objects.

```
        include 'mt.fi'

The thread function begins here

        subroutine ThreadFunc (param)
        include 'mt.fd'
        integer*4 param, waitResult, WaitForSingleObject
        integer*4 ThreadCounter
        integer*4 result, hMutex, hSemaphore, PreviousCount
        logical*4 release, ReleaseMutex, ReleaseSemaphore
        common result, hMutex, hSemaphore, ThreadCounter

Mutual Exclusion region begins here

        waitResult = WaitForSingleObject(hMutex, WAIT_INFINITE)

Modifying the global variables

        result = param + result
        ThreadCounter = ThreadCounter + 1

Release the sempahore if this is the last thread

        if (ThreadCounter .EQ. MAX_THREADS)
     +        release = ReleaseSemaphore(hSemaphore, 1,
                                        PreviousCount)

Mutual Exclusion region ends here

        release = ReleaseMutex(hMutex)
        return
        end

Main program begins here

        program test
        include 'mt.fd'
        external ThreadFunc
        integer*4 ThreadHandle, threadId
        integer*4 CreateSemaphore, CreateThread, CreateMutex
        integer*4 waitResult, WaitForSingleObject
        integer*4 loop
        integer*4 result, hMutex, hSemaphore, ThreadCounter
        integer*4 inarray
        dimension inarray(MAX_THREADS)
        common result, hMutex, hSemaphore, ThreadCounter
```

You can use an event object to trigger execution of other processes or other threads within a process. This is useful if one process provides data to many other processes. Using an event object frees the other processes from the trouble of polling to determine when new data is available. CreateEvent() creates either a manual reset event or an autoreset event, depending on the value of one of its parameters. CreateEvent() also sets the initial state of the event to either signaled (True) or not-signaled (False) state. When an event is not-signaled, any thread waiting on the event will block. You can set an event to the signaled state by calling SetEvent(), and reset to the not-signaled state by calling ResetEvent(). PulseEvent() sets the event to the signaled state and then immediately resets it to the not-signaled state. (I've used some of the APIs related to events in the following process-creation example.)

Process Creation

CreateProcess() creates a new process that runs independently of the creating process. CreateProcess() allows you to name the program to execute by specifying either the path name of the image file or a command line. This particular API call is prototyped, as in Figure 20.4.

Listing 20.4 (continued)

```
Initializing the global variables

    ThreadCounter = 0
    result = 0
    hMutex = CreateMutex(0, .FALSE. , 0)
    hSemaphore = CreateSemaphore(0, 0, 1, 0)

    do loop = 1, MAX_THREADS
       inarray(loop)= loop
       write(*,*) "Generating Thread #", loop
       ThreadHandle = CreateThread( 0, 0, ThreadFunc,
    +          inarray(loop), 0, threadId)
    end do

    write(*,*) 'Waiting for the semaphore release...'
    waitResult = WaitForSingleObject(hSemaphore, WAIT_INFINITE)
    write(*, '(1x, A, I4, A, I8)')
    +     'The sum of the first ', MAX_THREADS,' #s is', result
    end
```

In the kernel32 library, there are two occurrences of this function: _CreateProcessA@40 and _CreateProcessW@40. All calls that take a character string as at least one of their parameters are decorated with the trailing A (for ASCII) or W (for wide character, or Unicode). The Unicode implementation addresses the problem of multiple-character coding schemes and accommodates a more comprehensive set of characters.

CreateProcess() takes a long pointer to a C string as two of its arguments. In Fortran, the loc() values of the string can be passed to this function, and the arguments can be declared in the interface statement as being passed by value. These two are C strings, so they should have a null terminator or a char(0) at the end of the Fortran string. The creation-flags argument to CreateProcess() can control the way in which the process is created; for instance, whether it is a detached process or a suspended process. It is a DWORD in C, and an integer*4 value in Fortran. The last two parameters of this function call are long pointers to structures. The structures are STARTUPINFO and PROCESS_INFORMATION, and they are type defined in winbase.h; I've transliterated them into Fortran structures in mt.fd (Listing 20.2). The STARTUP-INFO structure requires initialization, and one of the members of this structure is initialized to the size of that structure. The C sizeof() can be implemented in Fortran by dynamically creating a two-element array of the structure and subtracting the loc() value of the first element from that of the second. However, I simply counted the number of bytes in that structure and specified it in the program.

Figure 20.4   CreateProcess() *prototype.*

```
BOOL WINAPI CreateProcessA(
        LPCSTR lpApplicationName,
        LPCSTR lpCommandLine,
        LPSECURITY_ATTRIBUTES lpProcessAttributes,
        LPSECURITY_ATTRIBUTES lpThreadAttributes,
        BOOL bInheritHandles,
        DWORD dwCreationFlags,
        LPVOID lpEnvironment,
        LPSTR lpCurrentDirectory,
        LPSTARTUPINFOA lpStartupInfo,
        LPPROCESS_INFORMATION lpProcessInformation
);
```

A child process can inherit the following properties and resources from its parent:

- Open handles that were opened with the inherit flag set to TRUE. The functions that create or open object handles [CreateEvent(), CreateFile(), CreateMutex(), CreateNamedPipe(), CreatePipe(), CreateProcess(), CreateThread()] take a security-attributes argument that includes this inherit flag. The mt.fd file (Listing 20.2) declares this structure in Fortran.

- Environment variables.

- Current directory.

- The I/O buffers for console applications (stdin and stdout).

Using Named Objects

CreateProcess() may allow sharing of its object handles through their names. In the following example, the parent process creates a couple of handles to event objects, with ReadEvent() and WriteEvent() as object names, and passes these names as command line arguments to the child process. The child process retrieves these arguments using the Microsoft Fortran Getarg() runtime function and uses the same names to open the handles to these objects. The names for each type of object exist in their own flat address space, and so a semaphore object could have the same name as a mutex object without collision. The child process usually specifies the desired access to the object. In this case, the child accesses the object with the attribute EVENT_ALL_ACCESS. This value is calculated by calling IOR() (the Microsoft Fortran Inclusive OR function) on STANDARD_RIGHTS_REQUIRED, SYNCHRONIZE, and 3h (0x3 in C and #3 in Microsoft Fortran).

The parent and child processes execute simultaneously after the CreateProcess() API call. However, the child process blocks at the WriteEvent until the parent writes the question onto the file named file.out. The parent then sets the WriteEvent, which is a green light for the child process. Subsequently, the parent process blocks at ReadEvent and waits for the cue from the child. The child opens the file, reads the question, writes its reply to the same file, and then sets the ReadEvent object, thus activating the parent process. The parent process then opens the file to read the answer given by the child process and writes it on the screen. The parent program is in Listing 20.5 and the child in Listing 20.6.

Listing 20.5   *Parent program (process) passing names of event objects to child process.*

```
        include 'mt.fi'

        program Parent
        include 'mt.fd'
        logical*4 procHandle, CreateProcess
        integer*4 CreateEvent, hReadEvent, hWriteEvent, SetEvent
        integer*4 waitResult, WaitForSingleObject
        character*255 buffer
        character*10 strReadEvent, strWriteEvent, FileName

        record /PROCESS_INFORMATION/ pi
        record /STARTUPINFO/ si

Initializing the strings

        strReadEvent = 'ReadEvent '
        strWriteEvent = 'WriteEvent '
        FileName = ' file.out '
        buffer = "child "//strReadEvent//strWriteEvent//FileName//" "C
        strReadEvent(10:10) = char(0)
        strWriteEvent(10:10) = char(0)

Initializing the STARTUPINFO structure

        si.cb = 68              ! sizeof (STARTUPINFO)
        si.lpReserved = 0
        si.lpDeskTop = 0
        si.lpTitle = 0
        si.dwFlags = 0
        si.cbReserved2 = 0
        si.lpReserved2 = 0
        si.hStdInput = 0
        si.hStdOutput = 0
        si.hStdError = 0

Creating Read and Write Event objects

        hReadEvent = CreateEvent(0, .FALSE., .FALSE., loc(strReadEvent))
        hWriteEvent = CreateEvent(0, .FALSE., .FALSE.,loc(strWriteEvent))

Spawning the child prcoess

        procHandle = CreateProcess( 0, loc(buffer), 0, 0, .TRUE. , 0, 0,
                             0, loc(si), loc(pi))
```

Inheriting Handles

A child process can inherit an open handle to a synchronization object if the Inher-itHandle attribute (in the security-attribute parameter) was set when the handle was created. The handle inherited by the child process has the same access as the parent's handle. The code fragments in Figure 20.5 describe this aspect and provide the required initialization for the security-attribute parameter. Note that the child process

---

Listing 20.5 (continued)

```
Providing a question for the child

        open (10, file= FileName)
        write(10, '(A)') "What issue of Dr. Dobb's is this?"
        close (10)

        write(*,*) 'Providing the green signal for child to continue...'
        waitResult = SetEvent(hWriteEvent)
        write(*,*) 'Waiting for the child to answer the question - '
        waitResult = WaitForSingleObject (hReadEvent, WAIT_INFINITE)

Writing the reply from the child on to the screen

        open (10, file= FileName)
        read(10, '(A)') buffer
        close (10)
        write(*,*) buffer
        end
```

Listing 20.6   Child program (process) accepting named objects from the parent.

```
    include 'mt.fi'

    program ChildProcess
    include 'mt.fd'

    character*255 buffer
    character*100 filename, strReadEvent, strWriteEvent
    integer*4 hReadEvent, hWriteEvent, OpenEvent, SetEvent
    integer*2 status
    integer*4 EVENT_ALL_ACCESS
    integer*4 waitResult, WaitForSingleObject
```

has no OpenEvent() calls, because the handles are inherited from the parent. To share an unnamed object between unrelated processes, the creating process must communicate the information necessary for the other process to duplicate the handle. Using DuplicateHandle(), the duplicating process can then open its handle with the same or more restricted access than the original handle.

Listing 20.6 (continued)

```
Retrieving the first command line parameter which is the name of the ReadEvent
      Call Getarg (1, buffer, status)
      strReadEvent(1:status) = buffer(1:status)
      status = status+1
      strReadEvent(status:status) = char(0) ! to make it a C string

Retrieving the second command line parameter which is the name of the WriteEvent
      Call Getarg (2, buffer, status)
      strWriteEvent(1:status) = buffer(1:status)
      status = status+1
      strWriteEvent(status:status) = char(0) ! to make it a C string

Setting the access privilege for the child
      EVENT_ALL_ACCESS = IOR (STANDARD_RIGHTS_REQUIRED, SYNCHRONIZE)
      EVENT_ALL_ACCESS = IOR (EVENT_ALL_ACCESS, #3)

Opening handles for event objects passed from parent as named objects
      hReadEvent=OpenEvent(EVENT_ALL_ACCESS, .FALSE., loc(strReadEvent))
      hWriteEvent=OpenEvent(EVENT_ALL_ACCESS, .FALSE., loc(strWriteEvent))

Wait until the parent signals the WriteEvent
      waitResult = WaitForSingleObject(hWriteEvent, WAIT_INFINITE)

Retrieve the file name which is the third argument
      Call Getarg (3, buffer, status)
      filename (1:status) = buffer(1:status)

Read the parent's question and then reply
      open (11, file= filename, mode ='readwrite')
      read(11, '(A)') buffer
      print *, buffer
      rewind 11
      write(11, '(A)') 'September 1993 issue'
      close (11)

Signal the parent to continue
      waitResult = SetEvent(hReadEvent)
      end
```

Figure 20.5   Parent and child code fragments showing handle inheritance.

A fragment of the parent program

Initialization of Security attributes for Read and Write Events

```
    ...

        record /SECURITY_ATTRIBUTES/ saR
        record /SECURITY_ATTRIBUTES/ saW

        saR.nLength = 12
        saR.lpSecurityDescriptor = 0
        saR.bInheritHandle = .TRUE.

        saW.nLength = 12
        saW.lpSecurityDescriptor = 0
        saW.bInheritHandle = .TRUE.

    ...

Creating events whose handles can be inherited

    ...

        hReadEvent = CreateEvent(loc(saR), .FALSE., .FALSE., 0)
        hWriteEvent = CreateEvent(loc(saW), .FALSE., .FALSE., 0)
    ...

---------------------------------------------------------------------

A fragment of the child program.
Retrieve the handle to Read and Write Events from the command line using
Getarg, and assign them to integer variables through Internal Read

    ...

        CALL GETARG(1, buffer, status)
        read(buffer(1:status), '(i4)') hReadEvent
        CALL GETARG(2, buffer, status)
        read(buffer(1:status), '(i4)') hWriteEvent

        waitResult = WaitForSingleObject(hWriteEvent, WAIT_INFINITE)

    ...
```

Conclusion

The C prototypes for the Win32 API can be found in the header files winbase.h and winnt.h shipped with the Microsoft Win32 SDK for Windows NT. The functions are actually defined in kernel32.lib and ntdll.lib. The description for some of these APIs can be found in the *Programmer's Reference: Overviews* manual and the api32wh.hlp file shipped with the NT SDK. All the programs listed here were compiled from the command line by invoking fl32.exe, which automatically links the object modules with the required libraries: libf.lib, libc.lib, ntdll.lib, and kernel32.lib.

In mt.fi, I've provided the interface statements for almost the entire set of Win32 APIs related to processes, threads, and synchronization, and the corresponding data structure declarations are in mt.fd. This includes DuplicateHandle() and other calls associated with attributes, priority, suspension, resumption, and termination of threads and processes. I've also written interface statements for all the APIs associated with thread local storage (TLS). With TLS, one thread can allocate an index that can be used by any thread of the process to store and retrieve a different value for each thread.

With mt.fi and other information provided in this chapter, you should be able to roll up your sleeves and create a killer multithreading/multitasking/multiprocessing Fortran application under Windows NT.

Chapter 21

Context Switch Performance on NT and Win95

Piaw Na

Windows 3.x offered what some people dubbed "one-at-a-time multitasking" — the scheduler could not guarantee that any Windows task but the foreground task would get much CPU time. The Win32 API allows for more robust schedulers, making it more feasible to break a large program into multiple processes. Windows 95 and Windows NT also offer the ability to create multiple threads of control within a single process (sometimes called "lightweight processes"), which provides another option for structuring control in an application.

Processes and threads do not come free, however. When one process passes control to another, the operating system has to switch from one process context to another. For example, the operating system may have to change various page tables so that the memory claimed by one process is not visible in the address space of another. All threads within a single process share the same address space, but they do have some register state, so thread context switching is not free either. As more programmers take advantage of multiple processes or multiple threads to structure their applications (perhaps implicitly, via OLE interprocess communications), it is important that they understand the overhead of context switching. In this chapter, I present benchmarks for measuring context switching performance, and describe the results of running the benchmarks on various configurations and processors. [For a dissection of part of the Win95 context switch code, see Pietrek (1995, p.305)].

Why Does Performance Matter?

Because it is sometimes easier to engineer many small executables rather than a simple big one, many products (such as Microsoft Visual C++) really consist of multiple processes communicating with each other. These processes may need to communicate large amounts of data among themselves, and file I/O is generally a slow way to accomplish that. Interprocess communication (IPC) on a single machine is best accomplished via shared memory in Win32. Named pipes and mailslots are not available in Windows 95 — only the client side is implemented, the assumption being that the server will be a Windows NT machine. TCP/IP pipes are available and the prevalence of Internet providers is making TCP/IP installations more and more common, but TCP/IP requires a lengthy and complicated installation. (How many people know the IP number of their DNS server?) Furthermore, TCP/IP performance is slow — in the milliseconds performance range, which is much higher than the overhead of a function call; whereas, accessing shared memory can be done almost instantaneously, making full use of virtual memory and the paging system.

The problem with using shared memory for IPC then becomes that of signaling the other process when valid data has been placed in the shared memory, and then waiting for the reply. If one process tries to read data while another process is in the middle of modifying that data, incorrect data might be used for a computation. In the worst case, if two processes are trying to modify the same piece of data in shared memory simultaneously, data corruption can occur. To eliminate these possibilities, many programs use the remote procedure call paradigm, where one process calls a function in another process. Each call/reply pair requires two interprocess context switches. For multiple threads running in the same process, every synchronization whereby a thread blocks while waiting for a mutex or semaphore held by another thread also requires two thread-level context switches. In fact, a common multithreading paradigm, the producer–consumer relationship, can be viewed as two threads calling each other via IPC as needed. The speed of the operating system in performing context switches is a major factor in determining how readily IPC or multiple threads can be used by an application.

Synchronization Constructs

Win32 provides three major synchronization constructs: events, semaphores, and mutexes. Events are objects that can be signaled. An auto-reset event automatically resets after a process that's been waiting for it has been signaled. Semaphores are counted synchronization constructs that allow multiple threads/processes access to a resource. Each thread that does not get immediate access to the semaphore is placed in a queue. Semaphores are frequently used to limit the number of threads attempting to grab a limited resource. Mutexes are like semaphores, but only one thread is allowed to a own a mutex at a time.

Windows lets you easily acquire any of these synchronization constructs by using a `WaitForSingleObject()` or `WaitForMultipleObjects()` API call. This allows a program to wait for an event or grab a semaphore or mutex using the same API — a kind of C-level polymorphism possible because all system objects are referred to via a Windows handle.

Event Context-Switching Benchmark

The benchmark programs I wrote to measure the overhead of context switching in Windows 95 and Windows NT is in `send.c` (Listing 21.1) and `catch.c` (Listing 21.2). The first program (`send.exe`) creates three events and then waits for the first one, which is the rendezvous event. The second program (`catch.exe`) starts up and obtains handles to the same events by calling `OpenEvent()` then signals the rendezvous event by calling `SetEvent()`. This unblocks `send.exe` and allows the initial benchmark to begin.

Listing 21.1 `send.c`*— The sender side of the benchmark.*

```
HexWeb HTML

// For interesting results, you must compile with
// optimization off:
// cl /Zi /MT -DWIN32 <file>
// bcc32 <file>

#include <windows.h>
#include <stdio.h>
```

Listing 21.1 *(continued)*

```c
/* Borland v4.5 needs a fix */
#if defined(__BORLANDC__) && (__BORLANDC__ <= 0x0460)
typedef struct FOO_LARGE_INTEGER {
        DWORD LowPart;
        LONG    HighPart;
} FOO_LARGE_INTEGER;

#define LARGE_INTEGER     FOO_LARGE_INTEGER
#endif

HANDLE event;
HANDLE recevent, ackevent;
LARGE_INTEGER        freq;

void receive(void)
{
    LARGE_INTEGER    start;
    LARGE_INTEGER    end;
    int              i;
    double           tks;

    SetEvent(event);
    QueryPerformanceCounter(&start);
    for (i = 0; i < 10000; i++) {
        WaitForSingleObject(recevent, INFINITE);
        SetEvent(ackevent);
        WaitForSingleObject(recevent, INFINITE);
        SetEvent(ackevent);
        WaitForSingleObject(recevent, INFINITE);
        SetEvent(ackevent);
    }
    QueryPerformanceCounter(&end);
    tks = ((end.LowPart - start.LowPart) / 3.0)/ 10000.0;
    fprintf(stderr, "Receiver: Average # of microseconds "
            "context switch with threads = %f\n",
            (tks / (double) freq.LowPart)*1000000.0);
    SetEvent(event);
}

void f(void) {}

#ifdef __BORLANDC__
#       pragma argsused
#endif
```

The first benchmark measures the speed of using events to synchronize control between two processes. The sender signals an event that unblocks the receiver, then waits for an acknowledgment event to be signaled. The receiver waits on an event and, when the sender signals that event, signals the acknowledgment event. Thus, control ping-pongs back and forth between the two processes as fast as possible. The programs measure the time required to do this 30,000 times.

Listing 21.1 (continued)

```
int main(int argc, char **argv)
{
    HANDLE sem1, sem2, sem3;
    HANDLE mu1, mu2, mu3;
    LARGE_INTEGER    start;
    LARGE_INTEGER    end;
    int              i;
    double           tks;
    DWORD            foo;

    // Figure out performance counter frequency
    QueryPerformanceFrequency(&freq);
    fprintf(stderr, "Performance counter frequency = low: "
            "%d high: %d\n", freq.LowPart, freq.HighPart);

    // create main syncrhonization event
    event = CreateEvent(0, FALSE, FALSE, "Start");

    // now do context switch using events
    recevent = CreateEvent(0, FALSE, FALSE, "RecSync");
    ackevent = CreateEvent(0, FALSE, FALSE, "AckSync");
    WaitForSingleObject(event, INFINITE);

    QueryPerformanceCounter(&start);
    for (i = 0; i < 10000; i++) {
        SetEvent(recevent);
        WaitForSingleObject(ackevent, INFINITE);
        SetEvent(recevent);
        WaitForSingleObject(ackevent, INFINITE);
        SetEvent(recevent);
        WaitForSingleObject(ackevent, INFINITE);
    }
    QueryPerformanceCounter(&end);
    tks = ((end.LowPart - start.LowPart) / 3.0)/ 10000.0;
    fprintf(stderr, "Average # of microseconds context "
            "switch using events = %f\n",
            (tks / (double) freq.LowPart)*1000000.0);
```

Listing 21.1 (continued)

```
// now for semaphores
sem1 = CreateSemaphore(0, 0, 1, "Sem1");
sem2 = CreateSemaphore(0, 0, 1, "Sem2");
sem3 = CreateSemaphore(0, 0, 1, "Sem3");
SetEvent(event);
ReleaseSemaphore(sem2, 1, 0);
WaitForSingleObject(event, INFINITE);

QueryPerformanceCounter(&start);
for (i = 0; i < 10000; i++) {
    ReleaseSemaphore(sem1, 1, 0);
    WaitForSingleObject(sem2, INFINITE);
    ReleaseSemaphore(sem3, 1, 0);
    WaitForSingleObject(sem1, INFINITE);
    ReleaseSemaphore(sem2, 1, 0);
    WaitForSingleObject(sem3, INFINITE);
}
QueryPerformanceCounter(&end);
tks = ((end.LowPart - start.LowPart) / 3.0)/ 10000.0;
QueryPerformanceFrequency(&freq);
fprintf(stderr, "Average # of microseconds context "
    "switch using semaphores = %f\n",
    (tks / (double) freq.LowPart)*1000000.0);

// mutexes
mu1 = CreateMutex(0, TRUE, "Mutex1");
mu2 = CreateMutex(0, TRUE, "Mutex2");
mu3 = CreateMutex(0, TRUE, "Mutex3");
SetEvent(event);
ReleaseMutex(mu2);
WaitForSingleObject(event, INFINITE);

QueryPerformanceCounter(&start);
for (i = 0; i < 10000; i++) {
    ReleaseMutex(mu1);
    WaitForSingleObject(mu2, INFINITE);
    ReleaseMutex(mu3);
    WaitForSingleObject(mu1, INFINITE);
    ReleaseMutex(mu2);
    WaitForSingleObject(mu3, INFINITE);
}
QueryPerformanceCounter(&end);
tks = ((end.LowPart - start.LowPart) / 3.0)/ 10000.0;
QueryPerformanceFrequency(&freq);
fprintf(stderr, "Average # of microseconds context "
    "switch using mutexes = %f\n",
    (tks / (double) freq.LowPart)*1000000.0);
```

When all the iterations are finished, the performance counter is read again, and the elapsed time per context switch is calculated. The discrepancies between the numbers reported by the sender and the receiver can be attributed to the printf() that could happen between processes, before the second process gets control and reads the performance counter. I consistently use the lower number of the two when using these benchmarks. However, the differences should be negligible, given the relatively large number of ping-pongs that occur.

Listing 21.1 (continued)

```
// the "catch" program will now terminate ---
// we'll continue and investigate
// inter-thread context switching
CreateThread(0, 0, (LPTHREAD_START_ROUTINE) receive,
             0, 0, &foo);
WaitForSingleObject(event, INFINITE) ;

QueryPerformanceCounter(&start);
for (i = 0; i < 10000; i++) {
    SetEvent(recevent);
    WaitForSingleObject(ackevent, INFINITE);
    SetEvent(recevent);
    WaitForSingleObject(ackevent, INFINITE);
    SetEvent(recevent);
    WaitForSingleObject(ackevent, INFINITE);
}
QueryPerformanceCounter(&end);
WaitForSingleObject(event, INFINITE);
tks = ((end.LowPart - start.LowPart) / 3.0)/ 10000.0;
fprintf(stderr, "Sender: Average # of microseconds "
        "context switch with threads = %f\n",
        (tks / (double) freq.LowPart)*1000000.0);

// check out system call performance
QueryPerformanceCounter(&start);
for (i = 0; i < 10000; i++) {
    GetTickCount();
    GetTickCount();
    GetTickCount();
}
QueryPerformanceCounter(&end);
tks = ((end.LowPart - start.LowPart) / 3.0)/ 10000.0;
fprintf(stderr, "Average # of microseconds system "
        "call = %f\n",
        (tks / (double) freq.LowPart)*1000000.0);
```

Listing 21.1 (continued)

```
            // null function call performance
            QueryPerformanceCounter(&start);
            for (i = 0; i < 10000; i++) {
                    f();            f();            f();
            }
            QueryPerformanceCounter(&end);
            tks = ((end.LowPart - start.LowPart) / 3.0)/ 10000.0;
            fprintf(stderr, "Average # of microseconds = %f\n",
                    (tks / (double) freq.LowPart)*1000000.0);
}
```

Listing 21.2 catch.c — The receiver side of the benchmark.

```
// run this after running send.exe

#include <windows.h>
#include <stdio.h>

/* Borland v4.5 needs a fix */
#if defined(__BORLANDC__) && (__BORLANDC__ <= 0x0460)
typedef struct FOO_LARGE_INTEGER {
        DWORD  LowPart;
        LONG   HighPart;
} FOO_LARGE_INTEGER;

#define LARGE_INTEGER    FOO_LARGE_INTEGER

#endif
#ifdef __BORLANDC__
#       pragma argsused
#endif
int main(int argc, char **argv)
{
        HANDLE  event;
        HANDLE  recevent, ackevent;
        HANDLE  sem1, sem2, sem3;
        HANDLE  mu1, mu2, mu3;
        LARGE_INTEGER   start;
        LARGE_INTEGER   end;
        LARGE_INTEGER   freq;
        int     i;
        double  tks;

        QueryPerformanceFrequency(&freq);
```

The performance counter is a 64-bit integer. The unit of the performance is a clock "tick," which varies between implementations of Win32. However, you can get the number of ticks in one second by calling QueryPerformanceFrequency(). If you run any of the benchmarks for such a long time that the lower 32-bit counter overflows, then you will get a negative number for the average context switch time. You would really have to run the benchmark for hours before this would occur.

After measuring the overhead of context switches using events, the programs perform similar loops using semaphores and then mutexes and the synchronization object. Finally, the receiver program terminates, but the sender creates a new thread and uses that to measure the overhead of thread context switches.

Why Three Mutexes?

You may wonder why three mutexes (and three semaphores) were used in the semaphore and mutex portions of the benchmarks. Indeed, when I first wrote the mutex version of the benchmark, I used just two mutexes. Unfortunately, two mutexes are not enough to force a context switch between two processes. To understand why requires a little thought.

Listing 21.2 (continued)

```
// open syncrhonization event
event = OpenEvent(EVENT_ALL_ACCESS, FALSE, "Start");

// now for event-based context switching
recevent = OpenEvent(EVENT_ALL_ACCESS, FALSE, "RecSync");
ackevent = OpenEvent(EVENT_ALL_ACCESS, FALSE, "AckSync");
SetEvent(event);
QueryPerformanceCounter(&start);
for (i = 0; i < 10000; i++) {
    WaitForSingleObject(recevent, INFINITE);
    SetEvent(ackevent);
    WaitForSingleObject(recevent, INFINITE);
    SetEvent(ackevent);
    WaitForSingleObject(recevent, INFINITE);
    SetEvent(ackevent);
}
QueryPerformanceCounter(&end);
tks = ((end.LowPart - start.LowPart) / 3.0)/ 10000.0;
fprintf(stderr, "Average # of microseconds context "
        "switch using events = %f\n",
        (tks / (double) freq.LowPart)*1000000.0);
```

Listing 21.2 *(continued)*

```
// semaphore based context switching
WaitForSingleObject(event, INFINITE);
sem1 = OpenSemaphore(SEMAPHORE_ALL_ACCESS, FALSE, "Sem1");
sem2 = OpenSemaphore(SEMAPHORE_ALL_ACCESS, FALSE, "Sem2");
sem3 = OpenSemaphore(SEMAPHORE_ALL_ACCESS, FALSE, "Sem3");
SetEvent(event);
WaitForSingleObject(sem2, INFINITE);
QueryPerformanceCounter(&start);
for (i = 0; i < 10000; i++) {
    WaitForSingleObject(sem1, INFINITE);
    ReleaseSemaphore(sem2, 1, 0);
    WaitForSingleObject(sem3, INFINITE);
    ReleaseSemaphore(sem1, 1, 0);
    WaitForSingleObject(sem2, INFINITE);
    ReleaseSemaphore(sem3, 1, 0);
}
QueryPerformanceCounter(&end);
tks = ((end.LowPart - start.LowPart) / 3.0)/ 10000.0;
fprintf(stderr, "Average # of microseconds context "
    "switch using semaphores = %f\n",
    (tks / (double) freq.LowPart)*1000000.0);

// mutex oriented context switching
WaitForSingleObject(event, INFINITE);
mu1 = OpenMutex(MUTEX_ALL_ACCESS, FALSE, "Mutex1");
mu2 = OpenMutex(MUTEX_ALL_ACCESS, FALSE, "Mutex2");
mu3 = OpenMutex(MUTEX_ALL_ACCESS, FALSE, "Mutex3");
WaitForSingleObject(mu2, INFINITE);
SetEvent(event);
QueryPerformanceCounter(&start);
for (i = 0; i < 10000; i++) {
    WaitForSingleObject(mu1, INFINITE);
    ReleaseMutex(mu2);
    WaitForSingleObject(mu3, INFINITE);
    ReleaseMutex(mu1);
    WaitForSingleObject(mu2, INFINITE);
    ReleaseMutex(mu3);
}
QueryPerformanceCounter(&end);
tks = ((end.LowPart - start.LowPart) / 3.0)/ 10000.0;
fprintf(stderr, "Average # of microseconds context "
    "switch using mutexes = %f\n",
    (tks / (double) freq.LowPart)*1000000.0);
}
```

Suppose you use two mutexes, called `mutex1` and `mutex2`, to force control to transfer between two processes, `process1` and `process2`. Initially, `process1` owns `mutex1`, and `process2` owns `mutex2` and is waiting for `mutex1`, so `process2` is blocked. Here is how the initial events might happen:

```
process1 releases mutex1
// now process2 is not blocked
process1 waits for mutex2
// now process1 is blocked, so
// control WILL switch to process2
process2 acquires mutex1
```

That's where things go wrong. Although this sequence of events forces the operating system to transfer control to `process2`, once `process2` owns both mutexes, there is no way to force control back to `process1`, because at that point `process1` owns no synchronization objects that `process2` can wait on.

I was puzzled by this, and, after I found out what was wrong, I tried various ways of rearranging the order of releasing and acquiring the two mutexes, but to no avail. A colleague and I then sat down and drew out a state diagram representing the two processes, proving that a repeating context switch could not be forced to occur using just two mutexes. We came to the conclusion that at least three mutexes (or semaphores) were required to force a context switch between the two processes.

Function Calls and System Calls

To compare the costs of performing IPC with other system-level functions, I've included the basic cost of a system call as well as that of a procedure call. For the procedure call, I chose an empty function that returned nothing. It is important that you turn optimization off when you compile this program. If optimization is turned on, the most likely result is that the function would get in-lined (and in fact, probably the entire loop would be eliminated), and the results would become meaningless.

For a system call, I picked `GetTickCount()`, which simply reads off a timer that changes infrequently. This causes no extra work for the operating system, but does not allow `kernel32.dll` to cache the result without signalling the OS.

Results

I ran my programs on a variety of machines and collected the results (Table 21.1) with all timing numbers in microseconds. As expected, the function call timings remained much the same between Windows 95 and Windows NT. The system calls exhibit strange results, particularly on the P90 running Windows 95, where `GetTickCount()`

Table 21.1 Context switching overhead (μsec) under Win32.*

	Event	Semaphore	Mutex	Thread	Function	Syscall
P90 W95	222.28	221.79	245.92	172.83	0.26	0.21
P90 NT 1057	83.62	81.24	94.06	56.56	0.26	0.32
W95/NT ratio	2.66	2.73	2.61	3.06	1.00	0.66
486/100 W95	202.91	208.08	227.01	202.00	0.32	0.40
486/100 NT 944	74.88	78.11	76.88	75.04	0.32	0.34
W95/NT ratio	27.1	2.66	2.95	2.69	1.00	1.18
DP W95	216.18	240.07	237.10	154.37	0.26	0.21
DP NT 1057	106.85	103.08	105.31	1116.02	0.26	0.32
W95/NT ratio	2.02	2.33	2.25	1.33	1.00	0.66
P66 W95	309.46	316.31	356.28	311.8	0.44	0.96
P66 NT 1057	113.83	111.37	120.38	99.96	0.43	0.86
W95/NT ratio	2.72	2.84	2.96	3.12	1.02	1.12
386/40 W95	1344.29	1372.16	1495.24	1283.36	4.66	5.72
386/40 NT 1057	604.12	610.59	636.87	591.67	3.5	3.62
W95/NT ratio	2.23	2.25	2.35	2.17	1.33	1.58

*Systems were configured as follows:
The P90 — Dell Dimension XPS (Pentium 90)
- 486 is an Intel DX4/100
- DP is a Dell PowerEdge Sp 590-2, a dual-processor Pentium
- P66 is a Dell Dimension XPS 466V (Pentium 60)
- 386/40 is a Domain 386 clone with 20Mb of RAM

Except where noted, all machines had 32Mb RAM and 256Kb external caches. Both external and internal caches were activated during the test. The complete specifications for the Domain 386 are unknown. Windows NT Build 1057 was used on all runs except those on the 486, which used Build 944. (Build 944 was the beta version of Windows NT v3.51, and I believe there were no substantial changes between Build 944 and Build 1057.)

actually seems faster than a standard function call. I suspect that this may be because GetTickCount() in Windows 95 is in kernel32.dll, which could be in page-locked memory across all processes and thus always remain in the cache. Or it could be that GetTickCount() uses a nonstandard calling sequence that is smaller and faster than that generated for normal C functions.

Because NT is a multiprocessor operating system, it naturally tries to schedule both threads to run on different processors simultaneously. Unfortunately, blocking between processors on a shared bus seems to be slower than switching contexts within the same processor, and the benchmarks actually run slower on a multiprocessor NT workstation than on a uniprocessor workstation running the same version of the operating system. Furthermore, in the thread-only context switch benchmark, in which both processors have to share the same address space, the snooping that has to happen over the bus (to verify cache coherency) apparently causes the benchmark to run more slowly than any of the other benchmarks running on the same multiprocessor workstation; the benchmark typically runs faster on uniprocessor workstations.

Conclusions

For each operating system, there is little difference in performance between any of the interprocess synchronization constructs. However, it takes about two and a half times as long on average to perform a cross-address-space context switch on Windows 95 than on Windows NT. I originally bought Microsoft's line about Windows 95 being rewritten from the ground up, and this result surprised me.

Windows 95 did not have to be portable and did not have to worry about multiprocessing, hence it should perform better on basic operating system benchmarks than Windows NT. I discussed the result with Andrew Schulman on CompuServe, and he suggested that Windows 95 might have to dig all the way down to DOS to switch PSPs (Program Segment Prefixes), even when switching contexts between two Win32 processes. This would account for the large differences in context-switch performance between Windows 95 and Windows NT. That the ratio differences are so consistent across implementations of the Intel x86 architecture is also remarkable.

Another interesting point is that the 486DX4/100 seems to be better at context switching than the P90. It is possible that the simpler pipeline structure of the 486 allows context switches to happen faster than on the Pentium, but at this point, any guess is as good as mine.

What do all of these numbers mean for the average application? In general, Windows 95 multithreads and operating system context switches are worse than those of Windows NT, so if you're developing on Windows NT and switching to Windows 95 only occasionally, you might be in for a big shock if your program has many threads that synchronize frequently, or if you have multiple processes all talking to each other. Any "hot spots" of mutex or semaphore contention will have a larger effect under

Windows 95 than on Windows NT. These benchmarks are small and don't swap at all while they are running; if the working set sizes of your applications are larger than available physical memory, the machine might start to thrash. If you don't need threads, don't use them. Also, if you have multiple processes synchronizing on some common synchronization objects, consider making the multiple processes different threads in one process. Thread context switches perform a lot better under Windows NT than process context switches, and perform no worse under Windows 95.

For multiprocessor NT machines and applications running on such machines, it might turn out to be faster to spawn off multiple processes and synchronize between them than to spawn off multiple threads within the same process. However, given the artificial nature of these benchmarks, it is difficult to say if this rule applies to real-world applications.

Finally, I should point out that the numbers I'm seeing for context switches are amazingly good. A 133MHz DEC Alpha workstation, considered a faster machine in all respects, performs round-trip context switches in about 100 microseconds when running Mach, a UNIX-like microkernel operating system. The efficiency of Windows NT on a Pentium more than makes up for the slower hardware it has to run on.

Acknowledgments

I would like to thank my colleagues at Pure for their valuable input on early versions of this chapter.

References

Pietrek, Matt. *Windows 95 System Programming Secrets*. IDG Books Worldwide, 1995.

Chapter 22

Writing a Control Panel Applet for Windows NT

Paula Tomlinson

The Control Panel in Windows NT, like its predecessor in Windows 3.x, gives users a graphical way to configure and customize their hardware and system-level software environment (e.g., to configure ports for printers or customize Desktop settings). The Control Panel client area displays an individual icon for each category of device or function, providing a consistent location for user modification of these settings. You might think of the Control Panel program (`control.exe`) as a slate for displaying and launching Control Panel applets.

Creating a Control Panel applet to add system-level visibility and support of a new device type is relatively simple. This chapter outlines the steps necessary to create a simple Control Panel applet for scanners. The Scanners applet provides general scanner device functions and exports a standard API that allows manufacturers of vendor-specific devices to add their own value-added features.

Before writing a Control Panel applet, review the installable driver interface and the standard "Drivers" Control Panel applet, both of which are documented in the Microsoft DDK documentation. The installable driver interface provides a standard interface for accessing multimedia devices, whereas the Drivers applet includes installation and configuration features for such devices. If your device falls into the multimedia category, you should strongly consider using this interface rather than building a custom Control Panel applet.

The `CPlApplet()` *Entry Point*

Control Panel applets are supported by Control Panel Libraries (CPLs). A CPL can support multiple Control Panel applets, each having its own icon on the Control Panel client area. For example, `main.cpl` contains the applets for Color, Fonts, Ports, Mouse, Desktop, Keyboard, Printers, International, Date/Time, and Networks. A CPL is essentially just a DLL that contains the following special callback routine:

```
LONG CALLBACK CPlApplet(HWND, WORD, DWORD, DWORD)
```

The Control Panel uses this routine to communicate with each applet. You must define it in your CPL and export it, either with the `_export` keyword or by listing it in your module definition file. The first `CPlApplet()` parameter is the handle to the Control Panel window. The second parameter is a message ID that the Control Panel uses to notify each applet of events and requests for information. The third and fourth parameters vary depending on the message ID. The Control Panel may send eight different messages to a CPL via `CPlApplet()`. These messages can be categorized as initialization messages, user-initiated messages, and termination messages.

Initialization Messages

When invoked, the Control Panel loads each applet it finds and immediately begins sending initialization messages to the `CPlApplet()` function in each CPL. The messages are sent in the order in which I discuss them here.

The Control Panel sends the first message, `CPL_INIT`, only once to each CPL. This message gives each CPL a chance to perform any necessary CPL-wide initialization tasks. If the CPL's initialization is successful, it should return `TRUE`. If `CPlApplet()` returns `FALSE`, the Control Panel terminates communication with that CPL. Returning `FALSE` to this message is the only way to prevent a CPL's applets from being loaded.

The Control Panel also sends the next message, `CPL_GETCOUNT`, only once to each CPL. This message asks the CPL how many applets it contains. The value returned by `CPlApplet()` determines how many icons to display on the Control Panel's client area for this CPL and thus how many times the `CPL_NEWINQUIRE` and `CPL_STOP` messages (described next) are sent.

The Control Panel sends `CPL_NEWINQUIRE` once for each applet the CPL contains. Your CPL's `CPlApplet()` should fill in a `NEWCPLINFO` structure with information pertaining to each of its applets. The third parameter is an index value used to identify that applet in subsequent messages: Control Panel passes 0 for the first applet in your CPL, 1 for the second applet, and so on. You should perform applet-specific initialization when you receive this message.

Windows 3.0 used the CPL_INQUIRE message rather than the CPL_NEWINQUIRE message. Although CPL_INQUIRE still exists for backwards compatibility, new Control Panel applets should respond to CPL_NEWINQUIRE. The Control Panel sends the CPL_NEWINQUIRE message first. If the CPL returns FALSE, the Control Panel then sends the CPL_INQUIRE message. Returning a valid response to CPL_NEWINQUIRE ensures that CPL_INQUIRE won't be sent.

User-Initiated Messages

User-initiated messages signify that a user has selected or executed — either directly or through another program — an applet contained in your CPL.

The CPL_SELECT message is sent if the user selects (single-clicks) an applet icon that is contained in your CPL. This message isn't extremely useful, so most CPLs don't process it.

The CPL_DBLCLK message is sent when the user executes (double-clicks) an applet icon that is contained in your CPL. The third parameter is an index value that specifies which one of the applets was selected. In response to this message, your CPL should display its dialog box for that applet.

Termination Messages

The last two messages — CPL_STOP and CPL_EXIT — notify the CPL that the Control Panel is closing.

CPL_STOP is sent once for every applet contained in the CPL and is sent just before the Control Panel is terminated. Its third parameter is an index value that specifies which applet contained in the CPL is being terminated. Any resources allocated for particular applets should be freed when this message is sent.

CPL_EXIT is sent to each CPL only once. This is your last chance to perform any CPL-wide cleanup. After this message is processed, the Control Panel calls FreeLibrary() to unload your CPL.

Choosing the Features for the Scanner Applet

One of the first decisions to be made in designing a CPL is whether to partition the applet functionality into general device features and vendor-specific features. If all devices of this type provide the same basic functionality — as is the case with the mouse, for example — then you can probably get away with a single dialog box that allows users to control these basic functions. Because scanners vary quite drastically in the capabilities they provide, I chose to create a general scanner applet and an API for adding modules to provide vendor-specific scanner features.

I tried to model the functionality of my Scanners applet loosely after the standard Drivers applet. Like the Drivers applet, my scanner applet does not provide vendor-specific features and has no vendor-specific knowledge. It simply lists currently installed scanner drivers (as with printers, it is possible to install drivers for scanners that you don't currently have!). From the Scanners applet dialog box, you can add additional scanner drivers, remove existing scanner drivers, and configure existing scanners and/or drivers.

I also decided that installing drivers is inherently a vendor-specific process. For instance, using the Hewlett-Packard scanners with 16-bit Windows applications under Windows NT requires the installation of a DOS stub device driver in config.nt and the presence of an NT Virtual Device Driver in the Windows NT System directory. Another recent trend in setup programs is to provide uninstall capabilities.

To implement these capabilities while still maintaining a very generic scanner applet, I defined the following three routines and "capability" values to notify vendor-specific modules of events occurring in the Scanners applet:

```
CPL_ScannerConfigure(HWND, ULONG, LPTSTR)
CPL_ScannerInstall(HWND, ULONG, LPTSTR)
CPL_ScannerUninstall(HWND, ULONG, LPTSTR)
#define CPL_SCANNER_SUPPORT_CONFIGURE    0x01
#define CPL_SCANNER_SUPPORT_INSTALL      0x02
#define CPL_SCANNER_SUPPORT_UNINSTALL    0x04
```

By exporting these routines in the vendor-specific modules, scanner vendors can provide their own configuration, install, and uninstall code.

All the information the Scanners applet needs concerning a new scanner driver is specified in scanaplt.inf, which I have defined to have the following format. Remember to be careful with case sensitivity in filenames. Under the NT file system (NTFS), SCANAPLT.INF is not the same file as scanaplt.inf!

```
[CPL_Scanner]
Scanners=3
Scanner1=Hewlett-Packard ScanJet IIc,
        HPSCANAP.DLL,HPSCANIIC,7
Scanner2=Hewlett-Packard ScanJet IIp,
        HPSCANAP.DLL,HPSCANIIP,7
Scanner3=ACME Scanner,ACMESCAN.DLL,ACME,6
```

The Scanners entry specifies how many scanner drivers are included in this scanaplt.inf file. The ScannerN entries contain a comma-delimited string specifying all the information the Scanners applet needs for that particular scanner/driver. The first field is the description that will appear in the listbox of the Scanners applet. The second field is the name of the vendor-specific module (DLL). The third field is a unique label that will be used to store the entire string in the Registry for later retrieval. The fourth field is a numerical value that logical ORs all the capabilities that this vendor-specific DLL supports. The maximum length of the entire string is 128 bytes. To add a new scanner driver, a vendor provides a `scanaplt.inf` file and instructs the user to select the Add button in the Scanners applet.

Applet User Interface Design

The Control Panel applet icon should, at a glance, convey clearly the category of device that it supports, so for the Scanners applet I designed a fairly simple icon that resembles a typical desktop scanner. Microsoft has established a precedent by using somewhat muted colors in their standard applet icons — with so many icons stacked in a row, the Control Panel would resemble a comic strip if the icons were too flashy. In keeping with this precedent, I used only shades of gray to draw my scanner icon. Figure 22.1 shows the Windows NT Control Panel, including my Scanners applet.

I also tried to model the user interface of my Scanners applet after the standard Drivers applet. This helps make the applet look as if it really belongs in the Control Panel client area, rather than having just been dropped there by some program (even though, of course, that is exactly what I am doing!). The "look" of a common applet

Figure 22.1   Windows NT control panel with sample Scanners applet.

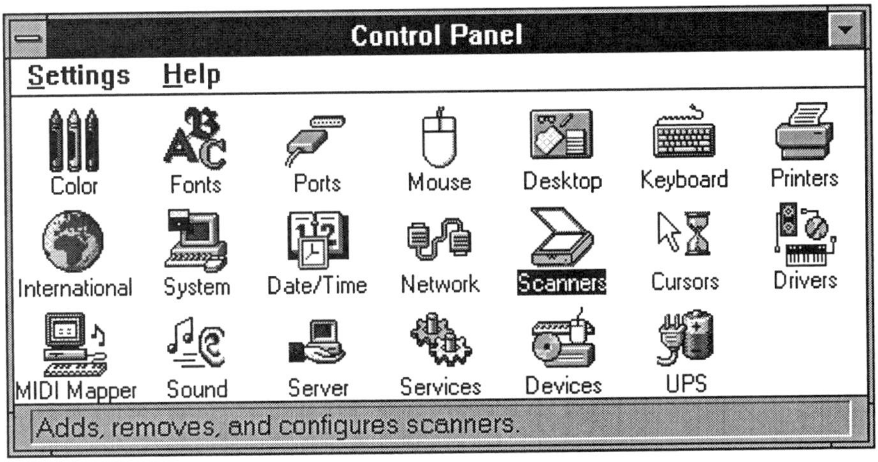

calls for a listbox on the left side and buttons along the right side. Typically, you would include a Cancel button to easily close the applet; a Help button to provide information on the Scanners applet itself (not vendor-specific help); an Add button to add additional drivers; a Remove button to remove an existing driver; and a button to provide vendor-specific features (usually called Configure or Setup). Figure 22.2 shows the dialog box for my Scanners applet.

Creating the Scanner CPL

The source code for the sample scanner Control Panel applet resides in `scanaplt.c` (Listing 22.1), `scanaplt.h` (Listing 22.2), `scanaplt.rc` (Listing 22.3), `scanaplt.def` (Listing 22.4), and `scanaplt.mak` (Listing 22.5). `CPlApplet()` contains a `case` statement for each of the eight messages sent by the Control Panel. This applet does not require special initialization or cleanup, so the only real action occurs during the `CPL_NEWINQUIRE` and `CPL_DBLCLK` messages.

When the Control Panel sends the `CPL_NEWINQUIRE` message, it passes a pointer to a `NEWCPLINFO` structure in `lParam2`. It is the CPL's responsibility to completely and accurately fill in this structure. `hIcon` contains the handle of the icon that I want displayed in the Control Panel client area, and the `szName` string should contain the string to be displayed immediately under the icon and in the Settings menu. The `szInfo` string will appear in the status bar area when a user selects the icon.

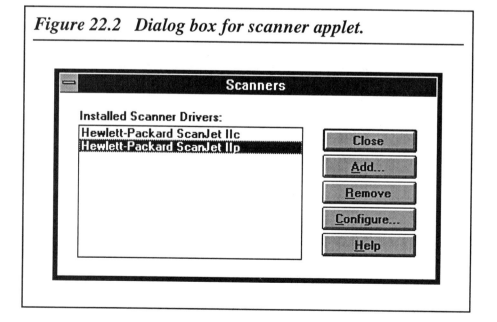

Figure 22.2   Dialog box for scanner applet.

Listing 22.1   scanaplt.c — *Windows NT control panel applet.*

```
/**-------------------------------------------------------**
** SCANAPLT.C:  Main entry-points for the Windows NT
**              scanner Control Panel Applet.
** Environment: Windows NT.
** (C) Hewlett-Packard Company 1993.  PLT.
**-------------------------------------------------------**/

/**----------------- Include Files --------------------**/
#include <windows.h>
#include <cpl.h>                    /* control panel defines */
#include <winreg.h>                  /* registry prototypes */
#include <stdlib.h>                   /* prototype for atoi */
#include "scanaplt.h"

/**-------------- Public Function Prototypes ------------**/
INT APIENTRY LibMain(HANDLE, ULONG, LPVOID);
LONG CALLBACK CPlApplet(HWND, UINT, LPARAM, LPARAM);

/**-------------- Private Function Prototypes -----------**/
BOOL WriteScannerRegistry(HWND, LPTSTR);
BOOL ReadScannerRegistry(HWND, int);
BOOL DeleteScannerRegistry(HWND, LPTSTR);
BOOL ReadInfFile(HWND, LPTSTR);
void ReplaceCommasWithTabs(LPTSTR);
int GetVendorCapabilities(LPTSTR);
void GetVendorModule(LPTSTR, LPTSTR);
void GetVendorValue(LPTSTR, LPTSTR);

/**------------------ Global Data ---------------------**/
HINSTANCE hInst;
int iCap=0, index=0;
char lpBuffer[MAX_STR_LEN+1];


/**********************************************************
** Routine:  LibMain
**    Called by Windows when a DLL is loaded. Perform your
**    process or thread specific initialization tasks here.
** Return:  Return 1 if initialization successful.
**********************************************************/
INT APIENTRY LibMain(HINSTANCE hModule, ULONG ulReason,
    LPVOID lpReserved)
{
    hInst = hModule;
    return 1;
} /* LibMain */
```

When the CPL_DBLCLK message is sent, I bring up the dialog box for the Scanners applet, specifying ScannerDlgProc as the dialog box procedure. During the WM_INITDIALOG message, the dialog procedure reads from the Registry and displays in the listbox any previously installed scanner drivers. Before explaining the procedure, however, I want to describe how a scanner driver gets added to the Scanners applet.

Listing 22.1 *(continued)*

```
/*************************************************************
** Routine:  CPlApplet
**     Standard callback entry point for the Control Panel.
*************************************************************/
LONG CALLBACK CPlApplet(HWND hWndCPL, UINT msg,
    LPARAM lParam1, LPARAM lParam2)
{
    LPNEWCPLINFO lpNewCPlInfo;

    switch (msg)
    {
        case CPL_INIT:
            /* Sent (once) immediately after DLL loaded */
            return TRUE;

        case CPL_GETCOUNT:
            /* Sent after CPL_INIT message, return # of apps */
            return NUM_SCANNER_APPS;

        case CPL_INQUIRE:
            /* obsoleted by CPL_NEWINQUIRE, just return FALSE */
            return FALSE;

        case CPL_NEWINQUIRE:
            /* Sent after CPL_GETCOUNT, once for each applet */
            lpNewCPlInfo = (LPNEWCPLINFO)lParam2;
            lpNewCPlInfo->dwSize = (DWORD)sizeof(NEWCPLINFO);
            lpNewCPlInfo->dwFlags = 0;
            lpNewCPlInfo->dwHelpContext = 0;
            lpNewCPlInfo->lData = 0;
            lpNewCPlInfo->hIcon = LoadIcon(hInst,
                (LPCTSTR)MAKEINTRESOURCE(ICO_SCANNER));
            lpNewCPlInfo->szHelpFile[0] = '\0';
            strcpy(lpNewCPlInfo->szName, "Scanners");
            strcpy(lpNewCPlInfo->szInfo,
                "Adds, removes, and configures scanners.");
            break;

        case CPL_SELECT:
            /* Sent when user selects your applet icon */
            break;
```

Listing 22.1 (continued)

```
    case CPL_DBLCLK:
        /* sent when user double-clicks your applet icon */
        DialogBox(hInst, MAKEINTRESOURCE(SCANNER_DLG),
            hWndCPL, (DLGPROC)ScannerDlgProc);
        break;

    case CPL_STOP:
        /* Sent once for each app before Cont-Panel ends */
        break;

    case CPL_EXIT:
        /* Sent after last CPL_STOP message */
        break;

    default:  break;
    } /* switch on msg */
  return TRUE;
} /* CPlApplet */

/************************************************************
** Routine:  ScannerDlgProc
**     Dialog box procedure for SCANNER_DLG
************************************************************/
BOOL APIENTRY ScannerDlgProc(HWND hDlg, UINT msg,
   WPARAM wParam, LPARAM lParam)
{
   HINSTANCE hLib = 0;
   FARPROC lpfn = 0;
   static int tabstops[] = { 400, 500, 600 };
   static char lpEntry[MAX_STR_LEN+1];

   switch (msg)
   {
      case WM_INITDIALOG:
         SendDlgItemMessage(hDlg, ID_SCANNER_LIST,
            LB_SETTABSTOPS, 3, (long)(int *)tabstops);
         ReadScannerRegistry(hDlg, ID_SCANNER_LIST);
         return TRUE;

      case WM_SYSCOMMAND:
         if (wParam == SC_CLOSE) EndDialog(hDlg, TRUE);
         return FALSE;

      case WM_COMMAND:
         switch(LOWORD(wParam))
         {
            case IDOK:
               EndDialog(hDlg, TRUE);
               return TRUE;
```

When a user presses the Add button, the dialog box in Figure 22.3 is displayed. This dialog box allows the user to specify the path where scanaplt.inf can be found. ReadInfFile() parses scanaplt.inf using the private profile string APIs. WriteScannerRegistry() then stores the information strings found in scanaplt.inf in the Registry. This routine opens the Control Panel\Scanners subkey of the HKEY_CURRENT_USER key. The Control Panel key is where most Control Panel

---

Listing 22.1 (continued)

```
        case ID_SCANNER_LIST:
            if (HIWORD(wParam) != LBN_SELCHANGE) break;
            if ((index = SendMessage((HWND)lParam,
                LB_GETCURSEL, 0, 0L)) != -1L)
            {
                SendMessage((HWND)lParam, LB_GETTEXT, index,
                    (LONG)(LPTSTR)lpBuffer);
                iCap = GetVendorCapabilities(lpBuffer);
                if ((iCap & CPL_SCANNER_SUPPORT_CONFIGURE) == 0)
                    EnableWindow(GetDlgItem(ID_SCANNER_CONFIGURE), 0);
                else EnableWindow(GetDlgItem(ID_SCANNER_CONFIGURE), 1);
            }
            return TRUE;

        case ID_SCANNER_HELP:       /* call WinHelp */
            MessageBox(hDlg, (LPTSTR)"You're doing fine!",
                (LPTSTR)"Scanners", MB_OK);
            return TRUE;

        case ID_SCANNER_ADD:
            DialogBox(hInst, MAKEINTRESOURCE(ADD_DLG),
                hDlg, (DLGPROC)AddDlgProc);
            ReadScannerRegistry(hDlg, ID_SCANNER_LIST);
            break;

        case ID_SCANNER_CONFIGURE:
            SendDlgItemMessage(hDlg, ID_SCANNER_LIST,
                LB_GETTEXT, index, (LONG)(LPTSTR)lpEntry);
            GetVendorModule(lpEntry, lpBuffer);

            if ((hLib = LoadLibrary(lpBuffer)) == NULL)
            {
                MessageBox(hDlg, "Couldn't find library "Scanners", MB_OK);
                break;
            }
            lpfn = GetProcAddress(hLib, "CPL_ScannerConfigure");
            (*lpfn)(hDlg, 0, (LPTSTR)lpEntry);
            FreeLibrary(hLib);
            break;
```

Listing 22.1 (continued)

```
                case ID_SCANNER_REMOVE:
                    SendDlgItemMessage(hDlg, ID_SCANNER_LIST,
                        LB_GETTEXT, index, (LONG)(LPTSTR)lpEntry);
                    if (DeleteScannerRegistry(hDlg, lpEntry))
                        ReadScannerRegistry(hDlg, ID_SCANNER_LIST);
                    break;

                default:
                    return TRUE;
            }
            break;
    }
    return FALSE;
} /* ScannerDlgProc */

/**********************************************************
** Routine:  AddDlgProc - dialog box procedure for ADD_DLG
**********************************************************/
BOOL APIENTRY AddDlgProc(HWND hDlg, UINT msg, WPARAM wParam, LPARAM lParam)
{
    static char lpFilename[MAX_STR_LEN+1];

    switch (msg)
    {
        case WM_INITDIALOG:
            SendDlgItemMessage(hDlg, ID_EDIT_DRIVESRC,
                EM_LIMITTEXT, MAX_STR_LEN, OL);
            SetDlgItemText(hDlg, ID_EDIT_DRIVESRC, "A:\\");
            return TRUE;

        case WM_COMMAND:
            switch(LOWORD(wParam))
            {
                case IDOK:
                    GetDlgItemText(hDlg, ID_EDIT_DRIVESRC,
                        lpFilename, MAX_STR_LEN);
                    if (lpFilename[strlen(lpFilename)-1] != '\\')
                        strcat(lpFilename, "\\");
                    strcat(lpFilename, "SCANAPLT.INF");
                    EndDialog(hDlg, ReadInfFile(hDlg, lpFilename));
                    return TRUE;

                case ID_ADD_HELP:       /* call WinHelp */
                    MessageBox(NULL, (LPTSTR)"You're doing fine!",
                        (LPTSTR)"Scanners", MB_OK);
                    return TRUE;
```

Listing 22.1 (continued)

```
                case IDCANCEL:
                    EndDialog(hDlg, FALSE);
                    return TRUE;

                default:
                    return TRUE;
            }
            break;
    }
    return FALSE;
} /* AddDlgProc */


/**-------------------------------------------------------**/
BOOL ReadScannerRegistry(HWND hDlg, int iListID)
{
    HKEY hKey;
    DWORD i, status;
    CHAR cValueName[MAX_STR_LEN+1], cDataString[MAX_STR_LEN+1];
    DWORD dwValueLen = MAX_STR_LEN, dwDataLen = MAX_STR_LEN;

    SendDlgItemMessage(hDlg, iListID, LB_RESETCONTENT, 0, 0L);

    if ((status = RegOpenKeyEx(HKEY_CURRENT_USER,
            "Control Panel\\Scanners", 0, KEY_QUERY_VALUE, &hKey))
            != ERROR_SUCCESS)
    {
        /* "Scanners" key doesn't exist, create it */
        RegCreateKeyEx(HKEY_CURRENT_USER, "Control Panel\\Scanners",
            0, "\0", REG_OPTION_NON_VOLATILE, KEY_ALL_ACCESS |
            KEY_WRITE, NULL, &hKey, &status);
        RegCloseKey(hKey);
        EnableWindow(GetDlgItem(hDlg, ID_SCANNER_REMOVE), 0);
        EnableWindow(GetDlgItem(hDlg, ID_SCANNER_CONFIGURE), 0);
        return FALSE;
    }

    for (i=0, status=ERROR_SUCCESS; status==ERROR_SUCCESS; I++)
    {
        dwValueLen = MAX_STR_LEN;    /* must reset max length */
        dwDataLen = MAX_STR_LEN;     /* must reset max length */
        status = RegEnumValue(hKey, i, cValueName, &dwValueLen,
            NULL, NULL, cDataString, &dwDataLen);
        if (status == ERROR_SUCCESS)
        {
            ReplaceCommasWithTabs(cDataString);
            SendDlgItemMessage(hDlg, iListID, LB_ADDSTRING, 0,
                (long)(LPTSTR)cDataString);        }
    }
    RegCloseKey(hKey);
```

information is stored. I include several small support routines at the end of `scan-aplt.c` to parse out individual fields from the comma-delimited string. Information is always stored in the Registry in the form of a value field, data type, and the actual data. I use the unique label in the information string as the value field and `REG_SZ` to indicate that the data is a null-terminated string. Finally, I store the information string itself as the data in the Registry. After a scanner has been added with the sample `scanaplt.inf` shown earlier, the Registry contains the following values in the `HKEY_CURRENT_USER\Control Panel\Scanners` key:

Listing 22.1 (continued)

```c
    SendDlgItemMessage(hDlg, iListID, LB_SETCURSEL, 0, 0L);
    SendDlgItemMessage(hDlg, iListID, LB_GETTEXT, 0,
        (LONG)(LPTSTR)lpBuffer);
    iCap = GetVendorCapabilities(lpBuffer);
    if ((iCap & CPL_SCANNER_SUPPORT_CONFIGURE) == 0)
        EnableWindow(GetDlgItem(hDlg, ID_SCANNER_CONFIGURE), 0);
    else EnableWindow(GetDlgItem(hDlg, ID_SCANNER_CONFIGURE), 1);
    EnableWindow(GetDlgItem(hDlg, ID_SCANNER_REMOVE), 1);

    return TRUE;
} /* ReadScannerRegistery */

/**-----------------------------------------------------**/
BOOL DeleteScannerRegistry(HWND hDlg, LPTSTR lpEntry)
{
    HKEY hKey;
    HINSTANCE hLib = 0;
    FARPROC lpfn = 0;

    if (MessageBox(hDlg, "Remove the selected scanner driver?",
        "Scanners", MB_YESNO | MB_ICONQUESTION) == IDNO)
        return FALSE;

    if (RegOpenKeyEx(HKEY_CURRENT_USER, "Control Panel\\Scanners", 0,
        KEY_WRITE, &hKey) != ERROR_SUCCESS) return FALSE;
    GetVendorValue(lpEntry, lpBuffer);
    RegDeleteValue(hKey, lpBuffer);
    RegCloseKey(hKey);

    if ((iCap & CPL_SCANNER_SUPPORT_UNINSTALL) != 0)
    {
        GetVendorModule(lpEntry, lpBuffer);
        if ((hLib = LoadLibrary(lpBuffer)) == NULL) return FALSE;
        lpfn = GetProcAddress(hLib, "CPL_ScannerUninstall");
        (*lpfn)(hDlg, 0, (LPTSTR)lpEntry);
        FreeLibrary(hLib);
    }
    return TRUE;
} /* DeleteScannerRegistry */
```

Listing 22.1 *(continued)*

```c
/**-----------------------------------------------------**/
BOOL WriteScannerRegistry(HWND hDlg, LPTSTR lpEntry)
{
   HKEY hKey;
   HINSTANCE hLib = 0;
   FARPROC lpfn = 0;

   if (RegOpenKeyEx(HKEY_CURRENT_USER, "Control Panel\\Scanners",
       0, KEY_WRITE, &hKey) != ERROR_SUCCESS) return FALSE;
   GetVendorValue(lpEntry, lpBuffer);
   RegSetValueEx(hKey, lpBuffer, 0, (DWORD)REG_SZ,
       (LPBYTE)lpEntry, strlen(lpEntry));
   RegCloseKey(hKey);

   iCap = GetVendorCapabilities(lpEntry);
   if ((iCap & CPL_SCANNER_SUPPORT_INSTALL) != 0)
   {
       GetVendorModule(lpEntry, lpBuffer);
       if ((hLib = LoadLibrary(lpBuffer)) == NULL) return FALSE;
       lpfn = GetProcAddress(hLib, "CPL_ScannerInstall");
       (*lpfn)(hDlg, 0, (LPTSTR)lpEntry);
       FreeLibrary(hLib);
   }
   return TRUE;
} /* WriteScannerRegistry */


/**-----------------------------------------------------**/
BOOL ReadInfFile(HWND hDlg, LPTSTR lpFilename)
{
   WORD wDrivers=0, i=0;
   char lpEntry[MAX_STR_LEN+1];

   wDrivers = GetPrivateProfileInt("CPL_Scanner", "Scanners", 0, lpFilename);

   for (i=1; i <= wDrivers; i++)
   {
      wsprintf(lpBuffer, "Scanner%d", i);
      GetPrivateProfileString("CPL_Scanner", lpBuffer, "0",
          lpEntry, MAX_STR_LEN, lpFilename);
      WriteScannerRegistry(hDlg, lpEntry);
   } /* for i */
   return TRUE;
} /* ReadInfFile */


/**-----------------------------------------------------**/
void ReplaceCommasWithTabs(LPTSTR lpEntry)
{
   int i;
   for (i=0; lpEntry[i] != '\0'; i++)
      if (lpEntry[i] == ',') lpEntry[i] = '\t';
} /* ReplaceCommasWithTabs */
```

```
HPSCANAPIIC:REG_SZ:Hewlett-Packard ScanJet IIc,
        HPSCANAP.DLL,HPSCANIIC,7
HPSCANAPIIP:REG_SZ:Hewlett-Packard ScanJet IIp,
        HPSCANAP.DLL,HPSCANIIP,7
ACME:REG_SZ:ACME Scanner,ACMESCAN.DLL,ACME,6
```

Finally, `WriteScannerRegistry()` checks the capabilities field of the information string. If the `CPL_SCANNER_SUPPORT_INSTALL` bit is turned on, I call `CPL_ScannerInstall()` in the DLL specified in the information string.

Similarly, if a user selects "Remove," `DeleteScannerRegistry()` uses the value label in the information string to determine which value in the Registry to delete. In this case, if the `CPL_SCANNER_SUPPORT_UNINSTALL` bit is turned on in the capabilities field, I call `CPL_ScannerUninstall()` in the specified DLL.

Listing 22.1 (continued)

```
/**---------------------------------------------------------**/
int GetVendorCapabilities(LPTSTR lpEntry)
{
   LPTSTR lp = lpEntry + strlen(lpEntry) - 1;
   while (*lp != '\0' && *lp != '\t' && *lp != ',') lp--;
   return atoi(++lp);
} /* GetVendorCapabilities */


/**---------------------------------------------------------**/
void GetVendorModule(LPTSTR lpEntry, LPTSTR lpModule)
{
   LPTSTR lp1 = lpEntry, lp2 = lpModule;

   while (*lp1 != '\0' && *lp1 != '\t' && *lp1 != ',') lp1++;
   lp1++;
   while (*lp1 != '\0' && *lp1 != '\t' && *lp1 != ',')
   *lp2++ = *lp1++;
   *lp2 = '\0';
} /* GetVendorModule */


/**---------------------------------------------------------**/
void GetVendorValue(LPTSTR lpEntry, LPTSTR lpValue)
{
   LPTSTR lp1 = lpEntry, lp2 = lpValue;

   while (*lp1 != '\0' && *lp1 != '\t' && *lp1 != ',') lp1++;    lp1++;
   while (*lp1 != '\0' && *lp1 != '\t' && *lp1 != ',') lp1++;    lp1++;
   while (*lp1 != '\0' && *lp1 != '\t' && *lp1 != ',') *lp2++ = *lp1++;
   *lp2 = '\0';
} /* GetVendorValue */
```

Listing 22.2   *scanaplt.h*— *Header file for* *scanaplt.c.*

```
/**-------------------------------------------------------**
** SCANAPLT.H: Defines and Prototypes for SCANAPLT.CPL
** Environment: Windows NT.
** (C) Hewlett-Packard Company 1993.  PLT.
**-------------------------------------------------------**/


/**--------------- General Defines --------------------**/
#define IDNULL              -1
#define MAX_STR_LEN         128
#define NUM_SCANNER_APPS     1
#define ICO_SCANNER         999


/**-------------- Vendor Capability Flags ---------------**/
#define CPL_SCANNER_SUPPORT_CONFIGURE    0x01
#define CPL_SCANNER_SUPPORT_INSTALL      0x02
#define CPL_SCANNER_SUPPORT_UNINSTALL    0x04


/**----------------- SCANNER_DLG ----------------------**/
#define SCANNER_DLG             4000
#define ID_SCANNER_LIST         4001
#define ID_SCANNER_ADD          4002
#define ID_SCANNER_REMOVE       4003
#define ID_SCANNER_CONFIGURE    4004
#define ID_SCANNER_HELP         4005


/**------------------ ADD_DLG -------------------------**/
#define ADD_DLG             4100
#define ID_EDIT_DRIVESRC    4101
#define ID_ADD_HELP         4102


/**-------------- Prototypes for SCANAPLT.C ------------**/
LONG CALLBACK CPlApplet(HWND, UINT, LPARAM, LPARAM);
BOOL APIENTRY ScannerDlgProc(HWND, UINT, WPARAM, LPARAM);
BOOL APIENTRY AddDlgProc(HWND, UINT, WPARAM, LPARAM);


/**------ Entry-point for Scanner Specific Options ------**/
ULONG APIENTRY CPL_ScannerConfigure(HWND, ULONG, LPTSTR);
ULONG APIENTRY CPL_ScannerInstall(HWND, ULONG, LPTSTR);
ULONG APIENTRY CPL_ScannerUninstall(HWND, ULONG, LPTSTR);
```

Whenever an entry in the listbox is selected, I check the capabilities value and determine whether or not to gray out the Configure button. If the user selects the Configure button, I call `CPL_ScannerConfigure()` in the specified DLL. This instructs the vendor-specific DLL to bring up its own dialog box and present its own configuration options.

Listing 22.3 `scanaplt.rc` *— Resource definitions for* `scanaplt.c`

```
/**--------------------------------------------------------**
** SCANAPLT.RC:    Resources information for SCANAPLT.CPL
** Environment: Windows NT.
** (C) Hewlett-Packard Company 1993.  PLT.
**--------------------------------------------------------**/

/**----------------- Include Files --------------------**/
#include <windows.h>
#include "scanaplt.h"

ICO_SCANNER ICON SCANAPLT.ICO

/**------- add the standard version resource info -------**/

/**-------------------- SCANNER_DLG --------------------*/
SCANNER_DLG DIALOG LOADONCALL MOVEABLE DISCARDABLE
   20, 20, 220, 112
STYLE DS_MODALFRAME | WS_POPUP | WS_VISIBLE | WS_CAPTION | WS_SYSMENU
CAPTION "Scanners"
FONT 8, "Helv"
BEGIN
   CONTROL "Installed Scanner Drivers:", IDNULL, "static",
      SS_LEFT | WS_CHILD, 12, 10, 191, 8
   CONTROL "", ID_SCANNER_LIST, "listbox", LBS_STANDARD |
      LBS_USETABSTOPS | WS_TABSTOP | WS_CHILD,
      12, 20, 130, 78
   CONTROL "Close", IDOK, "button", BS_DEFPUSHBUTTON |
      WS_TABSTOP | WS_CHILD, 154, 20, 54, 14
   CONTROL "&Add...", ID_SCANNER_ADD, "button",
      BS_PUSHBUTTON | WS_TABSTOP | WS_CHILD, 154, 36, 54, 14
   CONTROL "&Remove", ID_SCANNER_REMOVE, "button",
      BS_PUSHBUTTON | WS_TABSTOP | WS_CHILD, 154, 52, 54, 14
   CONTROL "&Configure...", ID_SCANNER_CONFIGURE, "button",
      BS_PUSHBUTTON | WS_TABSTOP | WS_CHILD, 154, 68, 54, 14
   CONTROL "&Help", ID_SCANNER_HELP, "button",
      BS_PUSHBUTTON | WS_TABSTOP | WS_CHILD, 154, 84, 54, 14
END
```

When the Scanners applet is first launched, I enumerate all of the values in the Scanners key of the Registry and display them in the listbox. To keep this example simple, I also re-enumerate the Registry values whenever a scanner driver is added or removed. Rather than define a complicated method for storing all the fields for each installed scanner driver that maps into the listbox index, I use the simple trick of replacing commas with tabs and adding the entire string to the listbox. All fields except the description are safely tabbed out of the client area of the listbox, so users will never see them. This trick makes it very easy to retrieve information about a selected scanner driver.

Listing 22.3 (continued)

```
/**--------------- Add... Dialog Box -------------------*/
ADD_DLG DIALOG LOADONCALL MOVEABLE DISCARDABLE
    30, 30, 257, 62 STYLE DS_MODALFRAME | WS_POPUP |
    WS_VISIBLE | WS_CAPTION | WS_SYSMENU
CAPTION "Add Scanner"
FONT 8, "Helv"
BEGIN
    CONTROL "Insert disk containing Scanner Driver in:",
        IDNULL, "static", SS_LEFT | WS_CHILD, 12, 18, 129, 8
    CONTROL "", ID_EDIT_DRIVESRC, "edit", ES_LEFT | WS_BORDER |
        ES_AUTOHSCROLL | WS_TABSTOP | WS_CHILD, 12, 32, 158, 12
    CONTROL "OK", IDOK, "button", BS_DEFPUSHBUTTON |
        WS_TABSTOP | WS_CHILD, 194, 8, 52, 14
    CONTROL "Cancel", IDCANCEL, "button",
        BS_PUSHBUTTON | WS_TABSTOP | WS_CHILD, 194, 24, 52, 14
    CONTROL "&Help", ID_ADD_HELP, "button",
        BS_PUSHBUTTON | WS_TABSTOP | WS_CHILD, 194, 40, 52, 14
END
```

Listing 22.4   scanaplt.def — Linker definitions for scanaplt.c

```
;SCANAPLT.DEF - module definition file for SCANAPLT.CPL

LIBRARY    ScanAplt

CODE       PRELOAD MOVEABLE DISCARDABLE
DATA       PRELOAD SINGLE

EXPORTS
    CPlApplet          @2
    ScannerDlgProc     @10
    AddDlgProc         @11
```

Listing 22.5 *scanaplt.mak — Makefile for* scanaplt.c.

```
# Nmake macros for building Windows 32-Bit apps
!include <win32.mak>

all: hpscanap.dll scanaplt.dll

.c.obj:
  $(cc) $(cdebug) $(cflags) $(cvarsdll) $*.c

hpscanap.res: hpscanap.rc hpscanap.h
    $(rc) $(rcflags) $(rcvars) -r hpscanap.rc

scanaplt.res: scanaplt.rc scanaplt.h
    $(rc) $(rcflags) $(rcvars) -r scanaplt.rc

hpscanap.dll: hpscanap.obj hpscanap.res hpscanap.def
    $(link) $(linkdebug) $(dllflags) \
    hpscanap.obj hpscanap.res $(guilibsdll) version.lib \
    -dll                    \
    -def:hpscanap.def       \
    -entry:LibMain$(DLLENTRY) \
    -out:hpscanap.dll $(MAPFILE)

scanaplt.dll: scanaplt.obj scanaplt.res scanaplt.def
    $(link) $(linkdebug) $(dllflags) \
    scanaplt.obj scanaplt.res $(guilibsdll) version.lib \
    -dll                    \
    -def:scanaplt.def       \
    -entry:LibMain$(DLLENTRY) \
    -out:scanaplt.dll $(MAPFILE)
```

Figure 22.3 Add dialog box for Scanner applet.

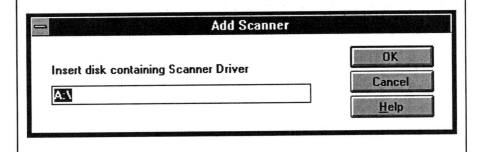

Windows NT Differences

Don't forget that DLL entry points don't have to be named `LibMain()` anymore; you can specify the DLL initialization function in the link statement of your makefile. Another important Windows NT difference is in the return values of `LoadLibrary()`. In Windows 3.x, `LoadLibrary()` returns a value between 0 and 32 if it fails. In Windows NT, `LoadLibrary()` returns `NULL` on failures. You must call `GetLastError()` to determine the exact cause of the failure.

Creating a Sample Vendor-Specific DLL

The complete source code for a vendor-specific DLL template that uses the Hewlett-Packard scanners as examples resides on the code disk. Most of the source code is shown in `hpscanap.c` (Listing 22.6). By specifying a value of 7 in the `scanaplt.inf` file for these scanners, I declare that I want to provide configuration support and that I want to be notified if my scanner drivers are installed or uninstalled. This requires exporting `CPL_ScannerConfigure()`, `CPL_ScannerInstall()`, and `CPL_ScannerUninstall()`.

Listing 22.6   `hpscanap.c` — Vendor-specific DLL template.

```
/**-------------------------------------------------------**
** HPSCANAP.C: Entry-points for the HP scanners.
** Environment: Windows NT.
** (C) Hewlett-Packard Company 1993.  PLT.
**-------------------------------------------------------**/

/**----------------- Include Files --------------------**/
#include <windows.h>
#include "scanaplt.h"
#include "hpscanap.h"

/**----------------- Global Data ---------------------**/
HINSTANCE hInst;
char lpTitle[64];

/***********************************************************
** Routine:  LibMain
**     Called by Windows when a DLL is loaded. Perform your
**     process or thread specific initialization tasks here.** Return:  Return 1
if initialization successful.
***********************************************************/
```

Listing 22.6 (continued)

```c
INT APIENTRY LibMain(HINSTANCE hModule, ULONG ulReason,
   LPVOID lpReserved)
{
   hInst = hModule;
   return 1;
} /* LibMain */

/***********************************************************
** Routine:  CPL_ScannerConfigure
**    Entry-point for vendor-specific configuration options.
**    Called when "Configure..." selected for an HP scanner.
** Return:  Return TRUE if successful, else return FALSE.
***********************************************************/
ULONG APIENTRY CPL_ScannerConfigure(HWND hWndApplet,
   ULONG ulData, LPTSTR lpScannerTitle)
{
   strcpy(lpTitle, lpScannerTitle);
   DialogBox(hInst, MAKEINTRESOURCE(CONFIGURE_DLG),
     hWndApplet, (DLGPROC)ConfigureDlgProc);
   return TRUE;
} /* CPL_ScannerConfigure */

/***********************************************************
** Routine:  CPL_ScannerInstall
**    Scanner Applet will call if user adds an HP scanner
**    (and capabilities indicate that install is supported).
** Return:  Return TRUE if successful, else return FALSE.
***********************************************************/
ULONG APIENTRY CPL_ScannerInstall(HWND hWndApplet,
   ULONG ulData, LPTSTR lpScannerTitle)
{
   /* copy/create files, add custom entries to registry */
   return TRUE;
} /* CPL_ScannerInstall */

/***********************************************************
** Routine:  CPL_ScannerUninstall
**    Scanner Applet will call if user removes an HP scanner
**    (and capabilities indicate uninstall is supported).
** Return:  Return TRUE if successful, else return FALSE.
***********************************************************/
ULONG APIENTRY CPL_ScannerUninstall(HWND hWndApplet,
   ULONG ulData, LPTSTR lpScannerTitle)
{
   /* delete files, remove custom entries from registry */
   return TRUE;
} /* CPL_ScannerUninstall */
```

CPL_ScannerInstall() and CPL_ScannerUninstall() just return TRUE in this simple example. Typically, for CPL_ScannerInstall(), you would copy any necessary driver files to disk, and update any configuration files or Registry entries. Likewise, for CPL_ScannerUninstall(), you would typically delete any files that you copied and remove your specific entries in configuration files or the Registry.

A scanner vendor would typically use CPL_ScannerConfigure() to display a dialog box offering vendor-specific options such as configuring the scanner driver and performing scanner diagnostics. Even though I use a single DLL to support two different scanners, I can use the string passed into CPL_ScannerConfigure() to determine

---

Listing 22.6 (continued)

```
/***********************************************************
** Routine:  ConfigureDlgProc
**     Dialog box procedure for CONFIGURE_DLG
***********************************************************/
BOOL APIENTRY ConfigureDlgProc(HWND hDlg, UINT msg,
   WPARAM wParam, LPARAM lParam)
{
   switch (msg)
   {
      case WM_INITDIALOG:
         SetDlgItemText(hDlg, ID_CONFIG_SCANNER, lpTitle);
         if (strstr(lpTitle, "IIc") == NULL)
            EnableWindow(GetDlgItem(hDlg, ID_CONFIG_CAL),
               FALSE);
         return TRUE;

      case WM_COMMAND:
         switch(wParam)
         {
            case ID_CONFIG_DRV:
               /* add code for configuring the drivers! */
               MessageBox(hDlg, (LPTSTR)"Configured!",
                  (LPTSTR)"HP Scanner Configuration", MB_OK);
               return TRUE;

            case ID_CONFIG_TEST:
               /* add code for testing the scanner */
               MessageBox(hDlg, (LPTSTR)"Tested!",
                  (LPTSTR)"HP Scanner Configuration", MB_OK);
               return TRUE;

            case ID_CONFIG_CAL:
               /* add code for doing color calibration */
               MessageBox(hDlg, (LPTSTR)"Calibrated!",
                  (LPTSTR)"HP Scanner Configuration", MB_OK);
               return TRUE;
```

which scanner was specified. For example, if the ScanJet IIp was specified, I gray out the Color Calibration button, because this is a gray-scale scanner. Figure 22.4 shows the dialog box for my vendor-specific DLL.

Listing 22.6 (continued)

```
            case ID_CONFIG_HELP:
               /* call WinHelp with HLP file and topic */
               MessageBox(hDlg, (LPTSTR)"You're doing fine!",
                 (LPTSTR)"HP Scanner Configuration", MB_OK);
               return TRUE;

            case IDOK:
               EndDialog(hDlg, TRUE);
               return TRUE;

            default:  return TRUE;
         } /* switch on wParam */
         break;

   } /* switch on msg */
   return FALSE;
} /* OptionsDlgProc */
```

Figure 22.4   Vendor-specific DLL dialog box.

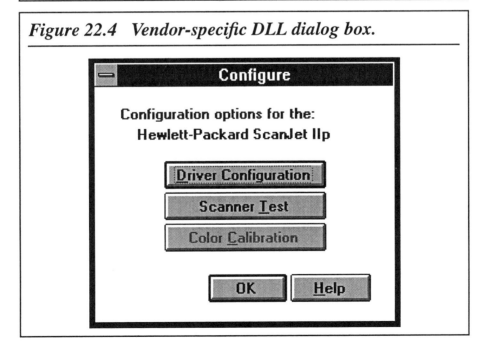

464 — Windows NT in Practice

Adding a CPL

There are several ways to register an applet with the Control Panel, and because there is some debate about the order in which the Control Panel performs its search, you should not rely too heavily on the load order of your applet. The Control Panel searches for applets in the following locations and in roughly this order:

- The Control Panel first loads the standard applets located in main.cpl.

- The Control Panel then checks the MMCPL key of the HKEY_CURRENT_USER key in the Registry (in Windows 3.x, this information was contained in the [MMCPL] section of control.ini). This may be the best place to specify your applet if the CPL has other functions besides supporting Control Panel applets.

- The Control Panel next looks for *.cpl files in the directory where control.exe is located.

- Finally, the Control Panel looks for any files with the *.cpl extension in the Windows NT System directory (winnt\system32).

Be sure to use the standard API functions, such as GetSystemDirectory(), to locate the System directory.

I am not particularly concerned about the order that my Scanners applet loads, so for this example I chose the fourth and simplest method. To register an applet this way, I need only rename my .dll to .cpl and copy it to the Windows NT System directory.

Starting a Control Panel Applet

There are three ways to start a Control Panel applet:

- A user can open the Control Panel and start an applet by double-clicking the applet icon or by choosing the name of the applet in the Settings menu.

- A user can open an applet by running control.exe with the name of the applet as a command-line parameter. When the Control Panel applet closes, the Control Panel automatically closes. An application can accomplish the same thing by using the following line of code:

```
WinExec("control.exe scanaplt", SW_SHOWNORMAL)
```

- An application can send a WM_CPL_LAUNCH message to the Control Panel while the Control Panel is running. When the applet closes, the Control Panel sends back a WM_CPL_LAUNCHED confirmation message and then closes automatically. (Refer to the code fragment in Figure 22.5 for an example of starting a Control Panel applet using this method.)

Figure 22.5 Code fragment for starting Control Panel applet.

```
#include <windows.h>
#include <cpl.h>

    HWND hCplWnd = NULL;
    WORD wStart = FALSE;
    HGLOBAL hName;
    LPSTR lpName;

    /* allocate a shareable memory block for applet name */
    hName = GlobalAlloc(GMEM_MOVEABLE, 9);
    if (hName == NULL) return FALSE;
    lpName = GlobalLock(hName);
    strcpy(lpName, "Scanners");
    GlobalUnlock(hName);

    /* see if Control Panel already running */
    if ((hCplWnd = FindWindow("CtlPanelClass", "Control Panel")) == NULL)
    {
        /* Control Panel not running, so start it now */
        WinExec("control.exe", SW_SHOWNA);
        hCplWnd = FindWindow("CtlPanelClass", "Control Panel");
        if (hCplWnd == NULL)
        {
            GlobalFree(hName);
            return FALSE;
        }
        wStart = TRUE;
    }

    /* start applet, I'll get back WM_CPL_LAUNCHED message */
    SendMessage(hCplWnd, WM_CPL_LAUNCH, (WPARAM)hMyWnd, (LPARAM)lpName);

    /* if I opened Control Panel, close it now */
    if (wStart) SendMessage(hCplWnd, WM_CLOSE, 0, 0);
    GlobalFree(hName);
```

Where to Go from Here

This sample CPL and vendor-specific module are really intended to be used as a template and to help flush out some of the specific development tasks and issues involved in writing CPLs. To keep the sample as brief and simple as possible, I do very little error checking. In practice, though, the scanner CPL should copy over the vendor-specific module when it performs an "Add" to ensure that it can be found when `CPL_ScannerInstall()` is called! A better solution would also allow vendors to specify `NONE` in place of the module name if they did not want to support configure, install, and uninstall. And, of course, additional capabilities could be added. Finally, it is always a good idea to add the standard version structures to your resource file so that other applications can obtain information about your DLL.

Although this is a 32-bit native Windows NT sample, the Control Panel interface has changed very little from Windows 3.x, so it should be a fairly simple job to port this sample to Windows 3.x. In that case, of course, you would use `*.ini` files rather than the Registry for storing information.

References

Custer, Helen. *Inside Windows NT.* Redmond, WA: Microsoft Press, 1992.
Microsoft Corp. Win32 SDK and DDK. Redmond, WA: October 1992.
Microsoft Corp. Preliminary Windows NT Device Driver Kit. Redmond, WA: October 1992.

## Chapter 23

Windows NT Virtual Device Drivers

Paula Tomlinson

As you are no doubt aware, not all 16-bit applications run under Windows NT without modification. In particular, 16-bit applications (both Windows- and DOS-based) that directly access hardware pose a problem because direct hardware access is considered a privileged operation in Windows NT; this is the realm of kernel-mode device drivers. But even if you have written a kernel-mode device driver to support your device (for example, Windows NT already provides very rich support for many common SCSI-based devices and SCSI-based adapters), you still may not be ready to roll all your 16-bit applications completely to 32-bit applications. The VDD interface was designed to solve this specific problem by providing a bridge between 16-bit applications and kernel-mode drivers.

In the first section of this chapter, I'll briefly describe the concepts behind Windows NT VDDs and show how easily they can be used to allow access to the Win32 API from a 16-bit application. In the second and third sections, I'll present examples of the two methods for using VDDs to allow 16-bit applications to access hardware under Windows NT. In the final section, I will present a detailed case study of how a VDD is used to support a 16-bit hardware-dependent application.

Using a VDD to Give a 16-bit Application Access to the Win32 API

The Windows NTVDM (NT Virtual DOS Machine) creates an environment that allows your 16-bit DOS and Windows applications (via the WOW layer or Windows on Win32) to run as if they were still in the old 16-bit environment they expect. The NTVDM also does all the work necessary to provide a context for running your VDD, which is essentially just a 32-bit DLL.

The VDD interface is essentially a back door into the NTVDM. Your 16-bit applications can use this back door to specify a 32-bit user-mode DLL (a VDD) and send information to this DLL in the form of requests or commands. The NTVDM takes care of all the work necessary to create a context in which this 32-bit DLL can run. So really, a VDD is nothing more than a 32-bit DLL with some special, predefined, entry points and with no more privilege than your average 32-bit DLL, whereas Windows 3.x Virtual Device Drivers (commonly referred to as VxDs) have a reputation for "being able to do anything."

The NTVDM provides two mechanisms for communicating between 16-bit applications and their companion VDDs (Figure 23.1). The first method is called application intercept. In this method, the 16-bit application is modified to call a special backdoor interface into the NTVDM. If you were trying to convert an application that performed direct access to a port, for instance, you would replace that code (the IN and OUT instructions) with calls to your VDD via this backdoor interface.

The second method is called *NTVDM intercept*. With this method, the VDD traps access to a particular port or memory address range. Then when a 16-bit application attempts to access that port or memory range, the VDD is called. Windows NT ships with NTVDM intercept VDDs preinstalled for the basic hardware devices (parallel port, serial port, keyboard, mouse, etc.). In this way, when your 16-bit application tries to directly access those hardware devices, the appropriate VDD is invoked and that VDD in turn routes requests on to the appropriate kernel-mode driver.

Trapping hardware access at a lower level means that the NTVDM intercept method is typically slower than using an application intercept implementation, but it has the advantage of not requiring any modifications in the original 16-bit code (just the addition of a VDD). The application intercept method, on the other hand, can be used in a general, non-device-specific way to give 16-bit applications access to the Win32 API.

Even though the original intention of Windows NT VDDs was to provide hardware access to 16-bit applications, there is nothing to prevent a 16-bit application from using an application intercept VDD to provide access to a 32-bit DLL and thus the Win32 API! I'll demonstrate the flexibility of the application intercept method by providing a VDD that can be called by a 16-bit application to provide access to the new Win32 extended registry functions.

The NTVDM Backdoor Interface

A VDD is really nothing more than a 32-bit DLL with some special, predefined entry points. An application intercept VDD must export both an initialization routine and a dispatch routine. You can call these routines anything you like, but the calling 16-bit application must know the names of these entry points. NTVDM intercept VDDs also require other routines that are called when a port or memory address being trapped by the VDD is accessed. Some NTVDM intercept VDDs also require a termination routine. Although I don't know of any circumstances where a termination routine is required in an application intercept VDD, I often include (and export) a termination routine just to be safe.

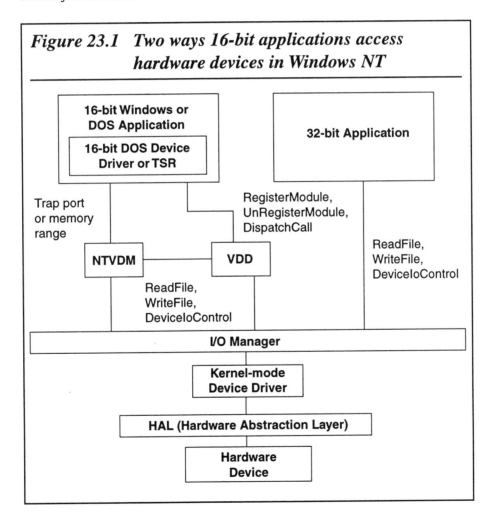

Figure 23.1   Two ways 16-bit applications access hardware devices in Windows NT

As I mentioned, the application intercept method takes advantage of a backdoor interface into the NTVDM to allow the 16-bit application to more or less "directly" call a VDD. This backdoor interface consists of three routines: RegisterModule(), UnRegisterModule(), and DispatchCall(). When a 16-bit application calls RegisterModule(), it passes the name of the VDD it wants to "Register" and the names of the VDD's initialization and dispatch routines. Registering a VDD essentially causes the NTVDM to load the DLL. When the calling application is finished using the VDD, it should let the NTVDM know that it is safe to be unloaded by calling UnRegisterModule(). The DispatchCall() interface is the only direct interface into the VDD from the calling application. All direct requests to the VDD must go through this interface and all parameters passed to the VDD must be passed via registers.

RegVDD, a Sample VDD

To demonstrate using a VDD in a general, non-device-related way, I wrote a simple VDD that can be used by a 16-bit application to access the Windows NT Registry. Although the 16-bit Windows API has routines to modify and read from the Registry, they are extremely limiting. For instance, the 16-bit routines only support value types of SZ_REG, and of course the APIs don't allow for accessing various root keys. This sample VDD, RegVDD, supports five registry operations: creating a subkey, deleting a subkey, writing a value, reading a value, and deleting a value. On the code disk you will find the complete source code for this sample VDD (RegVDD) and a 16-bit application that talks to it (WTest16).

The first step in writing an application intercept VDD is determining what information needs to be passed from the 16-bit application to the VDD and what information should be returned back to the 16-bit application. The VDD exports only one entrypoint to carry out requests, and any parameters must be passed in registers. It is usually best to create a data structure with fields for all the information that must be passed back and forth between the application and the VDD. The following data structure contains all the information the VDD needs to perform any of the five registry operations and to return any pertinent information to the calling application.

```
typedef struct {
    DWORD dwCmd;
    DWORD dwRootKey;
    DWORD dwVolatility;
    DWORD dwAccess;
    char szSubkey[128];
    DWORD dwValueType;
    char szValueName[128];
    BYTE szValueData[128];
    DWORD dwValueDataSize;
    DWORD dwStatus;
} REGVDD_INFO;
```

The dwCmd field specifies which of the five registry operations should be performed, and the dwStatus field indicates whether the operation was completed successfully. All the other fields are parameters used directly in calls to the Win32 registry routines. The following values are arbitrary values distinguishing the operations or commands.

```
#define REGVDD_CMD_CREATESUBKEY    1
#define REGVDD_CMD_DELETESUBKEY    2
#define REGVDD_CMD_WRITEVALUE      3
#define REGVDD_CMD_READVALUE       4
#define REGVDD_CMD_DELETEVALUE     5
```

There are two entry points, in addition to the DLL entry point itself, that all VDDs must export: an initialization routine and a dispatch routine. As shown in the third section of this chapter, some VDDs also require a termination routine. For consistency, I typically just export all three routines in my VDDs. In an application intercept VDD, the initialization routine is called when the calling application calls the VDD interface routine RegisterModule(). You may do initialization tasks here, but you should set the carry flag to indicate whether your initialization was successful. To get or set register contents from a VDD, you should always use the register manipulation routines provided by the NTVDM. These routines use the virtual registers of the x86 emulator on RISC machines. I don't need to do any initialization tasks in RegVDD, so I just clear the carry flag and return. Likewise, in the termination routine, I just return.

```
VOID RegVDDRegisterInit(VOID)
{
    setCF(0);              // Clear flags to indicate success
    return;
} // RegVDDRegisterInit

VOID RegVDDTerminateVDM(VOID)
{
    return;
} // RegVDDTerminateVDM
```

The dispatch routine is the real meat of the VDD. However, before writing this routine, we must decide which registers to use when passing information from the 16-bit application to the VDD. The first point to keep in mind is that when the application calls DispatchCall(), it must place the VDD handle [returned from the call to RegisterModule()] in the AX register, so the AX register isn't available for general use. I arbitrarily chose to place the address of the REGVDD_INFO data structure in ES:BX and the size of this data structure in CX. The VDD needs one more important piece of information: whether the calling application is passing a segment:offset or selector:offset type of address in ES:BX. The VDD uses the GetVDMPointer() routine to convert the address in ES:BX into a linear address usable by this 32-bit DLL. One of the parameters passed to GetVDMPointer() specifies whether the address is in the segment or selector format. I decided to pass TRUE in the DX register if ES is a selector and FALSE if ES is a segment. This makes RegVDD accessible from both protected- and real-mode 16-bit applications. On return from the dispatch routine, in addition to setting the dwStatus value of the data structure, I also set the carry flag. This allows the VDD to return an error status even if it couldn't access the data structure at all. Now the RegVDDDispatch() routine (Listing 23.1) simply needs to extract the information sent in the registers and, based on the dwCmd field, carry out one of the registry operations using the rest of the values sent in the REGVDD_INFO structure.

Building RegVDD

The VDD requires a typical module definition. You just need to make sure that the initialization and dispatch routines are exported (and the termination routine if you have one) and the library name is VDD. I used the BUILD tool that comes with the Windows NT SDK to build the RegVDD DLL. In section two, I'll discuss using the Visual C++ compiler to build VDDs. The BUILD tool requires a SOURCES file along with the standard makefile that comes with the NT DDK (see REGVDD.DEF, SOURCES, and MAKEFILE on the code disk). VDDs are typically copied to the windows\system32 directory.

Listing 23.1   The dispatch routine.

```
VOID RegVDDDispatch(VOID)
{
    USHORT usSize, usSel;
    REGVDD_INFO * pData;
    ULONG ulAddr;
    HKEY hKey;
    DWORD dwData;
    char szBase[128], szKey[128];
    int i;

    // get data passed in by client
    usSize = getCX();
    usSel = getDX();
    ulAddr = (ULONG)MAKELONG(getBX(), getES());
    pData = (REGVDD_INFO *)GetVDMPointer(ulAddr, usSize, usSel);

    // if don't have valid REGVDD_INFO structure, set carry
    if (pData == NULL) {
        setCF(1);
        return;
    }
```

Listing 23.1 (continued)

```c
pData->dwStatus = TRUE;

switch (pData->dwCmd)
{
   case REGVDD_CMD_CREATESUBKEY:
       // if exists already, it will be opened
       if (RegCreateKeyEx((HKEY)pData->dwRootKey,
           pData->szSubkey, 0, "\0", pData->dwVolatility,
           (REGSAM)pData->dwAccess, NULL, &hKey, &dwData)
           == ERROR_SUCCESS)
               RegCloseKey(hKey);
       else pData->dwStatus = FALSE;
       break;

   case REGVDD_CMD_DELETESUBKEY:
       // split szSubkey into base and key values
       strcpy(szBase, pData->szSubkey);
       for (i=strlen(szBase); i>=0 && szBase[i] != '\\'; i--);
       strcpy(szKey, &(szBase[i+1]));
       szBase[i] = '\0';

       if (RegOpenKeyEx((HKEY)pData->dwRootKey, szBase, 0,
           (REGSAM)pData->dwAccess, &hKey) == ERROR_SUCCESS)
       {
           if (!(RegDeleteKey(hKey, szKey) == ERROR_SUCCESS))
               pData->dwStatus = FALSE;
           RegCloseKey(hKey);
       }
       else pData->dwStatus = FALSE;
       break;

   case REGVDD_CMD_WRITEVALUE:
       if (RegCreateKeyEx((HKEY)pData->dwRootKey,
           pData->szSubkey, 0, "\0", pData->dwVolatility,
           (REGSAM)pData->dwAccess, NULL, &hKey, &dwData) ==
           ERROR_SUCCESS)
       {
           if (!(RegSetValueEx(hKey, pData->szValueName, 0,
               pData->dwValueType, (BYTE *)(pData->szValueData),
               pData->dwValueDataSize) == ERROR_SUCCESS))
               pData->dwStatus = FALSE;
           RegCloseKey(hKey);
       }
       else pData->dwStatus = FALSE;
       break;
```

WTest16, a Sample 16-bit Calling Application

Now that we have RegVDD built, we can turn our attention to the 16-bit application that will be using the VDD to perform registry operations on its behalf. First we need to take a closer look at the three VDD interface routines: RegisterModule(), DispatchCall(), and UnregisterModule(). In ISVBOP.H and ISVBOP.INC, included in the NT DDK, you'll notice that these routines are defined in the following way:

Listing 23.1 (continued)

```
        case REGVDD_CMD_READVALUE:
            if (RegOpenKeyEx((HKEY)pData->dwRootKey,
                pData->szSubkey, 0, (REGSAM)pData->dwAccess,
                &hKey) == ERROR_SUCCESS)
            {
                if (!(RegQueryValueEx(hKey, pData->szValueName, 0,
                    &(pData->dwValueType), (LPBYTE)(pData->szValueData),
                    &(pData->dwValueDataSize)) == ERROR_SUCCESS))
                        pData->dwStatus = FALSE;
                RegCloseKey(hKey);
            }
            else pData->dwStatus = FALSE;
            break;

        case REGVDD_CMD_DELETEVALUE:
            if (RegOpenKeyEx((HKEY)pData->dwRootKey,
                pData->szSubkey, 0, (REGSAM)pData->dwAccess,
                &hKey) == ERROR_SUCCESS)
            {
                if (!(RegDeleteValue(hKey, pData->szValueName)
                    == ERROR_SUCCESS)) pData->dwStatus = FALSE;
                RegCloseKey(hKey);
            }
            else pData->dwStatus = FALSE;
            break;
    }

    // Clear carry if success, set if error
    if (pData->dwStatus == FALSE) setCF(0);
    else setCF(1);

    // Deallocate VDM Pointer
    FreeVDMPointer(ulAddr, (ULONG)usSize, (PBYTE)pData, usSel);
    return;
} // RegVDDDispatch
```

```
#define RegisterModule()    _asm db 0xC4, 0xC4, 0x58, 0x0
#define UnRegisterModule() _asm db 0xC4, 0xC4, 0x58, 0x1
#define DispatchCall()      _asm db 0xC4, 0xC4, 0x58, 0x2
```

The reason we need to insert this information in the form of immediate data is because no assembler worth its salt would accept the instruction represented by 0xC4, 0xC4! Those two bytes decode into the instruction LES AX, SP, which is an invalid instruction. This is the backdoor interface into the NTVDM. When your 16-bit application, running under Windows NT, attempts to execute this invalid instruction, the exception handler in the NTVDM first checks the byte immediately following the offending instruction. If the value is 0x58, it knows that you intentionally executed an invalid instruction for the express purpose of calling a VDD. The following byte is used by the NTVDM to determine whether you were attempting a RegisterModule(), UnRegisterModule(), or DispatchCall() operation.

Unfortunately, some compilers have fairly limited inline assembly capabilities. For instance, Visual C++ does not accept the DB directive. After some searching, I discovered that Visual C++ will accept the _emit directive to specify immediate data a byte at a time. I created the following ISVBOPX.H file for use with the Visual C++ compiler, which I used to compile the sample WTest16 program (Listing 23.2).

```
#define RegisterModule      \
    _asm _emit 0xC4 _asm _emit 0xC4 _asm _emit 0x58 _asm _emit 0
#define UnregisterModule  \
    _asm _emit 0xC4 _asm _emit 0xC4 _asm _emit 0x58 _asm _emit 1
#define DispatchCall        \
    _asm _emit 0xC4 _asm _emit 0xC4 _asm _emit 0x58 _asm _emit 2
```

Listing 23.2 WTest16 — a 16-bit Windows application.

```
// Global variables
REGVDD_INFO regInfo;
REGVDD_INFO far *p = &regInfo;
int iSize = sizeof(REGVDD_INFO);
WORD VDDHandle;
char szVDDName[128] = "REGVDD.DLL";
char szVDDInit[128] = "RegVDDRegisterInit";
char szVDDDisp[128] = "RegVDDDispatch";
BOOL bWinNT;
char szNotNT[] = "Sorry, only available on Windows NT!";
char szCap[] = "WTEST16";
```

The WTest16 program is just a simple little 16-bit Windows application. It has a single menu called Test that contains five menu items: Create Subkey, Delete Subkey, Write Value, Read Value, and Delete Value. The program calls RegVDD.DLL in response to any of these menu items being selected. However, the first thing WTest16 does, during it's WinMain processing, is check whether it is running on Windows NT. If WTest16 tries to execute one of the macros defined in ISVBOPX.H while running under Windows 3.x, the results are very predictable — an application error due to executing an invalid instruction! For this reason, your 16-bit calling applications should always check whether they are running under Windows NT before enabling any operations that involve using the companion VDD. Note that you only use GetVersion() from a 32-bit application to determine whether you are running on Windows NT or Win32s. From a 16-bit application you should compare the value returned from GetWinFlags() with 0x4000. (See Chapter 5, "The Ultimate Windows Version Detector.")

Listing 23.2 (continued)

```
//... in MainWndProc

case WM_CREATE:
   // initialize REGVDD_INFO structure, etc.
   regInfo.dwCmd = REGVDD_CMD_CREATESUBKEY;
   regInfo.dwRootKey = 0x80000001;   //current user
   regInfo.dwVolatility = 0x00000001;
   regInfo.dwAccess = 0x000f003f;   //all access|write
   lstrcpy(regInfo.szSubkey, (LPSTR)"Software\\Microsoft\\RegVDD");
   regInfo.dwValueType = 1;          //REG_SZ;
   lstrcpy(regInfo.szValueName, (LPSTR)"DefaultSetting");
   lstrcpy(regInfo.szValueData, (LPSTR)"Stuff");
   regInfo.dwValueDataSize =        lstrlen(regInfo.szValueData);
   regInfo.dwStatus = 0;

   if (bWinNT) {
       _asm  mov si, offset szVDDName
       _asm  mov di, offset szVDDInit
       _asm  mov bx, offset szVDDDisp
       _asm  RegisterModule
       _asm  mov VDDHandle, ax
   }
   break;

case WM_DESTROY:
   if (bWinNT) {
       _asm  mov ax, VDDHandle
       _asm  UnregisterModule
   }
   PostQuitMessage(0);
   break;
```

```
// check GetWinFlags for a 16-bit app, NOT GetVersion!
bWinNT = (BOOL)(GetWinFlags() & 0x4000);
```

During processing of the WM_CREATE message, WTest16 initializes the REGVDD_INFO structure and calls RegisterModule(), passing the name of the VDD, the name of the initialization routine, and the name of the dispatch routine. A handle to this VDD is returned in the AX register and must be specified in subsequent calls to DispatchCall() and UnregisterModule(). During WM_DESTROY processing, WTest16 calls UnregisterModule() to let the NTVDM know that it can now safely unload RegVDD.DLL.

To demonstrate calling DispatchCall(), take a look at the Read Value registry operation. All the values initialized in the REGVDD_INFO structure during WM_CREATE are still valid except for the dwCmd field. In this case, I set the dwCmd field to REGVDD_CMD_READVALUE. Of course, before calling DispatchCall(), I first check the bWinNT flag. The AX register must contain the VDD handle that was returned by RegisterModule(). The other register contents were the arbitrary decisions I made earlier and are now the values that RegVDD expects. DispatchCall() results in the dispatch routine for the VDD specified by the VDD handle in AX to be called, in my case the RegVDDDispatch() routine in RegVDD.DLL. On return from RegVDDDispatch(), the szValueData field contains the data read from the value and key specified in the REGVDD_INFO structure.

```
case WM_COMMAND:
   switch(wParam)
   {
      case IDM_READVALUE:
         regInfo.dwCmd = REGVDD_CMD_READVALUE;
         if (bWinNT) {
            _asm  mov   ax, VDDHandle
            _asm  les   bx, p         // regInfo
            _asm  mov   cx, iSize     // sizeof regInfo
            _asm  mov   dx, TRUE      // selector
            _asm  DispatchCall
            MessageBox(hWnd, regInfo.szValueData,
               szCap, MB_OK);
         } else MessageBox(hWnd, szNotNT, szCap, MB_OK);
         break;
   //...
   }
```

Summary

All the source code necessary to build RegVDD and WTest16 are included on the code disk. As you can see, it's really not that difficult to use a Windows NT Virtual Device Driver to give your 16-bit applications access to the Win32 API. In the next two sections, you'll see that VDDs can also be used in the more traditional way, by allowing your 16-bit applications to access hardware devices via the appropriate kernel-mode driver.

Writing an Application Intercept VDD

In the previous section, I demonstrated using the application intercept method to essentially connect a Win32 DLL to your 16-bit Windows/DOS application and thus give your 16-bit program limited access to the Win32 API. In this section, I'll demonstrate a more common use for application intercept VDDs, allowing 16-bit applications to access hardware devices. In Windows NT, only kernel-mode drivers are allowed to directly access hardware (ports, memory ranges, etc.). Because most 16-bit applications access a set of common devices (display, parallel port, serial port, keyboard, etc.), built-in VDDs are provided to route requests from 16-bit applications to the appropriate kernel-mode driver to these devices.

If your 16-bit Windows/DOS application needs to access hardware that doesn't already have built-in VDD support, then you'll need to write your own VDD. Furthermore, if a kernel-mode driver for the device isn't already provided, you will need to write one of those too. Take the fairly common case of a 16-bit application that uses its own custom DOS device driver to communicate with a device. Because, in this example, the hardware I/O is isolated in a separate module (the DOS device driver), it is an excellent candidate for using the application intercept method. It really isn't that much effort to modify the DOS device driver (the 16-bit application does not require modification) to call the NTVDM–VDD backdoor directly. Besides, using the application intercept method generally yields better performance. We will replace the original DOS device driver with a stub DOS device driver that merely routes requests on to a companion VDD via the NTVDM–VDD backdoor interface. Then the VDD routes the request on to the kernel-mode driver for that device. I will look at each of these modules in detail, starting at the lowest level — the kernel-mode driver (Figure 23.2).

Figure 23.2 The application intercept method.

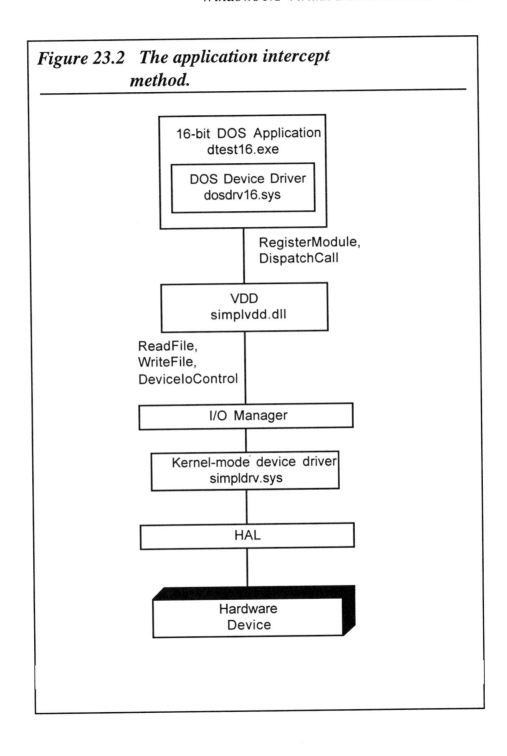

The Kernel-Mode Device Driver — simpldrv.sys

The point of this chapter is not to learn how to write kernel-mode drivers, so I chose a very simple kernel-mode driver sample from the Windows NT DDK (Device Driver Kit): simpldrv.sys. The source code for simpldrv.sys is in the q_a\samples\ddk\instdrv directory of the DDK CD-ROM. I added only three lines of source code to the SimplDrvDispatch() routine in simpldrv.c, which is really just a template for a kernel-mode driver; it really doesn't do anything. I added three lines of code so that the custom I/O Control (IOCTL) code will return a single byte with the value 13 to the 16-bit application when all four components are working properly. I bracketed the three lines of code that I added between pairs of "//".

```
NTSTATUS
SimplDrvDispatch(
    IN PDEVICE_OBJECT DeviceObject,
    IN PIRP           Irp
  )
{
    ...

    // added by PLT
    unsigned char ucValue = 13;
    //
    ...

    switch (irpStack->MajorFunction)
    {
     ...
     case IRP_MJ_DEVICE_CONTROL:
        ...
        switch (ioControlCode)
        {

        case IOCTL_SIMPLDRV_HELLO:
           // Some app is saying hello

           // added by PLT
           RtlMoveMemory(ioBuffer, &ucValue, sizeof(ucValue));
           Irp->IoStatus.Information = sizeof(ucValue);
           //
           break;
        }
        ...
    }
    ...
}
```

I rebuilt `simpldrv.sys` using the BUILD program (shipped with the NT DDK) and the SOURCES file from the original SimplDrv sample code, then I copied it to the `\system32\drivers` directory (the standard location for kernel-mode device drivers in Windows NT). Kernel-mode drivers are typically auto-started via entries in the Registry or started by an application that uses the Session Manager services to demand-load it. As shown later, our kernel-mode driver needs to be available before the first DOS Virtual Machine is created, so I chose to have it loaded and started during system startup. I created the `simpldrv.ini` file that can be used with the RegIni program (in the `ddk\bin` directory) to add the necessary entries to the Registry.

Before continuing, note the symbolic name for this driver. Kernel-mode drivers typically create a symbolic link object in the NT object namespace so that Win32 modules can access them via the Win32 file I/O interface. In this case, SimplDrv creates a symbolic link using the Unicode version of the literal string "\\DosDevices\\SIMPLDRV". Suffice it to say, this translates into Win32 code that opens a file called `\\\\.\\simpldrv`.

```
WCHAR        deviceLinkBuffer[]  = L"\\DosDevices\\SIMPLDRV";
...
    //
    // Create a symbolic link that Win32 apps can specify to gain access
    // to this driver/device
    //

    RtlInitUnicodeString (&deviceLinkUnicodeString,
                          deviceLinkBuffer
                          );

    ntStatus = IoCreateSymbolicLink (&deviceLinkUnicodeString,
                                     &deviceNameUnicodeString
                                     );
```

The Application Intercept VDD — `simplvdd.dll`

The next link in our device driver chain is the VDD. As was the case for the RegVDD VDD from the previous section, most of the work in SimplVDD is in its dispatch routine (Listing 23.3). Because the dispatch routine is always called to carry out a request, the first thing I do is open the file "\\\\.\\simpldrv." The file handle returned from `CreateFile()` can be used to read, write, and send IOCTL requests to SimplDrv.

Listing 23.3 `simplvdd.dll` *— The SimplVDD dispatch routine.*

```
VOID VDDDispatch(VOID)
{
   PCHAR pBuffer;
   USHORT cb;
   ULONG ulAddr;
   DWORD bytes=0L;

   hDevice = CreateFile((LPTSTR)"\\\\.\\simpldrv", GENERIC_READ |
      GENERIC_WRITE, 0, NULL, OPEN_EXISTING, FILE_ATTRIBUTE_NORMAL, NULL);

   cb = getCX();
   ulAddr = (ULONG)MAKELONG(getBX(), getES());
   pBuffer = (PCHAR)GetVDMPointer(ulAddr, (ULONG)cb, FALSE);

   switch (getDX())      // command code is in dx
   {
      case CMD_READ:
         ReadFile(hDevice, pBuffer, (ULONG)cb, &bytes, 0);
         setDI(STAT_OK);
         setCX((USHORT)bytes);
         break;

      case CMD_WRITE:

      case CMD_WRITE_VFY:
         WriteFile(hDevice, pBuffer, (ULONG)cb, &bytes, 0);
         setDI(STAT_OK);
         setCX((USHORT)bytes);
         break;

      case CMD_IN_IOCTL:
         if (DeviceIoControl(hDevice, IOCTL_SIMPLDRV_HELLO,
            NULL, 0, pBuffer, cb, &bytes, NULL))
setDI(STAT_OK);
         else setDI(STAT_GF);
         break;

      default:
         setDI(STAT_CE);         // unsupported command
         break;
   }

   FreeVDMPointer(ulAddr, (ULONG)cb, (PCHAR)pBuffer, FALSE);
   CloseHandle(hDevice);
   return;
} // VDDDispatch
```

I'll make an arbitrary decision that the companion DOS device driver will pass a command code in the DX register, the transfer length in the CX register, the address of a buffer in ES:BX, and receive status back in DI. Furthermore, I'll map command codes into the codes that DOS device drivers receive from DOS. For simplicity, I will only support read, write (and write-with-verify), and input IOCTL. For a truly functional kernel-mode device driver, read and write requests would be passed on to the kernel-mode driver using the Win32 ReadFile() and WriteFile() routines as I've shown. Of course, the SimplDrv driver doesn't really handle read and write requests. It only processes the custom I/O Control code IOCTL_SIMPLDRV_HELLO. When an input IOCTL request comes into the dispatch routine, I route it to SimplDrv using the Win32 DeviceIoControl() routine.

As you recall from the example in section one, you must use the register manipulation routines provided by NTVDM to access register contents passed in from the 16-bit calling code. Also, any pointers passed in from the 16-bit code must be converted into a linear address usable by the 32-bit VDD code. GetVDMPointer() is used for that purpose. Note that I've made an assumption that the address passed in ES:BX is in segment:offset form rather than selector:offset form [by passing FALSE as the last parameter to GetVDMPointer()]. If the VDD needs to handle both scenarios, you could pass a flag in one of the registers (as I did in the RegVDD example).

I built simplvdd.dll and copied it to the \system32 directory. (You also may copy it to the \system32\drivers directory if you prefer.)

The Stub DOS Device Driver — dosdrv16.sys

The stub DOS device driver is almost trivially simple. Any hardware I/O that existed in the original DOS device driver is stripped out and replaced by calls to the NTVDM–VDD backdoor interface [RegisterModule() and DispatchCall()]. When dosdrv16.sys (Listing 23.4) initializes, it loads the name of the VDD in DS:SI, the name of the VDD dispatch routine in DS:BX, the name of the VDD initialization function in DS:SI, and then calls RegisterModule(), which returns a handle in AX that is used for subsequent calls to DispatchCall().

I should note an odd discrepancy in the DDK documentation for RegisterModule(). The reference manual implies that the initialization routine of the VDD is an optional parameter; you can omit specifying it by setting both DS and SI to zero. Well, because the VDD name and the VDD dispatch routine are also passed in DS:SI and DS:BX (and are certainly not optional), I hardly think that setting DS to zero is a valid option! There was talk of changing the specification so that the VDD initialization routine would be passed in ES:SI instead, but I've not heard that such a change has been implemented in any shipping versions of Windows NT. Just to be safe, I load the ES register with the value of the DS register before calling RegisterModule().

When any command other than initialization is sent to dosdrv16.sys, it just loads the command code, the transfer length, and the buffer in the registers I specified in SimplVDD and then calls DispatchCall().

```
xor   dx,dx               ;some other command
mov   dl,RH.RHC_CMD        ;dx = command code
mov   cx,RH.RHC_CNT        ;cx = count
mov   ax,RH.RHC_SEG        ;es:bx = addr of data
mov   bx,RH.RHC_OFF
mov   es,ax                ;finally, load VDD handle
mov   ax,word ptr cs:[VDD_hVDD]
DispatchCall               ;call Dispatch in VDD
                           ;returns with status in di
```

Windows NT creates a virtual DOS environment for 16-bit applications to run in. Any DOS device drivers or TSRs that you want loaded automatically in that DOS environment should be listed in the config.nt file in the \system32 directory. Copy dosdrv16.sys to the system32\drivers directory and add the following line to the config.nt file:

Listing 23.4   dosdrv16.sys — *The Stub DOS device driver.*

```
DH_NAME db 'DRV16   '          ;char device name
...
VDD_DllName      db  "SIMPLVDD.DLL", 0
VDD_InitFunc     db  "VDDInit", 0
VDD_DispFunc     db  "VDDDispatch", 0
...

BOOTUP:
    ...
    mov  si,offset VDD_DllName  ;load regs for VDD
    mov  bx,offset VDD_DispFunc
    mov  di,offset VDD_InitFunc
    mov  ax,ds
    mov  es,ax                  ;just to be save
    RegisterModule              ;calls the VDD
    jnc  save_hVDD              ;if NC then success
    mov  di,STAT_GF             ;set failure status
    jmp  EXIT                   ;return via common exit

save_hVDD:
    mov  [VDD_hVDD],ax          ;save handle in ax
    mov  di,STAT_OK             ;load OK status
    jmp  EXIT                   ;return via common exit
```

```
device=%SystemRoot%\system32\drivers\dosdrv16.sys
```

A Sample 16-bit Application — dtest16.exe

Now, finally, we need a 16-bit Windows/DOS application to complete the chain. dtest16.exe (Listing 23.5) is a simple little DOS application. It opens the stub DOS device driver and sets the device to raw mode using interrupt 21h function 44h. To perform read or write requests, simply call the C library _read() and _write() routines with the handle of the opened DOS device driver. To request an input IOCTL, call interrupt 21h function 44h subfunction 2h. The input IOCTL expects the device handle in BX, the transfer length in CX, and the address of a buffer in DS:DX. Because we know the kernel-mode SimplDrv driver will only be passing back a single byte value, I set the transfer length to a value of one.

Once all three drivers (dosdrv16.sys, simplvdd.dll, and simpldrv.sys) have been built and installed, you need to do a complete system shutdown and restart for all the changes to take effect. After that, dtest16.exe produces the predicted results.

```
Open succeeded.
Device IOCTL data = 13
```

Summary

By adding an application intercept VDD and making a few changes to your original 16-bit application, even your favorite old hardware-dependent DOS and Windows 3.x applications can run under NT without too much effort. Of course, if a kernel-mode driver doesn't already exist for your device, then it is a bit more involved.

In the next section, I'll demonstrate a VDD that uses the NTVDM intercept method. Although this method is not usually as efficient as the application intercept method, it has the advantage of requiring no changes to the original 16-bit application. All the source code necessary to build simpldrv.sys, simplvdd.dll, dosdrv16.sys, and dtest16.exe are included on the code disk.

Writing an NTVDM Intercept VDD

In Windows NT, only kernel-mode drivers are allowed to directly access hardware (ports, memory ranges, etc.). Because the VDD is just a special-purpose 32-bit DLL, it doesn't have sufficient privilege to access hardware either. NTVDM intercept VDDs are used to trap these privileged operations and route them to the appropriate kernel-mode driver. To support 16-bit applications that access custom hardware on Windows NT requires writing both a VDD and a kernel-mode driver. NTVDM intercept

VDDs generally produce poorer performance than application intercept VDDs, because the VDM traps the device access at a lower level. However, the NTVDM intercept method does not required any changes to the original 16-bit application.

Accessing Devices

Applications use three very common methods to communicate with devices: port I/O, memory-mapped I/O, and DMA. The NTVDM provides services to allow a VDD and companion kernel-mode driver to support each of these methods of I/O (Figure 23.3). A VDD can also be used to translate real-mode addresses into flat 32-bit addresses and to simulate hardware interrupts. Although DMA is a common and efficient means of transferring data between physical memory and the device, it is a little beyond the

---

Listing 23.5   dtest16.exe — A 16-bit application.

```
// open the dos device driver by name and set to raw mode
if ((hDriver = _open("DRV16", O_BINARY | O_RDWR)) == -1) {
   printf("Couldn't open device driver\n");
   return;
} else printf("Open succeeded.\n");

inregs.x.ax = 0x4400;
inregs.x.bx = hDriver;
_intdos(&inregs, &outregs);        // int21 DOS ioctl

if ((outregs.x.dx & 0x80) > 0) {   // if character device
   inregs.h.al = 1;
   inregs.h.dh = 0;
   inregs.h.dl = outregs.h.dl | 0x20;
   _intdos(&inregs, &outregs);     // set to raw mode
}

// could read and write to the device using
// _write(hDriver,..) and _read(hDriver,..)

// do a device I/O Control Input from the device
inregs.x.ax = 0x4402;
inregs.x.bx = hDriver;
inregs.x.cx = 1;                // just one byte
_segread(&sregs);
inregs.x.dx = (unsigned int)(&ucData);
_intdosx(&inregs,&outregs,&sregs);

printf("Device IOCTL data = %d\n", ucData);
_close(hDriver);
```

Figure 23.3   The NTVDM intercept method.

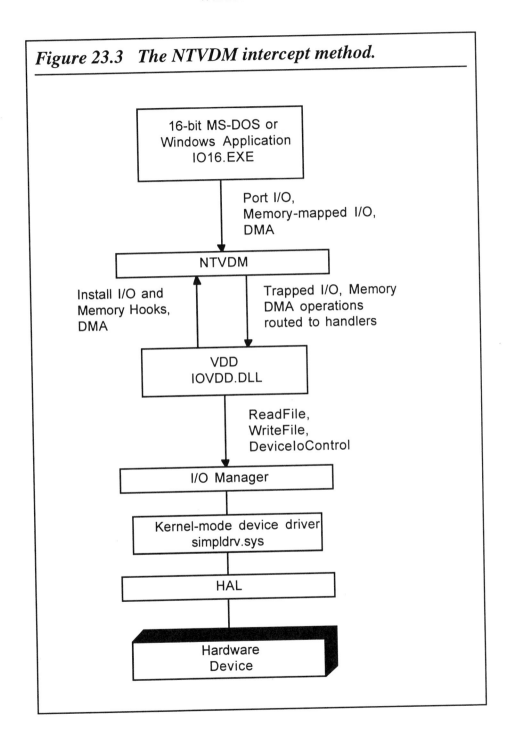

scope of this chapter. Instead I'll provide a working example of a VDD that handles both port I/O and memory-mapped I/O.

It is somewhat common for devices to use both port I/O and memory-mapped I/O. For instance, an adapter card might assign its registers to a range of port addresses so that applications can read and write to the registers using in and out instructions. It might also claim some memory in the range between C000h and DFFFh that is normally reserved for adapter ROM. Applications would access that range of memory just like any other range of memory (using instructions such as mov and cmp).

To make the sample as simple as possible and usable on systems without special hardware devices, I decided to invent a fictitious adapter card and make up an I/O protocol to go with it. Imagine this adapter card has five 8-bit registers that it assigned to I/O port addresses 300h–304h. The adapter also uses a 128-byte area of memory starting at address CC00h to transfer data between the adapter and the PC. Ordinarily adapters provide jumpers to allow users to adjust the port locations and memory locations that it uses, but our simple adapter is not that generous.

The five registers correspond to IDENTIFY, READ, WRITE, COUNT, and STATUS operations. To determine if my adapter is installed, an application can read from the IDENTIFY register (port 300h) and compare the result with the known ID of my adapter (which happens to be 13). To let the adapter know that you want to read or write from its memory, an application writes an arbitrary value to the READ (port 301h) or WRITE register (port 302h). The COUNT register (port 303h) is used to let the adapter know how many bytes the application wants to transfer for reads and writes. The application can also read from the COUNT register after the transfer is complete to see how many bytes were actually transferred. Applications read from the STATUS register (port 304h) to determine when the transfer is complete.

A Sample 16-bit Application — io16.exe

I wrote a simple 16-bit DOS application, io16.exe, to demonstrate this I/O protocol. I created some definitions for the port and memory addresses that io16.c uses.

```
#define PORT_IDENTIFY    0x300
#define PORT_READ        0x301
#define PORT_WRITE       0x302
#define PORT_COUNT       0x303
#define PORT_STATUS      0x304
#define MIO_SEG          0xCC00
#define MIO_RANGE        128
```

The first thing I do is check if the adapter is installed by reading from the IDENTIFY register. If my adapter is installed, it will return an ID value of 13.

```
// Check that the card is responding
_asm  mov  dx, PORT_IDENTIFY
_asm  in   al, dx
_asm  mov  byteID, al

printf("Port I/O: ID %d read from port 0x%x\n", byteID, PORT_IDENTIFY);
```

Next, I write a small buffer of data (64 bytes) to address CC00h. To let the driver know I'm doing a write operation, I output the number of bytes (64) to the COUNT register and output a value of 1 (the value is arbitrary) to the WRITE register. Now the adapter knows that I've transferred some data to it and it can now process it in whatever way it sees fit. The application polls the value in the STATUS register until it returns a value of 1, signifying that the operation is complete. Once the transfer is done I can read from the COUNT register to find out how many bytes were actually written.

```
unsigned char byteID, byteCount, i;
char dataBuffer[64];
char far *pMIOAddress;

// initialize output data buffer
pMIOAddress = (char far *)(((unsigned long)MIO_SEG) << 16);
for (i=0; i < 64; i++) dataBuffer[i]=i;

// copy to memory-mapped I/O area
_fmemcpy(pMIOAddress, dataBuffer, 64);

// set the data byte count
_asm  mov  dx, PORT_COUNT
_asm  mov  al, 64
_asm  out  dx, al

// send the write command signifying data ready
_asm  mov  dx, PORT_WRITE
_asm  mov  al, 1
_asm  out  dx, al

// wait until transfer complete
_asm  mov  dx, PORT_STATUS
_asm  WriteLoop:
_asm  in   al, dx
_asm  cmp  al, 1
_asm  jne  WriteLoop

// check how many bytes actually written
_asm  mov  dx, PORT_COUNT
_asm  in   al, dx
_asm  mov  byteCount, al

printf("%d bytes written.\n", byteCount);
```

The read operation follows a similar path. I output the maximum number of bytes I want to read to the COUNT register and write a value of 1 (again arbitrary) to the READ register. I poll the STATUS register until it returns a value of 1, indicating that the data has been transferred from the adapter. Then I read from the COUNT register to see how many bytes were successfully transferred.

```
// set the data byte count
_asm  mov  dx, PORT_COUNT
_asm  mov  al, 64
_asm  out  dx, al

// send the read command
_asm  mov  dx, PORT_READ
_asm  mov  al, 1
_asm  out  dx, al

// wait until transfer complete
_asm  mov  dx, PORT_STATUS
_asm  ReadLoop:
_asm  in   al, dx
_asm  cmp  al, 1
_asm  jne  ReadLoop

// check how many bytes actually available
_asm  mov  dx, PORT_COUNT
_asm  in   al, dx
_asm  mov  byteCount, al

// copy memory-mapped I/O area to local buffer
_fmemcpy(dataBuffer, pMIOAddress, byteCount);

printf("%d bytes read.\n", byteCount);
for (i=0; i < byteCount; i++) printf("%c", dataBuffer[i]);
printf("\n");
```

Of course, under Windows NT, the in and out instructions as well as the attempt to copy memory from address CC00h are privileged and thus will fail. To accommodate the 16-bit application io16.exe, I need to write an NTVDM intercept VDD.

VDD Main Entry Point

An NTVDM intercept VDD is not called or initialized explicitly by the 16-bit application, so any initialization work must be done in its main DLL entry point. My VDD, iovdd.dll, needs to tell the VDM which I/O ports it uses and where the adapter memory is located. The main entry point of an NTVDM intercept VDD is called (with the DLL_PROCESS_ATTACH notification) each time a VDM is created (Listing 23.6). This happens each time a user logs onto a Windows NT session and the first time a 16-bit application is started in any DOS shells that are running. The main entry point is only called with DLL_PROCESS_DETACH when each DOS shell is closed.

Listing 23.6   iovdd.dll — *VDD main entry point.*

```
// Globals
HANDLE hVDD = NULL;
VDD_IO_PORTRANGE portRange;
ULONG ulAddr;
PBYTE pMem;
BYTE byteStatus = 0;
BYTE byteCount = 0;
BOOLEAN bIoHooked = FALSE;
BOOLEAN bMemHooked= FALSE;
BOOLEAN bMemAllocated = FALSE;
BOOLEAN bDebug = TRUE;

...
VDD_IO_HANDLERS ioHandlers;
hVDD = hInst;

...
case DLL_PROCESS_ATTACH:
    Debug("IOVDD: VDDLibMain - Attach\n");

    portRange.First = IOVDD_PORT_START;
    portRange.Last  = IOVDD_PORT_END;

    ioHandlers.inb_handler   = IoVDD_ReadByte;
    ioHandlers.inw_handler   = NULL;
    ioHandlers.insb_handler  = NULL;
    ioHandlers.insw_handler  = NULL;
    ioHandlers.outb_handler  = IoVDD_WriteByte;
    ioHandlers.outw_handler  = NULL;
    ioHandlers.outsb_handler = NULL;
    ioHandlers.outsw_handler = NULL;
```

In response to the DLL_PROCESS_ATTACH, I fill out a VDD_IO_PORTRANGE structure that specifies the starting and ending I/O port address used by my adapter. I call the VDDInstallIOHook() routine to install my own handler for that range of ports. I also fill out an VDD_IO_HANDLERS structure with pointers to my own port handler routines. A VDD must provide at least the byte-in and byte-out routines. The word and string handlers are optional; if they are not provided, the VDM will emulate them by calling the VDD's byte handlers multiple times. If your device uses noncontiguous ranges of port locations, then you can pass multiple VDD_IO_PORTRANGE structures to VDDInstallIOHook(). You can only specify one set of port handlers to support all the ports that are hooked by your VDD. If the ports that I'm attempting to hook have already been hooked by a different VDD, then my attempt to hook them will fail — only one VDD can hook any given port or memory range.

Listing 23.6 *(continued)*

```
        if (!(bIoHooked = VDDInstallIOHook(hVDD,
            1, &portRange, &ioHandlers)))
        {
            Debug("IOVDD: Port hook failed");
            return FALSE;
        }


        ulAddr = (ULONG)MAKELONG(0, 0xCC00);
        pMem = (PBYTE)GetVDMPointer(ulAddr, IOVDD_MIO_RANGE, 0);
        if (!(bMemHooked = VDDInstallMemoryHook(
            hVDD, pMem, IOVDD_MIO_RANGE,
            (PVDD_MEMORY_HANDLER)IoVDD_Memory)))
        {
            Debug("IOVDD: Memory hook failed");
            return FALSE;
        }
        break;

case DLL_PROCESS_DETACH:
        Debug("IOVDD: VDDLibMain - Detach\n");
        if (bIoHooked)
            VDDDeInstallIOHook(hVDD, 1, &portRange);
        if (bMemHooked)
            VDDDeInstallMemoryHook(hVDD, pMem, IOVDD_MIO_RANGE);
        if (bMemAllocated)
            VDDFreeMem(hVDD, (PVOID)pMem, IOVDD_MIO_RANGE);
        if (pMem)
            FreeVDMPointer(ulAddr, IOVDD_MIO_RANGE, pMem, FALSE);
        break;
```

I create a 32-bit flat memory address for the adapter memory [using `GetVDM-Pointer()`] and install a memory handler for those addresses using the `VDDInstall-MemoryHook()` routine.

In response to the `DLL_PROCESS_DETACH`, I deinstall any I/O or memory hooks that I installed during `DLL_PROCESS_ATTACH`. I also release the memory that my memory handler allocated (as we'll see later).

VDD Memory Handler

Applications aren't allowed to access physical memory addresses under Windows NT. In particular, the memory region normally used by adapter cards is initially marked invalid so attempts to access that memory result in page faults. When the memory manager detects this it asks the VDM to check whether any VDDs have hooked the range of memory that is being accessed. If so, the VDM calls the memory handler installed for that memory range. The memory handler usually either allocates a buffer of memory to be used for that range of addresses or increments the `CS:IP` of the 16-bit application so that it doesn't continue to generate page faults.

In the first case, the memory handler allocates a buffer of memory for that memory range. The next time the 16-bit application attempts to access that memory, instead of generating a page fault it accesses the buffer of memory that was allocated. Because the memory hook is not called again, this scheme works well only if the VDD has a method for determining when to write the buffer to the device and when to refresh the buffer with data read from the device. My I/O protocol uses port I/O addresses to control the read and write operations, so I can use the simple method of allocating a buffer of memory to cover the hooked memory range. When my port I/O handlers receive output requests to the `WRITE` and `READ` registers, they know it is time to write the allocated buffer to the device or read from the device into the buffer. This lets the application access my buffer as if it was directly accessing memory on the adapter card.

```
VOID IoVDD_Memory(ULONG ulAddress, ULONG RWFlags)
{
    Debug("IOVDD: IoVDD_Memory\n");
    bMemAllocated = VDDAllocMem(hVDD, pMem,
        IOVDD_MIO_RANGE);
    return;
} // IoVDD_Memory
```

If the I/O protocol doesn't provide enough information to use the scheme I described, then you may have to use a more brute force approach. For instance, instead of allocating a buffer of memory to cover the adapter memory range, continue to let your memory hook receive notifications that the memory was accessed. Then the memory hook could decode the instruction that caused the page fault [by using the GetCS( ) and GetIP( ) routines to find the instruction and using GetVDMPointer( ) to translate it into a flat 32-bit address] and take some appropriate action based on the instruction and its operands.

VDD Port I/O Handler Routines

When a 16-bit application executes an in or out instruction, the VDM intercepts it and checks if any VDDs have registered a handler for that port. So, when io16.exe executes an in instruction to a port in the range 300h–304h, my IoVDD_ReadByte( ) routine is called (Listing 23.7). Likewise, when io16.exe executes an out instruction to a port in the same range, my IoVDD_WriteByte( ) routine is called (Listing 23.8).

Listing 23.7   Read handler routine.

```
VOID IoVDD_ReadByte(WORD wPort, PBYTE byteData)
{
    HANDLE hDevice=NULL;
    DWORD dwCount=0L;

    // handle ports that apps reads from
    switch(wPort)
    {
        case IOVDD_PORT_IDENTIFY:
            Debug("IOVDD: IOVDD_PORT_IDENTIFY\n");
            hDevice = CreateFile((LPTSTR)"\\\\.\\simpldrv", GENERIC_READ |
                GENERIC_WRITE, 0, NULL, OPEN_EXISTING, FILE_ATTRIBUTE_NORMAL, NULL);
            DeviceIoControl(hDevice, (DWORD)IOCTL_SIMPLDRV_HELLO,
                NULL, 0, byteData, 1, &dwCount, NULL);
            CloseHandle(hDevice);
            break;

        case IOVDD_PORT_STATUS:
            Debug("IOVDD: IOVDD_PORT_STATUS\n");
            *byteData = byteStatus;
            break;

        case IOVDD_PORT_COUNT:
            Debug("IOVDD: IOVDD_PORT_COUNT\n");
            *byteData = byteCount;
            break;

        default:
            Debug("IOVDD: Unsupported port read\n");
            break;
    }
    return;
} // IoVDD_ReadByte
```

Listing 23.8 Write handler routine.

```
VOID IoVDD_WriteByte(WORD wPort, BYTE byteData)
{
    HANDLE hDevice=NULL;
    DWORD dwCount=0L;

    // handle ports that apps write to
    switch(wPort)
    {
        case IOVDD_PORT_READ:
            Debug("IOVDD: IOVDD_PORT_READ\n");
            byteStatus = FALSE;
            // request kernel-mode driver to read,
            // when read completes, set status
            if (byteCount > 35) byteCount = 35;
            memcpy(pMem,
                "This would be data read from device",
                byteCount);
            byteStatus = TRUE;
            break;

        case IOVDD_PORT_WRITE:
            Debug("IOVDD: IOVDD_PORT_WRITE\n");
            byteStatus = FALSE;
            // request kernel-mode driver to write,
            // when write request completes, set status
            byteStatus = TRUE;
            break;

        case IOVDD_PORT_COUNT:
            Debug("IOVDD: IOVDD_PORT_COUNT\n");
            // this is how many bytes to write
            byteCount = byteData;
            if (byteCount > IOVDD_MIO_RANGE)
                byteCount = IOVDD_MIO_RANGE;
            break;

        default:
            Debug("IOVDD: Unsupported port write\n");
            break;
    }

    return;
} // IoVDD_WriteByte
```

The byte-in handler receives as parameters the specific port address that was accessed and a pointer to the memory location where the data was to be copied to. The byte-in handler then translates that request into calls to its companion kernel-mode driver, typically by either using the ReadFile() or DeviceIoControl() Win32 routines. To demonstrate this, I translate read requests to the IDENTIFY port into calls to SimplDrv's I/O control dispatch routine. SimplDrv always returns a value of 13 when sent an IOCTL_SIMPLDRV_HELLO request.

The other two registers that are read by application programs are the STATUS and COUNT registers. In each case, I return the value of a global variable that is set during write operations.

The byte-out handler needs to do a little more work. When an application writes a value to the READ register, the VDD would normally call the kernel-mode device driver to transfer information from the adapter into the data buffer. When this operation is complete, it sets the byteStatus global variable to TRUE. The next time the application reads from the STATUS register it will know that the transfer is complete. Likewise, when a value is written to the WRITE register, the VDD knows to write out the data in its buffer to the kernel-mode driver.

I don't have a fully functional kernel-mode driver (or adapter card!), so I just ignore the write request and fill the buffer with some hard-code information on read requests.

Building and Installing iovdd.dll

The module definition file for iovdd.dll only needs to export the main entry point of the DLL, VDDLibMain. I included a SOURCES file for building the DLL using the DDK BUILD tool. The iovdd.dll file needs to be copied to the windows\system32 directory.

Because NTVDM intercept VDDs aren't explicitly loaded by an application [such as when an application calls RegisterModule() for an application intercept VDD], I need to reference my VDD in the HKEY_LOCAL_MACHINE\SYSTEM\CurrentControlSet\Control\VirtualDeviceDrivers key in the Registry. This will ensure that my VDD gets loaded whenever a new VDM is created. To do this, I add the name of my VDD to the "VDD" value. If multiple VDDs are listed, their names are separated by a single NULL character.

```
VDD:REG_MULTI_SZ:IOVDD.DLL
```

Running IO16.EXE

After all the components (io16.exe, iovdd.dll, and simpldrv.sys) have been built and the drivers have been installed, you need to shutdown and restart your system before running io16.exe. When io16.exe is run on my system, it displays the following output, which is just what we expect.

```
Port I/O: ID 13 read from port 0x300
64 bytes written.
35 bytes read.
This would be data read from device
```

I sprinkled calls to OutputDebugString() (via my private Debug procedure) throughout iovdd.dll. I captured the following output to my secondary system running the kernel debugger. You can see that each time the 16-bit application executed an in or out instruction or attempted to access the physical memory range used by my adapter, the IOVDD handler routines were called.

```
IOVDD: VDDLibMain - Attach
IOVDD: VDDLibMain - Attach
IOVDD: IOVDD_PORT_IDENTIFY
SIMPLDRV.SYS: IRP_MJ_CREATE
SIMPLDRV.SYS: IRP_MJ_DEVICE_CONTROL
SIMPLDRV.SYS: IRP_MJ_CLOSE
IOVDD: IoVDD_Memory
IOVDD: IOVDD_PORT_COUNT
IOVDD: IOVDD_PORT_WRITE
IOVDD: IOVDD_PORT_STATUS
IOVDD: IOVDD_PORT_COUNT
IOVDD: IOVDD_PORT_COUNT
IOVDD: IOVDD_PORT_READ
IOVDD: IOVDD_PORT_STATUS
IOVDD: IOVDD_PORT_COUNT
```

Summary

Trying these samples on a system running NT shouldn't cause problems because iovdd.dll isn't really accessing the physical ports or the memory at CC00h. Running io16.exe under DOS, however, could cause problems if you have adapters that are also using those ports or memory locations.

NTVDM intercept VDDs are convenient in that they do not require that 16-bit applications be modified. However, it is generally slower to trap the I/O at this lower level. If the I/O code is fairly isolated and it would not be too difficult to replace with direct calls to an application intercept VDD, then this method is best for performance. Still, many powerful NTVDM services make it easy to write sophisticated VDDs that do not require any modification on the part of the 16-bit application at all.

All the source code necessary to build io16.exe, iovdd.dll, and simpldrv.sys are included on the code disk.

Supporting a 16-bit Hardware-Dependent Application

As a developer of applications for the HP ScanJet family of scanners, have encountered a large body of third-party 16-bit applications already in use. I want a solution that allows all of these applications to run unmodified under Windows NT. One bit of good fortune is that our current family of scanners uses a SCSI interface, and Windows NT provides a rich set of kernel-mode device drivers for the SCSI interface, in addition to parallel and serial interfaces.

The Windows NTVDM and Device Drivers

DOS and 16-bit Windows applications can run under Windows NT because of the emulation provided by the Windows NT Virtual DOS Machine (NTVDM or just VDM) environment subsystem. The VDM is actually a multithreaded Win32 application that provides a complete virtual DOS machine environment. When the user starts a DOS or 16-bit Windows application, the Win32 subsystem detects the DOS executable, starts a VDM process, loads drivers from the config.nt file, and loads the application into the VDM's virtual address space and executes it. Each DOS application is placed in its own VDM process with a private virtual address space containing DOS emulation code and any DOS device drivers that were loaded. For 16-bit Windows applications, the VDM loads the WOW (Windows on Win32) environment, essentially a multithreaded VDM, where all 16-bit Windows applications are loaded and executed as separate threads of a single VDM process. The VDM calls the Win32 subsystem — and occasionally the NT executive — to perform tasks on its behalf, such as windowing operations.

This architecture allows all 16-bit Windows applications to run in the same virtual address space (as they must to be compatible with Windows 3.1) and gives DOS applications the illusion of having a DOS environment all to themselves. Windows NT also provides for process isolation, which is fundamental to protecting the integrity of Windows NT processes. This VDM layer allows "most" 16-bit applications to run under Windows NT without modification.

The problem is the hardware-dependent 16-bit applications, such as a DOS program that directly accesses a scanner or other nonstandard hardware device. Under Windows NT, only kernel-mode drivers have sufficient privilege to perform DMA, or directly access I/O ports or perform memory-mapped I/O. Therefore, when 16-bit applications attempt these operations, the VDM intercepts the attempt and routes it to the kernel-mode driver that is allowed to perform the direct hardware access. The Virtual Device Driver (VDD) interface, with the help of the VDM, provides a way for hardware-dependent 16-bit applications to work under both 16-bit environments

(Windows 3.1 and DOS) and Windows NT. The VDD serves as a bridge between the 16-bit application and the 32-bit kernel-mode driver. When 16-bit applications attempt a privileged hardware access, the operation is typically intercepted by the VDM and sent to the VDD, where it is translated into a request for the appropriate kernel-mode driver. Windows NT provides standard VDDs for the mouse, keyboard, parallel ports, serial ports, and the display. Additional VDDs can be created fairly easily.

Windows NT supports the SCSI interface through a layered set of kernel-mode drivers, as shown in Figure 23.4. Win32 applications access SCSI devices at the "Class" driver layer by using the Win32 file API. Each SCSI Class driver supports a specific category of device types, such as hard disks, CD-ROMs, or scanners. Supporting a new type of SCSI device typically requires writing only a Class driver. The next layer is the SCSI Port driver. There is a single SCSI Port driver for each platform (e.g., one for Intel platforms, one for MIPS platforms, and so on). The Port driver is responsible for all synchronization operations and for any operating system or platform-dependent operations. This allows the Class and Miniport drivers to be portable

Figure 23.4   Windows NT SCSI interface support.

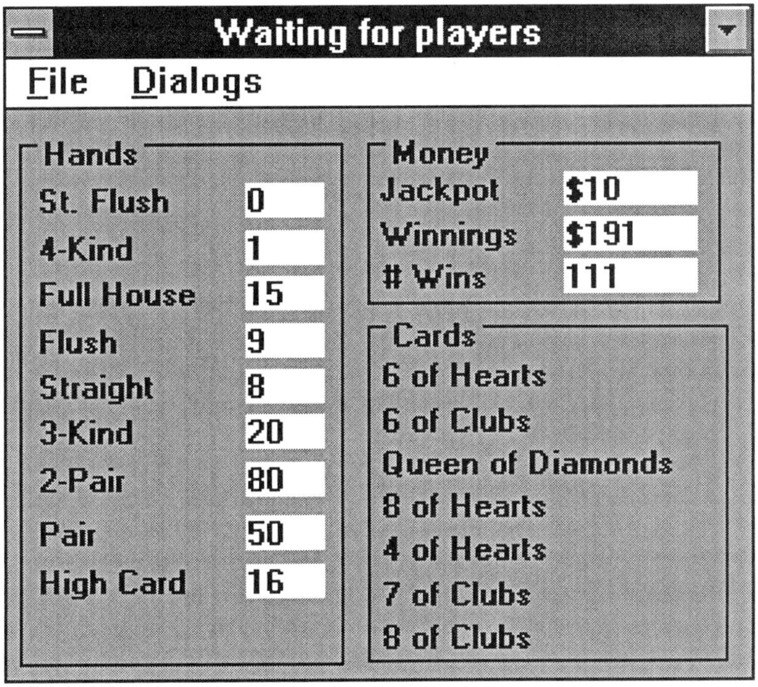

across platforms. The Miniport drivers support specific host bus adapters (HBAs), such as the Adaptec 154x series and the NCR 53c700 series. The Miniport drivers isolate the Port and Class drivers from any HBA-specific details.

When you first boot Windows NT, it calls each Miniport driver's initialization routine. The Miniport driver calls the Port driver's initialization routine and its own HwFindAdapter() routine to look for any corresponding HBAs installed. The Port driver scans through all possible targets and gathers inquiry data for each logical unit. When the Class drivers initialize, they access this INQUIRY information and claim any devices that match their device type. For instance, the newly developed SCSI Scanner Class driver claims any Scanner device types (06h) or Processor device types (03h). Notice that devices are found and claimed at initialization time, so all SCSI devices must be powered on when Windows NT boots, or they won't be recognized.

Deciding Which VDD Intercept Method to Use

There are two methods for implementing VDDs, again as shown in Figure 23.4. The methods are distinguished by what intercepts the hardware access — the VDM or a portion of the 16-bit application (typically a 16-bit driver).

In the first method, modify the 16-bit application or driver to replace any direct hardware access with calls to its companion VDD, which then routes these requests to the appropriate kernel-mode driver. The intercept in this case occurs at a high level as compared to intercepting attempts to directly manipulate the hardware. This typically results in better performance but requires rewriting part of the application or, at the very least, replacing the 16-bit driver with a stub driver that calls the VDD.

In the second method, let the VDM intercept the hardware access at a very low level. The VDD hooks the unique range of I/O ports and/or memory areas it uses. When the application or driver tries to access these ports or memory locations, the VDM intercepts the operation and routes it to the appropriate VDD. The VDD then calls the kernel-mode driver to perform the actual hardware access. Although performance usually suffers with this method, no portion of the 16-bit application or driver requires modifications.

Finally, you could use a combination of application and NTVDM-based intercept methods, which would allow you to intercept time-critical operations at a higher level in the stub driver, and use the NTVDM intercept method for the remaining, less performance-driven, operations.

Because most applications supporting the HP scanners use a common DOS device driver to communicate with the scanner, I chose the first method. This method yields better performance and is really no more difficult to implement than the second method. It required writing a replacement stub DOS device driver and an application-based intercept VDD. The 16-bit applications themselves required no changes, because the stub DOS device driver supplied the same interface as the original DOS device driver. VDDs are implemented as 32-bit DLLs, so you can also use them to export a 32-bit device API for your future Win32 applications. Remember that the three kernel-mode SCSI driver layers I needed already existed — it's a bit more work if you need to add a SCSI Class driver.

Creating the Stub DOS Device Driver

I'll briefly describe the source code for hpscan16.sys, the stub DOS device driver shown in hpscan16.asm (Listing 23.9) and hpscan16.inc (Listing 23.10). In the description, I'll refer to DOS, because it is Windows NT's job to accurately and fully simulate any DOS operations the DOS device driver relies on. It isn't necessary to be a DOS device driver expert; this driver is truly a "stub."

Listing 23.9   hpscan16.asm— Stub DOS device driver.

```
.MODEL small
;**************************************************
;
; Filename: hpscan16.asm
; Purpose:  Stub DOS Device Driver. Pass device
;   "HPSCAN" requests to the VDD, hpscan32.dll.
; Environment: MSDOS, Windows NT.
; (C) Hewlett-Packard Company 1993.
;**************************************************
;
INCLUDE hpscan16.inc    ;private
INCLUDE isvbop.inc      ;NT DDK

SUBTTL Segment and data definitions
        ASSUME  CS:CSEG,DS:NOTHING,ES:NOTHING
CSEG    SEGMENT


;-------------------------------------------------
; Resident data area - variables needed after init
;-------------------------------------------------

;**--- Device Header, must be at offset zero ---**
SCAN_HEADER:
        dd -1           ;becomes ptr to next req hdr
        dw 0C000H       ;character, supports IOCTL
        dw offset STRAT     ;Strategy routine
        dw offset IDVR      ;Interrupt routine
DH_NAME db 'HPSCAN  '       ;char device name

;**---- Request Header addr, saved by STRAT ----**
RH_PTRA LABEL   DWORD
RH_PTRO         dw  ?   ;offset
RH_PTRS         dw  ?   ;segment
```

Listing 23.9 (continued)

```
;**------------- Define Stack Space ------------**
STK_SEG  dw  ?          ;Save original stack segment
STK_PTR  dw  ?          ;Save original stack pointer
STACK    dw  200 DUP (0)    ;Local stack
TOP_STK  dw  ?          ;Top of local stack


;**--------------- VDD information -------------**
VDD_DllName      db  "HPSCAN32.DLL", 0
VDD_InitFunc     db  "VDDInit", 0
VDD_DispFunc     db  "VDDDispatch", 0
VDD_hVDD         dw  ?


;**-------------- Copyright Info --------------**
  db '(C) Copyright Hewlett-Packard Company 1993.'
  db 'All rights reserved.'

SUBTTL Device Strategy & Interrupt entry points

;**--------------- STRAT routine --------------**
STRAT  proc  far          ;Strategy routine
    mov  cs:RH_PTRO,bx     ;save offset address
    mov  cs:RH_PTRS,es     ;save segment address
    ret                   ;end Strategy routine
STRAT  endp

;**--------------- IDVR routine --------------**
IDVR  proc  far       ;Interrupt routine
    push  ds          ;save all modified registers
    push  es          ;DOS has stack for 20 pushes
    push  ax
    push  bx
    push  cx
    push  dx
    push  di
    push  si
    push  bp

    mov  cs:STK_PTR,sp   ;save original stack ptr
    mov  cs:STK_SEG,ss   ;save original stack seg
    cli                  ;disable for stack ops
    mov  ax,cs           ;setup new stack ptr
    mov  ss,ax           ;setup new stack seg
    mov  sp,offset TOP_STK
    sti                  ;restore flags back
    cld                  ;all moves are forward
```

At offset zero, all DOS device drivers are required to have a Device Header structure, which I have called SCAN_HEADER. The Device Header defines five key values for DOS. The first double-word value is initialized to -1. DOS will fill it in at runtime with a pointer that forms a linked list of all the DOS device drivers. The second word field describes attributes of the driver; in particular, it specifies whether it is a character- or block-mode device. My scanner driver is a character-mode device (it transfers data one byte at a time) and supports I/O controls (IOCTLs), so I have set bits 15 and 14, resulting in a value of 0C000h. The next two word fields specify the offsets of the "strategy" and "interrupt" routines for the driver. The last value contains an 8-byte

---

Listing 23.9 (continued)

```
        les  bx,cs:RH_PTRA   ;load req hdr adr in es:bx
        mov  al,RH.RHC_CMD
        cmp  al,0             ;check for init command
        je   BOOTUP           ;command 0 = init

        xor  dx,dx            ;some other command
        mov  dl,RH.RHC_CMD    ;dx = command code
        mov  cx,RH.RHC_CNT    ;cx = count
        mov  ax,RH.RHC_SEG    ;es:bx = addr of data
        mov  bx,RH.RHC_OFF
        mov  es,ax            ;finally, load VDD handle
        mov  ax,word ptr cs:[VDD_hVDD]
        DispatchCall          ;call Dispatch in VDD
                              ;returns with status in di
EXIT:
        les  bx,cs:RH_PTRA    ;restore ES:BX
        or   di,STAT_DONE     ;add "DONE" bit to status
        mov  RH.RHC_STA,di    ;save status in requ hdr
        cli                   ;disable ints for stack op
        mov  ss,cs:STK_SEG    ;restore stack seg
        mov  sp,cs:STK_PTR    ;restore stack ptr
        sti                   ;re-enable interrupts

        pop  bp               ;restore registers
        pop  si
        pop  di
        pop  dx
        pop  cx
        pop  bx
        pop  ax
        pop  es
        pop  ds
        ret                   ;far return
IDVR endp
```

Listing 23.9 (continued)

```
;**--------- jump here for Init Command --------**
BOOTUP:
    mov  ax,offset EndDriver
    mov  RH.RHC_OFF,ax   ;address of end of driver
    mov  RH.RHC_SEG,CS   ;reference from code seg

    mov  si,offset VDD_DllName  ;load regs for VDD
    mov  di,offset VDD_InitFunc
    mov  bx,offset VDD_DispFunc
    RegisterModule       ;calls the VDD
    jnc  save_hVDD       ;if NC then success
    mov  di,STAT_GF      ;set failure status
    jmp  EXIT            ;return via common exit

save_hVDD:
    mov  [VDD_hVDD],ax   ;save handle in ax
    mov  di,STAT_OK      ;load OK status
    jmp  EXIT            ;return via common exit

EndDriver db ?
CSEG    ENDS
        END  SCAN_HEADER ;REQUIRED BY EXE2BIN
```

Listing 23.10   `hpscan16.inc` — *Defines for stub DOS device driver.*

```
;**************************************************
; Name:        HPSCAN16.INC
; Description: Defines for HPSCAN16.ASM
;**************************************************

;**----------- Segment Declarations ------------**
CSEG    segment word public 'CODE'
CSEG    ends    ;header segment

;**-------------- Status Values ---------------**
STAT_OK      equ  0000h     ;ok
STAT_DONE    equ  0100h     ;function complete
STAT_GF      equ  800Ch     ;general failure

RH  EQU  ES:[BX]  ;request header
```

unique name that applications use to access the driver. Because my goal is to require no changes to any 16-bit applications that access my original DOS device driver, the stub's device header must be identical to my original DOS device driver's Device Header.

DOS device drivers are called twice to process each command. The first time, the strategy routine specified in the Device Header is called; the second time, the interrupt routine is called. This two-call scheme was based on the design of UNIX device drivers, but the strategy routine in DOS device drivers invariably does next to nothing.

The strategy routine (STRAT) in my device driver stub just saves the request header address that DOS placed in ES:BX. The Include file in Listing 23.10 sets up a general structure (RHC) for the request header (the actual contents of the request header depend on the command requested by the calling DOS application). The request header contains all the information necessary to carry out the requested command, including the command code.

The interrupt routine (IDVR) examines the request header and determines what command (such as a read or write) the DOS application is requesting. I chose to make the stub driver as generic as possible, so the IDVR routine passes all commands to the VDD except for the initialization command DOS sends when it first loads the device driver. This means that if I add extensions later, I only have to change the VDD, not the DOS device driver stub.

For the initialization command, the IDVR routine loads the name of the VDD in DS:SI, the address of the VDD initialization routine (the routine called when the VDD loads) in DS:DI, and the address of the VDD dispatch routine (the routine that handles requests) in DS:BX. Then the IDVR routine executes the RegisterModule macro (to review how these macros work, see "The NTVDM Backdoor Interface" and "WTest16, a Sample 16-bit Calling Application" in the first section of this chapter). On return from the macro, the IDVR routine saves the handle to the VDD that was

---

Listing 23.10 (continued)

```
;**------ Common Request Header Structure ------**
RHC      struc      ;common to all commands
         db   ?     ;length of request header
         db   ?     ;unit code of device
RHC_CMD  db   ?     ;command code
RHC_STA  dw   ?     ;completion status, 16-bits
         dq   ?     ;reserved for DOS
         db   ?     ;this field varies with command
RHC_OFF  dw   ?     ;offset of data
RHC_SEG  dw   ?     ;segment of data
RHC_CNT  dw   ?     ;byte count (length) of data
RHC      ends       ;end of common portion
```

placed in AX. The carry flag is set if an error occurred. If there are opportunities for your driver to fail initialization after RegisterModule is called, then the driver should call UnRegisterModule before it exits.

For all other commands, the IDVR routine loads the handle of the VDD in AX and executes the DispatchCall macro. The stub driver and the VDD can agree on using any other registers as private parameters. I chose to load the command code in DX, the transfer length in CX, and the address of the request header in ES:BX. The Dispatch-Call macro transfers control to the dispatch routine in my VDD. The VDD returns a status value in DI and the transfer length in CX. Finally, the stub driver cleans up and returns to the calling DOS application.

I used the following commands to build a stub driver that incorporates my 16-bit tools:

```
masm /mx hpscan16.asm,,nul.lst,nul.crf;
link /M /L hpscan16;
exe2bin hpscan16.exe hpscan16.sys
```

When a VDM loads, it checks config.nt for 16-bit DOS device drivers that might be required by 16-bit applications running in the VDM. To ensure that my stub DOS device driver is available to all 16-bit applications, I added the following line to the config.nt file:

```
device={path}hpscan16.sys
```

Creating the Application-Based Intercept VDD

The source code for the HP Scanner VDD, hpscan32.dll, is in hpscan32.c (Listing 23.11), hpscan32.h (Listing 23.12), hpscan32.def (Listing 23.13), and Sources (Listing 23.14). A VDD is really just a Win32 DLL that exports some specific routines known by the stub DOS device driver.

Listing 23.11 hspcan32.c — Windows NT VDD for HP scanner.

```
/**---------------------------------------------------**
** HPSCAN32.C:  HP Scanner Application-based VDD.
** Environment: Windows NT.
** (C) Hewlett-Packard Company 1993.
**---------------------------------------------------**/
```

Listing 23.11 (continued)

```c
#include <windows.h>
#include <devioctl.h>
#include <ntddscsi.h>
#include <vddsvc.h>
#include <stdio.h>          /* prototype for sprintf */
#include "hpscan32.h"

/**-------------------- Globals ----------------------**/
HANDLE hScanner=NULL;   /* handle to scanner driver */
PASS_THROUGH_STRUCT PassThru;

/**----------------------------------------------------
** VDDLibMain - serves as LibMain for this DLL.
**--------------------------------------------------**/
BOOL VDDLibMain(HINSTANCE hInst, ULONG ulReason,
   LPVOID lpReserved)
{
   switch (ulReason)
   {
      case DLL_PROCESS_ATTACH:
         if ((hScanner = HPScannerOpen()) ==
            INVALID_HANDLE_VALUE) return FALSE;
         break;

      case DLL_PROCESS_DETACH:
         HPScannerClose(hScanner);
         break;

      default: break;
   }
   return TRUE;
} /* VDDLibMain */

/**----------------------------------------------------
** VDDInit - Called when HPSCAN16.SYS initializes, via
**     the BIOS Operation Manager.
**--------------------------------------------------**/
VOID VDDInit(VOID)
{
   setCF(0);               /* Clear flags to indicate success */
   return;
} /* VDDInit */
```

The only entry point parameter I care about, in this case, is Reason. This parameter can have the following values: DLL_PROCESS_ATTACH, DLL_PROCESS_DETACH, DLL_THREAD_ATTACH, or DLL_THREAD_DETACH. Threads inherit handles from their parent process, so I am only interested in processes attaching and detaching. When a pro-

---

Listing 23.11 (continued)

```
/**---------------------------------------------------------
** VDDDispatch - called when HPSCAN16.SYS sends a request.
** Arguments:
**      Client (DX) = Command code
**      Client (CX) = Buffer size
**      Client (ES:BX) = Request Header
** Returns:
**      (CX) = Count transfered
**      (DI) = status
**--------------------------------------------------------**/
VOID VDDDispatch(VOID)
{
    PCHAR Buffer, DrvBuffer;
    USHORT cb, i=0;
    ULONG bytes=0L, ulAddr, ulIoAddr;
    PHPSCAN_IOCTL pIoctl;

    if (hScanner == NULL) return;

    /* client put the count in cx, request header in es:bx */
    cb = getCX();
    ulAddr = (ULONG)MAKELONG(getBX(), getES());
    Buffer = (PCHAR)GetVDMPointer(ulAddr, (ULONG)cb, FALSE);

    switch (getDX())        /* command code is in dx */
    {
        case CMD_READ:
            if ((bytes = HPScannerRead(hScanner, Buffer,
                (ULONG)cb)) == NULL) setDI(STAT_GF);
            else setDI(STAT_OK);
            setCX((USHORT)bytes);
            break;

        case CMD_WRITE:
        case CMD_WRITE_VFY:
            if ((bytes = HPScannerWrite(hScanner, Buffer,
                (ULONG)cb)) == NULL) setDI(STAT_GF);
            else setDI(STAT_OK);
            setCX((USHORT)bytes);
            break;
```

Listing 23.11 (continued)

```
      case CMD_OUT_IOCTL:
          pIoctl = (PHPSCAN_IOCTL)Buffer;
          ulIoAddr = (ULONG)MAKELONG(pIoctl->Offset,
              pIoctl->Segment);
          DrvBuffer = (PCHAR)GetVDMPointer(ulIoAddr,
              (ULONG)pIoctl->Count, FALSE);
          if ((pIoctl->Count = (USHORT)HPScannerIOCTL(hScanner,
              pIoctl->Command, DrvBuffer, (ULONG)pIoctl->Count))
              != NULL) setDI(STAT_OK);
          else setDI(STAT_CE);
          FreeVDMPointer(ulIoAddr, (ULONG)pIoctl->Count, DrvBuffer,
              FALSE);
          break;

      default:
          setDI(STAT_CE);          /* unsupported command */
          break;
   }
   FreeVDMPointer(ulAddr, (ULONG)cb, Buffer, FALSE);
   return;
} /* VDDDispatch */

/**----------------------------------------------------------
** VDDScannerCommand - 32-bit private API
**----------------------------------------------------------**/
ULONG APIENTRY VDDScannerCommand(USHORT usCommand,
   PCHAR pcBuffer, ULONG ulLength)
{
   switch(usCommand)
   {
      case CMD_READ:
          return HPScannerRead(hScanner, pcBuffer, ulLength);

      case CMD_WRITE:
          return HPScannerWrite(hScanner, pcBuffer, ulLength);

      case CMD_IOCTL_READBUFFER:
      case CMD_IOCTL_WRITEBUFFER:
      case CMD_IOCTL_SCSIINQ:
          return HPScannerIOCTL(hScanner, usCommand, pcBuffer,
              ulLength);

      default: return NULL;
   }
   return NULL;
} /* VDD_ScannerCommand */
```

Listing 23.11 (continued)

```
/**----------------- private routines ----------------**/

/**----------------------------------------------------------
** HPScannerOpen - returns handle to scanner device
**--------------------------------------------------------**/
HANDLE HPScannerOpen(VOID)
{
    /* for simplicity, we'll assume only one scanner */
    return CreateFile((LPTSTR)"\\\\.\\Scanner0",
        GENERIC_READ | GENERIC_WRITE, 0, NULL,
        OPEN_EXISTING, FILE_ATTRIBUTE_NORMAL, NULL);
} /* HPScannerOpen */


/**----------------------------------------------------------
** HPScannerClose - close handle passed in
**--------------------------------------------------------**/
BOOL HPScannerClose(HANDLE handle)
{
    return CloseHandle(handle);
} /* HPScannerClose */


/**----------------------------------------------------------
** HPScannerRead
**--------------------------------------------------------**/
ULONG HPScannerRead(HANDLE handle, PCHAR buffer, ULONG len)
{
    DWORD cnt=0;

    if (!(ReadFile(handle, buffer, len, &cnt, NULL)))
        return NULL;
    else return cnt;
} /* HPScannerRead */


/**----------------------------------------------------------
** HPScannerWrite
**--------------------------------------------------------**/
ULONG HPScannerWrite(HANDLE handle, PCHAR buffer, ULONG len)
{
    DWORD cnt=0;

    if (!(WriteFile(handle, buffer, len, &cnt, NULL)))
        return NULL;
    else return cnt;
} /* HPScannerWrite */
```

cess attaches, I attempt to open the scanner device, and when a process detaches, I close the scanner device.

VDDInit() and VDDDispatch() are called when the DOS stub device driver initializes and sends requests respectively. VDDInit() would be a good place to allocate any necessary resources. VDDDispatch() deciphers the register contents agreed on by the stub driver and sends a read, write, or IOCTL command to the hardware device. VDM provides a complete set of register manipulation routines, such as getAX(). (On

Listing 23.11 (continued)

```
/**-------------------------------------------------------------
** HPScannerIOCTL
**-----------------------------------------------------------**/
ULONG HPScannerIOCTL(HANDLE handle, USHORT usCommand,
    PCHAR pBuffer, ULONG ulLength)
{
    USHORT i=0;
    DWORD bytes=0L;

    /* clear CDB and data buffer before IOCTL call */
    memset(PassThru.ucDataBuf, 0, sizeof(PassThru.ucDataBuf));
    for (i=0; i <= 16; i++) PassThru.sptCmd.Cdb[i] = 0;

    PassThru.sptCmd.Length = sizeof(SCSI_PASS_THROUGH_DIRECT);
    PassThru.sptCmd.SenseInfoLength =
        sizeof(PassThru.ucSenseBuf);
    PassThru.sptCmd.DataTransferLength = ulLength;
    PassThru.sptCmd.TimeOutValue = 10;
    PassThru.sptCmd.DataBuffer = pBuffer;
    PassThru.sptCmd.SenseInfoOffset = PassThru.ucSenseBuf
        - (UCHAR*)&PassThru;

    switch(usCommand)
    {
        case CMD_IOCTL_READBUFFER:
            PassThru.sptCmd.CdbLength = 10;
            PassThru.sptCmd.DataIn = TRUE;
            PassThru.sptCmd.Cdb[0] = 0x3c;
            PassThru.sptCmd.Cdb[1] = 2;
            PassThru.sptCmd.Cdb[7] = HIBYTE(ulLength);
            PassThru.sptCmd.Cdb[8] = LOBYTE(ulLength);

            DeviceIoControl(hScanner, IOCTL_SCSI_MINIPORT_DIRECT,
                &PassThru, sizeof(SCSI_PASS_THROUGH), &PassThru,
                sizeof(PassThru), &bytes, FALSE);
            return PassThru.sptCmd.DataTransferLength;
```

RISC machines, these routines use virtual registers maintained by the x86 emulator.) You should use these routines to access any registers set by the stub driver. Another complication arises because the address in ES:BX is in segment:offset form. GetVDM-Pointer() translates DOS segment:offset- or selector:offset-style pointers to 32-bit linear addresses.

Now that I have a Win32 DLL that knows how to communicate with the SCSI kernel-mode drivers to access an HP scanner, I might as well add a 32-bit API so that any new Win32 applications I write can also easily access the scanner. The VDD exports the VDDScannerCommand() routine for this purpose. It requires only three simple parameters: an ID to identify the command (CMD_READ, CMD_WRITE, or CMD_IOCTL), an address of a buffer, and the length of a buffer. The command requested indicates what action to take with the buffer.

Listing 23.11 (continued)

```
    case CMD_IOCTL_WRITEBUFFER:
        PassThru.sptCmd.CdbLength = 10;
        PassThru.sptCmd.DataIn = TRUE;
        PassThru.sptCmd.Cdb[0] = 0x3b;
        PassThru.sptCmd.Cdb[1] = 2;
        PassThru.sptCmd.Cdb[7] = HIBYTE(ulLength);
        PassThru.sptCmd.Cdb[8] = LOBYTE(ulLength);

        DeviceIoControl(hScanner, IOCTL_SCSI_MINIPORT_DIRECT,
            &PassThru, sizeof(PassThru), &PassThru,
            sizeof(PassThru), &bytes, FALSE);
        return PassThru.sptCmd.DataTransferLength;

    case CMD_IOCTL_SCSIINQ:
        PassThru.sptCmd.CdbLength = 6;
        PassThru.sptCmd.DataIn = TRUE;
        PassThru.sptCmd.Cdb[0] = 0x12;
        PassThru.sptCmd.Cdb[4] = (UCHAR)ulLength;

        DeviceIoControl(hScanner, IOCTL_SCSI_MINIPORT_DIRECT,
            &PassThru, sizeof(PassThru), &PassThru,
            sizeof(PassThru), &bytes, FALSE);
        return PassThru.sptCmd.DataTransferLength;

    default: return NULL;                /* invalid command */
    } /* switch */
    return NULL;
} /* HPScannerIOCTL */
```

Listing 23.12 *hpscan32.h — Defines for Windows NT VDD.*

```
/**--------------------------------------------------**
** HPSCAN32.H:  HP Scanner Application-based VDD.
** Environment: Windows NT.
** (C) Hewlett-Packard Company 1993.
**--------------------------------------------------**/


/**-------- DOS Device Driver Status Codes ---------**/
#define STAT_OK         0x0000    /* SUCCESS */
#define STAT_CE         0x8003    /* invalid command */
#define STAT_GF         0x800C    /* general failure */


/**------- DOS Device Driver Command Codes ---------**/
#define CMD_READ        4     /* read command */
#define CMD_WRITE       8     /* write command */
#define CMD_WRITE_VFY   9     /* write with verify */
#define CMD_OUT_IOCTL   12    /* output I/O control */


/**------- DOS Device Driver SubCommand Codes -------**/
#define CMD_IOCTL_READBUFFER    0x09
#define CMD_IOCTL_WRITEBUFFER   0x0A
#define CMD_IOCTL_SCSIINQ       0x0D


/**---------- PASS_THROUGH_STRUCT -----------------**/
typedef struct
{
    SCSI_PASS_THROUGH sptCmd;
    UCHAR             ucSenseBuf[32];
} PASS_THROUGH_STRUCT;


/**---- IOCTL Structure from the DOS Stub driver ---**/
typedef struct
{
    USHORT Command;
    USHORT Status;
    USHORT Count;
    USHORT Offset;
    USHORT Segment;
} HPSCAN_IOCTL;
typedef HPSCAN_IOCTL *PHPSCAN_IOCTL;
```

HPScannerOpen() uses CreateFile() (a Win32 function) to open a handle to the device. A value of zero for the ShareMode parameter prevents the file/device from being shared. To simplify the example, I am assuming that only one scanner exists and that it is an HP scanner. A better solution is to attempt opening Scanner0 through ScannerN (the name the Class driver registers for itself) and check the INQUIRY data for each scanner found to determine if it is your scanner.

HPScannerClose(), HPScannerRead(), and HPScannerWrite() routines just call the corresponding Win32 API function, using the handle to the open scanner device and the buffer passed by the calling program.

HPScannerIOCTL() uses DeviceIoControl() (a Win32 function) to send IOCTL requests to the scanner device. Some very common SCSI IOCTLs, such as "Inquiry," are supported by a common SCSI Class driver. Some SCSI Class drivers support additional IOCTLs that are pertinent to that category of device. The SCSI Scanner Class driver is very generic and does not support any IOCTLs itself. The SCSI kernel-mode

---

Listing 23.12 (continued)

```
/**-------- HPSCAN32.C, private prototypes ---------**/
HANDLE HPScannerOpen(VOID);
BOOL HPScannerClose(HANDLE);
ULONG HPScannerRead(HANDLE, PCHAR, ULONG);
ULONG HPScannerWrite(HANDLE, PCHAR, ULONG);
ULONG HPScannerIOCTL(HANDLE, USHORT, PCHAR, ULONG);


/**-------- HPSCAN32.C, public prototypes ----------**/
BOOL VDDLibMain(HINSTANCE, ULONG, LPVOID);
VOID VDDInit(VOID);
VOID VDDDispatch(VOID);
ULONG APIENTRY VDDScannerCommand(USHORT, PCHAR, ULONG);
```

Listing 23.13   hpscan32.def — Module definition file for Windows NT VDD.

```
LIBRARY HPSCAN32

DESCRIPTION 'Application-based VDD for HP Scanners.'

EXPORTS
    VDDInit
    VDDDispatch
    VDDScannerCommand
```

drivers provide a method, called "Pass Through," to allow applications to send a command to a SCSI device. The HP scanners support many IOCTLs that aren't explicitly supported. For simplicity, I have included only the "Read Buffer," "Write Buffer," and "Inquiry" IOCTLs using the "Pass Through" mechanism (I could have used a direct IOCTL command, IOCTL_SCSI_GET_INQUIRY_DATA, for the "Inquiry" IOCTL).

I fill in a structure called PASS_THROUGH_STRUCT (defined in hpscan32.h) which has a SCSI_PASS_THROUGH structure (defined in NT's ntddscsi.h) embedded in it.

You could create a makefile for building the VDD, but just for fun, I am using the new BUILD tool that comes with the NT DDK. The BUILD program uses a standard makefile and a custom Sources file to build the sources in the current directory. The makefile contains only a reference to a makefile.def file and should never be edited. I started with a Sources file from one of the DDK samples and just modified it for my needs. You can use the Sources file in Listing 23.14 as a template for your VDD.

Listing 23.14 Sources file for NT build command.

```
INDENTED_DIRECTIVES=1

MAJORCOMP=hpscan32
MINORCOMP=hpscan32

TARGETNAME=hpscan32
TARGETPATH=$(BASEDIR)\lib
TARGETTYPE=DYNLINK
TARGETLIBS=$(BASEDIR)\lib\*\$(DDKBUILDENV)\kernel32.lib \
           $(BASEDIR)\lib\*\$(DDKBUILDENV)\ntvdm.lib

DLLENTRY=VDDLibMain
DLLBASE=0x2000000

INCLUDES=$(BASEDIR)\inc;$(BASEDIR)\src\storage\inc

SOURCES=hpscan32.c

I386_SOURCES=
MIPS_SOURCES=

C_DEFINES=-DWIN_32 -DDEBUG

UMTYPE=windows
UMTEST=
UMLIBS=
```

There are two ways to load a VDD. By calling `RegisterModule()` in my stub DOS device driver, I am in effect performing a `LoadLibrary()` on the VDD name specified in `DS:SI`. As long as the VDD is somewhere in the path, it will be loaded whenever my stub loads. A second method for loading a VDD involves adding a reference to it in the Registry (Figure 23.5). This causes the VDD to be loaded any time a new VDM is started. Therefore, if for any reason this VDD fails to load, the user will get an ominous message, and in some cases the entire VDM will be affected. You should use this method only if your VDD is essential to all VDMs. Multiple VDDs can be specified by separating them with a `NULL` (\0). For more information about the Windows NT Registry, see the sidebar "The Windows NT Registry".

Sample Programs

`test32.c` (Listing 23.15) and `test32.h` (Listing 23.16) contain the source for a very simple Win32 program. Test32 links with `hpscan32.lib` so that it can access the scanner via `VDDScannerCommand()`. First, it requests SCSI Inquiry information and displays the device type field in a dialog box. Then, it tests reading and writing to the device by writing data to the scanner in the form of an inquiry command for the scanner's model number, then reading the response string. The model number is also displayed in the dialog box. The module definition file is in `test32.def` (Listing 23.17), the dialog box definition is in `test32.rc` (Listing 23.18), and the makefile is in `test32.mak` (Listing 23.19).

The code disk also contains source files for a Win32 Console program that does basically the same thing as Test32. The Console interface allows you to write simple 32-bit character-mode programs. Don't let the `printf()` statements and lack of `WinMain()` fool you. This is a Win32 program and has no difficulty linking with and using `hpscan32.dll`.

I have also placed on the code disk source files for a 16-bit program that performs reads, writes, and IOCTLs via the "HPSCAN" DOS device driver. If you plan to convert your 16-bit applications to the DOS device driver model, this may be a helpful example. Again, it performs the same three device commands as the previous two examples. Remember that for character-mode device drivers, you must set the device to raw (binary) mode after opening it, and you must use the DOS INT 21 function 44h to send IOCTL requests to a DOS device driver.

Figure 23.5 Sample specification of a VDD in the Registry.

```
HKEY_LOCAL_MACHINE\SYSTEM\CurrentControlSet|Control|VirtualDevice Drivers
   VDD:REG_MULTI_SZ:{path}hpscan32.dll
```

Figure 23.6   Adding a driver to the Registry.

```
HKEY_LOCAL_MACHINE\SYSTEM\CurrentControlSet\Services\Scsiscan
    DependOnGroup:REG_MULTI_SZ:SCSI miniport
    ErrorControl:REG_DWORD:0x1
    Group:REG_REG_SZ:SCSI class
    Start:REG_DWORD:0x1
    Type:REG_DWORD:0x1
```

The Windows NT Registry

The registration database that first appeared in Windows 3.1 contained information only for SHELL and OLE applications. At that time, Microsoft introduced an API for querying and setting values in the registration database. In Win32, the new database is called "the Registry" and has been expanded significantly. You can still use the Windows 3.1 API, but Microsoft has added some extended versions of these routines. The Win32 Registry is intended to provide a single, consolidated source for configuration information, thus replacing the `config.sys` file and the proliferation of `*.ini files`.

The Win32 Registry contains a list of drivers that should be loaded, as well as configuration information about each of those drivers. Each driver is represented by a subkey under the `KHEY_LOCAL_MACHINE\SYSTEM\CurrentControlSet\Services` key (Figure 23.6). These driver-specific subkeys contain certain predefined registry values that control how the driver is loaded.

The `DependOnGroup` field specifies that the Scanner Class driver won't load unless at least on eSCSI Miniport driver has already loaded. The `ErrorControl` value of `0x1` specifies that the system will still boot even if the Scanner Class driver fails to load. The `Group` value specifies that this driver is a SCSI Class type of driver. The `Start` value of `0x1` specifies that this driver is not needed during the boot process, it will be loaded afterwards during the initialization process. The `Type` value of `0x1` specifies that this driver is a kernel-mode driver rather than a user-mode driver.

To confirm that the Class, Port, and Miniport drivers are all loaded properly, you can browse through the `HKEY_LOCAL_MACHINE\HARDWARE\DEVICEMAP\Scsi` key. This key contains subkeys for each valid SCSI target ID and logical unit number. Inquiry information is displayed for each device found. The Hewlett-Packard Scanners should report a string that contains the initials "HP" and the model number of your scanner. Many changes to the Registry don't take effect until you reboot. Also, keep in mind that the exact name of some keys and values in the Registry are considered proprietary by Microsoft and may change between versions of the operating system.

Listing 23.15 `test32.c`— *Windows NT test program for scanner VDD.*

```
/********* TEST32.C - source file for test32.exe **********/

#include "windows.h"
#include "test32.h"


/**---------------- WinMain ----------------------------**/
int APIENTRY WinMain(HINSTANCE hInst, HINSTANCE hPrevInst,
   LPSTR lpCmdLine, int nShow)
{
   DialogBox(hInst, MAKEINTRESOURCE(DISPLAY_DLG), NULL,
      DisplayDlgProc);
   return 0;
} /* WinMain */


/**----------------- DisplayDlgProc --------------------**/
BOOL CALLBACK DisplayDlgProc(HWND hDlg, UINT uMsg,
   WPARAM wParam, LPARAM lParam)
{
   char Buffer[64+1], TmpBuffer[64+1], i;

   switch (uMsg)
   {
      case WM_INITDIALOG:
         VDDScannerCommand(CMD_IOCTL_SCSIINQ, Buffer, 64);
         wsprintf(TmpBuffer, "%c", Buffer[0]+'0');
         SetDlgItemText(hDlg, ID_SCSIINQ, TmpBuffer);

         VDDScannerCommand(CMD_WRITE, "\x01B*s10E", 64);
         VDDScannerCommand(CMD_READ, Buffer, (ULONG)64);
         for (i=8; i <=12; i++) TmpBuffer[i-8] = Buffer[i];
         TmpBuffer[i-8] = '\0';
         SetDlgItemText(hDlg, ID_MODELNUM, TmpBuffer);
         return TRUE;

      case WM_COMMAND:
         if (wParam == IDOK) EndDialog(hDlg, TRUE);
         return TRUE;

      default:  return FALSE;
   }
   return TRUE;
} /* DisplayDlgProc */
```

Conclusion

As you can see, if your interface protocol is already supported at the kernel-mode level by Windows NT (as SCSI, serial, and parallel are), supporting 16-bit and 32-bit hardware-dependent applications under Windows NT is a fairly straightforward task. In the case of SCSI, even if your category of device requires you to write a new Class

---

Listing 23.16 `test32.h` — *Header file for* `test32.c`

```
/********* TEST32.H - include file for test32.exe *********/

#define IDNULL              -1
#define DISPLAY_DLG         2000
#define ID_SCSIINQ          2001
#define ID_MODELNUM         2002


/**------- DOS Device Driver Command Codes -------------**/
#define CMD_READ            4
#define CMD_WRITE           8
#define CMD_WRITE_VFY       9
#define CMD_OUT_IOCTL       12

/**------ DOS Device Driver SubCommand Codes -----------**/
#define CMD_IOCTL_READBUFFER    0x09
#define CMD_IOCTL_WRITEBUFFER   0x0A
#define CMD_IOCTL_SCSIINQ       0x0D

BOOL CALLBACK DisplayDlgProc(HWND, UINT, WPARAM, LPARAM);
ULONG APIENTRY VDDScannerCommand(USHORT, PCHAR, ULONG);
```

Listing 23.17 `test32.def` — *Module definition file for* `test32.c`

```
NAME            Test32
DESCRIPTION     "32-bit Test Program"
EXETYPE         WINDOWS
STUB            "WINSTUB.EXE"

CODE            PRELOAD MOVEABLE DISCARDABLE
DATA            PRELOAD MOVEABLE MULTIPLE
HEAPSIZE        1024
STACKSIZE       5120

EXPORTS
```

Listing 23.18 `test32.rc` — *Resource definitions for* `test32.c`

```
/****** TEST32.RC - resource file for TEST32.EXE *****/

#include <windows.h>
#include "test32.h"

DISPLAY_DLG DIALOG 40, 40, 140, 64
STYLE WS_POPUP | DS_MODALFRAME | WS_VISIBLE | WS_CAPTION
CAPTION "HP Scanner Test32"
BEGIN
    CONTROL "Device Type:", IDNULL, "static",
        SS_LEFT | WS_CHILD, 20, 12, 70, 8
    CONTROL "", ID_SCSIINQ, "static",
        SS_LEFT | WS_CHILD, 92, 12, 40, 8
    CONTROL "HP Scanner Model #:", IDNULL, "static",
        SS_LEFT | WS_CHILD, 20, 24, 70, 8
    CONTROL "", ID_MODELNUM, "static",
        SS_LEFT | WS_CHILD, 92, 24, 40, 8
    CONTROL "&OK", IDOK, "button", BS_DEFPUSHBUTTON |
        WS_TABSTOP | WS_CHILD, 50, 42, 40, 14
END
```

Listing 23.19 `test32.mak` — *Makefile for* `test32.exe`

```
# Nmake macros for building Windows 32-Bit apps
!include <ntwin32.mak>

all: test32.exe

test32.rbj: test32.rc test32.h
    rc -r test32.rc
    cvtres -$(CPU) test32.res -o test32.rbj

test32.obj: test32.c test32.h
    $(cc) $(cflags) $(cvars) $(cdebug) test32.c

test32.exe: test32.obj test32.rbj test32.def hpscan32.lib
    $(cvtobj) $(cvtdebug) *.obj
    $(link) $(linkdebug) $(guiflags) -out:test32.exe\
        test32.obj test32.rbj hpscan32.lib $(guilibs)
```

driver, at least you can take advantage of the lower level Port and Miniport drivers provided by Windows NT. If you have an entirely different interface protocol, then your only option is to provide a complete (monolithic) kernel-mode driver, which is not nearly as straightforward. This is the realm of asynchronous I/O and "spin-locks."

The source code described here is intended to be used as an example. It is not supported, in any way, by Hewlett-Packard.

References

Custer, Helen. *Inside Windows NT*. Redmond, WA: Microsoft Press, 1993.

Intel Corp. "Enhanced Small Computer System Interface (SCSI-2)" in *Intel 386™ DX Microprocessor Programmer's Reference Manual*.

Lai, Robert S. *Writing DOS Device Drivers*, 2nd ed. The Waite Group Press.

Microsoft Corp. Preliminary Win32 Software Development Kit for Windows NT. October 1992.

Microsoft Corp. Preliminary Windows NT Device Driver Kit. October 1992.

Chapter 24

Direct Port I/O and Windows NT

Undocumented features for direct control of hardware devices

Dale Roberts

Port I/O instructions allow all 80x86 CPUs to communicate with other hardware devices in the system. For low-level, direct control of a hardware device, the C functions _inp() and _outp() (implemented using the 80x86 processor's IN and OUT instructions) let you read from or write to an I/O port. However, inserting _inp() or _outp() in a Windows NT application gives you a privileged-instruction exception message and the option of terminating or debugging the offending application. If you attempt port I/O from a 16-bit DOS application in an NT console window, the I/O is either ignored or emulated by NT's virtual device drivers — you don't get an exception, but you don't get the direct I/O either.

This isn't a bug; NT is supposed to work this way. The NT architects decided that it would be too risky to allow applications to directly access the system hardware. With unrestricted I/O access, an application could turn off all interrupts, take over the system, and trash the display or the hard drive. A buggy program could unintentionally do the same. NT's architecture requires that all hardware be accessed via kernel-mode device drivers — special, trusted pieces of software that essentially become part of the operating system when loaded. These device drivers have complete access to the entire system memory, all hardware devices, and all privileged processor instructions. In contrast, applications run in user mode, where they have restricted access to memory and where the CPU can't execute certain privileged operating-system instructions, including I/O instructions.

The restriction on I/O port access is both a blessing and a curse. On one hand, it makes NT exceptionally stable. Generally, application programmers can write and crash and debug programs all day long without shaking NT. Several applications can run without adversely affecting one another. On the other hand, I/O restrictions prevent you from communicating directly and quickly with the hardware without taking the relatively large amount of time required for a call to a device driver. Whenever you want to communicate with a device driver, you must send a request through NT's I/O subsystem. This can take thousands of processor clock cycles. A port I/O instruction would take about 30 clock cycles.

Why would you ever need to put I/O instructions in user-mode code? When writing a device driver, a test program that interacts with the device via printf()s and getchar()s among port I/O instructions could verify that you are driving the device correctly before you put the code into an actual device driver and chance a system lockup. Or you may want to write a portion of a driver in a user-mode DLL (as with video drivers, for instance) to achieve a desired level of performance. One of my favorite uses of I/O is for an oscilloscope, used to debug programs and time sections of code. To do this, I need to set and clear a bit in a digital output port and monitor the voltage on a scope.

Because direct, user-mode port I/O in NT seems so useful, you'd think there would be an accepted way to achieve it. A quick look through the sample source code in the Windows NT Device Driver Kit (DDK) reveals a program called PORTIO. Initially, I thought this would provide direct port I/O from an application. However, PORTIO is merely an example showing how to use Win32 DeviceIoControl() calls to a kernel-mode device driver, which implements the actual I/O. Using PORTIO, each I/O operation requires a costly, time-consuming call to the device driver. This was useless for my oscilloscope timings. I needed a better way.

Accomplishing I/O Protection in NT

To figure out how to grant I/O access to a user-mode application, you have to understand how I/O protection is implemented in Windows NT. NT does not actually implement the I/O protection on its own. Because the CPU can trap attempted I/O port accesses, NT depends on this 80x86 feature. The first mechanism that must be understood is the privilege-level system used by the 80x86 processors. Four privilege levels are defined by the processor — 0, 1, 2, and 3 — and the CPU always operates at one of these levels. The most privileged level is 0; the least privileged, 3. NT uses only levels 0 and 3. Privilege level 0 is used for the full-access kernel mode, and 3 for the more restrictive user mode. The current privilege level (CPL) of the processor is stored in the two least significant bits of the CS (code segment) register.

Rather than statically defining which privilege levels can have I/O access, the CPU defines an I/O privilege level (IOPL) value, which is compared against the CPL to determine if I/O instructions can be used freely. The IOPL is stored in 2 bits of the processor's EFLAGS register. Any process with a CPL that is numerically greater than the IOPL must go through the I/O protection mechanism when attempting port I/O access. Because the IOPL cannot be less than 0, programs running at privilege level 0 (like kernel-mode device drivers) will always have direct port I/O access. NT sets the IOPL to 0. User-mode code always has a CPL of 3, which is larger than the IOPL. Therefore, user-mode port I/O access attempts must go through the protection mechanism.

Determining if CPL > IOPL is the first step in the protection mechanism. I/O protection is not all-or-nothing. The processor uses a flexible mechanism that allows the operating system to grant direct access to any subset of I/O ports on a task-by-task basis.

The CPU accomplishes this by using a bitmask array, where each bit corresponds to an I/O port. If the bit is a 1, access is disallowed and an exception occurs whenever access to the corresponding port is attempted. If the bit is a 0, direct and unhampered access is granted to that particular port. The I/O address space of the 80x86 processors encompasses 65,536 8-bit ports. The bitmask array is 8,192 (0x2000) bytes long, because the bitmask array is packed so that each byte holds 8 bits of the array. There is even flexibility in how much of the bitmask array must be provided. You can provide anywhere from 0 to the full 8,192 bytes of the table. The table always starts from I/O address 0, but you can choose not to provide the bitmask for upper I/O addresses. Any part of the bitmask that you do not provide is assumed to be 1, and therefore access is not granted to those ports.

The bitmask array, called the I/O Permission bit Map (IOPM), is stored in the Task State Segment (TSS) structure in main memory, which is contained in a special segment referenced by the segment selector in the processor's Task Register (TR). The location of the IOPM within the TSS is flexible. The offset of the IOPM within the TSS is stored in a 2-byte integer at location 0x66 in the TSS (Figure 24.1).

Figure 24.1** **The segment selector in the processor's TR points to the segment descriptor in the global table descriptor (GDT), which defines the location and size of theTSS in memory. The IOPM is stored as part of the TSS. Its offset is stored in a 2-byte integer at location 0x66 in the TSS.

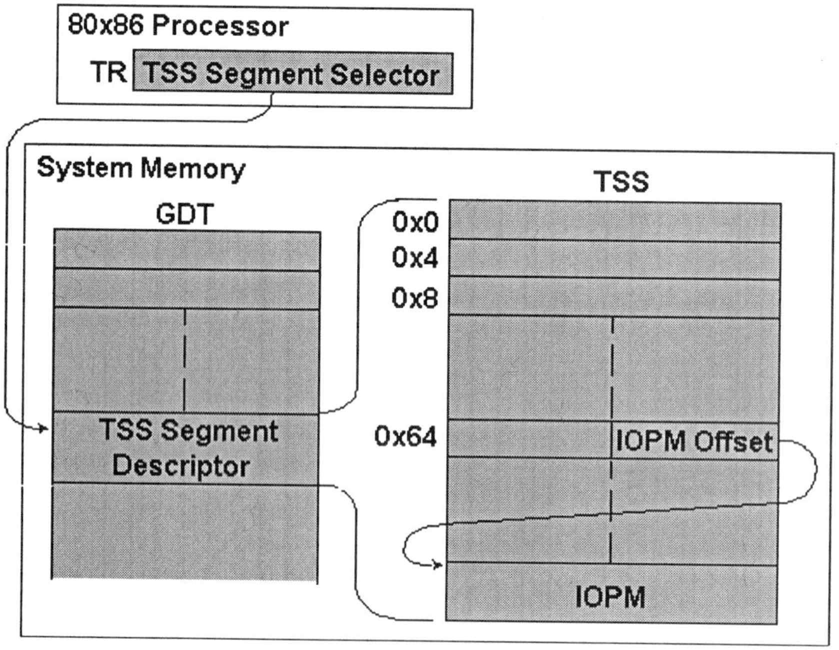

NT TSS Specifics

The 80x86 TSS was designed so that each task in the system could have its own TSS. In NT, however, the TSS is not fully used. The TR, which points to the TSS segment descriptor, is never modified. Each process uses the same copy of the TSS, so each process uses the same copy of the IOPM.

In NT, the default IOPM offset points beyond the end of the TSS. This effectively denies access by user-mode processes to all I/O ports. To grant access to I/O ports for user-mode processes, you must modify the IOPM offset so that it is within the TSS, or extend the TSS so that the original default offset falls within the TSS.

The Video Port Routines

Because I didn't want to reinvent the wheel, I looked through the NT DDK documentation to see if there was a facility to deal with user-mode I/O access. In the Kernel Mode Driver Reference Manual, I came across the video driver support routines `VideoPortMapMemory()` and `VideoPortSetTrappedEmulatorPorts()`. The former grants direct access of memory and I/O ports to user-mode portions of video drivers, presumably for performance. Source code examples in the DDK show user-mode portions of the VGA video drivers using the `IN` and `OUT` port I/O instructions. The latter video port function grants full-screen DOS-mode programs direct access to a subset of the VGA I/O ports. The description given in the DDK documentation for this second routine even makes reference to the IOPM and notes that it is shared by all of the virtual DOS machines (more accurately, it is shared across all NT processes).

The video port routines suggest that there is a mechanism within NT for allowing user-mode access to I/O ports. Initially, I tried to use the video routines in a kernel-mode driver to grant I/O access to my user-mode test program, but this turned out to be complicated. The kernel-mode device driver has to pretend that it is a video driver to use these routines. Video header files must be included, the video library must be linked to, and video initialization routines must be called.

The presence of these two routines demonstrates why user-mode I/O can be useful, and their descriptions in the DDK documentation are enlightening. But the functions are intended to be used only with video drivers. Using the video routines with a nonvideo driver was messy, so I dropped this as an option.

Delving Further

The video port functions are the only documented method for enabling direct-port I/O. Because I found them difficult to use, I decided to create my own. I first tried increasing the size of the TSS so that the default IOPM offset would land within the TSS (Figure 24.2). I had to modify the TSS segment descriptor in the global descriptor table (GDT) directly and change the default segment size of 0x20AB to 0x20AB + 0xF00 to allow access to the first 0xF00 I/O ports. The processor's TR then had to be reloaded for the change in the TSS descriptor to take effect. It isn't a good idea to extend segments in a haphazard fashion, because all memory must be accounted for by the 80x86 paging system. A page fault could occur during a reference to the IOPM, which would crash the system. But because the physical page size is 4Kb, and I did not extend the TSS beyond the end of a physical page, there was no trouble. Because there were only zeros beyond the original end of the TSS, increasing its size granted universal I/O access across all applications. The TotalIO device driver in Listing 24.1 illustrates this.

Figure 24.2   The default TSS size is 0x20AB. **We need to extend it to** 0x2FAB **so that the IOPM offset falls within the TSS.**

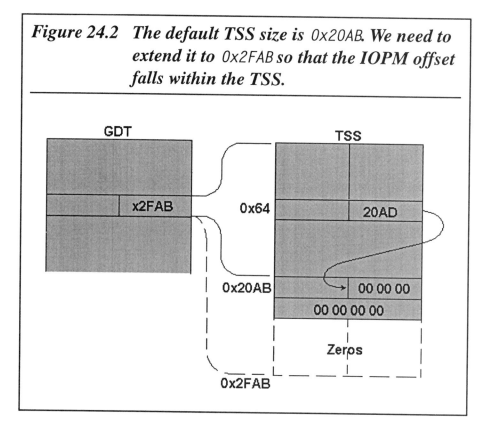

Listing 24.1 `totalio.sys` — *Give direct port I/O access to the whole system.*

```
/***********************************************************************
TOTALIO.SYS -- by Dale Roberts
Compile: Use DDK BUILD facility
Purpose: Give direct port I/O access to the whole system. This driver grants
total system-wide I/O access to all applications. Very dangerous, but useful
for short tests.  Note that no test application is required. Just use control
panel or "net start totalio" to start the device driver.  When the driver is
stopped, total I/O is removed.  Because no Win32 app needs to communicate with
the driver, we don't have to create a device object. So we have a tiny driver
here. Since we can safely extend the TSS only to the end of the physical memory
page in which it lies, the I/O access is granted only up to port 0xf00.
Accesses beyond this port address will still generate exceptions.
***********************************************************************/
#include <ntddk.h>
/* Make sure our structure is packed properly, on byte boundary, not
 * on the default doubleword boundary. */#pragma pack(push,1)
/* Structures for manipulating the GDT register and a GDT segment
 * descriptor entry.  Documented in Intel processor handbooks. */
typedef struct {
    unsigned short  limit;
    GDTENT  *base;
} GDTREG;
typedef struct {
    unsigned limit : 16;
    unsigned baselo : 16;
    unsigned basemid : 8;
    unsigned type : 4;
    unsigned system : 1;
    unsigned dpl : 2;
    unsigned present : 1;
    unsigned limithi : 4;
    unsigned available : 1;
    unsigned zero : 1;
    unsigned size : 1;
    unsigned granularity : 1;
    unsigned basehi : 8;
} GDTENT;
```

Listing 24.1 (continued)

```
#pragma pack(pop)
/* This is the lowest level for setting the TSS segment descriptor limit field.
 * We get the selector ID from the STR instruction, index into the GDT, and
 * poke in the new limit.  In order for the new limit to take effect, we must
 * then read the task segment selector back into the task register (TR).  */
void SetTSSLimit(int size)
{
    GDTREG gdtreg;
    GDTENT *g;
    short TaskSeg;
    _asm cli;                             // don't get interrupted!
    _asm sgdt gdtreg;                     // get GDT address
    _asm str TaskSeg;                     // get TSS selector index
    g = gdtreg.base + (TaskSeg >> 3);     // get ptr to TSS descriptor
    g->limit = size;                      // modify TSS segment limit
//
//  MUST set selector type field to 9, to indicate the task is
//  NOT BUSY.  Otherwise the LTR instruction causes a fault.
//
    g->type = 9;                          // mark TSS as "not busy"
//  We must do a load of the Task register, else the processor
//  never sees the new TSS selector limit.
    _asm ltr TaskSeg;                     // reload task register (TR)
    _asm sti;                             // let interrupts continue
}
/* This routine gives total I/O access across the whole system. It does this
 * by modifying the limit of the TSS segment by direct modification of the TSS
 * descriptor entry in the GDT. This descriptor is set up just once at system
 * init time. Once we modify it, it stays untouched across all processes.  */
void GiveTotalIO(void)
{
    SetTSSLimit(0x20ab + 0xf00);
}
/* This returns the TSS segment to its normal size of 0x20ab, which
 * is two less than the default I/O map base address of 0x20ad. */
void RemoveTotalIO(void)
{
    SetTSSLimit(0x20ab);
}
/****** Release all memory 'n' stuff. ******/
VOID TotalIOdrvUnload(
    IN  PDRIVER_OBJECT  DriverObject
    )
{
    RemoveTotalIO();
}
```

At first, this may seem like the best possible method to grant I/O access – set it once and you don't need to grant access to each process individually. However, this method is dangerous and unrestrictive. It would allow, for instance, DOS programs to directly access the video registers, even if they were not running in full-screen mode. It would allow DOS disk utilities to access the hard drive directly and wreak havoc on NTFS partitions. NT device drivers keep information on the state of the devices they control, and TotalIO would allow applications to completely violate this arrangement. As soon as you start up a DOS program, or any other program with port I/O, you risk trashing the whole system.

Granting Access to a Single Process

Because TotalIO is risky, I looked for a method that would allow a kernel-mode driver to grant I/O access to a single process.

Using a debugger, I examined the NT TSS and found a block of 0xFFs extending from offset 0x88 to the end of the TSS. I assumed that in NT, the block of 0xFFs was where the IOPM was intended to sit, even though the default IOPM offset points beyond this area. There were 0x2004 bytes of 0xFF. The extra 4 bytes are present because the 80x86 requires at least 1 byte extra of 0xFF at the end of the IOPM. The 80x86 requires the extra byte because it always accesses 2 bytes of the IOPM at a time.

Listing 24.1 (continued)

```
/****** Entry routine.  Set everything up. *****/
NTSTATUS DriverEntry(
    IN PDRIVER_OBJECT DriverObject,
    IN PUNICODE_STRING RegistryPath
    )
{
    DriverObject->DriverUnload = TotalIOdrvUnload;
    GiveTotalIO();
    return STATUS_SUCCESS;
}
```

Figure 24.3 *NT places the IOPM at offset* 0x88 *in the TSS. We need to modify the IOPM offset to point to this area.*

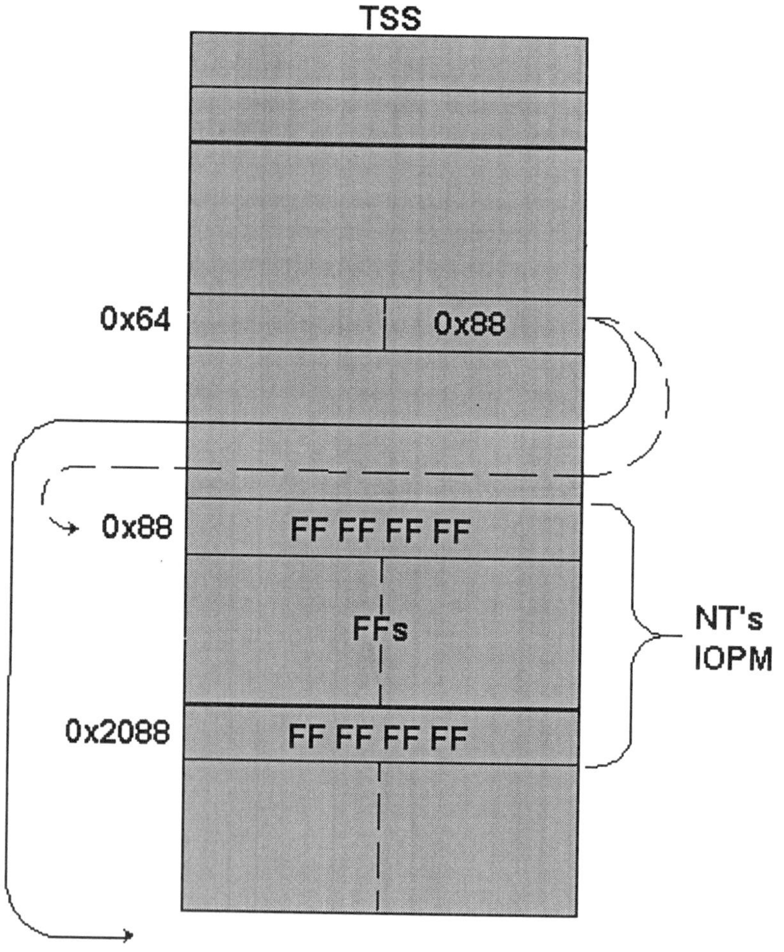

I moved the IOPM offset to point to the start of the 0xFFs, as in Figure 24.3. I zeroed a few bytes of the IOPM and tried to access ports. Nothing happened. My application still caused exceptions. The kernel-mode device-driver fragment in Listing 24.2 illustrates this attempt.

What was wrong? A visual inspection of a memory dump of an NT process structure showed that NT stores the IOPM offset in a location of its own, within the process structure. The actual IOPM offset in the TSS is loaded from the value in the process structure whenever a process gains control, so changing the TSS directly is of no use. To change the IOPM base address, the value in the process structure must be changed. Once the IOPM offset in the process structure is changed, user-mode I/O access is granted to that process for all ports whose corresponding IOPM access bit is 0. Listing 24.3 illustrates direct modification of the process structure.

Listing 24.2   A fragment of a kernel-mode device driver.

```
/****************************************************************************
This code fragment illustrates the unsuccessful attempt to directly modify the
IOPM base address. This code would appear in a kernel-mode device driver. Refer
to the GIVEIO.C listing for a complete device driver example.
****************************************************************************/
/* Make sure our structure is packed properly, on byte boundary, not
 * on the default doubleword boundary. */
#pragma pack(push,1)
/* Structure of a GDT (global descriptor table) entry; from processor manual.*/
typedef struct {
    unsigned limit : 16;
    unsigned baselo : 16;
    unsigned basemid : 8;
    unsigned type : 4;
    unsigned system : 1;
    unsigned dpl : 2;
    unsigned present : 1;
    unsigned limithi : 4;
    unsigned available : 1;
    unsigned zero : 1;
    unsigned size : 1;
    unsigned granularity : 1;
    unsigned basehi : 8;
} GDTENT;
/* Structure of the 48 bits of the GDT register that are stored
 * by the SGDT instruction. */
typedef struct {
    unsigned short  limit;
    GDTENT  *base;
} GDTREG;
```

Listing 24.2 (continued)

```
#pragma pack(pop)
/* This code demonstrates the brute force approach to modifying the IOPM base.
 * The IOPM base is stored as a two byte integer at offset 0x66 within the TSS,
 * as documented in the processor manual. In Windows NT, the IOPM is stored
 * within the TSS starting at offset 0x88, and going for 0x2004 bytes. This is
 * not documented anywhere, and was determined by inspection. The code here
 * puts some 0's into the IOPM so that we can try to access some I/O ports,
 * then modifies the IOPM base address. This code is unsuccessful because NT
 * overwrites the IOPM base on each process switch. */
void GiveIO()
{
    GDTREG gdtreg;
    GDTENT *g;
    short TaskSeg;
    char *TSSbase;
    int i;
    _asm str TaskSeg;                    // get the TSS selector
    _asm sgdt gdtreg;                    // get the GDT address
    g = gdtreg.base + (TaskSeg >> 3);    // get the TSS descriptor
                                         // get the TSS address
    TSSbase = (PVOID)(g->baselo | (g->basemid << 16)
                    | (g->basehi << 24));
    for(i=0; i < 16; ++i)                // poke some 0's into the
        TSSbase[0x88 + i] = 0;           //    IOPM
    *((USHORT *)(TSSbase + 0x66)) = 0x88;
}
```

Listing 24.3   Direct modification of the process structure.

```
/* From inpection of the TSS we know that NT's default IOPM offset is 0x20AD.
 * From an inspection of a dump of a process structure, we can find the bytes
 * 'AD 20' at offset 0x30.  This is where NT stores the IOPM offset for each
 * process, so that I/O access can be granted on a process-by-process basis.
 * This portion of the process structure is not documented in the DDK.
 * This kernel mode driver fragment illustrates the brute force
 * method of poking the IOPM base into the process structure. */
void GiveIO()
{
    char *CurProc;
    CurProc = IoGetCurrentProcess();
    *((USHORT *)(CurProc + 0x30)) = 0x88;
}
```

Yet Another Way

Early on, I ran across some kernel-mode function names in the NTOSKRNL library (which contains kernel-mode device driver support routines) that weren't documented in the DDK. Among these functions were `Ke386SetIoAccessMap()`, `Ke386QueryIoAccessMap()`, and `Ke386IoSetAccessProcess()`. From their names, these functions sounded like they might do what I needed, but because they were not documented, I initially had difficulty getting them to work. Only after I completely understood the 80x86 I/O protection mechanism and had my own implementation working, did I have the knowledge to go back and decipher them.

`Ke386SetIoAccessMap()` takes two arguments: an integer, which must be set to 1 in order for the function to work, and a buffer pointer. It copies a supplied I/O access bitmap of length 0x2000 from the buffer into the TSS at offset 0x88. `Ke386QueryIoAccessMap()` takes the same arguments but does the opposite, copying the current IOPM from the TSS into a buffer of length 0x2000. If the integer argument is set to 0, the Set function copies 0xFFs to the IOPM, and the Query function copies 0xFFs to the user's buffer.

`Ke386IoSetAccessProcess()` takes two arguments: a pointer to a process structure obtained from a call to `PsGetCurrentProcess()` and an integer that must be set to 1 to grant I/O access or to 0 to remove I/O access. When the integer argument is 0, the function disables I/O access by setting the IOPM offset of the passed process to point beyond the end of the TSS. When the integer argument is 1, the function enables I/O access by setting the IOPM offset of the passed process to point to the start of the IOPM at offset 0x88 in the TSS.

Using Set and Query together, it is possible to read, modify, and write back the IOPM, adding access to the desired ports by setting their respective permission bits to zero. `Ke386IoSetAccessProcess()` then enables the IOPM lookup for the desired process. The kernel-mode device driver in Listing 24.4, `giveio.c`, sets the IOPM to 0s to allow full user-mode access to all I/O ports. Listing 24.5, a user-mode test application called `testio.c`, uses direct port I/O to exercise the PC's internal speaker.

Listing 24.4 `giveio.sys` — Give direct port I/O access to a user-mode process.

```
/************************************************************
GIVEIO.SYS -- by Dale Roberts
Compile:    Use DDK BUILD facility
Purpose:    Give direct port I/O access to a user mode process.
************************************************************/
#include <ntddk.h>
#include <mondebug.h>
/* The name of our device driver. */
#define DEVICE_NAME_STRING L"giveio"
```

Direct — for Real?

Once a user-mode process is given permission to access an I/O port, the I/O access proceeds without further help from the device driver. The purpose of the device driver is to modify the IOPM and the process' copy of the IOPM offset. Once that's done, the application's I/O port accesses proceed unhindered. In fact, the device driver could be unloaded once the IOPM is modified, and the application could still do direct I/O. Listing 24.5 illustrates this by opening and closing the GiveIO driver, giving the application I/O access before it performs the port I/O.

Listing 24.4 (continued)

```c
/* This is the "structure" of the IOPM.  It is just a simple character array
 * of length 0x2000. This holds 8K * 8 bits -> 64K bits of the IOPM, which
 * maps the entire 64K I/O space of the x86 processor.  Any 0 bits will give
 * access to the corresponding port for user mode processes. Any 1
 * bits will disallow I/O access to the corresponding port. */
#define IOPM_SIZE    0x2000
typedef UCHAR IOPM[IOPM_SIZE];
/* This will hold simply an array of 0's which will be copied into our actual
 * IOPM in the TSS by Ke386SetIoAccessMap(). The memory is allocated at
 * driver load time. */
IOPM *IOPM_local = 0;
/* These are the two undocumented calls that we will use to give the calling
 * process I/O access. Ke386IoSetAccessMap() copies the passed map to the TSS.
 *  Ke386IoSetAccessProcess() adjusts the IOPM offset pointer so that the newly
 * copied map is actually used.  Otherwise, the IOPM offset points beyond the
 * end of the TSS segment limit, causing any I/O access by the user-mode
 * process to generate an exception. */
void Ke386SetIoAccessMap(int, IOPM *);
void Ke386QueryIoAccessMap(int, IOPM *);
void Ke386IoSetAccessProcess(PEPROCESS, int);
/***** Release any allocated objects. ******/
VOID GiveioUnload(IN PDRIVER_OBJECT DriverObject)
{
    WCHAR DOSNameBuffer[] = L"\\DosDevices\\" DEVICE_NAME_STRING;
    UNICODE_STRING uniDOSString;
    if(IOPM_local)
        MmFreeNonCachedMemory(IOPM_local, sizeof(IOPM));
    RtlInitUnicodeString(&uniDOSString, DOSNameBuffer);
    IoDeleteSymbolicLink (&uniDOSString);
    IoDeleteDevice(DriverObject->DeviceObject);
}
/**************************************************************************
Set the IOPM (I/O permission map) of the calling process so that it is given
full I/O access. Our IOPM_local[] array is all zeros, so IOPM will be all 0s.
If OnFlag is 1, process is given I/O access. If it is 0, access is removed.
**************************************************************************/
VOID SetIOPermissionMap(int OnFlag)
{
    Ke386IoSetAccessProcess(PsGetCurrentProcess(), OnFlag);
    Ke386SetIoAccessMap(1, IOPM_local);
}
void GiveIO(void)
{
    SetIOPermissionMap(1);
}
```

Listing 24.4 (continued)

```c
/********************************************************************
Service handler for a CreateFile() user mode call. This routine is entered in
the driver object function call table by DriverEntry(). When the user-mode
application calls CreateFile(), this routine gets called while still in the
context of the user-mode application, but with the CPL (the processor's Current
Privelege Level) set to 0. This allows us to do kernel-mode operations.
GiveIO() is called to give the calling process I/O access. All the user-mode
app needs do to obtain I/O access is open this device with CreateFile(). No
other operations are required. ***********************************************/
NTSTATUS GiveioCreateDispatch(
    IN  PDEVICE_OBJECT  DeviceObject,
    IN  PIRP            Irp
    )
{
    GiveIO();               // give the calling process I/O access
    Irp->IoStatus.Information = 0;
    Irp->IoStatus.Status = STATUS_SUCCESS;
    IoCompleteRequest(Irp, IO_NO_INCREMENT);
    return STATUS_SUCCESS;

}
/********************************************************************
Driver Entry routine. This routine is called only once after the driver is
initially loaded into memory. It allocates everything necessary for the
driver's operation. In our case, it allocates memory for our IOPM array, and
creates a device which user-mode applications can open. It also creates a
symbolic link to the device driver. This allows a user-mode application to
access our driver using the \\.\giveio notation. **************************/
NTSTATUS DriverEntry(
    IN  PDRIVER_OBJECT DriverObject,
    IN  PUNICODE_STRING RegistryPath
    )
{
    PDEVICE_OBJECT deviceObject;
    NTSTATUS status;
    WCHAR NameBuffer[] = L"\\Device\\" DEVICE_NAME_STRING;
    WCHAR DOSNameBuffer[] = L"\\DosDevices\\" DEVICE_NAME_STRING;
    UNICODE_STRING uniNameString, uniDOSString;
    //  Allocate a buffer for the local IOPM and zero it.
    IOPM_local = MmAllocateNonCachedMemory(sizeof(IOPM));
    if(IOPM_local == 0)
        return STATUS_INSUFFICIENT_RESOURCES;
    RtlZeroMemory(IOPM_local, sizeof(IOPM));
    //  Set up device driver name and device object.
    RtlInitUnicodeString(&uniNameString, NameBuffer);
    RtlInitUnicodeString(&uniDOSString, DOSNameBuffer);
    status = IoCreateDevice(DriverObject, 0, &uniNameString,
                FILE_DEVICE_UNKNOWN, 0, FALSE, &deviceObject);
    if(!NT_SUCCESS(status))
        return status;
    status = IoCreateSymbolicLink (&uniDOSString, &uniNameString);
    if (!NT_SUCCESS(status))
        return status;
    //  Initialize the Driver Object with driver's entry points.
    // All we require are the Create and Unload operations.
    DriverObject->MajorFunction[IRP_MJ_CREATE] = GiveioCreateDispatch;
    DriverObject->DriverUnload = GiveioUnload;
    return STATUS_SUCCESS;
}
```

Listing 24.5 `testio.c` — *Direct port I/O accesses the PC's internal speaker.*

```c
/************************************************************
TESTIO.C -- by Dale Roberts
Compile:   cl -DWIN32 tstio.c
Purpose:   Test the GIVEIO device driver by doing some direct
           port I/O.  We access the PC's internal speaker.
************************************************************/
#include <stdio.h>
#include <windows.h>
#include <math.h>
#include <conio.h>
typedef struct {
    short int pitch;
    short int duration;
} NOTE;
/* Table of notes. Given in half steps. Communication from "other side." */
NOTE notes[] = {{14, 500}, {16, 500}, {12, 500}, {0, 500}, {7, 1000}};
/***** Set PC's speaker frequency in Hz.  The speaker is controlled by an
 ***** Intel 8253/8254 timer at I/O port addresses 0x40-0x43. *****/
void setfreq(int hz)
{
    hz = 1193180 / hz;                   // clocked at 1.19MHz
    _outp(0x43, 0xb6);                   // timer 2, square wave
    _outp(0x42, hz);
    _outp(0x42, hz >> 8);
}
/************************************************************
Pass a note, in half steps relative to 400 Hz.  The 12 step scale is an
exponential thing. Speaker control is at port 0x61. Setting lowest two bits
enables timer 2 of the 8253/8254 timer and turns on the speaker.
************************************************************/
void playnote(NOTE note)
{
    _outp(0x61, _inp(0x61) | 0x03);      // start speaker going
    setfreq((int)(400 * pow(2, note.pitch / 12.0)));
    Sleep(note.duration);
    _outp(0x61, _inp(0x61) & ~0x03);     // stop that racket!
}
```

I/O Timing

Using port I/O from an application isn't a free ride. There's overhead in the protection mechanism, so the 80x86 IN and OUT instructions take longer in user mode, where CPL > IOPL. The number of processor clock cycles it takes to execute the IN and OUT instructions varies depending on the CPU mode. In so-called real mode (plain vanilla, nonextended DOS), an OUT instruction takes 16 processor clock cycles to execute on a 486; in virtual 8086 mode (a DOS program running in a Windows DOS box or an NT console window), it takes 29 cycles. In protected mode, the execution time depends on whether CPL > IOPL. In the context of NT, this means that it depends on whether a process is executing in kernel mode or user mode. In kernel mode, an OUT instruction takes a mere ten cycles. In user mode it takes a whopping 30 cycles! So the execution time of a "direct" I/O operation is in fact three times longer for a user-mode process, but it is still tiny compared to a device-driver call, which might take on the order of 6,000 to 12,000 clocks (somewhere in the 100–200msec range on my 486). The extra time taken when CPL > IOPL, and when the processor is in virtual 8086 mode, is the time it takes the processor to check the bits in the IOPM.

Listing 24.5 (continued)

```
/********************************************************************
   Open and close the GIVEIO device.  This should give us direct I/O
access.  Then try it out by playin' our tune.
 ********************************************************************/
int main()
{
    int i;
    HANDLE h;
    h = CreateFile("\\\\.\\giveio", GENERIC_READ, 0, NULL,
                    OPEN_EXISTING, FILE_ATTRIBUTE_NORMAL, NULL);
    if(h == INVALID_HANDLE_VALUE) {
        printf("Couldn't access giveio device\n");
        return -1;
    }
    CloseHandle(h);
    for(i=0; i < sizeof(notes)/sizeof(int); ++i)
        playnote(notes[i]);
    return 0;
}
```

Careful with that Axe, Eugene!

Pardon the Pink Floyd reference, but it seems appropriate to provide warnings about this potentially dangerous tool.

With I/O access knowledge, you may be tempted to start using it for everything, but remember that I/O protection exists in NT for good reasons. I/O protection helps give the operating system its seemingly bullet-proof stability by forcing all access to a device to go through a single, controlled channel. Frivolous use of user-mode port I/O would tend to erode NT's stability. Circumventing an existing kernel-mode device driver is a bad idea. Device drivers maintain information about the state of the devices they control. Bypassing a driver and accessing hardware directly may cause the driver and the hardware to get out of sync, with unpredictable results. Imagine the chaos that would result if every application tried to directly access the network card.

User-mode I/O may be useful for developing device drivers. It might serve as a development tool for quickly testing new hardware. Direct I/O from user-mode processes should find very little use in software that is distributed to end users. It should never occur in an application. If you are accessing a device, you should be doing it from a device driver. User-mode port I/O might occasionally be useful in user-mode portions of a device driver to achieve better overall performance for the driver.

Having ruled out its use in applications, it is likely that even most device drivers would not benefit from user-mode port I/O. Although it may be tempting to use it in every device driver, just to squeeze out that last bit of performance, most devices would not become appreciably faster by using user-mode port I/O. In many devices, the time delays perceived by the user are not in the calls to the device driver, but in the action of the device. The user isn't usually waiting for the device driver call itself to complete, but rather for the disk drive to spin, the read/write head to move, or the paper to feed through the printer. User-mode I/O should only be used if there is a definite bottleneck in port I/O access from applications, and then, only if direct user-mode I/O access would improve the driver by making a noticeable and significant difference to the user. Even Microsoft uses this technique sparingly. The only device driver in the system's `drivers` directory that references the three undocumented routines is the `videoprt.sys` driver, which contains the `VideoPort...` functions.

If I/O access is done in the user-mode section of a driver, kernel mode may still be needed for, among other things, servicing interrupts and controlling DMA. User-mode port I/O does not remove the necessity of writing kernel-mode device drivers.

If you decide that you want to use port I/O in the user-mode portion of your device driver, your kernel-mode driver should modify only the IOPM permission bits that correspond to the I/O ports required by the user-mode portion of the driver. You should use the `Ke386QueryIoAccessMap()` to get the current IOPM, zero each of the permission bits required by the driver, then use the `Ke386SetIoAccessMap()` routine to write the IOPM back. If and when your driver is unloaded, it should set each permission bit back to 1. Only one IOPM is used by all processes in the system, including, possibly, the video driver. For this reason it is important that the IOPM is not simply written with `0xFF`s when access is no longer needed. Of course, the usual device driver rules given in the DDK manual for allocating I/O ports and keeping track of them in the Registry still apply.

Is system security and integrity violated by user-mode port I/O access? No, because a device driver is still required to grant the I/O access to the application, so it is not possible for an application to gain access to I/O ports on its own. The granting of I/O access may be done on a per-process basis, and the kernel-mode device driver that grants I/O access could be modified to grant access only to those processes that it trusts. Only a user running with administrator privileges can load device drivers, so in general, a user-mode application cannot load a device driver and grant itself I/O access unless the administrator is running it. Granting I/O access to a user-mode process is not directly related to NT's security system and does not make any attempt to foil it.

Granting I/O access to a process is a very specific action. It does not enable the use of the other protected 80x86 instructions, such as `STI` (enable interrupts) and `CLI` (disable interrupts). These, and the other privileged instructions, can be executed only by a kernel-mode driver.

Portability

The technique described here is specific to 80x86-compatible CPUs. Still, NT runs on several other platforms, including the DEC Alpha, MIPS, and PowerPC. Although this specific implementation is not portable to those processors, there should be no reason why the same effect could not be achieved on them. None of the other processors have I/O instructions; all hardware is memory mapped. Because any physical memory can be mapped into a user-mode process's memory space (see the Mapmem example program in the DDK), it should be possible to make any hardware accessible to a user-mode process.

None of the techniques presented here are documented by Microsoft, so portability across releases of NT, even on the same processor platform, could be problematic. It is not likely that the whole mechanism would be removed, because the video drivers rely on it. But the names and functionality of specific undocumented routines could change, or the routines could go away altogether and perhaps become embedded in the video port library.

It appears that the undocumented functions were added to NT to increase video driver performance. On the 80x86 platform, increasing video performance required allowing access to some of the video I/O ports in user mode. Because this is the only use of the mechanism, and because it is documented indirectly through the VideoPort... routines, there was no reason for the underlying Ke386... routines to be documented.

Another reason Microsoft may have chosen not to document this mechanism is that it is not fully implemented. Currently, the IOPM is shared by all user-mode processes in the system. To be safer and more useful, the system should maintain a separate IOPM for each process. One way to do this would be to save the IOPM (or a pointer to one) in the process structure and copy it into the TSS each time a process changes. But copying 8,192 bytes would add a large amount of overhead to a task switch. Another way to give each process its own IOPM would be to give each process its own TSS. NT's process structure could be stored in the TSS, because Intel reserves only the first 0x68 bytes of the TSS for the processor's use and allows the rest to be used by the operating system. Switching the TSS for each process requires reloading the TR. The LTR instruction, which loads the 80x86 task register, has only a tiny overhead of 20 clocks on a 486. Each TSS could have its own segment descriptor in the GDT. Or, because segment descriptors are a commodity, the segment descriptor for the TSS could be modified for each process switch. In any case, keeping the entire IOPM would require an overhead of 8Kb for each process. An alternative would be to store only as much of the IOPM as is needed and to only create a new TSS and store the IOPM for processes that require user-mode I/O access. Most I/O devices exist below the 0x400 port address, so this would require only 0x80 (128) bytes of storage. To achieve full generality, NT could just save as much of the IOPM as is necessary to map the highest I/O address that needs to be accessed.

Conclusion

The availability of direct port I/O in user-mode processes opens new doors for NT programmers. Hopefully this technique will prove useful in dealing with hardware devices in an 80x86 NT environment.